REVISED & EXPANDED

PROCLAIMING JUSTICE & PEACE

Papal Documents
from *Rerum Novarum*
through *Centesimus Annus*

Edited by Michael Walsh
and Brian Davies

XXIII
TWENTY-THIRD PUBLICATIONS
Mystic, Connecticut

The publisher gratefully acknowledges permission to publish English translations of these documents:

America Press: *Gaudium et Spes,* from Walter Abbott, *Documents of Vatican II;* Doubleday & Co.: *Rerum Novarum,* from Etienne Gilson, *The Church Speaks to the World;* Our Sunday Visitor: *Mater et Magistra, Pacem in Terris, Populorum Progressio;* United States Catholic Conference: *Quadragesimo Anno,* from *On Reconstructing the Social Order;* Vatican Polyglot Press: *Dives in Misericordia, Evangelii Nuntiandi, Justice in the World, Laborem Exercens, Octagesimo Adveniens, Redemptor Hominis, Sollicitudo Rei Socialis; Centesimus Annus.*

Expanded, North American Edition 1991

Twenty-Third Publications
185 Willow Street
P.O. Box 180
Mystic, CT 06355
(203) 536-2611
800-321-0411

Originally published in England (without the 1991 encyclical *Centesimus Annus*) by Flame, an imprint of HarperCollins Religious, part of Harper-Collins Publishers, 77-85 Fulham Palace Road, London W6 8JB.

ISBN 0-89622-481-3
Library of Congress Catalog Card No. 91-65007

Foreword

In his *Images of Faith* (1973), William J. Lynch, S.J., has described the "sequence of faith" with just enough of a syntactical jolt to provide a fresh perspective on an age-old reality. Faith "does not see; then it hears (the word of God or man); then it inserts this paradigm of hearing into its seeing; its imagining; its experiencing the world" In sum, "Faith does not see; it hears from another."

It has been said that without faith Scripture is an unlighted torch. It might also be said today that without faith the documents of the teaching church have no special claim on the assent of the reader.

The reader of the documents assembled here under title of *Proclaiming Justice & Peace* may or may not be a person of faith. Some of these official documents are explicitly addressed to all persons of good will, not exclusively to the Catholic "faithful" or a larger population of "believers" in Jesus Christ. Any citizen of the human community can find here principles and policy-proposals capable of contributing to the advancement of human welfare and strengthening of societal bonds. The believer, however, recognizing that he or she does not always see the way toward a just society, will be prepared to listen to the teaching church with more than open ears and open mind, indeed with more than ordinary respect. Since faith does not "see" but rather "hears from another," the believer depends on words from certain significant others for guidance on the journey along the path of faith.

When God speaks through Scripture, God enables the hearing believer to see through darkness, doubt, and ambiguity, but even then what is seen is only "a dim reflection in a mirror" (1 Cor. 13:12). When the church speaks through papal encyclicals, conciliar and synodal documents, the hearing believer receives varying measures of reliable, dependable, authoritative guidance. Such documents are not the word of God; they are rather the work of those whose leadership in the church is exercised whenever they attempt to examine the contemporary human condition in the light of God's word and the teaching tradition of the church.

The documents presented here are not, therefore, to be taken simply "on faith." Indeed they can be profitably taken, even by believers, "on reason," in response to the intrinsic force of their moral arguments. They do not carry the authority of Scripture. They need not be read "in faith." But it is important to note that official church teaching, even in its fallibility, does carry doctrinal weight. The believer should approach these documents with respect, "listen" to them carefully and then, in the sequence outlined by William Lynch, insert what has been heard into one's view of the world —not simply one's view as a passive observer, but into one's imagining of a better world and into one's experiencing of a world believed to be on its way to the kingdom proclaimed by Jesus, a kingdom characterized by peace and justice.

Although most of the documents assembled here originated during the past three decades, the whole collection is rooted in the encyclical *Rerum*

Novarum, not included in the first edition of this volume, but reprinted here one hundred years after Pope Leo XIII issued it in 1891. In it the social question relates to the protection of the rights and dignity of workers in an industrializing society within the nation state. This encyclical is the bedrock of modern Catholic social doctrine. Also added to this edition are Pope Pius XI's vision for the reconstruction of the social order, *Quadragesimo Anno* (1931), and Pope John Paul II's *Centesimus Annus* (1991), the encyclical written to commemorate the centenary of *Rerum Novarum* and to address contemporary social concerns. *Mater et Magistra,* published seventy years after *Rerum Novarum,* was written by Pope John XXIII to assist in resolving "the social question" in ways that the pontiff thought to be "more in accord with the needs of the present time." In *Laborem Exercens,* Pope John Paul specifies the social question as the issue of "making life more human" for men and women everywhere. And in making this specification, he is simply repeating the Second Vatican Council's Constitution on the Church in the Modern World (1965), which is included in the present volume under its Latin title *Gaudium et Spes.*

A major document in this collection is *Populorum Progressio,* the 1967 encyclical letter of Pope Paul VI. Acknowledging that his predecessors "did not fail in the duty of their office of shedding the light of the Gospel on the social questions of their time," Pope Paul asserted that the "principal fact" to be recognized in his time "is that the social question has become world-wide."

The social question—the question of the development of human persons in full human dignity, not alone but in true human community—is the reference point from which reflection on these documents should begin. For the person of faith, a reflective reading is not enough. These documents call for a faith-based listening. They "proclaim" justice and peace. They invite a faith-committed response.

The response, of course, must be to the right question, to the social question as specified by the circumstances of our day. Without experience of the world and awareness of the human condition, even the most faith-committed reader is unlikely to be a part of an effective response. If a sufficient number of believers combine awareness and experience with commitment to the principles documented here, then there is hope that peace and justice proclaimed by the church will become policies and programs at work for the well-being of the world. If a sufficient number of non-believers are also moved by the moral reasonings found in these documents, that hope will rise accordingly.

What I refer to as moral reasonings in these documents are enhanced and elucidated by the inclusion, in this second edition, of John Paul II's *Sollicitudo Rei Socialis* (1988). Here the notion of "solidarity," mentioned in earlier documents, particularly *Populorum Progressio,* is raised to the level of a moral category. Solidarity, in the mind of John Paul II, refers to true interrelatedness and interdependence among nations. For Paul VI, development was the new word for peace. For John Paul II, solidarity functions as a path to both development and peace. We cannot have one without the other. We will have neither without the moral impetus these documents were written to encourage.

William J. Byron, S.J.
President, The Catholic University of America

Contents

Editorial Note

The basis upon which the documents included in this collection have been chosen will be explained in the Introduction. The definitive texts appeared, in Latin, in the Catholic Church's official publication *Acta Apostolicae Sedis*. In the case of some of the documents there are available a number of different translations into English: those printed here seemed the most readily comprehensible. In order to make reference back to the Latin text somewhat simpler, the paragraphs of the English versions as they are printed here correspond to the paragraphs as they appear in the *Acta*.

In this collection every paragraph has been numbered. Any enumeration which appeared in the Latin text is retained, but where it is clearly insufficient it has been added to. For example, if a paragraph is numbered 3, and then there are four further unnumbered paragraphs before paragraph 4, the enumeration runs 3, 3.1, 3.2, 3.3, 3.4, 4 and so on. The particular system used, together with the reference by date and volume number to the definitive text in the *Acta*, are given in the brief introduction to each document.

The usual practice of the Vatican is to refer to documents by the opening two or three words of the Latin text. That practice has been retained here (except for *Justice in the World* which is more commonly known by its English title), and the abbreviations have been based upon the Latin title. Each document is preceded by a short note setting it in context and drawing attention to one or two important aspects of its content, and by a summary which attempts to outline the main points of the document. Footnotes have been printed at the back.

Introduction

This volume contains twelve complete and two excerpted documents which together constitute the most authoritative and most recent social teaching of the Roman Catholic Church. All but four of them are encyclical letters. Of these four, two are statements prepared by bishops meeting in Rome. Of the remaining two, one is called an 'Apostolic Letter', the other an 'Apostolic Exhortation'. Both were written by Pope Paul VI, whose last formal encyclical was *Humanae Vitae*, published in 1968: after that he appears to have chosen forms of communication other than encyclicals. The documents stretch over a hundred years all but a day or two, and are being published in this new edition of *Proclaiming Justice & Peace* to commemorate the centenary in 1991 of what is generally recognized as the first social encyclical, Pope Leo XIII's *Rerum Novarum*.

That the Church should have a social teaching is nowadays taken for granted. In some ways Christianity has always had one. Saint Paul reflected upon the relationship between Christians and the State in his Letter to the Romans. The Fathers of the Church were deeply concerned about the morality of warfare and the ownership of property. Medieval schoolmen dwelt at length on the propriety of charging interest on loans. In the sixteenth century Bartolomé de las Casas and Francisco Vitoria, both of them Spanish Dominicans, wrote vigorously about the problems of colonization, and about the treatment of the indigenous populations in territories newly conquered by Spain. One could instance many more examples. The problems presented to the Church by the world have constantly been addressed both by saints and by scholars, confronted by missionaries and debated by academics.

It should have come as no surprise, therefore, when the Catholic Church, in the person of the Bishop of Rome, the Pope, began to speak out on social issues. Yet it did. Although Pope Leo XIII attacked socialism, his encyclical was itself regarded as socialist. As one commentator has described it, the shock waves produced by *Rerum Novarum* in 1891 were like those which would no doubt be produced today if the Pope were suddenly to publish an encyclical unequivocally condemning nuclear weapons.

Not only has it proved to be the first in a long series, many of the later documents were composed explicitly to commemorate its publication, as some of their titles bear witness. It was inevitable that there would appear an encyclical to celebrate *Rerum Novarum*'s hundredth birthday, and that its title, *Centesimus Annus*, should reflect that anniversary. It is important, then, to understand the reasons for the appearance of Leo's encyclical with, behind it, all the authority—short of the then recently defined dogma of papal infallibility—of the Vicar of Christ.

History

Looking back over nearly a century it is difficult to understand, not why *Rerum Novarum* was published at all, but why it had not been published much earlier. Nearly fifty years separated its appearance from the publication of the *Communist Manifesto*. Some Church leaders had long been aware of the challenge by socialism for the leadership of the working-class. In 1864, the same year that Marx established the First International, Wilhelm von Ketteler, the Bishop of Mainz, produced a book entitled *The Worker-Question and Christianity*. His ideas were influenced more by somewhat romanticized notions of the structures of medieval Germany than by his experience of industrial society, but they were more in sympathy with the ideals of socialism than with the ideology of economic liberalism then prevailing. In France the *Conseil des Études* followed similar reasoning, and arrived at similar conclusions. There was rather less theory in England, but some practice. Along with other continental reformers, Bishop von Ketteler was a correspondent of Cardinal Manning, who won considerable fame both at home and abroad for his arbitration in the London dock strike of 1889. He also made valiant efforts to rally English Catholics to the side of Labour. His successor as Archbishop of Westminster, Cardinal Herbert Vaughan, attributed this latter to senility.

At the local level, then, there was wide involvement of the Church in social problems. And although *Rerum Novarum*, as an encyclical letter, was theoretically universal in its scope, it, too, reflected local concerns: the situation in Italy after the fall of Rome in 1870, and the final unification of that country.

The creation of the new Kingdom of Italy, the country's growing industrialization, and the expansion of the suffrage, all meant that the traditional Italian ruling class, particularly the landowners and the nobility, no longer had the power to which they were accustomed. Debarred from politics—even if they had a taste for it—by the *Non Expedit* ('It is not fitting') decree of 1868, many turned to concern for the poor, especially the rural poor. In a restoration of the *ancien régime* they looked for both a means of improving social conditions, and a restoration of their own lost authority. Welfare was for them associated with piety: it had little to do with democracy. Political reform was, however, slowly taking place. In 1882 the franchise was extended from two to ten per cent of the population, and although by modern standards it still remained small, it was sufficient to bring the socialists into parliament in coalition with the radicals. Then in 1891 the Italian Socialist Party was formally constituted. That was the year *Rerum Novarum* was published.

Rerum Novarum

With its condemnation of socialism and its defence of workers' rights, with its regret for the passing of the guilds and its insistence that, in the new workers' associations, spiritual and temporal concerns should be equally prominent, Leo's encyclical was not only criticizing the structures of a new, industrialized Italy, it was also giving support to the traditionalist groups eager to see the restoration of the *ancien régime*. At least, that is one possible interpretation. It would be unfair to see what came to be called 'the workers' charter' entirely in that light, but it would be unhistorical to ignore the Italian context within which the encyclical was composed.

A hundred years on, it is difficult to understand the impact of Leo's encyclical, so old-fashioned does it appear. It is not just a nostalgia for a medieval past. Leo was a great enthusiast for the recovery of the medieval theological and philosophical synthesis achieved by St Thomas Aquinas. Thomism—which admittedly is not quite the same thing as St Thomas himself—is the philosophical context in which the encyclical was composed. It decisively shaped social teaching down almost to the present day. Only Pope John Paul II has stepped outside it. Also part of the medieval vision was the link between guilds and religion: they were to be, at least in part, pious associations: Catholics were to have their own unions wherever possible. In some countries Catholic trade unionism still survives: its establishment at the turn of the century split the working-class movement.

This may not, of course, have been a conscious intention on the part of the papacy, but it certainly helped reinforce another of the Church's concerns, that there should be no 'class struggle'. This was an explicit theme of the next social encyclical, *Quadragesimo Anno*, or 'Forty years on', which was published on 15 May 1931 and was, as the name suggests, a document commemorating the fortieth anniversary of *Rerum Novarum*.

Quadragesimo Anno

We are in the unusual situation of knowing a great deal about the composition of this encyclical from the man who composed it. Pius XI asked for the help of the Jesuits, and the General of the Jesuits put the task in the hands of Oswald Nell-Breunning. Nell-Breunning wrote an account of the process in the German Jesuit periodical *Stimmen der Zeit* in 1971—translations of the article are readily available. This account, valuable though it be, dwells more on the intellectual than on the political and economic background to *Quadragesimo Anno*, but they too are important, and once again Italian domestic politics are to the fore.

Two years previously the Holy see had negotiated with Italy the Lateran Treaty which established the Vatican City State. Not all Vatican officials were sympathetic to the regime then ruling Italy—Mgr Montini, much later to be Pope Paul VI, was particularly opposed—but the tyranny of Mussolini had not yet been wholly revealed. The form of corporate state which he had created, and which was also at that time to be found in Portugal under Salazar, seemed to be consonant with the developing social teaching. At least it avoided the danger of class conflict. The Pope also recommended a form of economic structure which, he believed, avoided the pitfalls of socialism on the one hand and liberalism on the other, both of which he roundly condemned.

For, of course, the encyclical, being written in 1931, was composed after the collapse of the money markets in 1929, and in the context of economic recession with its inevitable growth of unemployment. Out of the grinding hardship of the working class one might have expected a new sense of strength in solidarity to develop. Pope Pius XI laid great emphasis, as had Leo XIII, on the need for there to continue to be Catholic trades unions.

[3]

However much the Pope might condemn the abuses of capitalism, and the condemnation is most certainly present in the encyclical, he was not in favour of workers reaching across denominational boundaries to oppose it.

One important element of *Quadragesimo Anno* that is occasionally overlooked is the 'principle of solidarity', the notion that a higher authority should not undertake a task which a subordinate one could perfectly well accomplish. It is a common-sense idea, though not one which the Church has applied to itself in any systematic way. But it can also be employed to justify in broad terms the very liberalism the Pope was condemning and, in Britain in the second half of the 1940s, it was used by Catholics to oppose the welfare legislation brought in by the Labour Government of the day.

There was a forty-year gap between *Rerum Novarum* and *Quadragesimo Anno*: there was to be a thirty-year one between the latter encyclical and *Mater et Magistra*. Leo's encyclical was dated 15 May 1891. *Mater et Magistra* did not appear on the seventieth anniversary, though the original intention was that it should do so. Paul VI's *Octagesimo Adveniens* was issued to mark the eightieth anniversary, as the title indicates, and *Laborem Exercens* to celebrate the ninetieth—though because of the assassination attempt on Pope John Paul II it appeared several months late. No matter how different his approach may be, each Pope likes to present his teaching as in direct continuity with that of his predecessors. He cannot challenge earlier teaching without calling his own authority into question. Hence the constant reference in these documents to what has gone before: Pope John Paul refers often to *Rerum Novarum* in *Laborem Exercens*, but Leo's letter does not merit a footnote.

If Pope John XXIII was marking the seventieth anniversary of the first great social encyclical, he also had some local, and very pressing, problems to which to attend. Under Pius XII the Vatican had been heavily involved in Italian political life. Pope John disapproved. As far as possible, and it could not be entirely possible, he wanted the Church to withdraw from this role. Meanwhile, Signor Aldo Moro, then the leader of the Italian Christian Democrat Party, was struggling to halt his party's drift to the right, and to reassert its original commitment to social justice and reform. In order to achieve this he needed to broaden the base of the government by associating the Christian Democrats with the Socialists. This 'opening to the left' was vigorously opposed by a number of high-ranking clerics in Italy. An article appeared in the Vatican's daily newspaper, *L'Osservatore Romano*, insisting upon the right of bishops to intervene in social and political matters and, in particular, to judge the morality of political alliances and coalitions. Part of Pope John's response to Cardinals Tardini, Ottaviani and Siri, all of whom had worked on the *Osservatore* article, was *Mater et Magistra*. So once again the Vatican's preoccupation with Italian affairs helped to shape, even if it did not dictate, the content of a papal encyclical.

Mater et Magistra

In the words of Donal Dorr, *Mater et Magistra* 'began the process of breaking the long alliance between Roman Catholicism and socially conservative forces'. It recommended, for example, that employees should have some share in the company for which they work, together with a say in its management. It also proposed that workers should have a part in determining policy at a national level. Pope John believed that the State should play a more active role in national life than his predecessors had generally been prepared to countenance. It should exercise control over major companies; it should own property in the name of the common good; it should play a larger part in coping with social problems. John XXIII viewed the onset of the welfare state with greater equanimity than had his predecessor. He had an optimistic view of the world, believing not only that people could, but also that they would, co-operate at all levels of society. He supposed that the (then) current economic expansion would achieve a greater distribution of wealth; he made the first major attempt by a pope to discuss aid to countries in process of development; he recommended improvements in social structures. But he did not propose means for bringing those improvements about. He relied very largely upon exhortation. He did not issue a serious challenge to the capitalist system then prevailing in the Western world.

Pacem in Terris

His next encyclical, however, raised some fundamental questions about that golden calf of liberal capitalism, human rights. *Pacem in Terris* was dated 11 April 1963. It was published in the course of the Second Vatican Council, an event which focused a good deal of attention upon Rome. Pope John had, in any case, become by this time a well-loved, highly respected figure and there was a ready-made audience for what he had to say: this was indeed the first such document to be addressed not simply to a Roman Catholic audience but to all those of good will. His emphasis now was upon rights and duties: of the individual in society, of individuals towards the State, of states towards each other and finally of both individuals and states within the entire world community. There is in *Pacem in Terris* a defence of human rights to an extent that was new in the official pronouncements of the Catholic Church. But Pope John was well aware that the exercise of rights on the part of some citizens might obstruct other citizens in the exercise of theirs. It was the duty of the State, he therefore wrote, to preserve a balance, and not to be so concerned about the rights of one group that the rights of another might be sacrificed. On the face of it this seems, as unhappily papal documents so often seem, to be a distinctly abstract statement. But there was plenty of basis for it. There were, and are, a number of countries, including some in which Roman Catholicism is the dominant religion, where the defence of an individual's rights is used to justify the failure of the State to intervene against manifest injustice. Human rights may be as readily invoked to defend the privileges of a minority as they can be to ameliorate the conditions of the disadvantaged.

Gaudium et Spes

What Pope John talked about in general terms, the Fathers at the Second Vatican Council addressed more specifically in *Gaudium et Spes*, their Pastoral Constitution on the Church in the Modern World. At the very beginning of the Council the Fathers composed a ringing 'Message to Humanity'. In it they insisted that the two great problems facing the Church were peace and social justice—and then they went on to talk of other things. That was not their fault. The Commissions which had prepared the Council's agenda had not seen the need for it to tackle these issues. It was belated pressure from those attending the sessions that brought about the compilation of this document, and it was not formally approved until 7 December 1965, the day before the Council ceremonially concluded its labours. On the two major topics mentioned in the Message, *Gaudium et Spes* was relatively successful. Peace was presented not merely as an absence of war, but as a consequence of the right ordering of society. And such an ordering does not just happen, it has to be worked for and then defended. So peace is bound up with justice. The fathers did not launch a radical attack upon the prevailing economic system. They were apparently confident, as Pope John had been, that the problems of the poorer nations would be progressively resolved through development. They were, on the other hand, prepared to see large estates broken up for the benefit of the landless poor. This was quite a concrete limitation upon an individual's right to property such as Pope John had spoken of in a rather more abstract fashion. It was a step forward, but it did not go very far. The passage speaks of estates which are 'only slightly cultivated or lie completely idle': there is no suggestion that by this means wealth might be more widely distributed within society. The rich might be expected to give up only what was superfluous after they had provided all they considered appropriate to their status in society.

Populorum Progressio

Though on developmental issues in general *Gaudium et Spes* is not always rated highly, at least it stressed the necessity of a change in the balance of trading relationships between rich and poor countries. This is a theme which recurs in Pope Paul VI's encyclical, *Populorum Progressio*, dated 26 March 1967. He asks why there is such a disparity of wealth among nations, and at least in part finds the answer in the heritage of colonialism, in new forms of colonialism, and in the imbalance of power which leads inevitably to an imbalance in contracts of trade. When one party to such a contract is weak and the other strong, it is very likely that the terms of the contract will favour the stronger of the two. Pope Paul therefore attacks the idea of totally free trade. He also lists some of the evils which arise from colonialism, though even-handedly he praises some of the colonial powers for having reduced ignorance and disease, and having improved communications and living conditions. It seems fairly clear from *Populorum Progressio* that Pope Paul believed the situation would change because of action by the rich nations. They would surrender some of their power out of an enlightened self-interest, if for no other reason. For as he points out, if nothing is done to redress the balance in favour of the poor, then the poor will be 'sorely tempted to redress these insults to their human nature by violent means'. In the paragraph which follows this statement the Pope seems to be applying the criteria for a just war, and to be on the point of coming down on the side of revolution. But at the last moment he backs away from giving even tacit approval to the use of violence to bring about a change in structures.

Octagesimo Adveniens

From *Mater et Magistra* onwards major documents on the social teaching of the Church had appeared at two-yearly intervals. Now there was a pause. Pope Paul VI went on his travels. Among other places he went to Colombia, to attend the Second General Conference of the Bishops of Latin America, held during the last week of August and the first week of September 1968 at Medellín. The purpose of the gathering was to apply the conclusions of the Council to the particular situation of Latin America. It was an outstanding, though distinctly controversial, success. The bishops spoke the language of liberation theology, and they were to have enormous influence upon documents later to come out of Rome. Their influence was clear in *Octagesimo Adveniens*, a letter addressed to Cardinal Maurice Roy in his dual capacity as head of the Pontifical Commission Justice and Peace and of the Council for the Laity, but obviously intended for Catholics throughout the world. It appeared on 14 May 1971, and marked a new departure in papal theorizing about world affairs. For one thing, it was very down to earth. Pope Paul mentioned the journeys he had undertaken and emphasized the knowledge these had given him of the diversity of the problems around the world. Hence he insists towards the end of his letter that individual Catholics have to learn to apply the general social teaching to the concrete situation in which they live. Problems relatively new to the social teaching are addressed: urbanization is one, industrialization another. Even environmental issues merit a mention. Paul is also aware of the failure of the developmental model for progress. There is, he admits, a 'radical limitation' to attempts to overcome injustice simply by way of economics: attention has also to be paid to the 'political dimension'. On the other hand Pope Paul wants to deny to unions any role in the political sphere. This would necessarily set class against class, and contradicts the consensus model of political life which papal social teaching tends to promote. Though the meeting at Medellín had for the most part a favourable influence on Paul's thinking, this was not necessarily true of the situation in Latin America in general. His criticism of Socialism and of Marxism was vigorous. He warned that although certain aspects of the latter might at first sight seem acceptable—and Marxist social analysis was having a profound effect upon Christian thinking in Latin America—ultimately the various strands of Marxism were tightly bound together in an unacceptable ideology. 'The most revolutionary ideologies', he warned, 'lead only to a change of masters.'

Justice in the World

In October and early November of the year in which *Octagesimo Adveniens* was published, a synod of bishops met in Rome. At its close it produced a document entitled *Justice in the World*. It is short and direct. Like the papal letter, it draws its inspiration rather less from the general social teaching of teaching of the Church, and relies to a greater extent upon reading the signs of the times. It admits that because the synod was drawn from bishops throughout the world its conclusion have to be universal rather than specific. It stresses that, if its conclusions are to mean anything, they must be interpreted and put into practice at the local level. The bishops, like Pope Paul, were influenced by Medellín, and give the language of liberation a prominent place. Again like Pope Paul the synodal fathers were aware that the 'developmental model' for progress was not a success. Not only had economic growth failed to bring about a more equitable distribution of wealth, it had militated against such a distribution. Much more than economics was necessary: 'It is impossible to conceive true progress without recognizing the necessity—within the political system chosen—of a development composed *both* of economic growth *and* participation' (my italics), and goes on to stress the latter rather than the former. One major step forward is the remarkable declaration that if the Church wishes to put itself on the side of the poor and to proclaim justice, then it must practice poverty and behave justly towards its own members. It is an obvious enough statement, but a courageous one nonetheless: the document contains some quite specific criticisms of ecclesiastical practice in a form that is unexpectedly frank in a statement from a Roman source.

Evangelii Nuntiandi

The next synod of bishops met towards the end of 1974 and was devoted to evangelization. It failed to produce more than a summary statement at the end of its discussions, and decided, as Pope Paul later wrote, 'to remit to the Pastor of the Universal Church, with great trust and simplicity, the fruits of all their labours, stating that they awaited from him a fresh forward impulse, capable of creating within a Church still more firmly rooted in the undying power and strength of Pentecost a new period of evangelization'. The Pope's response, from which that quotation is taken, was *Evangelii Nuntiandi*. It was published on 8 December 1975 and is an outstanding document. At the 1971 synod the bishops had declared, in a controversial sentence, that 'action on behalf of justice and participation in the transformation of the world fully appear to us as a *constitutive dimension* of the preaching of the gospel or, in other words, of the Church's mission for the redemption of the human race and its liberation from every oppressive situation' (my italics). Pope Paul echoed this. The kernel of the good news proclaimed by Christ is 'salvation, this great gift of God which is salvation from *everything* that oppresses man' (my italics). Pope Paul establishes a firm link between salvation and liberation, but he is concerned lest the former be reduced to the latter: that the Church's role be reduced to a purely temporal one. He is worried that his espousal of the language of liberation might be taken to imply approval of the use of violence. *Evangelii Nuntiandi* is no blue-print for action. It is nonetheless a profound theological statement of the Church's commitment to the struggle for justice.

Redemptor Hominis

The importance of *Evangelii Nuntiandi* can be gauged from the heavy reliance placed upon it by the January 1979 meeting of the Latin American bishops at Puebla in Mexico. Pope John Paul II gave the opening address at Puebla, and he, too, frequently turned to it. Shortly after his return to Rome he published *Redemptor Hominis*. This, his first encyclical letter, is a wide-ranging document, and only part of it is reproduced in this collection, but it contains a good deal of material for those concerned with the Church's social teaching. In common with *Justice in the World* and *Evangelii Nuntiandi*, the encyclical asserts that 'the Church considers an essential, unbreakably united element of her mission this solicitude for man, for his humanity, for the future of men on earth and therefore also for the course set for the whole of development and progress'. John Paul II, however, appears somewhat sceptical about the benefits of progress. He points constantly to its failures. He is characteristically vigorous—despite his tone being pessimistic—in defence of human rights, which he describes as the 'measure' by which social justice can be tested. At the heart of this message lies the freedom to seek the truth. It is, then, somewhat disappointing that he lays so much emphasis upon religious freedom which is surely only one aspect of that truth.

Dives in Misericordia

Redemptor Hominis was dated 4 March 1979. *Dives in Misericordia* appeared just under two years later, on 30 November 1980. It is a moving document, but little of it is directly concerned with social teaching. As in the case of Pope John Paul's first encyclical, only excerpts have been republished in this volume. The Pope returns to some of the themes he had discussed before. In particular he again speaks of the sense of unease experienced by human beings. He identifies one source of this unease as the remorse felt at the disparity of the distribution of wealth in the world, whether between individuals or among nations. And he makes a powerful case that justice alone is insufficient: 'The experience of the past and of our own time demonstrates that justice alone is not enough, that it can even lead to the negation and destruction of itself, if that deeper power, which is love, is not allowed to shape human life in its various dimensions'.

Laborem Exercens

The 'social question' was directly tackled by the present Pope in *Laborem Exercens*, which appeared in September 1981. Leo XIII's encyclical was primarily a critique of society and of the individual's relationship to it. Other popes had followed in the same tradition. Pope John Paul's letter, however, marked a definite break with the past. It does not so much discuss social issues as present a philosophy and theology of work cast either in biblical terms or in a philosophy which, despite occasional references to St Thomas Aquinas, depends very little upon the natural law type of argument hitherto common in Roman documents. As a Yugoslav theologian has pointed out, the Pope's approach is surprisingly phenomenological. Rather than producing a definition of work he describes it in its various manifestations. The Pope insists that work is not only an expression of human dignity but also that work increases it—a disturbing position to hold, for what then of the dignity of those who, for age or infirmity, cannot work? Or, more fundamentally, what of those who simply cannot find work? He does not seem to have responded to the contemporary reality of increasing unemployment. Though at times the Pope appears distinctly theoretical, some of the principles he insists upon have not yet been taken seriously, no matter how much lip service is paid them. Time and again he emphasizes the priority of labour over capital: though he appreciates the need, under certain circumstances, for nationalization he asserts that state capitalism is not an adequate response; he wants a true sharing in the ownership and management of industry by those who work in it; he insists on a criticism that is every bit as severe on Capitalism as it is on Marxism. It is also interesting to note what he says about the place of women. If at times he appears to suggest that the proper place for women is in the home, he also writes that 'the true advancement of women requires that labour should be structured in such a way that women do not have to pay for their advancement by abandoning what is specific to them'.

Sollicitudo Rei Socialis

'No encyclical of John Paul II's has stirred as much international controversy as "Concern for social reality"', Michael Novak has written. That may be true, but the controversy has largely come from Novak and those who sympathize with his neo-conservative views. Ronald Preston, Emeritus Professor of Social and Pastoral Theology at Manchester University, who thinks the encyclical 'wordy, repetitive and diffuse', remarks that it aroused little comment in the United Kingdom—*Populorum Progressio* having given rise to much more. What appears to have captured people's attention in the United States—apart, that is, from the throw-away passage on the Church selling off its riches to help the poor—is the 'moral equivalence', or moral parallelism, which the Pope appears to believe exists between the Eastern and the Western blocs: the letter, it should be noted, was written before the full impact of 'glasnost' had made itself felt in international relations. The rivalry between the blocs, Pope John Paul says, is one of the factors hindering the development of the Third World. The Third World is a major topic within the encyclical which was ostensibly written to mark the 20th anniversary of *Populorum Progressio*. But the letter is wide-ranging in scope and addresses a number of other themes, including ecology and homelessness, which are relatively new to the social doctrine. One important aspect of *Sollicitudo* is the use it makes of the language of liberation theology. It even espouses the notion of 'structural sin', at one time the real *bête noire* of liberation theology's critics. Indeed, after the two documents from the Congregation for the Doctrine of the Faith of 1984 and 1986 highly critical of liberation theology—the first, it must be said, rather more so than the second—*Sollicitudo* marks a turning point in the Vatican's attitude to this new approach to theological thinking. This change of heart was something Vatican-watchers had spotted earlier, but the encyclical gives it, as it were, official sanction. The encyclical also confirms that the Pope has broken with the Thomistic philosophical tradition in which his predecessors had couched their own documents, and instead embraced a more biblical and theological approach. This departure has been widely recognized and warmly welcomed. But whatever its merits, and they are considerable, it has at least one important drawback. Basing themselves on natural law theory, popes could claim in the past to be addressing all human kind, a claim sometimes made explicit in the opening of the document. 'All people of good will' are still among the addressees of *Sollicitudo*, but it is difficult to see how the creationist arguments which are employed can be expected to persuade anyone except Christians, and not all of them.

Centesimus Annus

Yet even the biblically-based theology fell into the background when Pope John Paul came to write the encyclical to commemorate the centenary of *Rerum Novarum*. *Centesimus Annus* quotes Leo's encyclical time and again, and John Paul's reflections are presented by him as a 're-reading' of that document, but it is a re-reading with a very contemporary air. For once there is little need to seek out the particular political situation which inspired it. The Pope is quite explicit. There is a chapter devoted to 'The Events of 1989' in which he reflects upon the sudden collapse of the Communist bloc (which, it could be argued, he had himself done a good deal to bring about), and provides reasons for it. Naturally he attributes it to 'the spiritual void brought about by atheism', but only after he has listed the violation of workers' rights and the inefficiency of the Communist economic system. This is a distinctly Eurocentric document, and there is a passionate call to the countries of Europe, which he sees as sharing a common culture, to aid the former socialist states in their emergence from the domination of Marxism. He praises the profit motive and capitalism in general, though with a number of *caveats*, and no one could accuse this statement of the 'moral equivalence' mentioned a moment ago. John Paul condemns consumerism, not least because of the harm it does to the environment both natural and human, and praises democracy while stressing, in the traditional manner, that the Church is not wedded to any one political structure. Nevertheless, so forthright an appreciation of democracy is not traditional: one looked in vain for any expression of regret that the Church has in the past so often identified itself with regimes which were anything but democratic. With his constant citing of other papal writings, especially his own, Pope John Paul stated his claim that *Centesimus Annus* was part of a developing 'social magisterium' going back, as he points to, to encyclicals Pope Leo XIII has written before *Rerum Novarum*. But in its topic and style it reads somewhat like the manifesto of someone determined to play a role of leader within Europe. And, at least on the issues of the class struggle and the nature of property, it consciously parts company with what had gone before.

Ideal versus ideology

What has been written above is a very cursory attempt to suggest something of the context and the flavour of the documents included in this volume, and briefly to show how they relate to one another. They represent that part of the Roman Catholic Church's social teaching as it has been expressed over the last century by the highest authority in the Church.

Sometimes the term 'social doctrine' is used in place of 'social teaching'. In *Centesimus Annus* Pope John Paul discusses these terms and uses them interchangeably, along with 'social *magisterium*'. The words may literally mean the same thing, but they are used rather differently. 'Teaching' is taken to be a neutral term. 'Doctrine' or *magisterium*, on the other hand, are often regarded as implying an 'ideology' in a pejorative sense: a set of autonomous beliefs which distort one's understanding of reality. José Miguez Bonino has described the history of Catholic social teaching as a gradual abandonment of ideology. He sees it as a move away from the natural law arguments with their basically deductive approach as enunciated by Leo XIII, to a teaching on social questions more rooted in a Christian reaction to the issues as they present themselves, informed by the light of the Gospel. The tone of the documents, he believes, has changed from moral exhortation to practical recommendation. Bonino is a Methodist, but in general terms his view is shared by the French Dominican priest, Marie-Dominique Chenu. It raises a question about the value of the social teaching, and has to be examined.

Bonino is obviously right about one thing: Catholic social ethics have been heavily influenced by the natural law tradition in philosophy. So strongly has this particular philosophy entered into Catholic social thinking there is almost an assumption that it enjoys something of a divine right to do so. And of course it does not. Of its very nature, philosophical truth is open to all to discover for themselves by use of reason alone. In matters philosophical the Church, or churchmen, can have no special authority. What churchmen propose on the basis of philosophical argument can by rejected by other philosophers, and could in no way form part of the Christian faith. Were the Church's social teaching solely a philosophy, then it would be very difficult to understand why there was any social teaching at all over and above the moral imperative to do good and avoid evil. But of course it has come to rest upon much more than a philosophy. In an important passage in *Evangelii Nuntiandi* (EN31) Pope Paul demonstrated the links between what he called the plan of creation and the plan of redemption. He based the Church's authority in social matters upon those links. As has been seen, this approach has been adopted and developed in recent encyclicals by Pope John Paul II. He has built his arguments around biblical texts, in the interpretation of which he has clearly been influenced by the problems which face today's world. The last document included in this edition, *Centesimus Annus*, is wholly issue-based: the amount of theologizing is modest, of philosophizing non-existent save when Pope John Paul takes Marxism to task.

Implied in the comment that the Church's social teaching constitutes an ideology, is the criticism that the natural law philosophy upon which it has been built is ahistorical: a pre-existing set of beliefs which is applied to very different historical situations in order to produce answers. Some of the exponents of natural law philosophy would not regard this so much as a criticism as a compliment. It could reasonably be argued, however, that the choice of the natural law theory was accidental. Had Pope Leo XIII not been so fervent an admirer of Thomas Aquinas another philosophical tradition might conceivably have informed the beginnings of modern Catholic social teaching. And even though Leo whole-heartedly embraced the natural law school of philosophy, interpretation of it had to be modified to suit circumstances. Early drafts of *Rerum Novarum* made clear the subordination of private property to the demands of the common good. But the implications for state ownership and state intervention brought Catholic teaching too close to socialism for comfort. The emphasis was changed away from the common good to private property. It has taken almost a century to recover, more or less unambiguously but without denying the value of private property, the primacy of the common good over individual rights. The problems entailed by an exaggerated defence of an individual's rights have been mentioned above. It ought also to be pointed out that an equally exaggerated insistence upon the primacy of the common good over an individual's rights may very well lead to the establishment of a national security state.

So not only can Pope Leo's choice of natural law philosophy as the basis of his social teaching be seen as historically conditioned, so too can his interpretation of it. As was suggested at the beginning of this Introduction, support for the Church in Italy at the time of Leo XIII came, to a very large extent, from the landowning classes. It is understandable, therefore, that the Pope had 'real estate' in mind when he wrote about property, and that has influenced the way in which his successors have written about social issues. But land is only one form of property. In the present generation it may not even be a very important form. Others, such as knowledge, say, or weapons, or the control of technology, or the ownership of the means of distributing information, are much more significant. It is upon these, rather than upon land, that power is based in an industrial society. Pope John Paul recognizes this in *Centesimus Annus*, adding that the lack of technological 'know-how' has created a new sort of poverty in the modern world. It is not so much the redistribution of land as the sharing of power that will alter the structures of society, and people who have the power are rarely eager to relinquish control of it. It is this which gives rise to class conflict.

The terminology of 'the class struggle' is Marxist. The whole notion appears to offend against Christian charity. The popes, therefore, have attempted to play down its significance in modern society, adopting as a model a 'functionalist' rather than a 'dialectical' sociology, to quote Bonino: 'The functionalist perspective is a vision "from the top", from the situation of those sectors of society (whether groups, classes or nations) which exercise power and control and which therefore perceive society as basically a satisfactory organic system that must be preserved and perfected. Dialectical sociologies, on the other hand, express a vision "from below", from those sectors to which society appears as inadequate, badly structured, full of conflict and in need of transformation'. Not only is it ahistorical to ignore the reality of class conflict, it is, it has been argued, attempting to avoid something which is inevitably part of a developing society.

One means of avoiding it is to present social relationships as if they were on a par with personal relationships. But in personal relations it is important to change the way people think—hence the popes have in the past resorted to a good deal of moral exhortation. In social relationship the first priority is to change the way people behave, and to modify behaviour society's structures have to be altered. Pope Paul VI faced this squarely in *Evangelii Nuntiandi* when he came down firmly on the side of first changing structures and afterwards converting hearts. Pope John Paul no doubt in introduces the notion of the 'indirect employer' into *Laborem Exercens* for good pedagogical reasons, but on the face of it one might suppose that he was once again attempting to reduce a complex social relationship to the terminology of personal relationships. 'Nations', says one recent critic referring to *Sollicitudo Rei Socialis*, 'are addressed as if they could behave as individuals'. Clearly, like his predecessors, Pope John Paul was not happy with the idea of class conflict. One might reasonably interpret his urging in *Laborem Exercens* of trade unions to stay out of politics as a means of preventing the class struggle from becoming institutionalized. But he understands it and, by *Centesimus Annus*, is prepared to admit that the clash of class interests is part of life. He recommends the 'socialization' of some forms of property. But he insists that the workers must be associated fully with the running of such socialized industries. It seems fairly clear that he is here reflecting upon his knowledge of the situation in Poland: his approach is anything but ahistorical. And though he undoubtedly wishes to play down class conflict, he does so by striking at its root, for he recommends the widest possible diffusion of power throughout society.

People in the liberal western democracies have tended to look sceptically upon the Church's social teaching. It has often seemed to be addressing issues which, at least in that part of the world ready to listen to the teaching, had already been resolved. As document has followed document such criticism has had less and less validity. In Pope John Paul's *Laborem Exercens* there is described a model of society which has nowhere yet been achieved. It is no utopian vision, but for its implementation it requires a thorough change in the structures of society, and a radical conversion of heart.

Michael J. Walsh
Heythrop College, University of London
Pentecost 1991

Rerum Novarum

An encyclical letter of Pope Leo XIII to our venerable brethren, the Patriarchs, Archbishops, and all Bishops of the Catholic world having peace and communion with the Apostolic See, on the Condition of Workers.

Introduction

In this, regarded as the first of the social encyclicals, Pope Leo is concerned with the harsh conditions under which many workers had to live. In urging that they be improved, he is careful not to allot to the state too great an authority in keeping the balance between classes, though he sees that as part of its role. He was clearly afraid of state intervention, a major tenet of the socialism which he condemns in the course of the letter. He advocates self-help on the part of the working class through the establishment of unions (though he prefers 'associations' which becomes the accepted term within Catholic social doctrine), but insists that they should have a religious, as well as a social, purpose. There is almost a medieval flavour to the Pope's picture of society—he laments the passing of the guild system and he draws much of his inspiration from medieval philosophy—which rather set the tone for successive papal writings.

The text of *Rerum Novarum* (RN) is unnumbered as it appears in *Leonis Papae XIII Allocutiones, Epistolae, Constitutiones, Aliaque Acta Praecipua,* volumen IV (1890-1891), pp. 177-209, published by Desclée de Brouwer et Soc., 1894. In the English version used here, the translator has frequently divided long paragraphs into smaller units. Numbers have been added to the English translation so that each group of numbers (e.g., paras 1, 1.1, 1.2, 1.3) represents an entire paragraph in the Latin version. Just occasionally, however, he amalgamated paragraphs: they have been separated out in this edition.

Paras. 1-2: In modern industrial society the conditions under which employees have to work is deteriorating, and they no longer have either the old guild system or religion to defend their interests.

Paras. 3-4: Socialism proposes as a cure the abolition of private property. This would lead, they believe, to an equitable distribution of wealth. But to do so would be to rob the workers of their freedom to use their wages as they wish.

Paras. 5-9: Such action is also unjust because there is a right to private property which arises out of human nature: people make the earth their own by their labour, which brings it to fruitfulness.

Paras. 10-14: Property is necessary to enable the head of the household to provide for his family—which includes leaving them an inheritance. The state must not interfere with this duty. The socialist doctrine of common ownership, therefore, harms the very people it is intended to help. On issues such as these the Church has a right and a duty to speak.

Paras. 15-17: Inequalities in society are unavoidable, but this should not lead to conflict: differentiation of roles is inevitable. Just as there are duties laid upon employees, so there are upon employers, who must render what is just to their work force.

Paras. 18-25: Wealth indeed brings with it great spiritual dangers; it is one thing rightfully to have wealth, it is another rightfully to use it. On the other hand the poor and unfortunate seem to be especially favoured by God. Both sorts of people are bound together as children of God.

Paras. 26-32: The Church commits itself to the reform of society, for society can only be healed by Christian life and teaching. The Church has also founded many institutions whose purpose it is directly to help the poor.

Paras. 33-36: The state has the duty to foster prosperity both public and private, to care for every class of citizen—even though not in the same way for all—and should have particular care for unpropertied workers.

Paras. 37-39: The state can intervene only when the public interest, or the interest of a particular class, is being harmed. There are a number of examples of this, but especial regard must be had for the protection by the State of the poor, of the weak, and of private property.

Paras. 40-47: The state should also intervene to prevent strikes by removing the causes of conflict, in particular by improving the conditions of labour. It should ensure, where necessary, a just wage—that is to say, one which allows workers not only to support their families but also to save money for the purposes of acquiring private property. Taxation must not be so high that this acquisition of property proves impossible.

Paras. 48-58: Workers and employers can do a good deal by founding associations such as mutual benefit societies, but more especially founding workers' associations. The state cannot forbid the establishment of these private societies because they spring from a natural right—including those societies formed for religious purposes which have been under attack. Some associations are inconsistent with Christian principles: Catholics have the choice either of putting their religion in danger by joining them, or of founding their own. Many Catholics have already bonded together in associations to improve the condition of the poor. Such organisations must be self-governing, operating under appropriate constitutions, and they should encourage their members to fulfil their religious duties, as well as to work for the improvement of conditions of work.

[16]

Paras. 59-61: A solution to the problem of the conditions of workers must be sought and found quickly. In this enterprise the Church will help.

Introduction

1. The nations of the world have for long been disturbed by the lust for revolution and it was to be expected that once eagerness for change had been aroused it would spread from the field of politics into the related sphere of economics.

1.1 The coming of new industrial growth with the application of new techniques; of changed relationships between employers and employed; of immense wealth for a small number and deepest poverty for the multitude; of greater self-reliance and closer collaboration of the workers among themselves; and, finally, of a worsening of morals; from all of these changes has come an explosive struggle. The desperate anxiety which has seized upon men's minds shows how much is at stake. In learned circles, in business meetings, in popular assemblies, in legislative bodies, in councils of government, everywhere men meet there is deep concern about what is happening. No question is of more pressing importance at the present time, none more strongly grips the attention of mankind.

1.2 And so, venerable brethren, just as on former occasions when, for the sake of the Church and the common weal, we thought it opportune to address to you letters on political power, human liberty, the Christian constitution of states, and other matters of a similar kind, so also now we find ourselves drawn to write in like manner about the condition of the workers.

1.3 We have already touched upon this question more than once, as occasion offered. However, consciousness of our apostolic office urges us to treat of it in this letter more fully and more explicitly. Our purpose is to make clear the principles by means of which the struggle can be broken off and ended, as equity and the facts of the case require. The case is a difficult one to disentangle and not without risk. It is not easy to assess the rights and duties which ought to govern relationships between the wealthy owners of the means of production, who supply capital, and the unpropertied workers, who supply labour, even without the danger presented by the unceasing efforts of violent and deceitful men to steer the masses away from right judgment and to foment civil discord. However that may be, it is clearly universally agreed that the interests of the people at the bottom of the social scale must be consulted promptly, as befits their plight.

2. For the most part, they are tossed about helplessly and disastrously in conditions of pitiable and utterly undeserved misery. The old working men's guilds were abolished in the last century and no other means of protection was provided in their place. At the same time, all trace of the religion of our fathers was stripped from government and the law. And so it comes about that working men are now left isolated and helpless, betrayed to the inhumanity of employers and the unbridled greed of competitors. Voracious usury makes matters worse, an evil condemned frequently by the Church but nevertheless still practised in deceptive ways by avaricious men. In addition to all this, the hiring of labour and the management of industry and trade

have become concentrated into the hands of a few, so that a tiny group of extravagantly rich men have been able to lay upon a great multitude of unpropertied workers a yoke little better than that of slavery itself.

Socialism

3. While inciting the needy to envy the wealthy owners of the means of production, the socialists argue that the remedy for this evil is the abolition of private property. Individual possessions should become common property, they say, to be administered either by local authorities or by central government. In this transference of property from the private to the public sphere they claim to have found a cure for present ills which will lead to an equitable distribution of capital and income. Their device is ill-adapted to its purpose. It will not end the conflict; it will do harm to the working class; and it is, moreover, greatly unjust. It will do violence to lawful owners, divert government from its proper tasks and cause utter confusion in the state.

4. It is easy to see that anyone who does anything of any kind for pay does it primarily to get something as his own, something that belongs to him and to nobody else. He hires out his strength and skill to get possession of what he must have to satisfy his human needs. In working for a wage he works also for a full and perfect right to use his earnings as seems good to him. If, therefore, a man spends less on consumption and uses what he saves to buy a farm, that farm is his wage in another form, as much at his disposal as was the wage itself. It is precisely in this power of disposal that ownership consists, whether the property be in real estate or in movable goods. It follows that when socialists endeavour to transfer privately owned goods into common ownership they worsen the condition of all wage-earners. By taking away from them freedom to dispose of their wages they rob them of all hope and opportunity of increasing their possessions and bettering their condition.

5. What is even more serious is that the remedy proposed is plainly unjust, since to possess property privately as his own is a right which a man receives from nature.

5.1 In this consideration is to be found one of the greatest differences between man and the rest of the animal creation. Brute beasts do not govern themselves. They are guided and controlled by two natural instincts: one keeps them on the alert, ready to display their strength and capacity for action; the other stimulates and at the same time regulates their individual desires. By one instinct they are led to protect their own lives, by the other to propagate their species. Both purposes are served by the use of things which lie ready to hand, a condition which prevents any further development since it is only by their senses and what their senses perceive that they are moved. Man's nature is very different. At least as much as the rest of the animal creation he has full and perfect possession of animal faculties and therefore also of the enjoyment of material things. But even at its highest level, animal nature cannot set bounds to human nature, so far inferior is the one to the other. The animal nature is made to answer the call of the human nature and be obedient to it. What is most remarkable about us and distinguishes us, what classifies man as man and sets him apart from the brute creation, is the possession of mind or reason. It is because he is the only animal possessed of

[18]

reason that there must be attributed to man the right not only to use things as all animals do, but also to have and to hold them in settled and permanent possession; and that applies not only to goods which are used up in their using, but also to goods which continue to give service over time.

The settled ownership of property is from the natural law

6. This becomes even clearer when we make a deeper study of human nature in itself. Man's ability to understand an indefinitely large number of objects enables him to link the present with the future. Since he also has mastery over his own acts, he can govern himself by his own foresight and judgment, subject always to the eternal law, the guidance of God whose providence extends to all things. It follows that he has freedom to choose whatever course of action he judges to be in his own best interest, not only for the passing moment but also into the future. And from that it follows that it is right and proper for a man to have ownership, not only of the fruits of the earth, but also of the earth itself, because of his awareness that the earth is the source from which his future needs will be supplied. Because his needs are forever recurring—satisfied today, they are as pressing tomorrow— nature must have given to man access to a stable source of supply, one that is always at his disposition and on which he might expect to draw perennially. It is only the earth with its fruitfulness which can satisfy this requirement of permanency.

7. There is no case for introducing the providence of the state. Man is older than the state. Before any state came into existence, man had already received from nature the right to make provision for his life and livelihood.

7.1 An objection to private ownership cannot be based upon the fact that God has given the earth to the whole human race for them to use and enjoy. In giving the earth to mankind in general he does not intend that all should exercise dominion over it indiscriminately. It is because he does not assign any part of it to anyone in particular, but leaves this question to be settled by man's industry and established national customs, that he is said to have given it in general. Besides, however it is distributed among individuals, the earth does not cease to serve the needs which are common to all men. There is no one who does not feed upon the produce of the fields. People without capital supply labour. Thus it may truly be said that the universal means of providing the necessities and comforts of life consists in labour, whether it is applied to a man's own land or in some type of industry, earning a wage which can have no other source than the manifold fruits of the earth, for which it is exchanged.

8. All this affords further proof that it is fully in accordance with nature to own property privately. The truth is that it is only when men cultivate it skilfully that the earth provides in plenty all that men need for the preservation of life and still more for its higher development. Thus, when a man expends the activity of his mind and the stength of his body in procuring the goods of nature he makes his own that part of nature's resources which he brings to completion, leaving on it, as it were, in some form, the imprint of himself. This being so, it cannot but be right for him to possess that part as his very own, nor can it be lawful for anyone to violate that right in any way.

[19]

9. It is amazing that some people dissent from arguments as powerful as these and seek to resurrect bad opinions long since outworn. Enjoyment only of the different products of the soil is all they are willing to concede to a private person. They flatly deny the existence of any right of freehold possession, whether of the land on which a man has built or of a farm which he has cultivated. They do not see that in making these denials they defraud a man of part of the produce of his labour. For the soil which is cultivated with toil and skill is greatly changed in condition: the wilderness is made productive, the infertile fruitful. That which has improved the soil becomes so completely mingled with it as to inhere in it and become to a large extent utterly inseparable from it. Does justice allow any man to seize and enjoy something which another man has stained with his sweat? As effects follow their cause, so is it right for the fruit of labour to belong to those who have given their labour. It is with good reason, then, that the common opinion of mankind has found no merit in the dissenting opinions of a few. Making a close study of nature, men have found in nature's law the basis for a distribution of goods and for private ownership and have been fully convinced that these are in the highest degree in conformity with the nature of man and with peace and tranquillity. Practice has sanctioned this conclusion throughout the ages. It is confirmed and enforced by the civil laws, which, when they are just, receive their binding force from the natural law. The authority of the Decalogue adds its sanction, with its strict prohibition against any coveting of what belongs to another: 'You shall not covet your neighbour's wife, nor shall you set your heart on his house, his field, his servant—man or woman—his ox, his donkey or anything which is his' (Deut 5:21).

10. The importance of rights of this kind which inhere in individual human beings is much better understood when they are looked at in the light of their connexion with and appropriateness to the obligations imposed on men by their family relationships. It is indisputable that everyone is completely free to choose between following Christ's counsel on virginity or committing himself to the bonds of matrimony when he decides upon a state of life. No human law can take away the original natural right of a man to marry or in any way impose limits on the principal purpose of marriage ordained by God's authority from the beginning: 'Increase and multiply' (Gen. 1:28). And so we have the family, the society of the household, which, small though it is, is a true society and older than any state; one therefore which must have its own rights and duties which depend not at all upon the state. Thus, the right of ownership, which we have seen to be given by nature to individual persons, must belong also to a man in his capacity of head of a family. That right is all the stronger inasmuch as the human personality is further developed in the family group.

11. A most sacred law of nature ordains that the head of a family should provide for the necessities and comforts of the children he has begotten. That same nature leads him to want to provide for his children—who recall and in some sense extend his personality—a reasonable degree of protection against ill-fortune in life's uncertain course. This he can do only by leaving income yielding property to his children as his heirs. As we have said, the family is a true society equally with the state and, like the state, it possesses its own source of government, the authority of the father. Provided that it stays

within the bounds set for it by its own special purpose, the family has for this reason at least equal rights with the state to choose and employ whatever is necessary for its rightful life and liberty. We say, at least equal rights. Inasmuch as the domestic household precedes the state, both as an idea and as a fact, it must also have prior rights and duties which are more immediately grounded in nature. Detestation of political society would quickly take the place of desire for it if citizens, families, found that when they entered upon it their rights were rendered less secure and they were hindered rather than helped.

12. It follows that to want to see the state's power arbitrarily at work within the intimacy of households is to make a great and pernicious mistake. Of course, when a family happens to be in a state of great distress, helpless and utterly unable to escape from its predictment, it is right that its pressing need be met by public aid. After all, every family is a part of the state. Similarly, when within a family there is grave dispute about mutual rights, it is for the public authority to insist upon each party giving to the other its due. In doing this the state does not rob citizens of their rights, but rather strengthens them and supports them as it should. However, rulers must stop at this point. Nature does not permit them to go further. Its origin being where human life itself begins, a father's authority is such that it can be neither abolished nor absorbed by the state. 'Children are something of the father' and in some sense an extension of his personality. Strictly speaking, it is not of themselves but by virtue of the family into which they are born that children enter into and partake in civil society. And precisely because 'children are naturally something of their father . . . they are held under the care of their parents until they acquire the use of free will' (St Thomas, *S. Theol.* II-II, Q.10, art.12). Thus, when socialists set aside parental care and put that of the state in its place they offend against natural justice and dissolve the bonds of family life.

13. The harm goes further than injustice. Exceedingly great disturbance and upset would afflict all classes. Close behind would come hard and hateful servitude for the citizens. The door would be thrown open to mutual envy, detraction and dissension. All incentive for individuals to exercise their ingenuity and skill would be removed and the very founts of wealth dry up. The dream of equality would become a reality of equal want and degradation for all. None would be spared. From this it is plain to see that the socialist doctrine of common ownership ought to be altogether repudiated. It harms those it is meant to help; it denies to individuals their rights; it throws the administration of public affairs into disorder; it disturbs the peace. The conclusion is inescapable. All who set out to improve the conditions of the masses must start from the fundamental principle that private possessions must be held inviolate. That being established, let us proceed to an explanation of where the sought-for remedy is to be found.

The action of the Church

14. We approach this matter with confidence, as we are fully entitled to do, since no good solution to the problem can be found without recourse to religion and the Church. Since the care of religion and of those matters for

which the Church has responsibility falls principally to us, continued silence on our part would be seen as neglect of duty. Undoubtedly, there is need for others besides ourselves to bend their efforts to the cause: members of governments, employers and wealthy owners of the means of production, and finally those whose cause we are pleading, the people without property. Nevertheless, we do not hesitate to insist that whatever men may choose to do will be in vain if they leave out the Church. Evidently it is the Church which draws from the Gospel teaching strong enough to end the conflict or, at the very least, make it less bitter; and she it is who tries by her injunctions not merely to inform men's minds, but also to guide the life and morals of every one of them. She has highly efficient organisations which promote better conditions for the unpropertied; she urges all classes to work together in thought and action to produce the best possible solution to the difficulties of the workers; she argues that the state ought to apply its administrative and legislative authority to the same end, to the extent that the situation requires.

Inequalities and the hardships of labour are unavoidable

15. The first point to be made is that men must put up with the human predicament : in civil society it is not possible for those at the bottom to be equal with those at the top. Socialists are violently opposed to this, but they struggle in vain against the nature of things. The differences which exist naturally between men are great and many. There is no equality in talent, or skill, or health, or strength, and these unavoidable differences lead of themselves to inequalities of fortune. This is clearly of advantage both to individuals and to society. A community needs to have within it different capacities for action and a variety of services at its disposal; and men are most impelled to supply these by the differences of their condition.

15.1 As regards manual work, even in the state of innocence men would not have been wholly idle; but what they would then have chosen freely for the pleasure it gave them became, after the Fall, something to which necessity compelled them to submit, in painful atonement for their sin. 'Accursed be the soil because of you. With suffering shall you get your food from it every day of your life' (Gen. 3:17). In like manner, men may not look for an end to their bitter legacy in this life. The burden of the ill-effects of sin lies heavily on them, harsh and difficult to bear. There is no escape for any man to the end of his days. To suffer and endure is the lot of men; and whatever means they use and however much they try, no art, no force can free their society from this painful condition. Anyone who claims to be able to rid the common people of all pain and sorrow and to bring them peace and a life of never-ending pleasure lies outrageously. He sets out a false prospectus which can lead only to an eruption of evils even greater than those men suffer now. The best course for men to follow is to accept reality and seek elsewhere for suitable means to alleviate their troubles, as we have pointed out.

16. In the subject under discussion it is a great mistake to imagine that class is spontaneously hostile to class, as if nature had matched together the wealthy owners of the means of production and the unpropertied workers to persist stubbornly in laying wildly about each other. This picture is so far removed

from truth and reason as to be directly contrary to both. Just as the different parts of the body unite to form a whole so well proportioned as to be called symmetrical, so also nature has decreed that in the state these twin classes should correspond to each other in concord and create an equilibrium. Each stands entirely in need of the other: there can be no capital without labour, nor labour without capital. Concord begets order and beauty, whereas a continuation of conflict leads inevitably to barbarity and wild confusion. Christian institutions are possessed of marvellous and many-sided strength which enables them to put an end to conflict and to cut away its roots.

Justice

17. By constantly recalling both parties to the duties they owe each other, and especially to their obligations in justice, the teaching of religion, of which the Church is the interpreter and guardian, is immensely well qualified to bring together the wealthy owners of the means of poduction and the men without property. Among the obligations of justice which bind the unpropertied worker are: to fulfil faithfully and completely whatever contract of employment he has freely and justly made; to do no damage to the property nor harm to the persons of his employers; to refrain from the use of force in defence of his interests and from inciting civil discord; to avoid the company of men of evil principles who use artful promises of great results to raise extravagant hopes which can end only in vain regrets and heavy loss. For his part, the rich employer must not treat his workers as though they were his slaves, but must reverence them as men who are his equals in personal dignity and made the more noble by their Christian calling. Both natural reason and Christian philosophy agree that it does not shame a man to engage in a profitable occupation. Rather does it do him credit, for it provides him with an honourable means of livelihood. What is truly shameful and inhuman is to misuse men as instruments for gain and to value them only as so much mere energy and strength. There is an obligation to keep in view the religious needs of unpropertied men and the good of their souls. Employers must see to it, therefore, that the worker has time for his religious duties; that he is not exposed to morally corrupting influences and occasions of sin; and that he is not seduced from his domestic duties and a wise use of his earnings. Furthermore, employers must not impose tasks which overtax a man's strength or are of a kind which is unfitted to a worker's age and sex.

17.1 However, among the major duties of employers the most important is to give to each and every man what is just. Of course, there are many matters to be kept in mind when a just standard of wages is being considered; but wealthy owners of the means of production and employers must never forget that both divine and human law forbid them to squeeze the poor and wretched for the sake of gain or to profit from the helplessness of others. To defraud a man of the wage which is his due is to commit a grievously sinful act which cries out to heaven for vengeance. 'Labourers mowed your fields, and you cheated them—listen to the wages that you kept back, calling out; realize that the cries of the reapers have reached the ears of the Lord of hosts' (James 5:4). Lastly, the wealthy owners of the means of production must take scrupulous care not to harm in any way the savings of the unpropertied, whether by force, or fraud, or usurious dealings; and this the more so both because their poverty makes them ill-equipped to counter injustice and because what few possessions they have should be held the more sacred the scantier they are.

17.2 Might not compliance with these rules of conduct be able of itself to rob these differences of their force and utterly to remove their causes?

Charity

18. But the Church, with Jesus Christ for teacher and guide, seeks persistently for more than justice. She warns men that it is by keeping a more perfect rule that class becomes joined to class in the closest neighbourliness and friendship. We cannot understand and value the goods of this mortal life unless we have a clear vision of that other life of immortality. If we lose sight of that, we lose also and at once the true sense of virtue. Everything to do with our material world becomes lost in a mystery which no human mind can fathom. Nature and Christian dogma concur in teaching us the truth which forms the base on which the whole concept of religion rests: that it is only after we have left this life that we shall really begin to live. It is not for the fleeting and the perishable, but for the heavenly and the eternal that God has created man. The earth he gives us as a place of exile, not a dwelling place. Abundance or lack of wealth and other things which men call good is of no importance for eternal happiness. How we use them is of the greatest importance. When Jesus Christ brought to us his plentiful redemption, he did not relieve us of the various sorrows which form so large a part of mortal life; he transformed them into incentives to virtue and occasions of merit. It is plain that no mortal being can come to possess the goods of eternity unless he follows in the blood-stained footprints of Jesus Christ. 'If we hold firm, then we shall reign with him' (2 Tim. 2:12). The labours and sufferings which he bore of his own free will have marvellously blunted the edge of all labour and suffering. He has made it easier to endure sorrows, not only by his example, but also by his grace and the hope of everlasting reward which he holds out to us. 'Yes, the troubles which are soon over, though they weigh little, train us for the carrying of a weight of eternal glory which is out of all proportion to them' (2 Cor. 4:17).

19. Therefore, the wealthy are warned that wealth brings neither freedom from sorrow nor help towards the happiness of eternity, to which indeed it is more of an obstacle (Mt. 19:23-4). Let the rich owners of the means of production tremble at the exceptional threats of Jesus Christ (Lk. 6:24-5): God will demand the strictest accounting for the use they make of their possessions.

The true advantage of riches

20. Most excellent and of the greatest importance is the teaching on the use to be made of wealth which philosophy discovers incompletely but the Church gives clearly and perfectly. Moreover, she does this in such a way as to influence men's conduct as well as inform their minds. The fundamental point of this teaching is that the rightful possession of riches is to be distinguished from their rightful use. As has just been established, to own

goods privately is a natural right of man; and to exercise that right, particularly in society, is not only good but entirely necessary. 'It is not only legitimate for a man to possess things as his own, it is even necessary for human life' (St Thomas, *S. Theol.* II-II, Q.66, art.2). And if the question be asked, 'How must possessions be used?', the Church replies without hesitation: 'No man is entitled to manage things merely for himself, he must do so in the interests of all, so that he is ready to share them with others in case of necessity. This is why Paul writes to Timothy: "As for the rich of this world, charge them to be liberal and generous' (St Thomas, *S. Theol.*, *ibid.*). True, no one is commanded to provide aid for others out of what is required for his own needs and those of his household; or, rather, to hand over to others what he needs to provide a fitting standard for himself: 'Nobody should live unbecomingly' (St Thomas, *S. Theol.* II-II, Q.32, art.6).

21. But when necessity and seemliness have been satisfied, there is the duty of using what is over to relieve the poor. 'Give alms from what you have' (Lk. 11:41). These are not duties of justice, except in extreme cases, but of Christian charity, duties which it is not right to have enforced by law. But prior to the laws and judgments of men there are the law and judgment of Christ, who in many ways recommends the habit of giving generously: 'There is more happiness in giving than in receiving' (Act 20:35); and who will judge a kindness done or refused to the poor as a kindness done or refused to himself: 'In so far as you did this to one of the least of these brothers of mine, you did it to me' (Mt. 25:40).

22. This teaching can be summarized thus: whoever has been generously supplied by God with either corporal and external goods or those of the spirit, possesses them for this purpose—to apply them equally to his own perfection and, in his role as a steward of divine providence, to the benefit of others. 'Let him who has a talent, therefore, be careful not to hide it; let him who enjoys abundance watch lest he fail in generosity to the poor; let him who possesses the skills of management be particularly careful to share them and their benefits with his neighbour' (St Gregory the Great, *Evang. Hom.* IX, n.7).

The innate dignity of poverty

23. As for the poor, the Church teaches insistently that God sees no disgrace in poverty, nor cause for shame in having to work for a living. Christ our Lord confirmed this by his way of life, when for our salvation he who 'was rich became poor for our sake' (2 Cor. 8:9). He chose to be seen and thought of as the son of a carpenter, despite his being the Son of God and very God himself; and having done so, made no objection to spending a large part of his life at the carpenter's trade. 'Surely, this is the carpenter, the son of Mary?' (Mk 8:3). Contemplation of this divine example makes it easier to understand that a man's worth and nobility are found in his way of life, that is to say, his virtue; that virtue is the common inheritance of mankind, within easy reach of high and low, rich and unpropertied alike; and that the reward of eternal happiness is earned only by acts of virtue and service, by whomsoever they are performed. Indeed, the will of God himself seems to give preference to people who are particularly unfortunate. Jesus Christ

proclaims formally that the poor are blessed ('Happy are the poor in spirit' Mt. 5:3); most lovingly he invites all those who labour and mourn to come to him, the source of comfort ('Come to me, all you who labour and are overburdened', Mt. 11:28); with loving care he clasps closely to himself the lowly and oppressed. Knowledge of all this cannot but lower the pride of the well-to-do and lift up the heart of the poor man who is full of misery, turning the one to fellowship and the other to moderation in his desires. Thus, the separation which pride tends to create will be lessened in extent and it will not be difficult for the two classes willingly to join themselves together in bonds of friendship.

Christian brotherhood

24. However, if they obey Christian teaching it will be the bond of brotherly love rather than of friendship that will unite them. They will then feel and understand the obvious truth that all men have the same Father, who is God the Creator; that all reach out for the same final good, who is God himself, who alone can bring absolutely perfect happiness to both men and angels; that by the action of Jesus Christ all alike are redeemed and re-established in the dignity of sons of God, so that all might be bound together in fraternal love, brothers to one another as they are to Christ our Lord, 'the first born among many brothers'. The same benefits of nature and gifts of divine grace belong in common to the whole human race, without distinction, and only those who are unworthy will be disinherited. 'If we are children we are heirs as well: heirs of God and co-heirs with Christ' (Rom. 8:17).

25. Such is the scheme of rights and duties which Christian philosophy teaches. Where this teaching flourishes will not all strife quickly end?

The spread of Christian teaching

26. Not content with merely pointing out the way to set things right, the Church herself takes reform in hand. She commits herself entirely to educating men by her teaching and forming them by her discipline, and by the work of her bishops and priests she seeks to spread the life-giving waters of her doctrine to the furthest possible extent. She strives to inform minds and direct wills so that men will allow themselves to be ruled and guided by the discipline of God's teaching. It is in this, the principal matter of importance because on it depends all the good that is sought for, that the action of the Church is peculiarly effective; and this because the instruments she most uses to influence men's minds are given to her for that very purpose by Jesus Christ and derive their effectiveness from God. It is only instruments of this kind which can touch the innermost reaches of the heart and lead a man to put his duty first, to control his appetites, to love God and his neighbour with his whole heart and soul and to stamp out courageously all that stands in the way of a life of virtue.

The renewal of society

27. In matters of this sort it is enough to glance briefly at the pattern of antiquity. There is not the slightest doubt about the events we bring to mind.

Civil society was renewed from its foundations by the teachings of Christianity. By virtue of this renewal the human race was lifted up to better things, called back indeed from death to life, to a life more perfect than any known before and as good as any yet to come. The first cause and final end of these benefits is Jesus Christ: as all things come from him, so all must be brought back to him. Undoubtedly, as by the light of the Gospel tidings of the great mystery of the incarnation of the Word and of the redemption of mankind were spread throughout the world, the societies of men were permeated by the life of Jesus Christ, God and man, and imbued with his faith, his teaching and his laws. If the society of mankind is to be healed, it can be done only by a recall to Christian life and teaching. If societies in decay wish to be restored, the truest starting point is a return to their origins. The perfection of all associations consists in seeking and attaining the end for which they were established, and this will be done when all social activity springs from the same cause as that which gave societies birth. It is for this reason that to fall away from the original principles is to suffer corruption and to return to them is to have wholeness restored. This is true, not only of the whole body of the state but also of that class of citizens, by far the largest, who work for their living.

The promotion of a better standard of living

28. It must not be thought that the Church's great concern with the care of souls leads her to neglect the affairs of this earthly and mortal life. She wants expressly to see the unpropertied workers emerge from their great poverty and better their condition; and what she wants, she works for. That she calls men to virtue and forms them in its practice is no small help of itself in that direction. Complete adherence to the code of Christian morals leads directly of itself to greater prosperity. It joins men with God, the ground and fount of all good things; it restrains an excessive appetite for material possessions and a thirst for pleasure, the twin plagues which often make even the rich man unhappy: 'The love of money is the root of all evils' (1 Tim. 6:10); it teaches contentment with a frugal standard of living, so that income from savings is available to meet misfortune and the vices which eat up not only small but exceedingly large fortunes and dissipate great inheritances are avoided. In addition to this, moreover, the Church takes direct action to bring prosperity to the unpropertied by founding and fostering institutions which she knows will be conducive to their escape from poverty.

29. In this she has always been successful enough to wring praise even from her enemies. So deeply did the first Christians love one another that very many among them who were well-to-do stripped themselves of wealth to bring aid to those worse off: 'None of their members was ever in want' (Acts 4:34). The Apostles instituted the order of deacons to take charge of the daily distribution; and dispite his burden of care for all the churches St Paul did not hesitate to undertake laborious journeys to bring alms to the poorer Christians. These sums of money, collected by the Christians by universal agreement, were called by Tertullian 'deposits of loving kindness' because 'they are used entirely to feed the needy when they are alive and bury them when they are dead, to care for poor orphans, aged servants and the shipwrecked' (*Apologia* II, 39).

[27]

30. Thus there came gradually into existence an inheritance which the Church has looked after with scrupulous care as the property of the poor. She has always tried to collect funds to help them so as to spare them the humiliation of begging. Acting as the mother of the rich owners of the means of production and of the poor alike and drawing upon the great fount of love which she everywhere creates, the Church has founded congregations of religious and many other useful institutions which have done their work so well that there is hardly any kind of need for which help is not provided. There are many today who follow the example of the heathens of old and find fault with the Church for showing such great charity. They argue that state welfare benefits should be provided instead. But there is no human device which can take the place of this Christian charity, which thinks of nothing other than to bring help where it is needed. The Church alone possesses such virtue because its source is the heart of Jesus Christ himself. There is none other. And whoever cuts himself off from the Church wanders far from Christ.

31. However, it is not to be doubted that to do what needs to be done calls for everything that lies within men's powers. It is necessary for all who have a part to play to work and strain to do their share. As with the providence which governs the world so also here, we see that effects which depend upon a number of causes come about only when all are at work together.

32. The next step to take, therefore, is to ask what part of the remedy is to be looked for from the action of the state, it being understood that in this context 'state' does not refer to such examples as we find in practice in this country or in that, but to that which sound reasoning congruent with nature and the lessons of divine wisdom show to be good. All of this has been clearly explained in encyclicals on the Christian constitution of states.

The right of the state to intervene

33. The first task of rulers is to make use of the whole system of laws and institutions to give assistance both generally and to particular classes. Statesmanship consists in making the structure and administrative functioning of the state conduce of themselves to public and private prosperity. Bringing this about is the particular function of those who govern. The prosperity of a state is best served where there are sound morals, well-ordered family life, regard for religion and justice, moderate taxes equitably levied, growing industry and trade, a flourishing agriculture, and other provisions of a like kind which it is generally agreed will contribute to the greater well-being and happiness of the citizens. By these means rulers can benefit other classes and at the same time be of the greatest help to the unpropertied. It is fully within their right to act thus and since by virtue of its office the state ought to care for the common good they are not to be accused of excessive interference. The greater the abundance of opportunities which arise out of this general care, the less will be the need to try other measures to help the workers.

Regard for the common good

34. But there is another aspect to be considered which is of very great

importance in this connection. The one purpose for which the state exists is common to the highest and the lowest within it. By nature, the right of the unpropertied men to citizenship is equal to that of the wealthy owners of the means of production, for they through their families are among the true and living parts which go to form the body of the state. Indeed, it can be added, in every actual state they are greatly in the majority. Since it would be utterly absurd to care for one section of citizens and neglect another, it is evident that the public authority ought to take proper care to safeguard the lives and well-being of the unpropertied class. To fail in this would be to violate justice which bids us give to every man his due. As St Thomas has wisely said: 'As a part and the whole are identical in a sense, so too in a sense that which is of the whole is also of a part' (*S. Theol.* II-II, Q.61, art.1, ad.2). Consequently, not the least nor the lightest of the duties which fall to rulers in their regard for the common good, but that which comes first of all, is to keep inviolate the justice which is called distributive by caring impartially for each and every class of citizen.

Regard for the interests of the workers

35. However much it is necessary for all citizens without exception to make some contribution to the common good, which of itself benefits every individual, each enjoying his share, it is not possible for everyone to contribute in the same way or to an equal extent. For a state to exist at all, or even be thought possible, there have to be differences of degree among its citizens and these will persist however much forms of government may change. It will always be necessary to find people who will devote themselves to public affairs, make the laws, dispense justice, and by their counsel and authority administer affairs of state and the conduct of war. Such people have a leading part to play and ought to be accorded pre-eminence in every state. Anyone can see that their labours make an immediate and invaluable contribution to the common good. Then there are those who are engaged in some kind of business. These do not serve the state in the same way and to the same extent and, valuable though their service is, it is less direct. Lastly, it is obvious that the social good is principally a moral good, since it ought to be of such a kind that in enjoyment of it men are made better.

36. Nevertheless a characteristic of a well constituted state is an abundance of material goods, 'the use of which is necessary to virtuous action' (St Thomas, *De Regimine Principum*, I, xv). Such goods cannot be provided without the highly productive, skilled and painstaking labour of the unpropertied workers who are employed in farms and factories. So great is their vigour and efficiency in this regard that it may truly be said that it is only by the labour of working-men that states grow rich. Equity requires of the state, therefore, that it have particular regard for the unpropertied workers, so that those who bring so much of advantage to the community should themselves be well housed and clothed, enjoy greater comfort and suffer less hardship. Whence it follows that measures ought to be supported which are seen in some way to offer an improvement of the condition of the workers. Such solicitude is far from being harmful to others. Rather, it is greatly beneficial to the whole community, for it is of great importance to the state that those from whom

such necessary goods proceed are not themselves made wretched in every way.

The principle of intervention

37. We have said already that the state has no authority to swallow up either the individual or the family. To the extent that the common good is not endangered or any person hurt, justice requires full freedom of action for both. On those who govern lies the duty of caring for both the community and its parts. The community, because nature's charge to the ruling authority to maintain it makes care of the public welfare not only the supreme law of the state, but also its entire cause and the sole reason for its existence; the parts, because management of the state is to be used for the advantage of those who are governed, not of those who govern. Philosophy and the Christian faith concur in this conclusion. Since the power to rule originates in God and might be termed a participation in his supreme authority, the example to be followed is that of God's dominion which cares like a father for each individual creature as much as for the whole universe. The public authority must intervene, therefore, whenever the public interest or that of a particular class is harmed or endangered, provided that this is the only way to prevent or remove the evil.

The application of the principle of intervention

37.1 The maintenance of peace and order is of as much importance to the public as to private good. Its requirements are: the regulation of family life in accordance with God's commands and the law of nature; respect for and the fostering of religion; insistence upon the integrity of public and private morals and on the sanctity of justice, so that no one shall hurt another with impunity; care for young citizens so that they can grow up strong enough to serve and, if need be, defend the state. Wherefore, should it happen that a strike or a lock-out threatens disorder; or the natural ties of the family are weakened among the unpropertied; or the practice of religion among the workers is harmed because time is not allowed to them for its observance; or the integrity of morality is endangered in the factories by indiscriminate mixing of the sexes or other evil practices which create occasions of sin; or the employing class imposes unjust burdens on the working class or afflicts them with conditions inconsistent with the dignity of the human person; or too great a burden of work damages health or has insufficient regard for sex and age; in all such cases it is plainly true that, within certain limits, the force and authority of the law must be brought to bear. The facts of each particular case determine the limits to the application of the law; but evidently, the law must not be asked to do more nor to proceed further than is necessary to put right what is wrong or to avert what threatens.

38. Rights must be held sacred wherever they exist. The public authority must enable every individual to maintain his right by providing for the prevention and punishment of transgressions. Where the protection of private rights is concerned, special regard must be had for the poor and weak. Rich people can use their wealth to protect themselves and have less need of the state's protection; but the mass of the poor have nothing of their

own with which to defend themselves and have to depend above all upon the protection of the state. Because the wage-earners are numbered among the multitude of the poor, the state owes them particular care and protection.

Protection of private property

39. Particular attention must now be given to certain very important matters. At the head of the list is the duty to use the strength and protection of the law to safeguard private possessions. At the present time, when greed is rampant, it is of the greatest importance to keep the masses in the way of duty. It is permissible for people to try to better themselves provided that in doing so they commit no injustice, but neither justice nor reasons of public advantage permit them to take what belongs to others and to pounce upon the fortunes of others in the name of some foolish uniformity. Of course, the great majority of the workers prefer to improve their condition by honest work without inflicting injury on any one; nevertheless, there are not a few who, steeped in false opinions and eager for revolution, seek by every means to foment trouble and urge others on to violence. The public authority should intervene to put a brake on the activities of rabble-rousers and thus protect workers from bad influences and legitimate owners of property from the risk of plunder.

Strikes

40. Hours that are too long, work that is too heavy, wages said to be too low, these are reasons usually given by workers when they go on strike. These stoppages are a frequent cause of serious inconvenience, hurt employers and employed alike, do harm to trade and damage the general public interest, bringing violence and disorder close and endangering peace. Everybody should be seeking a remedy. Much the best and most efficacious course is for the law to intervene in good time before trouble starts, to prevent it from erupting by removing the causes of conflict between employers and workers.

Conditions of labour

41. There are many matters of a like kind in which the worker needs the protection of the state. His spiritual good comes first. Good and desirable though this mortal life is in itself, it is not the ultimate end for which we are born. It is only the way and the means by which, through knowledge of the truth and love of the good, we reach the perfection of the life of the soul. It is upon the soul that is impressed the divine image and likeness and it is in it that resides the sovereignty by virtue of which man is commanded to rule over the whole of the lower creation and to use all the earth and the sea for his own needs. 'Be fruitful, multiply, fill the earth and conquer it. Be masters of the fish of the sea, the birds of heaven and all the living animals on earth' (Gen. 1:28). In this respect all men are equal. There is here no difference between rich and poor, between masters and servants, between rulers and ruled: 'all belong to the same Lord' (Rom. 10:12). Nor may anyone violate with impunity the dignity of man, whom God himself treats 'with great reverence', or to impede progress to that perfection which corresponds with the eternal life in heaven.

41.1 It follows that no man has the power freely to consent to treatment not in accordance with his nature and to deliver his soul into slavery. The rights which are at stake are not at a man's own disposition. They are duties owed to God and must be scrupulously observed.

42. Hence the necessity of rest from work on holy days. Such rest is not to be thought of as indulgence in mere idleness; much less is it, as many would like it to be, an opportunity for spending money on vicious pursuits. It is to be a real rest from labour, hallowed by religion. When it is joined with religion, it withdraws a man from the daily round of work and business dealings and leaves him free to think about heavenly goods and pay to God the debt of adoration which is owing. Such, above all, is the nature of the seventh day of rest and the reason for it. This is what God decreed among the principal laws of the Old Testament: 'Remember the sabbath day and keep it holy' (Ex. 20:8); and what he taught by his own action, the mysterious rest which he took immediately after he had created man: 'He rested on the seventh day after all the work he had been doing' (Gen. 2:2).

43. As regards protection of this world's goods, the first task is to save the wretched workers from the brutality of those who make use of human beings as mere instruments for the unrestrained acquisition of wealth. It is evident that neither justice nor common humanity permits some men to impose upon others such a heavy burden of labour as will stupefy their minds and exhaust their bodies. A man's ability to work is limited, as is his nature, and there is a point beyond which he cannot go. He can develop his strength by training and use, but only if he obeys the rule of limited spells and frequent periods of rest. Care must be taken, therefore, not to lengthen the working day beyond a man's capacity. How much time there must be for rest depends upon the type of work, the circumstances of time and place and, particularly, the health of the workers. There must be appropriately shorter hours of work in occupations, such as mining for coal and quarrying iron and the like, where the burden of labour is particularly heavy and also injurious to health. Account should be taken also of the seasons of the year, for often what can be done easily at one time becomes quite impossible or extremely difficult at another. Finally, it is unjust to ask of a woman or a child work which is well within the capacity of a strong and healthy adult man. Great care must be taken always to prevent the employment of children in factories until they are sufficiently mature in mind and body and character. Calls which are made too early upon the strength of youth can beat it down, like new-grown grass too tender to be trodden, and quite destroy all possibility of education. It is equally true that certain types of work are less suitable for women, who are adapted rather to domestic tasks. It is these which best safeguard their womanly virtue and most correspond to the bringing-up of children and the well-being of the family. The general rule is that the greater the burden of labour the greater must be the provision for rest and recuperation: what work has taken away, rest from work must restore. In any contract made between employers and employed there is always the explicit or implicit condition that opportunities must be provided for both rest and recuperation. Any other agreement would be unjust, for there is a duty never to ask on one side, nor

promise on the other, neglect of the duties which a man owes either to God or to himself.

The just wage

44. The subject we now approach is of equally great importance. It is one which must be properly understood if we are not to offend against one party or the other. It is argued that, given that the scale of wages is decided by free agreement, it would appear that the employer fulfils the contract by paying the wage agreed upon, that nothing further is due from him and that injustice will be done only if the employer does not pay the full price or the worker does not perform the whole of his task. In these cases and not otherwise it would be right for the political authority to intervene and require each party to give to the other his due. This is an argument which a balanced judgment can neither entirely agree with nor easily accept. It does not take every consideration into account; and there is one consideration of the greatest importance which is omitted altogether. This is that to work is to exert oneself to obtain those things which are necessary for the various requirements of life and most of all for life itself. 'With sweat on your brow shall you eat your bread' (Gen. 3:19). Thus, human work has stamped upon it by nature, as it were, two marks peculiar to it. First, it is *personal*, because the force acting adheres to the person acting; and therefore it belongs entirely to the worker and is intended for his advantage. Second, it is *necessary*, because a man needs the results of his work to maintain himself in accordance with a command of nature itself which he must take particular care to obey. Were we to confine our attention to the personal aspect, we could take it for granted that the worker is free to agree to any rate of pay, however small. Since he works of his own free will, he is free to offer his work for a small payment, or for none at all.

45. But this position changes radically when to the personal we join the necessary aspect of labour, as we must. For although they can be separated in theory, in practice the two are inseparable. The reality is that it is every man's duty to stay alive. To fail in that is a crime. Hence arises necessarily the right to obtain those things which are needed to sustain life; and it is only the wage for his labour which permits the man at the bottom of the ladder to exercise this right. Let workers and employer, therefore, make any bargains they like, and in particular agree freely about wages; nevertheless, there underlies a requirement of natural justice higher and older than any bargain voluntarily struck: the wage ought not to be in any way insufficient for the bodily needs of a temperate and well-behaved worker. If, having no alternative and fearing a worse evil, a workman is forced to accept harder conditions imposed by an employer or contractor, he is the victim of violence against which justice cries out.

46. In these and similar cases—such, for instance, as the regulation of hours of labour in different industries or measures to safeguard health and safety at work—it is important to prevent the public authorities from thrusting themselves forward inconsiderately. Particularly because of the great variety of circumstances, times and places, it will be better to reserve such matters to

the judgment of associations, of which more will be said later, or to find some other way by which the interests of wage-earners can be safeguarded. In the last resort appeal must be made to the help and protection of the state.

Zeal for the promotion of thrift

47. If a worker earns a wage which enables him to make ample provision for the needs of himself, his wife and his children, he will find it easy to practise thrift. If he is sensible, does what nature itself advises him to do and cuts out excessive expenditure, he can contrive to acquire some little property. We have seen that effective efforts to put an end to the troubles facing us must start from the principle that the right to own privately must be maintained absolutely. For that reason the law should support this right and do what it can to enable as many as possible of the people to choose to exercise it. Most valuable consequences must follow from such action, the foremost among them being a more equitable distribution of wealth. The forces of social change have split states between two classes separated by an enormous gulf. On one side stands the extremely powerful party, because extremely rich; which, being in possession of the whole of industry and trade, turns all means of production to the service of its own ends and is able to take no small part in the government of the state. On the other side stands the multitude of the weak, destitute of resources, filled with bitterness and ever ready to revolt. However, if the efforts of the people were aroused by the hope of acquiring something of what the soil contains, it would gradually come about that class would move closer to class and the gulf which separates the greatest wealth from the deepest poverty be removed. An additional benefit would be more abundant supplies of all goods of the earth. When men work on what they know to be their own, they do so with more readiness and greater care. Indeed, they fall wholly in love with the land they cultivate and which yields them food and an abundance of other things for them and theirs. It is obvious how greatly this quickening of the will can add to the volume of production and the revenues of the state. And there is a third advantage to be looked for from this. Men prefer to remain in the land in which they were born and reared and they are less likely to leave it for foreign parts when it provides them with the means to obtain a better life.

47.1 However, one condition which must be satisfied if these benefits are to be obtained is that private means must not be exhausted by excessive taxation. Because the right to possess property privately is given by nature and not by human law, that law has no power to abolish it. All that the public authority may do is to regulate the use of property in keeping with the requirements of the common good. To take from private citizens under the guise of taxation more than is equitable is unjust and inhuman.

48. Finally, employers and workers can do much themselves in this matter by means of institutions which can bring timely aid to the needy and draw class closer to class. Examples of these are mutual benefits societies; foundations of various kinds to provide security for workers and their widows and orphans in cases of sudden emergency, illness and death; and welfare organizations which provide for the protection of children, adolescents and older people.

48.1 But the most important are working-men's associations, the aims of which include almost all of those listed above. The good work done by the old guilds of artisans is well known. They brought benefit to the members themselves and also did much to develop the crafts, as many monuments show. Working-men's associations have to be adapted now to the greater demands which are made on people in an age of wider education and new ways of life. It is gratifying that everywhere societies of this kind are being formed, either by workers alone or by both classes together, and it is greatly to be desired that they should become both more numerous and more efficient. We have spoken of them more than once and this is the place to demonstrate that with their many advantages they exist of their own right and to discuss how they should be organized and what they ought to do.

There is a natural right of association

49. Experience of his own weakness both impels and encourages a man to ally his forces with those of another. As the Bible puts it: 'Better two than one by himself, since thus their work is really profitable. If one should fall, the other helps him up; but woe to the man by himself with no one to help him up when he falls down' (Eccles. 4:9-10); and in another place: 'Brother helped by brother is a fortress, friends are like the bars of a keep' (Prov. 18:19). Just as a man is led by this natural propensity to associate with others in a political society, so also he finds it advantageous to join with his fellows in other kinds of societies, which though small and not independent are nevertheless true societies.

Because of their different immediate objectives there are many differences between these societies and the great society we call the state. The purpose for which the state exists concerns all the citizens as a whole because it comprises the common good—a good in which all and each have a right to participate in a proportionate degree. It is called a *public* society because in it 'men join themselves together to form a state' (St Thomas Aquinas, *Contra impugnantes Dei cultum et religionem*, c.II). By contrast, societies which are formed within the state are said to be *private*, and rightly so because their immediate purpose is the particular interest peculiar to their own members.

50. A private society is one which is formed to attain private objects, as when two or three form an association to trade in common' (*ibid.*). Although private societies exist within the state as parts of it, as it were, the state does not possess the power to make a general order against their existence. It is by virtue of the law of nature that men may enter into private societies and it is for the defence of the law, not for its destruction, that the state comes into being. If the state forbids its citizens to associate together it obviously makes war upon itself, for both it and the private associations are born of one and the same principle, the natural sociability of men.

51. There will be occasions when the law may rightly intervene against private associations, as when some among them pursue policies which are plainly contrary to honesty, justice and the good of the state itself. In cases such as these the public authority may with justice prevent the formation of associations and dissolve them where they exist. However, great care must be taken lest the rights of the citizens be emptied of content and unreasonable

regulations made under the pretence of public benefit. For laws have to be obeyed only when they accord with right reason and the eternal law of God.[1]

52. Here we bring to mind the confraternities of various kinds, the associations and religious orders which the authority of the Church and the holy will of Christian people have brought into being. History tells us how much benefit they have been to the human race right up to our own day. Looked at solely in the light of reason, it is evident that societies of this kind have been formed by natural right because the purposes for which they have been established are good. As far as they affect religious matters it is to the Church alone that they are answerable. The rulers of the state, therefore, have no just ground on which to claim any right over them or to interfere in their administration. It is rather the duty of the state to defend and help them and shield them from harm when they have need of protection. However, what has been done, particularly in our own day, has been very different from this. By making them subject to civil law, denying their corporate status and seizing their property the state has in many places attacked communities of this nature and inflicted many injustices upon them. The Church had a right in that property, as also had the members of the associations, those who endowed them for their purposes and those for whose benefit they were endowed. We cannot withhold our objection to such unjust and wicked despoliation. We have all the more reason for complaint because the law proclaims freedom of association even while it is proscribing societies of Christian men and refusing to them, who are men of peace seeking only the general good, what it grants freely to others whose objectives are harmful to both religion and the state.

53. Associations in immense variety and especially unions of workers are now more common than they have ever been. This is not the place to enquire into the origins of most of them, their aims or the methods they employ. There is plenty of evidence to confirm the opinion that many are in the hands of secret leaders and are used for purposes which are inconsistent with both Christian principles and the social good. They do all that they can to ensure that those who will not join them shall not eat. In this state of affairs Christian workers have but two alternatives: they can join these associations and greatly endanger their religion; or they can form their own and, with united strength, free themselves courageously from such injustice and intolerable oppression. That the second alternative must be chosen cannot be doubted by those who have no desire to see men's highest good put into extreme danger.

54. High praise is due to the many Catholics who have informed themselves, seen what is needed and tried to learn from experience by what honourable means they might be able to lead unpropertied workers to a better standard of living. They have taken up the workers' cause, seeking to raise the incomes of families and individuals, introduce equity into the relations between workers and employers and strengthen among both groups regard for duty and the teaching of the Gospel—teaching which inculcates moderation, forbids excess and safeguards harmony in the state between very differently situated men and organizations. We see eminent men coming together to learn from each other about these things and unite their forces to deal with them as effectively as possible. Others encourage different groups

of workers to form useful associations, advise them, give them practical help and enable them to find suitable and well-paid employment. The bishops offer their goodwill and support; and under their authority and guidance many of the clergy, both secular and regular, work assiduously for the spiritual interests of the members of these associations. Nor is there any lack of help from Catholics who are rich. Many have voluntarily associated themselves with the wage-earners and have spent large sums in founding and widely extending fraternal societies by means of which it becomes easy for a worker to acquire by his labour not only present advantages but also provision for honourable support in later life. How greatly commmunity affairs have been helped by such varied and willing activity is too well known to require emphasis. These associations give ground for hope for the future, provided that they continue to develop and to be prudently conducted. The state should protect them and the right they embody, but it must not intrude itself into their conduct of their own affairs. For the spirit which moves to life and action is fed from within and external force can all too easily crush it.

The right to self-government

55. An association has to be harmoniously organized and carefully administered if it is to arrive at agreed courses of action and a union of wills. Since citizens are possessed of a power freely to join together in associations, they must also have a right to choose freely how they shall manage their affairs and how legislate so as to attain most effectively the purposes they have set before themselves.

56. We do not consider it possible to set forth detailed rules for the constitution and administration of these self-governing societies. These are to be largely determined in the light of careful consideration of national characteristics, past experience, the nature and efficacy of the work to be done, the stage of economic development, and many other features peculiar to the time and place. What can be done is to enunciate a general law which holds good at all times: the constitution and administration of self-governing unions of workers must be such as will enable the societies to serve their purposes most speedily and completely and thus bring to their members as great as possible an increase in physical and spiritual well-being and access to property. It is clear that perfection of faith and morals ought to be seen as being of the first importance and it is to this end that the conduct of union affairs ought to be principally aimed. Unions managed otherwise must degenerate and become like those other societies which have no place for religion. What does it profit a man if through his union he obtains a plentiful supply of material goods but finds his soul imperilled by a lack of spiritual food? 'What, then, will a man gain if he wins the whole world and ruins his life?' (Mt. 16:26). Christ our Lord teaches us that this is the mark by which the Christian is to be distinguished from the heathen: 'It is the pagans who set their hearts on all these things . . . Set your hearts on his kingdom first, and on his righteousness, and all these things will be given you as well' (Mt. 6:32-3). Therefore, with God as their starting point let the unions make ample provision for the religious instruction of their members to give them a thorough awareness of what is due to God—what they ought to believe, what to hope for and what to do for the sake of their eternal salvation. Particularly

great care must be taken to arm them against false ideas and corrupt men who would seduce them from their path. The worker is to be urged to the worship of God and the whole-hearted practice of religion, and in particular to the observance of the holy days. Let him be led to reverence and love the Church, the mother common to us all. Let him submit to her teaching and frequent the sacraments, the divine instruments for removing stains from the soul and preparing him for holiness.

Functions, duties and rights of associations

57. When societies found their laws upon religion they can easily establish mutual relations among their members which secure their peace and prosperity. Offices should be allocated so as best to serve the common purpose, particular care being taken to ensure that distinctions do not breed discord and that the duties are distributed intelligently and defined clearly. Harm to individuals will follow if this is not done. Common funds must be properly administered and the aid appropriate to the needs of individuals be settled beforehand. The rights and duties of employers are to be suitably reconciled with the rights and duties of workers. Should a member of either class think himself to be in any way injured, nothing would be better than that the laws of the association should provide for the appointment of a committee of honest and prudent men, members of the association, whose judgment will determine the issue. It is of the greatest importance also to provide for jobs to be readily obtainable at all times and for funds to be available to relieve the needs of individuals in cases of industrial accident, sickness, old age and any other cause of distress.

58. The willing adoption of these means will enable these Catholic societies to meet the needs of the poor suitably and sufficiently and to bring desirable aid to the prosperity of the state. It is not rash to make provision for the future in the light of past experience. Times change, but it is remarkable how far conditions remain the same because God's providence governs all. He rules the course of events and turns it to serve the end he set before himself when he created the human race. We are told that in the early days of the Church it was cause for reproach against the Christians that the majority of them had to live precariously by manual labour or by begging for half-pence. But destitute of wealth and power though they were, they won the love of the wealthy owners of capital and the advocacy of the powerful. They showed themselves to be energetic, hard-working, peaceful, tenacious of justice and above all of charity to an exemplary degree. In the presence of that mode of life and behaviour all prejudice vanished, the disparagement of the ill-willed was silenced and the untruths of long established superstition gave way gradually to Christian truth.

58.1 The condition of the workers is the question of the hour. It will be answered one way or another, rationally or irrationally, and which way it goes is of the greatest importance to the state. Christian workers can easily end matters by forming associations, choosing wise leaders and entering upon the same road as that which their fathers followed with singular advantage to themselves and to the whole community. Great though the power of prejudiced opinion and of greed may be, unless the sense of what is right be deliberately and wickedly stifled the good will of the citizens will come spontaneously to turn more and more towards those whom they see to be industrious and moderate, putting justice before gain and the sacredness of duty before all things else. A further advantage to be looked for from such a course of action is the hope and opportunity of a better life that will be offered to workers who now either altogether despise the Christian faith or live contrary to its requirements. These men know for the most part that they have been fooled by false hopes and lying appearances. They feel themselves to be treated with great inhumanity by their greedy employers who regard them as no more than so many instruments of gain; but if they are members of a union it will be of one which has no love and no affection at its heart and is torn apart by the internal strife which is the perpetual accompaniment of proud and unbelieving poverty. Broken in spirit, worn out in body, how many wish to free themselves from servitude and humiliation! But though their desire is stong, human respect or the fear of hunger holds them back. The self-governing unions of Catholics can be of immense benefit to all of these men if they will invite them, hesitant though they are, to join them in their search for a solution to their difficulties and will receive them with faith and aid and comfort as they do so.

Conclusion

59. You know, venerable brethren, who are the people who must work hard to settle this very difficult question and how they must act. Everyone must gird himself for his part of the work and act with the utmost despatch to prevent delay from making utterly irremediable what is already so great an evil. Those who govern the state must make use of its laws and institutions; wealthy owners of the means of production and employers must be mindful of their duties; the unpropertied workers must exert themselves in legitimate ways in what is primarily their affair; and since, as we said at the beginning, religion alone is able totally to eradicate the evil, all men must be persuaded that the first thing they must do is to renew Christian morals. If that is not done even the wisest measures that can be devised to fit the case will fall short of their purpose.

59.1 As for the Church, whatever the time and circumstance her aid will never be looked for in vain. Those in whose hands lies the care of the general welfare must understand that the greater the freedom she is allowed, the more efficacious will be her action. All who are in holy orders must bring to the work their full strength of mind and body. Acting under your authority and inspired by your example, venerable brethren, they must never cease from setting before men of every class the pattern of life given to us by the Gospel. They must do all they can for the good of the people, particularly by way of strenuous efforts to nourish in themselves and to inspire in others the practice of charity, mistress and queen of all the virtues. For indeed it is from a great outpouring of charity that the desired results are principally to be looked for. It is of Christian charity that we speak, the virtue which sums up the whole Gospel law. It is this which makes a man ever and entirely ready to sacrifice himself for the good of others. It is this which is man's most effective antidote against worldly pride and immoderate love of self. It is of this that the Apostle Paul spoke in these words expressing its function and divine likeness: 'Love is always patient and kind; it is never jealous; love is never boastful or conceited; it is never rude or selfish; it does not take offence, and is not resentful. Love takes no pleasure in other people's sins but delights in the truth; it is always ready to excuse, to trust, to hope, and to endure whatever comes' (1 Cor. 13:4-7).

60. As a pledge of God's mercies and a sign of our good-will towards each and every one of you, venerable brethren, and to your clergy and people, we lovingly bestow upon you the apostolic benediction in the Lord.

61. Given at St Peter's, Rome, the 15th day of May 1891, in the fourteenth year of our pontificate.

LEO PP. XIII

Quadragesimo Anno

An encyclical letter of Pope Pius XI to Our Venerable Brethren the Patriarchs, Primates, Archbishops, Bishops and other Ordinaries in peace and communion with the Apostolic See, and likewise to all the Faithful of the Catholic world, on the reconstruction of the social order and of bringing it into conformity with the law of the Gospel, on the fortieth anniversary of the publication of Pope Leo XIII's encyclical letter, "Rerum Novarum".

Introduction

Perhaps without *Quadragesimo Anno* there would have been no modern Catholic social doctrine. *Rerum Novarum* might have been a once-off, rather than the start of a tradition. But in 1931 Pius XI was moved to commemorate the fortieth anniversary of Leo's letter, just as, thirty years after that, John XXIII commemorated its seventieth. Though aware of the dangers of the free-market economy, Pius shows himself rather more concerned about the spread of socialism, especially in its Communist form. As with Leo's letter, much space is devoted to the establishment of 'associations'. The Pope was later accused of giving suport to a form of syndicalism which propped up the 'corporative state' in some European and Latin American countries, but though this is undoubtedly to be found in the letter it is not a major theme. Also briefly mentioned, but given considerable emphasis in the text, is the 'principle of subsidiarity', which has come to play a major role in Catholic social doctrine. It should be noted that when Pius talks of 'Catholic Action' he is thinking primarily, though not entirely, of an organisation of that name. Nonetheless he presents all forms of Catholic Action as being pursued under the close direction of the hierarchy.

For further discussion of *Quadragesimo Anno* (QA), see the *Introduction*, pp. xiii The Latin text appeared in AAS 23 (1931), 177-228. In the original the paragraphs were not numbered, though the text was divided into the three major sections indicated by Roman numerals. Enumeration has been added in accordance with the policy outlined in the Editorial Note (p. ix). The cross-headings are as they appear in the margin of the official text.

Summary

Paras. 1-11: This encyclical is being written forty years after Leo XIII's 'On the condition of workers'. That letter had been occasioned by the divisions then existing within society, and particularly by the wretched situation in which workers found themselves.

[41]

Paras. 12-14: It was not written in vain. It was received enthusiastically both by the workers themselves and by those striving to improve their situation. There were some, however, who treated it with suspicion because it attacked Liberalism, and because it was in advance of its time. Others regarded it as laying down an ideal, but one which was unattainable.

Paras. 15-16: It is apropriate to express gratitude for the encyclical and to develop further certain points it made. There are three chief benefits which arose out of Leo's encyclical:

Paras. 17-22: The Church has time and again proclaimed its teaching on social issues. This teaching has since been developed by scholars into a new Catholic social science which has been widely taught through courses and publications until it has reached out beyond the Church, even apparently influencing those who were responsible for restoring peace after the War.

Paras. 23-24: Leo's teaching has also had practical consequences as clergy have devoted themselves—alongside their pastoral duties—to raising the dignity of the working class. Not only have more charitable works been undertaken, but there has been a growth in workers' organisations, often under the leadership of priests.

Paras. 25-28: Since Leo's encyclical, sovereigns have shown themselves increasingly concerned with the welfare of their citizens, often assisted by Catholics imbued with the spirit of Leo's teaching, so that a whole new body of welfare law has sprung up—though admittedly not always in strict conformity to Leo's teaching.

Paras. 29-38: Leo's encyclical must also be given credit for the growth of workers, or workers' and employers' associations. These are of three types. Some devote themselves to defense of their members' interests in the labour market; others provide mutual economic aid; others again are devoted to religious and moral duties. In some countries Catholics have been unable to form their own unions and have had to join secular ones—but in that instance it is important that societies to foster religious ends should also be created. Other associations have also come into existence under the influence of Leo's encyclical, though regrettably not yet enough associations of employers.

Paras. 39-40: The encyclical has been called the *Magna Charta* of workers. Some doubts have arisen about it, however, which need to be addressed.

Paras. 41-43: There is a doubt about the right of the Church to speak on social issues. But such issues raise moral questions. They also involve the law of nature, through which we reach up to God.

Paras. 44-49: There has been much debate about Pope Leo's insistence on the right to private property. This right must be defended, while avoiding the twin perils of individualism and collectivism. But the ownership of private property gives rise to obligations, and can be subject to control by the State in the name of the common good.

Paras. 50-51: Superfluous income must be devoted to almsgiving, or to the creation of work for others.

Paras. 52-62: Titles to ownership arise either out of occupancy, or out of labour: but the labour of one and the property (or capital) of another are closely associated. The owners of capital must not demand so much that workers are left with little or nothing; or the workers claim that all the fruit of their labour belongs to them. Wealth must be distributed in society for the good of all, yet the number of the poor, both industrial and rural workers, is increasing while the wealth of the rich is growing. There must be a more equitable distribution, so that through their savings the workers may have a more secure future.

Paras. 63-68: Arriving at a just wage is not easy, and wage-contracts need to be modified by a partnership contract.

Paras. 69-75: There are social issues involved in calculating wages—the need to provide for a wife and children, the financial situation of the business in which a person is employed, that unemployment either through too high or too low a level of wages be avoided, and goods be produced that are reasonably priced.

Paras. 76-80: What has been said so far only indirectly touches the social order, but that, too, must be reconstituted because it is an injustice to assign to a higher association what a lesser one can do: it is the State's role to regulate this principle of 'subsidiary function'.

Paras. 81-90: The State must also avoid conflict between classes, promoting instead cooperation through associations in which interests common to the whole industry or profession have first place. Nor must the State allow unbridled free economic competition, but promote social justice and charity—and not only within but also between nations.

Paras. 91-98: A system has recently been developed in which workers belong to one syndicate, employers to another, and both syndicates are represented in corporations which direct a particular industry, the State only intervening when conflict arises. Though it has its dangers, this system has many benefits, and its dangers may be averted if people are imbued with Catholic social doctrine.

Paras. 99-110: One of the major changes since Leo XIII's time has been the spread of the capitalist economic system, with the regrettable concentration of wealth and therefore power into the hands of a very few: free competition must be kept within bounds and brought under public authority to ensure that human society conform to the needs of the common good.

Paras. 110-129: Another change is in the nature of socialism which, in the form of Communism, seeks class warfare and the abolition of private property, and has caused terrible destruction in Eastern Europe and Asia. A more moderate form has retained the name of Socialism, but nonetheless its concept of society is incompatible with Christian truth because it believes human association is solely for material advantage, that the individual must be subordinate to society and that the higher goods of humanity must be sacrificed to the most efficient production of goods: Christian socialism is a contradiction in terms. Socialism has come to pervade society and culture, and many, even Catholics, have been attracted to it, unjustly accusing the Church of always siding with the rich. Those who have deserted the Church are invited to return to help restore society on the basis of social justice and charity, according to the mind of the Church, for only a return to Christian life and institutions will heal society.

Paras. 130-135: Modern social and economic life puts obstacles in the way of people saving their souls, for they are strongly incited to prefer the goods of this world to those of heaven. Governments should act to restrain the moral evils that arise from the economic system, but they have too often failed to do so. Both employers and employees are at risk.

Paras. 136-140: The only remedy is a return to the teaching of the Gospel which requires wealth to be gained only in a just and lawful manner. But justice itself will not do, for alone it can never bring about a union of mind and hearts: for that charity is needed. Many are already engaged on the task of restoring human society in Christ, those in Catholic Action, young workers and the leaders of workers' organisations, and future leaders of society.

Paras. 141-149: A world largely fallen into paganism has to be won back: clergy must seek and teach new apostles among both workers and employers as auxiliary soldiers of the Church. But so that the effort be not dissipated they should be united under the leadership and teaching guidance of the Church.

Venerable Brethren and Beloved Children, Health and Apostolic Benediction.

1. Forty years have passed since Leo XIII's peerless Encyclical, *On the Condition of Workers*, first saw the light, and the whole Catholic world, filled with grateful recollection, is undertaking to commemorate it with befitting solemnity.

2. Other Encyclicals of Our Predecessor had in a way prepared the path for that outstanding document and proof of pastoral care: namely, those on the family and the Holy Sacrament of Matrimony as the source of human society,[1] on the origin of civil authority[2] and its proper relations with the Church,[3] on the chief duties of Christian citizens,[4] against the tenets of Socialism,[5] against false teachings on human liberty,[6] and others of the same nature fully expressing the mind of Leo XIII. Yet the Encyclical, *On the Condition of Workers*, compared with the rest had this special distinction that at a time when it was most opportune and actually necessary to do so, it laid down for all mankind the surest rules to solve aright that difficult problem of human relations called 'the social question.'

The occasion

3. For toward the close of the nineteenth century, the new kind of economic life that had arisen and the new developments of industry had gone to the point in most countries that human society was clearly becoming divided more and more into two classes. One class, very small in number, was enjoying almost all the advantages which modern inventions so abundantly

provided; the other, embracing the huge multitude of working people, oppressed by wretched poverty, was vainly seeking escape from the straits wherein it stood.

4. Quite agreeable, of course, was this state of things to those who thought it in their abundant riches the result of inevitable economic laws and accordingly, as if it were for charity to veil the violation of justice which lawmakers not only tolerated but at times sanctioned, wanted the whole care of supporting the poor committed to charity alone. The workers, on the other hand, crushed by their hard lot, were barely enduring it and were refusing longer to bend their necks beneath so galling a yoke; and some of them, carried away by the heat of evil counsel, were seeking the overturn of everything, while others, whom Christian training restrained from such evil designs, stood firm in the judgment that much in this had to be wholly and speedily changed.

5. The same feeling those many Catholics, both priests and laymen, shared, whom a truly wonderful charity had long spurred on to relieve the unmerited poverty of the non-owning workers, and who could in no way convince themselves that so enormous and unjust an inequality in the distribution of this world's goods truly conforms to the designs of the all-wise Creator.

6. Those men were without question sincerely seeking an immediate remedy for this lamentable disorganization of States and a secure safeguard against worse dangers. Yet such is the weakness of even the best of human minds that, now rejected as dangerous innovators, now hindered in the good work by their very associates advocating other courses of action, and, uncertain in the face of various opinions, they were at a loss which way to turn.

7. In such a sharp conflict of mind, therefore, while the question at issue was being argued this way and that, nor always with calmness, all eyes as often before turned to the Chair of Peter, to that sacred depository of all truth whence words of salvation pour forth to all the world. And to the feet of Christ's Vicar on earth were flocking in unaccustomed numbers, men well versed in social questions, employers, and workers themselves, begging him with one voice to point out, finally, the safe road to them.

8. The wise Pontiff long weighed all this in his mind before God; he summoned the most experienced and learned to counsel; he pondered the issues carefully and from every angle. At last, admonished 'by the consciousness of His Apostolic Office'[7] lest silence on his part might be regarded as failure in his duty[8] he decided, in virtue of the Divine Teaching Office entrusted to him, to address not only the whole Church of Christ but all mankind.

9. Therefore on the fifteenth day of May, 1891, that long awaited voice thundered forth; neither daunted by the arduousness of the problem nor weakened by age but with vigorous energy, it taught the whole human family to strike out in the social question upon new paths.

Chief headings

10. You know, Venerable Brethren and Beloved Children, and understand full well the wonderful teaching which has made the Encyclical, *On the*

Condition of Workers, illustrious forever. The Supreme Pastor in this Letter, grieving that so large a portion of mankind should 'live undeservedly in miserable and wretched conditions,'[9] took it upon himself with great courage to defend 'the cause of the workers whom the present age had handed over, each alone and defenseless, to the inhumanity of employers and the unbridled greed of competitors.'[10] He sought no help from either Liberalism or Socialism, for the one had proved that it was utterly unable to solve the social problem aright, and the other, proposing a remedy far worse than the evil itself, would have plunged human society into great dangers.

11. Since a problem was being treated 'for which no satisfactory solution' is found 'unless religion and the Church have been called upon to aid,'[11] the Pope, clearly exercising his right and correctly holding that the guardianship of religion and the stewardship over those things that are closely bound up with it had been entrusted especially to him and relying solely upon the unchangeable principles drawn from the treasury of right reason and Divine Revelation, confidently and *as one having authority*,[12] declared and proclaimed 'the rights and duties within which the rich and the proletariat—those who furnish material things and those who furnish work—ought to be restricted in relation to each other,'[13] and what the Church, heads of States and the people themselves directly concerned ought to do.

12. The Apostolic voice did not thunder forth in vain. On the contrary, not only did the obedient children of the Church hearken to it with marvelling admiration and hail it with the greatest applause, but many also who were wandering far from the truth, from the unity of the faith, and nearly all who since then either in private study or in enacting legislation have concerned themselves with the social and economic question.

13. Feeling themselves vindicated and defended by the Supreme Authority on earth, Christian workers received this Encyclical with special joy. So, too, did all those noble-hearted men who, long solicitous for the improvement of the condition of the workers, had up to that time encountered almost nothing but indifference from many, and even rankling suspicion, if not open hostility, from some. Rightly, therefore, have all these groups constantly held the Apostolic Encyclical from that time in such high honor that to signify their gratitude they are wont, in various places and in various ways, to commemorate it every year.

14. However, in spite of such great agreement, there were some who were not a little disturbed; and so it happened that the teaching of Leo XIII, so noble and lofty and so utterly new to worldly ears, was held suspect by some, even among Catholics, and to certain ones it even gave offense. For it boldly attacked and overturned the idols of Liberalism, ignored long-standing prejudices, and was in advance of its time beyond all expectation, so that the slow of heart disdained to study this new social philosophy and the timid feared to scale so lofty a height. There were some also who stood, indeed, in awe at its splendor, but regarded it as a kind of imaginary ideal of perfection more desirable than attainable.

Scope of the present encyclical

15. Venerable Brethren and Beloved Children, as all everywhere and especially Catholic workers who are pouring from all sides into this Holy City, are celebrating with such enthusiasm the solemn commemoration of the fortieth anniversary of the Encyclical *On the Condition of Workers*, We deem it fitting on this occasion to recall the great benefits this Encyclical has brought to the Catholic Church and to all human society; to defend the illustrious Master's doctrine on the social and economic question against certain doubts and to develop it more fully as to some points; and lastly, summoning to court the contemporary economic regime and passing judgment on Socialism, to lay bare the root of the existing social confusion and at the same time point the only way to sound restoration: namely, the Christian reform of morals. All these matters which we undertake to treat will fall under three main headings, and this entire Encyclical will be devoted to their development.

I. Benefits from Rerum Novarum

16. To begin with the topic which we have proposed first to discuss, We cannot refrain, following the counsel of St. Ambrose[14] who says that 'no duty is more important than that of returning thanks,' from offering our fullest gratitude to Almighty God for the immense benefits that have come through Leo's Encyclical to the Church and to human society. If indeed We should wish to review these benefits even cursorily, almost the whole history of the social question during the last forty years would have to be recalled to mind. These benefits can be reduced conveniently, however, to three main points, corresponding to the three kinds of help which Our Predecessor ardently desired for the accomplishment of his great work of restoration.

1. What the Church has done

17. In the first place Leo himself clearly stated what ought to be expected from the Church:[15] 'Manifestly it is the Church which draws from the Gospel the teachings through which the struggle can be composed entirely, or, after its bitterness is removed, can certainly become more tempered. It is the Church, again, that strives not only to instruct the mind, but to regulate by her precepts the life and morals of individuals, and that ameliorates the condition of the workers through her numerous and beneficent institutions.'

Doctrinal Matters

18. The Church did not let these rich fountains lie quiescent in her bosom, but from them drew copiously for the common good of the longed-for peace. Leo himself and his Successors, showing paternal charity and pastoral constancy always, in defense especially of the poor and the weak,[16] proclaimed and urged without ceasing again and again by voice and pen the teaching on the social and economic question which *On the Condition of Workers* presented, and adapted it fittingly to the needs of time and of cirucumstance. And many bishops have done the same, who in their

continual and able interpretation of this same teaching have illustrated it with commentaries and in accordance with the mind and instructions of the Holy See provided for its application to the conditions and institutions of diverse regions.[17]

19. It is not surprising, therefore, that many scholars, both priests and laymen, led especially by the desire that the unchanged and unchangeable teaching of the Church should meet new demands and needs more effectively, have zealously undertaken to develop, with the Church as their guide and teacher, a social and economic science in accord with the conditions of our time.

20. And so, with Leo's Encyclical pointing the way and furnishing the light, a true Catholic social science has arisen, which is daily fostered and enriched by the tireless efforts of those chosen men whom We have termed auxiliaries of the Church. They do not, indeed, allow their science to lie hidden behind learned walls. As the useful and well attended courses instituted in Catholic universities, colleges, and seminaries, the social congresses and 'weeks' that are held at frequent intervals with most successful results, the study groups that are promoted, and finally the timely and sound publications that are disseminated everywhere and in every possible way, clearly show, these men bring their science out into the full light and stress of life.

21. Nor is the benefit that has poured forth from Leo's Encyclical confined within these bounds; for the teaching which *On the Condition of Workers* contains has gradually and imperceptibly worked its way into the minds of those outside Catholic unity who do not recognize the authority of the Church. Catholic principles on the social question have as a result, passed little by little into the patrimony of all human society, and We rejoice that the eternal truths which Our Predecessor of glorious memory proclaimed so impressively have been frequently invoked and defended not only in non-Catholic books and journals but in legislative halls and also courts of justice.

22. Furthermore, after the terrible war, when the statesmen of the leading nations were attempting to restore peace on the basis of a thorough reform of social conditions, did not they, among the norms agreed upon to regulate in accordance with justice and equity the labor of the workers, give sanction to many points that so remarkably coincide with Leo's principles and instructions as to seem consciously taken therefrom? The Encyclical *On the Condition of Workers*, without question, has become a memorable document and rightly to it may be applied the words of Isaiah: 'He shall set up a standard to the nations.'[18]

Practical applications

23. Meanwhile, as Leo's teachings were being widely diffused in the minds of men, with learned investigations leading the way, they have come to be put into practice. In the first place, zealous efforts have been made, with active good will, to lift up that class which on account of the modern expansion of industry had increased to enormous numbers but not yet had obtained its rightful place or rank in human society and was, for that reason, all but neglected and despised—the workers, We mean—to whose improvement, to

the great advantage of souls, the diocesan and regular clergy, though burdened with other pastoral duties, have under the leadership of the Bishops devoted themselves. This constant work, undertaken to fill the workers' souls with the Christian spirit, helped much also to make them conscious of their true dignity and render them capable, by placing clearly before them the rights and duties of their class, of legitimately and happily advancing and even of becoming leaders of their fellows.

24. From that time on, fuller means of livelihood have been more securely obtained; for not only did works of beneficence and charity begin to multiply at the urging of the Pontiff, but there have also been established everywhere new and continuously expanding organizations in which workers, draftsmen, farmers and employees of every kind, with the counsel of the Church and frequently under the leadership of her priests, give and receive mutual help and support.

2. What civil authority has done

25. With regard to civil authority, Leo XIII, boldly breaking through the confines imposed by Liberalism, fearlessly taught that government must not be thought a mere guardian of law and of good order, but rather must put forth every effort so that 'through the entire scheme of laws and institutions ...both public and individual well-being may develop spontaneously out of the very structure and administration of the State.'[19] Just freedom of action must, of course, be left both to individual citizens and to families, yet only on condition that the common good be preserved and wrong to any individual be abolished. The function of the rulers of the State, moreover, is to watch over the community and its parts; but in protecting private individuals in their rights, chief consideration ought to be given to the weak and the poor. 'For the nation, as it were, of the rich is guarded by its own defences and is in less need of governmental protection, whereas the suffering multitude, without the means to protect itself relies especially on the protection of the State. Wherefore, since wage-workers are numbered among the great mass of the needy, the State must include them under its special care and foresight.'[20]

26. We, of course, do not deny that even before the Encyclical of Leo, some rulers of peoples have provided for certain of the more urgent needs of the workers and curbed more flagrant acts of injustice inflicted upon them. But after the Apostolic voice had sounded from the Chair of Peter throughout the world, rulers of nations, more fully alive at last to their duty, devoted their minds and attention to the task of promoting a more comprehensive and fruitful social policy.

27. And while the principles of Liberalism were tottering, which had long prevented effective action by those governing the State, the Encyclical *On the Condition of Workers* in truth impelled peoples themselves to promote a social policy on truer grounds and with greater intensity, and so strongly encouraged good Catholics to furnish valuable help to heads of States in this field that they often stood forth as illustrious champions of this new policy even in legislatures. Sacred ministers of the Church, thoroughly imbued with Leo's teaching, have, in fact, often proposed to the votes of the peoples'

representatives the very social legislation that has been enacted in recent years and have resolutely demanded and promoted its enforcement.

28. A new branch of law, wholly unknown to the earlier time, has arisen from this continuous and unwearied labor to protect vigorously the sacred rights of the workers that flow from their dignity as men and as Christians. These laws undertake the protection of life, health, strength, family, homes, workshops, wages and labor hazards, in fine, everything which pertains to the condition of wage workers, with special concern for women and children. Even though these laws do not conform exactly everywhere and in all respects to Leo's recommendations, still it is undeniable that much in them savors of the Encyclical, *On the Condition of Workers*, to which great credit must be given for whatever improvement has been achieved in the workers' condition.

3. What the concerned parties have done

29. Finally, the wise Pontiff showed that 'employers and workers themselves can accomplish much in this matter, manifestly through those institutions by the help of which the poor are opportunely assisted and the two classes of society are brought closer to each other.'[21] First place among these institutions, he declares, must be assigned to associations that embrace either workers alone or workers and employers together. He goes into considerable detail in explaining and commending these associations and expounds with a truly wonderful wisdom their nature, purpose, timeliness, rights, duties, and regulations.

30. These teachings were issued indeed most opportunely. For at that time in many nations those at the helm of State, plainly imbued with Liberalism, were showing little favor to workers' associations of this type; nay, rather they openly opposed them, and while going out of their way to recognize similar organizations of other classes and show favor to them, they were with criminal injustice denying the natural right to form associations to those who needed it most to defend themselves from ill treatment at the hands of the powerful. There were even some Catholics who looked askance at the efforts of workers to form associations of this type as if they smacked of a socialistic or revolutionary spirit.

Worker's associations

31. The rules, therefore, which Leo XIII issued in virtue of his authority, deserve the greatest praise in that they have been able to break down this hostility and dispel these suspicions; but they have even a higher claim to distinction in that they encouraged Christian workers to found mutual associations according to their various occupations, taught them how to do so, and resolutely confirmed in the path of duty a goodly number of those whom socialist organizations strongly attracted by claiming to be the sole defenders and champions of the lowly and oppressed.

32. With respect to the founding of these societies, the Encyclical *On the Condition of Workers* most fittingly declared that 'workers' associations ought to be so constituted and so governed as to furnish the most suitable and most convenient means to attain the object proposed, which consists in this,

that the individual members of the association secure, so far as is possible, an increase in the goods of body, of soul, and of property,' yet it is clear that 'moral and religious perfection ought to be regarded as their principal goal, and that their social organization as such ought above all to be directed completely by this goal.'[22] For 'when the regulations of associations are founded upon religion, the way is easy toward establishing the mutual relations of the members, so that peaceful living together and prosperity will result.'[23]

33. To the founding of these associations the clergy and many of the laity devoted themselves everywhere with truly praiseworthy zeal, eager to bring Leo's program to full realization. Thus associations of this kind have molded truly Christian workers who, in combining harmoniously the diligent practice of their occupation with the salutary precepts of religion, protect effectively and resolutely their own temporal interests and rights, keeping a due respect for justice and a genuine desire to work together with other classes of society for the Christian renewal of all social life.

34. These counsels and instructions of Leo XIII were put into effect differently in different places according to varied local conditions. In some places one and the same association undertook to attain all the ends laid down by the Pontiff; in others, because circumstances suggested or required it, a division of work developed and separate associations were formed. Of these, some devoted themselves to the defense of the rights and legitimate interests of their members in the labor market; others took over the work of providing mutual economic aid; finally still others gave all their attention to the fulfillment of religious and moral duties and other obligations of like nature.

35. This second method has especially been adopted where either the laws of a country, or certain special economic institutions, or that deplorable dissension of minds and hearts so widespread in contemporary society and an urgent necessity of combating with united purpose and strength the massed ranks of revolutionarists, have prevented Catholics from founding purely Catholic labor unions. Under these conditions, Catholics seem almost forced to join secular labor unions. These unions, however, should always profess justice and equity and give Catholic members full freedom to care for their own conscience and obey the laws of the Church. It is clearly the office of bishops, when they know that these associations are on account of circumstances necessary and are not dangerous to religion, to approve of Catholic workers joining them, keeping before their eyes, however, the principles and precautions laid down by Our Predecessor, Pius X of holy memory.[24] Among these precautions the first and chief is this: Side by side with these unions there should always be associations zealously engaged in imbuing and forming their members in the teaching of religion and morality so that they in turn may be able to permeate the unions with that good spirit which should direct them in all their activity. As a result, the religious associations will bear good fruit even beyond the circle of their own membership.

36. To the Encyclical of Leo, therefore, must be given this credit, that these associations of workers have so flourished everywhere that while, alas, still surpassed in numbers by socialist and communist organizations, they already

embrace a vast multitude of workers and are able, within the confines of each nation as well as in wider assemblies, to maintain vigorously the rights and legitimate demands of Catholic workers and insist also on the salutary Christian principles of society.

Associations in other classes

37. Leo's learned treatment and vigorous defense of the natural right to form associations began, furthermore, to find ready application to other associations also and not alone to those of the workers. Hence no small part of the credit must, it seems, be given to this same Encyclical of Leo for the fact that among farmers and others of the middle class most useful associations of this kind are seen flourishing to a notable degree and increasing day by day, as well as other institutions of a similar nature in which spiritual development and economic benefit are happily combined.

Associations of employers

38. But if this cannot be said of organizations which Our same Predecessor intensely desired established among employers and managers of industry—and We certainly regret that they are so few—the condition is not wholly due to the will of men but to far graver difficulties that hinder associations of this kind which We know well and estimate at their full value. There is, however, strong hope that these obstacles also will be removed soon, and even now We greet with the deepest joy of Our soul, certain by no means insignificant attempts in this direction, the rich fruits of which promise a still richer harvest in the future.[25]

Conclusion: Rerum Novarum
Magna Charta of the Social Order

39. All these benefits of Leo's Encyclical, Venerable Brethren and Beloved Children, which We have outlined rather than fully described, are so numerous and of such import as to show plainly that this immortal document does not exhibit a merely fanciful, even if beautiful, ideal of human society. Rather did our Predecessor draw from the Gospel and, therefore, from an ever-living and life-giving fountain, teachings capable of greatly mitigating, if not immediately terminating that deadly internal struggle which is rending the family of mankind. The rich fruits which the Church of Christ and the whole human race have, by God's favour, reaped therefrom unto salvation prove that some of this good seed, so lavishly sown forty years ago, fell on good ground. On the basis of the long period of experience, it cannot be rash to say that Leo's Encyclical has proved itself the *Magna Charta* upon which all Christian activity in the social field ought to be based, as on a foundation. And those who would seem to hold in little esteem this Papal Encyclical and its commemoration either blaspheme what they know not, or understand nothing of what they are only superficially acquainted with, or if they do understand convict themselves formally of injustice and ingratitude.

40. Yet since in the course of these same years, certain doubts have arisen concerning either the correct meaning of some parts of Leo's Encyclical or

conclusions to be deduced therefrom, which doubts in turn have even among Catholics given rise to controversies that are not always peaceful; and since, furthermore, new needs and changed conditions of our age have made necessary a more precise application of Leo's teaching or even certain additions thereto, We most gladly seize this fitting occasion, in accord with Our Apostolic Office through which We are debtors to all,[26] to answer, so far as in Us lies, these doubts and these demands of the present day.

II. The authority of the Church in social an economic matters

41. Yet before proceeding to explain these matters, that principle which Leo XIII so clearly established must be laid down at the outset here, namely, that there resides in Us the right and duty to pronounce with supreme authority upon social and economic matters.[27] Certainly the Church was not given the commission to guide men to an only fleeting and perishable happiness but to that which is eternal. Indeed 'the Church holds that it is unlawful for her to mix without cause in these temporal concerns'[28]; however, she can in no wise renounce the duty God entrusted to her to interpose her authority, not of course in matters of technique for which she is neither suitably equipped nor endowed by office, but in all things that are connected with the moral law. For as to these, the deposit of truth that God committed to Us and the grave duty of disseminating and interpreting the whole moral law, and of urging it in season and out of season, bring under and subject to Our supreme jurisdiction not only social order but economic activities themselves.

42. Even though economics and moral science employs each its own principles in its own sphere, it is, nevertheless, an error to say that the economic and moral orders are so distinct from and alien to each other that the former depends in no way on the latter. Certainly the laws of economics, as they are termed, being based on the very nature of material things and on the capacities of the human body and mind, determine the limits of what productive human effort cannot, and of what it can attain in the economic field and by what means. Yet it is reason itself that clearly shows, on the basis of the individual and social nature of things and of men, the purpose which God ordained for all economic life.

43. But it is only the moral law which, just as it commands us to seek our supreme and last end in the whole scheme of our activity, so likewise commands us to seek directly in each kind of activity those purposes which we know that nature, or rather God the Author of nature, established for that kind of action, and in orderly relationship to subordinate such immediate purposes to our supreme and last end. If we faithfully observe this law, then it will follow that the particular purposes, both individual and social, that are sought in the economic field will fall in their proper place in the universal order of purposes, and We, in ascending through them, as it were by steps, shall attain the final end of all things, that is God, to Himself and to us, the supreme and inexhaustible Good.

1. Right of property

44. But to come down to particular points, We shall begin with ownership or the right of property. Venerable Brethren and Beloved Children, you know

that Our Predecessor of happy memory strongly defended the right of property against the tenets of the Socialists of his time by showing that it abolition would result, not to the advantage of the working class, but to their extreme harm. Yet since there are some who calumniate the Supreme Pontiff, and the Church herself, as if she had taken and were still taking the part of the rich against the non-owning workers—certainly no accusation is more unjust than that—and since Catholics are at variance with one another concerning the true and exact mind of Leo, it has seemed best to vindicate this, that is, the Catholic teaching on this matter from calumnies and safeguard it from false interpretations.

Its individual and social character

45. First, then, let it be considered as certain and established that neither Leo nor those theologians who have taught under the guidance and authority of the Church have ever denied or questioned the twofold character of ownership, called usually individual or social according as it regards either separate persons or the common good. For they have always unanimously maintained that nature, rather the Creator Himself, has given man the right of private ownership not only that individuals may be able to provide for themselves and their families but also that the goods which the Creator destined for the entire family of mankind may through this institution truly serve this purpose. All this can be achieved in no wise except through the maintenance of a certain and definite order.

46. Accordingly, twin rocks of shipwreck must be carefully avoided. For, as one is wrecked upon, or comes close to, what is known as 'individualism' by denying or minimizing the social and public character of the right of property, so by rejecting or minimizing the private and individual character of this same right, one inevitably runs into 'collectivism' or at least closely approaches its tenets. Unless this is kept in mind, one is swept from his course upon the shoals of that moral, juridical, and social modernism which We denounced in the Encyclical issued at the beginning of Our Pontificate.[29] And, in particular, let those realize this who, in their desire for innovation, do not scruple to reproach the Church with infamous calumnies, as if she had allowed to creep into the teachings of her theologians a pagan concept of ownership which must be completely replaced by another that they with amazing ignorance call 'Christian.'

Obligations of ownership

47. In order to place definite limits on the controversies that have arisen over ownership and its inherent duties there must be first laid down as foundation a principle established by Leo XIII: The right of property is distinct from its use.[30] That justice called commutative commands sacred respect for the division of possessesions and forbids invasion of others' rights through the exceeding of the limits of one's own property; but the duty of owners to use their property only in a right way does not come under this type of justice, but under other virtues, obligations of which 'cannot be enforced by legal action.'[31] Therefore, they are in error who assert that ownership and its right use are limited by the same boundaries; and it is much farther still from the

truth to hold that a right to property is destroyed or lost by reason of abuse or non-use.

48. Those, therefore, are doing a work that is truly salutary and worthy of all praise who, while preserving harmony among themselves and the integrity of the traditional teaching of the Chuirch, seek to define the inner nature of these duties and their limits whereby either the right of property itself or its use, that is, the exercise of ownership, is circumscribed by the necessities of social living. On the other hand, those who seek to restrict the individual character of ownership to such a degree that in fact they destroy it are mistaken and in error.

Power of state in ownership

49. It follows from what We have termed the individual and at the same time social character of ownership, that men must consider in this matter not only their own advantage but also the common good. To define these duties in detail when necessity requires and the natural law has not done so, is the function of those in charge of the State. Therefore, public authority, under the guiding light always of the natural and divine law, can determine more accurately upon consideration of the true requirements of the common good, what is permitted and what is not permitted to owners in the use of their property. Moreover, Leo XIII wisely taught 'that God has left the limits of private possessions to be fixed by the industry of men and institutions of peoples.'[32] That history proves ownership, like other elements of social life, to be not absolutely unchanging, We once declared as follows: 'What divers forms has property had, from that primitive form among rude and savage peoples, which may be observed in some places even in our time, to the form of possession in the patriarchal age; and so further to the various forms under tyranny (We are using the word tyranny in its classical sense); and then through the feudal and monarchial forms down to the various types which are to be found in more recent times.'[33] That the State is not permitted to discharge its duty arbitrarily is, however, clear. The natural right itself both of owning goods privately and of passing them on by inheritance ought always to remain intact and inviolate, since this indeed is a right that the State cannot take away: 'For man is older than the State,'[34] and also 'domestic living together is prior both in thought and in fact to uniting into a polity.'[35] Wherefore the wise Pontiff declared that it is grossly unjust for a State to exhaust private wealth through the weight of imposts and taxes. 'For since the right of possessing goods privately has been conferred not by man's law, but by nature, public authority cannot abolish it, but can only control its exercise and bring it into conformity with the common weal.'[36] Yet when the State brings private ownership into harmony with the needs of the common good, it does not commit a hostile act against private owners but rather does them a friendly service; for it thereby effectively prevents the private possession of goods, which the Author of nature in His most wise providence ordained for the support of human life, from causing intolerable evils and thus rushing to its own destruction; it does not destroy private possessions, but safeguards them; and it does not weaken private property rights, but strengthens them.

[55]

Obligations regarding superfluous income

50. Furthermore, a person's superfluous income, that is, income which he does not need to sustain life fittingly and with dignity, is not left wholly to his own free determination. Rather the Sacred Scriptures and the Fathers of the Church constantly declare in the most explicit language that the rich are bound by a very grave precept to practice almsgiving, beneficence, and munificence.

51. Expending larger incomes so that opportunity for gainful work may be abundant, provided, however, that this work is applied to producing really useful goods, ought to be considered, as We deduce from the principles of the Angelic Doctor,[37] an outstanding exemplification of the virtue of munifience an one particularly suited to the needs of the times.

Titles in acquiring ownership

52. That ownership is originally acquired both by occupancy of a thing not owned by any one and by labour, or, as is said, by specification, the tradition of all ages as well as the teaching of Our Predecessor Leo clearly testifies. For, whatever some idly say to the contrary, no injury is done to any person when a thing is occupied that is available to all but belongs to no one; however, only that labour which a man performs in his own name and by virtue of which a new form or increase has been given to a thing grants him title to these fruits.

2. Property ('capital') and labour

53. Far different is the nature of work that is hired out to others and expended on the property of others. To this indeed especially applies what Leo XIII says is 'incontestible,' namely, that 'the wealth of nations originates from no other source than from the labour of workers.'[38] For is it not plain that the enormous volume of goods that makes up human wealth is produced by and issues from the hands of the workers that either toil unaided or have their efficiency marvelously increased by being equipped with tools or machines? Every one knows, too, that no nation has ever risen out of want and poverty to a better and nobler condition save by the enormous and combined toil of all the people, both those who manage work and those who carry out directions. But it is no less evident that, had not God the Creator of all things, in keeping with His goodness, first generously bestowed natural riches and resouces—the wealth and forces of nature—such supreme efforts would have been idle and vain, indeed could never even have begun. For what else is work but to use or exercise the energies of mind and body on or through these very things? And in the application of natural resources to human use the law of nature, or rather God's will promulgated by it, demands that right order be observed. This order consists in this: that each thing have its proper owner. Hence it follows that unless a man is expending labour on his own property, the labour of one person and the property of another must be associated, for neither can produce anything without the other. Leo XIII certainly had this in mind when he wrote: 'Neither capital can do without labour, nor labour without capital.'[39] Wherefore it is wholly false to ascribe to property alone or to labour alone whatever has been

obtained through the combined effort of both, and it is wholly unjust for either, denying the efficacy of the other, to arrogate to itself whatever has been produced.

Unjust claims of 'capital'

54. Property, that is,'capital,' has undoubtedly long been able to appropriate too much to itself. Whatever was produced, whatever returns accrued, capital claimed for itself, hardly leaving to the worker enough to restore and renew his strength. For the doctrine was preached that all accumulation of capital falls by an absolutely insuperable economic law to the rich, and that by the same law the workers are given over and bound to perpetual want, to the scantiest of livelihoods. It is true, indeed, that things have not always and everywhere corresponded with this sort of teaching of the so-called Manchesterian Liberals; yet it cannot be denied that economic-social institutions have moved steadily in that direction. That these false ideas, these erroneous suppositions, have been vigorously assailed, and not by those alone who through them were being deprived of their innate right to obtain better conditions, will surprise no one.

Unjust claims of labour

55. And therefore, to the harassed workers there have come 'intellectuals', as they are called, setting up in opposition to a fictitious law the equally fictitious moral principle that all products and profits, save only enough to repair and renew capital, belong by very right to the workers. This error, much more specious than that of certain of the socialists who hold that whatever serves to produce goods ought to be transferred to the State or, as they say 'socialized,' is consequently all the more dangerous and the more apt to deceive the unwary. It is an alluring poison which many have eagerly drunk whom open Socialism had not been able to deceive.

Principle of just distribution

56. Unquestionably, so as not to close against themselves the road to justice and peace through these false tenets, both parties ought to have been forewarned by the wise words of Our Predecessor: 'However the earth may be apportioned among private owners, it does not cease to serve the common interests of all.'[40] This same doctrine We ourselves also taught above in declaring that the division of goods which results from private ownership was established by nature itself in order that created things may serve the needs of mankind in fixed and stable order. Lest one wander from the straight path of truth, this is something that must be continually kept in mind.

57. But not every distribution among human beings of property and wealth is of a character to attain either completely or to a satisfactory degree of perfection the end which God intends. Therefore, the riches that economic-social developments constantly increase ought to be so distributed among individual persons and classes that the common advantage of all, which Leo XIII had praised, will be safeguarded; in other words, that the common good of all society will be kept inviolate. By this law of social justice, one class is forbidden to exclude the other from sharing in the benefits. Hence the class

of the wealthy violates this law no less, when, as if free from care on account of its wealth, it thinks it the right order of things for it to get everything and the worker nothing, than does the non-owning working class when, angered deeply at outraged justice and too ready to assert wrongly the one right it is conscious of, it demands for itself everything as if produced by its own hands, and attacks and seeks to abolish, therefore, all property and returns or incomes, of whatever kind they are or whatever the function they perform in human society, that have not been obtained by labour, and for no other reason save that they are of such a nature. And in this connection We must not pass over the unwarranted and unmerited appeal made by some to the Apostle when he said: 'If any man will not work neither let him eat.'[41] For the Apostle is passing judgment on those who are unwilling to work, although they can and ought to, and he admonishes us that we ought diligently to use our time and energies of body and mind and not be a burden to others when we can provide for ourselves. But the Apostle in no wise teaches that labor is the sole title to a living or an income.[42]

58. To each, therefore, must be given his own share of goods, and the distribution of created goods, which, as every discerning person knows, is laboring today under the gravest evils due to the huge disparity between the few exceedingly rich and the unnumbered propertyless, must be effectively called back to and brought into conformity with the norms of the common good, that is, social justice.

3. Redemption of the non-owning workers

59. The redemption of the non-owning workers—this is the goal that Our Predecessor declared must necessarily be sought. And the point is the more emphatically to be asserted and more insistently repeated because the commands of the Pontiff, salutary as they are, have not infrequently been consigned to oblivion either because they were deliberately suppressed by silence or thought impracticable although they both can and ought to be put into effect. And these commands have not lost their force and wisdom for our time because that 'pauperism' which Leo XIII beheld in all its horror is less widespread. Certainly the condition of the workers has been improved and made more equitable especially in the more civilized and wealthy countries where the workers can no longer be considered universally overwhelmed with misery and lacking the necessities of life. But since manufacturing and industry have so rapidly pervaded and occupied countless regions, not only in the countries called new, but also in the realms of the Far East that have been civilized from antiquity, the number of the non-owning working poor has increased enormously and their groans cry to God from the earth. Added to them is the huge army of rural wage workers, pushed to the lowest level of existence and deprived of all hope of ever acquiring 'some property in land,'[43] and, therefore, permanently bound to the status of non-owning worker unless suitable and effective remedies are applied.

Conditions to be overcome by wage earner ownership

60. Yet while it is true that the status of non-owning worker is to be carefully distinguished from pauperism, nevertheless the immense multitude of the

non-owning workers on the one hand and the enormous riches of certain very wealthy men on the other establish an unanswerable argument that the riches which are so abundantly produced in our age of 'industrialism', as it is called, are not rightly distributed and equitably made available to the various classes of the people.

61. Therefore, with all our strength and effort we must strive that at least in the future the abundant fruits of production will accrue equitably to those who are rich and will be distributed in ample sufficiency among the workers—not that these may become remiss in work, for man is born to labor as the bird to fly—but that they may increase their property by thrift, that they may bear, by wise management of this increase in property, the burdens of family life with greater ease and security, and that, emerging from the insecure lot in life in whose uncertainties non-owning workers are cast, they may be able not only to endure the vicissitudes of earthly existence but have also assurance that when their lives are ended they will provide in some measure for those they leave after them.

62. All these things which Our Predecessor has not only suggested but clearly and openly proclaimed, We emphasize with renewed insistence in our present Encyclical; and unless utmost efforts are made without delay to put them into effect, let no one persuade himself that public order, peace, and the tranquillity of human society can be effectively defended against agitators of revolution.

4. Just wages and salaries

63. As We have already indicated, following in the footsteps of Our Predecessor, it will be impossible to put these principles into practice unless the non-owning workers through industry and thrift advance to the state of possessing some little property. But except from pay for work, from what source can a man who has nothing else but work from which to obtain food and the necessaries of life set anything aside for himself through practicing frugality? Let us, therefore, explaining and developing wherever necessary Leo XIII's teachings and precepts, take up this question of wages and salaries which he called one 'of very great importance.'[44]

Working for wages not essentially wrong

64. First of all, those who declare that a contract of hiring and being hired is unjust of its own nature, and hence a partnership-contract must take its place, are certainly in error and gravely misrepresent Our Predecessor whose Encyclical not only accepts working for wages or salaries but deals at some length with its regulation in accordance with the rules of justice.

65. We consider it more advisable, however, in the present condition of human society that, so far as is possible, the work-contract be somewhat modified by a partnership-contract, as is already being done in various ways and with no small advantage to workers and owners. Workers and the employees thus become sharers in ownership or management or participate in some fashion in the profits received.

66. The just amount of pay, however, must be calculated not on a single basis

but on several, as Leo XIII already wisely declared in these words: 'To establish a rule of pay in accord with justice, many factors must be taken into account.'[45]

67. By this statement he plainly condemned the shallowness of those who think that this most difficult matter is easily solved by the application of a single rule or measure—and one quite false.

68. For they are greatly in error who do not hesitate to spread the principle that labour is worth and must be paid as much as its products are worth, and that consequently the one who hires out his labour has the right to demand all that is produced through his labour. How far this is from the truth is evident from that We have already explained in treating of property and labour.

Individual and social character of work

69. It is obvious that, as in the case of ownership, so in the case of work, especially work hired out to others, there is a social aspect also to be considered in addition to the personal or individual aspect. For man's productive effort cannot yield its fruits unless a truly social and organic body exists, unless a social and juridical order watches over the exercise of work, unless the various occupations, being interdependent, cooperate with and mutually complete one another, and, what is still more important, unless mind, material things, and work combine and form as it were a single whole. Therefore, where the social and individual nature of work is neglected, it will be impossible to evaluate work justly and pay it according to justice.

Three points to be considered

70. Conclusions of the greatest importance follow from this twofold character which nature has impressed on human work, and it is in accordance with these that wages ought to be regulated and established.

a) Support of the worker and his family

71. In the first place, the worker must be paid a wage sufficient to support him and his family.[46] That the rest of the family should also contribute to the common support, according to the capacity of each, is certainly right, as can be observed especially in the families of farmers, but also in the families of many craftsmen and small shopkeepers. But to abuse the years of childhood and the limited strength of women is grossly wrong. Mothers, concentrating on household duties, should work primarily in the home or in its immediate vicinity. It is an intolerable abuse, and to be abolished at all cost, for mothers on account of the father's low wage to be forced to engage in gainful occupations outside the home to the neglect of their proper cares and duties, especially the training of children. Every effort must therefore be made that fathers of families receive a wage large enough to meet ordinary family needs adequately. But if this cannot always be done under existing circumstances, social justice demands that changes be introduced as soon as possible whereby such a wage will be assured to every adult workingman. It will not be out of place here to render merited praise to all, who with a wise and useful purpose, have tried and tested various ways of adjusting the pay for

work to family burdens in such a way that, as these increase, the former may be raised and indeed, if the contingency arises, there may be enough to meet extraordinary needs.

b) Condition of the business

72. In determining the amount of the wage, the condition of a business and of the one carrying it on must also be taken into account; for it would be unjust to demand excessive wages which a business cannot stand without its ruin and consequent calamity to the workers. If, however, a business makes too little money, because of lack of energy or lack of initiative or because of indifference to technical and economic progress, that must not be regarded a just reason for reducing the compensation of the workers. But if the business in question is not making enough money to pay the workers an equitable wage because it is being crushed by unjust burdens or forced to sell its product at less than a just price, those who are thus the cause of the injury are guilty of grave wrong, for they deprive workers of their just wage and force them under the pinch of necessity to accept a wage less than fair.

73. Let, then, both workers and employers strive with united strength and counsel to overcome the difficulties and obstacles and let a wise provision on the part of public authority aid them in so salutary a work. If, however, matters come to an extreme crisis, it must be finally considered whether the business can continue or the workers are to be cared for in some other way. In such a situation, certainly most serious, a feeling of close relationship and a Christian concord of minds ought to prevail and function effectively among employers and workers.

c) Requirements of the common good

74. Lastly, the amount of the pay must be adjusted to the public economic good. We have shown above how much it helps the common good for workers and other employees, by setting aside some part of their income which remains after necessary expenditures, to attain gradually to the possession of a moderate amount of wealth. But another point, scarcely less important, and especially vital in our times, must not be overlooked: namely, that the opportunity to work be provided to those who are able and willing to work. This opportunity depends largely on the wage and salary rate, which can help as long as it is kept within proper limits, but which on the other hand can be an obstacle if it exceeds these limits. For everyone knows that an excessive lowering of wages, or their increase beyond due measure, causes unemployment. This evil indeed, especially as we see it prolonged and injuring so many during the years of Our Pontificate, has plunged workers into misery and temptations, ruined the prosperity of nations, and put in jeopardy the public order, peace, and tranquillity of the whole world. Hence it is contrary to social justice when, for the sake of personal gain and without regard for the common good, wages and salaries are excessively lowered or raised; and this same social justice demands that wages and salaries be so managed, through agreement of plans and wills, in so far as can be done, as to offer to the greatest possible number the opportunity of getting work and obtaining suitable means of livelihood.

75. A right proportion among wages and salaries also contributes directly to the same result; and with this is closely connected a right proportion in the prices at which the goods are sold that are produced by the various occupations, such as agriculture, manufacturing, and others. If all these relations are properly maintained, the various occupations will combine and coalesce into, as it were, a single body and like members of the body mutually aid and complete one another. For then only will the social economy be rightly established and attain its purposes when all and each are supplied with all the goods that the wealth and resources of nature, technical achievement, and the social organization of economic life can furnish. And these goods ought indeed to be enough both to meet the demands of necessity and decent comfort and to advance people to that happier and fuller condition of life which, when it is wisely cared for, is not only no hindrance to virtue but helps it greatly.[47]

5. Reconstruction of the social order

76. What We have thus far stated regarding an equitable distribution of property and regarding just wages concerns individual persons and only indirectly touches social order, to the restoration of which according to the principles of sound philosophy and to its perfection according to the sublime precepts of the law of the Gospel, Our Predecessor, Leo XIII, devoted all his thought and care.

77. Still, in order that what he so happily initiated may be solidly established, that what remains to be done may be accomplished, and that even more copious and richer benefits may accrue to the family of mankind, two things are especially necessary: reform of institutions and correction of morals.

78. When we speak of the reform of institutions, the State comes chiefly to mind, not as if universal well-being were to be expected from its activity, but because things have come to such a pass through the evil of what we have termed 'individualism' that, following upon the overthrow and near extinction of that rich social life which was once highly developed through associations of various kinds, there remain virtually only individuals and the State. This is to the great harm of the State itself; for, with a structure of social governance lost, and with the taking over of all the burdens which the wrecked associations once bore, the State has been overwhelmed and crushed by almost infinite tasks and duties.

79. As history abundantly proves, it is true that on account of changed conditions many things which were done by small associations in former times cannot be done now save by large associations. Still, that most weighty principle, which cannot be set aside or changed, remains fixed and unshaken in social philosophy: Just as it is gravely wrong to take from individuals what they can accomplish by their own initiative and industry and give it to the community, so also it is an injustice and at the same time a grave evil and disturbance of right order to assign to a greater and higher association what lesser and subordinate organizations can do. For every social activity ought of its very nature to furnish help to the members of the body social, and never destroy and absorb them.

80. The supreme authority of the State ought, therefore, to let subordinate groups handle matters and concerns of lesser importance, which would otherwise dissipate its efforts greatly. Thereby the State will more freely, powerfully, and effectively do all those things that belong to it alone because it alone can do them: directing, watching, urging, restraining, as occasion requires and necessity demands. Therefore, those in power should be sure that the more perfectly a graduated order is kept among the various associations, in observance of the principle of 'subsidiary function,' the stronger social authority and effectiveness will be the happier and more prosperous the condition of the State.

Mutual cooperation

81. First and foremost, the State and every good citizen ought to look to and strive toward this end: that the conflict between the hostile classes be abolished and harmonious cooperation of the Industries and Professions be encouraged and promoted.

82. The social policy of the State, therefore, must devote itself to the reestablishment of the Industries and Professions. In actual fact, human society now, for the reason that it is founded on classes with divergent aims and hence opposed to one another and therefore inclined to enmity and strife, continues to be in a violent condition and is unstable and uncertain.

83. Labour, as Our Predecessor explained well in his Encyclical,[48] is not a mere commodity. On the contrary, the worker's human dignity in it must be recognized. It therefore cannot be bought and sold like a commodity. Nevertheless, as the situation now stands, hiring and offering for hire in the so-called labour market separate men into two divisions, as into battle lines, and the contest between these divisions turns the labour market itself almost into a battlefield where, face to face, the opposing lines struggle bitterly. Everyone understands that this grave evil which is plunging all human society to destruction must be remedied as soon as possible. But complete cure will not come until this opposition has been abolished and well-ordered members of the social body—Industries and Professions—are constituted in which men may have their place, not according to the position each has in the labour market but according to the respective social functions which each performs. For under nature's guidance it comes to pass that just as those who are joined together by nearness of habitation establish towns, so those who follow the same industry or profession—whether in the economic or other field—form guilds or associations, so that many are wont to consider these self-governing organizations, if not essential, at least natural to civil society.

84. Because order, as St. Thomas well explains,[49] is unity arising from the harmonious arrangement of many objects, a true, genuine social order demands that the various members of a society be united together by some strong bond. This unifying force is present not only in the producing of goods or the rendering of services—in which the employers and employees of an identical Industry or Profession collaborate jointly—but also in that common good, to achieve which all Industries and Professions together ought, each to the best of its ability, to cooperate amicably. And this unity will be the

stronger and more effective, the more faithfully individuals and the Industries and Professions themselves strive to do their work and excel in it.

85. It is easily deduced from what has been said that the interests common to the whole Industry or Profession should hold first place in these guilds. The most important among these interests is to promote the cooperation in the highest degree of each industry and profession for the sake of the common good of the country. Concerning matters, however, in which particular points, involving advantage or detriment to employers or workers, may require special care and protection, the two parties, when these cases arise, can deliberate separately or as the situation requires reach a decision separately.

86. The teaching of Leo XIII on the form of political government, namely, that men are free to choose whatever form they please, provided that proper regard is had for the requirements of justice and of the common good, is equally applicable in due proportion, it is hardly necessary to say, to the guilds of the various industries and professions.[50]

87. Moreover, just as inhabitants of a town are wont to found associations with the widest diversity of purposes, which each is quite free to join or not, so those engaged in the same industry or profession will combine with one another into associations equally free for purposes connected in some manner with the pursuit of the calling itself. Since these free associations are clearly and lucidly explained by Our Predecessor of illustrious memory, We consider it enough to emphasize this one point: People are quite free not only to found such associations, which are a matter of private order and private right, but also in respect to them 'freely to adopt the organization and the rules which they judge most appropriate to achieve their purpose.'[51] The same freedom must be asserted for founding associations that go beyond the boundaries of individual callings. And may these free organizations, now flourishing and rejoicing in their salutary fruits, set before themselves the task of preparing the way, in conformity with the mind of Christian social teaching, for those larger and more important guilds, Industries and Professions, which We mentioned before, and make every possible effort to bring them to realization.

Restoration of guiding principles of economics

88. Attention must be given also to another matter that is closely connected with the foregoing. Just as the unity of human society cannot be founded on an opposition of classes, so also the right ordering of economic life cannot be left to a free competition of forces. For from this source, as from a poisoned spring, have originated and spread all the errors of individualist economic teaching. Destroying through forgetfulness or ignorance the social and moral character of economic life, it held that economic life must be considered and treated as altogether free from and independent of public authority, because in the market, i.e., in the free struggle of competitors, it would have a principle of self-direction which governs it much more perfectly than would the intervention of any created intellect. But free competition, while justified and certainly useful provided it is kept within certain limits, clearly cannot direct economic life—a truth which the outcome of the application in practice

of the tenets of this evil individualistic spirit has more than sufficiently demonstrated. Therefore, it is most necessary that economic life be again subjected to and governed by a true and effective directing principle. This function is one that the economic dictatorship which has recently displaced free competition can still less perform, since it is a headstrong power and a violent energy that, to benefit people, needs to be strongly curbed and wisely ruled. But it cannot curb and rule itself. Loftier and nobler principles—social justice and social charity—must, therefore, be sought whereby this dictatorship may be governed firmly and fully. Hence, the institutions themselves of peoples and, particularly those of all social life, ought to be penetrated with this justice, and it is most necessary that it be truly effective, that is, establish a juridical and social order which will, as it were, give form and shape to all economic life. Social charity, moreover, ought to be as the soul of this order, an order which public authority ought to be ever ready effectively to protect and defend. It will be able to do this the more easily as it rids itself of those burdens which, as We have stated above, are not properly its own.

89. Furthermore, since the various nations largely depend on one another in economic matters and need one another's help, they should strive with a united purpose and effort to promote by wisely conceived pacts and institutions a prosperous and happy international cooperation in economic life.

90. If the members of the body social are, as was said, reconstituted, and if the directing principle of economic-social life is restored, it will be possible to say in a certain sense even of this body what the Apostle says of the mystical body of Christ: 'The whole body (being closely joined and knit together through every joint of the system according to the functioning in due measure of each single part) derives its increase to the building up of itself in love.'[52]

91. Recently, as all know, there has been inaugurated a special system of syndicates and corporations of the various callings which in view of the theme of this Encyclical it would seem necessary to describe here briefly and comment upon appropriately.

92. The civil authority itself constitutes the syndicate as a juridical personality in such a manner as to confer on it simultaneously a certain monopoly-privilege, since only such a syndicate, when thus approved, can maintain the rights (according to the type of syndicate) of workers or employers, and since it alone can arrange for the placement of labor and conclude so-termed labor agreements. Anyone is free to join a syndicate or not, and only within these limits can this kind of syndicate be called free; for syndical dues and special assessments are exacted of absolutely all members of every specified calling or profession, whether they are workers or employers; likewise all are bound by the labor agreements made by the legally recognized syndicate. Nevertheless, it has been officially stated that this legally recognized syndicate does not prevent the existence, without legal status, however, of other associations made up of persons following the same calling.

93. The associations, or corporations, are composed of delegates from the two syndicates (that is, of workers and employers) respectively of the same industry or profession and, as true and proper organs and institutions of the

State, they direct the syndicates and coordinate their activities in matters of common interest toward one and the same end.

94. Strikes an lock-outs are forbidden; if the parties cannot settle their dispute, public authority intervenes.

95. Anyone who gives even slight attention to the matter will easily see what are the obvious advantages in the system We have thus summarily described: The various classes work together peacefully, socialist organizations and their activities are repressed, and a special magistracy exercises a governing authority. Yet lest We neglect anything in a matter of such great importance and that all points treated may be properly connected with the more general principles which We mentioned above and with those which We intend shortly to add, We are compelled to say that to Our certain knowledge there are not wanting some who fear that the State, instead of confining itself as it ought to the furnishing of necessary and adequate assistance, is substituting itself for free activity; that the new syndical and corporative order savors too much of an involved and political system of administration; and that (in spite of those more general advantages mentioned above, which are of course fully admitted) it rather serves particular political ends than leads to the reconstruction and promotion of a better social order.

96. To achieve this latter lofty aim, and in particular to promote the common good truly and permanently, We hold it is first and above everything wholly necessary that God bless it and, secondly, that all men of good will work with united effort toward that end. We are further convinced, as a necessary consequence, that this end will be attained the more certainly the larger the number of those ready to contribute toward it their technical, occupational, and social knowledge and experience; and also, what is more important, the greater the contribution made thereto of Catholic principles and their application, not indeed by Catholic Action (which excludes strictly syndical or political activities from its scope) but by those sons of Ours whom Catholic Action imbues with Catholic principles and trains for carrying on an apostolate under the leadership and teaching guidance of the Church—of that Church which in this field also that We have described, as in every other field where moral questions are involved and discussed, can never forget or neglect through indifference its divinely imposed mandate to be vigilant and to teach.

97. What We have taught about the reconstruction and perfection of social order can surely in no wise be brought to realization without reform of morality, the very record of history clearly shows. For there was a social order once which, although indeed not perfect or in all respects ideal, nevertheless, met in a certain measure the requirements of right reason, considering the conditions and needs of the time. If that order has long since perished, that surely did not happen because the order could not have accommodated itself to changed conditions and needs by development and by a certain expansion, but rather because men, hardened by too much love of self, refused to open the order to the increasing masses as they should have done, or because, deceived by allurements of a false freedom and other errors, they became impatient of every authority and sought to reject every form of control.

98. There remains to Us, after again calling to judgment the economic system now in force and its most bitter accuser, Socialism, and passing explicit and just sentence upon them, to search out more thoroughly the root of these many evils and to point out that the first and most necessary remedy is a reform of morals.

III. The Great Changes Since Leo's Time

99. Important indeed have the changes been which both the economic system and Socialism have undergone since Leo XIII's time.

100. That, in the first place, the whole aspect of economic life is vastly altered, is plain to all. You know, Venerable Brethren and Beloved Children, that the Encyclical of Our Predecessor of happy memory had in view chiefly that economic system, wherein, generally, some provide capital while others provide labour for a joint economic activity. And in a happy phrase he described it thus: 'Neither capital can do without labour, nor labour without capital.'[53]

1. Changes in economic Life

101. With all his energy Leo XIII sought to adjust this economic system according to the norms of right order; hence, it is evident that this system is not to be condemned in itself. And surely it is not of its own nature vicious. But is does violate right order when capital hires workers, that is, the non-owning working class, with a view to and under such terms that it directs business and even the whole economic system according to its own will and advantage, scorning the human dignity of the workers, the social character of economic activity and social justice itself, and the common good.

102. Even today this is not, it is true, the only economic system in force everywhere; for there is another system also, which still embraces a huge mass of humanity, significant in numbers and importance, as for example, agriculture wherein the greater portion of mankind honorably and honestly procures its livelihood. This group, too, is being crushed with hardships and with difficulties, to which Our Predecessor devotes attention in several places in his Encyclical and which We Ourselves have touched upon more than once in Our present Letter.

103. But, with the diffusion of modern industry throughout the whole world, the 'capitalist' economic regime has spread everywhere to such a degree, particularly since the publication of Leo XIII's Encyclical, that it has invaded and pervaded the economic and social life of even those outside its orbit and is unquestionably impressing on it its advantages, disadvantages and vices, and, in a sense, is giving it its own shape and form.

104. Accordingly, when directing Our special attention to the changes which the capitalist economic system has undergone since Leo's time, We have in mind the good not only of those who dwell in regions given over to 'capital' and industry, but of all mankind.

Domination has succeeded free competition

105. In the first place, it is obvious that not only is wealth concentrated in our times but an immense power and despotic economic dictatorship is consolidated in the hands of a few, who often are not owners but only the trustees and managing directors of invested funds which they administer according to their own arbitrary will and pleasure.

106. The dictatorship is being most forcibly exercised by those who, since they hold the money and completely control it, control credit also and rule the lending of money. Hence they regulate the flow, so to speak, of the life-blood whereby the entire economic system lives, and have so firmly in their grasp the soul, as it were, of economic life that no one can breathe against their will.

107. This concentration of power and might, the characteristic mark, as it were, of contemporary economic life, is the fruit that the unlimited freedom of struggle among competitors has of its own nature produced, and which lets only the strongest survive; and this is often the same as saying, those who fight the most violently, those who give least heed to their conscience.

108. This accumulation of might and of power generates in turn three kinds of conflict. First, there is the struggle for economic supremacy itself; then there is the bitter fight to gain supremacy over the State in order to use in economic struggles its resources and authority; finally there is conflict between States themselves, not only because countries employ their power and shape their policies to promote every economic advantage of their citizens, but also because they seek to decide political controversies that arise among nations through the use of their economic supremacy and strength.

Tragic consequences

109. The ultimate consequences of the individualist spirit in economic life are those which you yourselves, Venerable Brethren and Beloved Children, see and deplore: Free competition has destroyed itself; economic dictatorship has supplanted the free market; unbridled ambition for power has likewise succeeded greed for gain; all economic life has become tragically hard, inexorable, and cruel. To these are to be added the grave evils that have resulted from an intermingling and shameful confusion of the functions and duties of public authority with those of the economic sphere—such as, one of the worst, the virtual degradation of the majesty of the State, which although it ought to sit on high like a queen and supreme arbitress, free from all partiality and intent upon the one common good and justice, is become a slave, surrendered and delivered to the passions and greed of men. And as to international relations, two different streams have issued from the one fountain-head: On the one hand, economic nationalism or even economic imperialism; on the other, a no less deadly and accursed internationalism of finance or international imperialism whose country is where profit is.

Remedies

110. In the second part of this Encyclical where We have presented Our teaching, We have described the remedies for these great evils so explicitly

that We consider it sufficient at this point to recall them briefly. Since the present system of economy is founded chiefly upon ownership and labor, the principles of right reason, that is, of Christian social philosophy, must be kept in mind regarding ownership and labor and their association together, and must be put into actual practice. First, so as to avoid the reefs of individualism and collectivism, the two-fold character, that is individual and social, both of capital or ownership and of work or labour must be given due and rightful weight. Relations of one to the other must be made to conform to the laws of strictest justice—commutative justice, as it is called—with the support, however, of Christian charity. Free competition, kept within definite and due limits, and still more economic dictatorship, must be effectively brought under public authority in these matters which pertain to the latter's function. The public institutions themselves, of peoples, moreover, ought to make all human society conform to the needs of the common good; that is, to the norm of social justice. If this is done, that most important division of social life, namely, economic activity, cannot fail likewise to return to right and sound order.

2. Changes of Socialism

111. Socialism, against which Our Predecessor, Leo XIII, had especially to inveigh, has since his time changed no less profoundly than the form of economic life. For Socialism, which could then be termed almost a single system and which maintained definite teachings reduced into one body of doctrine, has since then split chiefly into two sections, often opposing each other and even bitterly hostile, without either one however abandoning a position fundamentally contrary to Christian truth that was characteristic of Socialism.

a) The more violent section: Communism

112. One section of Socialism has undergone almost the same change that the capitalistic economic system, as We have explained above, has undergone. It has sunk into Communism. Communism teaches and seeks two objectives: Unrelenting class warfare and absolute extermination of private ownership. Not secretly or by hidden methods does it do this, but publicly, openly, and by employing every and all means, even the most violent. To achieve these objectives there is nothing which it does not dare, nothing for which it has respect or reverence; and when it has come to power, it is incredible and portentlike in its cruelty and inhumanity. The horrible slaughter and destruction through which it has laid waste vast regions of eastern Europe and Asia are the evidence; how much an enemy and how openly hostile it is to Holy Church and to God Himself is, alas, too well proved by facts and fully known to all. Although We, therefore, deem it superfluous to warn upright and faithful children of the Church regarding the impious and iniquitous character of Communism, yet We cannot without deep sorrow contemplate the heedlessness of those who apparently make light of these impending dangers, and with sluggish inertia allow the widespread propagation of doctrine which seeks by violence and slaughter to destroy society altogether. All the more gravely to be condemned is the folly of those who

neglect to remove or change the conditions that inflame the minds of peoples, and pave the way for the overthrow and destruction of society.

b) The more moderate section: Socialism

113. The other section, which has kept the name Socialism, is surely more moderate. It not only professes the rejection of violence but modifies and tempers to some degree, if it does not reject entirely, the class struggle and the abolition of private ownership. One might say that, terrified by its own principles and by the conclusions drawn therefrom by Communism, Socialism inclines toward and in a certain measure approaches the truths which Christian tradition has always held sacred; for it cannot be denied that its demands at times come very near those that Christian reformers of society justly insist upon.

Class struggle and abolition of ownership diminished

114. For if the class struggle abstains from enmities and mutual hatred, it gradually changes into an honest discussion of differences founded on a desire for justice, and if this is not that blessed social peace which we all seek, it can and ought to be the point of departure from which to move forward to the mutual cooperation of the Industries and Professions. So also the war declared on private ownership, more and more abated, is being so restricted that now, finally, not the possession itself of the means of production is attacked but rather a kind of sovereignty over society which ownership has, contrary to all right, seized and usurped. For such sovereignty belongs in reality not to owners but to the public authority. If the foregoing happens, it can come even to the point that imperceptibly these ideas of the more moderate socialism will no longer differ from the desires and demands of those who are striving to remold human society on the basis of Christian principles. For certain kinds of property, it is rightly contended, ought to be reserved to the State since they carry with them a dominating power so great that cannot without danger to the general welfare be entrusted to private individuals.

115. Such just demands and desire have nothing in them now which is inconsistent with Christian truth, and much less are they special to Socialism. Those who work solely toward such ends have, therefore, no reason to become socialists.

Is a middle course possible?

116. Yet let no one think that all the socialist groups or factions that are not communist have, without exception, recovered their senses to this extent either in fact or in name. For the most part they do not reject the class struggle or the abolition of ownership, but only in some degree modify them. Now if these false principles are modified and to some extent erased from the program, the question arises, or rather is raised without warrant by some, whether the principles of Christian truth cannot perhaps be also modified to some degree and be tempered so as to meet Socialism half-way and, as it were, by a middle course, come to agreement with it. There are some allured

by the foolish hope that socialists in this way will be drawn to us. A vain hope! Those who want to be apostles among socialists ought to profess Christian truth whole and entire, openly and sincerely, and not connive at error in any way. If they truly wish to be heralds of the Gospel, let them above all strive to show to socialists that socialist claims, so far as they are just, are far more strongly supported by the principles of Christian faith and much more effectively promoted through the power of Christian charity.

117. But what if Socialism has really been so tempered and modified as to the class struggle and private ownership that there is in it no longer anything to be censured on these points? Has it thereby renounced its contradictory nature to the Christian religion? This is the question that holds many minds in suspense. And numerous are the Catholics who, although they clearly understand that Christian principles can never be abandoned or diminished seem to turn their eyes to the Holy See and earnestly beseech Us to decide whether this form of Socialism has so far recovered from false doctrines that it can be accepted without the sacrifice of any Christian principle and in a certain sense be baptized. That We, in keeping with Our fatherly solicitude, may answer their petitions, We make this pronouncement: Whether considered as a doctrine, or an historical fact, or a movement, Socialism, if it remains truly Socialism, even after it has yielded to truth and justice on the points which we have mentioned, cannot be reconciled with the teachings of the Catholic Church because its concept of society itself is utterly foreign to Christian truth.

Socialist concept of society and of man's social character foreign to christian truth

118. For, according to Christian teaching, man, endowed with a social nature, is placed on this earth so that by leading a life in society and under an authority ordained of God[54] he may fully cultivate and develop all his faculties unto the praise and glory of his Creator; and that by faithfully fulfilling the duties of his craft or other calling he may obtain for himself temporal and at the same time eternal happiness. Socialism, on the other hand, wholly ignoring and indifferent to this sublime end of both man and society, affirms that human association has been instituted for the sake of material advantage alone.

119. Because of the fact that goods are produced more efficiently by a suitable division of labour than by the scattered efforts of individuals, socialists infer that economic activity, only the material ends of which enter into their thinking, ought of necessity to be carried on socially. Because of this necessity, they hold that men are obliged, with respect to the producing of goods, to surrender and subject themselves entirely to society. Indeed, possession of the greatest possible supply of things that serve the advantages of this life is considered of such great importance that the higher goods of man, liberty not excepted, must take a secondary place and even be sacrificed to the demands of the most efficient production of goods. This damage to human dignity, undergone in the 'socialized' process of production, will be easily offset, they say, by the abundance of socially produced goods which will pour out in profusion to individuals to be used freely at their

pleasure for comforts and cultural development. Society, therefore, as Socialism conceives it, can on the one hand neither exist nor be thought of without an obviously excessive use of force; on the other hand, it fosters a liberty no less false, since there is no place in it for true social authoriy, which rests not on temporal and material advantages but descends from God alone, the Creator and last end of all things.[55]

Catholic and socialist: contradictory terms

120. If Socialism, like all errors, contains some truth (which, moreover, the Supreme Pontiffs have never denied), it is based nevertheless on a theory of human society peculiar to itself and irreconcilable with true Christianity. Religious socialism, Christian socialism, are contradictory terms; no one can be at the same time a good Catholic and a true socialist.

Socialism pervading morality and culture

121. All these admonitions which have been renewed and confirmed by Our solemn authority must likewise be applied to a certain new kind of socialist activity, hitherto little known but now carried on among many socialist groups. It devotes itself above all to the training of the mind and character. Under the guise of affection it tries in particular to attract children of tender age and win them to itself, although it also embraces the whole population in its scope in order finally to produce true socialists who would shape human society to the tenets of Socialism.

122. Since in Our Encyclical, *The Christian Education of Youth*,[56] We have fully taught the principles that Christian education insists on and the ends it pursues, the contradiction between these principles and ends and the activities and aims of this Socialism that is pervading morality and culture is so clear and evident that no demonstration is required here. But they seem to ignore or underestimate the grave dangers that it carries with it who think it of no importance courageously and zealously to resist them according to the gravity of the situation. It belongs to Our Pastoral Office to warn these persons of the grave and imnminent evil: let all remember that Liberalism is the father of this Socialism that is pervading morality and culture and that Bolshevism will be its heir.

Catholic deserters to Socialism

123. Accordingly, Venerable Brethren, you can well understand with what great sorrow We observe that not a few of Our sons, in certain regions especially, although We cannot be convinced that they have given up the true faith and right will, have deserted the camp of the Church and gone over to the ranks of Socialism, some to glory openly in the name of socialist and to profess socialist doctrines, others through thoughtlessness or even, almost against their wills to join associations which are socialist by profession or in fact.

124. In the anxiety of Our paternal solicitude, We give Ourselves to reflection and try to discover how it could happen that they should go so far astray and We seem to hear what many of them answer and plead in excuse:

The Church and those proclaiming attachment to the Church favour the rich, neglect the workers and have no concern for them; therefore, to look after themselves they had to join the ranks of Socialism.

125. It is certainly most lamentable, Venerable Brethren, that there have been, nay, that even now there are men who, although professing to be Catholics, are almost completely unmindful of that sublime law of justice and charity that binds us not only to render to everyone what is his but to succour brothers in need as Christ the Lord Himself,[57] and—what is worse— out of greed for gain do not scruple to exploit the workers. Even more, there are men who abuse religion itself, and under its name try to hide their unjust exactions in order to protect themselves from the manifestly just demands of the workers. The conduct of such We shall never cease to censure gravely. For they are the reason why the Church could, even though undeservedly, have the appearance of and be charged with taking the part of the rich and with being quite unmoved by the necessities and hardships of those who have been deprived, as it were, of their natural inheritance. The whole history of the Church plainly demonstrates that such appearances are unfounded and such charges unjust. The Encyclical itself, whose anniversary we are celebrating, is clearest proof that it is the height of injustice to hurl these calumnies and reproaches at the Church and her teaching.

Invitation to return

126. Although pained by the injustice and downcast in fatherly sorrow, it is so far from Our thought to repulse or to disown children who have been miserably deceived and have strayed so far from the truth and salvation that We cannot but invite them with all possible solicitude to return to the maternal bosom of the Church. May they lend ready ears to Our voice, may they return whence they have left, to the home that is truly their Father's, and may they stand firm there where their own place is, in the ranks of those who, zealously following the admonitions which Leo promulgated and We have solemnly repeated, are striving to restore society according to the mind of the Church on the firmly established basis of social justice and social charity. And let them be convinced that nowhere, even on earth, can they find full happiness save with Him who, being rich, became poor for our sakes that through His poverty we might become rich,[58] Who was poor an in labours from His youth, Who invited to Himself all that labour and are heavily burdened that He might refresh them fully in the love of His heart,[59] and Who, lastly, without any respect for persons will require more of them to whom more has been given[60] and 'will render to everyone according to his conduct.'[61]

3. Moral renovation

127. Yet, if we look into the matter more carefully and more thoroughly, we shall clearly perceive that, preceding this ardently desired social restoration, there must be a renewal of the Christian spirit, from which so many immersed in economic life have, far and wide, unhappily fallen away, lest all our efforts be wasted and our house be builded not on a rock but on shifting sand.[62]

[73]

128. And so, Venerable Bethren and Beloved Sons, having surveyed the present economic system, We have found it labouring under the gravest of evils. We have also summoned Communism and Socialism again to judgment and have found all their forms, even the most modified, to wander far from the precepts of the Gospel.

129. 'Wherefore,' to use the words of Our Predecessor, 'if human society is to be healed, only a return to Christian life and institutions will heal it.'[63] For this alone can provide effective remedy for that excessive care for passing things that is the origin of all vices; and this alone can draw away men's eyes, fascinated by and wholly fixed on the changing things of the world, and raise them toward Heaven. Who would deny that human society is in most urgent need of this cure now?

Chief form of disorder: loss of souls

130. Minds of all, it is true, are affected almost solely by temporal upheavals, disasters, and calamities. But if we examine things critically with Christian eyes, as we should, what are all these compared with the loss of souls? Yet it is not rash by any means to say that the whole scheme of social and economic life is now such as to put in the way of vast numbers of mankind most serious obstacles which prevent them from caring for the one thing necessary; namely, their eternal salvation.

131. We, made Shepherd and Protector by the Prince of Shepherds, Who Redeemed them by His Blood, of a truly innumerable flock, cannot hold back Our tears when contemplating this greatest of their dangers. Nay rather, fully mindful of Our pastoral office aNd with paternal solicitude, We are continually meditating on how We can help them; and We have summoned to Our aid the untiring zeal of others who are concerned on grounds of justice or charity. For what will it profit men to become expert in more wisely using their wealth, even to gaining the whole world, if thereby they suffer the loss of their souls?[64] What will it profit to teach them sound principles of economic life if in unbridled and sordid greed they let themselves be swept away by their passion for property, so that 'hearing the commandments of the Lord they do all things contrary.'[65]

Causes of this loss

132. The root and font of this defection in economic and social life from the Christian law, and of the consequent apostasy of great numbers of workers from the Catholic faith, are the disordered passions of the soul, the sad result of original sin which has so destroyed the wonderful harmony of man's faculties that, easily led astray by his evil desires, he is strongly incited to prefer the passing goods of this world to the lasting goods of Heaven. Hence arises that unquenchable thirst for riches and temporal goods, which has at all times impelled men to break God's laws and trample upon the rights of their neighbors but which, on account of the present system of economic life, is laying far more numerous snares for human frailty. Since the instability of economic life, and especially of its structure, exacts of those engaged in it most intense and unceasing effort, some have become so hardened to the stings of conscience as to hold that they are allowed, in any manner

whatsoever, to increase their profits and use means, fair or foul, to protect their hard-won wealth against sudden changes of fortune. The easy gains that a market unrestricted by any law opens to everybody attracts large numbers to buying and selling goods, and they, their one aim being to make quick profits with the least expenditure of work, raise or lower prices by their uncontrolled business dealings so rapidly according to their own caprice and greed that they nullify the wisest forecast of producers. The laws passed to promote corporate business, while dividing and limiting the risk of business, have given occasion to the most sordid license. For We observe that consciences are little affected by this reduced obligation of accountability; that furthermore, by hiding under the shelter of a joint name, the worst of injustices and frauds are penetrated; and that, too, directors of business companies, forgetful of their trust, betray the rights of those whose savings they have undertaken to administer. Lastly, We must not omit to mention those crafty men who, wholly unconcerned about any honest usefulness of their work, do not scruple to stimulate the baser human desires and, when they are aroused, use them for their own profit.

133. Strict and watchful moral restraint enforced vigorously by governmental authority could have banished these enormous evils and even forestalled them; this restraint, however, has too often been sadly lacking. For since the seeds of a new form of economy were bursting forth just when the principles of rationalism had been implanted and rooted in many minds, there quickly developed a body of economic teaching far removed from the true moral law, and, as a result, completely free rein was given to human passions.

134. Thus it came to pass that many, much more than ever before, were solely concerned with increasing their wealth by any means whatsoever, and that in seeking their own selfish interests before everything else they had no conscience about committing even the gravest of crimes against others. Those first entering upon this broad way that leads to destruction[66] easily found numerous imitators of their iniquity by the example of their manifest success, by their insolent display of wealth, by their ridiculing the conscience of others, who, as they said, were troubled by silly scruples, or lastly by crushing more conscientious competitors.

135. With the rulers of economic life abandoning the right road, it was easy for the rank and file of workers everywhere to rush headlong also into the same chasm; and all the more so, because very many managements treated their workers like mere tools, with no concern at all for their souls, without indeed even the least thought of spiritual things. Truly the mind shudders at the thought of the grave dangers to which the morals of workers (particularly younger workers) and the modesty of girls and women are exposed in modern factories; when we recall how often the present economic scheme, and particularly the shameful housing conditions, create obstacles to the family bond and normal family life; when we remember how many obstacles are put in the way of the proper observance of Sundays and Holy Days; and when we reflect upon the universal weakening of that truly Christian sense through which even rude and unlettered men were wont to value higher things, and upon its substitution by the single preoccupation of getting in any way whatsoever one's daily bread. And thus bodily labour, which Divine

[75]

Providence decreed to be performed, even after original sin, for the good at once of man's body and soul, is being everywhere changed into an instrument of perversion; for dead matter comes forth from the factory ennobled, while men there are corrupted and degraded.

Remedies: a) Christian principles of Economics

136. No genuine cure can be furnished for this lamentable ruin of souls, which, so long as it continues, will frustrate all efforts to regenerate society, unless men return openly and sincerely to the teaching of the Gospel, to the precepts of Him Who alone has the words of everlasting life,[67] words which will never pass away, even if Heaven and earth will pass away.[68] All experts in social problems are seeking eagerly a structure so fashioned in accordance with the norms of reason that it can lead economic life back to sound and right order. But this order, which We Ourselves ardently long for and with all Our efforts promote, will be wholly defective and incomplete unless all the activities of men harmoniously unite to imitate and attain, in so far as it lies within human strength, the marvelous unity of the Divine plan. We mean that perfect order which the Church with great force and power preaches and which right human reason itself demands, that all things be directed to God as the first and supreme end of all created activity, and that all created good under God be considered as mere instruments to be used only in so far as they conduce to the attainment of the supreme end. Nor is it to be thought that gainful occupations are thereby belittled or judged less consonant with human dignity; on the contrary, we are taught to recognize in them with reverence the manifest will of the Divine Creator Who placed man upon the earth to work it and use it in a multitude of ways for his needs. Those who are engaged in producing goods, therefore, are not forbidden to increase their fortune in a just and lawful manner; for it is only fair that he who renders service to the community and makes it richer should also, through the increased wealth of the community, be made richer himself according to his position, provided that all these things be sought with due respect for the laws of God and without impairing the rights of others and that they be employed in accordance with faith and right reason. If these principles are observed by everyone, everywhere, and always, not only the production and acquisition of goods but also the use of wealth, which now is seen to be so often contrary to right order, will be brought back soon within the bounds of equity and just distribution. The sordid love of wealth, which is the shame and great sin of our age, will be opposed in actual fact by the gentle yet effective law of Christian moderation which commands man to seek first the Kingdom of God and His justice, with the assurance that, by virtue of God's kindness and unfailing promise, temporal goods also, in so far as he has need of them, shall be given him besides.[69]

b) Role of charity

137. But in effecting all this, the law of charity, 'which is the bond of perfection,'[70] must always take a leading role. How completely deceived, therefore, are those rash reformers who concern themselves with the

enforcement of justice alone—and this, commutative justice—and in their pride reject the assistance of charity! Admittedly, no vicarious charity can substitute for justice which is due as an obligation and is wrongfully denied. Yet even supposing that everyone should finally receive all that is due him, the widest field for charity will always remain open. For justice alone can, if faithfully observed, remove the causes of social conflict but can never bring about union of minds and hearts. Indeed all the institutions for the establishment of peace and the promotion of mutual help among men, however perfect these may seem, have the principal foundation of their stability in the mutual bond of minds and hearts whereby the members are united with one another. If this bond is lacking, the best of regulations come to naught, as we have learned by too frequent experience. And so, then only will true cooperation be possible for a single common good when the constituent parts of society deeply feel themselves members of one great family and children of the same Heavenly Father; nay, that they are one body in Christ, 'but severally members one of another,'[71] so that 'if one member suffers anything, all the members suffer with it.'[72] For then the rich and others in positions of power will change their former indifference toward their poorer brothers into a solicitous and active love, listen with kindliness to their just demands, and freely forgive their possible mistakes and faults. And the workers, sincerely putting aside every feeling of hatred or envy which the promoters of social conflict so cunningly exploit, will not only accept without rancour the place in human society assigned them by Divine Providence, but rather will hold it in esteem, knowing well that everyone according to his function and duty is toiling usefully and honorably for the common good and is following closely in the footsteps of Him Who, being in the form of God, willed to be a carpenter among men and be known as the son of a carpenter.

Difficult task

138. Therefore, out of this new diffusion throughout the world of the spirit of the Gospel, which is the spirit of Christian moderation and universal charity, We are confident there will come that longed-for and full restoration of human society in Christ, and that 'Peace of Christ in the Kingdom of Christ,' to accomplish which, from the very beginning of Our Pontificate, We firmly determined and resolved within Our heart to devote all Our care and all Our pastoral solicitude,[73] and toward this same highly important and most necessary end now, you also, Venerable Brethren, who with Us rule the Church of God under the mandate of the Holy Ghost,[74] are earnestly toiling with wholly praiseworthy zeal in all parts of the world, even in the regions of the holy missions to the infidels. Let well-merited acclamations of praise be bestowed upon you and at the same time upon all those, both clergy and laity, who We rejoice to see, are daily participating and valiantly helping in this same great work, Our beloved sons engaged in Catholic Action, who with a singular zeal are undertaking with Us the solution of the social problems in so far as by virtue of her divine institution this is proper to and devolves upon the Church. All these We urge in the Lord, again and again, to spare no labours and let no difficulties conquer them, but rather to become day by day more courageous and more valiant.[75] Arduous indeed is the task

which We propose to them, for We know well that on both sides, both among the upper and the lower classes of society, there are many obstacles and barriers to be overcome. Let them not, however, lose heart; to face bitter combats is a mark of Christians, and to endure grave labours to the end is a mark of them who, as good soldiers of Christ,[76] follow Him closely.

139. Relying therefore solely on the all-powerful aid of Him 'Who wishes all men to be saved,'[77] let us strive with all our strength to help those unhappy souls who have turned from God and, drawing them away from the temporal cares in which they are too deeply immersed, let us teach them to aspire with confidence to the things that are eternal. Sometimes this will be achieved much more easily then seems possible at first sight to expect. For if wonderful spiritual forces lie hidden, like sparks beneath ashes, within the secret recesses of even the most abandoned man—certain proof that his soul is naturally Christian—how much the more in the hearts of those many upon many who have been led into error rather through ignorance or environment.

140. Moreover, the ranks of the workers themselves are already giving happy and promising signs of a social reconstruction. To Our souls' great joy, We see in these ranks also the massed companies of young workers, who are receiving the counsel of Divine Grace with willing ears and striving with marvelous zeal to gain their comrades for Christ. No less praise must be accorded to the leaders of workers' organizations who, disregarding their own personal advantage and concerned solely about the good of their fellow members, are striving prudently to harmonize the just demands of their members with the prosperity of their whole occupation and also to promote these demands, and who do not let themselves be deterred from so noble a service by any obstacle or suspicion. Also, as anyone may see, many young men, who by reason of their talent or wealth will soon occupy high places among the leaders of society, are studying social problems with deeper interest, and they arouse the joyful hope that they will dedicate themselves wholly to the restoration of society.

Way to proceed

141. The present state of affairs, Venerable Brethren, clearly indicates the way in which We ought to proceed. For We are now confronted, as more than once before in the history of the Church, with a world that in large part has almost fallen back into paganism. That these whole classes of men may be brought back to Christ Whom they have denied, we must recruit and train from among them, themselves, auxiliary soldiers of the Church who know them well and their minds and wishes, and can reach their hearts with a tender brotherly love. The first and immediate apostles to the workers ought to be workers; the apostles to those who follow industry and trade ought to be from among them themselves.

142. It is chiefly your duty, Venerable Brethren, and of your clergy, to search diligently for these lay apostles both of workers and of employers, to select them with prudence, and to train and instruct them properly. A difficult task, certainly, is thus imposed on priests, and to meet it, all who are growing up as the hope of the Church, must be duly prepared by an intensive study of the social question. Especially is it necessary that those whom you intend to

assign in particular to this work should demonstrate that they are men possessed of the keenest sense of justice, who will resist with true manly courage the dishonest demands or the unjust acts of anyone, who will excel in the prudence and judgment which avoids every extreme, and, above all, who will be deeply permeated by the charity of Christ, which alone has the power to subdue firmly but gently the hearts and wills of men to the laws of justice and equity. Upon this road so often tried by happy experience, there is no reason why we should hesitate to go forward with all speed.

143. These Our Beloved Sons who are chosen for so great a work, We earnestly exhort in the Lord to give themselves wholly to the training of the men committed to their care, and in the discharge of this eminently priestly and apostolic duty to make proper use of the resources of Christian education by teaching youth, forming Christian organizations, and founding study groups guided by principles in harmony with the Faith. But above all, let them hold in high esteem and assiduously employ for the good of their disciples that most valuable means of both personal and social restoration which, as We taught in Our Encyclical, *Mens Nostra*,[78] is to be found in the Spiritual Exercises. In that Letter We expressly mentioned and warmly recommended not only the Spiritual Exercises for all the laity, but also the highly beneficial Workers' Retreats. For in that school of the spirit, not only are the best of Christians developed but true apostles also are trained for every condition of life and are enkindled with the fire of the heart of Christ. From this school they will go forth as did the Apostles from the Upper Room of Jerusalem, strong in faith, endowed with an invincible steadfastness in persecution, burning with zeal, interested solely in spreading everywhere the Kingdom of Christ.

144. Certainly there is the greatest need now of such valiant soldiers of Christ who will work with all their strength to keep the human family safe from the dire ruin into which it would be plunged were the teachings of the Gospel to be flouted, and that order of things permitted to prevail which tramples underfoot no less the laws of nature than those of God. The Church of Christ, built upon an unshakable rock, has nothing to fear for herself, as she knows for a certainty that the gates of hell shall never prevail against her.[79] Rather, she knows full well, through the experience of many centuries, that she is wont to come forth from the most violent storms stronger than ever and adorned with new triumphs. Yet her maternal heart cannot but be moved by the countless evils with which so many thousands would be afflicted during storms of this kind, and above all by the consequent enormous injury to spiritual life which would work eternal ruin to so many souls redeemed by the Blood of Jesus Christ.

145. To ward off such great evils from human society nothing, therefore, is to be left untried; to this end may all our labors turn, to this all our energies, to this our fervent and unremitting prayers to God! For with the assistance of Divine Grace the fate of the human family rests in our hands.

146. Venerable Brethren and Beloved Sons, let us not permit the children of this world to appear wiser in their generation than we who by the Divine Goodness are the children of the light.[80] We find them, indeed, selecting and training with the greatest shrewdness alert and resolute devotees who spread

their errors ever wider day by day through all classes of men and in every part of the world. And whenever they undertake to attack the Church of Christ more violently, We see them put aside their internal quarrels, assembling in full harmony in a single battle line with a completely united effort, and work to achieve their common purpose.

Close union and cooperation urged

147. Surely there is not one that does not know how many and how great are the works that the tireless zeal of Catholics is striving everywhere to carry out, both for social and economic welfare as well as in the fields of education and religion. But this admirable and unremitting activity not infrequently shows less effectiveness because of the dispersion of its energies in too many different directions. Therefore, let all men of good will stand united, all who under the Shepherds of the Church wish to fight this good and peaceful battle of Christ; and under the leadership and teaching guidance of the Church let all strive according to the talent, powers, and position of each to contribute something to the Christian reconstruction of human society which Leo XIII inaugurated through his immortal Encyclical, *On the Condition of Workers*, seeking not themselves and their own interests, but those of Jesus Christ,[81] not trying to press at all costs their own counsels, but ready to sacrifice them, however excellent, if the greater common good should seem to require it, so that in all and above all Christ may reign, Christ may command to Whom be 'honour and glory and dominion forever and ever.'[82]

148. That this may happily come to pass, to all of you, Venerable Brethren and Beloved Children, who are members of the vast Catholic family entrusted to Us, but with the especial affection of Our heart to workers and to all others engaged in manual occupations, committed to us more urgently by Divine Providence, and to Christian employers and managements, with paternal love We impart the Apostolic Benediction.

149. Given at Rome, at Saint Peter's, the fifteenth day of May, in the year 1931, the tenth year of Our Pontificate.

Mater et Magistra

Encyclical letter of His Holiness John XXIII by divine providence pope to his venerable brothers the patriarchs, primates, archbishops, bishops, and all other local ordinaries that are at peace and in communion with the Apostolic See, and to the clergy and faithful of the entire Catholic world concerning a re-evaluation of the social question in the light of Christian teaching.

Introduction

This encyclical letter is dated 15 May 1961 and celebrates the seventieth anniversary of the publication of Leo XIII's *Rerum Novarum* and the thirtieth of Pius XI's *Quadragesimo Anno*. Popes make a point of establishing links with the past. They want to demonstrate that they are part of a long tradition of teaching, in this instance on social matters. So Pope John is claiming that he will be discussing traditional issues in the light of changed circumstances.

In practice, however, *Mater et Magistra* marked a quite decisive break with the past. It is indeed true that the encyclical treats of some fairly traditional topics—the just wage, for example, and the right to private property. But it also treats of some less traditional subjects. There is a lengthy section on agriculture and its problems, and Pope John was the first Roman pontiff to raise a subject which has since become a major element in papal social teaching: aid to underdeveloped countries.

But perhaps the most important innovation in this encyclical was a change in attitude towards the State. John saw the State as having a much larger role to play in the lives of its citizens, particularly in matters of welfare, than his predecessors had done, and some commentators have taken *Mater et Magistra* as an implicit endorsement of socialism. This is going far too far. If he endorses anything it is the kind of liberal capitalism which, in 1961, was the economic system prevailing in western Europe and the United States. Even so, he calls for a far greater participation by the workers in the management of the industry than was normal then or has been achieved since.

For a longer discussion of *Mater et Magistra* (MM) see the Introduction, pp.xiii. The Latin text is to be found in AAS 53 (1961), 401-464. In the original the paragraphs were not numbered: the enumeration has been added in accordance with the policy outlined in the Editorial Note (p.ix), as have the cross-headings.

Summary

Paras. 1-26: Though the Church's first concern must be for souls, it must also, in imitation of Christ, be concerned about the demands of people's daily lives. This concern is expressed in the Church's social teaching of which Leo XIII's encyclical *Rerum Novarum* was an outstanding example. He wrote it at a time when there was a great deal of protest among the working class about the conditions under which they had to live. Leo addressed himself in particular to the problems of fair wages, private property, the role of the State, the right of association and Christian brotherhood.

Paras. 27-50: Forty years later Pius XI published *Quadragesimo Anno*, clarifying parts of Leo's teaching, especially on private property and the just wage. He also stressed the opposition of the Church to communism and to socialism. Pius noted that economic power had come to be concentrated in the hands of a few, and called upon the State to promote the good of all. Pius XII reiterated the teachings of his predecessors, but all the time the situation is changing, technologically, socially and politically. It is the intention of this new encyclical to make church teaching more specific in the light of the new developments.

Paras. 51-67: Public authority has an increasing power to influence the economy, but this must never be at the cost of depriving the individual of freedom of action. It is to the advantage of individuals that they should come together in associations to promote their interests, but once again this must not be at the expense of individual freedom.

Paras. 68-103: It is the pope's duty to insist that wages should not simply be left to market forces, but be determined in accordance with justice and equity. In some cases workers ought to receive shares in the firms for which they work. The common good, both national and international, should be taken into account when assessing the level of reasonable profit. Workers should be allowed a greater say in the conduct of the firms for which they work and, through their professional groups and workers' associations, about the economy of their countries.

Paras. 104-121: Private property, a right vigorously defended by the popes, is today of less consequence than it used to be, but private property remains a guarantee of an individual's freedom and is an indispensable element in social order. Property ought to be widely distributed and not over-concentrated in public hands. It must be remembered that though the Gospels sanction private property, they also contain an invitation to convert material goods into spiritual ones by transferring material goods to the poor.

Paras. 122-149: The move of workers from agriculture to industry often has causes other than economic expansion: agriculture has become a depressed occupation. The State should provide better services for the farming community, and help it to modernize its methods. In the financial sphere, the State should recognize the special needs of farmers. Industries, especially those allied to agriculture, ought to be established in rural areas to provide alternative employment. But farmers could also help themselves by linking up in various organizations.

Paras. 150-184: The State, assisted by private enterprise, should strive to ensure an economic and social balance within the community. The solidarity of the human race and common Christianity require that imbalances among nations also as far as possible be eliminated. Nations of the world are becoming more dependent upon each other, and there is an obligation to help those less well-off. International aid and co-operation are increasing, but they should not be used to exercise control over the developing nations. It is a source of satisfaction to find Catholics deeply involved in this work.

Paras. 185-199: There is rapid population growth in less developed countries. Though there is no imminent world crisis arising from the disproportion between food supply and population growth, there is certainly a problem for poorer countries. No solution is acceptable which does violence to human dignity—it has to be found in world-wide co-operation. God has given the human race adequate means to find a solution to problems arising from the transmission of life.

Paras. 200-217: Nations must work together for their mutual benefit, but people in public life seem incapable of bringing this about. Ideological differences lie at the heart of the mistrust among rulers: trust cannot grow except out of respect for a moral order which has its source in God. As it is, people are losing their belief in an earthly paradise, and increasingly are asserting human, inviolable rights. There will be no peace or justice until people return to a sense of their dignity as children of God.

Paras. 218-247: The Church's social teaching, formulated over the last 100 years, points a sure way to social reconstruction. It is essential that this doctrine be better known. It must also be put into practice, and in this the laity has an important role. There are three stages in putting social principles into action—usually called 'See, Judge and Act'. The Church has the right and duty not merely to be the custodian of ethical and religious principles, but to declare authoritatively how they should be implemented. Progress, and the resultant material well-being, mark an important stage in human development, but it must be remembered that they are only means to an end.

Paras. 248-264: Religious, moral and physical well-being all require Sunday rest which, regrettably, is being eroded. It is the Church's task to humanize and Christianize the modern world. Members of the Church are called to a share in Christ's divine life, and their work is a continuation of his, even when they are simply engaged on the affairs of the world. There are immense possibilities for those who work with the Church. May all nations enjoy true prosperity, happiness and peace.

Venerable brothers and dearest sons and daughters, greetings and apostolic benediction.

The task of the Church

1. Mother and teacher of all nations—such is the Catholic Church in the mind of her founder, Jesus Christ; to hold the world in an embrace of love, that men, in every age, should find in her their own completeness in a higher order of living, and their ultimate salvation. She is 'the pillar and ground of the truth'.[1] To her was entrusted by her holy founder the twofold task of giving life to her children and of teaching them and guiding them—both as individuals and as nations—with maternal care. Great is their dignity, a dignity which she has always guarded most zealously and held in the highest esteem.

2. Christianity is the meeting point of earth and heaven. It lays claim to the whole man, body and soul, intellect and will, inducing him to raise his mind above the changing conditions of this earthly existence and reach upwards for the eternal life of heaven, where one day he will find his unfailing happiness and peace.

3. Hence, though the Church's first care must be for souls, how she can sanctify them and make them share in the gifts of heaven, she concerns herself too with the exigencies of man's daily life, with his livelihood and education, and his general, temporal welfare and prosperity.

4. In all this she is but giving effect to those principles which Christ himself established in the church he founded. When he said 'I am the way, and the truth, and the life,'[2] 'I am the light of the world,'[3] it was doubtless man's eternal salvation that was uppermost in his mind, but he showed his concern for the material welfare of his people when, seeing the hungry crowd of his followers, he was moved to exclaim: 'I have compassion on the multitude.'[4] And these were no empty words of our divine redeemer. Time and again he proved them by his actions, as when he miraculously multiplied bread to alleviate the hunger of the crowds.

5. Bread it was for the body, but it was intended also to foreshadow that other bread, that heavenly food of the soul, which he was to give them on 'the night before he suffered'.

6. Small wonder, then, that the Catholic Church, in imitation of Christ and in fulfilment of his commandment, relies not merely upon her teaching to hold aloft the torch of charity, but also upon her own widespread example. This has been her course now for nigh on two thousand years, from the early ministrations of her deacons right down to the present time. It is a charity which combines the precepts and practice of mutual love. It holds fast to the twofold aspect of Christ's command to *give*, and summarizes the whole of the Church's social teaching and activity.

The effect of Rerum Novarum

7. An outstanding instance of this social teaching and action carried on by the Church throughout the ages is undoubtedly that magnificent encyclical on the christianizing of the conditions of the working classes, *Rerum Novarum*, published seventy years ago by our predecessor, Leo XIII.[5]

8. Seldom have the words of a pontiff met with such universal acclaim. In the weight and scope of his arguments, and in the forcefulness of their expression, Pope Leo XIII can have but few rivals. Beyond any shadow of doubt, his directives and appeals have established for themselves a position of such high importance that they will never, surely, sink into oblivion. They opened out new horizons for the activity of the universal Church, and the supreme shepherd, by giving expression to the hardships and sufferings and aspirations of the lowly and oppressed, made himself the champion and restorer of their rights.

9. The impact of this remarkable encyclical is still with us even today, so many years after it was written. It is discernible in the writings of the popes who succeeded Pope Leo. In their social and economic teaching they have frequent recourse to the Leonine encyclical, either to draw inspiration from it and clarify its application, or to find in it a stimulus to Catholic action. It is discernible too in the subsequent legislation of a number of states. What further proof need we of the permanent validity of the solidly grounded principles, practical directives and fatherly appeals contained in this masterly encyclical? It also suggests new and vital criteria by which men can judge the magnitude of the social question as it presents itself today, and decide on the course of action they must take.

I

The background to Rerum Novarum

10. Leo XIII spoke in a time of social and economic upheaval, of heightening tensions and actual revolt. Against this dark background, the brilliance of his teaching stands out in clear relief.

11. As is well known, the outlook that prevailed on economic matters was for the most part a purely naturalistic one, which denied any correlation between economics and morality. Personal gain was considered the only valid motive for economic activity. In business the main operative principle was that of free and unrestricted competition. Interest on capital, prices—whether of goods or of services—profits and wages, were to be determined by the purely mechanical application of the laws of the market place. Every precaution was to be taken to prevent the civil authority from intervening in any way in economic matters. The status of trade unions varied in different countries. They were either forbidden, tolerated, or recognized as having private legal personality only.

12. In an economic world of this character, it was the might of the strongest which not only arrogated to itself the force of law, but also dominated the ordinary business relationships between individuals, and thereby undermined the whole economic structure.

13. Enormous riches accumulated in the hands of a few, while large numbers of working men found themselves in conditions of ever increasing hardship. Wages were insufficient even to the point of reaching starvation level, and working conditions were often of such a nature as to be injurious alike to health, morality and religious faith. Especially inhuman were the working conditions to which women and children were sometimes subjected. There was also the constant spectre of unemployment and the progressive disruption of family life.

14. The natural consequence of all this was a spirit of indignation and open protest on the part of the working man, and a widespread tendency to subscribe to extremist theories far worse in their effects than the evils they purported to remedy.

15. It was at such a time and under pressure of such circumstances as these that Leo XIII wrote his social encyclical, *Rerum Novarum*, based on the needs of human nature itself and animated by the principles and spirit of the gospel. His message, not unnaturally, aroused opposition in some quarters, but was received by the majority of people with the greatest admiration and enthusiasm. It was not, of course, the first occasion on which the Apostolic See had come out strongly in defence of the earthly interests of the poor; indeed, Leo himself had made other pronouncements which in a sense had prepared the way for his encyclical. But here for the first time was a complete synthesis of social principles, formulated with such historical insight as to be of permanent value to Christendom. It is rightly regarded as a compendium of Catholic social and economic teaching.

16. In this Leo XIII showed his complete mastery of the situation. There were those who presumed to accuse the Church of taking no interest in social matters other than to preach resignation to the poor and generosity to the rich, but Leo XIII had no hesitation in proclaiming and defending the legitimate rights of the workers. As he said at the beginning of his exposition of the principles and precepts of the Church in social matters: 'We approach the subject with confidence, and in the exercise of the rights which manifestly appertain to us, for no practical solution of this question will be found apart from the counsel of religion and of the Church.'[6]

The principles of Rerum Novarum

17. You know well enough, venerable brothers, the basic economic and social principles for the reconstruction of human society enunciated so clearly and authoritatively by this great pope.

18. They concern first of all the question of work, which must be regarded not merely as a commodity, but as a specifically human activity. In the majority of cases a man's work is his sole means of livelihood. Its remuneration, therefore, cannot be made to depend on the state of the market. It must be determined by the laws of justice and equity. Any other procedure would be a clear violation of justice, even supposing the contract of work to have been freely entered into by both parties.

19. Secondly, private ownership of property, including that of productive

goods, is a natural right which the State cannot suppress. But it naturally entails a social obligation as well. It is a right which must be exercised not only for one's own personal benefit but also for the benefit of others.

20. As for the State, its whole *raison d'être* is the realization of the common good in the temporal order. It cannot, therefore, hold aloof from economic matters. On the contrary, it must do all in its power to promote the production of a sufficient supply of material goods, 'the use of which is necessary for the practice of virtue'.[7] It has also the duty to protect the rights of all its people, and particularly of its weaker members, the workers, women and children. It can never be right for the State to shirk its obligation to work actively for the betterment of the condition of the working man.

21. It is furthermore the duty of the State to ensure that terms of employment are regulated in accordance with justice and equity, and to safeguard the human dignity of workers by making sure that they are not required to work in an environment which may prove harmful to their material and spiritual interests. It was for this reason that the Leonine encyclical enunciated those general principles of rightness and equity which have been assimilated into the social legislation of many a modern state, and which, as Pope Pius XI declared in the encyclical *Quadragesimo Anno*,[8] have made no small contribution to the rise and development of that new branch of jurisprudence called labour law.

22. Pope Leo XIII also defended the worker's natural right to enter into association with his fellows. Such associations may consist either of workers alone or of workers and employers, and should be structured in a way best calculated to safeguard the workers' legitimate professional interest. And it is the natural right of the workers to work without hindrance, freely, and on their own initiative within these associations for the achievement of these ends.

23. Finally, both workers and employers should regulate their mutual relations in accordance with the principle of human solidarity and Christian brotherhood. Unrestricted competition in the *liberal* sense, and the Marxist creed of class warfare, are clearly contrary to Christian teaching and the nature of man.

24. These venerable brethren, are the basic principles upon which a genuine social and economic order must be built.

25. The response of good Catholics to this appeal and the enterprise they showed in reducing these principles into practice is hardly surprising. But others too, men of good will from every nation in the world, were impelled, under pressure of human necessity, to pursue the same course.

26. Hence, the Leonine encyclical is rightly regarded, even today, as the *Magna Charta*[9] of social and economic reconstruction.

The teaching of Quadragesimo Anno

27. Forty years after the appearance of this magnificent summary of Christian social principles, our predecessor, Pius XI, published his own encyclical, *Quadragesimo Anno*.[10]

28. In it the supreme pontiff confirmed the right and duty of the Catholic Church to work for an equitable solution of the many pressing problems weighing upon human society and calling for a joint effort by all the people. He reiterated the principles of the Leonine encyclical and stressed those directives which were applicable to modern conditions. In addition, he took the opportunity not only to clarify certain points of this teaching which had given rise to difficulties even in the minds of Catholics, but also to reformulate Christian social thought in the light of changed conditions.

29. The difficulties referred to principally concerned the Catholic's attitude to private property, the wage system, and moderate socialism.

30. With regard to private property, our predecessor reaffirmed its origin in natural law, and enlarged upon its social aspect and the obligations of ownership.

31. As for the wage system, while rejecting the view that it is unjust of its very nature, he condemned the inhuman and unjust way in which it is so often implemented, and specified the terms and conditions to be observed if justice and equity are not to be violated.

32. In this connection, as our predecessor clearly points out, it is advisable in the present circumstances that the wage contract be somewhat modified by applying to it elements taken from the contract of partnership, so that 'wage-earners and other employees participate in the ownership or the management, or in some way share in the profits'.[11]

33. Of special doctrinal and practical importance is his affirmation that 'if the social and individual character of work be overlooked, it can be neither justly valued nor equitably recompensed'.[12] In determining wages, therefore, justice demands that account be taken not only of the needs of the individual workers and their families, but also of the financial state of the business concern for which they work and of 'the economic welfare of the whole people'.[13]

34. Pope Pius XI further emphasized the fundamental opposition between communism and Christianity, and made it clear that no Catholic could subscribe even to moderate socialism. The reason is that socialism is founded on a doctrine of human society which is bounded by time and takes no account of any objective other than that of material well-being. Since, therefore, it proposes a form of social organization which aims solely at production, it places too severe a restraint on human liberty, at the same time flouting the true notion of social authority.

35. Pius XI was not unaware of the fact that in the forty years that had supervened since the publication of the Leonine encyclical the historical scene had altered considerably. It was clear, for example, that unregulated competition had succumbed to its own inherent tendencies to the point of practically destroying itself. It had given rise to a great accumulation of wealth, and, in the process, concentrated a despotic economic power in the hands of a few 'who for the most part are not the owners, but only the trustees and directors of invested funds, which they administer at their own good pleasure'.[14]

36. Hence, as the pope remarked so discerningly, 'economic domination has taken the place of the open market. Unbridled ambition for domination has succeeded the desire for gain; the whole economic regime has become hard, cruel and relentless in frightful measure.'[15] As a consequence, even the public authority was becoming the tool of plutocracy, which was thus gaining a stranglehold on the entire world.

37. Pius XI saw the re-establishment of the economic world within the framework of the moral order and the subordination of individual and group interests to the interest of the common good as the principal remedies for these evils. This, he taught, necessitated an orderly reconstruction of society, with the establishment of economic and vocational bodies which would be autonomous and independent of the State. Public authority should resume its duty of promoting the common good of all. Finally, there should be co-operation on a world scale for the economic welfare of all nations.

38. Thus Pius XI's teaching in this encyclical can be summed up under two heads. First he taught what the supreme criterion in economic matters ought *not* to be. It must not be the special interests of individuals or groups, nor unregulated competition, economic despotism, national prestige or imperialism, nor any other aim of this sort.

39. On the contrary, all forms of economic enterprise must be governed by the principles of social justice and charity.

40. The second point which we consider basic in the encyclical is his teaching that man's aim must be to achieve in social justice a national and international juridical order, with its network of public and private institutions, in which all economic activity can be conducted not merely for private gain but also in the interests of the common good.

The teaching of Pope Pius XII

41. For all that he did to render more precise the Christian definition of social rights and duties, no small recognition is due to our late predecessor, Pius XII. On Pentecost Sunday, 1 June 1941, he broadcast his message 'to call to the attention of the Catholic world a memory worthy of being written in letters of gold on the Church's calendar: the fiftieth anniversary of the publication of the epoch-making social encyclical of Leo XIII, *Rerum Novarum*,'[16] and 'to render to Almighty God from the bottom of our heart, our humble thanks for the gift, which...he bestowed on the Church in that encyclical of his vicar on earth, and to praise him for the life-giving breath of the Spirit which through it, in ever-growing measure from that time on, has blown on all mankind'.[17]

42. In that broadcast message the great pontiff claimed for the Church 'the indisputable competence' to 'decide whether the bases of a given social system are in accord with the unchangeable order which God our creator and redeemer has shown us through the natural law and revelation'.[18] He confirmed the perennial validity and inexhaustible worth of the teaching of *Rerum Novarum*, and took occasion 'to give some further directive moral

principles on three fundamental values of social and economic life. These three fundamental values, which are closely connected one with the other, mutually complementary and dependent, are: the use of material goods, work, and the family'.[19]

43. Concerning the use of material goods, our predecessor declared that the right of every man to use these for his own sustenance is prior to every other economic right, even that of private property. The right to the private possession of material goods is admittedly a natural one; nevertheless, in the objective order established by God, the right to property cannot stand in the way of the axiomatic principle that 'the goods which were created by God for all men should flow to all alike, according to the principles of justice and charity.'[20]

44. On the subject of work, Pius XII repeated the teaching of the Leonine encyclical, maintaining that a man's work is at once his duty and his right. It is for individuals, therefore, to regulate their mutual relations where their work is concerned. If they cannot do so, or will not do so, then, and only then, does 'it fall back on the State to intervene in the division and distribution of work, and this must be according to the form and measure that the common good properly understood demands.'[21]

45. In dealing with the family the supreme pontiff affirmed that the private ownership of material goods has a great part to play in promoting the welfare of family life. It 'secures for the father of a family the healthy liberty he needs in order to fulfil the duties assigned him by the creator regarding the physical, spiritual and religious welfare of the family'.[22] It is in this that the right of families to migrate is rooted. And so our predecessor, in speaking of migration, admonished both parties involved, namely the country of departure and the country receiving the newcomers, to seek always 'to eliminate as far as possible all obstacles to the birth and growth of real confidence'[23] between the nations. In this way both will contribute to, and share in, the increased welfare of man and the progress of culture.

New political, social and economic developments

46. But in the twenty years which have elapsed since the changing economic climate noted at that time by Pius XII the economic scene has undergone a radical transformation, both in the internal structure of the various states and in their relations with one another.

47. In the field of science, technology and economics we have the discovery of nuclear energy, and its application first to the purposes of war and later, increasingly, to peaceful ends; the practically limitless possibilities of chemistry in the production of synthetic materials; the growth of automation in industry and public services; the modernization of agriculture; the easing of communications, especially by radio and television; faster transportation and the initial conquest of interplanetary space.

48. In the social field we have the development of social insurance and, in the more economically advanced communities, the introduction of social

security systems. Men in labour unions are showing a more responsible awareness of the major social and economic problems. There is a progressive improvement in basic education, a wider distribution of essential commodities, greater opportunities for advancement in industry and the consequent breaking down of class barriers, and a keener interest in world affairs shown by people of average education. At the same time, however, this assessment of the increased efficiency of social and economic systems in a growing number of communities serves also to bring to light certain glaring discrepancies. There is, in the first place, a progressive lack of balance between agriculture on the one hand, and industry and public services on the other. Secondly, there are areas of varying economic prosperity within the same political communities. Finally—to take a world view—one observes a marked disparity in the economic wealth possessed by different countries.

49. To turn to the political field, we observe many changes. In a number of countries all classes of citizens are taking a part in public life, and public authorities are injecting themselves more each day into social and economic matters. We are witnessing the break away from colonialism and the attainment of political independence by the peoples of Asia and Africa. Drawn together by their common needs nations are becoming daily more interdependent. There is, moreover, an ever extending network of societies and organizations which set their sights beyond the aims and interests of individual countries and concentrate on the economic, social, cultural and political welfare of all nations throughout the world.

50. As we pass all this in review, we are aware of our responsibility to take up this torch which our great predecessors lighted, and hand it on with undiminished flame. It is a torch to lighten the pathways of all who would seek appropriate solutions to the many social problems of our times. Our purpose, therefore, is not merely to commemorate in a fitting manner the Leonine encyclical, but also to confirm and make more specific the teaching of our predecessors, and to determine clearly the mind of the Church on the new and important problems of the day.

II

The State and the individual

51. It should be stated at the outset that in the economic order first place must be given to the personal initiative of private citizens working either as individuals or in association with each other in various ways for the furtherance of common interests.

52. But—for reasons explained by our predecessors—the civil power must also have a hand in the economy. It has to promote production in a way best calculated to achieve social progress and the well-being of all citizens.

53. And in this work of directing, stimulating, co-ordinating, supplying and integrating, its guiding principle must be the 'principle of subsidiary function' formulated by Pius XI in *Quadragesimo Anno*.[24] 'This is a fundamental

principle of social philosophy, unshaken and unchangeable... Just as it is wrong to withdraw from the individual and commit to a community what private enterprise and industry can accomplish, so too it is an injustice, a grave evil and a disturbance of right order, for a larger and higher association to arrogate to itself functions which can be performed efficiently by smaller and lower societies. Of its very nature the true aim of all social activity should be to help members of the social body, but never to destroy or absorb them.'[25]

54. The present advance in scientific knowledge and productive technology clearly puts it within the power of the public authority to a much greater degree than ever before to reduce imbalances which may exist between different branches of the economy or between different regions within the same country or even between the different peoples of the world. It also puts into the hands of public authority a greater means for limiting fluctuations in the economy and for providing effective measures to prevent the recurrence of mass unemployment. Hence the insistent demands on those in authority—since they are responsible for the common good—to increase the degree and scope of their activities in the economic sphere, and to devise ways and means and set the necessary machinery in motion for the attainment of this end.

55. But however extensive and far reaching the influence of the State on the economy may be, it must never be exerted to the extent of depriving the individual citizen of his freedom of action. It must rather augment his freedom while effectively guaranteeing the protection of his essential personal rights. Among these is a man's right and duty to be primarily responsible for his own upkeep and that of his family. Hence every economic system must permit and facilitate the free development of productive activity.

56. Moreover, as history itself testifies with ever increasing clarity, there can be no such thing as a well-ordered and prosperous society unless individual citizens and the State co-operate in the economy. Both sides must work together in harmony, and their respective efforts must be proportioned to the needs of the common good in the prevailing circumstances and conditions of human life.

57. Experience has shown that where personal initiative is lacking, political tyranny ensues and, in addition, economic stagnation in the production of a wide range of consumer goods and of services of the material and spiritual order—those, namely, which are in a great measure dependent upon the exercise and stimulus of individual creative talent.

58. Where, on the other hand, the good offices of the State are lacking or deficient, incurable disorder ensues: in particular, the unscrupulous exploitation of the weak by the strong. For men of this stamp are always in evidence, and, like cockle among the wheat, thrive in every land.

The growth of associations

59. Certainly one of the principal characteristics which seem to be typical of our age is an increase in social relationships,* in those mutual ties, that is,

*Asterisk indicates editor's note, which will be found at the end of each document.

which grow daily more numerous and which have led to the introduction of many and varied forms of associations in the lives and activities of citizens, and to their acceptance within our legal framework. Scientific and technical progress, greater productive efficiency and a higher standard of living are among the many present-day factors which would seem to have contributed to this trend.

60. This development in the social life of man is at once a symptom and a cause of the growing intervention of the State, even in matters which are of intimate concern to the individual, hence of great importance and not devoid of risk. We might cite as examples such matters as health and education, the choice of a career, and the care and rehabilitation of the physically and mentally handicapped. It is also partly the result, partly the expression of a natural, well-nigh irresistible urge in man to combine with his fellows for the attainment of aims and objectives which are beyond the means or the capabilities of single individuals. In recent times, this tendency has given rise to the formation everywhere of both national and international movements, associations and institutions with economic, cultural, social, sporting, recreational, professional and political ends.

61. Clearly, this sort of development in social relationships brings many advantages in its train. It makes it possible for the individual to exercise many of his personal rights, especially those which we call economic and social and which pertain to the necessities of life, health care, education on a more extensive and improved basis, a more thorough professional training, housing, work, and suitable leisure and recreation. Furthermore, the progressive perfection of modern methods of thought-diffusion—the press, cinema, radio, television—makes it possible for everyone to participate in human events the world over.

62. At the same time, however, this multiplication and daily extension of forms of association brings with it a multiplicity of restrictive laws and regulations in many departments of human life. As a consequence, it narrows the sphere of a person's freedom of action. The means often used, the methods followed, the atmosphere created, all conspire to make it difficult for a person to think independently of outside influences, to act on his own initiative, exercise his responsibility and express and fulfil his own personality. What then? Must we conclude that these increased social relationships necessarily reduce men to the condition of being mere automatons? By no means.

63. For actually this growth in the social life of man is not a product of natural forces working, as it were, by blind impulse. It is, as we saw, the creation of men who are free and autonomous by nature—though they must, of course, recognize and, in a sense, obey the laws of economic development and social progress, and cannot altogether escape from the pressure of environment.

64. The development of these social relationships, therefore, can and ought to be realized in a way best calculated to promote its inherent advantages and to preclude, or at least diminish, its attendant disadvantages.

Associations and the individual

65. To this end, a sane view of the common good must be present and operative in men invested with public authority. They must take account of all those social conditions which favour the full development of human personality. Moreover, we consider it altogether vital that the numerous intermediary bodies and corporate enterprises—which are, so to say, the main vehicle of this social growth—be really autonomous, and loyally collaborate in pursuit of their own specific interests and those of the common good. For these groups must themselves necessarily present the form and substance of a true community, and this will only be the case if they treat their individual members as human persons and encourage them to take an active part in the ordering of their lives.

66. As these mutual ties binding the men of our age one to the other grow and develop, governments will the more easily achieve a right order the more they succeed in striking a balance between the autonomous and active collaboration of individuals and groups, and the timely co-ordination and encouragement by the State of these private undertakings.

67. So long as social relationships do in fact adhere to these principles within the framework of the moral order, their extension does not necessarily mean that individual citizens will be gravely discriminated against or excessively burdened. On the contrary, we can hope that they will help him to develop and perfect his own personal talents, and lead to that organic reconstruction of society which our predecessor Pius XI advocated in his encyclical *Quadragesimo Anno* as the indispensable prerequisite for the fulfilment of the rights and obligations of social life.[26]

Fair wages

68. We are filled with an overwhelming sadness when we contemplate the sorry spectacle of millions of workers in many lands and entire continents condemned through the inadequacy of their wages to live with their families in utterly subhuman conditions. This is probably due to the fact that the process of industrialization in these countries is only in its initial stages, or is still not sufficiently developed.

69. Nevertheless, in some of these lands the enormous wealth, the unbridled luxury, of the privileged few stands in violent, offensive contrast to the utter poverty of the vast majority. In some parts of the world men are being subjected to inhuman privations so that the output of the national economy can be increased at a rate of acceleration beyond what would be possible if regard were had to social justice and equity. And in other countries a notable percentage of income is absorbed in building up an ill-conceived national prestige, and vast sums are spent on armaments.

70. In economically developed countries, relatively unimportant services, and services of doubtful value, frequently carry a disproportionately high rate of remuneration, while the diligent and profitable work of whole classes of

honest, hard-working men gets scant reward. Their rate of pay is quite inadequate to meet the basic needs of life. It in no way corresponds to the contribution they make to the good of the community, to the profits of the company for which they work, and to the general national economy.

71. We therefore consider it our duty to reaffirm that the remuneration of work is not something that can be left to the laws of the marketplace; nor should it be a decision left to the will of the more powerful. It must be determined in accordance with justice and equity; which means that workers must be paid a wage which allows them to live a truly human life and to fulfil their family obligations in a worthy manner. Other factors too enter into the assessment of a just wage: namely, the effective contribution which each individual makes to the economic effort, the financial state of the company for which he works, the requirements of the general good of the particular country—having regard especially to the repercussions on the overall employment of the working force in the country as a whole—and finally the requirements of the common good of the universal family of nations of every kind, both large and small.

72. The above principles are valid always and everywhere. So much is clear. But their degree of applicability to concrete cases cannot be determined without reference to the quantity and quality of available resources; and these can—and in fact do—vary from country to country, and even, from time to time, within the same country.

Shared ownership

73. In view of the rapid expansion of national economies, particularly since the war, there is one very important social principle to which we would draw your attention. It is this: economic progress must be accompanied by a corresponding social progress, so that all classes of citizens can participate in the increased productivity. The utmost vigilance and effort is needed to ensure that social inequalities, so far from increasing, are reduced to a minimum.

74. As our predecessor Pius XII observed with evident justification: 'Likewise the national economy, as it is the product of the men who work together in the community of the State, has no other end than to secure without interruption the material conditions in which the individual life of the citizens may fully develop. Where this is secured in a permanent way, a people will be, in a true sense, economically rich, because the general well-being, and consequently the personal right of all to the use of worldly goods, is thus actuated in conformity with the purpose willed by the creator.'[27] From this it follows that the economic prosperity of a nation is not so much its total assets in terms of wealth and property, as the equitable division and distribution of this wealth. This it is which guarantees the personal development of the members of society, which is the true goal of a nation's economy.

75. We must notice in this connection the system of self-financing adopted in many countries by large, or comparatively large firms. Because these

[95]

companies are financing replacement and plant expansion out of their own profits, they grow at a very rapid rate. In such cases we believe that the workers should be allocated shares in the firms for which they work, especially when they are paid no more than a minimum wage.

76. We should recall here the principle enunciated by Pius XI in *Quadragesimo Anno*: 'It is entirely false to ascribe to the property alone or to the work alone whatever has been obtained through the combined effort of both, and it is wholly unjust for either, denying the efficacy of the other, to arrogate to itself whatever has been produced.'[28]

77. Experience suggests many ways in which the demands of justice can be satisfied. Not to mention other ways, it is especially desirable today that workers gradually come to share in the ownership of their company, by ways and in the manner that seem most suitable. For today, even more than in the time of our predecessor, 'every effort must be made that at least in future a just share only of the fruits of production be permitted to accumulate in the hands of the wealthy, and that an ample sufficiency be supplied to the workers.'[29]

Taking account of the common good

78. But a further point needs emphasizing: any adjustment between wages and profits must take into account the demands of the common good of the particular country and of the whole human family.

79. What are these demands? On the national level they include: employment of the greatest possible number of workers; care lest privileged classes arise, even among the workers; maintenance of equilibrium between wages and prices; the need to make goods and services accessible to the greatest number; elimination, or at least the restriction, of inequalities in the various branches of the economy—that is, between agriculture, industry and services; creation of a proper balance between economic expansion and the development of social services, especially through the activity of public authorities; the best possible adjustment of the means of production to the progress of science and technology; seeing to it that the benefits which make possible a more human way of life will be available not merely to the present generation but to the coming generations as well.

80. The demands of the common good on the international level include: the avoidance of all forms of unfair competition between the economies of different countries; the fostering of mutual collaboration and good will; and effective co-operation in the development of economically less advanced communities.

81. These demands of the common good, both on a national and a world level, must also be borne in mind when assessing the rate of return due as compensation to the company's management, and as interest or dividends to investors.

Worker participation

82. Justice is to be observed not only in the distribution of wealth, but also in regard to the conditions in which men are engaged in producing this wealth. Every man has, of his very nature, a need to express himself in his work and thereby to perfect his own being.

83. Consequently, if the whole structure and organization of an economic system is such as to compromise human dignity, to lessen a man's sense of responsibility or rob him of opportunity for exercising personal initiative, then such a system, we maintain, is altogether unjust—no matter how much wealth it produces, or how justly and equitably such wealth is distributed.

84. It is not possible to give a concise definition of the kind of economic structure which is most consonant with man's dignity and best calculated to develop in him a sense of responsibility. Pius XII, however, comes to our rescue with the following directive: 'The small and average-sized undertakings in agriculture, in the arts and crafts, in commerce and industry, should be safeguarded and fostered. Moreover, they should join together in co-operative associations to gain for themselves the benefits and advantages that usually can be gained only from large organizations. In the large concerns themselves there should be the possibility of moderating the contract of work by one of partnership.'[30]

85. Hence the craftsman's business and that of the family farm, as well as the co-operative enterprise which aims at the completion and perfection of both these concerns—all these are to be safeguarded and encouraged in harmony with the common good and technical progress.

86. We shall return shortly to the question of the family farm. Here we consider it appropriate to say something about artisan and co-operative enterprises.

87. First of all it is necessary to emphasize that if these two kinds of undertaking are to thrive and prosper they must be prepared constantly to adjust their productive equipment and their productive methods to meet new situations created by the advance of science and technology and the changing demands and preferences of the consumer. This adaptation must be effected principally by the workers themselves and the members of the co-operatives.

88. Both these groups, therefore, need a thoroughgoing technical and general education, and should have their own professional organizations. It is equally important that the government take the proper steps regarding their training, taxation, credit, social security and insurance.

89. Furthermore, these two categories of citizens—craftsmen and members of co-operatives—are fully entitled to these watchful measures of the State, for they are upholding true human values and contributing to the advance of civilization.

90. We therefore paternally invite our beloved sons—craftsmen and members of co-operatives throughout the world—to realize the greatness of this task which is theirs in the State. By the force of their example they are helping to

keep alive in their own community a true sense of responsibility, a spirit of co-operation, and the constant desire to create new and original work of outstanding merit.

91. We, no less than our predecessors, are convinced that employees are justified in wishing to participate in the activity of the industrial concern for which they work. It is not of course, possible to lay down hard and fast rules regarding the manner of such participation, for this must depend upon prevailing conditions, which vary from firm to firm and are frequently subject to rapid and substantial alteration. But we have no doubt as to the need for giving workers an active part in the business of the company for which they work—be it a private or a public one. Every effort must be made to ensure that the enterprise is indeed a true human community, concerned about the needs, the activities and the standing of each of its members.

92. This demands that the relations between management and employees reflect understanding, appreciation and good will on both sides. It demands, too, that all parties co-operate actively and loyally in the common enterprise, not so much for what they can get out of it for themselves, but as discharging a duty and rendering a service to their fellow men. All this implies that the workers have their say in, and make their own contribution to, the efficient running and development of the enterprise. As Pius XII remarked, 'the economic and social function which every man aspires to fulfil, demands that the carrying on of the activity of each one is not completely subjected to the others.'[31] Obviously, any firm which is concerned for the human dignity of its workers must also maintain a necessary and efficient unity of direction. But it must not treat those employees who spend their days in service with the firm as though they were mere cogs in the machinery, denying them any opportunity of expressing their wishes or bringing their experience to bear on the work in hand, and keeping them entirely passive in regard to decisions that regulate their activity.

93. We would observe, finally, that the present demand for workers to have a greater say in the conduct of the firm accords not only with man's nature, but also with recent progress in the economic, social and political spheres.

94. For although many unjust and inhuman economic and social imbalances still exist in our day, and there are still many errors affecting the activity, aims, structure and operation of economies the world over, it is an undeniable fact that, thanks to the driving impulse of scientific and technical advance, productive systems are today rapidly becoming more modernized and efficient—more so than ever before. Hence a greater technical skill is required of the workers, and more exacting professional qualifications. Which means that they must be given more assistance, and more free time in which to complete their vocational training as well as try out more fittingly their cultural, moral and religious education.

95. As a further consequence, the modern youth is enabled to devote a longer time to his basic schooling in the arts and sciences.

96. All this serves to create an environment in which workers are encouraged to assume greater responsibility in their own sphere of employment. In

politics, too, it is of no small consequence that citizens are becoming daily more aware of their responsibility for furthering the common good in all spheres of life.

Associations and the economy

97. In modern times we have seen an extensive increase in the number of workers' associations, and their general recognition in the juridical codes of single states and on the international level. Members are no longer recruited in order to agitate, but rather to co-operate, principally by the method of collective bargaining. But it is worthwhile stressing here how timely and imperative it is that workers be given the opportunity to exert their influence throughout the State, and not just within the limits of their own spheres of employment.

98. The reason for this is that the individual productive concerns, regardless of their size, efficiency and importance in the State, form but a part—an integral part—of a nation's entire economic and social life, upon which their own prosperity must depend.

99. Hence it is not the decisions made within the individual productive units which have the greatest bearing on the economy, but those made by public authorities and by institutions which tackle the various economic problems on a national or international basis. It is therefore very appropriate, or even necessary, that these public authorities and institutions bring the workers into their discussions, and those who represent the rights, demands and aspirations of the working men; and not confine their deliberations to those who merely represent the interests of management.

100. It is our prerogative to be a father, and there is a special place in our thoughts and in our heart for those professional groups and Christian associations of workers which exist and operate in so many parts of the world. We know the nature and extent of the difficulties under which these dearest sons of ours are labouring, as they strive continually and effectually to promote in their own countries and throughout the world the material and moral interests of the working people.

101. They are fully deserving of our praise. The importance of their work must be gauged not merely by its immediate and obvious results, but also by its effect on the working world as a whole, where it helps to spread sound principles of action and the wholesome influence of the Christian religion.

102. We wish further to praise those dear sons of ours who in a true Christian spirit collaborate with other professional groups and workers' associations which respect the natural law and the freedom of conscience of the members.

103. We must also express here our heartfelt appreciation of the work that is being done by the International Labour Organization—popularly known in various countries as the OIL or ILO or OIT. For many years now it has been making an effective and valued contribution to the establishment in the world of an economics and social order marked by justice and humanity, an order which recognizes and safeguards the lawful rights of the working man.

[99]

The right to private property

104. It is well-known that in recent years in the larger industrial concerns distinction has been growing between the ownership of productive goods and the responsibility of company managers. This has created considerable problems for public authorities, whose duty it is to see that the aims pursued by the leaders of the principal organizations—especially those which have an important part to play in the national economy—do not conflict in any way with the interests of the common good. Experience shows that these problems arise whether the capital which makes possible these vast undertakings belongs to private citizens or to public corporations.

105. It is also true that more and more people today, through belonging to insurance groups and systems of social security, find that they can face the future with confidence—the sort of confidence which formerly resulted from their possession of a certain amount of property.

106. And another thing happening today is that people are aiming at proficiency in their trade or profession rather than the acquisition of private property. They think more highly of an income which derives from capital and the rights of capital.

107. And this is as it should be. Work, which is the immediate expression of a human personality, must always be rated higher than the possession of external goods which of their very nature are merely instrumental. This view of work is certainly an indication of an advance that has been made in our civilization.

108. What, then, of that social and economic principle so vigorously asserted and defended by our predecessors: man's natural right to own private property, including productive goods? Is this no longer operative today, or has it lost some of its validity in view of the economic conditions we have described above? This is the doubt that has arisen in many minds.

109. There is no reason for such a doubt to persist. The right of private ownership of goods, including productive goods, has permanent validity. It is part of the natural order, which teaches that the individual is prior to society and society must be ordered to the good of the individual. Moreover, it would be quite useless to insist on free and personal initiative in the economic field, while at the same time withdrawing man's right to dispose freely of the means indispensable to the achievement of such initiative. Further, history and experience testify that in those political regimes which do not recognize the rights of private ownership of goods, productive included, the exercise of freedom in almost every other direction is suppressed or stifled. This suggests, surely, that the exercise of freedom finds its guarantee and incentive in the right of ownership.

110. This explains why social and political movements for the harmonizing of justice and freedom in society, though until recently opposed to the private ownership of productive goods, are today reconsidering their position in the light of a clearer understanding of social history, and are in fact now declaring themselves in favour of this right.

111. Accordingly, we make our own the directive of our predecessor Pius XII: 'In defending the principle of private ownership the Church is striving after an important ethico-social end. She does not intend merely to uphold the present condition of things as if it were an expression of the divine will, or to protect on principle the rich and plutocrats against the poor and indigent... The Church aims rather at securing that the institution of private property be such as it should be according to the plan of the divine wisdom and the dispositions of nature.'[32] Hence private ownership must be considered as a guarantee of the essential freedom of the individual, and at the same time an indispensable element in a true social order.

112. Moreover, in recent years, as we have seen, the productive efficiency of many national economies has been increasing rapidly. Justice and fairness demand, therefore, that, within the limits of the common good, wages too shall increase. This means that workers are able to save more and thus acquire a certain amount of property of their own. In view of this it is strange that the innate character of a right which derives its force and validity from the fruitfulness of work should ever be called in question—a right which constitutes so efficacious a means of asserting one's personality and exercising responsibility in every field, and an element of solidity and security for family life and of greater peace and prosperity in the state.

113. But it is not enough to assert that the right to own private property and the means of production is inherent in human nature. We must also insist on the extension of this right in practice to all classes of citizens.

114. As our predecessor Pius XII so rightly affirmed: the dignity of the human person 'normally demands the right to the use of the goods of the earth, to which corresponds the fundamental obligation of granting an opportunity to possess property to all if possible'.[33] This demand arises from the moral dignity of work. It also guarantees 'the conservation and perfection of a social order which makes possible a secure, even if modest, property to all classes of people'.[34]

115. Now, if ever, is the time to insist on a more widespread distribution of property, in view of the rapid economic development of an increasing number of states. It will not be difficult for the body politic, by the adoption of various techniques of proved efficiency, to pursue an economic and social policy which facilitates the widest possible distribution of private property in terms of durable consumer goods, houses, land, tools and equipment (in the case of craftsmen and owners of family farms), and shares in medium and large business concerns. This policy is in fact being pursued with considerable success by several of the socially and economically advanced nations.

The limitations of public ownership

116. This, of course, is not to deny the lawfulness of state and public ownership of productive goods, especially those which 'carry with them a power too great to be left to private individuals without injury to the community at large'.[35]

117. State and public ownership of property is very much on the increase today. This is explained by the exigencies of the common good, which demand that public authority broaden its sphere of activity. But here, too, the 'principle of subsidiary function' must be observed. The State and other agencies of public law must not extend their ownership beyond what is clearly required by considerations of the common good properly understood, and even then there must be safeguards. Otherwise private ownership could be reduced beyond measure, or, even worse, completely destroyed.

118. It is important, too, not to overlook the fact that the economic enterprises of the State and other agencies of public law must be entrusted to men of good reputation who have the necessary experience and ability and a keen sense of responsibility towards their country. Furthermore, a strict check should constantly be kept upon their activity, so as to avoid any possibility of the concentration of undue economic power in the hands of a few state officials, to the detriment of the best interests of the community.

The obligations of ownership

119. Our predecessors have insisted time and again on the social function inherent in the right of private ownership, for it cannot be denied that in the plan of the creator all of this world's goods are primarily intended for the worthy support of the entire human race. Hence, as Leo XIII so wisely taught in *Rerum Novarum*: 'whoever has received from the divine bounty a large share of temporal blessings, whether they be external and corporeal, or gifts of the mind, has received them for the purpose of using them for the perfecting of his own nature, and, at the same time, that he may employ them, as the steward of God's providence, for the benefit of others. "He that hath a talent," says St Gregory the Great, "let him see that he hide it not; he that hath abundance, let him quicken himself to mercy and generosity; he that hath art and skill, let him do his best to share the use and the utility thereof with his neighbour." '[36]

120. In recent years the State and other agencies of public law have extended, and are continuing to extend, the sphere of their activity and initiative. But this does not mean that the doctrine of the social function of private ownership is out of date, as some would maintain. It is inherent in the very right of private ownership. Then, too, a further consideration arises. Tragic situations and urgent problems of an intimate and personal nature are continually arising which the State with all its machinery is unable to remedy or assist. There will always remain, therefore, a vast field for the exercise of human sympathy and the Christian charity of individuals. We would observe, finally, that the efforts of individuals, or of groups of private citizens, are definitely more effective in promoting spiritual values than is the activity of public authority.

121. We should notice at this point that the right of private ownership is clearly sanctioned by the gospel. Yet at the same time, the divine master frequently extends to the rich the insistent invitation to convert their material goods into spiritual ones by conferring them on the poor. 'Lay not up to

yourselves treasures on earth; where the rust and moth consume and where thieves break through and steal. But lay up to yourselves treasures in heaven; where neither the rust nor moth doth consume, and where thieves do not break through nor steal.'[37] And the Lord will look upon the charity given to the poor as given to himself. 'Amen, I say to you, as long as you did it to one of these my least brethren, you did it to me.'[38]

III

Problems of farmers

122. History shows with ever increasing clarity that it is not only the relations between workers and managers that need to be re-established on the basis of justice and equity, but also those between the various branches of the economy, between areas of varying productivity within the same political community, and between countries with a different degree of social and economic development.

123. First, with regard to agriculture, it would not appear that the rural population as a whole is decreasing, but it is an undeniable fact that many people are moving away from their farms into more thickly populated areas as well as into the cities themselves. When we realize that this movement of population is going on in nearly every part of the world, often on a large scale, we begin to appreciate the complexity of the human problems involved and their difficulty of solution.

124. We know that as an economy develops, the number of people engaged in agriculture decreases, while the percentage employed in industry and the various services rises. Nevertheless, we believe that very often this movement of population from farming to industry has other causes besides those dependent upon economic expansion. Among these there is the desire to escape from confining surroundings which offer little prospect of a more comfortable way of life. There is the lure of novelty and adventure which has taken such a hold on the present generation, the attractive prospect of easy money, of greater freedom and the enjoyment of all the amenities of town and city life. But a contributory cause of this movement away from the country is doubtless the fact that farming has become a depressed occupation. It is inadequate both in productive efficiency and in the standard of living it provides.

125. Nearly every country, therefore, is faced with this fundamental problem: what can be done to reduce the disproportion in productive efficiency between agriculture on the one hand, and industry and services on the other; and to ensure that agricultural living standards approximate as closely as possible those enjoyed by city-dwellers who draw their resources either from industry or from the services in which they are engaged? What can be done to persuade agricultural workers that, far from being inferior to other people, they have every opportunity of developing their personality through their work, and can look forward to the future with confidence?

How the State could help

126. It seems to us opportune to indicate certain directives that can contribute to a solution of this problem: directives which we believe have value whatever may be the historical environment in which one acts—on condition, obviously, that they be applied in the manner and to the degree allowed, suggested, or even demanded by the circumstances.

127. In the first place, considerable thought must be given, especially by public authorities, to the suitable development of essential facilities in country areas—such as roads; transportation; means of communication; drinking water; housing; health services; elementary, technical and professional education; religious and recreational facilities; and the supply of modern installations and furnishings for the farm residence. Such services as these are necessary nowadays if a becoming standard of living is to be maintained. In those country areas where they are lacking, economic and social progress is either prevented or greatly impeded, with the result that nothing can be done to retard the drift of population away from the land, and it even becomes difficult to make a good appraisal of the numbers involved.

128. If a country is to develop economically, it must do so gradually, maintaining an even balance between all sectors of the economy. Agriculture, therefore, must be allowed to make use of the same reforms in the method and type of production and in the conduct of the business side of the venture as are permitted or required in the economic system as a whole. All such reforms should correspond as nearly as possible with those introduced in industry and the various services.

129. In this way, agriculture will absorb a larger amount of industrial goods and require a better system of services. But at the same time it will provide both industry and the services and the country as a whole with the type of products which, in quantity and quality, best meet the needs of the consumer and contribute to the stability of the purchasing power of money—a major consideration in the orderly development of the entire economic system.

130. One advantage which would result from the adoption of this plan would be that it would be easier to keep track of the movement of the working force set free by the progressive modernization of agriculture. Facilities could then be provided for the training of such people for their new kind of work, and they would not be left without economic aid and the mental and spiritual assistance they need to ensure their proper integration in their new social milieu.

131. In addition, a sound agricultural programme is needed if public authority is to maintain an evenly balanced progress in the various branches of the economy. This must take into account tax policies, credit, social insurance, prices, the fostering of ancillary industries and the adjustment of the structure of farming as a business enterprise.

132. In a system of taxation based on justice and equity it is fundamental that the burdens be proportioned to the capacity of the people contributing.

133. But the common good also requires that public authorities, in assessing the amount of tax payable, take cognizance of the peculiar difficulties of farmers. They have to wait longer than most people for their returns, and these are exposed to greater hazards. Consequently, farmers find greater difficulty in obtaining the capital necessary to increase returns.

134. For this reason, too, investors are more inclined to put their money in industry rather than agriculture. Farmers are unable to pay high rates of interest. Indeed, they cannot as a rule make the trading profit necessary to furnish capital for the conduct and development of their own business. It is therefore necessary, for reasons of the common good, for public authorities to evolve a special credit policy and to form credit banks which will guarantee such capital to farmers at a moderate rate of interest.

135. In agriculture the existence of two forms of insurance may be necessary: one concerned with agricultural produce, the other with the farm workers and their families. We realize that agricultural workers earn less per capita than workers in industry and the services, but that is no reason why it should be considered socially just and equitable to set up systems of social insurance in which the allowances granted to farm workers and their families are substantially lower than those payable to other classes of workers. Insurance programmes that are established for the general public should not differ markedly whatever be the economic sector in which the individuals work or the source of their income.

136. Systems of social insurance and social security can make a most effective contribution to the overall distribution of national income in accordance with the principles of justice and equity. They can therefore be instrumental in reducing imbalances between the different classes of citizens.

137. Given the special nature of agricultural produce, modern economists must devise a suitable means of price protection. Ideally, such price protection should be enforced by the interested parties themselves, though supervision by the public authority cannot be altogether dispensed with.

138. On this subject it must not be forgotten that the price of agricultural produce represents, for the most part, the reward of the farmer's labour rather than a return on invested capital.

139. Hence, in *Quadragesimo Anno* Pope Pius XI rightly observed that 'a proper proportion between different wages is also a matter of importance.' He continued: 'And intimately connected with this is a proper proportion between the prices charged for the products of the various economic groups, agricultural, industrial, and so forth.'[39]

140. While it is true that farm produce is mainly intended for the satisfaction of man's primary needs, and the price should therefore be within the means of all consumers, this cannot be used as an argument for keeping a section of the population—farm workers—in a permanent state of economic and social inferiority, depriving them of the wherewithal for a decent standard of living. This would be diametrically opposed to the common good.

141. Moreover, the time has come to promote in agricultural regions the

establishment of those industries and services which are concerned with the preservation, processing and transportation of farm products. Enterprises relating to other sectors of the economy might also be established there. In this case the rural population would have another means of income at their disposal, a means which they could exploit in the social milieu to which they are accustomed.

142. It is not possible to determine *a priori* what the structure of farm life should be, since rural conditions vary so much from place to place and from country to country throughout the world. But if we hold to a human and Christian concept of man and the family, we are bound to consider as an ideal that form of enterprise which is modelled on the basis of a community of persons working together for the advancement of their mutual interests in accordance with the principles of justice and Christian teaching. We are bound above all to consider as an ideal the kind of farm which is owned and managed by the family. Every effort must be made in the prevailing circumstances to give effective encouragement to farming enterprises of this nature.

143. But if the family farm is not to go bankrupt it must make enough money to keep the family in reasonable comfort. To ensure this, farmers must be given up-to-date instruction on the latest methods of cultivation, and the assistance of experts must be put at their disposal. They should also form a flourishing system of co-operative undertakings, and organize themselves professionally to take an effective part in public life, both on the administrative and the political level.

How farmers could help themselves

144. We are convinced that the farming community must take an active part in its own economic advancement, social progress and cultural betterment. Those who live on the land can hardly fail to appreciate the nobility of the work they are called upon to do. They are living in close harmony with nature—the majestic temple of creation. Their work has to do with the life of plants and animals, a life that is inexhaustible in its expression, inflexible in its laws, rich in allusions to God the creator and provider. They produce food for the support of human life, and the raw materials of industry in ever richer supply.

145. Theirs is a work which carries with it a dignity all its own. It brings into its service many branches of engineering, chemistry and biology, and is itself a cause of the continued practical development of these sciences in view of the repercussions of scientific and technical progress on the business of farming. It is a work which demands a capacity for orientation and adaptation, patient waiting, a sense of responsibility, and a spirit of perseverance and enterprise.

146. It is important also to bear in mind that in agriculture, as in other sectors of production, association is a vital need today—especially in the case of family farms. Rural workers should feel a sense of solidarity with one another, and should unite to form co-operatives and professional associations. These are very necessary if farm workers are to benefit from

scientific and technical methods of production and protect the prices of their products. They are necessary, too, if they are to attain an equal footing with other professional classes who, in most cases, have joined together in associations. They are necessary, finally, if farm workers are to have their proper voice in political circles and in public administration. The lone voice is not likely to command much of a hearing in times such as ours.

147. In using their various organizations, agricultural workers—as indeed all other classes of workers—must always be guided by moral principles and respect for the civil law. They must try to reconcile their rights and interests with those of other classes of workers, and even subordinate the one to the other if the common good demands it. If they show themselves alive to the common good and contribute to its realizations, they can legitimately demand that their efforts for the improvement of agricultural conditions be seconded and complemented by public authority.

148. We therefore desire here to express our satisfaction with those sons of ours the world over who are actively engaged in co-operatives, in professional groups and in worker movements intent on raising the economic and social standards of the agricultural community.

149. In the work on the farm the human personality finds every incentive for self-expression, self-development and spiritual growth. It is a work, therefore, which should be thought of as a vocation, a God-given mission, an answer to God's call to actuate his providential, saving plan in history. It should be thought of, finally, as a noble task, undertaken with a view to raising oneself and others to a higher degree of civilization.

A balanced economy

150. Among citizens of the same political community there is often a marked degree of economic and social inequality. The main reason for this is the fact that they are living and working in different areas, some of which are more economically developed than others. Where this situation obtains, justice and equity demand that public authority try to eliminate or reduce such imbalances. It should ensure that the less developed areas receive such essential public services as their circumstances require, in order to bring the standard of living in these areas into line with the national average. Furthermore, a suitable economic and social policy must be devised which will take into account the supply of labour, the drift of population, wages, taxes, credit, and the investing of money, especially in expanding industries. In short, it should be a policy designed to promote useful employment, enterprising initiative, and the exploitation of local resources.

151. But the justification of all government action is the common good. Public authority, therefore, must bear in mind the interests of the state as a whole; which means that it must promote all three areas of production—agriculture, industry and services—simultaneously and evenly. Everything must be done to ensure that citizens of the less developed areas are treated as responsible human beings, and are allowed to play the major role in achieving their own economic, social and cultural advancement.

152. Private enterprise too must contribute to an economic and social balance in the different areas of the same political community. Indeed, in accordance with 'the principle of subsidiary function', public authority must encourage and assist private enterprise, entrusting to it, wherever possible, the continuation of economic development.

Collaboration among nations

153. It is not out of place to remark here on a problem which exists in quite a number of countries, namely, a gross disproportion between land and population. In some countries arable land abounds, but there is a scarcity of population; whereas in other countries the position is reversed: the population is large, arable land scarce.

154. Again, some countries use primitive methods of agriculture, with the result that, for all their abundance of natural resources, they are not able to produce enough food to feed their population; whereas other countries, using modern methods of agriculture, produce a surplus of food which has an adverse effect on the economy.

155. It is therefore obvious that the solidarity of the human race and Christian brotherhood demand the elimination as far as possible of these discrepancies. With this object in view, people all over the world must co-operate actively with one another in all sorts of ways, so as to facilitate the movement of goods, capital and men from one country to another. We shall have more to say on this point later on.

156. Here we would like to express our sincere appreciation of the work which the FAO* has undertaken to establish effective collaboration among nations, to promote the modernization of agriculture especially in less developed countries, and to alleviate the suffering of hunger-striken peoples.

157. Probably the most difficult problem today concerns the relationship between political communities that are economically advanced and those in the process of development. Whereas the standard of living is high in the former, the latter are subject to extreme poverty. The solidarity which binds all men together as members of a common family makes it impossible for wealthy nations to look with indifference upon the hunger, misery and poverty of other nations whose citizens are unable to enjoy even elementary human rights. The nations of the world are becoming more and more dependent on one another and it will not be possible to preserve a lasting peace so long as glaring economic and social imbalances persist.

158. Mindful of our position as the father of all peoples, we feel constrained to repeat here what we said on another occasion: 'We are all equally responsible for the undernourished peoples.[40] [Hence], it is necessary to educate one's conscience to the sense of responsibility which weighs upon each and every one, especially upon those who are more blessed with this world's goods.'[41]

159. The Church has always emphasized that this obligation of helping those who are in misery and want should be felt most strongly by Catholics, in view

of the fact that they are members of the mystical body of Christ. 'In this we have known the charity of God,' says St John, 'because he has laid down his life for us; and we ought to lay down our lives for the brethren. He that hath the substance of this world and shall see his brother in need and shall shut up his bowels from him; how doth the charity of God abide in him?'[42]

160. It is therefore a great source of joy to us to see those nations which enjoy a high degree of economic wealth helping the nations not so well provided, so that they may more effectively raise their standard of living.

International aid

161. Justice and humanity demand that those countries which produce consumer goods, especially farm products, in excess of their own needs should come to the assistance of those other countries where large sections of the population are suffering from want and hunger. It is nothing less than an outrage to justice and humanity to destroy or to squander goods that other people need for their very lives.

162. We are, of course, well aware that over-production, especially in agriculture, can cause economic harm to a certain section of the population. But it does not follow that one is thereby exonerated from extending emergency aid to those who need it. On the contrary, everything must be done to minimize the ill effects of over-production, and to spread the burden equitably over the entire population.

163. Of itself, however, emergency aid will not go far in relieving want and famine when these are caused—as they so often are—by the primitive state of a nation's economy. The only permanent remedy for this is to make use of every possible means of providing these citizens with the scientific, technical and professional training they need, and to put at their disposal the necessary capital for speeding up their economic development with the help of modern methods.

164. We are aware how deeply the public conscience has been affected in recent years by the urgent need of supporting the economic development and social progress of those countries which are still struggling against poverty and economic disabilities.

165. International and regional organizations, national and private societies, all are working towards this goal, increasing day to day the measure of their own technical co-operation in all productive spheres. By their combined efforts thousands of young people are being given facilities for attending the universities of the more advanced countries, and acquiring an up-to-date scientific, technical and professional training. World banking institutes, individual states and private persons are helping to furnish the capital for an ever richer network of economic enterprises in the less wealthy countries. It is a magnificent work that they are doing, and we are most happy to take this occasion of giving it the praise that it deserves. It is a work, however, which needs to be increased, and we hope that the years ahead will see the wealthier nations making even greater efforts for the scientific, technical and economic

advancement of those political communities whose development is still only in its initial stages.

166. We consider it our duty to give further advice on this matter.

167. In the first place, those nations which are still only at the beginning of their journey along the road to economic development would do well to consider carefully the experiences of the wealthier nations which have traversed this road before them.

168. Increase in production and productive efficiency is, of course, sound policy, and indeed a vital necessity. However, it is no less necessary—and justice itself demands—that the riches produced be distributed fairly among all members of the political community. This means that everything must be done to ensure that social progress keeps pace with economic progress. Again, every sector of the economy—agriculture, industry and the services—must progress evenly and simultaneously.

169. The developing nations, obviously, have certain unmistakable characteristics of their own, resulting from the nature of the particular region and the natural dispositions of their citizens, with their time-honoured traditions and customs.

170. In helping these nations, therefore, the more advanced communities must recognize and respect this individuality. They must beware of making the assistance they give an excuse for forcing these people into their own national mould.

171. There is also a further temptation which the economically developed nations must resist: that of giving technical and financial aid with a view to gaining control over the political situation in the poorer countries, and furthering their own plans for world domination.

172. Let us be quite clear on this point. A nation that acted from these motives would in fact be introducing a new form of colonialism—cleverly disguised, no doubt, but actually reflecting that older, outdated type from which many nations have recently emerged. Such action would, moreover, have harmful impact on international relations, and constitute a menace to world peace.

173. Necessity, therefore, and justice demand that all such technical and financial aid be given without thought of domination, but rather for the purpose of helping the less developed nations to achieve their own economic and social growth.

174. If this can be achieved, then a precious contribution will have been made to the formation of a world community, in which each individual nation, conscious of its rights and duties, can work on terms of equality with the rest for the attainment of universal prosperity.

175. Scientific and technical progress, economic development and the betterment of living conditions, are certainly valuable elements in a civilization. But we must realize that they are essentially instrumental in character. They are not supreme values in themselves.

176. It pains us, therefore, to observe the complete indifference to the true hierarchy of values shown by so many people in the economically developed countries. Spiritual values are ignored, forgotten or denied, while the progress of science, technology and economics is pursued for its own sake, as though material well-being were the be-all and end-all of life. This attitude is contagious, especially when it infects the work that is being done for the less developed countries, which have often preserved in their ancient traditions an acute and vital awareness of the more important human values, on which the moral order rests.

177. To attempt to undermine this national integrity is clearly immoral. It must be respected and as far as possible clarified and developed, so that it may remain what it is: a foundation of true civilization.

The role of the Church

178. The Church is by divine right universal. History itself bears this out, for the Church is present everywhere on earth, doing all that she can to embrace all peoples.

179. Now, in bringing people to Christ, the Church has invariably—both now and in the past—brought them many social and economic advantages. For true Christians cannot help feeling obliged to improve their own temporal institutions and environment. They do all they can to prevent these institutions from doing violence to human dignity. They encourage whatever is conducive to honesty and virtue, and strive to eliminate every obstacle to the attainment of this aim.

180. Moreover, in becoming as it were the life-blood of these people, the Church is not, nor does she consider herself to be, a foreign body in their midst. Her presence brings about the rebirth, the resurrection, of each individual in Christ; and the man who is reborn and rises again in Christ never feels himself constrained from without. He feels himself free in the very depth of his being, and freely raised up to God. And thus he affirms and develops that side of his nature which is noblest and best.

181. 'The Church of Jesus Christ', as our predecessor Pius XII observed with such penetration, 'is the repository of his wisdom; she is certainly too wise to discourage or belittle those peculiarities and differences which mark out one nation from another. It is quite legitimate for nations to treat those differences as a sacred inheritance and guard them at all costs. The Church aims at unity, a unity determined and kept alive by that supernatural love which should be actuating everybody; she does not aim at a uniformity which would only be external in its effects and would cramp the natural tendencies of the nations concerned. Every nation has its own genius, its own qualities, springing from the hidden roots of its being. The wise development, the encouragement within limits, of that genius, those qualities, does no harm; and if a nation cares to take precautions, to lay down rules, for that end, it has the Church's approval. She is mother enough to befriend such projects with her prayers.'[43]

182. It is a source of profound satisfaction to us to see the prominent part which is being played by Catholic citizens of the less wealthy countries in the economic and social development of their own state.

183. Then, too, the Catholics of the wealthier states are doing all they can to increase the effectiveness of the social and economic work that is being done for the poorer nations. We would give our special approval to the increasing assistance they are giving, in all sorts of ways, to African and Asian students scattered throughout the universities of Europe and America; and to the care that is being devoted to the training of those persons who are prepared to go to the less wealthy areas in order to engage in work of a technical and professional nature.

184. To these our beloved sons in every land who, in promoting genuine progress and civilization, are a living proof of the Church's perennial vitality, we wish to extend our kind and fatherly word of appreciation and encouragement.

Solving the problems of population growth

185. How can economic development and the supply of food keep pace with the continual rise in population? This is a question which constantly obtrudes itself today—a world problem, as well as one for the poverty-stricken nations.

186. As a world problem, the case is put thus: according to sufficiently reliable statistics the next few decades will see a very great increase in human population, whereas economic development will proceed at a slower rate. Hence, we are told, if nothing is done to check this rise in population, the world will be faced in the not-too-distant future with an increasing shortage in the necessities of life.

187. As it affects the less developed countries, the problem is stated thus: the resources of modern hygiene and medicine will very shortly bring about a notable decrease in the mortality rate, especially among infants, while the birth rate—which in such countries is unusually high—will tend to remain more or less constant, at least for a considerable period. The excess of births over deaths will therefore show a steep rise, whereas there will be no corresponding increase in the productive efficiency of the economy. Accordingly, the standard of living in these poorer countries cannot possibly improve. It must surely worsen, even to the point of extreme hardship. Hence there are those who hold the opinion that, in order to prevent a serious crisis from developing, the conception and birth of children should be secretly avoided, or, in any event, curbed in some way.

188. Truth to tell, we do not seem to be faced with any immediate or imminent world problem arising from the disproportion between the increase of population and the supply of food. Arguments to this effect are based on such unreliable and controversial data that they can only be of very uncertain validity.

189. Besides, the resources which God in his goodness and wisdom has

implanted in nature are well-nigh inexhaustible, and he has at the same time given man the intelligence to discover ways and means of exploiting these resources for his own advantage and his own livelihood. Hence, the real solution of the problem is not to be found in expedients which offend against the divinely established moral order and which attack human life at its very source, but in a renewed scientific and technical effort on man's part to deepen and extend his dominion over nature. The progress of science and technology that has already been achieved opens up almost limitless horizons in this field.

190. As for the problems which face the poorer nations in various parts of the world, we realize, of course, that these are very real. They are caused, more often than not, by a deficient economic and social organization, which does not offer living conditions proportionate to the increase in population. They are caused, also, by the lack of effective solidarity among such peoples.

191. But granting this, we must nevertheless state most emphatically that no statement of the problem and no solution to it is acceptable which does violence to man's essential dignity; those who propose such solutions base them on an utterly materialistic conception of man himself and his life.

192. The only possible solution to this question is one which envisages the social and economic progress both of individuals and of the whole of human society, and which respects and promotes true human values. First consideration must obviously be given to those values which concern man's dignity generally, and the immense worth of each individual human life. Attention must then be turned to the need for worldwide co-operation among men, with a view to a fruitful and well-regulated interchange of useful knowledge, capital and manpower.

193. We must solemnly proclaim that human life is transmitted by means of the family, and the family is based upon a marriage which is one and indissoluble and, with respect to Christians, raised to the dignity of a sacrament. The transmission of human life is the result of a personal and conscious act, and, as such, is subject to the all-holy, inviolable and immutable laws of God, which no man may ignore or disobey. He is not therefore permitted to use certain ways and means which are allowable in the propagation of plant and animal life.

194. Human life is sacred—all men must recognize that fact. From its very inception it reveals the creating hand of God. Those who violate his laws not only offend the divine majesty and degrade themselves and humanity, they also sap the vitality of the political community of which they are members.

195. It is of the utmost importance that parents exercise their right and obligation towards the younger generation by securing for their children a sound cultural and religious formation. They must also educate them to a deep sense of responsibility in life, especially in such matters as concern the foundation of a family and the procreation and education of children. They must instil in them an unshakeable confidence in divine providence and a determination to accept the inescapable sacrifices and hardships involved in so noble and important a task as the co-operation with God in the

transmitting of human life and the bringing up of children. To the attainment of this end nothing can be more effective than those principles and that supernatural aid which the Church supplies. On this score alone the right of the Church to full liberty in the exercise of her mission must be recognized.

196. Genesis relates how God gave two commandments to our first parents: to transmit human life—'Increase and multiply'[44]—and to bring nature into their service—'Fill the earth, and subdue it.'[45] These two commandments are complementary.

197. Nothing is said in the second of these commandments about destroying nature. On the contrary, it must be brought into the service of human life.

198. We are sick at heart, therefore, when we observe the contradiction which has beguiled so much modern thinking. On the one hand we are shown the fearful spectre of want and misery which threatens to extinguish human life, and on the other hand we find scientific discoveries, technical inventions and economic resources being used to provide terrible instruments of ruin and death.

199. A provident God grants sufficient means to the human race to find a dignified solution to the problems attendant upon the transmission of human life. But these problems can become difficult of solution, or even insoluble, if man, led astray in mind and perverted in will, turns to such means as are opposed to right reason, and seeks ends that are contrary to his social nature and the intentions of providence.

The need for international co-operation

200. The progress of science and technology in every aspect of life has led, particularly today, to increased relationships between nations, and made the nations more and more dependent on one another.

201. As a rule no single commonwealth has sufficient resources at its command to solve the more important scientific, technical, economic, social, political and cultural problems which confront it at the present time. These problems are necessarily the concern of a whole group of nations, and possibly of the whole world.

202. Individual political communities may indeed enjoy a high degree of culture and civilization. They may have a large and industrious population, an advanced economic structure, great natural resources and extensive territories. Yet, even so, in isolation from the rest of the world they are quite incapable of finding an adequate solution to their major problems. The nations, therefore, must work with each other for their mutual development and perfection. They can help themselves only in so far as they succeed in helping one another. That is why international understanding and co-operation are so necessary.

203. Yet although individuals and nations are becoming more and more convinced of this twofold necessity, it would seem that men in general, and particularly those with high responsibility in public life, are showing

themselves quite incapable of achieving it. The root of such inability is not to be sought in scientific, technical or economic reasons, but in the absence of mutual trust. Men, and consequently states, are in mortal fear of each other. Each fears that the other harbours plans of conquest and is only waiting for a favourable moment to put these plans into effect. Hence each organizes its own defence and builds up munitions of war as a deterrent against the would-be aggressor.

204. The result is a vast expenditure of human energy and natural resources on projects which are disruptive of human society rather than beneficial to it; while a growing uneasiness gnaws at men's hearts and makes them less responsive to the call of nobler enterprises.

The primacy of moral values

205. The root cause of so much mistrust is the presence of ideological differences between nations, and more especially between their rulers. There are some indeed who go so far as to deny the existence of a moral order which is transcendent, absolute, universal and equally binding upon all. And where the same law of justice is not adhered to by all, men cannot hope to come to open and full agreement on vital issues.

206. Yes, both sides speak of *justice* and *the demands of justice*, but these words frequently take on different or opposite meanings according to which side uses them. Hence, when rulers of nations appeal to *justice* and *the demands of justice*, they not only disagree on terms, but often increase the tension that exists between their states. And so the belief is engendered that if a nation is to assert its rights and pursue its own interests, there is only one way open to it: to have recourse to violence; ignoring the fact that violence is the source of the very greatest evils.

207. Mutual trust among rulers of states cannot begin nor increase except by recognition of, and respect for, the moral order.

208. But the moral order has no existence except in God; cut off from God it must necessarily disintegrate. Moreover, man is not just a material organism. He consists also of spirit; he is endowed with reason and freedom. He demands, therefore, a moral and religious order; and it is this order—and not considerations of a purely extraneous, material order—which has the greatest validity in the solution of problems relating to his life as an individual and as a member of society, and problems concerning individual states and their interrelations.

209. It has been claimed that in an era of scientific and technical triumphs such as ours man can well afford to rely on his own powers, and construct a very good civilization without God. But the truth is that these very advances in science and technology frequently involve the whole human race in such difficulties as can only be solved in the light of a sincere faith in God, the creator and ruler of man and his world.

210. The almost limitless horizons opened up by scientific research only go to confirm this truth. More and more men are beginning to realize that science

has so far done little more than scratch the surface of nature and reality. There are vast hidden depths still to be explored and adequately explained. Such men are appalled when they consider how these gigantic forces for good can be turned by science into engines of destruction. They realize then the supreme importance of spiritual and moral values, if scientific and technical progress is to be used in the service of civilization, and not involve the whole human race in irremediable disaster.

211. Furthermore, the increasing sense of dissatisfaction with worldly goods which is making itself felt among citizens of the wealthier nations, is rapidly destroying the treasured illusion of an earthly paradise. Men, too, are becoming more and more conscious of their rights as human beings, rights which are universal and inviolable; and they are aspiring to more just and more human relations with their fellows. The effect of all this is to make the modern man more deeply aware of his own limitations, and to create in him a striving for spiritual values. All of which encourages us in the hope that individuals and nations will one day learn to unite in a spirit of sincere understanding and profitable co-operation.

IV

Rebuilding society

212. After all this scientific and technical progress, and even because of it, the problem remains: how to build up a new order of society based on a more balanced human relationship between political communities on a national and international level?

213. The attempt to find a solution to this problem has given birth to a number of theories. Some of these were little more than ephemeral; others have undergone, and are still undergoing, substantial change; others again are proving themselves less and less attractive to modern man. Why is this? It is because these ideologies do not take account of the whole man, nor even of his most important part. In particular, they take little account of certain inevitable human weaknesses such as sickness and suffering, weaknesses which even the most advanced economic and social systems cannot completely eliminate. Finally, they fail to take account of that deep-rooted sense of religion which exists in all men everywhere, and which nothing, neither violence nor cunning, can eradicate.

214. The most fundamental modern error is that of imagining that man's natural sense of religion is nothing more than the outcome of feeling or fantasy, to be eradicated from his soul as an anachronism and an obstacle to human progress. And yet this very need for religion reveals a man for what he is: a being created by God and tending always toward God. As we read in St Augustine: 'Lord, you have made us for yourself, and our hearts can find no rest until they rest in you.'[46]

215. Let men make all the technical and economic progress they can, there will be no peace nor justice in the world until they return to a sense of their

dignity as creatures and sons of God, who is the first and final cause of all created being. Separated from God a man is but a monster, in himself and toward others; for the right ordering of human society presupposes the right ordering of man's conscience with God, who is himself the source of all justice, truth and love.

216. Here is a spectacle for all the world to see: thousands of our sons and brothers, whom we love so dearly, suffering years of bitter persecution in many lands, even those of an ancient Christian culture. And will not men who see clearly and compare the superior dignity of the persecuted with that refined barbarity of their oppressors, soon return to their senses, if indeed they have not already done so?

217. The most perniciously typical aspect of the modern era consists in the absurd attempt to reconstruct a solid and fruitful temporal order divorced from God, who is, in fact, the only foundation on which it can endure. In seeking to enhance man's greatness, men fondly imagine that they can do so by drying up the source from which that greatness springs and from which it is nourished. They want, that is, to restrain and, if possible, to eliminate the soul's upward surge toward God. But today's experience of so much disillusionment and bloodshed only goes to confirm those words of scripture: 'Unless the Lord build the house, they labour in vain that build it.'[47]

The Church's social teaching

218. The permanent validity of the Catholic Church's social teaching admits of no doubt.

219. This teaching rests on one basic principle: individual human beings are the foundation, the cause and the end of every social institution. That is necessarily so, for men are by nature social beings. This fact must be recognized, as also the fact that they are raised in the plan of providence to an order of reality which is above nature.

220. On this basic principle, which guarantees the sacred dignity of the individual, the Church constructs her social teaching. She has formulated, particularly over the past hundred years, and through the efforts of a very well-informed body of priests and laymen, a social doctrine which points out with clarity the sure way to social reconstruction. The principles she gives are of universal application, for they take human nature into account, and the varying conditions in which man's life is lived. They also take into account the principle characteristics of contemporary society, and are thus acceptable to all.

221. But today, more than ever, it is essential that this doctrine be known, assimilated, and put into effect in the form and manner that the different situations allow and demand. It is a difficult task indeed, yet a most noble one. To the performance of it we call, not only our own sons and brothers scattered throughout the world, but also men of good will everywhere.

222. First, we must reaffirm most strongly that this Catholic social doctrine is an integral part of the Christian conception of life.

223. It is therefore our urgent desire that this doctrine be studied more and more. First of all it should be taught as part of the daily curriculum in Catholic schools of every kind, particularly seminaries, although we are not unaware that in some of these latter institutions, this has been done for a long time now and in an outstanding way. We would also like to see it added to the religious instruction programmes of parishes and of associations of the lay apostolate. It must be spread by every modern means at our disposal: daily newspapers, periodicals, popular and scientific publications, radio and television.

224. Our beloved sons, the laity, can do much to help this diffusion of Catholic social doctrine by studying it themselves and putting it into practice, and by zealously striving to make others understand it.

225. They should be convinced that the best way of demonstrating the truth and efficacy of this teaching is to show that it can provide the solution to present-day difficulties. They will thus win those people who are opposed to it through ignorance of it. Who knows, but a ray of its light may one day enter their minds.

226. It is not enough merely to formulate a social doctrine. It must be translated into reality. And this is particularly true of the Church's social doctrine, the light of which is truth, justice its objective, and love its driving force.

227. It is vitally important, therefore, that our sons learn to understand this doctrine. They must be educated to it.

228. No Christian education can be considered complete unless it covers every kind of obligation. It must therefore aim at implanting and fostering among the faithful an awareness of their duty to carry on their economic and social activities in a Christian manner.

229. The transition from theory to practice is of its very nature difficult; and it is especially so when one tries to reduce to concrete terms a social doctrine such as that of the Church. There are several reasons why this is so; among them we can mention man's deep-rooted selfishness, the materialism in which modern society is steeped, and the difficulty of determining sometimes what precisely the demands of justice are in a given instance.

230. Consequently, a purely theoretical instruction in man's social and economic obligations is inadequate. People must also be shown ways in which they can properly fulfil these obligations.

231. In our view, therefore, formal instruction, to be successful, must be supplemented by the students' active co-operation in their own training. They must gain an experimental knowledge of the subject, and that by their own positive action.

232. It is practice which makes perfect, even in such matters as the right use of liberty. Thus one learns Christian behaviour in social and economic matters by actual Christian action in those fields.

233. The lay apostolate, therefore, has an important role to play in social

education—especially those associations and organizations which have as their specific objective the Christianization of contemporary society. The members of these associations, besides profiting personally from their own day-to-day experience in this field, can also help in the social education of the rising generation by giving it the benefit of the experience they have gained.

234. But we must remind you here of an important truth: the Christian conception of life demands of all—whether high-born or lowly—a spirit of moderation and sacrifice. That is what God calls us to by his grace.

235. There is, alas, a spirit of hedonism abroad today which beguiles men into thinking that life is nothing more than the quest for pleasure and the satisfaction of human passions. This attitude is disastrous. Its evil effects on soul and body are undeniable. Even on the natural level, temperance and simplicity of life are the dictates of sound policy. On the supernatural level, the Gospels and the whole ascetic tradition of the Church require a sense of mortification and penance which assures the rule of the spirit over the flesh, and offers an efficacious means of expiating the punishment due to sin, from which no one, except Jesus Christ and his immaculate mother, is exempt.

Putting the teaching into practice

236. There are three stages which should normally be followed in the reduction of social principles into practice. First, one reviews the concrete situation; secondly, one forms a judgement on it in the light of these same principles; thirdly, one decides what in the circumstances can and should be done to implement these principles. These are the three stages that are usually expressed in the three terms: *look, judge, act.*

237. It is important for our young people to grasp this method and to practise it. Knowledge acquired in this way does not remain merely abstract, but is seen as something that must be translated into action.

238. Differences of opinion in the application of principles can sometimes arise even among sincere Catholics. When this happens, they should be careful not to lose their respect and esteem for each other. Instead, they should strive to find points of agreement for effective and suitable action, and not wear themselves out in interminable arguments, and, under pretext of the better or the best, omit to do the good that is possible and therefore obligatory.

239. In their economic and social activities, Catholics often come into contact with others who do not share their view of life. In such circumstances, they must, of course, bear themselves as Catholics and do nothing to compromise religion and morality. Yet at the same time they should show themselves animated by a spirit of understanding and unselfishness, ready to co-operate loyally in achieving objects which are good in themselves, or can be turned to good. Needless to say, when the hierarchy has made a decision on any point Catholics are bound to obey their directives. The Church has the right and obligation not merely to guard ethical and religious principles, but also to declare its authoritative judgment in the matter of putting these principles into practice.

240. These, then, are the educational principles which must be put into effect. It is a task which belongs particularly to our sons, the laity, for it is their lot to live an active life in the world and organize themselves for the attainment of temporal ends.

241. In performing this task, which is a noble one, they must not only be well qualified in their trade or profession and practise it in accordance with its own proper laws, they must also bring their professional activity into conformity with the Church's social teaching. Their attitude must be one of loyal trust and filial obedience to ecclesiastical authority. They must remember, too, that if in the transaction of their temporal affairs they take no account of those social principles which the Church teaches, and which we now confirm, then they fail in their obligations and may easily violate the rights of others. They may even go so far as to bring discredit on the Church's teaching, lending substance to the opinion that, in spite of its intrinsic value, it is in fact powerless to direct men's lives.

Getting priorities right

242. As we have noted already, modern man has greatly deepened and extended his knowledge of nature's laws, and has harnessed the forces of nature, making them subservient to his ends. The magnitude of his achievements deserves ungrudging admiration; nor is he yet at the end of his resources. Nevertheless, in his striving to master and transform the world around him he is in danger of forgetting and of destroying himself. As our predecessor, Pope Pius XI, lamented in *Quadragesimo Anno*: 'And so bodily labour, which even after original sin was decreed by providence for the good of man's body and soul, is in many instances changed into an instrument of perversion; for from the factory dead matter goes out improved, whereas men there are corrupted and degraded.'[48]

243. Similarly, our predecessor, Pius XII, rightly asserted that our age is marked by a clear contrast between the immense scientific and technical progress and the fearful human decline shown by 'its monstrous masterpiece...transforming man into a giant of the physical world at the expense of his spirit, which is reduced to that of a pygmy in the supernatural and eternal world'.[49]

244. And so the words of the psalmist about the worshippers of false gods are strikingly verified today. Men are losing their own identity in their works, which they admire to the point of idolatry: 'The idols of the gentiles are silver and gold, the works of the hands of men.'[50]

245. In our paternal care as universal pastor of souls, we earnestly beg our sons, immersed though they be in the business of this world, not to allow their consciences to sleep; not to lose sight of the true hierarchy of values.

246. Certainly, the Church teaches—and has always taught—that scientific and technical progress and the resultant material well-being are good things and mark an important phase in human civilization. But the Church teaches,

too, that goods of this kind must be valued according to their true nature: as instruments used by man for the better attainment of his end. They help to make him a better man, both in the natural and the supernatural order.

247. May these warning words of the divine master ever sound in men's ears: 'For what doth it profit a man, if he gain the whole world and suffer the loss of his own soul? Or what exchange shall a man give for his soul?'[51]

The importance of Sunday

248. Allied to what we have said so far is the question of the Sunday rest.

249. To safeguard man's dignity as a creature of God endowed with a soul in the image and likeness of God, the Church has always demanded a diligent observance of the third commandment: 'Remember that thou keep holy the sabbath day.'[52] God certainly has the right and power to command man to devote one day a week to his duty of worshipping the eternal majesty. Free from mundane cares, he should lift up his mind to the things of heaven, and look into the depths of his conscience, to see how he stands with God in respect of those necessary and inviolable relationships which must exist between the creature and his creator.

250. In addition, man has a right to rest a while from work, and indeed a need to do so if he is to renew his bodily strength and to refresh his spirit by suitable recreation. He has also to think of his family, the unity of which depends so much on frequent contact and the peaceful living together of all its members.

251. Thus, religion and moral and physical well-being are one in demanding this periodic rest, and for many centuries now the Church has set aside Sunday as a special day of rest for the faithful, on which they participate in the holy sacrifice of the Mass, the memorial and application of Christ's redemptive work for souls.

252. Heavy in heart, we cannot but deplore the growing tendency in certain quarters to disregard this sacred law, if not to reject it outright. This attitude must inevitably impair the bodily and spiritual health of the workers, whose welfare we have so much at heart.

253. In the name of God, therefore, and for the sake of the material and spiritual interests of men, we call upon all, public authorities, employers and workers, to observe the precepts of God and his Church and to remember their grave responsibilities before God and society.

The Christian value of work

254. We have only been able to touch lightly upon this matter, but our sons, the laity especially, must not suppose that they would be acting prudently to lessen their personal Christian commitment in this passing world. On the contrary, we insist that they must intensify it and increase it continually.

255. In his solemn prayer for the Church's unity, Christ our Lord did not ask

his father to remove his disciples from the world: 'I pray not that thou shouldst take them out of the world, but that thou shouldst keep them from evil.'[53] Let no man therefore imagine that a life of activity in the world is incompatible with spiritual perfection. The two can very well be harmonized. It is a gross error to suppose that a man cannot perfect himself except by putting aside all temporal activity, on the plea that such activity will inevitably lead him to compromise his personal dignity as a human being and a Christian.

256. That a man should develop and perfect himself through his daily work—which in most cases is of a temporal character—is perfectly in keeping with the plan of divine providence. The Church today is faced with an immense task: to humanize and to Christianize this modern civilization of ours. The continued development of this civilization, indeed its very survival, demand and insist that the Church do her part in the world. That is why, as we said before, she claims the co-operation of her laity. In conducting their human affairs to the best of their ability, they must recognize that they are doing a service to humanity, in intimate union with God through Christ, and to God's greater glory. And St Paul insisted: 'Whether you eat or drink, or whatsoever else you do, do all to the glory of God.'[54] 'All whatsoever you do in word or in work, do all in the name of the Lord Jesus Christ, giving thanks to God and the Father by him.'[55]

257. To search for spiritual perfection and eternal salvation in the conduct of human affairs and institutions is not to rob these of the power to achieve their immediate, specific ends, but to enhance this power. The words of our divine master are true for all time: 'Seek ye therefore first the kingdom of God and his justice; and all these things shall be added unto you.'[56] The man who is 'light in the Lord'[57] and who walks as a 'child of the light'[58] has a sure grasp of the fundamental demands of justice in all life's difficulties and complexities, obscured though they may be by so much individual, national and racial selfishness. Animated, too, by the charity of Christ, he finds it impossible not to love his fellow men. He makes his own their needs, their sufferings and their joys. There is a sureness of touch in all his activity in every field. It is energetic, generous and considerate. For 'charity is patient, is kind; charity envieth not, dealeth not perversely, is not puffed up, is not ambitious, seeketh not her own, is not provoked to anger, thinketh no evil; rejoiceth not in iniquity, but rejoiceth with the truth; beareth all things, believeth all things, hopeth all things, endureth all things.'[59]

The work of Christ continued

258. In conclusion, venerable brethren, we would remind you of that sublime truth of Catholic doctrine: our incorporation as living members in Christ's mystical body, the Church, 'For as the body is one and hath many members; and all the members of the body, whereas they are many, yet are one body; so also is Christ.'[60]

259. We most earnestly beg all our sons the world over, clergy and laity, to be deeply conscious of the dignity, the nobility, which is theirs through being

grafted on to Christ as shoots on a vine: 'I am the vine; you the branches.'[61] They are thus called to a share in his own divine life; and since they are united in mind and spirit with the divine redeemer even when they are engaged in the affairs of the world, their work becomes a continuation of his work, penetrated with redemptive power. 'He that abideth in me, and I in him, the same beareth much fruit.'[62] Thus is man's work exalted and ennobled—so highly exalted that it leads to his own personal perfection of soul, and helps to extend to others the fruits of redemption, all over the world. It becomes a means whereby the Christian way of life can leaven this civilization in which we live and work—leaven it with the ferment of the gospel.

260. This era in which we live is in the grip of deadly errors; it is torn by deep disorders. But it is also an era which offers to those who work with the Church immense possibilities in the field of the apostolate. And therein lies our hope.

261. Venerable brethren and dear sons, we began with that wonderful encyclical of Pope Leo, and passed in review before you the various problems of our modern social life. We have given principles and directives which we exhort you earnestly to think over, and now, for your part, to put into effect. Your courageous co-operation in this respect will surely help to bring about the realization of Christ's kingdom in this world, 'a kingdom of truth and life; a kingdom of holiness and grace; a kingdom of justice, of love and of peace',[63] which assures the enjoyment of those heavenly blessings for which we were created and for which we long most ardently.

262. For here our concern is with the doctrine of the Catholic and Apostolic Church. She is the mother and teacher of all nations. Her light illumines, enkindles and enflames. No age but hears her warning voice, vibrant with heavenly wisdom. She is ever powerful to offer suitable, effective remedies for the increasing needs of men, and the sorrows and anxieties of this present life. Her words re-echo those of the psalmist of old—words which never fail to raise our fainting spirits and give us courage: 'I will hear what the Lord God will speak in me: for he will speak peace unto his people. And unto his saints: and unto them that are converted to the heart. Surely his salvation is near to them that fear him: that glory may dwell in our land. Mercy and truth have met each other: justice and peace have kissed. Truth is sprung out of the earth: and justice hath looked down from heaven. For the Lord will give goodness: and our earth shall yield her fruit. Justice shall walk before him: and shall set his steps in the way.'[64]

263. For some considerable time now, venerable brethren, our solicitude for the universal Church has been directed into the writing of this letter; and we wish to conclude it by voicing the following desires: may man's divine redeemer 'who of God is made unto us wisdom and justice and sanctification and redemption',[65] reign and triumph gloriously throughout all ages, in all and over all. And, with the right ordering of human society, may all nations at last enjoy true prosperity, happiness and peace.

264. In earnest of these wishes, and as a pledge of our fatherly good will, may the apostolic blessing, which we give in the Lord with all our heart,

descend upon you, venerable brethren, and upon all the faithful entrusted to your care, and especially upon those who respond with generosity to our appeals.

Given in Rome, at St Peter's on 15 May 1961, the third year of our pontificate.

Editor's Notes

MM 59: For this expression, see the Introduction, p.xx, and footnote 26.

MM 156: Food and Agriculture Organization—an agency of the United Nations, based in Rome.

Pacem in Terris

*Encyclical letter of Pope John XXIII to his venerable
brothers the patriarchs, primates, archbishops, bishops and
other local ordinaries that are at peace and in
communion with the Apostolic See, to the clergy
and faithful of the whole world and to all
men of good will, about establishing universal peace
in truth, justice, charity and liberty.*

Introduction

The encyclical is dated 11 April 1963 and was therefore published in the
course of the Second Vatican Council. This was significant. Pope John, who
was to die a few months later, had already made an enormous impact by the
force of his personality upon the world at large and was a highly popular
figure. But the council which he had summoned had attracted hosts of
journalists to Rome so that not only was there a much broader audience for
Pacem in Terris than there had been for *Mater et Magistra*, there were also
people more skilled at interpreting it for the world's press. The pope was
clearly aware of this. *Mater et Magistra* had been addressed 'to the clergy and
faithful of the entire Catholic world'. *Pacem in Terris* included in its
salutation 'all men of good will'.

This social encyclical was, perhaps, not quite as innovative as Pope John's
earlier letter and is somewhat more theoretical, with a long discussion of
human rights in the context of the natural law. The pope does, however, treat
of the problem of the arms race and he also sees the need in some instances
for human rights to be restricted when their exercise conflicts with the rights
of others less able to look after themselves: the Church's stress on an
individual's freedom was not to be used as an excuse for oppression (cf. PT
62 and 65).

In an important paragraph (PT 159) Pope John seems to be moving
towards some sort of an accommodation with communist governments—or
at least parties—when he distinguishes between 'false philosophy', as
something to be rejected, and 'undertakings [which] draw their origin and
inspiration from that philosophy'.

For a longer discussion of *Pacem in Terris* (PT) see the Introduction, pp.xiv.
The Latin text is to be found in AAS 55 (1963), 257-304. In the original the
paragraphs were not numbered: enumeration has been added in accordance
with the policy outlined in the Editorial Note (p.ix), as have the
cross-headings.

Summary

Paras. 1-10: Peace requires the observance of the divinely established order. There is disunity among individuals and among nations which is out of keeping with the perfect order of the universe. The father of the universe has inscribed upon hearts the laws which are to govern human beings, how they should relate to each other in society and in the State, and also how states should relate to each other.

Paras. 11-38: Human beings have a right to bodily integrity and to the means necessary to preserve and develop life. They have a right to respect and to freedom, to education and to worship, to choose freely a state of life and to have support in bringing up a family. There is a right to work, to the ownership of property, and to association, to travel freely and to take part in public life. But such rights have corresponding duties, above all the duty to respect the rights of others, and these must be observed if a society is to be considered well ordered. The foundation of that order is truth, put into effect by justice and animated by love. Such an order finds its source in God.

Paras. 39-45: Three things characterize the modern age: an improvement in the economic and social conditions of workers; the greater role in society taken by women; the establishment of newly independent states. All of these are of great significance in the formation of a society along the lines outlined.

Paras. 46-66: Well-ordered society requires within it some ruling authority. Government is required by the moral order and derives from God. But laws which are in contradiction to the moral order have no binding force: the sole purpose of civil authority is the attainment of the common good. The authorities must promote that good in the interests of all, not favouring any individual, or category of, citizen—though paying more attention to the disadvantaged. The chief concern of the State must be to guarantee personal rights and duties, to ensure they are recognized, respected, co-ordinated, defended and promoted. Heads of states must act to create a climate in which individuals can safeguard their rights and fulfil their duties, through the provision of essential services and suitable employment.

Paras. 67-79: It is not possible to lay down what is the best form of government, but it is proper that the State should take a form which embodies the threefold division of legislative, administrative and judicial function. Each of the functions needs to have a clear idea of the nature and limits of its competence, and it is a natural consequence of human dignity that people have a right to take an active part in government. To meet demands concerning the juridical nature of states, each should have as part of its constitution a charter of fundamental human rights and each constitution should clearly lay down the spheres of competence of public officials. Relations between citizens and the authorities should be clearly described in terms of rights and duties.

Paras. 80-107: The law of nature that regulates the lives of individuals must also regulate the lives of political communities in their relations with each other, and political leaders are bound by the natural law which governs all moral conduct. The mutual ties between states must be governed by truth, and truth requires the abolition of every trace of racial discrimination and the recognition that all states are by nature equal in dignity. The more developed nations have no right to unjust political domination over others, but they have an obligation to make a greater contribution to social progress. Truth and justice must also be evident in the dissemination of information. States must not pursue their own development by methods which involve injury or unjust oppression towards others. Clashes of interest must be settled in a human manner and not by resorting to force. A special instance of this clash of interest is the treatment of minorities and ethnic groups, especially those who have left their own countries in search of work. The policy ought to be to bring work to the workers, not *vice versa*. People also have to go into exile for political reasons, and at present there are a great number of refugees. These, too, are people with rights which must be recognized—including the right to enter a country to start a new life.

Paras. 108-129: Because of the arms race, and particularly because of atomic weapons, people live in constant fear. Nuclear weapons must be banned, but without mutual trust disarmament cannot be complete. No country has a right to take any action which would constitute unjust oppression of another country, or unwarranted interference in its affairs. People must be helped in a way which preserves their freedom. The conviction that disputes must be settled by negotiations arises from fear of the use of modern weapons, and though the same fear causes vast sums of money to be spent on armaments, yet the negotiations themselves can help to build up better relations.

Paras. 130-145: Progress in science and technology has been a spur to collaboration among peoples. There is also a growing economic interdependence. The universal common good presents problems which are world-wide: the moral order therefore demands the establishment of some general form of public authority, the purpose of which is to create world conditions in which the public authorities of individual nations can carry out their tasks. The United Nations Organization, and in particular its Declaration on Human Rights, is an approach to the establishment of a juridical and political ordering of the world community.

Paras. 146-156: Christians should involve themselves in political, economic and cultural development. Christians have contributed to the creation of civil institutions in traditionally Christian states, and yet often these institutions are only slightly affected by the Christian spirit. There is too great a cleavage between faith and practice, coupled with too little education in Christian morality. It is essential that religious training should be complete and continuous, and keep pace with scientific knowledge and technical progress.

Paras. 157-173: The principles laid down above derive from human rights. Putting them into practice entails co-operation between Catholics and other Christians, with other believers and indeed with non-believers, should prudence so decide. Work must be done slowly and gradually to build up new relationships in human society. Peace is an empty word if it does not rest upon an order founded on truth, built on justice, animated by charity and brought into effect in freedom.

Venerable brothers and dearest sons and daughters, greetings and apostolic benediction.

God's order, the world's disorder

1. Peace on earth—which man throughout the ages has so longed for and sought after—can never be established, never guaranteed, except by the diligent observance of the divinely established order.

2. That a marvellous order predominates in the world of living beings and in the forces of nature, is the plain lesson which the progress of modern research and the discoveries of technology teach us. And it is part of the greatness of man that he can appreciate that order, and devise the means for harnessing those forces for his own benefit.

3. But what emerges first and foremost from the progress of scientific knowledge and the inventions of technology is the infinite greatness of God himself, who created both man and the universe. Yes; out of nothing he made all things, and, filled them with the fullness of his own wisdom and goodness. Hence, these are the words the holy psalmist used in praise of God: 'O Lord, our Lord: how admirable is thy name in the whole earth!'[1] And elsewhere he says: 'How great are thy works, O Lord! Thou hast made all things in wisdom.'[2] Moreover, God created man 'in his own image and likeness',[3] endowed him with intelligence and freedom, and made him lord of creation. All this the psalmist proclaims when he says: 'Thou hast made him a little less than the angels: thou hast crowned him with glory and honour, and hast set him over the works of thy hands. Thou hast subjected all things under his feet.'[4]

4. And yet there is a disunity among individuals and among nations which is in striking contrast to this perfect order in the universe. One would think that the relationships that bind men together could only be governed by force.

5. But the world's creator has stamped man's inmost being with an order revealed to man by his conscience; and his conscience insists on his preserving it. Men 'show the work of the law written in their hearts. Their conscience bears witness to them.'[5] And how could it be otherwise? All created being reflects the infinite wisdom of God. It reflects it all the more clearly, the higher it stands in the scale of perfection.[6]

6. But the mischief is often caused by erroneous opinions. Many people think that the laws which govern man's relations with the State are the same as those which regulate the blind, elemental forces of the universe. But it is not

so; the laws which govern men are quite different. The Father of the universe has inscribed them in man's nature, and that is where we must look for them; there and nowhere else.

7. These laws clearly indicate how a man must behave toward his fellows in society, and how the mutual relationships between the members of a state and its officials are to be conducted. They show too what principles must govern the relations between states; and finally, what should be the relations between individuals or states on the one hand, and the world-wide community of nations on the other. Men's common interests make it imperative that at long last a world-wide community of nations be established.

I

8. We must devote our attention first of all to that order which should prevail among men.

9. Any well-regulated and productive association of men in society demands the acceptance of one fundamental principle: that each individual man is truly a person. His is a nature, that is, endowed with intelligence and free will. As such he has rights and duties, which together flow as a direct consequence from his nature. These rights and duties are universal and inviolable, and therefore altogether inalienable.[7]

10. When, furthermore, we consider man's personal dignity from the standpoint of divine revelation, inevitably our estimate of it is incomparably increased. Men have been ransomed by the blood of Jesus Christ. Grace has made them sons and friends of God, and heirs to eternal glory.

Human rights

11. But first we must speak of man's rights. Man has the right to live. He has the right to bodily integrity and to the means necessary for the proper development of life, particularly food, clothing, shelter, medical care, rest, and, finally, the necessary social services. In consequence, he has the right to be looked after in the event of ill-health; disability stemming from his work; widowhood; old age; enforced unemployment; or whenever through no fault of his own he is deprived of the means of livelihood.[8]

12. Moreover, man has a natural right to be respected. He has a right to his good name. He has a right to freedom in investigating the truth, and—within the limits of the moral order and the common good—to freedom of speech and publication, and to freedom to pursue whatever profession he may choose. He has the right, also, to be accurately informed about public events.

13. He has the natural right to share in the benefits of culture, and hence to receive a good general education, and a technical or professional training consistent with the degree of educational development in his own country. Furthermore, a system must be devised for affording gifted members of society the opportunity of engaging in more advanced studies, with a view to

their occupying, as far as possible, positions of responsibility in society in keeping with their natural talent and acquired skill.[9]

14. Also among man's rights is that of being able to worship God in accordance with the right dictates of his own conscience, and to profess his religion both in private and in public. According to the clear teaching of Lactantius, 'this is the very condition of our birth, that we render to the God who made us that just homage which is his due; that we acknowledge him alone as God, and follow him. It is from this *ligature* of piety, which binds us and joins us to God, that religion derives its name.'[10] Hence, too, Pope Leo XIII declared that 'true freedom, freedom worthy of the sons of God, is that freedom which most truly safeguards the dignity of the human person. It is stronger than any violence or injustice. Such is the freedom which has always been desired by the Church, and which she holds most dear. It is the sort of freedom which the apostles resolutely claimed for themselves. The apologists defended it in their writings; thousands of martyrs consecrated it with their blood.'[11]

15. Human beings have also the right to choose for themselves the kind of life which appeals to them: whether it is to found a family—in the founding of which both the man and the woman enjoy equal rights and duties—or to embrace the priesthood or the religious life.[12]

16. The family, founded upon marriage freely contracted, one and indissoluble, must be regarded as the natural, primary cell of human society. The interests of the family, therefore, must be taken very specially into consideration in social and economic affairs, as well as in the spheres of faith and morals. For all of these have to do with strengthening the family and assisting it in the fulfilment of its mission.

17. Of course, the support and education of children is a right which belongs primarily to the parents.[13]

18. In the economic sphere, it is evident that a man has the inherent right not only to be given the opportunity to work, but also to be allowed the exercise of personal initiative in the work he does.[14]

19. The conditions in which a man works form a necessary corollary to these rights. They must not be such as to weaken his physical or moral fibre, or militate against the proper development of adolescents to manhood. Women must be accorded such conditions of work as are consistent with their needs and responsibilities as wives and mothers.[15]

20. A further consequence of man's personal dignity is his right to engage in economic activities suited to his degree of responsibility.[16] The worker is likewise entitled to a wage that is determined in accordance with the precepts of justice. This needs stressing. The amount a worker receives must be sufficient, in proportion to available funds, to allow him and his family a standard of living consistent with human dignity. Pope Pius XII expressed it in these terms: 'Nature imposes work upon man as a duty, and man has the corresponding natural right to demand that the work he does shall provide him with the means of livelihood for himself and his children. Such is nature's categorical imperative for the preservation of man'.[17]

21. As a further consequence of man's nature, he has the right to the private ownership of property, including that of productive goods. This, as we have said elsewhere, is 'a right which constitutes so efficacious a means of asserting one's personality and exercising responsibility in every field, and an element of solidity and security for family life, and of greater peace and prosperity in the state.'[18]

22. Finally, it is opportune to point out that the right to own private property entails a social obligation as well.[19]

23. Men are by nature social, and consequently they have the right to meet together and to form associations with their fellows. They have the right to confer on such associations the type of organization which they consider best calculated to achieve their objectives. They have also the right to exercise their own initiative and act on their own responsibility within these associations for the attainment of the desired results.[20]

24. As we insisted in our encyclical *Mater et Magistra*, the founding of a great many such intermediate groups or societies for the pursuit of aims which it is not within the competence of the individual to achieve efficiently, is a matter of great urgency. Such groups and societies must be considered absolutely essential for the safeguarding of man's personal freedom and dignity, while leaving intact a sense of responsibility.[21]

25. Again, every human being has the right to freedom of movement and of residence within the confines of his own state. When there are just reasons in favour of it, he must be permitted to emigrate to other countries and take up residence there.[22] The fact that he is a citizen of a particular state does not deprive him of membership in the human family, nor of citizenship in that universal society, the common, world-wide fellowship of men.

26. Finally, man's personal dignity involves his right to take an active part in public life, and to make his own contribution to the common welfare of his fellow citizens. As Pope Pius XII said, 'man as such, far from being an object or, as it were, an inert element in society, is rather its subject, its basis and its purpose; and so must he be esteemed.'[23]

27. As a human person he is entitled to the legal protection of his rights, and such protection must be effective, unbiased, and strictly just. To quote again Pope Pius XII: 'In consequence of that juridical order willed by God, man has his own inalienable right to juridical security. To him is assigned a certain, well-defined sphere of law, immune from arbitrary attack.'[24]

Human duties

28. The natural rights of which we have so far been speaking are inextricably bound up with as many duties, all applying to one and the same person. These rights and duties derive their origin, their sustenance, and their indestructibility from the natural law, which in conferring the one imposes the other.

29. Thus, for example, the right to live involves the duty to preserve one's life; the right to a decent standard of living, the duty to live in a becoming fashion; the right to be free to seek out the truth, the duty to devote oneself to an ever deeper and wider search for it.

30. Once this is admitted, it follows that in human society one man's natural right gives rise to a corresponding duty in other men; the duty, that is, of recognizing and respecting that right. Every basic human right draws its authoritative force from the natural law, which confers it and attaches to it its respective duty. Hence, to claim one's rights and ignore one's duties, or only half fulfil them, is like building a house with one hand and tearing it down with the other.

31. Since men are social by nature, they must live together and consult each other's interests. That men should recognize and perform their respective rights and duties is imperative to a well-ordered society. But the result will be that each individual will make his whole-hearted contribution to the creation of a civic order in which rights and duties are ever more diligently and more effectively observed.

32. For example, it is useless to admit that a man has a right to the necessities of life, unless we also do all in our power to supply him with means sufficient for his livelihood.

33. Hence society must not only be well ordered, it must also provide men with abundant resources. This postulates not only the mutual recognition and fulfilment of rights and duties, but also the involvement and collaboration of all men in the many enterprises which our present civilization makes possible, encourages or indeed demands.

34. Man's personal dignity requires besides that he enjoy freedom and be able to make up his own mind when he acts. In his association with his fellows, therefore, there is every reason why his recognition of rights, observance of duties, and many-sided collaboration with other men, should be primarily a matter of his own personal decision. Each man should act on his own initiative, conviction, and sense of responsibility, not under the constant pressure of external coercion or enticement. There is nothing human about a society that is welded together by force. Far from encouraging, as it should, the attainment of man's progress and perfection, it is merely an obstacle to his freedom.

35. Hence, before a society can be considered well-ordered, creative, and consonant with human dignity, it must be based on truth. St Paul expressed this as follows: 'Putting away lying, speak ye the truth every man with his neighbour, for we are members one of another.'[25] And so will it be, if each man acknowledges sincerely his own rights and his own duties toward others. Human society, as we here picture it, demands that men be guided by justice, respect the rights of others and do their duty. It demands, too, that they be animated by such love as will make them feel the needs of others as their own, and induce them to share their goods with others, and to strive in the world to make all men alike heirs to the noblest of intellectual and spiritual values. Nor is this enough; for human society thrives on freedom, namely, on the use of

means which are consistent with the dignity of its individual members, who, being endowed with reason, assume responsibility for their own actions.

The moral order

36. And so, dearest sons and brothers, we must think of human society as being primarily a spiritual reality. By its means enlightened men can share their knowledge of the truth, can claim their rights and fulfil their duties, receive encouragement in their aspirations for the goods of the spirit, share their enjoyment of all the wholesome pleasures of the world, and strive continually to pass on to others all that is best in themselves and to make their own the spiritual riches of others. It is these spiritual values which exert a guiding influence on culture, economics, social institutions, political movements and forms, laws, and all the other components which go to make up the external community of men and its continual development.

37. Now the order which prevails in human society is wholly incorporeal in nature. Its foundation is truth, and it must be brought into effect by justice. It needs to be animated and perfected by men's love for one another, and, while preserving freedom intact, it must make for an equilibrium in society which is increasingly more human in character.

38. But such an order—universal, absolute and immutable in its principles—finds its source in the true, personal and transcendent God. He is the first truth, the sovereign good, and as such the deepest source from which human society, if it is to be properly constituted, creative, and worthy of man's dignity, draws its genuine vitality.[26] This is what St Thomas means when he says: 'Human reason is the standard which measures the degree of goodness of the human will, and as such it derives from the eternal law, which is divine reason...Hence it is clear that the goodness of the human will depends much more on the eternal law than on human reason.'[27]

Characteristics of modern society

39. There are three things which characterize our modern age.

40. In the first place we notice a progressive improvement in the economic and social condition of working men. They began by claiming their rights principally in the economic and social spheres, and then proceeded to lay claim to their political rights as well. Finally, they have turned their attention to acquiring the more cultural benefits of society. Today, therefore, working men all over the world are loud in their demands that they shall in no circumstances be subjected to arbitrary treatment, as though devoid of intelligence and freedom. They insist on being treated as human beings, with a share in every sector of human society: in the socio-economic sphere, in government, and in the realm of learning and culture.

41. Secondly, the part that women are now playing in political life is everywhere evident. This is a development that is perhaps of swifter growth among Christian nations, but it is also happening extensively, if more slowly, among nations that are heirs to different traditions and imbued with a

different culture. Women are gaining an increasing awareness of their natural dignity. Far from being content with a purely passive role or allowing themselves to be regarded as a kind of instrument, they are demanding both in domestic and in public life the rights and duties which belong to them as human persons.

42. Finally, we are confronted in this modern age with a form of society which is evolving on entirely new social and political lines. Since all peoples have either attained political independence or are on the way to attaining it, soon no nation will rule over another and none will be subject to an alien power.

43. Thus all over the world men are either the citizens of an independent state, or are shortly to become so; nor is any nation nowadays content to submit to foreign domination. The long-standing inferiority complex of certain classes because of their economic and social status, sex, or position in the state, and the corresponding superiority complex of other classes, is rapidly becoming a thing of the past.

44. Today, on the contrary the conviction is widespread that all men are equal in natural dignity; and so, on the doctrinal and theoretical level, at least, no form of approval is being given to racial discrimination. All this is of supreme significance for the formation of a human society animated by the principles we have mentioned above, for man's awareness of his rights must inevitably lead him to the recognition of his duties. The possession of rights involves the duty of implementing those rights, for they are the expression of a man's personal dignity. And the possession of rights also involves their recognition and respect by other people.

45. When society is formed on a basis of rights and duties, men have an immediate grasp of spiritual and intellectual values, and have no difficulty in understanding what is meant by truth, justice, charity and freedom. They become, moreover, conscious of being members of such a society. And that is not all. Inspired by such principles, they attain to a better knowledge of the true God—a personal God transcending human nature. They recognize that their relationship with God forms the very foundation of their life—the interior life of the spirit, and the life which they live in the society of their fellows.

II

The origin of the State's authority

46. Human society can be neither well ordered nor prosperous without the presence of those who, invested with legal authority, preserve its institutions and do all that is necessary to sponsor actively the interests of all its members. And they derive their authority from God, for, as St Paul teaches, 'there is no power but from God.'[28] In his commentary on this passage, St John Chrysostom writes: 'What are you saying? Is every ruler appointed by God? No, that is not what I mean, he says, for I am not now talking about individual rulers, but about authority as such. My contention is that the

existence of a ruling authority—the fact that some should command and others obey, and that all things should not come about as the result of blind chance—this is a provision of divine wisdom.'[29] God has created men social by nature, and a society cannot 'hold together unless someone is in command to give effective direction and unity of purpose. Hence every civilized community must have a ruling authority, and this authority, no less than society itself, has its source in nature, and consequently has God for its author.'[30]

47. But it must not be imagined that authority knows no bounds. Since its starting point is the permission to govern in accordance with right reason, there is no escaping the conclusion that it derives its binding force from the moral order, which in turn has God as its origin and end. Hence, to quote Pope Pius XII, 'The absolute order of living beings, and the very purpose of man—an autonomous being, the subject of duties and inviolable rights, and the origin and purpose of human society—have a direct bearing upon the State as a necessary community endowed with authority. Divest it of this authority, and it is nothing, it is lifeless...But right reason, and above all Christian faith, make it clear that such an order can have no other origin but in God, a personal God, our creator. Hence it is from him that state officials derive their dignity, for they share to some extent in the authority of God himself.'[31]

48. Hence, a regime which governs solely or mainly by means of threats and intimidation or promises of reward, provides men with no effective incentive to work for the common good. And even if it did, it would certainly be offensive to the dignity of free and rational human beings. Authority is before all else a moral force. For this reason the appeal of rulers should be to the individual conscience, to the duty which every man has of voluntarily contributing to the common good. But since all men are equal in natural dignity, no man has the capacity to force internal compliance on another. Only God can do that, for he alone scrutinizes and judges the secret counsels of the heart.

49. Hence, representatives of the State have no power to bind men in conscience, unless their own authority is tied to God's authority, and is a participation in it.[32]

50. The application of this principle likewise safeguards the dignity of citizens. Their obedience to civil authorities is never an obedience paid to them as men. It is in reality an act of homage paid to God, the provident creator of the universe, who has decreed that men's dealings with one another be regulated in accordance with that order which he himself has established. And we men do not demean ourselves in showing due reverence to God. On the contrary, we are lifted up and ennobled in spirit, for to serve God is to reign.[33]

51. Governmental authority, therefore, is a postulate of the moral order and derives from God. Consequently, laws and decrees passed in contravention of the moral order, and hence of the divine will, can have no binding force in conscience, since 'it is right to obey God rather than men.'[34] Indeed, the

passing of such laws undermines the very nature of authority and results in shameful abuse. As St Thomas teaches: 'In regard to the second proposition, we maintain that human law has the *rationale* of law in so far as it is in accordance with right reason, and as such it obviously derives from eternal law. A law which is at variance with reason is to that extent unjust and has no longer the *rationale* of law. It is rather an act of violence.'[35]

52. The fact that authority comes from God does not mean that men have no power to choose those who are to rule the state, or to decide upon the type of government they want, and determine the procedure and limitations of rulers in the exercise of their authority. Hence the above teaching is consonant with any genuinely democratic form of government.[36]

The purpose of the State's authority

53. Men, both as individuals and as intermediate groups, are required to make their own specific contributions to the general welfare. The main consequence of this is that they must harmonize their own interests with the needs of others, and offer their goods and services as their rulers shall direct—assuming, of course, that justice is maintained and the authorities are acting within the limits of their competence. Those who have authority in the state must exercise that authority in a way which is not only morally irreproachable, but also best calculated to ensure or promote the state's welfare.

54. The attainment of the common good is the sole reason for the existence of civil authorities. In working for the common good, therefore, the authorities must obviously respect its nature, and at the same time adjust their legislation to meet the requirements of the given situation.[37]

55. Among the essential elements of the common good one must certainly include the various characteristics distinctive of each individual people.[38] But these by no means constitute the whole of it. For the common good, since it is intimately bound up with human nature, can never exist fully and completely unless the human person is taken into account at all times. Thus, attention must be paid to the basic nature of the common good and what it is that brings it about.[39]

56. We must add, therefore, that it is in the nature of the common good that every single citizen has the right to share in it—although in different ways, depending on his tasks, merits and circumstances. Hence every civil authority must strive to promote the common good in the interest of all, without favouring any individual citizen or category of citizen. As Pope Leo XIII insisted: 'The civil power must not be subservient to the advantage of any one individual, or of some few persons; in as much as it was established for the common good of all.'[40] Nevertheless, considerations of justice and equity can at times demand that those in power pay more attention to the weaker members of society, since these are at a disadvantage when it comes to defending their own rights and asserting their legitimate interests.[41]

57. In this connection, we would draw the attention of our own sons to the

fact that the common good is something which affects the needs of the whole man, body and soul. That, then, is the sort of good which rulers of states must take suitable measures to ensure. They must respect the hierarchy of values, and aim at achieving the spiritual as well as the material prosperity of their subjects.[42]

58. These principles are clearly contained in that passage in our encyclical *Mater et Magistra* where we emphasized that the common good 'must take account of all those social conditions which favour the full development of human personality'.[43]

59. Consisting, as he does, of body and immortal soul, man cannot in this mortal life satisfy his needs or attain perfect happiness. Thus, the measures that are taken to implement the common good must not jeopardize his eternal salvation; indeed, they must even help him to obtain it.[44]

60. It is generally accepted today that the common good is best safeguarded when personal rights and duties are guaranteed. The chief concern of civil authorities must therefore be to ensure that these rights are recognized, respected, co-ordinated, defended and promoted, and that each individual is enabled to perform his duties more easily. For 'to safeguard the inviolable rights of the human person, and to facilitate the performance of his duties, is the principal duty of every public authority.'[45]

61. Thus any government which refused to recognize human rights or acted in violation of them, would not only fail in its duty; its decrees would be wholly lacking in binding force.[46]

The State and human rights

62. One of the principal duties of any government, moreover, is the suitable and adequate superintendence and co-ordination of men's respective rights in society. This must be done in such a way (1) that the exercise of their rights by certain citizens does not obstruct other citizens in the exercise of theirs; (2) that the individual, standing upon his own rights, does not impede others in the performance of their duties; (3) that the rights of all be effectively safeguarded, and completely restored if they have been violated.[47]

63. In addition, heads of states must make a positive contribution to the creation of an overall climate in which the individual can both safeguard his own rights and fulfil his duties, and can do so readily. For if there is one thing we have learned in the school of experience, it is surely this: that, in the modern world especially, political, economic and cultural inequities among citizens become more and more widespread when public authorities fail to take appropriate action in these spheres. And the consequence is that human rights and duties are thus rendered totally ineffective.

64. The public administration must therefore give considerable care and thought to the question of social as well as economic progress, and to the development of essential services in keeping with the expansion of the productive system. Such services include road-building, transportation, communications, drinking-water, housing, medical care, ample facilities for

the practice of religion and aids to recreation. The government must also see to the provision of insurance facilities, to obviate any likelihood of a citizen's being unable to maintain a decent standard of living in the event of some misfortune, or greatly increased family responsibilities. The government is also required to show no less energy and efficiency in the matter of providing opportunities for suitable employment, graded to the capacity of the workers. It must make sure that working men are paid a just and equitable wage, and are allowed a sense of responsibility in the industrial concerns for which they work. It must facilitate the formation of intermediate groups, so that the social life of the people may become more fruitful and less constrained. And finally, it must ensure that everyone has the means and opportunity of sharing as far as possible in cultural benefits.

65. The common welfare further demands that in their efforts to co-ordinate and protect, and their efforts to promote, the rights of citizens, the civil authorities preserve a delicate balance. An excessive concern for the rights of any particular individuals or· groups might well result in the principal advantages of the state being in effect monopolized by these citizens. Or again, the absurd situation can arise where the civil authorities, while taking measures to protect the rights of citizens, themselves stand in the way of the full exercise of these rights. 'For this principle must always be retained: that however extensive and far-reaching the influence of the State on the economy may be, it must never be exerted to the extent of depriving the individual citizen of his freedom of action. It must rather augment his freedom, while effectively guaranteeing the protection of everyone's essential, personal rights.'[48]

66. And the same principle must be adopted by civil authorities in their various efforts to facilitate the exercise of rights and performance of duties in every department of social life.

Structures of the State

67. For the rest, it is not possible to give a general ruling on the most suitable form of government, or the ways in which civil authorities can most effectively fulfil their legislative, administrative, and judicial functions.

68. In determining what form a particular government shall take, and the way in which it shall function, a major consideration will be the prevailing circumstances and the condition of the people; and these are things which vary in different places and at different times. We think, however, that it is in keeping with human nature for the state to be given a form which embodies a threefold division of public office properly corresponding to the three main functions of public authority. In such a state a precise legal framework is provided, not only for the official functions of government, but also for the mutual relations between citizens and public officials. This will obviously afford sure protection to citizens, both in the safeguarding of their rights and in the fulfilment of their duties.

69. If, however, this juridical and political structure is to realize its potential benefits, it is absolutely essential that public officials do their utmost to solve

the problems that arise; and they must do so by using policies and techniques which it is within their competence to implement, and which suit the actual condition of the state. It is also essential that, despite constantly changing conditions, legislators never disregard the moral law or constitutional provision, nor act at variance with the exigencies of the common good. And as justice must be the guiding principle in the administration of the state, and executives must thoroughly understand the law and carefully weigh all attendant circumstances, so too in the courts: justice must be administered impartially, and judges must be wholly incorrupt and uninfluenced by the solicitations of interested parties. The good order of society also requires that individuals and subsidiary groups within the state be effectively protected by law in the affirmation of their rights and the performance of their duties, both in their relations with each other and with government officials.[49]

70. There can be no doubt that a state juridical system which conforms to the principles of justice and rightness, and corresponds to the degree of civic maturity evinced by the state in question, is highly conducive to the attainment of the common good.

71. And yet social life is so complex, varied and active in this modern age, that even a juridical system which has been established with great prudence and foresight often seems inadequate to the need.

72. Moreover, the relations of citizens with each other, of citizens and intermediate groups with public authorities, and the relations between public authorities of the same state, are sometimes seen to be of so ambiguous and explosive a nature, that they are not susceptible of being regulated by any hard and fast system of laws. In such cases, if the authorities want to preserve the state's juridical system intact—in itself and in its application to specific cases—and if they want to minister to the principal needs of society, adapt the laws to the conditions of modern life and seek solutions to new problems, then it is essential that they have a clear idea of the nature and limits of their own legitimate spheres of action. Their calmness, integrity, clearsightedness and perseverance must be such that they will recognize at once what is needed in a given situation, and act with promptness and efficiency.[50]

73. A natural consequence of men's dignity is unquestionably their right to take an active part in government, though their degree of participation will necessarily depend on the stage of development reached by the political community of which they are members.

74. For the rest, this right to take part in government opens out to men a new and extensive field of opportunity for service. A situation is created in which civic authorities can, from the greater frequency of their contacts and discussions with the citizens, gain a clearer idea of what policies are in fact effectual for the common good; and in a system which allows for a regular succession of public officials, the authority of these officials, far from growing old and feeble, takes on a new vitality in keeping with the progressive development of human society.[51]

75. There is every indication at the present time that these aims and ideals are giving rise to various demands concerning the juridical organization of states.

The first is this: that a clear and precisely worded charter of fundamental human rights be formulated and incorporated into the state's general constitutions.

76. Secondly, each state must have a public constitution, couched in juridical terms, laying down clear rules relating to the designation of public officials, their reciprocal relations, spheres of competence and prescribed methods of operation.

77. The final demand is that relations between citizens and public authorities be described in terms of rights and duties. It must be clearly laid down that the principal function of public authorities is to recognize, respect, co-ordinate, safeguard and promote citizens' rights and duties.

78. We must, however, reject the view that the will of the individual or the group is the primary and only source of a citizen's rights and duties, and of the binding force of political constitutions and the government's authority.[52]

79. But the aspirations we have mentioned are a clear indication of the fact that men, increasingly aware nowadays of their personal dignity, have found the incentive to enter government service and demand constitutional recognition for their own inviolable rights. Not content with this, they are demanding, too, the observance of constitutional procedures in the appointment of public authorities, and are insisting that they exercise their office within this constitutional framework.

III

State-to-state relations

80. With respect to states themselves, our predecessors have constantly taught, and we wish to lend the weight of our own authority to their teaching, that nations are the subjects of reciprocal rights and duties. Their relationships, therefore, must likewise be harmonized in accordance with the dictates of truth, justice, willing co-operation, and freedom. The same law of nature that governs the life and conduct of individuals must also regulate the relations of political communities with one another.

81. This will be readily understood when one reflects that it is quite impossible for political leaders to lay aside their natural dignity while acting in their country's name and in its interests. They are still bound by the natural law, which is the rule that governs all moral conduct, and they have no authority to depart from its slightest precepts.

82. The idea that men, by the fact of their appointment to public office, are compelled to lay aside their own humanity, is quite inconceivable. Their very attainment to this high-ranking office was due to their exceptional gifts and intellectual qualities, which earned for them their reputation as outstanding representatives of the body politic.

83. Moreover, a ruling authority is indispensable to civil society. That is a

fact which follows from the moral order itself. Such authority, therefore, cannot be misdirected against the moral order. It would immediately cease to exist, being deprived of its whole *raison d'être*. God himself warns us of this: 'Hear, therefore, ye kings, and understand: learn, ye that are judges of the ends of the earth. Give ear, you that rule the people, and that please yourselves in multitudes of nations. For power is given you by the Lord, and strength by the Most High, who will examine your works, and search out your thoughts.'[53]

84. And lastly one must bear in mind that, even when it regulates the relations between states, authority must be exercised for the promotion of the common good. That is the primary reason for its existence.

85. But one of the principal imperatives of the common good is the recognition of the moral order and the unfailing observance of its precepts. 'A firmly established order between political communities must be founded on the unshakeable and unmoving rock of the moral law, that law which is revealed in the order of nature by the creator himself, and engraved indelibly on men's hearts... Its principles are beacon lights to guide the policies of men and nations. They are also warning lights—providential signs—which men must heed if their laborious efforts to establish a new order are not to encounter perilous storms and shipwreck.'[54]

86. The first point to be settled is that mutual ties between states must be governed by truth. Truth calls for the elimination of every trace of racial discrimination, and the consequent recognition of the inviolable principle that all states are by nature equal in dignity. Each of them accordingly has the right to exist, to develop, and to possess the necessary means and accept a primary responsibility for its own development. Each is also legitimately entitled to its good name and to the respect which is its due.

87. As we know from experience, men frequently differ widely in knowledge, virtue, intelligence and wealth, but that is no valid argument in favour of a system whereby those who are in a position of superiority impose their will arbitrarily on others. On the contrary, such men have a greater share in the common responsibility to help others to reach perfection by their mutual efforts.

88. So, too, on the international level: some nations may have attained to a superior degree of scientific, cultural and economic development. But that does not entitle them to exert unjust political domination over other nations. It means that they have to make a greater contribution to the common cause of social progress.

89. The fact is that no one can be by nature superior to his fellows; since all men are equally noble in natural dignity. And consequently there are no differences at all between political communities from the point of view of natural dignity. Each state is like a body, the members of which are human beings. And, as we know from experience, nations can be highly sensitive in matters in any way touching their dignity and honour; and with good reason.

90. Truth further demands an attitude of unruffled impartiality in the use of

the many aids to the promotion and spread of mutual understanding between nations which modern scientific progress has made available. This does not mean that people should be prevented from drawing particular attention to the virtues of their own way of life, but it does mean the utter rejection of ways of disseminating information which violate the principles of truth and justice, and injure the reputation of another nation.[55]

91. Relations between states must furthermore be regulated by justice. This necessitates both the recognition of their mutual rights, and, at the same time, the fulfilment of their respective duties.

92. States have the right to existence, to self-development, and to the means necessary to achieve this. They have the right to play the leading part in the process of their own development, and the right to their good name and due honours. Consequently, states are likewise in duty bound to safeguard all such rights effectively, and to avoid any action that could violate them. And just as individual men may not pursue their own private interests in a way that is unfair and detrimental to others, so too it would be criminal in a state to aim at improving itself by the use of methods which involve other nations in injury and unjust oppression. There is a saying of St Augustine which has particular relevance in this context: 'Take away justice, and what are kingdoms but mighty bands of robbers?'

93. There may be, and sometimes is, a clash of interests among states, each striving for its own development. When differences of this sort arise, they must be settled in a truly human way, not by armed force nor by deceit or trickery. There must be a mutual assessment of the arguments and feelings on both sides, a mature and objective investigation of the situation, and an equitable reconciliation of opposing views.

Problems between states

94. A special instance of this clash of interests is furnished by that political trend (which since the nineteenth century has become widespread throughout the world and has gained in strength) as a result of which men of similar ethnic background are anxious for political autonomy and unification into a single nation. For many reasons this cannot always be effected, and consequently minority peoples are often obliged to live within the territories of a nation of a different ethnic origin. This situation gives rise to serious problems.

95. It is quite clear that any attempt to check the vitality and growth of these ethnic minorities is a flagrant violation of justice; the more so if such perverse efforts are aimed at their very extinction.

96. Indeed, the best interests of justice are served by those public authorities who do all they can to improve the human conditions of the members of these minority groups, especially in what concerns their language, culture, ancient traditions, and their economic activity and enterprise.[57]

97. It is worth noting, however, that these minority groups, in reaction, perhaps, to the enforced hardships of their present situation, or to historical

[142]

circumstances, frequently tend to magnify unduly characteristics proper to their own people. They even rate them above those human values which are common to all mankind, as though the good of the entire human family should subserve the interests of their own particular groups. A more reasonable attitude for such people to adopt would be to recognize the advantages, too, which accrue to them from their own special situation. They should realize that their constant association with a people steeped in a different civilization from their own has no small part to play in the development of their own particular genius and spirit. Little by little they can absorb into their very being those virtues which characterize the other nation. But for this to happen these minority groups must enter into some kind of association with the people in whose midst they are living, and learn to share their customs and way of life. It will never happen if they sow seeds of disaffection which can only produce a harvest of evils, stifling the political development of nations.

98. Since relationships between states must be regulated in accordance with the principles of truth and justice, states must further these relationships by taking positive steps to pool their material and spiritual resources. In many cases this can be achieved by all kinds of mutual collaboration; and this is already happening in our own day in the economic, social, political, educational, health and athletic spheres—and with beneficial results. We must bear in mind that of its very nature civil authority exists, not to confine men within the frontiers of their own nations, but primarily to protect the common good of the state, which certainly cannot be divorced from the common good of the entire human family.

99. Thus, in pursuing their own interests, civil societies, far from causing injury to others, must join plans and forces whenever the efforts of particular states cannot achieve the desired goal. But in doing so great care must be taken. What is beneficial to some states may prove detrimental rather than advantageous to others.

100. Furthermore, the universal common good requires the encouragement in all nations of every kind of reciprocation between citizens and their intermediate societies. There are many parts of the world where we find groupings of people of more or less different ethnic origin. Nothing must be allowed to prevent reciprocal relations between them. Indeed such a prohibition would flout the very spirit of an age which has done so much to nullify the distances separating peoples. Nor must one overlook the fact that whatever their ethnic background, men possess, besides the special characteristics which distinguish them from other men, other very important elements in common with the rest of mankind. And these can form the basis of their progressive development and self-realization especially in regard to spiritual values. They have, therefore, the right and duty to carry on their lives with others in society.

101. As everyone is well aware, there are some countries where there is an imbalance between the amount of arable land and the number of inhabitants; others where there is an imbalance between the richness of the resources and the instruments of agriculture available. It is imperative, therefore, that

nations enter into collaboration with each other, and facilitate the circulation of goods, capital and manpower.[58]

102. We advocate in such cases the policy of bringing the work to the workers, wherever possible, rather than bringing workers to the scene of the work. In this way many people will be afforded an opportunity of increasing their resources without being exposed to the painful necessity of uprooting themselves from their own homes, settling in a strange environment, and forming new social contacts.

103. The deep feelings of paternal love for all mankind which God has implanted in our heart make it impossible for us to view without bitter anguish of spirit the plight of those who for political reasons have been exiled from their own homelands. There are great numbers of such refugees at the present time, and many are the sufferings—the incredible sufferings—to which they are constantly exposed.

104. Here surely is our proof that, in defining the scope of a just freedom within which individual citizens may live lives worthy of their human dignity, the rulers of some nations have been far too restrictive. Sometimes in states of this kind the very right to freedom is called in question, and even flatly denied. We have here a complete reversal of the right order of society, for the whole *raison d'être* of public authority is to safeguard the interests of the community. Its sovereign duty is to recognize the noble realm of freedom and protect its rights.

105. For this reason, it is not irrelevant to draw the attention of the world to the fact that these refugees are persons and all their rights as persons must be recognized. Refugees cannot lose these rights simply because they are deprived of citizenship of their own states.

106. And among man's personal rights we must include his right to enter a country in which he hopes to be able to provide more fittingly for himself and his dependants. It is therefore the duty of state officials to accept such immigrants and—so far as the good of their own community, rightly understood, permits—to further the aims of those who may wish to become members of a new society.

107. We therefore take this opportunity of giving our public approval and commendation to every undertaking, founded on the principles of human solidarity or of Christian charity, which aims at relieving the distress of those who are compelled to emigrate from their own country to another.

108. And we must indeed single out for the praise of all right-minded men those international agencies which devote all their energies to this most important work.

The arms race

109. On the other hand, we are deeply distressed to see the enormous stocks of armaments that have been, and continue to be, manufactured in the economically more developed countries. This policy is involving a vast outlay

of intellectual and material resources, with the result that the people of these countries are saddled with a great burden, while other countries lack the help they need for their economic and social development.

110. There is a common belief that under modern conditions peace cannot be assured except on the basis of an equal balance of armaments and that this factor is the probable cause of this stockpiling of armaments. Thus, if one country increases its military strength, others are immediately roused by a competitive spirit to augment their own supply of armaments. And if one country is equipped with atomic weapons, others consider themselves justified in producing such weapons themselves, equal in destructive force.

111. Consequently people are living in the grip of constant fear. They are afraid that at any moment the impending storm may break upon them with horrific violence. And they have good reasons for their fear, for there is certainly no lack of such weapons. While it is difficult to believe that anyone would dare to assume responsibility for initiating the appalling slaughter and destruction that war would bring in its wake, there is no denying that the conflagration could be started by some chance and unforeseen circumstance. Moreover, even though the monstrous power of modern weapons does indeed act as a deterrent, there is reason to fear that the very testing of nuclear devices for war purposes can, if continued, lead to serious danger for various forms of life on earth.

112. Hence justice, right reason, and the recognition of man's dignity cry out insistently for a cessation to the arms race. The stockpiles of armaments which have been built up in various countries must be reduced all round and simultaneously by the parties concerned. Nuclear weapons must be banned. A general agreement must be reached on a suitable disarmament programme, with an effective system of mutual control. In the words of Pope Pius XII: 'The calamity of a world war, with the economic and social ruin and the moral excesses and dissolution that accompany it, must not on any account be permitted to engulf the human race for a third time.'[59]

113. Everyone, however, must realize that, unless this process of disarmament be thorough-going and complete, and reach men's very souls, it is impossible to stop the arms race, or to reduce armaments, or—and this is the main thing—ultimately to abolish them entirely. Everyone must sincerely co-operate in the effort to banish fear and the anxious expectation of war from men's minds. But this requires that the fundamental principles upon which peace is based in today's world be replaced by an altogether different one, namely, the realization that true and lasting peace among nations cannot consist in the possession of an equal supply of armaments but only in mutual trust. And we are confident that this can be achieved, for it is a thing which not only is dictated by common sense, but is in itself most desirable and most fruitful of good.

114. Here, then, we have an objective dictated first of all by reason. There is general agreement—or at least there should be—that relations between states, as between individuals, must be regulated not by armed force, but in accordance with the principles of right reason: the principles, that is, of truth, justice and vigorous and sincere co-operation.

115. Secondly, it is an objective which we maintain is more earnestly to be desired. For who is there who does not feel the craving to be rid of the threat of war, and to see peace preserved and made daily more secure?

116. And finally it is an objective which is rich with possibilities for good. Its advantages will be felt everywhere, by individuals, by families, by nations, by the whole human race. The warning of Pope Pius XII still rings in our ears: 'Nothing is lost by peace; everything may be lost by war.'[60]

117. We therefore consider it our duty as the vicar on earth of Jesus Christ—the saviour of the world, the author of peace—and as interpreter of the most ardent wishes of the whole human family, in the fatherly love we bear all mankind, to beg and beseech mankind, and above all the rulers of states, to be unsparing of their labour and efforts to ensure that human affairs follow a rational and dignified course.

118. In their deliberations together, let men of outstanding wisdom and influence give serious thought to the problem of achieving a more human adjustment of relations between states throughout the world. It must be an adjustment that is based on mutual trust, sincerity in negotiation, and the faithful fulfilment of obligations assumed. Every aspect of the problem must be examined, so that eventually there may emerge some point of agreement from which to initiate treaties which are sincere, lasting, and beneficial in their effects.

119. We, for our part, will pray unceasingly that God may bless these labours by his divine assistance, and make them fruitful.

Preserving freedom

120. Furthermore, relations between states must be regulated by the principle of freedom. This means that no country has the right to make any action that would constitute an unjust oppression of other countries, or an unwarranted interference in their affairs. On the contrary, all should help to develop in others an increasing awareness of their duties, an adventurous and enterprising spirit, and the resolution to take the initiative for their own advancement in every field of endeavour.

121. All men are united by their common origin and fellowship, their redemption by Christ, and their supernatural destiny. They are called to form one Christian family. In our encyclical *Mater et Magistra*, therefore, we appealed to the more wealthy nations to render every kind of assistance to those states which are still in the process of economic development.[61]

122. It is no small consolation to us to be able to testify here to the wide acceptance of our appeal, and we are confident that in the years that lie ahead it will be accepted even more widely. The result we look for is that the poorer states shall in as short a time as possible attain to a degree of economic development that enables their citizens to live in conditions more in keeping with their human dignity.

123. Again and again we must insist on the need for helping these peoples in a way which guarantees to them the preservation of their own freedom. They must be conscious that they are themselves playing the major role in their economic and social development; that they are themselves to shoulder the main burden of it.

124. Hence the wisdom of Pope Pius XII's teaching: 'A new order founded on moral principles is the surest bulwark against the violation of the freedom, integrity and security of other nations, no matter what may be their territorial extension or their capacity for defence. For although it is almost inevitable that the larger states, in view of their greater power and vaster resources, will themselves decide on the norms governing their economic associations with small states, nevertheless these smaller states cannot be denied their right, in keeping with the common good, to political freedom, and to the adoption of a position of neutrality in the conflicts between nations. No state can be denied this right, for it is a postulate of the natural law itself, as also of international law. These smaller states have also the right of assuring their own economic development. It is only with the effective guaranteeing of these rights that smaller nations can fittingly promote the common good of all mankind, as well as the material welfare and the cultural and spiritual progress of their own people.'[62]

125. The wealthier states, therefore, while providing various forms of assistance to the poorer, must have the highest possible respect for the latter's national characteristics and time-honoured civil institutions. They must also repudiate any policy of domination. If this can be achieved, then 'a precious contribution will have been made to the formation of a world community, in which each individual nation, conscious of its rights and duties, can work on terms of equality with the rest for the attainment of universal prosperity.'[63]

126. Men nowadays are becoming more and more convinced that any disputes which may arise between nations must be resolved by negotiation and agreement, and not by recourse to arms.

127. We acknowledge that this conviction owes its origin chiefly to the terrifying destructive force of modern weapons. It arises from fear of the ghastly and catastrophic consequences of their use. Thus, in this age which boasts of its atomic power, it no longer makes sense to maintain that war is a fit instrument with which to repair the violation of justice.

128. And yet, unhappily, we often find the law of fear reigning supreme among nations and causing them to spend enormous sums on armaments. Their object is not aggression, so they say—and there is no reason for disbelieving them—but to deter others from aggression.

129. Nevertheless, we are hopeful that, by establishing contact with one another and by a policy of negotiation, nations will come to a better recognition of the natural ties that bind them together as men. We are hopeful, too, that they will come to a fairer realization of one of the cardinal duties deriving from our common nature: namely, that love, not fear, must dominate the relationships between individuals and between nations. It is principally characteristic of love that it draws men together in all sorts of

ways, sincerely united in the bonds of mind and matter; and this is a union from which countless blessings can flow.

IV

Collaboration towards the universal common good

130. Recent progress in science and technology has had a profound influence on man's way of life. This progress is a spur to men all over the world to extend their collaboration and association with one another in these days when material resources, travel from one country to another, and technical information have so vastly increased. This has led to a phenomenal growth in relationships between individuals, families and intermediate associations belonging to the various nations, and between the public authorities of the various political communities. There is also a growing economic interdependence between states. National economies are gradually becoming so interdependent that a kind of world economy is being born from the simultaneous integration of the economies of individual states. And finally, each country's social progress, order, security and peace are necessarily linked with the social progress, order, security and peace of every other country.

131. From this it is clear that no state can fittingly pursue its own interests in isolation from the rest, nor, under such circumstances, can it develop itself as it should. The prosperity and progress of any state is in part consequence, and in part cause, of the prosperity and progress of all other states.

132. No era will ever succeed in destroying the unity of the human family, for it consists of men who are all equal by virtue of their natural dignity. Hence there will always be an imperative need—born of man's very nature—to promote in sufficient measure the universal common good; the good, that is, of the whole human family.

133. In the past rulers of states seem to have been able to make sufficient provision for the universal common good through the normal diplomatic channels, or by top-level meetings and discussions, treaties and agreements; by using, that is, the ways and means suggested by the natural law, the law of nations, or international law.

134. In our own day, however, mutual relationships between states have undergone a far-reaching change. On the one hand, the universal common good gives rise to problems of the utmost gravity, complexity and urgency—especially as regards the preservation of the security and peace of the whole world. On the other hand, the rulers of individual nations, being all on an equal footing, largely fail in their efforts to achieve this, however much they multiply their meetings and their endeavours to discover more fitting instruments of justice. And this is no reflection on their sincerity and enterprise. It is merely that their authority is not sufficiently influential.

135. We are thus driven to the conclusion that the shape and structure of

political life in the modern world, and the influence exercised by public authority in all the nations of the world are unequal to the task of promoting the common good of all peoples.

136. Now, if one considers carefully the inner significance of the common good on the one hand, and the nature and function of public authority on the other, one cannot fail to see that there is an intrinsic connection between them. Public authority, as the means of promoting the common good in civil society, is a postulate of the moral order. But the moral order likewise requires that this authority be effective in attaining its end. Hence the civil institutions in which such authority resides, becomes operative and promotes its ends, are endowed with a certain kind of structure and efficacy: a structure and efficacy which make such institutions capable of realizing the common good by ways and means adequate to the changing historical conditions.

137. Today the universal common good presents us with problems which are world-wide in their dimensions; problems, therefore, which cannot be solved except by a public authority with power, organization and means co-extensive with these problems, and with a world-wide sphere of activity. Consequently the moral order itself demands the establishment of some such general form of public authority.

138. But this general authority equipped with world-wide power and adequate means for achieving the universal common good cannot be imposed by force. It must be set up with the consent of all nations. If its work is to be effective, it must operate with fairness, absolute impartiality, and with dedication to the common good of all peoples. The forcible imposition by the more powerful nations of a universal authority of this kind would inevitably arouse fears of its being used as an instrument to serve the interests of the few or to take the side of a single nation, and thus the influence and effectiveness of its activity would be undermined. For even though nations may differ widely in material progress and military strength, they are very sensitive as regards their juridical equality and the excellence of their own way of life. They are right, therefore, in their reluctance to submit to an authority imposed by force, established without their co-operation, or not accepted of their own accord.

139. The common good of individual states is something that cannot be determined without reference to the human person, and the same is true of the common good of all states taken together. Hence the public authority of the world community must likewise have as its special aim the recognition, respect, safeguarding and promotion of the rights of the human person. This can be done by direct action, if need be, or by the creation throughout the world of the sort of conditions in which rulers of individual states can more easily carry out their specific functions.

140. The same principle of subsidiarity which governs the relations between public authorities and individuals, families and intermediate societies in a single state, must also apply to the relations between the public authority of the world community and the public authorities of each political community. The special function of this universal authority must be to evaluate and find a

solution to economic, social, political and cultural problems which affect the universal common good. These are problems which, because of their extreme gravity, vastness and urgency, must be considered too difficult for the rulers of individual states to solve with any degree of success.

141. But it is no part of the duty of universal authority to limit the sphere of action of the public authority of individual states, or to arrogate any of their functions to itself. On the contrary, its essential purpose is to create world conditions in which the public authorities of each nation, its citizens and intermediate groups, can carry out their tasks, fulfil their duties and claim their rights with greater security.[64]

The United Nations

142. The United Nations Organization (UN) was established, as is well known, on 26 June 1945. To it were subsequently added lesser organizations consisting of members nominated by the public authority of the various nations and entrusted with highly important international functions in the economics, social, cultural, educational and health fields. The United Nations Organization has the special aim of maintaining and strengthening peace between nations, and of encouraging and assisting friendly relations between them, based on the principles of equality, mutual respect, and extensive co-operation in every field of human endeavour.

143. A clear proof of the far-sightedness of this organization is provided by the Universal Declaration of Human Rights passed by the United Nations General Assembly on 10 December 1948. The preamble of this declaration affirms that the genuine recognition and complete observance of all the rights and freedoms outlined in the declaration is a goal to be sought by all peoples and all nations.

144. We are, of course, aware that some of the points in the declaration did not meet with unqualified approval in some quarters; and there was justification for this. Nevertheless, we think the document should be considered a step in the right direction, an approach toward the establishment of a juridical and political ordering of the world community. It is a solemn recognition of the personal dignity of every human being; an assertion of everyone's right to be free to seek out the truth, to follow moral principles, discharge the duties imposed by justice, and lead a fully human life. It also recognized other rights connected with these.

145. It is therefore our earnest wish that the United Nations Organization may be able progressively to adapt its structure and methods of operation to the magnitude and nobility of its tasks. May the day be not long delayed when every human being can find in this organization an effective safeguard of his personal rights; those rights, that is, which derive directly from his dignity as a human person, and which are therefore universal, inviolable and inalienable. This is all the more desirable in that men today are taking an ever more active part in the public life of their own nations, and in doing so they are showing an increased interest in the affairs of all peoples. They are

becoming more and more conscious of being living members of the universal family of mankind.

V

Christian commitment to human progress

146. Here once more we exhort our sons to take an active part in public life, and to work together for the benefit of the whole human race, as well as for their own political communities. It is vitally necessary for them to endeavour, in the light of Christian faith, and with love as their guide, to ensure that every institution, whether economic, social, cultural or political, be such as not to obstruct but rather to facilitate man's self-betterment, both in the natural and in the supernatural order.

147. And yet, if they are to imbue civilization with right ideals and Christian principles, it is not enough for our sons to be illumined by the heavenly light of faith and to be fired with enthusiasm for a cause; they must involve themselves in the work of these institutions, and strive to influence them effectively from within.

148. But in a culture and civilization like our own, which is so remarkable for its scientific knowledge and its technical discoveries, clearly no one can insinuate himself into public life unless he be scientifically competent, technically capable, and skilled in the practice of his own profession.

149. And yet even this must be reckoned insufficient to bring the relationships of daily life into conformity with a more human standard, based, as it must be, on truth, tempered by justice, motivated by mutual love, and holding fast to the practice of freedom.

150. If these policies are really to become operative, men must first of all take the utmost care to conduct their various temporal activities in accordance with the laws which govern each and every such activity, observing the principles which correspond to their respective natures. Secondly, men's actions must be made to conform with the precepts of the moral order. This means that their behaviour must be such as to reflect their consciousness of exercising a personal right or performing a personal duty. Reason has a further demand to make. In obedience to the providential designs and commands of God respecting our salvation and neglecting the dictates of conscience, men must conduct themselves in their temporal activity in such a way as to effect a thorough integration of the principal spiritual values with those of science, technology and the professions.

151. In traditionally Christian states at the present time, civil institutions evince a high degree of scientific and technical progress and possess abundant machinery for the attainment of every kind of objective. And yet it must be owned that these institutions are often but slightly affected by Christian motives and a Christian spirit.

152. One may well ask the reason for this, since the men who have largely

contributed—and who are still contributing—to the creation of these institutions are men who are professed Christians, and who live their lives, at least in part, in accordance with the precepts of the gospels. In our opinion the explanation lies in a certain cleavage between faith and practice. Their inner, spiritual unity must be restored, so that faith may be the light and love the motivating force of all their actions.

153. We consider too that a further reason for this very frequent divorce between faith and practice in Christians is an inadequate education in Christian teaching and Christian morality. In many places the amount of energy devoted to the study of secular subjects is all too often out of proportion to that devoted to the study of religion. Scientific training reaches a very high level, whereas religious training generally does not advance beyond the elementary stage. It is essential, therefore, that the instruction given to our young people be complete and continuous, and imparted in such a way that moral goodness and the cultivation of religious values may keep pace with scientific knowledge and continually advancing technical progress. Young people must also be taught how to carry out their own particular obligations in a truly fitting manner.[65]

154. In this connection we think it opportune to point out how difficult it is to understand clearly the relation between the objective requirements of justice and concrete situations; to define, that is, correctly to what degree and in what form doctrinal principles and directives must be applied in the given state of human society.

155. The definition of these degrees and forms is all the more difficult in an age such as ours, driven forward by a fever of activity. And yet this is the age in which each one of us is required to make his own contribution to the universal common good. Daily is borne in on us the need to make the reality of social life conform better to the requirements of justice. Hence our sons have every reason for not thinking that they can relax their efforts and be satisfied with what they have already achieved.

156. What has so far been achieved is insufficient compared with what needs to be done; all men must realize that. Every day provides a more important, a more fitting enterprise to which they must turn their hands—industry, trade unions, professional organizations, insurance, cultural institutions, the law, politics, medical and recreational facilities, and other such activities. The age in which we live needs all these things. It is an age in which men, having discovered the atom and achieved the breakthrough into outer space, are now exploring other avenues, leading to almost limitless horizons.

The framework for Christian collaboration

157. The principles we have set out in this document take their rise from the very nature of things. They derive, for the most part, from the consideration of man's natural rights. Thus the putting of these principles into effect frequently involves extensive co-operation between Catholics and those Christians who are separated from this Apostolic See. It even involves the co-operation of Catholics with men who may not be Christians but who

nevertheless are reasonable men, and men of natural moral integrity. 'In such circumstances they must, of course, bear themselves as Catholics, and do nothing to compromise religion and morality. Yet at the same time they should show themselves animated by a spirit of understanding and unselfishness, ready to co-operate loyally in achieving objects which are good in themselves, or conducive to good.'[66]

158. It is always perfectly justifiable to distinguish between error as such and the person who falls into error—even in the case of men who err regarding the truth or are led astray as a result of their inadequate knowledge, in matters either of religion or of the highest ethical standards. A man who has fallen into error does not cease to be a man. He never forfeits his personal dignity; and that is something that must always be taken into account. Besides, there exists in man's very nature an undying capacity to break through the barriers of error and seek the road to truth. God, in his great providence, is ever present with his aid. Today, maybe, a man lacks faith and turns aside into error; tomorrow, perhaps, illumined by God's light, he may indeed embrace the truth. Catholics who, in order to achieve some external good, collaborate with unbelievers or with those who through error lack the fullness of faith in Christ, may possibly provide the occasion or even the incentive for their conversion to the truth.

159. Again it is perfectly legitimate to make a clear distinction between a false philosophy of the nature, origin and purpose of men and the world, and economic, social, cultural, and political undertakings, even when such undertakings draw their origin and inspiration from that philosophy. True, the philosophic formula does not change once it has been set down in precise terms, but the undertakings clearly cannot avoid being influenced to a certain extent by the changing conditions in which they have to operate. Besides, who can deny the possible existence of good and commendable elements in these undertakings, elements which do indeed conform to the dictates of right reason, and are an expression of man's lawful aspirations?

160. It may sometimes happen, therefore, that meetings arranged for some practical end—though hitherto they were thought to be altogether useless—may in fact be fruitful at the present time, or at least offer prospects of success. But whether or not the moment for such co-operation has arrived, and the manner and degree of such co-operation in the attainment of economic, social, cultural and political advantages—these are matters for prudence to decide; prudence, the queen of all the virtues which rule the lives of men both as individuals and in society. As far as Catholics are concerned, the decision rests primarily with those who take a leading part in the life of the community, and in these specific fields. They must, however, act in accordance with the principles of the natural law, and observe the Church's social teaching and the directives of ecclesiastical authority. For it must not be forgotten that the Church has the right and duty not only to safeguard her teaching on faith and morals, but also to exercise her authority over her sons by intervening in their external affairs whenever a judgement has to be made concerning the practical application of this teaching.[67]

The scale of the challenge

161. There are indeed some people who, in their generosity of spirit, burn with a desire to institute wholesale reforms whenever they come across situations which show scant regard for justice or are wholly out of keeping with its claims. They tackle the problem with such impetuosity that one would think they were embarking on some political revolution.

162. We would remind such people that it is the law of nature that all things must be of gradual growth. If there is to be any improvement in human institutions, the work must be done slowly and deliberately from within. Pope Pius XII expressed it in these terms: 'Salvation and justice consist not in the uprooting of an outdated system, but in a well-designed policy of development. Hotheadedness was never constructive; it has always destroyed everything. It has inflamed passions, but never assuaged them. It sows no seeds but those of hatred and destruction. Far from bringing about the reconciliation of contending parties, it reduces men and political parties to the necessity of laboriously redoing the work of the past, building on the ruins that disharmony has left in its wake.'[68]

163. Hence among the very serious obligations incumbent upon men of high principles, we must include the task of establishing new relationships in human society, under the mastery and guidance of truth, justice, charity and freedom—relations between individual citizens, between citizens and their respective states, between states, and finally between individuals, families, intermediate associations and states on the one hand, and the world community on the other. There is surely no one who will not consider this a most exalted task, for it is one which is able to bring about true peace in accordance with divinely established order.

164. Considering the need, the men who are shouldering this responsibility are far too few in number, yet they are deserving of the highest recognition from society, and we rightfully honour them with our public praise. We call upon them to persevere in their ideals, which are of such tremendous benefit to mankind. At the same time we are encouraged to hope that many more men, Christians especially, will join their cause, spurred on by love and the realization of their duty. Everyone who has joined the ranks of Christ must be a glowing point of light in the world, a nucleus of love, a leaven of the whole mass. He will be so in proportion to his degree of spiritual union with God.

In search of true peace

165. The world will never be the dwelling-place of peace, till peace has found a home in the heart of each and every man, till every man preserves in himself the order ordained by God to be preserved. That is why St Augustine asks the question: 'Does your mind desire the strength to gain the mastery over your passions? Let it submit to a greater power, and it will conquer all beneath it. And peace will be in you—true, sure, most ordered peace. What is that order? God as ruler of the mind; the mind as ruler of the body. Nothing could be more orderly.'[69]

166. Our concern here has been with problems which are causing men extreme anxiety at the present time; problems which are intimately bound up with the progress of human society. Unquestionably, the teaching we have given has been inspired by a longing which we feel most keenly, and which we know is shared by all men of good will: that peace may be assured on earth.

167. We who, in spite of our inadequacy, are nevertheless the vicar of him whom the prophet announced as the *Prince of Peace*,[70] conceive of it as our duty to devote all our thoughts and care and energy to further this common good of all mankind. Yet peace is but an empty word, if it does not rest upon that order which our hope prevailed upon us to set forth in outline in this encyclical. It is an order that is founded on truth, built up on justice, nurtured and animated by charity, and brought into effect under the auspices of freedom.

168. So magnificent, so exalted is this aim that human resources alone, even though inspired by the most praiseworthy good will, cannot hope to achieve it. God himself must come to man's aid with his heavenly assistance, if human society is to bear the closest possible resemblance to the kingdom of God.

169. The very order of things therefore, demands that during this sacred season we pray earnestly to him who by his bitter passion and death washed away men's sins, which are the fountainhead of discord, misery and inequality; to him who shed his blood to reconcile the human race to the heavenly Father, and bestowed the gifts of peace 'For he is our peace, who hath made both one... And coming, he preached peace to you that were afar off; and peace to them that were nigh.'[71]

170. The sacred liturgy of these days re-echoes the same message: 'Our Lord Jesus Christ, after his resurrection stood in the midst of his disciples and said: Peace be upon you, alleluia. The disciples rejoiced when they saw the Lord.'[72] It is Christ, therefore, who brought us peace; Christ who bequeathed it to us: 'Peace I leave with you: my peace I give unto you: not as the world giveth, do I give unto you.'[73]

171. Let us, then, pray with all fervour for this peace which our divine redeemer came to bring us. May he banish from the souls of men whatever might endanger peace. May he transform all men into witnesses of truth, justice and brotherly love. May he illumine with his light the minds of rulers, so that, besides caring for the proper material welfare of their peoples, they may also guarantee them the fairest gift of peace. Finally, may Christ inflame the desires of all men to break through the barriers which divide them, to strengthen the bonds of mutual love, to learn to understand one another, and to pardon those who have done them wrong. Through his power and inspiration may all peoples welcome each other to their hearts as brothers, and may the peace they long for ever flower and ever reign among them.

172. And so, dear brothers, with the ardent wish that peace may come upon the flocks committed to your care, for the special benefit of those who are most lowly and in the greatest need of help and defence, lovingly in the Lord we bestow on you, on our priests both secular and regular, on religious both

men and women, on all the faithful and especially those who give wholehearted obedience to these our exhortations, our apostolic blessing. And upon all men of good will, to whom we also address this encyclical, we implore from God health and prosperity.

173. Given in Rome, at St Peter's, on Holy Thursday, 11 April 1963, the fifth year of our pontificate.

Gaudium et Spes

Pastoral Constitution on the Church in the Modern World

Introduction

In their 'Message to Humanity' with which they opened the Second Vatican Council, the bishops of the Catholic Church gathered in Rome drew attention to 'two issues of special urgency' which confronted them: peace and social justice. That was in October 1962. The Pastoral Constitution on the Church in the Modern World which concerned itself with those topics was not formally approved until 7 December 1965. The council's closure came the following day. There had indeed been no provision made for a document such as *Gaudium et Spes* in the preparatory work for Vatican II, and it might not have been put together at all but for an intervention by Cardinal Léon-Joseph Suenens in the December following the opening of the council.

Critics have said that the pastoral constitution was, in the end, too rushed, too repetitious, too long and too general, and that it was not well knit together. It is indeed unusually lengthy, and there is no doubt that it does not stand in the very first rank of conciliar documents, but it is nonetheless in some important respects an advance on earlier papal social teaching—on peace and war for example—and it is sometimes quite surprisingly radical. The Fathers of the Council went as far as suggesting that, in order to give greater witness to the world the Church ought to abandon the privileged position which it held in certain countries. What this was in practice to mean became clear in the decade which followed, and nowhere more dramatically, perhaps, than in Spain.

The Latin text of *Gaudium et Spes* (GS) is to be found in AAS 58 (1966), 1025-1120. It is unusual for a Vatican document in having a large number of cross-headings—indeed, there is a heading for every main paragraph. All except these paragraph headings have been retained, and none added. The main paragraphs were also numbered, but subordinate paragraphs, where they existed, were not. The paragraph numbering has been retained, but subordinate paragraphs have been given subordinate numbers in accordance with the policy outlined in the Editorial Note. (p.ix). A fuller discussion of *Gaudium et Spes* (GS) is to be found in the Introduction, pp.xiv.

Summary

Paras. 1-10: The council focuses its attention on the world, the theatre of human kind's history, and on the Church's role in fostering fellowship at a time of profound and rapid change. Never have people had such wealth, yet huge numbers still go hungry; there is a keen understanding of freedom, yet new kinds of slavery appear; never has there been greater need for solidarity, yet the world is torn into opposing camps. The human race has passed from a somewhat static concept of reality to a more dynamic one, and this brings changes which in turn call into question accepted values. Many are demanding these benefits of which they judge themselves deprived. The discords in society flow from divisions within individuals. The council wishes to shed light on the mystery of the individual and to help in finding solutions to modern problems.

Paras. 11-22: God created male and female. This companionship produces the primary form of interpersonal communion, so human beings are social by their innermost being. But they have destroyed their proper relationship with God and as a result all human life is a struggle between good and evil. In the depth of their consciences people detect a law which they do not impose upon themselves, and which enjoins them to search for truth. Only in freedom can they direct themselves towards goodness. The basic source of human dignity lies in the call to communion with God. Many, however, have never recognized this link with God and atheism is one of the most serious problems of the age, for which believers must take some of the blame. The Church strives to detect the hidden causes for the denial of God and holds that recognition of God is not hostile to human dignity. The remedy for atheism is the proper presentation of the Church's teaching, and the life of the Church and its members. The Church wants dialogue, so that believers and unbelievers alike can work for a better world. Christ died for all, so the Holy Spirit offers to all the possibility of being associated with the paschal mystery.

Paras. 23-32: There has been an increase in interdependence, chiefly promoted by modern technological advances. God has willed that all should constitute one family, but even while individuals may be aided by life within society, they are often diverted from pursuing the good by their social circumstances. When structures are flawed by the consequences of sin there are new inducements to sin. Social order and development should always work to the benefit of the individual, and they require constant improvement. Respect and love ought to be extended to those who think differently from oneself in social, political and religious matters, and though that will not render us indifferent to the truth we must distinguish between the error and the person who errs, never losing sight of the latter's dignity. Human institutions, private and public, must work to minister to human dignity and oppose any kind of slavery. Praise is due to those nations where the largest possible number of citizens are freely involved in public affairs.

Paras. 33-39: When men and women labour for the benefit of society they are not only providing substance for themselves but contributing to the realization of God's plan in history. And whoever humbly strives to penetrate the secrets of reality is being guided by God. But while human progress is a great advantage, it brings strong temptations and is imperilled by pride and deranged self-love. It has therefore to be purified and perfected through the power of the Spirit at work in human hearts. Earthly progress is to be distinguished from the growth of Christ's kingdom, but in so far as it can contribute to the better ordering of society it is of vital concern to the kingdom of God.

Paras. 40-45: The Church believes that it can contribute to making the human family and its history more humane, and esteems what other churches and ecclesial communities are doing in pursuit of the same goal. Personal dignity and liberty cannot be safeguarded as well by human laws as they can by the gospel entrusted to the Church. The Church has no proper role in the political, economic or social order, but its religious mission can serve to structure and consolidate the human community according to divine law. The promotion of unity belongs to the Church's innermost nature especially because it is bound to no particular culture or political or economic system. The Christian who neglects his temporal duties jeopardizes his salvation. These duties belong properly, though not exclusively, to lay people. Pastors cannot give concrete solutions to every problem, and the Church is aware of the gulf between its message and the human failings of those to whom the gospel is entrusted. The Church requires help to express the gospel in the diverse cultures in which it is preached, and its structure can be enriched by developments in social life.

Paras. 46-52: The council wishes to offer guidance and support to all Christians trying to preserve the holiness, dignity and value of marriage, which is a permanent relationship of life and love established by God. The Christian family springing from marriage will show Christ's living presence to all. The transmission of human life and the education of children is the proper mission of parents, but marriage is not instituted solely for procreation but also for the growth of mutual love. The welfare of the family should be protected by the State, and properly trained priests should offer couples spiritual assistance.

Paras. 53-62: Culture in a general sense includes everything which helps in the development of bodily and spiritual qualities and helps to bring the world under control through knowledge and through work. There is a growing realization that people are themselves creators of the culture of their own community. There is a danger of people putting too much trust in modern discoveries, but that does not detract from the positive value of scientific study. Culture is subordinate to the integral perfection of the whole person, but it also requires that, within the boundaries of morality and common utility, people can freely search for truth and express their opinions. Everything must be done to make all conscious of their right to culture and their duty to develop themselves. While the Church has contributed to the development of culture, it should also use the findings, especially of psychology and sociology, in its pastoral theology. Theologians should collaborate with others versed in the secular sciences, while the laity are urged to dedicate themselves ever more professionally to the study of the sacred sciences.

Paras. 63-72: Economic growth is not to be allowed to continue mechanically: strenuous efforts must be made to remove economic inequalities. The agricultural community, in particular, must not be allowed to remain as lower-class citizens, as often happens. Migrant labour must be given fair treatment. Everyone has the duty to work faithfully, and the right to work and to adequate remuneration for it. The right to found unions is a basic one and unions should be allowed to contribute towards the organization of economic life. The strike remains a necessary means for the defence of workers' rights, but peaceful means of settlement should first be tried. Private ownership in some form is wholly necessary for personal autonomy, but public authority has the right to prevent the misuse of private property to the detriment of the common good.

Paras. 73-76: People realize that they cannot achieve a fully human life on their own—a wider community is needed. The political community exists to serve the common good. Political authority, which must always be exercised within the limits of the moral order, is designed by God. It can take a number of forms, but it is inhuman for public authority to fall back on dictatorial methods which violate people's rights. The Church is not in any way identified with the political community, yet both are devoted to the personal and social vocation of the same people, and the Church should have freedom to preach the faith.

Paras. 77-93: The council calls upon Christians to work for a peace based on justice. But peace is also a fruit of love, which goes beyond what justice can provide. The council praises those who renounce the use of violence as a means of vindicating their rights. The horror of war is magnified by the number of weapons, and any act of war aimed at the destruction of large areas with their populations is condemned. If war is to be outlawed some universal public authority must be established, but in the meantime efforts must be made to eliminate the danger of war, a danger which sometimes stems from the excessive economic inequality and at other times from the desire for domination. There is need for greater co-operation in the economic field, and for the advanced nations to help the developing ones. There is special need for help with the problem of demographic growth. The Council welcomes the involvement of Catholics in aid programmes, and urges them to active co-operation with non-Catholics. The Church should be a sign of fellowship. In order for it to be so, mutual esteem, reverence and harmony ought to be fostered within the Church. The Church desires dialogue with all those who acknowledge God, for all can and should work together to build up the world in genuine peace.

Paul, bishop, servant of the servants of God, together with the Fathers of the Sacred Council, for everlasting memory.

PREFACE

1. The joys and the hopes, the griefs and the anxieties of the men of this age, especially those who are poor or in any way afflicted, these are the joys and hopes, the griefs and anxieties of the followers of Christ. Indeed, nothing genuinely human fails to raise an echo in their hearts. For theirs is a community composed of men. United in Christ, they are led by the Holy Spirit in their journey to the kingdom of their father and they have welcomed the news of salvation which is meant for every man. That is why this community realizes that it is truly linked with mankind and its history by the deepest of bonds.

2. Hence this Second Vatican Council, having probed more profoundly into the mystery of the Church, now addresses itself without hesitation, not only to the sons of the Church and to all who invoke the name of Christ, but to the whole of humanity. For the council yearns to explain to everyone how it conceives of the presence and activity of the Church in the world of today.

2.1. Therefore, the council focuses its attention on the world of men, the whole human family along with the sum of those realities in the midst of which it lives; that world which is the theatre of man's history, and the heir of his energies, his tragedies and his triumphs; that world which the Christian sees as created and sustained by its maker's love, fallen indeed into the bondage of sin, yet emancipated now by Christ, who was crucified and rose again to break the stranglehold of personified evil, so that the world might be fashioned anew according to God's design and reach its fulfilment.

3. Though mankind is stricken with wonder at its own discoveries and its power, it often raises anxious questions about the current trend of the world, about the place and role of man in the universe, about the meaning of its individual and collective strivings, and about the ultimate destiny of reality and of humanity. Hence, giving witness and voice to the whole people of God gathered together by Christ, this council can provide no more eloquent proof of its solidarity with, as well as its respect and love for the entire human family with which it is bound up, than by engaging with it in conversation about these various problems. The council brings to mankind light kindled from the gospel, and puts at its disposal those saving resources which the Church herself, under the guidance of the Holy Spirit, receives from her founder. For the human person deserves to be preserved; human society deserves to be renewed. Hence the focal point of our total presentation will be man himself, whole and entire, body and soul, heart and conscience, mind and will.

3.1. Therefore, this sacred synod, proclaiming the noble destiny of man and championing the Godlike seed which has been sown in him, offers to mankind the honest assistance of the Church in fostering that brotherhood of all men which corresponds to this destiny of theirs. Inspired by no earthly ambition, the Church seeks but a solitary goal: to carry forward the work of Christ under the lead of the befriending Spirit. And Christ entered this world to give witness to the truth, to rescue and not to sit in judgement, to serve and not to be served.[1]

INTRODUCTORY STATEMENT

The situation of men in the modern world

4. To carry out such a task, the Church has always had the duty of scrutinizing the signs of the times and of interpreting them in the light of the gospel. Thus, in language intelligible to each generation, she can respond to the perennial questions which men ask about this present life and the life to come, and about the relationship of the one to the other. We must therefore recognize and understand the world in which we live, its expectations, its longings, and its often dramatic characteristics. Some of the main features of the modern world can be sketched as follows.

4.1. Today, the human face is involved in a new stage of history. Profound and rapid changes are spreading by degrees around the whole world. Triggered by the intelligence and creative energies of man, these changes recoil upon him, upon his decisions and desires, both individual and collective, and upon his manner of thinking and acting with respect to things and to people. Hence we can already speak of a true cultural and social transformation, one which has repercussions on man's religious life as well.

4.2. As happens in any crisis of growth, this transformation has brought serious difficulties in its wake. Thus while man extends his power in every direction, he does not always succeed in subjecting it to his own welfare. Striving to probe more profoundly into the deeper recesses of his own mind, he frequently appears more unsure of himself. Gradually and more precisely he lays bare the laws of society, only to be paralysed by uncertainty about the direction to give it.

4.3. Never has the human race enjoyed such an abundance of wealth, resources and economic power, and yet a huge proportion of the world's citizens are still tormented by hunger and poverty, while countless numbers suffer from total illiteracy. Never before has man had so keen an understanding of freedom, yet at the same time, new forms of social and psychological slavery make their appearance. Although the world of today has a very vivid awareness of its unity and of how one man depends on another in needful solidarity, it is most grievously torn into opposing camps by conflicting forces. For political, social, economic, racial and ideological disputes still continue bitterly, and with them the peril of a war which would reduce everything to ashes. True, there is a growing exchange of ideas, but the very words by which key concepts are expressed take on quite different meanings in diverse ideological systems. Finally, man painstakingly searches for a better world, without a corresponding spiritual advancement.

4.4. Influenced by such a variety of complexities, many of our contemporaries are kept from accurately identifying permanent values and adjusting them properly to fresh discoveries. As a result, buffeted between hope and anxiety and pressing one another with questions about the present course of events, they are burdened down with uneasiness. This same course of events leads men to look for answers; indeed, it forces them to do so.

5. Today's spiritual agitation and the changing conditions of life are part of a

broader and deeper revolution. As a result of the latter, intellectual formation is ever increasingly based on the mathematical and natural sciences and on those dealing with man himself, while in the practical order the technology which stems from these sciences takes on mounting importance. This scientific spirit has a new kind of impact on the cultural sphere and on modes of thought. Technology is now transforming the face of the earth, and is already trying to master outer space.

5.1. To a certain extent, the human intellect is also broadening its dominion over time: over the past by means of historical knowledge; over the future, by the art of projecting and by planning. Advances in biology, psychology and the social sciences not only bring men hope of improved self-knowledge; in conjunction with technical methods, they are helping men exert direct influence on the life of social groups. At the same time, the human race is giving steadily increasing thought to forecasting and regulating its own population growth.

5.2. History itself speeds along on so rapid a course that an individual person can scarcely keep abreast of it. The destiny of the human community has become all of a piece, where once the various groups of men had a kind of private history of their own. Thus, the human race has passed from a rather static concept of reality to a more dynamic, revolutionary one. In consequence there has arisen a new series of problems, a series as numerous as can be, calling for new efforts of analysis and synthesis.

6. By this very circumstance, the traditional local communities such as families, clans, tribes, villages, various groups and associations stemming from social contacts, experience more thorough changes every day.

6.1. The industrial type of society is gradually being spread, leading some nations to economic affluence, and radically transforming ideas and social conditions established for centuries. Likewise, the cult and pursuit of city living has grown, either because of a multiplication of cities and their inhabitants, or by a transplantation of city life to rural settings.

6.2. New and more efficient media of social communication are contributing to the knowledge of events; by setting off chain reactions they are giving the swiftest and widest possible circulation to styles of thought and feeling.

6.3. It is also noteworthy how many men are being induced to migrate on various counts, and are thereby changing their manner of life.

6.4. Thus a man's ties with his fellows are constantly being multiplied, and at the same time 'socialization'* brings further ties, without, however, always promoting appropriate personal development and truly personal relationships.

6.5. This kind of evolution can be seen more clearly in those nations which already enjoy the conveniences of economic and technological progress, though it is also astir among peoples still striving for such progress and eager to secure for themselves the advantages of an industrialized and urbanized society. These peoples, especially those among them who are attached to older traditions, are simultaneously undergoing a movement toward more mature and personal exercise of liberty.

7. A change in attitudes and in human structures frequently calls accepted values into question, especially among young people, who have grown

impatient on more than one occasion, and indeed become rebels in their distress. Aware of their own influence in the life of society, they want a part in it sooner. This frequently causes parents and educators to experience greater difficulties day by day in discharging their tasks.

7.1. The institutions, laws and modes of thinking and feeling as handed down from previous generations do not always seem to be well adapted to the contemporary state of affairs; hence arises an upheaval in the manner and even the norms of behaviour.

7.2. Finally, these new conditions have their impact on religion. On the one hand, a more critical ability to distinguish religion from a magical view of the world and from the superstitions which still circulate purifies it and exacts day by day a more personal and explicit adherence to faith. As a result many persons are achieving a more vivid sense of God. On the other hand, growing numbers of people are abandoning religion in practice. Unlike former days, the denial of God or of religion, or the abandonment of them, are no longer unusual and individual occurrences. For today it is not rare for such things to be presented as requirements of scientific progress or of a certain new humanism. In numerous places these views are voiced not only in the teachings of philosophers, but on every side they influence literature, the arts, the interpretation of the humanities and of history and civil laws themselves. As a consequence, many people are shaken.

8. This development coming so rapidly and often in a disorderly fashion, combined with keener awareness itself of the inequalities in the world beget or intensify contradictions and imbalances.

8.1. Within the individual person there develops rather frequently an imbalance between an intellect which is modern in practical matters, and a theoretical system of thought which can neither master the sum total of its ideas, nor arrange them adequately into a synthesis. Likewise an imbalance arises between a concern for practicality and efficiency, and the demands of moral conscience; also very often between the conditions of collective existence and the requisites of personal thought, and even of contemplation. At length there develops an imbalance between specialized human activity and a comprehensive view of reality.

8.2. As for the family, discord results from population, economic and social pressures, or from difficulties which arise between succeeding generations, or from new social relationships between men and women.

8.3. Differences crop up too between races and between various kinds of social orders; between wealthy nations and those which are less influential or are needy; finally, between international institutions born of the popular desire for peace, and the ambition to propagate one's own ideology, as well as collective greed existing in nations or other groups.

8.4. What results is mutual distrust, enmities, conflicts and hardships. Of such is man at once the cause and the victim.

9. Meanwhile the conviction grows not only that humanity can and should increasingly consolidate its control over creation, but even more, that it devolves on humanity to establish a political, social and economic order which will increasingly serve man and help individuals as well as groups to affirm and develop the dignity proper to them.

9.1. As a result many persons are quite aggressively demanding those benefits of which with vivid awareness they judge themselves to be deprived either through injustice or unequal distribution. Nations on the road to progress, like those recently made independent, desire to participate in the goods of modern civilization, not only in the political field but also economically, and to play their part freely on the world scene. Still they continually fall behind while very often their economic and other forms of dependence on wealthier nations increases more rapidly. People hounded by hunger call upon those better off. Where they have not yet won it, women claim for themselves an equity with men before the law and in fact. Labourers and farmers seek not only to provide for the necessities of life, but to develop the gifts of their personality by their labours and indeed to take part in regulating economic, social, political and cultural life. Now, for the first time in human history all people are convinced that the benefits of culture ought to be and actually can be extended to everyone.

9.2. Still, beneath all these demands lies a deeper and more widespread longing: persons and societies thirst for a full and free life worthy of man; one in which they can subject to their own welfare all that the modern world can offer them so abundantly. In addition, nations try harder every day to bring about a kind of universal community.

9.3. Since all these things are so, the modern world shows itself at once powerful and weak, capable of the noblest deeds or the foulest; before it lies the path to freedom or to slavery, to progress or retreat, to brotherhood or hatred. Moreover, man is becoming aware that it is his responsibility to guide aright the forces which he has unleashed and which can enslave him or minister to him. That is why he is putting questions to himself.

10. The truth is that the imbalances under which the modern world labours are linked with that more basic imbalance which is rooted in the heart of man. For in man himself many elements wrestle with one another. Thus, on the one hand, as a creature he experiences his limitations in a multitude of ways; on the other he feels himself to be boundless in his desires and summoned to a higher life. Pulled by manifold attractions he is constantly forced to choose among them and to renounce some. Indeed, as a weak and sinful being, he often does what he would not, and fails to do what he would.[2] Hence he suffers from internal divisions, and from these flow so many and such great discords in society. No doubt many whose lives are infected with a practical materialism are blinded against any sharp insight into this kind of dramatic situation; or else, weighed down by unhappiness they are prevented from giving the matter any thought. Thinking they have found serenity in an interpretation of reality everywhere proposed these days, many look forward to a genuine and total emancipation of humanity wrought solely by human effort; they are convinced that the future rule of man over the earth will satisfy every desire of his heart. Nor are there lacking men who despair of any meaning to life and praise the boldness of those who think that human existence is devoid of any inherent significance and strive to confer a total meaning on it by their own ingenuity alone. Nevertheless, in the face of the modern development of the world, the number constantly swells of the people who raise the most basic questions or recognize them with a new sharpness: what is man? What is this sense of sorrow, of evil, of death, which continues

to exist despite so much progress? What purpose have these victories secured at so high a cost? What can man offer to society, what can he expect from it? What follows this earthly life?

10.1. The Church firmly believes that Christ, who died and was raised up for all,[3] can through his Spirit offer man the light and the strength to measure up to his supreme destiny. Nor has any other name under heaven been given to man by which it is fitting for him to be saved.[4] She likewise holds that in her most benign Lord and master can be found the key, the focal point and the goal of man, as well as of all human history. The Church also maintains that beneath all changes there are many realities which do not change and which have their ultimate foundation in Christ, who is the same yesterday and today, yes and forever.[5] Hence under the light of Christ, the image of the unseen God, the first-born of every creature,[6] the council wishes to speak to all men in order to shed light on the mystery of man and to co-operate in finding the solution to the outstanding problems of our time.

PART I

The Church and man's calling

11. The people of God believes that it is led by the Lord's Spirit, who fills the earth. Motivated by this faith, it labours to decipher authentic signs of God's presence and purpose in the happenings, needs and desires in which this people has a part along with other men of our age. For faith throws a new light on everything, manifests God's design for man's total vocation, and thus directs the mind to solutions which are fully human.

11.1. This council, first of all, wishes to assess in this light those values which are most highly prized today and to relate them to their divine source. In so far as they stem from endowments conferred by God on man, these values are exceedingly good. Yet they are often wrenched from their rightful function by the taint in man's heart, and hence stand in need of purification.

11.2. What does the Church think of man? What needs to be recommended for the upbuilding of contemporary society? What is the ultimate significance of human activity throughout the world? People are waiting for an answer to these questions. From the answers it will be increasingly clear that the people of God and the human race in whose midst it lives render service to each other. Thus the mission of the Church will show its religious, and by that very fact, its supremely human character.,

CHAPTER I

The dignity of the human person

12. According to the most unanimous opinion of believers and unbelievers alike, all things on earth should be related to man as their centre and crown.

12.1. But what is man? About himself he has expressed, and continues to express, many divergent and even contradictory opinions. In these he often exalts himself as the absolute measure of all things or debases himself to the point of despair. The result is doubt and anxiety. The Church certainly understands these problems. Endowed with light from God, she can offer solutions to them, so that man's true situation can be portrayed and his defects explained, while at the same time his dignity and destiny are justly acknowledged.

12.2. For sacred scripture teaches that man was created 'to the image of God', is capable of knowing and loving his creator, and was appointed by him as master of all earthly creatures[7] that he might subdue them and use them to God's glory.[8] 'What is man that you should care for him? You have made him little less than the angels, and crowned him with glory and honour. You have given him rule over the works of your hands, putting all things under his feet.' (Ps. 8:5-7).

12.3. But God did not create man to be alone, for from the beginning 'male and female he created them' (Gen. 1:27). Their companionship produces the primary form of interpersonal communion. For by his innermost nature man is a social being, and unless he relates himself to others he can neither live nor develop his potential.

12.4. Therefore, as we read elsewhere in holy scripture, God saw 'all that he had made, and it was very good' (Gen. 1:31).

13. Although he was made by God in a state of holiness, from the very beginning of his history man abused his liberty, at the urging of the evil one. Man set himself against God and sought to attain his goal apart from God. Although they knew God, they did not glorify him as God, but their senseless minds were darkened and they served the creature rather than the creator.[9] What divine revelation makes known to us conforms with experience. Examining his heart, man finds that he has inclinations towards evil too, and is engulfed by manifold ills which cannot come from his good creator. Often refusing to acknowledge God as his beginning, man has disrupted also his proper relationship to his own ultimate goal as well as his whole relationship toward himself and others and all created things.

13.1. Therefore man is split within himself. As a result, all of human life, whether individual or collective, shows itself to be a dramatic struggle between good and evil, between light and darkness. Indeed, man finds that by himself he is incapable of battling the assaults of evil successfully, so that everyone feels as though he is bound by chains. But the Lord himself came to free and strengthen man, renewing him inwardly and casting out that 'prince of this world' (John 12:31) who held him in the bondage of sin.[10] For sin has diminished man, blocking his path to fulfilment.

13.2. The call to grandeur and the depths of misery, both of which are a part of human experience, find their ultimate and simultaneous explanation in the light of this revelation.

14. Though made of body and soul, man is one. Through his bodily composition he gathers to himself the elements of the material world; thus they reach their crown through him, and through him raise their voice in free praise of the creator.[11] For this reason man is not allowed to despise his bodily life; rather he is obliged to regard his body as good and honourable since God has created it and will raise it up on the last day. Nevertheless,

wounded by sin, man experiences rebellious stirrings in his body. But the very dignity of man postulates that man glorify God in his body[12] and forbids it to serve the evil inclinations of his heart.

14.1. Now, man is not wrong when he regards himself as superior to bodily concerns, and as more than a speck of nature or a nameless constituent of the city of man. For by his interior qualities he outstrips the whole sum of mere things. He plunges into the depths of reality whenever he enters into his own heart; God, who probes the heart,[13] awaits him there; there he discerns his proper destiny beneath the eyes of God. Thus, when he recognizes in himself a spiritual and immortal soul, he is not being mocked by a fantasy born only of physical or social influences, but is rather laying hold of the proper truth of the matter.

15. Man judges rightly that by his intellect he surpasses the material universe, for he shares in the light of the divine mind. By relentlessly employing his talents through the ages he has indeed made progress in the practical sciences and in technology and the liberal arts. In our times he has won superlative victories, especially in his probing of the material world and in subjecting it to himself. Still he has always searched for more penetrating truths, and finds them. For his intelligence is not confined to observable data alone, but can with genuine certitude attain to reality itself as knowable, though in consequence of sin that certitude is partly obscured and weakened.

15.1 The intellectual nature of the human person is perfected by wisdom and needs to be, for wisdom gently attracts the mind of man to a quest and a love for what is true and good. Steeped in wisdom, man passes through visible realities to those which are unseen.

15.2. Our era needs such wisdom more than bygone ages if the discoveries made by man are to be further humanized. For the future of the world stands in peril unless wiser men are forthcoming. It should also be pointed out that many nations, poorer in economic goods, are quite rich in wisdom and can offer noteworthy advantages to others.

15.3. It is, finally, through the gift of the Holy Spirit that man comes by faith to the contemplation and appreciation of the divine plan.[14]

16. In the depths of his conscience, man detects a law which he does not impose upon himself, but which holds him to obedience. Always summoning him to love good and avoid evil, the voice of conscience when necessary speaks to his heart: do this, shun that. For man has in his heart a law written by God; to obey it is the very dignity of man; according to it he will be judged.[15] Conscience is the most secret core and sanctuary of a man. There he is alone with God, whose voice echoes in his depths.[16] In a wonderful manner conscience reveals that law which is fulfilled by love of God and neighbour.[17] In fidelity to conscience, Christians are joined with the rest of men in the search for truth, and for the genuine solution to the numerous problems which arise in the life of individuals and from social relationships. Hence the more correct conscience holds sway, the more persons and groups turn aside from blind choice and strive to be guided by the objective norms of morality. Conscience frequently errs from invincible ignorance without losing its dignity. The same cannot be said for a man who cares but little for truth and goodness, or for a conscience which by degrees grows practically sightless as a result of habitual sin.

17. Only in freedom can man direct himself toward goodness. Our contemporaries make much of this freedom and pursue it eagerly; and rightly to be sure. Often, however, they foster it perversely as a licence for doing whatever pleases them, even if it is evil. For its part, authentic freedom is an exceptional sign of the divine image within man. For God has willed that man remain 'under the control of his own decisions',[18] so that he can seek his creator spontaneously, and come freely to utter and blissful perfection through loyalty to him. Hence man's dignity demands that he act according to a knowing and free choice that is personally motivated and prompted from within, not under blind internal impulse nor by mere external pressure. Man achieves such dignity when, emancipating himself from all captivity to passion, he pursues his goal in a spontaneous choice of what is good and procures for himself, through effective and skilful action, aids to that end. Since man's freedom has been damaged by sin, only by the aid of God's grace can he bring such a relationship with God into full flower. Before the judgement seat of God each man must render an account of his own life, whether he has done good or evil.[19]

18. It is in the face of death that the riddle of human existence grows most acute. Not only is man tormented by pain and by the advancing deterioration of his body, but even more so by a dread of perpetual extinction. He rightly follows the intuition of his heart when he abhors and repudiates the utter ruin and total disappearance of his own person. He rebels against death because he bears in himself an eternal seed which cannot be reduced to sheer matter. All the endeavours of technology, though useful in the extreme, cannot calm his anxiety; for a prolongation of biological life is unable to satisfy that desire for a higher life which is inescapably lodged in his breast.

18.1. Although the mystery of death utterly beggars the imagination, the Church has been taught by divine revelation and firmly teaches that man has been created by God for a blissful purpose beyond the reach of earthly misery. In addition, that bodily death from which man would have been immune had he not sinned[20] will be vanquished, according to the Christian faith, when man who was ruined by his own doing is restored to wholeness by an almighty and merciful saviour. For God has called man and still calls him so that with his entire being he might be joined to him in an endless sharing of a divine life beyond all corruption. Christ won this victory when he rose to life, for by his death he freed man from death.[21] Hence to every thoughtful man a solidly established faith provides the answer to his anxiety about what the future holds for him. At the same time faith gives him the power to be united in Christ with his loved ones who have already been snatched away by death; faith arouses the hope that they have found true life with God.

19. The basic source of human dignity lies in man's call to communion with God. From the very circumstance of his origin man is already invited to converse with God. For man would not exist were he not created by God's love and constantly preserved by it; and he cannot live fully according to truth unless he freely acknowledges that love and devotes himself to his creator. Still, many of our contemporaries have never recognized this

intimate and vital link with God, or have explicitly rejected it. Thus atheism must be accounted among the most serious problems of this age, and is deserving of closer examination.

19.1. The word atheism is applied to phenomena which are quite distinct from one another. For while God is expressly denied by some, others believe that man can assert absolutely nothing about him. Still others use such a method to scrutinize the question of God as to make it seem devoid of meaning. Many, unduly transgressing the limits of the positive sciences, contend that everything can be explained by this kind of scientific reasoning alone or, by contrast, they altogether disallow the fact that there is any absolute truth. Some laud man so extravagantly that their faith in God lapses into a kind of anaemia, though they seem more inclined to affirm man than to deny God. Again some form for themselves such a fallacious idea of God that when they repudiate this figment they are by no means rejecting the God of the gospel. Some never get to the point of raising questions about God, since they seem to experience no religious stirrings nor do they see why they should trouble themselves about religion. Moreover, atheism results not rarely from a violent protest against the evil in this world, or from the absolute character with which certain human values are unduly invested, and which thereby already accords them the stature of God. Modern civilization itself often complicates the approach to God not for any essential reason but because it is so heavily engrossed in earthly affairs.

19.2. Undeniably, those who wilfully shut out God from their hearts and try to dodge religious questions are not following the dictates of their consciences, and hence are not free of blame; yet believers themselves frequently bear some responsibility for this situation. For, taken as a whole, atheism is not a spontaneous development but stems from a variety of causes, including a critical reaction against religious beliefs, and in some places against the Christian religion in particular. Hence believers can have more than a little to do with the birth of atheism. To the extent that they neglect their own training in the faith, or teach erroneous doctrine, or are deficient in their religious, moral or social life, they must be said to conceal rather than reveal the authentic face of God and religion.

20. Modern atheism often takes on a systematic expression which, in addition to other causes, stretches the desire for human independence to such a point that it poses difficulties against any kind of dependence on God. Those who profess atheism of this sort maintain that it gives man freedom to be an end unto himself, the sole artisan and creator of his own history. They claim that this freedom cannot be reconciled with the affirmation of a Lord who is author and purpose of all things, or at least that this freedom makes such an affirmation altogether superfluous. The sense of power which modern technical progress generates in man can nourish this belief.

20.1. Not to be overlooked among the forms of modern atheism is that which anticipates the liberation of man especially through his economic and social emancipation. This form argues that by its nature religion thwarts this liberation by arousing man's hope for a deceptive future life, thereby diverting him from the constructing of the earthly city. Consequently when the proponents of this doctrine gain governmental power they vigorously fight against religion, and promote atheism by using, especially in the education of youth, those means of pressure which public power has at its disposal.

21. In her loyal devotion to God and men, the Church has already repudiated[22] and cannot cease repudiating, sorrowfully but as firmly as possible, those poisonous doctrines and actions which contradict reason and the common experience of humanity, and dethrone man from his native excellence.

21.1. Still, she strives to detect in the atheistic mind the hidden causes for the denial of God; conscious of how weighty are the questions which atheism raises, and motivated by love for all men, she believes these questions ought to be examined seriously and more profoundly.

21.2. The Church holds that the recognition of God is in no way hostile to man's dignity, since this dignity is rooted and perfected in God. For man was made an intelligent and free member of society by the God who created him; but even more important, he is called as a son to commune with God and share in his happiness. She further teaches that a hope related to the end of time does not diminish the importance of intervening duties but rather undergirds the acquittal of them with fresh incentives. By contrast, when a divine substructure and the hope of life eternal are wanting, man's dignity is most grievously lacerated, as current events often attest; the riddles of life and death, of guilt and of grief go unsolved, with the frequent result that men succumb to despair.

21.3. Meanwhile every man remains to himself an unsolved puzzle, however obscurely he may perceive it. For on certain occasions no one can entirely escape the kind of self-questioning mentioned earlier, especially when life's major events take place. To this questioning only God fully and most certainly provides an answer as he summons man to higher knowledge and humbler probing.

21.4. The remedy which must be applied to atheism, however, is to be sought in a proper presentation of the Church's teaching as well as in the integral life of the Church and her members. For it is the function of the Church, led by the Holy Spirit who renews and purifies her ceaselessly,[23] to make God the father and his incarnate son present and in a sense visible. This result is achieved chiefly by the witness of a living and mature faith, namely, one trained to see difficulties clearly and to master them. Many martyrs have given luminous witness to this faith and continue to do so. This faith needs to prove its fruitfulness by penetrating the believer's entire life, including its worldly dimensions, and by activating him towards justice and love, especially regarding the needy. What does the most reveal God's presence, however, is the brotherly charity of the faithful who are united in spirit as they work together for the faith of the gospel[24] and who prove themselves a sign of unity.

21.5. While rejecting atheism, root and branch, the Church sincerely professes that all men, believers and unbelievers alike, ought to work for the rightful betterment of this world in which all alike live; such an ideal cannot be realized, however, apart from sincere and prudent dialogue. Hence the Church protests against the distinction which some state authorities make between believers and unbelievers, with prejudice to the fundamental rights of the human person. The Church calls for the active freedom of believers to build up in this world God's temple too. She courteously invites atheists to examine the gospel of Christ with an open mind.

21.6. Above all the Church knows that her message is in harmony with the most secret desires of the human heart when she champions the dignity of the human vocation, restoring hope to those who have already despaired of anything higher than their present lot. Far from diminishing man, her message brings to his development light, life and freedom. Apart from this message nothing will avail to fill up the heart of man: 'Thou hast made us for thyself,' O Lord, 'and our hearts are restless till they rest in thee.'[25]

22. The truth is that only in the mystery of the incarnate word does the mystery of man take on light. For Adam, the first man, was a figure of him who was to come,[26] namely Christ the Lord. Christ, the final Adam, by the revelation of the mystery of the father and his love, fully reveals man to man himself and makes his supreme calling clear. It is not surprising, then, that in him all the aforementioned truths find their root and attain their crown.

22.1. He who is 'the image of the invisible God' (Col. 1:15),[27] is himself the perfect man. To the sons of Adam he restores the divine likeness which had been disfigured from the first sin onward. Since human nature as he assumed it was not annulled.[28] by that very fact it has been raised up to a divine dignity in our respect too. For by his incarnation the son of God has united himself in some fashion with every man. He worked with human hands, he thought with a human mind, acted by human choice[29] and loved with a human heart. Born of the Virgin Mary, he has truly been made one of us, like us in all things except sin.[30]

22.2. As an innocent lamb he merited for us life by the free shedding of his own blood. In him God reconciled us[31] to himself and among ourselves; from bondage to the devil and sin he delivered us, so that each one of us can say with the apostle: the son of God 'loved me and gave himself up for me' (Gal. 2:20). By suffering for us he not only provided us with an example for our imitation,[32] he blazed a trail, and if we follow it, life and death are made holy and take on a new meaning.

22.3. The Christian man, conformed to the likeness of that son who is the firstborn of many brothers,[33] received 'the first fruits of the Spirit' (Rom. 8:23) by which he becomes capable of discharging the new law of love.[34] Through this Spirit, who is 'the pledge of our inheritance' (Eph. 1:14), the whole man is renewed from within, even to the achievement of 'the redemption of the body' (Rom. 8:23): 'If the Spirit of him who raised Jesus from the dead dwells in you, then he who raised Jesus Christ from the dead will also bring to life your mortal bodies because of his Spirit who dwells in you' (Rom. 8:11).[35] Pressing upon the Christian to be sure, are the need and the duty to battle against evil through manifold tribulations and even to suffer death. But, linked with the paschal mystery and patterned after the dying Christ, he will hasten forward to resurrection in the strength which comes from hope.[36]

22.4. All this holds true not only for Christians, but for all men of good will in whose hearts grace works in an unseen way.[37] For, since Christ died for all men,[38] and since the ultimate vocation of man is in fact one, and divine, we ought to believe that the Holy Spirit in a manner known only to God offers to every man the possibility of being associated with this paschal mystery.

22.5. Such is the mystery of man, and it is a great one, as seen by believers in the light of Christian revelation. Through Christ and in Christ, the riddles of sorrow and death grow meaningful. Apart from his gospel, they overwhelm us. Christ has risen, destroying death by his death; he has lavished life upon us[39] so that, as sons in the son, we can cry out in the Spirit: Abba, Father![40]

CHAPTER II

The community of mankind

23. One of the salient features of the modern world is the growing interdependence of men one on the other, a development promoted chiefly by modern technical advances. Nevertheless brotherly dialogue among men does not reach its perfection on the level of technical progress, but on the deeper level of interpersonal relationships. These demand a mutual respect for the full spiritual dignity of the person. Christian revelation contributes greatly to the promotion of this communion between persons, and at the same time leads us to a deeper understanding of the laws of social life which the creator has written into man's moral and spiritual nature.

23.1. Since rather recent documents of the Church's teaching authority have dealt at considerable length with Christian doctrine about human society,[41] this council is merely going to call to mind some of the more basic truths, treating their foundations under the light of revelation. Then it will dwell more at length on certain of their implications having special significance for our day.

24. God, who has fatherly concern for everyone, has willed that all men should constitute one family and treat one another in a spirit of brotherhood. For having been created in the image of God, who 'from one man has created the whole human race and made them live all over the face of the earth' (Acts 17:26), all men are called to one and the same goal, namely God himself.

24.1. For this reason, love for God and neighbour is the first and greatest commandment. Sacred scripture, however, teaches us that the love of God cannot be separated from love of neighbour: 'If there is any other commandment, it is summed up in this saying: Thou shalt love thy neighbour as thyself...Love therefore is the fulfilment of the law' (Rom. 13:9, 10; cf. I John 4:20). To men growing daily more dependent on one another, and to a world becoming more unified every day, this truth proves to be of paramount importance.

24.2. Indeed, the Lord Jesus, when he prayed to the father, 'that all may be one...as we are one' (John 17:21, 22) opened up vistas closed to human reason, for he implied a certain likeness between the union of the divine persons, and the unity of God's sons in truth and charity. This likeness reveals that man, who is the only creature on earth which God willed for itself, cannot fully find himself except through a sincere gift of himself.[42]

25. Man's social nature makes it evident that the progress of the human person and the advance of society itself hinge on one another. For the beginning, the subject and the goal of all social institutions is and must be the human person, which for its part and by its very nature stands completely in need of social life.[43] Since this social life is not something added on to man, through his dealings with others, through reciprocal duties, and through fraternal dialogue he develops all his gifts and is able to rise to his destiny.

25.1. Among those social ties which man needs for his development some, like the family and political community, relate with greater immediacy to his innermost nature; others originate rather from his free decision. In our era, for various reasons, reciprocal ties and mutual dependencies increase day by day and give rise to a variety of associations and organizations, both public and private. This development, which is called socialization, while certainly not without its dangers, brings with it many advantages with respect to consolidating and increasing the qualities of the human person, and safeguarding his rights.[44]

25.2. But if by this social life the human person is greatly aided in responding to his destiny, even in its religious dimensions, it cannot be denied that men are often diverted from doing good and spurred towards evil by the social circumstances in which they live and are immersed from their birth. To be sure the disturbances which so frequently occur in the social order result in part from the natural tensions of economic, political and social forms. But at a deeper level they flow from man's pride and selfishness, which contaminate even the social sphere. When the structure of affairs is flawed by the consequences of sin, man, already born with a bent towards evil, finds there new inducements to sin, which cannot be overcome without strenuous efforts and the assistance of grace.

26. Every day human interdependence tightens and spreads by degrees over the whole world. As a result the common good, that is, the sum of those conditions of social life which allow social groups and their individual members relatively thorough and ready access to their own fulfilment, today takes on an increasingly universal complexion and consequently involves rights and duties with respect to the whole human race. Every social group must take account of the needs and legitimate aspirations of other groups, and even of the general welfare of the entire human family.[45]

26.1. At the same time, however, there is a growing awareness of the exalted dignity proper to the human person, since he stands above all things, and his rights and duties are universal and inviolable. Therefore, there must be made available to all men everything necessary for leading a life truly human, such as food, clothing, and shelter; the right to choose a state of life freely and to found a family, the right to education, to employment, to a good reputation, to respect, to appropriate information, to activity in accord with the upright norm of one's own conscience, to protection of privacy and to rightful freedom, even in matters religious.

26.2. Hence, the social order and its development must always work to the benefit of the human person if the disposition of affairs is to be subordinate to the personal realm and not contrariwise, as the Lord indicated when he said that the sabbath was made for man, and not man for the sabbath.[46] This social order requires constant improvement. It must be founded on truth, built on justice and animated by love; in freedom it should grow every day towards a more humane balance.[47] An improvement in attitudes and numerous changes in society will have to take place if these objectives are to be gained.

26.3 God's Spirit, who with a marvellous providence directs the unfolding of time and renews the face of the earth, is not absent from this development. The ferment of the gospel too has aroused and continues to arouse in man's heart the irresistible requirements of his dignity.

27. Coming down to practical and particularly urgent consequences, this council lays stress on reverence for man; everyone must consider his every neighbour without exception as another self, taking into account first of all his life and the means necessary to living it with dignity,[48] so as not to imitate the rich man who had no concern for the poor man Lazarus.[49]

27.1. In our times a special obligation binds us to make ourselves the neighbour of every person without exception, and of actively helping him when he comes across our path, whether he be an old person abandoned by all, a foreign labourer unjustly looked down upon, a refugee, a child born of an unlawful union and wrongly suffering for a sin he did not commit, or a hungry person who disturbs our conscience by recalling the voice of the Lord, 'As long as you did it for one of these the least of my brethren, you did it for me' (Matt. 25:40).

27.2. Furthermore, whatever is opposed to life itself, such as any type of murder, genocide, abortion, euthanasia or wilful self-destruction, whatever violates the integrity of the human person, such as mutilation, torments inflicted on body or mind, attempts to coerce the will itself; whatever insults human dignity, such as subhuman living conditions, arbitrary imprisonment, deportation, slavery, prostitution, the selling of women and children; as well as disgraceful working conditions, where men are treated as mere tools for profit, rather than as free and responsible persons; all these things and others of their like are infamies indeed. They poison human society, but they do more harm to those who practise them than those who suffer from the injury. Moreover, they are a supreme dishonour to the creator.

28. Respect and love ought to be extended also to those who think or act differently from us in social, political and even religious matters. In fact, the more deeply we come to understand their ways of thinking through such courtesy and love, the more easily will we be able to enter into dialogue with them.

28.1. This love and good will, to be sure, must in no way render us indifferent to truth and goodness. Indeed love itself impels the disciples of Christ to speak the saving truth to all men. But it is necessary to distinguish between error, which always merits repudiation, and the person in error, who never loses the dignity of being a person even when he is flawed by false or inadequate religious notions.[50] God alone is the judge and searcher of hearts; for the reason he forbids us to make judgements about the internal guilt of anyone.[51]

28.2. The teaching of Christ even requires that we forgive injuries[52] and extends the law of love to include every enemy, according to the command of the new law: 'You have heard that it was said: Thou shalt love thy neighbour and hate thy enemy. But I say to you: love your enemies, do good to those who hate you, and pray for those who persecute and calumniate you' (Matt. 5:43, 44).

29. Since all men possess a rational soul and are created in God's likeness, since they have the same nature and origin, have been redeemed by Christ and enjoy the same divine calling and destiny, the basic equality of all must receive increasingly greater recognition.

29.1. True, all men are not alike from the point of view of varying physical power and the diversity of intellectual and moral resources. Nevertheless, with respect to the fundamental rights of the person, every type of discrimination, whether social or cultural, whether based on sex, race, colour, social condition, language or religion, is to be overcome and eradicated as contrary to God's intent. For in truth it must still be regretted that fundamental personal rights are not yet being universally honoured. Such is the case of a woman who is denied the right to choose a husband freely, to embrace a state of life or to acquire an education or cultural benefits equal to those recognized for men.

29.2. Therefore, although rightful differences exist between men, the equal dignity of persons demands that a more humane and a just condition of life be brought about. For excessive economic and social differences between the members of the one human family or population groups cause scandal, and militate against social justice, equity, the dignity of the human person, as well as social and international peace.

29.3. Human institutions, both private and public, must labour to minister to the dignity and purpose of man. At the same time let them put up a stubborn fight against any kind of slavery, whether social or political, and safeguard the basic rights of man under every political system. Indeed human institutions themselves must be accommodated by degrees to the highest of all realities, spiritual ones, even though meanwhile, a long enough time will be required before they arrive at the desired goal.

30. Profound and rapid changes make it more necessary that no one ignoring the trend of events or drugged by laziness, content himself with a merely individualistic morality. It becomes increasingly true that the obligations of justice and love are fulfilled only if each person, contributing to the common good, according to his own abilities and the needs of others, also promotes and assists the public and private institutions dedicated to bettering the conditions of human life. Yet there are those who, while professing grand and rather noble sentiments, nevertheless in reality live always as if they cared nothing for the needs of society. Many in various places even make light of social laws and precepts, and do not hesitate to resort to various frauds and deceptions in avoiding just taxes or other debts due to society. Others think little of certain norms of social life, for example those designed for the protection of health, or laws establishing speed limits; they do not even avert to the fact that by such indifference they imperil their own life and that of others.

30.1. Let everyone consider it his sacred obligation to esteem and observe social necessities as being among the primary duties of modern man. For the more unified the world becomes, the more plainly do the offices of men extend beyond particular groups and spread by degrees to the whole world. But this development cannot occur unless individual men and their associations cultivate in themselves the moral and social virtues, and promote them in society; thus, with the needed help of divine grace men who are truly new and artisans of a new humanity can be forthcoming.

31. Individual men, in order to discharge with great exactness the obligations of their conscience toward themselves and the various groups to which they belong, must be carefully educated to a higher degree of culture through the use of the immense resources available today to the human race. Above all the education of youth from every social background has to be undertaken, so that there can be produced not only men and women of refined talents, but those great-souled persons who are so desperately required by our times.

31.1. Now a man can scarcely arrive at the needed sense of responsibility, unless his living conditions allow him to become conscious of his dignity, and to rise to his destiny by spending himself for God and for others. But human freedom is often crippled when a man encounters extreme poverty, just as it withers when he indulges in too many of life's comforts and imprisons himself in a kind of splendid isolation. Freedom acquires new strength, by contrast, when a man consents to the unavoidable requirements of social life, takes on the manifold demands of human partnership, and commits himself to the service of the human community.

31.2. Hence, the will to play one's role in common endeavours should be everywhere encouraged. Praise is due to those national processes which allow the largest possible number of citizens to participate in public affairs with genuine freedom. Account must be taken, to be sure, of the actual conditions of each people and the firmness required by public authority. If every citizen is to feel inclined to take part in the activities of the various groups which make up the social body, these must offer advantages which will attract members and dispose them to serve others. We can justly consider that the future of humanity lies in the hands of those who are strong enough to provide coming generations with reasons for living and hoping.

32. As God did not create man for life in isolation, but for the formation of social unity, so also 'it has pleased God to make men holy and save them not merely as individuals, without bond or link between them, but by making them into a single people, a people which acknowledges him in truth and serves him in holiness.'[53] So from the beginning of salvation history he has chosen men not just as individuals but as members of a certain community. Revealing his mind to them, God called these chosen ones 'his people' (Ex. 3:7,12), and even made a covenant with them on Sinai.[54]

32.1. This communitarian character is developed and consummated in the work of Jesus Christ. For the very Word made flesh willed to share in the human fellowship. He was present at the wedding of Cana, visited the house of Zachaeus, ate with publicans and sinners. He revealed the love of the father and the sublime vocation of man in terms of the most common of social realities and by making use of the speech and the imagery of plain everyday life. Willingly obeying the laws of his country, he sanctified those human ties, especially family ones, which are the foundation of social structures. He chose to lead the life proper to an artisan of his time and place.

32.2. In his preaching he clearly taught the sons of God to treat one another as brothers. In his prayers he pleaded that all his disciples might be 'one'. Indeed as the redeemer of all, he offered himself for all even to the point of death. 'Greater love than this no one has, that one lay down his life for his friends' (John 15:13). He commanded his apostles to preach to all peoples the gospel's message that the human race was to become the family of God, in which the fullness of the law would be love.

32.3. As the first-born of many brethren and by the giving of his Spirit, he founded after his death and resurrection a new brotherly community composed of all those who receive him in faith and in love. This he did through his body, which is the Church. There everyone, as members one of the other, would render mutual service according to the different gifts bestowed on each.

32.4. This solidarity must be constantly increased until that day on which it will be brought to perfection. Then, saved by grace, men will offer flawless glory to God as a family beloved of God and of Christ their brother.

CHAPTER III

Man's activity throughout the world

33. Through his labours and his native endowments man has ceaselessly striven to better his life. Today, however, especially with the help of science and technology, he has extended his mastery over nearly the whole of nature and continues to do so. Thanks to increased opportunities for many kinds of social contact among nations, the human family is gradually recognizing that it comprises a single world community and is making itself so. Hence many benefits once looked for, especially from heavenly powers, man has now enterprisingly procured for himself.

33.1. In the face of these immense efforts which already preoccupy the whole human race, men raise numerous questions among themselves. What is the meaning and value of this feverish activity? How should all these things be used? To the achievement of what goal are the strivings of individuals and societies heading? The Church guards the heritage of God's word and draws from it moral and religious principles without always having at hand the solution to particular problems. As such she desires to add the light of revealed truth to mankind's store of experience, so that the path which humanity has taken in recent times will not be a dark one.

34. Throughout the course of the centuries, men have laboured to better the circumstances of their lives through a monumental amount of individual and collective effort. To believers, this point is settled: considered in itself, this human activity accords with God's will. For man, created to God's image, received a mandate to subject to himself the earth and all it contains, and to govern the world with justice and holiness;[55] a mandate to relate himself and

the totality of things to him who was to be acknowledged as the lord and creator of all. Thus, by the subjection of all things to man, the name of God would be wonderful in all the earth.[56]

34.1. This mandate concerns the whole range of everyday activity as well. For while providing the substance of life for themselves and their families, men and women are performing their activities in a way which appropriately benefits society. They can justly consider that by their labour they are unfolding the creator's work, consulting the advantages of their brother men, and are contributing by their personal industry to the realization in history of the divine plan.[57]

34.2. Thus, far from thinking that works produced by man's own talent and energy are in opposition to God's power, and that the rational creature exists as a kind of rival to the creator, Christians are convinced that the triumphs of the human race are a sign of God's grace and the flowering of his own mysterious design. For the greater man's power becomes, the further his individual and community responsibility extends. Hence it is clear that men are not deterred by the Christian message from building up the world, or impelled to neglect the welfare of their fellows, but that they are rather more stringently bound to do these very things.[58]

35. Human activity, to be sure, takes its significance from its relationship to man. Just as it proceeds from man, so it is ordered towards man. For when a man works he not only alters things and society, he develops himself as well. He learns much, he cultivates his resources, he goes outside himself and beyond himself. Rightly understood, this kind of growth is of greater value than any external riches which can be garnered. A man is more precious for what he is than for what he has.[59] Similarly, all that men do to obtain greater justice, wider brotherhood, a more humane ordering of social relationships has greater worth than technical advances. For these advances can supply the material for human progress, but of themselves alone they can never actually bring it about.

35.1. Hence, the norm of human activity is this: that in accord with the divine plan and will, it harmonize with the genuine good of the human race, and that it allow men as individuals and as members of society to pursue their total vocation and fulfil it.

36. Now many of our contemporaries seem to fear that a closer bond between human activity and religion will work against the independence of men, of societies, or of the sciences.

36.1. If by the autonomy of earthly affairs we mean that created things and societies themselves enjoy their own laws and values which must be gradually deciphered, put to use, and regulated by men, then it is entirely right to demand that autonomy. This is not merely required by modern man, but harmonizes also with the will of the creator. For by the very circumstance of their having been created, all things are endowed with their own stability, truth, goodness, proper laws and order. Man must respect these as he isolates them by the appropriate methods of the individual sciences or arts. Therefore, if methodical investigation within every branch of learning is carried out in a genuinely scientific manner and in accord with moral norms, it never truly conflicts with faith, for earthly matters and the concerns of faith derive from the same God.[60] Indeed whoever labours to penetrate the secrets of reality with a humble and steady mind, even though he is unaware of the fact, is nevertheless being led by the hand of God, who holds all things in existence, and gives them their identity. Consequently, we cannot but deplore certain habits of mind, which are sometimes found too among Christians, which do not sufficiently attend to the rightful independence of science and which, from the arguments and controversies they spark, lead many minds to conclude that faith and science are mutually opposed.[61]

36.2. But if the expression, the autonomy of temporal affairs, is taken to mean that created things do not depend on God, and that man can use them without any reference to their creator, anyone who acknowledges God will see how false such a meaning is. For without the creator the creature would disappear. For their part, however, all believers of whatever religion always hear his revealing voice in the discourse of creatures. When God is forgotten, however, the creature itself grows unintelligible.

37. Sacred scripture teaches the human family what the experience of the ages confirms: that while human progress is a great advantage to man, it brings with it a strong temptation. For when the order of values is jumbled and bad is mixed with the good, individuals and groups pay heed solely to their own interests, and not to those of others. Thus it happens that the world ceases to be a place of true brotherhood. In our own day, the magnified power of humanity threatens to destroy the race itself.

37.1. For a monumental struggle against the powers of darkness pervades the whole history of man. The battle was joined from the very origins of the world and will continue until the last day, as the Lord has attested.[62] Caught in this conflict, man is obliged to wrestle constantly if he is to cling to what is good, nor can he achieve his own integrity without great efforts and the help of God's grace.

37.2. That is why Christ's Church, trusting in the design of the creator, acknowledges that human progress can serve man's true happiness, yet she cannot help echoing the apostle's warning 'Be not conformed to this world' (Rom. 12:2). Here by the world is meant that spirit of vanity and malice which transforms into an instrument of sin those human energies intended for the service of God and man.

37.3. Hence if anyone wants to know how this unhappy situation can be overcome, Christians will tell him that all human activity, constantly imperilled by man's pride and deranged self-love, must be purified and perfected by the power of Christ's cross and resurrection. For redeemed by Christ and made a new creature in the Holy Spirit, man is able to love the things themselves created by God, and ought to do so. He can receive them from God and respect and reverence them as flowing constantly from the hand of God. Grateful to his benefactor for these creatures, using and enjoying them in detachment and liberty of spirit, man is led forward into a true possession of them, as having nothing, yet possessing all things.[63] 'All are yours, and you are Christ's, and Christ is God's' (I Cor. 3:22-23).

38. For God's Word, through whom all things were made, was himself made flesh and dwelt on man's earth.[64] Thus he entered the world's history as a perfect man, taking that history up into himself and summarizing it.[65] He

himself revealed to us that 'God is love' (I John 4:8) and at the same time taught us that the new command of love was the basic law of human perfection and hence of the world's transformation. To those, therefore, who believe in divine love, he gives assurance that the way of love lies open to men and that the effort to establish a universal brotherhood is not a hopeless one. He cautions them at the same time that this love is not something to be reserved for important matters, but must be pursued chiefly in the ordinary circumstances of life. Undergoing death itself for all of us sinners,[66] he taught us by example that we too must shoulder that cross which the world and the flesh inflict upon those who search after peace and justice. Appointed Lord by his resurrection and given all power in heaven and on earth,[67] Christ is now at work in the hearts of men through the energy of his Spirit, arousing not only a desire for the age to come, but by that very fact animating, purifying and strengthening those noble longings too by which the human family makes its life more human and strives to render the whole earth submissive to this goal. Now, the gifts of the Spirit are diverse: while he calls some to give clear witness to the desire for a heavenly home and to keep that desire fresh among the human family, he summons others to dedicate themselves to the earthly service of men and to make ready the material of the celestial realm by this ministry of theirs. Yet he frees all of them so that by putting aside love of self and bringing all earthly resources into the service of human life they can devote themselves to that future when humanity itself will become an offering accepted by God.[68]

38.1. The Lord left behind a pledge of this hope and strength for life's journey in that sacrament of faith where natural elements refined by man are gloriously changed into his body and blood, providing a meal of brotherly solidarity and a foretaste of the heavenly banquet.

39. We do not know the time for the consummation of the earth and of humanity,[69] nor do we know how all things will be transformed. As deformed by sin, the shape of this world will pass away;[70] but we are taught that God is preparing a new dwelling place and a new earth where justice will abide,[71] and whose blessedness will answer and surpass all the longings for peace which spring up in the human heart.[72] Then, with death overcome, the sons of God will be raised up in Christ, and what was sown in weakness and corruption will be clothed with incorruptibility.[73] Enduring with charity and its fruits,[74] all that creation[75] which God made on man's account will be unchained from the bondage of vanity.

39.1. Therefore, while we are warned that it profits a man nothing if he gain the whole world and lose himself,[76] the expectation of a new earth must not weaken but rather stimulate our concern for cultivating this one. For here grows the body of a new human family, a body which even now is able to give some kind of foreshadowing of the new age. Hence, while earthly progress must be carefully distinguished from the growth of Christ's kingdom, to the extent that the former can contribute to the better ordering of human society, it is of vital concern to the kingdom of God.[77]

39.2. For after we have obeyed the Lord, and in his Spirit nurtured on earth the values of human dignity, brotherhood and freedom, and indeed all the good fruits of our nature and enterprise, we will find them again, but freed of stain, burnished and transfigured, when Christ hands over to the father: 'a kingdom eternal and universal, a kingdom of truth and life, of holiness and grace, of justice, love and peace'.[78] On this earth that kingdom is already present in mystery. When the Lord returns it will be brought into full flower.

CHAPTER IV

The role of the Church in the modern world

40. Everything we have said about the dignity of the human person, and about the human community and the profound meaning of human activity, lays the foundation for the relationship between the Church and the world, and provides the basis for dialogue between them.[79] In this chapter, presupposing everything which has already been said by this council concerning the mystery of the Church, we must now consider this same Church in as much as she exists in the world, living and acting with it.

40.1. Coming forth from the eternal father's love,[80] founded in time by Christ the redeemer and made one in the Holy Spirit,[81] the Church has a saving and an eschatological purpose which can be fully attained only in the future world. But she is already present in this world, and is composed of men, that is, of members of the earthly city who have a call to form the family of God's children during the present history of the human race, and to keep increasing it until the Lord returns. United on behalf of heavenly values and enriched by them, this family has been 'constituted and structured as a society in this world'[82] by Christ, and is equipped 'by appropriate means for visible and social union'.[83] Thus the Church, at once 'a visible association and a spiritual community',[84] goes forward together with humanity and experiences the same earthly lot which the world does. She serves as a leaven and as a kind of soul for human society[85] as it is to be renewed in Christ and transformed into God's family.

40.2. That the earthly and the heavenly city penetrate each other is a fact accessible to faith alone; it remains a mystery of human history, which sin will keep in great disarray until the splendour of God's sons is fully revealed. Pursuing the saving purpose which is proper to her, the Church does not only communicate divine life to men but in some way casts the reflected light of that life over the entire earth, most of all by its healing and elevating impact on the dignity of the person, by the way in which it strengthens the seams of human society and imbues the everyday activity of men with a deeper meaning and importance. Thus through her individual members and her whole community, the Church believes she can contribute greatly towards making the family of man and its history more human.

40.3. In addition, the Catholic Church gladly holds in high esteem the things which other Christian churches and ecclesial communities have done or are doing co-operatively by way of achieving the same goal. At the same time, she is convinced that she can be abundantly and variously helped by the world in the matter of preparing the ground for the gospel. This help she gains from the talents and industry of individuals and from human society as a whole.

The council now sets forth certain general principles for the proper fostering of this mutual exchange and assistance in concerns which are in some way common to the world and the Church.

41. Modern man is on the road to a more thorough development of his own personality, and to a growing discovery and vindication of his own rights. Since it has been entrusted to the Church to reveal the mystery of God, who is the ultimate goal of man, she opens up to man at the same time the meaning of his own existence, that is, the innermost truth about himself. The Church truly knows that only God, whom she serves, meets the deepest longings of the human heart, which is never fully satisfied by what this world has to offer. She also knows that man is constantly worked upon by God's Spirit, and hence can never be altogether indifferent to the problems of religion. The experience of past ages proves this, as do numerous indications in our own times. For man will always yearn to know, at least in an obscure way, what is the meaning of his life, of his activity, of his death. The very presence of the Church recalls these problems to his mind. But only God, who created man to his own image and ransomed him from sin, provides a fully adequate answer to these questions, and this he does through what he has revealed in Christ his son, who became man. Whoever follows after Christ, the perfect man, becomes himself more of a man. For by his incarnation the father's Word assumed, and sanctified through his cross and resurrection, the whole of man, body and soul, and through that totality the whole of nature created by God for man's use.

41.1. Thanks to this belief, the Church can anchor the dignity of human nature against all tides of opinion, for example those which undervalue the human body or idolize it. By no human law can the personal dignity and liberty of man be so aptly safeguarded as by the gospel of Christ which has been entrusted to the Church. For this gospel announces and proclaims the freedom of the sons of God, and repudiates all the bondage which ultimately results from sin (cf. Rom. 8:14-17);[86] it has a sacred reverence for the dignity of conscience and its freedom of choice, constantly advises that all human talents be employed in God's service and men's and, finally, commends all to the charity of all (cf. Matt. 22:39).[87] This agrees with the basic law of Christian dispensation. For though the same God is saviour and creator, lord of human history as well as of salvation history, in the divine arrangement itself, the rightful autonomy of the creature, and particularly of man, is not withdrawn, but is rather re-established in its own dignity and strengthened in it.

41.2. The Church, therefore, by virtue of the gospel committed to her, proclaims the rights of man; she acknowledges and greatly esteems the dynamic movements of today by which these rights are everywhere fostered. Yet these movements must be penetrated by the spirit of the gospel and protected against any kind of false autonomy. For we are tempted to think that our personal rights are fully ensured only when we are exempt from every requirement of divine law. But this way lies not the maintenance of the dignity of the human person, but its annihilation.

42. The union of the human family is greatly fortified and fulfilled by the unity, founded on Christ,[88] of the family of God's sons.

42.1. Christ, to be sure, gave his Church no proper mission in the political, economic or social order. The purpose which he set before her is a religious one.[89] But out of this religious mission itself come a function, a light and an energy which can serve to structure and consolidate the human community according to the divine law. As a matter of fact, when circumstances of time and place produce the need, she can and indeed should initiate activities on behalf of all men, especially those designed for the needy, such as the works of mercy and similar undertakings.

42.2. The Church recognizes that worthy elements are found in today's social movements, especially an evolution towards unity, a process of wholesome socialization and of association in civic and economic realms. The promotion of unity belongs to the innermost nature of the Church, for she is, 'thanks to her relationship with Christ, a sacramental sign and an instrument of intimate union with God, and of the unity of the whole human race'.[90] Thus she shows the world that an authentic union, social and external, results from a union of minds and hearts, namely from that faith and charity by which her own unity is unbreakably rooted in the Holy Spirit. For the force which the Church can inject into the modern society of man consists in that faith and charity put into vital practice, not in any external dominion exercised by merely human means.

42.3. Moreover, since in virtue of her mission and nature she is bound to no particular form of human culture, nor to any political, economic or social system, the Church by her very universality can be a very close bond between diverse human communities and nations, provided these trust her and truly acknowledge her right to true freedom in fulfilling her mission. For this reason, the Church admonishes her own sons, but also humanity as a whole, to overcome all strife between nations and races in this family spirit of God's children, and in the same way, to give internal strength to human associations which are just.

42.4. Therefore, this council regards with great respect all the true, good and just elements inherent in the very wide variety of institutions which the human race has established for itself and constantly continues to establish. The council affirms, moreover, that the Church is willing to assist and promote all these institutions to the extent that such a service depends on her and can be associated with her mission. She has no fiercer desire than that in pursuit of the welfare of all she may be able to develop herself freely under any kind of government which grants recognition to the basic rights of person and family, to the demands of the common good and to the free exercise of her own mission.

43. This council exhorts Christians, as citizens of two cities, to strive to discharge their earthly duties conscientiously and in response to the gospel spirit. They are mistaken who, knowing that we have here no abiding city but seek one which is to come,[91] think that they may therefore shirk their earthly responsibilities. For they are forgetting that by the faith itself they are more obliged than ever to measure up to these duties, each according to his proper vocation.[92] Nor, on the contrary, are they any less wide of the mark who think that religion consists in acts of worship alone and in the discharge of certain moral obligations, and who imagine they can plunge themselves into

earthly affairs in such a way as to imply that these are altogether divorced from the religious life. This split between the faith which many profess and their daily lives deserves to be counted among the more serious errors of our age. Long since, the prophets of the Old Testament fought vehemently against this scandal[93] and even more so did Jesus Christ himself in the New Testament threaten it with grave punishments.[94] Therefore, let there be no false opposition between professional and social activities on the one part, and religious life on the other. The Christian who neglects his temporal duties, neglects his duties toward his neighbour and even God, and jeopardizes his eternal salvation. Christians should rather rejoice that, following the example of Christ who worked as an artisan, they are free to exercise all their earthly activities by gathering their humane, domestic, professional, social and technical enterprises into one vital synthesis with religious values, under whose supreme direction all things are harmonized unto God's glory.

43.1. Secular duties and activities belong properly although not exclusively to laymen. Therefore acting as citizens in the world, whether individually or socially, they will observe the laws proper to each discipline, and labour to equip themselves with a genuine expertise in their various fields. They will gladly work with men seeking the same goals. Acknowledging the demands of faith and endowed with its force, they will unhesitatingly devise new enterprises, where they are appropriate, and put them into action. Laymen should also know that it is generally the function of their well-formed Christian conscience to see that the divine law is inscribed in the life of the earthly city; from priests they may look for spiritual light and nourishment. Let the layman not imagine that his pastors are always such experts, that to every problem which arises, however complicated, they can readily give him a concrete solution, or even that such is their mission. Rather enlightened by Christian wisdom and giving close attention to the teaching authority of the Church,[95] let the layman take on his own distinctive role.

43.2. Often enough the Christian view of things will itself suggest some specific solution in certain circumstances. Yet it happens rather frequently, and legitimately so, that with equal sincerity some of the faithful will disagree with others on a given matter. Even against the intentions of their proponents, however, solutions proposed on one side or another may be easily confused by many people with the gospel message. Hence it is necessary for people to remember that no one is allowed in the aforementioned situations to appropriate the Church's authority for his opinion. They should always try to enlighten one another through honest discussion, preserving mutual charity and caring above all for the common good.

43.3. Since they have an active role to play in the whole life of the Church, laymen are not only bound to penetrate the world with a Christian spirit, but are also called to be witnesses to Christ in all things in the midst of human society.

43.4. Bishops, to whom is assigned the task of ruling the Church of God, should, together with their priests, so preach the news of Christ that all the earthly activities of the faithful will be bathed in the light of the gospel. All pastors should remember too that by their daily conduct and concern[96] they are revealing the face of the Church to the world, and men will judge the power and truth of the Christian message thereby. By their lives and speech, in union with religious and their faithful, may they demonstrate that even now the Church, by her presence alone and by all the gifts which she contains, is an unspent fountain of those virtues which the modern world needs the most. By unremitting study they should fit themselves to do their part in establishing dialogue with the world and with men of all shades of opinion. Above all let them take to heart the words which this council has spoken: 'Since humanity today increasingly moves toward civil, economic and social unity, it is more than ever necessary that priests, with joint concern and energy, and under the guidance of the bishops and the supreme pontiff, erase every cause of division, so that the whole human race may be led to the unity of God's family.'[97]

43.5. Although by the power of the Holy Spirit the Church will remain the faithful spouse of her lord and will never cease to be the sign of salvation on earth, still she is very well aware that among her members,[98] both clerical and lay, some have been unfaithful to the Spirit of God during the course of many centuries; in the present age, too, it does not escape the Church how great a distance lies between the message she offers and the human failings of those to whom the gospel is entrusted. Whatever be the judgement of history on these defects, we ought to be conscious of them, and struggle against them energetically, lest they inflict harm on spread of the gospel. The Church also realizes that in working out her relationship with the world she always has great need of the ripening which comes with the experience of the centuries. Led by the Holy Spirit, Mother Church unceasingly exhorts her sons 'to purify and renew themselves so that the sign of Christ can shine more brightly on the face of the Church'.[99]

44. Just as it is in the world's interest to acknowledge the Church as a historical reality, and to recognize her good influence, so the Church herself knows how richly she has profited by the history and development of humanity.

44.1. The experience of past ages, the progress of the sciences, and the treasures hidden in the various forms of human culture, by all of which the nature of man himself is more clearly revealed and new roads to truth are opened, these profit the Church, too. For, from the beginning of her history she has learned to express the message of Christ with the help of the ideas and terminology of various philosophers, and has tried to clarify it with their wisdom, too. Her purpose has been to adapt the gospel to the grasp of all as well as to the needs of the learned, in so far as such was appropriate. Indeed this accommodated preaching of the revealed Word ought to remain the law of all evangelization. For thus the ability to express Christ's message in its own way is developed in each nation, and at the same time there is fostered a living exchange between the Church and the diverse cultures of people.[100] To promote such exchange, especially in our days, the Church requires the special help of those who live in the world, are versed in different institutions and specialities, and grasp their innermost significance in the eyes of both believers and unbelievers. With the help of the Holy Spirit, it is the task of the entire people of God, especially pastors and theologians, to hear, distinguish and interpret the many voices of our age, and to judge them in the light of the divine word, so that revealed truth can always be more deeply penetrated, better understood and set forth to greater advantage.

44.2. Since the Church has a visible and social structure as a sign of her unity in Christ, she can and ought to be enriched by the development of human social life, not that there is any lack in the constitution given her by Christ, but that she can understand it more penetratingly, express it better, and adjust it more successfully to our times. Moreover, she gratefully understands that in her community life no less than in her individual sons, she receives a variety of helps from men of every rank and condition, for whoever promotes the human community at the family level, culturally, in its economic, social and political dimensions, both nationally and internationally, such a one, according to God's design, is contributing greatly to the Church as well, to the extent that she depends on things outside herself. Indeed, the Church admits that she has greatly profited and still profits from the antagonism of those who oppose or who persecute her.[101]

45. While helping the world and receiving many benefits from it, the Church has a single intention: that God's kingdom may come, and that the salvation of the whole human race may come to pass. For every benefit which the people of God during its earthly pilgrimage can offer to the human family stems from the fact that the Church is 'the universal sacrament of salvation',[102] simultaneously manifesting and exercising the mystery of God's love for man.

45.1. For God's Word, by whom all things were made, was himself made flesh so that as perfect man he might save all men and sum up all things in himself. The Lord is the goal of human history, the focal point of the longings of history and of civilization, the centre of the human race, the joy of every heart and the answer to all its yearnings.[103] He it is whom the father raised from the dead, lifted on high and stationed at his right hand, making him judge of the living and the dead. Enlivened and united in his Spirit, we journey toward the consummation of human history, one which fully accords with the counsel of God's love: 'To re-establish all things in Christ, both those in the heavens and those on the earth' (Eph. 11:10).

45.2. The Lord himself speaks: 'Behold I come quickly! And my reward is with me, to render to each one according to his works. I am the alpha and the omega, the first and the last, the beginning and the end' (Apoc. 22:12-13).

PART II

Some problems of special urgency

46. This council has set forth the dignity of the human person and the work which men have been destined to undertake throughout the world both as individuals and as members of society. There are a number of particularly urgent needs characterizing the present age, needs which go to the roots of the human race. To a consideration of these in the light of the gospel and of human experience, the council would now direct the attention of all.

46.1. Of the many subjects arousing universal concern today, it may be helpful to concentrate on these: marriage and the family, human progress, life in its economic, social and political dimensions, the bonds between the family of nations, and peace. On each of these may there shine the radiant ideals proclaimed by Christ. By these ideals may Christians be led, and all mankind enlightened, as they search for answers to questions of such complexity.

CHAPTER I

Fostering the nobility of marriage and the family

47. This well-being of the individual person and of human and Christian society is intimately linked with the healthy condition of that community produced by marriage and family. Hence Christians and all men who hold this community in high esteem sincerely rejoice in the various ways by which men today find help in fostering this community of love and perfecting its life, and by which parents are assisted in their lofty calling. Those who rejoice in such aids look for additional benefits from them and labour to bring them about.

47.1. Yet the excellence of this institution is not everywhere reflected with equal brilliance, since polygamy, the plague of divorce, so-called free love and other disfigurements have an obscuring effect. In addition, married love is too often profaned by excessive self-love, the worship of pleasure and illicit practices against human generation. Moreover, serious disturbances are caused in families by modern economic conditions, by influences at once social and psychological, and by the demands of civil society. Finally, in certain parts of the world problems resulting from population growth are generating concern. All these situations have produced anxiety of conscience. Yet, the power and strength of the institution of marriage and family can also be seen in the fact that time and again, despite the difficulties produced, the profound changes in modern society reveal the true character of this institution in one way or another.

47.2. Therefore, by presenting certain key points of Church doctrine in a clearer light, this sacred synod wishes to offer guidance and support to those Christians and other men who are trying to preserve the holiness and to foster the natural dignity of the married state and its superlative value.

48. The intimate partnership of married life and love has been established by the creator and qualified by his laws, and is rooted in the conjugal covenant of irrevocable personal consent. Hence by that human act whereby spouses mutually bestow and accept each other a relationship arises which by divine will and in the eyes of society too is a lasting one. For the good of the spouses and their offspring as well as of society, the existence of the sacred bond no longer depends on human decisions alone. For God himself is the author of matrimony, endowed as it is with various benefits and purposes.[104] All of these have a very decisive bearing on the continuation of the human race, on the personal development and eternal destiny of the individual members of a family, and on the dignity, stability, peace and prosperity of the family itself

and of human society as a whole. By their very nature, the institution of matrimony itself and conjugal love are ordained for the procreation and education of children, and find in them their ultimate crown. Thus a man and a woman, who by their compact of conjugal love 'are no longer two, but one flesh' (Matt. 19:6), render mutual help and service to each other through an intimate union of their persons and of their actions. Through this union they experience the meaning of their oneness and attain to it with growing perfection day by day. As a mutual gift of two persons, this intimate union and the good of the children impose total fidelity on the spouses and argue for an unbreakable oneness between them.[105]

48.1. Christ the Lord abundantly blessed this many-faceted love, welling up as it does from the fountain of divine love and structured as it is on the model of his union with his Church. For as God of old made himself present[106] to his people through a covenant of love and fidelity, so now the saviour of men and the spouse[107] of the Church comes into the lives of married Christians through the sacrament of matrimony. He abides with them thereafter so that, just as he loved the Church and handed himself over on her behalf,[108] the spouses may love each other with perpetual fidelity through mutual self-bestowal. Authentic married love is caught up into divine love and is governed and enriched by Christ's redeeming power and the saving activity of the Church, so that this love may lead the spouses to God with powerful effect and may aid and strengthen them in the sublime office of being a father or a mother.[109] For this reason Christian spouses have a special sacrament by which they are fortified and receive a kind of consecration in the duties and dignity of their state.[110] By virtue of this sacrament, as spouses fulfil their conjugal and family obligations, they are penetrated with the spirit of Christ, which suffuses their whole lives with faith, hope and charity. Thus they increasingly advance the perfection of their own personalities, as well as their mutual sanctification, and hence contribute jointly to the glory of God.

48.2. As a result, with their parents leading the way by example and family prayer, children and indeed everyone gathered around the family hearth will find a readier path to human maturity, salvation and holiness. Graced with the dignity and office of fatherhood and motherhood, parents will energetically acquit themselves of a duty which devolves primarily on them, namely education and especially religious education.

48.3. As living members of the family, children contribute in their own way to making their parents holy. For they will respond to the kindness of their parents with sentiments of gratitude, with love and trust. They will stand by them as children should when hardships overtake their parents and old age brings its loneliness. Widowhood, accepted bravely as a continuation of the marriage vocation, should be esteemed by all.[111] Families too will share their spiritual riches generously with other families. Thus the Christian family, which springs from marriage as a reflection of the loving covenant uniting Christ with the Church,[112] and as a participation in that covenant, will manifest to all men Christ's living presence in the world, and the genuine nature of the Church. This family will do by the mutual love of the spouses, by their generous fruitfulness, their solidarity and faithfulness, and by the loving way in which all members of the family assist one another.

49. The biblical word of God several times urges the betrothed and the married to nourish and develop their wedlock by pure conjugal love and undivided affection.[113] Many men of our own age also highly regard true love between husband and wife as it manifests itself in a variety of ways depending on the worthy customs of various peoples and times. This love is an eminently human one since it is directed from one person to another through an affection of the will; it involves the good of the whole person, and therefore can enrich the expressions of the body and mind with a unique dignity, ennobling these expressions as special ingredients and signs of the friendship distinctive of marriage. This love God has judged worthy of special gifts, healing, perfecting and exalting gifts of grace and of charity. Such love, merging the human with the divine, leads the spouses to a free and mutual gift of themselves, a gift proving itself by gentle affection and by deed; such love pervades the whole of their lives:[114] indeed by its active generosity it grows better and grows greater. Therefore it far excels mere erotic inclination, which, selfishly pursued, soon enough fades wretchedly away.

49.1. This love is uniquely expressed and perfected in the special area of matrimony. The actions within marriage by which the couple are united intimately and chastely are noble and worthy ones. Expressed in a manner which is truly human, these actions promote that mutual self-giving by which spouses enrich each other with a joyful and ready will. Sealed by mutual faithfulness and hallowed above all by Christ's sacrament, this love remains steadfastly true in body and in mind, in bright days or dark. It will never be profaned by adultery or divorce. Firmly established by the Lord, the unity of marriage will radiate from the equal personal dignity of wife and husband, a dignity acknowledged by mutual and total love. The constant fulfilment of the duties of this Christian vocation demands notable virtue. For this reason, strengthened by grace for holiness of life, the couple will painstakingly cultivate and pray for steadfastness of love, large-heartedness and the spirit of sacrifice.

49.2. Authentic conjugal love will be more highly prized, and wholesome public opinion created regarding it if Christian couples give outstanding witness to faithfulness and harmony in their love, and to their concern for educating their children; also, if they do their part in bringing about the needed cultural, psychological and social renewal on behalf of marriage and the family. Especially in the heart of their own families, young people should be aptly and seasonably instructed in the dignity, duty and work of married love. Trained thus in the cultivation of chastity, they will be able at a suitable age to enter a marriage of their own after an honourable courtship.

50. Marriage and conjugal love are by their nature ordained toward the begetting and educating of children. Children are really the supreme gift of marriage and contribute very substantially to the welfare of their parents. The God himself who said, 'it is not good for man to be alone' (Gen. 2:18) and 'Who made man from the beginning male and female' (Matt. 19:4), wishing to share with man a certain special participation in his own creative work, blessed male and female, saying: 'Increase and multiply' (Gen. 1:28). Hence, while not making the other purposes of matrimony of less account, the true practice of conjugal love, and the whole meaning of the family life which

results from it, have this aim: that the couple be ready with stout hearts to co-operate with the love of the creator and the saviour, who through them will enlarge and enrich his own family day by day.

50.1. Parents should regard as their proper mission the task of transmitting human life and educating those to whom it has been transmitted. They should realize that they are thereby co-operators with the love of God the creator, and are, so to speak, the interpreters of that love. Thus they will fulfil their task with human and Christian responsibility, and, with docile reverence towards God, will make decisions by common counsel and effort. Let them thoughtfully take into account both their own welfare and that of their children, those already born and those which the future may bring. For this accounting they need to reckon with both the material and the spiritual conditions of the times as well as of their state in life. Finally, they should consult the interests of the family group, of temporal society, and of the Church herself. The parents themselves should ultimately make this judgement in the sight of God. But in their manner of acting, spouses should be aware that they cannot proceed arbitrarily, but must always be governed according to a conscience dutifully conformed to the divine law itself, and should be submissive toward the Church's teaching office, which authentically interprets that law in the light of the gospel. That divine law reveals and protects the integral meaning of conjugal love, and impels it toward a truly human fulfilment. Thus, trusting in divine providence and refining the spirit of sacrifice,[115] married Christians glorify the creator and strive toward fulfilment in Christ when with a generous human and Christian sense of responsibility they acquit themselves of the duty to procreate. Among the couples who fulfil their God-given task in this way, those merit special mention who with a gallant heart, and with wise and common deliberation, undertake to bring up suitably even a relatively large family.[116]

50.2 Marriage to be sure is not instituted solely for procreation; rather, its very nature as an unbreakable contact between persons, and the welfare of the children, both demand that the mutual love of the spouses be embodied in a rightly ordered manner, that it grow and ripen. Therefore, marriage persists as a whole manner and communion of life, and maintains its value and indissolubility, even when, despite the often intense desire of the couple, offspring are lacking.

51. This council realizes that certain modern conditions often keep couples from arranging their married lives harmoniously, and that they find themselves in circumstances where at least temporarily the size of their families should not be increased. As a result, the faithful exercise of love and the full intimacy of their lives is hard to maintain. But where the intimacy of married life is broken off, its faithfulness can sometimes be imperilled and its quality of fruitlessness ruined, for then the upbringing of the children and the courage to accept new ones are both endangered.

51.1. To these problems there are those who presume to offer dishonourable solutions indeed; they do not recoil even from the taking of life. But the Church issues the reminder that a true contradiction cannot exist between the divine laws pertaining to the transmission of life and those pertaining to authentic conjugal love.

51.2. For God, the lord of life, has conferred on men the surpassing ministry of safeguarding life in a manner which is worthy of man. Therefore from the moment of its conception life must be guarded with the greatest care. The sexual characteristics of man and the human faculty of reproduction wonderfully exceed the dispositions of lower forms of life. Hence the acts themselves which are proper to conjugal love and which are exercised in accord with genuine human dignity must be honoured with great reverence. Hence when there is question of harmonizing conjugal love with the responsible transmission of life, the moral aspect of any procedure does not depend solely on sincere intentions or on an evaluation of motives, but must be determined by objective standards. These, based on the nature of the human person and his acts preserve the full sense of mutual self-giving and human procreation in the context of true love. Such a goal cannot be achieved unless the virtue of conjugal chastity is sincerely practised. Relying on these principles, sons of the Church may not undertake methods of birth regulation which are found blameworthy by the teaching authority of the Church in its unfolding of the divine law.[117]

51.3. All should be persuaded that human life and the task of transmitting it are not realities bound up with this world alone. Hence they cannot be measured or perceived only in terms of it, but always have a bearing on the eternal destiny of men.

52. The family is a kind of school of deeper humanity. But if it is to achieve the full flowering of its life and mission, it needs the kindly communion of minds and the joint deliberation of spouses, as well as the painstaking co-operation of parents in the education of their children. The active presence of the father is highly beneficial to their formation. The children, especially the younger among them, need the care of their mother at home. This domestic role of hers must be safely preserved, though the legitimate social progress of women should not be underrated on that account. Children should be so educated that as adults they can follow their vocation, including a religious one, with a mature sense of responsibility and can choose their state of life; if they marry, they can thereby establish their family in favourable moral, social and economic conditions. Parents or guardians should by prudent advice provide guidance to their young with respect to founding a family, and the young ought to listen gladly. At the same time no pressure, direct or indirect, should be put on the young to make them enter marriage or choose a specific partner.

52.1. Thus the family, in which the various generations come together and help one another grow wiser and harmonize personal rights with the other requirements of social life, is the foundation of society. All those, therefore, who exercise influence over communities and social groups should work effectively for the welfare of marriage and the family. Public authority should regard it as a sacred duty to recognize, protect and promote their authentic nature, to shield public morality and to favour the prosperity of home life. The right of parents to beget and educate their children in the bosom of the family must be safeguarded. Children too who unhappily lack the blessing of a family should be protected by prudent legislation and various undertakings and assisted by the help they need.

52.2. Christians, redeeming the present time[118] and distinguishing eternal realities from their changing expressions, should actively promote the values of marriage and the family, both by the example of their own lives and by co-operation with other men of good will. Thus when difficulties arise, Christians will provide on behalf of family life those necessities and helps which are suitably modern. To this end the Christian instincts of the faithful, the upright moral consciences of men, and the wisdom and experience of persons versed in the sacred sciences will have much to contribute.

52.3. Those too who are skilled in other sciences, notably the medical, biological, social and psychological, can considerably advance the welfare of marriage and the family along with peace of conscience if by pooling their efforts they labour to explain more thoroughly the various conditions favouring a proper regulation of births.

52.4. It devolves on priests duly trained about family matters to nurture the vocation of spouses by a variety of pastoral means, by preaching God's word, by liturgical worship, and by other spiritual aids to conjugal and family life; to sustain them sympathetically and patiently in difficulties, and to make them courageous through love, so that families which are truly illustrious can be formed.

52.5. Various organizations, especially family associations, should try by their programmes of instruction and action to strengthen young people and spouses themselves, particularly those recently wed, and to train them for family, social and apostolic life.

52.6. Finally, let the spouses themselves, made to the image of the living God and enjoying the authentic dignity of persons, be joined to one another[119] in equal affection, harmony of mind and the work of mutual sanctification. Thus, following Christ who is the principle of life,[120] by the sacrifices and joys of their vocation and through their faithful love, married people can become witnesses of the mystery of love which the Lord revealed to the world by his dying and his rising up to life again.[121]

CHAPTER II

The proper development of culture

53. Man comes to a true and full humanity only through culture, that is through the cultivation of the goods and values of nature. Wherever human life is involved, therefore, nature and culture are quite intimately connected one with the other.

53.1. The word 'culture' in its general sense indicates everything whereby man develops and perfects his many bodily and spiritual qualities; and strives by his knowledge and his labour, to bring the world itself under his control. He renders social life more human both in the family and the civic community, through improvement of customs and institutions. Throughout the course of time he expresses, communicates and conserves in his works, great spiritual experiences and desires, that they might be of advantage to the progress of many, even of the whole human family.

53.2. Thence it follows that human culture has necessarily a historical and social aspect and the word 'culture' also often assumes a sociological and ethnological sense. According to this sense we speak of a plurality of cultures. Different styles of life and multiple scales of values arise from the diverse manner of using things, of labouring, of expressing oneself, of practising religion, of forming customs, of establishing laws and juridical institutions, of cultivating the sciences, the arts and beauty. Thus the customs handed down to it form the patrimony proper to each human community. It is also in this way that there is formed the definite, historical milieu which enfolds the man of every nation and age and from which he draws the values which permit him to promote civilization.

Section 1. The circumstances of culture in the world today
54. The circumstances of the life of modern man have been so profoundly changed in their social and cultural aspect, that we can speak of a new age of human history.[122] New ways are open, therefore, for the perfection and the further extension of culture. These ways have been prepared by the enormous growth of natural, human and social sciences, by technical progress, and advances in developing and organizing means whereby men can communicate with one another. Hence the culture of today possesses particular characteristics: sciences which are called exact greatly develop critical judgement; the more recent psychological studies more profoundly explain human activity; historical studies make it much easier to see things in their mutable and evolutionary aspects; customs and usages are becoming more and more uniform; industrialization, urbanization, and other causes which promote community living create a mass-culture from which are born new ways of thinking, acting and making use of leisure. The increase of commerce between the various nations and groups of men opens more widely to all the treasures of different civilizations and thus, little by little, there develops a more universal form of human culture, which better promotes and expresses the unity of the human race to the degree that it preserves the particular aspects of the different civilizations.

55. From day to day, in every group or nation, there is an increase in the number of men and women who are conscious that they themselves are the authors and the artisans of the culture of their community. Throughout the whole world there is a mounting increase in the sense of autonomy as well as of responsibility. This is of paramount importance for the spiritual and moral maturity of the human race. This becomes more clear if we consider the unification of the world and the duty which is imposed upon us, that we build a better world based upon truth and justice. Thus we are witnesses of the birth of a new humanism, one in which man is defined first of all by this responsibility to his brothers and to history.

56. In these conditions, it is no cause of wonder that man, who senses his responsibility for the progress of culture, nourishes a high hope but also looks with anxiety upon many contradictory things which he must resolve:
    56.1. What is to be done to prevent the increased exchanges between cultures, which should lead to a true and fruitful dialogue between groups and nations, from disturbing the life of communities, from destroying the wisdom received from ancestors, or from placing in danger the character proper to each people?

56.2. How is the dynamism and expansion of a new culture to be fostered without losing a living fidelity to the heritage of tradition? This question is of particular urgency when a culture which arises from the enormous progress of science and technology must be harmonized with a culture nourished by classical studies according to various traditions.

56.3. How can we quickly and progressively harmonize the proliferation of particular branches of study with the necessity of forming a synthesis of them, and of preserving among men the faculties of contemplation and observation which lead to wisdom?

56.4. What can be done to make all men partakers of cultural values in the world, when the human culture of those who are more competent is constantly becoming more refined and more complex?

56.5. Finally how is the autonomy which culture claims for itself to be recognized as legitimate without generating a notion of humanism which is merely terrestial, and even contrary to religion itself?

56.6. In the midst of these conflicting requirements, human culture must evolve today in such a way that it can both develop the whole human person and aid man in those duties to whose fulfilment all are called, especially Christians fraternally united in one human family.

Section 2. Some principles for the proper development of culture
57. Christians, on pilgrimage toward the heavenly city, should seek and think of those things which are above.[123] This duty in no way decreases, rather it increases, the importance of their obligation to work with all men in the building of a more human world. Indeed, the mystery of the Christian faith furnishes them with an excellent stimulus and aid to fulfil this duty more courageously and especially to uncover the full meaning of this activity, one which gives to human culture its eminent place in the integral vocation of man.

57.1. When man develops the earth by the work of his hands or with the aid of technology, in order that it might bear fruit and become a dwelling worthy of the whole human family and when he consciously takes part in the life of social groups, he carries out the design of God manifested at the beginning of time, that he should subdue[124] the earth, perfect creation and develop himself. At the same time he obeys the commandment of Christ that he place himself at the service of his brethren.

57.2. Furthermore, when man gives himself to the various disciplines of philosophy, history and of mathematical and natural sciences, and when he cultivates the arts, he can do very much to elevate the human family to a more sublime understanding of truth, goodness, and beauty, and to the formation of considered opinions which have universal value. Thus mankind may be more clearly enlightened by that marvellous wisdom which was with God from all eternity, composing all things with him, rejoicing in the earth, delighting in the sons of men.[125]

57.3. In this way, the human spirit, being less subjected to material things, can be more easily drawn to the worship and contemplation of the creator. Moreover, by the impulse of grace, he is disposed to acknowledge the Word of God, who before he became flesh in order to save all and to sum up all in himself was already 'in the world' as 'the true light which enlightens every man' (John 1:9-10).[126]

57.4. Indeed today's progress in science and technology can foster a certain exclusive emphasis on observable data, and an agnosticism about everything else. For the methods of investigation which these sciences use can be wrongly considered as the supreme rule of seeking the whole truth. By virtue of their methods these sciences cannot penetrate to the intimate notion of things. Indeed the danger is present that man, confiding too much in the discoveries of today, may think that he is sufficient unto himself and no longer seek the higher things.

57.5. These unfortunate results, however, do not necessarily follow from the culture of today, nor should they lead us into the temptation of not acknowledging its positive values. Among these values are included: scientific study and fidelity towards truth in scientific enquiries, the necessity of working together with others in technical groups, a sense of international solidarity, a clearer awareness of the responsibility of experts to aid and even to protect men, the desire to make the conditions of life more favourable for all, especially for those who are poor in culture or who are deprived of the opportunity to exercise responsibility. All of these provide some preparation for the acceptance of the message of the gospel—a preparation which can be animated by divine charity through him who has come to save the world.

58. There are many ties between the message of salvation and human culture. For God, revealing himself to his people to the extent of a full manifestation of himself in his incarnate son, has spoken according to the culture proper to each epoch.

58.1. Likewise the Church, living in various circumstances in the course of time, has used the discoveries of different cultures so that in her preaching she might spread and explain the message of Christ to all nations, that she might examine it and more deeply understand it, that she might give it better expression in liturgical celebration and in the varied life of the community of the faithful.

58.2. But at the same time, the Church, sent to all peoples of every time and place, is not bound exclusively and indissolubly to any race or nation, any particular way of life or any customary pattern of life recent or ancient. Faithful to her own tradition and at the same time conscious of her universal mission, she can enter into communion with the various civilizations, to their enrichment and the enrichment of the Church herself.

58.3. The gospel of Christ constantly renews the life and culture of fallen man; it combats and removes the errors and evils resulting from the permanent allurement of sin. It never ceases to purify and elevate the morality of peoples. By riches coming from above, it makes fruitful, as it were from within, the spiritual qualities and traditions of every people and of every age. It strengthens, perfects and restores[127] them in Christ. Thus the Church, in the very fulfilment of her own function[128] stimulates and advances human and civic culture; by her action, also by her liturgy, she leads men toward interior liberty.

59. For the above reasons, the Church recalls to the mind of all that culture is to be subordinated to the integral perfection of the human person, to the good of the community and of the whole society. Therefore it is necessary to

develop the human faculties in such a way that there results a growth of the faculty of wonder, of intuition, of contemplation, of making personal judgement, of developing a religious, moral and social sense.

59.1. Culture, because it flows immediately from the spiritual and social character of man, has constant need of a just freedom in order to develop; it needs also the legitimate possibility of exercising its autonomy according to its own principles. It therefore rightly demands respect and enjoys a certain inviolability within the limits of the common good, as long, of course, as it preserves the rights of the individual and the community, whether particular or universal.

59.2. This sacred synod, therefore, recalling the teaching of the first Vatican Council, declares that there are 'two orders of knowledge' which are distinct, namely faith and reason; and that the Church does not forbid that 'the human arts and disciplines use their own principles and their proper method, each in its own domain'; therefore 'acknowledging this just liberty', this sacred synod affirms the legitimate autonomy of human culture and especially of the sciences.[129]

59.3. All this supposes that, within the limits of morality and the common utility, man can freely search for the truth, express his opinion and publish it; that he can practise any art he chooses; that finally, he can avail himself of accurate information concerning events of a public nature.[130]

59.4. As for public authority, it is not its function to determine the character of the civilization, but rather to establish the conditions and to use the means which are capable of fostering the life of culture among all even within the minorities of a nation.[131] It is necessary to do everything possible to prevent culture from being turned away from its proper end and made to serve as an instrument of political or economic power.

Section 3. Some more urgent duties of Christians in regard to culture
60. It is now possible to free most of humanity from the misery of ignorance. Therefore the duty most consonant with our times, especially for Christians, is that of working diligently for fundamental decisions to be taken in economic and political affairs, both on the national and international level, which will everywhere recognize and satisfy the right of all to a human and social culture in conformity with the dignity of the human person without any discrimination based on race, sex, nation, religion or social condition. Therefore it is necessary to provide all with a sufficient quantity of cultural benefits, especially of those which constitute the so-called basic culture lest very many be prevented from co-operating in the promotion of the common good in a truly human manner because of illiteracy and a lack of responsible activity.

60.1. We must strive to provide for those men who are gifted the possibility of pursuing higher studies; and in such a way that, as far as possible, they may occupy in society those duties, offices and services which are in harmony with their natural aptitude and the competence they have acquired.[132] Thus each man and the social groups of every people will be able to attain the full development of their culture in conformity with their qualities and traditions.

60.2. Everything must be done to make everyone conscious of the right to culture and the duty he has of developing himself culturally and of helping others. Sometimes there exist conditions of life and of work which impede the cultural striving of men and destroy in them the eagerness for culture. This is especially true of farmers and workers. It is necessary to provide for them those working conditions which will not impede their human culture but rather favour it. Women now engage in almost all spheres of activity. It is fitting that they are able to assume their proper role in accordance with their own nature. It is incumbent upon all to acknowledge and favour the proper and necessary participation of women in cultural life.

61. Today it is more difficult to form a synthesis of the various disciplines of knowledge and the arts than it was formerly. For while the mass and the diversity of cultural factors are increasing, there is a decrease in each man's faculty of perceiving and unifying these things, so that the image of 'universal man' is being lost sight of more and more. Nevertheless it remains each man's duty to preserve an understanding of the whole human person in which the values of intellect, will, conscience and fraternity are pre-eminent. These values are all rooted in God the creator and have been wonderfully restored and elevated in Christ.

61.1. The family is, as it were, the primary mother and nurse of this education. There, the children, in an atmosphere of love, more easily learn the correct order of things, while proper forms of human culture impress themselves in an almost unconscious manner upon the mind of the developing adolescent.

61.2. Opportunities for the same education are to be found also in the societies of today, due especially to the increased circulation of books and to the new means of cultural and social communication which can foster a universal culture. With the more or less universal reduction of working hours, the leisure time of most men has increased. May this leisure be used properly to relax, to fortify the health of soul and body through spontaneous study and activity, through tourism which refines man's character and enriches him with understanding of others, through sports activity which helps to preserve an equilibrium of spirit even in the community, and to establish fraternal relations among men of all conditions, nations and races. Let Christians co-operate so that the cultural manifestations and collective activity characteristic of our time may be imbued with a human and a Christian spirit.

61.3 All these leisure activities however cannot bring man to a full cultural development unless there is at the same time a profound inquiry into the meaning of culture and science for the human person.

62. Although the Church has contributed much to the development of culture, experience shows that, because of circumstances, it is sometimes difficult to harmonize culture with Christian teaching.

62.1. These difficulties do not necessarily harm the life of faith, rather they can stimulate the mind to a deeper and more accurate understanding of the faith. The recent studies and findings of science, history and philosophy raise new questions which affect life and which demand new theological investigations. Furthermore, theologians, observing the requirements and methods proper to theology, are invited to seek continually for more suitable ways of communicating doctrine to the men of their times; for the deposit of faith or the truths are one thing and the manner in which they are enunciated, in the same meaning and understanding, is another.[133] In pastoral care, sufficient use must be made not only of theological principles, but also of the findings of the secular sciences, especially of psychology and sociology, so that the faithful may be brought to a more adequate and mature life of faith.

62.2. Literature and the arts are also, in their own way, of great importance to the life of the Church. They strive to make known the proper nature of man, his problems and his experiences in trying to know and perfect both himself and the world. They have much to do with revealing man's place in history and in the world; with illustrating the miseries and joys, the needs and strengths of man and with foreshadowing a better life for him. Thus they are able to elevate human life, expressed in manifold forms in various times and places.

62.3. Efforts must be made so that those who foster these arts feel that the Church recognizes their activity and so that, enjoying orderly freedom, they may initiate more friendly relations with the Christian community. The Church acknowledges also new forms of art which are adapted to our age and are in keeping with the characteristics of various nations and regions. They may be brought into the sanctuary since they raise the mind to God, once the manner of expression is adapted and they are conformed to liturgical requirements.[134]

62.4. Thus the knowledge of God is better manifested and the preaching of the gospel becomes clearer to human intelligence and shows itself to be relevant to man's actual conditions of life.

62.5. May the faithful, therefore, live in very close union with the other men of their time and judging, as expressed in their culture. Let them blend new sciences and theories and the understanding of the most recent discoveries with Christian morality and the teaching of Christian doctrine, so that their religious culture and morality may keep pace with their scientific knowledge and with the constantly progressing technology. Thus they will be able to interpret and evaluate all things in a truly Christian spirit.

62.6. Let those who teach theology in seminaries and universities strive to collaborate with men versed in the other sciences through a sharing of their resources and points of view. Theological inquiry should pursue a profound understanding of revealed truth; at the same time it should not neglect close contact with its own time that it may be able to help those men skilled in various disciplines to attain to a better understanding of the faith. This common effort will greatly aid the formation of priests, who will be able to present to our contemporaries the doctrine of the Church concerning God, man and the world, in a manner more adapted to them so that they may receive it more willingly.[135] Furthermore, it is to be hoped that many of the laity will receive a sufficient formation in the sacred sciences and that some will dedicate themselves professionally to these studies, developing and deepening them by their own labours. In order that they may fulfil their function, let it be recognized that all the faithful, whether clerics or laity, possess a lawful freedom of inquiry, freedom of thought and of expressing their mind with humility and fortitude in those matters on which they enjoy competence.[136]

CHAPTER III

Economic and social life

63. In the economic and social realms, too, the dignity and complete vocation of the human person and the welfare of society as a whole are to be respected and promoted. For man is the source, the centre, and the purpose of all economic and social life.

63.1. Like other areas of social life, the economy of today is marked by man's increasing domination over nature, by closer and more intense relationships between citizens, groups, and countries and their mutual dependence, and by the increased intervention of the State. At the same time progress in the methods of production and in the exchange of goods and services has made the economy an instrument capable of better meeting the intensified needs of the human family.

63.2. Reasons for anxiety, however, are not lacking. Many people, especially in economically advanced areas, seem, as it were, to be ruled by economics, so that almost their entire personal and social life is permeated with a certain economic way of thinking. Such is true both of nations that favour a collective economy and of others. At the very time when the development of economic life could mitigate social inequalities (provided that it be guided and co-ordinated in a reasonable and human way), it is often made to embitter them; or, in some places, it even results in a decline of the social status of the underprivileged and in contempt for the poor. While an immense number of people still lack the absolute necessities of life, some, even in less advanced areas, live in luxury or squander wealth. Extravagance and wretchedness exist side by side. While a few enjoy very great power of choice, the majority are deprived of almost all possibility of acting on their own initiative and responsibility, and often subsist in living and working conditions unworthy of the human person.

63.3. A similar lack of economic and social balance is to be noticed between agriculture, industry, and the services, and also between different parts of one and the same country. The contrast between the economically more advanced countries and other countries is becoming more serious day by day, and the very peace of the world can be jeopardized thereby.

63.4. Our contemporaries are coming to feel these inequalities with an ever sharper awareness, since they are thoroughly convinced that the ampler technical and economic possibilities which the world of today enjoys can and should correct this unhappy state of affairs. Hence, many reforms in the socio-economic realm and a change of mentality and attitude are required for all. For this reason the Church down through the centuries and in the light of the gospel has worked out the principles of justice and equity demanded by right reason both for individual and social life and for international life, and she has proclaimed them especially in recent times. This sacred council intends to strengthen these principles according to the circumstances of this age and to set forth certain guidelines, especially with regard to the requirements of economic development.[137]

Section 1. Economic development
64. Today more than ever before attention is rightly given to the increase of the production of agricultural and industrial goods and of the rendering of services, for the purpose of making provision for the growth of population and of satisfying the increasing desires of the human race. Therefore, technical progress, an inventive spirit, an eagerness to create and to expand enterprises, the application of methods of production, and the strenuous efforts of all who engage in production—in a word, all the elements making for such development—must be promoted. The fundamental purpose of this production is not the mere increase of products nor profit or control but rather the service of man, and indeed of the whole man with regard for the full range of his material needs and the demands of his intellectual, moral, spiritual, and religious life; this applies to every man whatsoever and to every group of men, of every race and of every part of the world. Consequently, economic activity is to be carried on according to its own methods and laws within the limits of the moral order,[138] so that God's plan for mankind may be realized.[139]

65. Economic development must remain under man's determination and must not be left to the judgement of a few men or groups possessing too much economic power or of the political community alone or of certain more powerful nations. It is necessary, on the contrary, that at every level the largest possible number of people and, when it is a question of international relations, all nations have an active share in directing that development. There is need as well of the co-ordination and fitting and harmonious combination of the spontaneous efforts of individuals and of free groups with the undertakings of public authorities.
65.1. Growth is not to be left solely to a kind of mechanical course of economic activity of individuals, nor to the authority of government. For this reason, doctrines which obstruct the necessary reforms under the guise of a false liberty, and those which subordinate the basic rights of individual persons and groups to the collective organization of production must be shown to be erroneous.[140]
65.2. Citizens, on the other hand, should remember that it is their right and duty, which is also to be recognized by the civil authority, to contribute to the true progress of their own community according to their ability. Especially in underdeveloped areas, where all resources must urgently be employed, those who hold back their unproductive resources or who deprive their community of the material or spiritual aid that it needs—saving the personal right of migration—gravely endanger the common good.

66. To satisfy the demands of justice and equity, strenuous efforts must be made, without disregarding the rights of persons or the natural qualities of each country, to remove as quickly as possible the immense economic inequalities, which now exist and in many cases are growing and which are connected with individual and social discrimination. Likewise, in many areas, in view of the special difficulties of agriculture relative to the raising and selling of produce, country people must be helped both to increase and to market what they produce, and to introduce the necessary development and renewal and also obtain a fair income. Otherwise, as too often happens, they

will remain in the condition of lower-class citizens. Let farmers themselves, especially young ones, apply themselves to perfecting their professional skill, for without it, there can be no agricultural advance.[141]

66.1. Justice and equity likewise require that the mobility which is necessary in a developing economy be regulated in such a way as to keep the life of individuals and their families from becoming insecure and precarious. When workers come from another country or district and contribute to the economic advancement of a nation or region by their labour, all discrimination as regards wages and working conditions must be carefully avoided. All the people, moreover, above all the public authorities, must treat them not as mere tools of production but as persons, and must help them to bring their families to live with them and to provide themselves with a decent dwelling; they must also see to it that these workers are incorporated into the social life of the country or region that receives them. Employment opportunities, however, should be created in their own areas as far as possible.

66.2. In economic affairs which today are subject to change, as in the new forms of industrial society in which automation, for example, is advancing, care must be taken that sufficient and suitable work and the possibility of the appropriate technical and professional formation are furnished. The livelihood and the human dignity especially of those who are in very difficult conditions because of illness or old age must be guaranteed.

Section 2. Certain principles governing socio-economic life as a whole
67. Human labour which is expended in the production and exchange of goods or in the performance of economic services is superior to the other elements of economic life, for the latter have only the nature of tools.

67.1. This labour, whether it is engaged in independently or hired by someone else, comes immediately from the person, who as it were stamps the things of nature with his seal and subdues them to his will. By his labour a man ordinarily supports himself and his family, is joined to his fellow men and serves them, and can exercise genuine charity and be a partner in the work of bringing divine creation to perfection. Indeed, we hold that through labour offered to God man is associated with the redemptive work of Jesus Christ, who conferred an eminent dignity on labour when at Nazareth he worked with his own hands. From this there follows for every man the duty of working faithfully and also the right to work. It is the duty of society, moreover, according to the circumstances prevailing in it, and in keeping with its role, to help the citizens to find sufficient employment. Finally, remuneration for labour is to be such that man may be furnished the means to cultivate worthily his own material, social, cultural, and spiritual life and that of his dependants, in view of the function and productiveness of each one, the conditions of the factory or workshop, and the common good.[142]

67.2. Since economic activity for the most part implies the associated work of human beings, any way of organizing and directing it which might be detrimental to any working men and women would be wrong and inhuman. It happens too often, however, even in our days, that workers are reduced to the level of being slaves to their own work. This is by no means justified by the so-called economic laws. The entire process of productive work, therefore, must be adapted to the needs of the person and to his way of life, above all to his domestic life, especially in respect to mothers of families, always with due regard for sex and age. The opportunity, moreover, should be granted to workers to unfold their own abilities and personality through the performance of their work. Applying their time and strength to their employment with a due sense of responsibility, they should also all enjoy sufficient rest and leisure to cultivate their familial, cultural, social and religious life. They should also have the opportunity freely to develop the energies and potentialities which perhaps they cannot bring to much fruition in their professional work.

68. In economic enterprises it is persons who are joined together, that is, free and independent human beings created to the image of God. Therefore, taking account of the prerogatives of each—owners or employers, management or labour—and without doing harm to the necessary unity of management, the active sharing of all in the administration and profits of these enterprises in ways to be properly determined should be promoted.[143] Since more often, however, decisions concerning economic and social conditions, on which the future lot of the workers and of their children depends, are made not within the business itself but by institutions on a higher level, the workers themselves should have a share also in determining these conditions—in person or through freely elected delegates.

68.1. Among the basic rights of the human person is to be numbered the right of freely founding unions for working people. These should be able truly to represent them and to contribute to the organizing of economic life in the right way. Included is the right of freely taking part in the activity of these unions without risk of reprisal. Through this orderly participation joined to progressive economic and social formation, all will grow day by day in the awareness of their own function and responsibility, and thus they will be brought to feel that they are comrades in the whole task of economic development and in the attainment of the universal common good according to their capacities and aptitudes.

68.2. When, however, socio-economic disputes arise, efforts must be made to come to a peaceful settlement. Although recourse must always be had first to a sincere dialogue between the parties, the strike, nevertheless, can remain even in present-day circumstances a necessary, though ultimate, means for the defence of the workers' own rights and fulfilment of their just desires. As soon as possible, however, ways should be sought to resume negotiations and discussions leading towards reconciliation.

69. God intended the earth with everything contained in it for the use of all human beings and peoples. Thus, under the guidance of justice together with charity, created goods should be in abundance for all in an equitable manner.[144] Whatever the forms of property may be, as adapted to the legitimate institutions of peoples, according to diverse and changeable circumstances, attention must always be paid to this universal goal of earthly goods. In using them, therefore, man should regard the external things that he legitimately possesses not only as his own but also as common in the sense that they should be able to benefit not only him but also others as well.[145] On the other hand, the right of having a share of earthly goods sufficient for

oneself and one's family belongs to everyone. The fathers and doctors of the Church held this opinion, teaching that men are obliged to come to the relief of the poor and to do so not merely out of their superfluous goods.[146] If one is in extreme necessity, he has the right to procure for himself what he needs out of the riches of others.[147] Since there are so many people prostrate with hunger in the world, this sacred council urges all, both individuals and governments to remember the aphorism of the fathers, 'Feed the man dying of hunger, because if you have not fed him, you have killed him,'[148] and really to share and use their earthly goods, according to the ability of each, especially by supporting individuals or peoples with the aid by which they may be able to help and develop themselves.

69.1. In economically less advanced societies the common destination of earthly goods is partly satisfied by means of the customs and traditions proper to the community, by which the absolute essentials are furnished to each member. An effort must be made, however, to avoid regarding certain customs as altogether unchangeable, if they no longer answer the new needs of this age. On the other hand, imprudent action should not be taken against respectable customs which, provided they are suitably adapted to present-day circumstances, do not cease to be very useful. Similarly in highly developed nations a body of social institutions dealing with protection and security can, for its own part, bring to reality the common destination of earthly goods. Family and social services, especially those that provide for culture and education, should be further promoted. When all these things are being organized, vigilance is necessary to prevent the citizens from being led into a certain inertia vis-à-vis society or from rejecting the burden of taking up office or from refusing to serve.

70. Investments, for their part, must be directed toward providing employment and sufficient income for the people both now and in the future. Whoever make decisions concerning these investments and the planning of the economy—whether they be individuals or groups or public authorities—are bound to keep these objectives in mind and to recognize their serious obligation of making sure, on the one hand, that provision be made for the necessities required for a decent life both of individuals and of the whole community and, on the other, of looking out for the future and of establishing a proper balance between the needs of present-day consumption, both individual and collective, and the demands of investing for the generation to come. They should also always bear in mind the urgent needs of underdeveloped countries or regions. In monetary matters they should beware of hurting the welfare of their own country or of other countries. Care should also be taken lest the economically weak countries unjustly suffer any loss from a change in the value of money.

71. Since property and other forms of private ownership of external goods contribute to the expression of the personality, and since, moreover, they furnish one an occasion to exercise his function in society and in the economy, it is very important that the access of both individuals and communities to some ownership of external goods be fostered.

71.1. Private property or some ownership of external goods confers on everyone a sphere wholly necessary for the autonomy of the person and the family, and it should be regarded as an extension of human freedom. Lastly, since it adds incentives for carrying on one's function and duty, it constitutes one of the conditions for civil liberties.[149]

71.2. The forms of such ownership of property are varied today and are becoming increasingly diversified. They all remain, however, a cause of security not to be underestimated, in spite of social funds, rights, and services provided by society. This is true not only of material goods but also of intangible goods such as professional skills.

71.3. The right of private ownership, however, is not opposed to the right inherent in various forms of public property. Goods can be transferred to the public domain only by the competent authority, according to the demands and within the limits of the common good, and with fair compensation. Furthermore, it is the right of public authority to prevent anyone from misusing his private property to the detriment of the common good.[150]

71.4. By its very nature private property has a social quality which is based on the law of the common destination of earthly goods.[151] If this social quality is overlooked, property often becomes an occasion of a passionate desire for wealth and serious disturbances, so that a pretext is given to those who attack private property for calling the right itself into question.

71.5. In many underdeveloped regions there are large or even extensive rural estates which are only slightly cultivated or lie completely idle for the sake of profit, while the majority of the people either are without land or have only very small fields, and, on the other hand, it is evidently urgent to increase the productivity of the fields. Not infrequently those who are hired to work for the landowners or who till a portion of the land as tenants receive a wage or income unworthy of a human being, lack decent housing and are exploited by middlemen. Deprived of all security, they live under such personal servitude that almost every opportunity of acting on their own initiative and responsibility is denied to them and all advancement in human culture and all sharing in social and political life is forbidden to them. According to different circumstances, therefore, reforms are necessary: that income may grow, working conditions should be improved, security in employment increased, and an incentive to working on one's own initiative given. Indeed, insufficiently cultivated estates should be distributed to those who can make these lands fruitful; in this case, the necessary ways and means, especially educational aids and the right facilities for co-operative organization, must be supplied. Whenever, nevertheless, the common good requires expropriation, compensation must be reckoned in equity after all the circumstances have been weighed.

72. Christians who take an active part in present-day socio-economic development and fight for justice and charity should be convinced that they can make a great contribution to the prosperity of mankind and to the peace of the world. In these activities let them, either as individuals or as members of groups, give a shining example. Having acquired the skills and experience which are absolutely necessary, they should observe the right order in their earthly activities in faithfulness to Christ and his gospel. Thus their whole life, both individual and social, will be permeated with the spirit of the beatitudes, notably with a spirit of poverty.

72.1. Whoever in obedience to Christ seeks first the kingdom of God, takes therefrom a stronger and purer love for helping all his brethren and for perfecting the work of justice under the inspiration of charity.[152]

CHAPTER IV

The life of the political community

73. In our day, profound changes are apparent also in the structure and institutions of peoples. These result from their cultural, economic and social evolution. Such changes have a great influence on the life of the political community, especially regarding the rights and duties of all in the exercise of civil freedom and in the attainment of the common good, and in organizing the relations of citizens among themselves and with respect to public authority.

73.1. The present keener sense of human dignity has given rise in many parts of the world to attempts to bring about a politico-juridical order which will give better protection to the rights of the person in public life. These include the right freely to meet and form associations, the right to express one's own opinion and to profess one's religion both publicly and privately. The protection of the rights of a person is indeed a necessary condition so that citizens, individually or collectively, can take an active part in the life and government of the state.

73.2. Along with cultural, economic and social development, there is a growing desire among many people to play a greater part in organizing the life of the political community. In the conscience of many there arises an increasing concern that the rights of minorities be recognized, without any neglect for their duties towards the political community. In addition, there is a steadily growing respect for men of other opinions or other religions. At the same time, there is wider co-operation to guarantee the actual exercise of personal rights to all citizens, and not only to a few privileged individuals.

73.3. However, those political systems, prevailing in some parts of the world, are to be reproved which hamper civic or religious freedom, victimize large numbers through avarice and political crimes, and divert the exercise of authority from the service of the common good to the interests of one or another faction or of the rulers themselves.

73.4. There is no better way to establish political life on a truly human basis than by fostering an inward sense of justice and kindliness, and of service to the common good, and by strengthening basic convictions as to the true nature of the political community and the purpose, right exercise, and sphere of action of public authority.

74. Men, families and the various groups which make up the civil community are aware that they cannot achieve a truly human life by their own unaided efforts. They see the need for a wider community, within which each one makes his specific contribution every day towards an ever broader realization of the common good.[153] For this purpose they set up a political community which takes various forms. The political community exists,

consequently, for the sake of the common good, in which it finds its full justification and significance, and the source of its inherent legitimacy. Indeed, the common good embraces the sum of those conditions of the social life whereby men, families and associations more adequately and readily may attain their own perfection.[154]

74.1. Yet the people who come together in the political community are many and diverse, and they have every right to prefer divergent solutions. If the political community is not to be torn apart while everyone follows his own opinion, there must be an authority to direct the energies of all citizens towards the common good, not in a mechanical or despotic fashion, but by acting above all as a moral force which appeals to each one's freedom and sense of responsibility.

74.2. It is clear, therefore, that the political community and public authority are founded on human nature and hence belong to the order designed by God, even though the choice of a political regime and the appointment of rulers are left to the free will of citizens.[155]

74.3. It follows also that political authority, both in the community as such and in the representative bodies of the state, must always be exercised within the limits of the moral order and directed towards the common good—with a dynamic concept of that good—according to the juridical order legitimately established or which should be established. When authority is so exercised, citizens are bound in conscience to obey.[156] Accordingly, the responsibility, dignity and importance of leaders are indeed clear.

74.4. But where citizens are oppressed by a public authority overstepping its competence, they should not protest against those things which are objectively required for the common good; but it is legitimate for them to defend their own rights and the rights of their fellow citizens against the abuse of this authority, while keeping within those limits drawn by the natural law and the Gospels.

74.5. According to the character of different peoples and their historic development, the political community can, however, adopt a variety of concrete solutions in its structures and the organization of public authority. For the benefit of the whole human family, these solutions must always contribute to the formation of a type of man who will be cultivated, peace-loving and well-disposed towards all his fellow men.

75. It is in full conformity with human nature that there should be juridico-political structures providing all citizens in an ever better fashion and without any discrimination with the practical possibility of freely and actively taking part in the establishment of the juridical foundations of the political community and in the direction of public affairs, in fixing the terms of reference of the various public bodies and in the election of political leaders.[157] All citizens, therefore, should be mindful of the right and also the duty to use their free vote to further the common good. The Church praises and esteems the work of those who for the good of men devote themselves to the service of the state and take on the burdens of this office.

75.1. If the citizens' responsible co-operation is to produce the good results which may be expected in the normal course of political life, there must be a statute of positive law providing for a suitable division of the functions and bodies of authority and an efficient and independent system for the protection of rights. The rights of all persons, families and groups, and their practical application, must be recognized, respected and furthered, together with the duties binding on all citizens.[158] Among the latter, it will be well to recall the duty of rendering the political community such material and personal services as are required by the common good. Rulers must be careful not to hamper the development of family, social or cultural groups, nor that of intermediate bodies or organizations, and not to deprive them of opportunities for legitimate and constructive activity; they should willingly seek rather to promote the orderly pursuit of such activity. Citizens, for their part, either individually or collectively, must be careful not to attribute excessive power to public authority, not to make exaggerated and untimely demands upon it in their own interests, lessening in this way the responsible role of persons, families and social groups.

75.2. The complex circumstances of our day make it necessary for public authority to intervene more often in social, economic and cultural matters in order to bring about favourable conditions which will give more effective help to citizens and groups in their free pursuit of man's total well-being. The relations, however, between socialization[159]* and the autonomy and development of the person can be understood in different ways according to various regions and the evolution of peoples. But when the exercise of rights is restricted temporarily for the common good, freedom should be restored immediately upon change of circumstances. Moreover, it is inhuman for public authority to fall back on dictatorial systems or totalitarian methods which violate the rights of the person or social groups.

75.3. Citizens must cultivate a generous and loyal spirit of patriotism, but without being narrow-minded. This means that they will always direct their attention to the good of the whole human family, united by the different ties which bind together races, people and nations.

75.4. All Christians must be aware of their own specific vocation within the political community. It is for them to give an example by their sense of responsibility and their service of the common good. In this way they are to demonstrate concretely how authority can be compatible with freedom, personal initiative with the solidarity of the whole social organism, and the advantages of unity with fruitful diversity. They must recognize the legitimacy of different opinions with regard to temporal solutions, and respect citizens, who, even as a group, defend their points of view by honest methods. Political parties, for their part, must promote those things which in their judgement are required for the common good; it is never allowable to give their interests priority over the common good.

75.5. Great care must be taken with regard to civic and political formation, which is of the utmost necessity today for the population as a whole, and especially for youth, so that all citizens can play their part in the life of the political community. Those who are suited or can become suited should prepare themselves for the difficult, but at the same time, the very noble art of politics,[160] and should seek to practise this art without regard for their own interests or for material advantages. With integrity and wisdom, they must take action against any form of injustice and tyranny, against arbitrary domination by an individual or a political party, and any intolerance. They should dedicate themselves to the service of all with sincerity and fairness, indeed, with the charity and fortitude demanded by political life.

76. It is very important, especially where a pluralistic society prevails, that there be a correct notion of the relationship between the political community and the Church, and a clear distinction between the tasks which Christians undertake, individually or as a group, on their own responsibility as citizens guided by the dictates of a Christian conscience, and the activities which, in union with their pastors, they carry out in the name of the Church.

76.1. The Church, by reason of her role and competence, is not identified in any way with the political community nor bound to any political system. She is at once a sign and a safeguard of the transcendent character of the human person.

76.2. The Church and the political community in their own fields are autonomous and independent from each other. Yet both, under different titles, are devoted to the personal and social vocation of the same men. The more that both foster healthier co-operation between themselves with due consideration for the circumstances of time and place, the more effectively will their service be exercised for the good of all. For man's horizons are not limited only to the temporal order: while living in the context of human history, he preserves intact his eternal vocation. The Church, for her part, founded on the love of the redeemer, contributes towards the reign of justice and charity within the borders of a nation and between nations. By preaching the truths of the gospel, and bringing to bear on all fields of human endeavour the light of her doctrine and of a Christian witness, she respects and fosters the political freedom and responsibility of citizens.

76.3. The apostles, their successors and those who co-operate with them, are sent to announce to mankind Christ, the saviour. Their apostolate is based on the power of God, who very often shows forth the strength of the gospel in the weakness of its witnesses. All those dedicated to the ministry of God's word must use the ways and means proper to the gospel which in a great many respects differ from the means proper to the earthly city.

76.4. There are, indeed close links between earthly things and those elements of man's condition which transcend the world. The Church herself makes use of temporal things in so far as her own mission requires it. She, for her part, does not place her trust in the privileges offered by civil authority. She will even give up the exercise of certain rights which have been legitimately acquired, if it becomes clear that their use will cast doubt on the sincerity of her witness or that new ways of life demand new methods. It is only right, however, that at all times and in all places, the Church should have true freedom to preach the faith, to teach her social doctrine, to exercise her role freely among men, and also to pass moral judgement in those matters which concern public order when the fundamental rights of a person or the salvation of souls requires it. In this, she should make use of all the means—but only those—which accord with the gospel and which correspond to the general good with due regard to the diverse circumstances of time and place.

76.5. While faithfully adhering to the gospel and fulfilling her mission to the world, the Church, whose duty it is to foster and elevate[161] all that is found to be true, good and beautiful in the human community, strengthens peace among men for the glory of God.[162]

CHAPTER V

The fostering of peace and the promotion of a community of nations

77. In our generation when men continue to be afflicted by acute hardships and anxieties arising from the ravages of war or the threat of it, the whole human family faces an hour of supreme crisis in its advance toward maturity. Moving gradually together and everywhere more conscious already of its unity, this family cannot accomplish its task of constructing for all men everywhere a world more genuinely human unless each person devotes himself to the cause of peace with renewed vigour. Thus it happens that the gospel message, which is in harmony with the loftier strivings and aspirations of the human race, takes on a new lustre in our day as it declares that the artisans of peace are blessed 'because they will be called the sons of God' (Matt. 5:9).

77.1. Consequently, as it points out the authentic and noble meaning of peace and condemns the frightfulness of war, the council wishes passionately to summon Christians to co-operate, under the help of Christ, the author of peace, with all men in securing among themselves a peace based on justice and love and in setting up the instruments of peace.

78. Peace is not merely the absence of war; nor can it be reduced solely to the maintenance of a balance of power between enemies; nor is it brought about by dictatorship. Instead, it is rightly and appropriately called an enterprise of justice (Is. 32:7). Peace results from that order structured into human society by its divine founder, and actualized by men as they thirst after ever greater justice. The common good of humanity finds its ultimate meaning in the eternal law. But since the concrete demands of this common good are constantly changing as time goes on, peace is never attained once and for all, but must be built up ceaselessly. Moreover, since the human will is unsteady and wounded by sin, the achievement of peace requires a constant mastering of passions and the vigilance of lawful authority.

78.1. But this is not enough. This peace on earth cannot be obtained unless personal well-being is safeguarded and men freely and trustingly share with one another the riches of their inner spirits and their talents. A firm determination to respect other men and peoples and their dignity, as well as the studied practice of brotherhood are absolutely necessary for the establishment of peace. Hence peace is likewise the fruit of love, which goes beyond what justice can provide.

78.2. That earthly peace which arises from love of neighbour symbolizes and results from the peace of Christ which radiates from God the father. For by the cross the incarnate son, the prince of peace reconciled all men with God. By thus restoring all men to the unity of one people and one body, he slew hatred in his own flesh;[163] and, after being lifted on high by his resurrection, he poured forth the spirit of love into the hearts of men.

78.3. For this reason, all Christians are urgently summoned to do in love what the truth requires (Eph. 4:15), and to join with all true peacemakers in pleading for peace and bringing it about.

78.4. Motivated by this same spirit, we cannot fail to praise those who renounce the use of violence in the vindication of their rights and who resort to methods of defence which are otherwise available to weaker parties too, provided this can be done without injury to the rights and duties of others or of the community itself.

78.5. In so far as men are sinful, the threat of war hangs over them, and hang over them it will until the return of Christ. But in so far as men vanquish sin by a union of love, they will vanquish violence as well and make these words come true: 'They shall turn their swords into plough-shares, and their spears into sickles. Nation shall not lift up sword against nation, neither shall they learn war any more' (Is. 2:4).

Section 1. The avoidance of war

79. In spite of the fact that recent wars have wrought physical and moral havoc on our world, war produces its devastation day by day in some part of the world. Indeed, now that every kind of weapon produced by modern science is used in war, the fierce character of warfare threatens to lead the combatants to a savagery far surpassing that of the past. Furthermore, the complexity of the modern world and the intricacy of international relations allow guerrilla warfare to be carried on by new methods of deceit and subversion. In many cases the use of terrorism is regarded as a new way to wage war.

79.1. Contemplating this melancholy state of humanity, the council wishes, above all things else, to recall the permanent binding force of universal natural law and its all-embracing principles. Man's conscience itself gives ever more emphatic voice to these principles. Therefore, actions which deliberately conflict with these same principles, as well as orders commanding such actions, are criminal, and blind obedience cannot excuse those who yield to them. The most infamous among these are actions designed for the methodical extermination of an entire people, nation or ethnic minority. Such actions must be vehemently condemned as horrendous crimes. The courage of those who fearlessly and openly resist those who issue such commands merits the highest commendation.

79.2. On the subject of war, quite a large number of nations have subscribed to international agreements aimed at making military activity and its consequences less inhuman. Their stipulations deal with such matters as the treatment of wounded soldiers and prisoners. Agreements of this sort must be honoured. Indeed they should be improved upon so that the frightfulness of war can be better and more workably held in check. All men, especially government officials and experts in these matters, are bound to do everything they can to effect these improvements. Moreover, it seems right that laws make humane provisions for the case of those who for reasons of conscience refuse to bear arms, provided however, that they agree to serve the human community in some other way.

79.3. Certainly, war has not been rooted out of human affairs. As long as the danger of war remains and there is no competent and sufficiently powerful authority at the international level, governments cannot be denied the right to legitimate defence once every means of peaceful settlement has been exhausted. Government authorities and others who share public responsibility have the duty to conduct such grave matters soberly and to protect the welfare of the people entrusted to their care. But it is one thing to undertake military action for the just defence of the people, and something else again to seek the subjugation of other nations. Nor, by the same token, does the mere fact that war has unhappily begun mean that all is fair between the warring parties.

79.4. Those too who devote themselves to the military service of their country should regard themselves as the agents of security and freedom of peoples. As long as they fulfil this role properly, they are making a genuine contribution to the establishment of peace.

80. The horror and perversity of war is immensely magnified by the increase in the number of scientific weapons. For acts of war involving these weapons can inflict massive and indiscriminate destruction, thus going far beyond the bounds of legitimate defence. Indeed, if the kind of instruments which can now be found in the armouries of the great nations were to be employed to their fullest, an almost total and altogether reciprocal slaughter of each side by the other would follow, not to mention the widespread devastation that would take place in the world and the deadly after-effects that would be spawned by the use of weapons of this kind.

80.1. All these considerations compel us to undertake an evaluation of war with an entirely new attitude.[164] The men of our time must realize that they will have to give a sombre reckoning of their deeds of war for the course of the future will depend greatly on the decisions they make today.

80.2. With these truths in mind, this most holy synod makes its own the condemnations of total war already pronounced by recent popes,[165] and issues the following declaration:

80.3. Any act of war aimed indiscriminately at the destruction of entire cities or extensive areas along with their population is a crime against God and man himself. It merits unequivocal and unhesitating condemnation.

80.4. The unique hazard of modern warfare consists in this: it provides those who possess modern scientific weapons with a kind of occasion for perpetrating just such abominations; moreover, through a certain inexorable chain of events, it can catapult men into the most atrocious decisions. That such may never happen in the future, the bishops of the whole world gathered together beg all men, especially government officials and military leaders, to give unremitting thought to their tremendous responsibility before God and the entire human race.

81. Scientific weapons, to be sure, are not amassed solely for use in war. Since the defensive strength of any nation is considered to be dependent upon its capacity for immediate retaliation, this accumulation of arms, which increases each year, likewise serves, in a way heretofore unknown, as a deterrent to possible enemy attack. Many regard this as the most effective way by which peace of a sort can be maintained between nations at the present time.

81.1. Whatever be the facts about this method of deterrence, men should be convinced that the arms race in which an already considerable number of countries are engaged is not a safe way to preserve a steady peace, nor is the so-called balance resulting from this race a sure and authentic peace. Rather than being eliminated thereby, the causes of war are in danger of being gradually aggravated. While extravagant sums are being spent for the furnishing of ever new weapons, an adequate remedy cannot be provided for the multiple miseries afflicting the whole modern world. Disagreements between nations are not really and radically healed; on the contrary, they spread the infection to other parts of the earth. New approaches based on reformed attitudes must be taken to remove this trap and to emancipate the world from its crushing anxiety through the restoration of genuine peace.

81.2. Therefore, we say it again: the arms race is an utterly treacherous trap for humanity, and one which ensnares the poor to an intolerable degree. It is much to be feared that if this race persists, it will eventually spawn all the lethal ruin whose path it is now making ready.

81.3. Warned by the calamities which the human race has made possible, let us make use of the interlude granted us from above and for which we are thankful, to become more conscious of our own responsibility and to find means for resolving our disputes in a manner more worthy of man. Divine providence urgently demands of us that we free ourselves from the age-old slavery of war. If we refuse to make this effort, we do not know where we will be led by the evil road we have set upon.

82. It is our clear duty, therefore, to strain every muscle in working for the time when all war can be completely outlawed by international consent. This goal undoubtedly requires the establishment of some universal public authority acknowledged as such by all and endowed with the power to safeguard on the behalf of all, security, regard for justice, and respect for rights. But before this hoped-for authority can be set up, the highest existing international centres must devote themselves vigorously to the pursuit of better means for obtaining common security. Since peace must be born of mutual trust between nations and not be imposed on them through fear of the available weapons, everyone must labour to put an end at last to the arms race, and to make a true beginning of disarmament, not unilaterally indeed, but proceeding at an equal pace according to agreement, and backed up by adequate and workable safeguards.[166]

82.1. In the meantime, efforts which have already been made and are still under way to eliminate the danger of war are not to be underrated. On the contrary, support should be given to the good will of the very many leaders who work hard to do away with war, which they abominate. These men, although burdened by the extremely weighty preoccupations of their high office, are nonetheless moved by the very grave peacemaking task to which they are bound, even if they cannot ignore the complexity of matters as they stand. We should fervently ask God to give these men the strength to go forward perseveringly and to follow through courageously on this work of building peace with vigour. It is a work of supreme love for mankind. Today it certainly demands that they extend their thoughts and their spirit beyond the confines of their own nation, that they put aside national selfishness and ambition to dominate other nations, and that they nourish a profound reverence for the whole of humanity, which is already making its way so laboriously toward greater unity.

82.2. The problems of peace and of disarmament have already been the subject of extensive, strenuous and constant examination. Together with international meetings dealing with these problems, such studies should be regarded as the first steps toward solving these serious questions, and should be promoted with even greater urgency by way of yielding concrete results in the future. Nevertheless, men should take heed not to entrust themselves only to the efforts of others, while not caring about their own attitudes. For government officials who must at one and the same time guarantee the good of their own people and promote the universal good are very greatly dependent on public opinion and feeling. It does them no good to work for peace as long as feelings of hostility, contempt and distrust, as well as racial hatred and unbending ideologies, continue to divide men and place them in opposing camps. Consequently there is above all a pressing need for a renewed education of attitudes and for new inspiration in public opinion. Those who are dedicated to the work of education, particularly of the young, or who mould public opinion, should consider it their most weighty task to instruct all in fresh sentiments of peace. Indeed, we all need a change of heart as we regard the entire world and those tasks which we can perform in unison for the betterment of our race.

82.3. But we should not let false hope deceive us. For unless enmities and hatred are put away and firm, honest agreements concerning world peace are reached in the future, humanity, which already is in the middle of a grave crisis, even though it is endowed with remarkable knowledge, will perhaps be brought to that dismal hour in which it will experience no peace other than the dreadful peace of death. But, while we say this, the Church of Christ, present in the midst of the anxiety of this age, does not cease to hope most firmly. She intends to propose to our age over and over again, in season and out of season, this apostolic message: 'Behold, now is the acceptable time for a change of heart; behold! now is the day of salvation.'[167]

Section 2. Setting up an international community
83. In order to build up peace the causes of discord among men, especially injustice, which foment wars must above all be rooted out. Not a few of these causes come from excessive economic inequalities and from putting off the steps needed to remedy them. Other causes of discord, however, have their source in the desire to dominate and in a contempt for persons. And, if we look for deeper causes, we find them in human envy, distrust, pride, and other egotistical passions. Man cannot bear so many ruptures in the harmony of things. Consequently, the world is constantly beset by strife and violence between men, even when no war is being waged. Besides, since these same evils are present in the relations between various nations as well, in order to overcome or forestall them and to keep violence once unleashed within limits, it is absolutely necessary for countries to co-operate to better advantage, to work together more closely, and jointly to organize international bodies and to work tirelessly for the creation of organizations which will foster peace.

84. In view of the increasingly close ties of mutual dependence today between all the inhabitants and peoples of the earth, the fitting pursuit and effective realization of the universal common good now require of the community of nations that it organize itself in a manner suited to its present responsibilities, especially towards the many parts of the world which are still suffering from unbearable want.

84.1. To reach this goal, organizations of the international community, for their part, must make provision for men's different needs, both in the fields of social life—such as food supplies, health, education, labour—and also in certain special circumstances which can crop up here and there, e.g., the need to promote the general improvement of developing countries, or to alleviate the distressing conditions in which refugees dispersed throughout the world find themselves, or also to assist migrants and their families.

84.2. International and regional organizations which are already in existence certainly deserve well of the human race. These are the first efforts at laying the foundations on an international level for a community of all men to work for the solution to the serious problems of our times, to encourage progress everywhere, and to obviate wars of whatever kind. In all of these activities the Church rejoices in the spirit of true brotherhood flourishing between Christians and non-Christians as it strives to make ever more strenuous efforts to relieve widespread misery.

85. The present solidarity of mankind also calls for a revival of greater international co-operation in the economic field. Although nearly all peoples have become autonomous, they are far from being free of every form of undue dependence, and far from escaping all danger of serious internal difficulties.

85.1. The development of a nation depends on human and financial aids. The citizens of each country must be prepared by education and professional training to discharge the various tasks of economic and social life. But this in turn requires the aid of foreign specialists who, when they give aid, will not act as overlords, but as helpers and fellow-workers. Developing nations will not be able to procure material assistance unless radical changes are made in the established procedures of modern world commerce. Other aid should be provided as well by advanced nations in the form of gifts, loans or financial investments. Such help should be accorded with generosity and without greed on the one side, and received with complete honesty on the other side.

85.2. If an authentic economic order is to be established on a world-wide basis, an end will have to be put to profiteering, to national ambition, to the appetite for political supremacy, to militaristic calculations, and to machinations for the purpose of spreading and imposing ideologies.

86. The following norms seem useful for such co-operation:

86.1 (a) Developing nations should take great pains to seek as the object of progress to express and secure the total human fulfilment of their citizens. They should bear in mind that progress arises and grows above all out of the labour and genius of the nations themselves because it has to be based, not only on foreign aid, but especially on the full utilization of their own resources, and on the development of their own culture and traditions. Those who exert the greatest influence on others should be outstanding in this respect.

86.2 (b) On the other hand, it is a very important duty of the advanced nations to help the developing nations in discharging their above-mentioned responsibilities. They should therefore gladly carry out on their own home front those spiritual and material readjustments that are required for the realization of this universal co-operation. Consequently, in business dealings with weaker and poorer nations, they should be careful to respect their welfare, for these countries need the income they receive on the sale of their homemade products to support themselves.

86.3 (c) It is the role of the international community to co-ordinate and promote development, but in such a way that the resources earmarked for this purpose will be allocated as effectively as possible, and with complete equity. It is likewise this community's duty, with due regard for the principle of subsidiarity, so to regulate economic relations throughout the world that these will be carried out in accordance with the norms of justice. Suitable organizations should be set up to foster and regulate international business affairs, particularly with the underdeveloped countries, and to compensate for losses resulting from an excessive inequality of power among the various nations. This type of organization, in unison with technical, cultural, and financial aid, should provide the help which developing nations need so that they can advantageously pursue their own economic advancement.

86.4. (d) In many cases there is an urgent need to revamp economic and social structures. But one must guard against proposed technical solutions that are untimely. This is particularly true of those solutions providing man with material conveniences, which are nevertheless contrary to man's spiritual nature and advancement. For 'not by bread alone does man live, but by every word which proceeds from the mouth of God' (Matt. 4:4). Every sector of the family of man carries within itself and in its best traditions some portion of the spiritual treasure entrusted by God to humanity, even though many may not be aware of the source from which it comes.

87. International co-operation is needed today especially for those peoples who, besides facing so many other difficulties, likewise undergo pressures due to a rapid increase in population. There is an urgent need to explore, with the full and intense co-operation of all, and especially of the wealthier nations, ways whereby the human necessities of food and a suitable education can be furnished and shared with the entire human community. But some peoples could greatly improve upon the conditions of their life if they would change over from antiquated methods of farming to the new technical methods, applying them with needed prudence according to their own circumstances. Their life would likewise be improved by the establishment of a better social order and by a fairer system for the distribution of land ownership.

87.1. Governments undoubtedly have rights and duties, within the limits of their proper competency, regarding the population problem in their respective countries, for instance, with regard to social- and family-life legislation, or with regard to information concerning the condition and needs of the country. Since men today are giving thought to this problem and are so greatly disturbed over it, it is desirable in addition that Catholic specialists, especially in the universities, skilfully pursue and develop studies and projects on all these matters.

87.2. But there are many today who maintain that the increase in world population, or at least the population increase in some countries, must be radically curbed by every means possible and by any kind of intervention on the part of public authority. In view of this contention, the council urges everyone to guard against solutions, whether publicly or privately supported, or at times even imposed, which are contrary to the moral law. For in keeping with man's inalienable right to marry and generate children, the decision concerning the number of children they will have depends on the correct judgement of the parents and it cannot in any way be left to the judgement of public authority. But since the judgement of the parents presupposes a rightly formed conscience, it is of the utmost importance that the way be open for everyone to develop a correct and genuinely human responsibility which respects the divine law and takes into consideration the circumstances of the place and the time. But sometimes this requires an improvement in educational and social conditions, and, above all, formation in religion or at least a complete moral training. Men should judiciously be informed, furthermore, of scientific advances in exploring methods whereby spouses can be helped in regulating the number of their children and whose safeness has been well proven and whose harmony with the moral order has been ascertained.

88. Christians should co-operate willingly and wholeheartedly in establishing an international order that includes a genuine respect for all freedoms and amicable brotherhoods between all. This is all the more pressing since the greater part of the world is still suffering from so much poverty that it is as if Christ himself were crying out in these poor to beg the charity of the disciples. Do not let men then be scandalized because some countries with a majority of citizens who are counted as Christians have an abundance of wealth, whereas others are deprived of the necessities of life and are tormented with hunger, disease, and every kind of misery. The spirit of poverty and charity are the glory and witness of the Church of Christ.

88.1. Those Christians are to be praised and supported, therefore, who volunteer their services to help other men and nations. Indeed, it is the duty of the whole people of God, following the word and example of the bishops, to alleviate as far as they are able the sufferings of the modern age. They should do this too, as was the ancient custom in the Church, out of the substance of their goods, and not only out of what is superfluous.

88.2. The procedure of collecting and distributing aid, without being inflexible and completely uniform, should nevertheless be carried out in an orderly fashion in dioceses, nations, and throughout the entire world. Wherever it seems fitting, this activity of Catholics should be carried on in unison with other Christian brothers. For the spirit of charity does not forbid, but on the contrary commands that charitable activity be carried out in a careful and orderly manner. Therefore, it is essential for those who intend to dedicate themselves to the service of the developing nations to be properly trained in appropriate institutes.

89. Since, in virtue of her mission received from God, the Church preaches the gospel to all men and dispenses the treasures of grace, she contributes to the ensuring of peace everywhere on earth and to the placing of the fraternal

exchange between men on solid ground by imparting knowledge of the divine and natural law. Therefore, to encourage and stimulate co-operation among men, the Church must be clearly present in the midst of the community of nations, both through her official channels and through the full and sincere collaboration of all Christians—a collaboration motivated solely by the desire to be of service to all.

89.1. This will come about more effectively if the faithful themselves, conscious of their responsibility as men and as Christians, will exert their influence in their own milieu to arouse a ready willingness to co-operate with the international community. Special care must be given, in both religious and civic education, to the formation of youth in this regard.

90. An outstanding form of international activity on the part of Christians is found in the joint efforts which, both as individuals and in groups, they contribute to institutes already established or to be established for the encouragement of co-operation among nations. There are also various Catholic associations on the international level which can contribute in many ways to the building up of a peaceful and fraternal community of nations. These should be strengthened by augmenting in them the number of well-qualified collaborators, by increasing needed resources, and by a suitable co-ordination of their forces. For today both effective action and the need for dialogue demand joint projects. Moreover, such associations contribute much to the development of a universal outlook—something certainly appropriate for Catholics. They also help to form an awareness of genuine universal solidarity and responsibility.

90.1. Finally, it is very much to be desired that Catholics, in order to fulfil their role properly in the international community, should seek to co-operate actively and in a positive manner both with their separated brothers, who together with them profess the gospel of charity, and with all men thirsting for true peace.

90.2. The council, considering the immensity of the hardships which still afflict the greater part of mankind today, regards it as most opportune that an organism of the universal Church be set up in order that both the justice and love of Christ towards the poor might be developed everywhere. The role of such an organism would be to stimulate the Catholic community to promote progress in needy regions and international social justice.

CONCLUSION

91. Drawn from the treasures of church teaching, the proposals of this sacred synod look to the assistance of every man of our time, whether he believes in God, or does not explicitly recognize him. If adopted, they will promote among men a sharper insight into their full destiny, and thereby lead them to fashion the world more to man's surpassing dignity, to search for a brotherhood which is universal and more deeply rooted, and to meet the urgencies of our age with a gallant and unified effort born of love.

91.2. Undeniably this conciliar programme is but a general one in several of its parts; and deliberately so, given the immense variety of situations and forms of human culture in the world. Indeed while it presents teaching already accepted in the Church, the programme will have to be followed up and amplified since it sometimes deals with matters in a constant state of development. Still, we have relied on the word of God and the spirit of the gospel. Hence we entertain the hope that many of our proposals will prove to be of substantial benefit to everyone, especially after they have been adapted to individual nations and mentalities by the faithful, under the guidance of their pastors.

92. By virtue of her mission to shed on the whole world the radiance of the gospel message, and to unify under one spirit all men of whatever nation, race or culture, the Church stands forth as a sign of that brotherhood which facilitates and invigorates sincere dialogue.

92.1. Such a mission requires in the first place that we foster within the Church itself mutual esteem, reverence and harmony, through the full recognition of lawful diversity. Thus all those who compose the one people of God, both pastors and the general faithful, can engage in dialogue with ever increasing effectiveness. For the bonds which unite the faithful are mightier than anything dividing them. Hence, let there be unity in essentials; freedom in doubtful matters; and in all things charity.

92.2. Our hearts embrace also those brothers and communities not yet living with us in full communion; to them we are linked nonetheless by our profession of the Father and the Son and the Holy Spirit, and by the bond of charity. We are not unmindful of the fact that the unity of Christians is today awaited and desired by many, too, who do not believe in Christ; for the further it advances toward truth and love under the powerful impulse of the Holy Spirit, the more this unity will be a harbinger of unity and peace for the world at large. Therefore, by common effort and in ways which are today increasingly appropriate for seeking this splendid goal effectively, let us take pains to pattern ourselves after the gospel more exactly every day, and thus work as brothers in rendering service to the human family. For, in Christ Jesus this family is constituted to the family of the sons of God.

92.3. We think cordially too of all who acknowledge God, and who preserve in their traditions precious elements of religion and humanity. We want frank conversation to compel us all to receive the impulses of the Spirit faithfully and to act on them energetically.

92.4. For our part, the desire for such dialogue, which can lead to truth through love alone, excludes no one, though an appropriate measure of prudence must undoubtedly be exercised. We include those who cultivate outstanding qualities of the human spirit, but do not yet acknowledge the source of these qualities. We include those who oppress the Church and harass her in manifold ways. Since God the Father is the origin and purpose of all men, we are all called to be brothers. Therefore, if we have been summoned to the same destiny, human and divine, we can and we should work together without violence and deceit in order to build up the world in genuine peace.

93. Mindful of the Lord's saying: 'by this will all men know that you are my disciples, if you have love for one another' (John 13:35), Christians cannot yearn for anything more ardently than to serve the men of the modern

world ever more generously and effectively. Therefore, by holding faithfully to the gospel and benefiting from its resources, by joining with every man who loves and practises justice, Christians have shouldered a gigantic task to be carried out in this world, a task concerning which they must give a reckoning to him who will judge every man on the last day. Not everyone who cries, 'Lord, Lord,' will enter into the kingdom of heaven, but those who do the Father's will[168] by taking a strong grip on the work at hand. Now, the Father wills that in all men we recognize Christ our brother and love him effectively, in word and in deed. By thus giving witness to the truth, we will share with others the mystery of the heavenly Father's love. As a consequence, men throughout the world will be aroused to a lively hope—the gift of the Holy Spirit—that finally they will be caught up in peace and utter happiness in that fatherland radiant with the glory of the Lord.

93.1. Now to him who is able to accomplish all things in a measure far beyond what we ask or conceive, in keeping with the power that is at work in us—to him be glory in the Church and in Christ Jesus, down through all the ages of time without end. Amen (Eph. 3:20-21).

93.2. The entire text and all the individual elements which have been set forth in this pastoral constitution have pleased the Fathers. And by the apostolic power conferred on us by Christ, we, together with the venerable Fathers, in the Holy Spirit, approve, decree and enact them; and we order that what has been thus enacted in council be promulgated, to the glory of God.

Given in Rome, at St Peter's, on 7 December 1965.

Editor's Note

GS 6.4: See Introduction, p.xxi, and footnote 26.
GS 75.2: See Introduction, p.xxi, and footnote 26.

Populorum Progressio

Encyclical letter of Pope Paul VI to the bishops, priests, religious, the faithful of the entire Catholic world, and to all men of good will on fostering the development of peoples.

Introduction

After the long gap of thirty years between the publication of *Quadragesimo Anno* and *Mater et Magistra*, major church documents on social issues came out with astonishing regularity, at intervals of approximately two years in the 1960s. *Populorum Progressio* kept up the impetus, being dated 26 March 1967, only just over fifteen months after the promulgation of *Gaudium et Spes*.

As its Latin title clearly indicates, it was concerned primarily with the relationships between rich and poor nations, and not with individuals. Pope Paul analyses why the inequality exists—the inheritance of a colonial past, forms of neo-colonialism and, above all perhaps, the imbalance of power between nations which affects their trading links. The pope recognizes that the international economic system as it exists does little to improve the conditions of the poorer nations, and indeed may very well exacerbate them. So he rejects the notion of entirely free trade, pointing out that the parties to trading agreements must be equal in status if the agreements are to be fair.

The pope is sometimes hortatory but often harshly pragmatic, pointing out to the rich that if the inequalities continue there is a distinct danger that the poor will resort to violence (PP 30). In the following paragraph there is even a very slight hint that violence might, in certain circumstances, be justified—but the pope hurriedly backs away from saying so explicitly.

One of the great strengths of this encyclical is the stress the pope laid upon *integral* development. Development was not seen as simply economic progress. There had also to be growth in knowledge, in culture and in the necessities of life—of the whole person, in other words.

The Latin text of *Populorum Progressio* (PP) is to be found in AAS 59 (1967) 257-299. The paragraph numbering is as in the Latin text, but cross-headings have been added.

Summary

Paras. 1-11: The Church is aware of the needs of the developing nations, of people with legitimate desires living under conditions which frustrate those desires. It is clear that in the past even beneficial colonialism failed to provide structures in the former colonies to cope with the harsh realities of today. There are flagrant inequalities of wealth, of food supply, in the exercise of power. Social unrest is fuelled by a clash between the new industrialized culture and the traditional one, made worse by a conflict between the generations.

Paras. 12-21: Through its missionary activity the Church has tried to help, but there is need for a universal, concentrated effort to achieve an authentic development, one which is not restricted to economics alone. Everyone is born to seek self-fulfilment, both personally and within society. This will be put at risk if a proper scale of values is not maintained, if there is no move from a less than human to a truly human condition of life.

Paras. 22-33: The world was intended by God to provide people with the necessities of life and tools for their progress. All rights are subordinated to that end, including the right to private property. The common good sometimes requires, for example, that improperly exploited land be expropriated or the transfer of funds be curtailed. Unbridled liberal capitalism is to be condemned. The present state of affairs, with all its injustices, must be overcome: continuing development calls for bold innovation. Public authorities, while avoiding the dangers of a planned economy, must lay down means and ends, and stimulate those involved in the common activity of economic progress.

Paras. 34-42: Economics and technology are pointless if they do not serve humanity. Economic growth is dependent on social progress, and lack of education is as serious as lack of food. The family is the first and most basic social structure in this task of development. Professional organizations and cultural institutions are also of assistance. The ultimate goal is the fulfilment of the whole person, and of every person. That is the true humanism which points towards God.

Paras. 43-60: There is a threefold obligation upon the wealthier nations: material aid, better trading relations with the developing world, universal charity. The need to build a better world calls for generosity, sacrifice and effort. The wealthier nations are called upon to set aside not only some of their own goods, but also some of their own experts in order to help the poorer ones: in doing so they will ultimately be serving their own interests. Could not part of military expenditure be used for the relief of poverty? Could not bilateral and multilateral agreements give way to world-wide collaboration which would avert the suspicion of some new form of colonialism? There must be dialogue between those who give aid and those who receive it, for when two parties are in very unequal positions mutual consent does not guarantee fair agreements.

Paras. 61-70: In order that international trade be more humane and moral, social justice requires that a certain equality of opportunity be restored to the participants. Nationalism and racism are also two obstacles to the establishment of a more just social order. World solidarity should allow all peoples to be the artisans of their own destinies, and international relationships should be marked by respect, friendship and co-operation. Travellers between nations, especially the young and emigrant workers, should be made welcome, businessmen travelling within the developing nations should exercise their power wisely.

Paras. 71-87: Technical experts are being sent to developing nations in increasing numbers, but though the expertise is essential, it must be accompanied by genuine love, and by sensitivity to the situation in which they find themselves. In this way solidarity endures after aid programmes have ended. People are growing anxious to establish closer ties, and international collaboration requires institutions to promote, co-ordinate and direct such ties. The pope appeals to all, recalling that progress and economic development are the only way to true peace. People in different walks of life have their own specific parts to play in this.

Venerable brothers and dearest sons and daughters, greetings and apostolic benediction.

The Church's concern for development

1. The progressive development of peoples is an object of deep interest and concern to the Church. This is particularly true in the case of those peoples who are trying to escape the ravages of hunger, poverty, endemic disease and ignorance; of those who are seeking a larger share in the benefits of civilization and a more active improvement of their human qualities; of those who are consciously striving for fuller growth. With an even clearer awareness, since the Second Vatican Council, of the demands imposed by Christ's gospel in this area, the Church judges it her duty to help all men explore this serious problem in all its dimensions, and to impress upon them the need for concerted action at this critical juncture.

2. Our recent predecessors did not fail to do their duty in this area. Their noteworthy messages shed the light of the gospel on contemporary social questions. There was Leo XIII's encyclical *Rerum Novarum,*[1] Pius XI's encyclical *Quadragesimo Anno,*[2] Pius XII's radio message to the world,[3] and John XXIII's two encyclicals, *Mater et Magistra*[4] and *Pacem in Terris.*[5]

3. Today it is most important for people to understand and appreciate that the social question ties all men together, in every part of the world. John XXIII stated this clearly,[6] and Vatican II confirmed it in its pastoral constitution on The Church in the World of Today.[7] The seriousness and urgency of these teachings must be recognized without delay. The hungry nations of the world cry out to the peoples blessed with abundance. And the Church, cut to the quick by this cry, asks each and every man to hear his brother's plea and answer it lovingly.

[223]

4. Before we became pope, we travelled to Latin America (1960) and Africa (1962). There we saw the perplexing problems that vex and besiege these continents, which are otherwise full of life and promise. On being elected pope, we became the father of all men. We made trips to Palestine and India, gaining first-hand knowledge of the difficulties that these age-old civilizations must face in their struggle for further development. Before the close of the Second Vatican Council, providential circumstances allowed us to address the United Nations and to plead the case of the impoverished nations before that distinguished assembly.

5. Even more recently, we sought to fulfil the wishes of the council and to demonstrate the Holy See's concern for the developing nations. To do this, we felt it was necessary to add another pontifical commission to the Church's central administration. The purpose of this commission is 'to awaken in the people of God full awareness of their mission today. In this way they can further the progress of poorer nations and international social justice, as well as help less developed nations to contribute to their own development.'[8] The name of this commission, Justice and Peace, aptly describes its programme and its goal. We are sure that all men of good will will want to join our fellow Catholics and fellow Christians in carrying out this programme. So today we earnestly urge all men to pool their ideas and their activities for man's complete development and the development of all mankind.

I

Problems facing developing countries

6. Today we see men trying to secure a sure food supply, cures for diseases, and steady employment. We see them trying to eliminate every ill, to remove every obstacle which offends man's dignity. They are continually striving to exercise greater personal responsibility; to do more, learn more, and have more so that they might increase their personal worth. And yet, at the same time, a large number of them live amid conditions which frustrate these legitimate desires. Moreover, those nations which have recently gained independence find that political freedom is not enough. They must also acquire the social and economic structures and processes that accord with man's nature and activity, if their citizens are to achieve personal growth and if their country is to take its rightful place in the international community.

7. Though insufficient for the immensity and urgency of the task, the means inherited from the past are not totally useless. It is true that colonizing nations were sometimes concerned with nothing save their own interests, their own power and their own prestige; their departure left the economy of these countries in precarious imbalance—the one-crop economy, for example, which is at the mercy of sudden, wide-ranging fluctuations in market prices. Certain types of colonialism surely caused harm and paved the way for further troubles. On the other hand, we must also reserve a word of praise for

those colonizers whose skills and technical know-how brought benefits to many untamed lands, and whose work survives to this day. The structural machinery they introduced was not fully developed or perfected, but it did help to reduce ignorance and disease, to promote communication, and to improve living conditions.

8. Granted all this, it is only too clear that these structures are no match for the harsh economic realities of today. Unless the existing machinery is modified, the disparity between rich and poor nations will increase rather than diminish; the rich nations are progressing with rapid strides while the poor nations move forward at a slow pace. The imbalance grows with each passing day: while some nations produce a food surplus, other nations are in desperate need of food or are unsure of their export market.

9. At the same time, social unrest has gradually spread throughout the world. The acute restlessness engulfing the poorer classes in countries that are now being industrialized has spread to other regions where agriculture is the mainstay of the economy. The farmer is painfully aware of his 'wretched lot'.[9] Then there are the flagrant inequalities not merely in the enjoyment of possessions, but even more in the exercise of power. In certain regions a privileged minority enjoys the refinements of life, while the rest of the inhabitants, impoverished and disunited, 'are deprived of almost all possibility of acting on their own initiative and responsibility, and often subsist in living and working conditions unworthy of the human person'.[10]

10. Moreover, traditional culture comes into conflict with the advanced techniques of modern industrialization; social structures out of tune with today's demands are threatened with extinction. For the older generation, the rigid structures of traditional culture are the necessary mainstay of one's personal and family life; they cannot be abandoned. The younger generation, on the other hand, regards them as useless obstacles, and rejects them to embrace new forms of societal life. The conflict between generations leads to a tragic dilemma: either to preserve traditional beliefs and structures and reject social progress; or to embrace foreign technology and foreign culture, and reject ancestral traditions with their wealth of humanism. The sad fact is that we often see the older moral, spiritual and religious values give way without finding any place in the new scheme of things.

11. In such troubled times some people are strongly tempted by the alluring but deceitful promises of would-be saviours. Who does not see the concomitant dangers: public upheavals, civil insurrection, the drift toward totalitarian ideologies? These are the realities of the question under study here, and their gravity must surely be apparent to everyone.

12. True to the teaching and example of her divine founder, who cited the preaching of the gospel to the poor as a sign of his mission,[11] the Church has never failed to foster the human progress of the nations to which she brings faith in Christ. Besides erecting sacred edifices, her missionaries have also promoted construction of hospitals, sanitoriums, schools and universities. By teaching the native population how to take full advantage of natural resources, the missionaries often protected them from the greed of foreigners.

We would certainly admit that this work was sometimes far from perfect, since it was the work of men. The missionaries sometimes intermingled the thought patterns and behaviour patterns of their native land with the authentic message of Christ. Yet, for all this, they did protect and promote indigenous institutions; and many of them pioneered in promoting the country's material and cultural progress. We need only mention the efforts of Père Charles de Foucauld: he compiled a valuable dictionary of the Tuareg language, and his charity won him the title, 'everyone's brother'. So we deem it fitting to praise those oft forgotten pioneers who were motivated by love for Christ, just as we honour their imitators and successors who today continue to put themselves at the generous and unselfish service of those to whom they preach the gospel.

13. In the present day, however, individual and group effort within these countries is no longer enough. The world situation requires the concerted effort of everyone, a thorough examination of every facet of the problem—social, economic, cultural and spiritual. The Church, which has long experience in human affairs and has no desire to be involved in the political activities of any nation, 'seeks but one goal: to carry forward the work of Christ under the lead of the befriending Spirit. And Christ entered this world to give witness to the truth; to save, not to judge; to serve, not to be served.'[12] Founded to build the kingdom of heaven on earth rather than to acquire temporal power, the Church openly avows that the two powers—Church and State—are distinct from one another; that each is supreme in its own sphere of competency.[13] But since the Church does dwell among men, she has the duty 'of scrutinizing the signs of the times and of interpreting them in the light of the gospel'.[14] Sharing the noblest aspirations of men and suffering when she sees these aspirations not satisfied, she wishes to help them attain their full realization. So she offers man her distinctive contribution: a global perspective on man and human realities.

Development of both individuals and communities

14. The development we speak of here cannot be restricted to economic growth alone. To be authentic, it must be well rounded; it must foster the development of each man and of the whole man. As an eminent specialist on this question has rightly said: 'We cannot allow economics to be separated from human realities, nor development from the civilization in which it takes place. What counts for us is man—each individual man, each human group, and humanity as a whole.'[15]

15. In God's plan, every man is born to seek self-fulfilment, for every human life is called to some task by God. At birth a human being possesses certain aptitudes and abilities in germinal form, and these qualities are to be cultivated so that they may bear fruit. By developing these traits through formal education of personal effort, the individual works his way towards the goal set for him by the creator. Endowed with intellect and free will, each man is responsible for his self-fulfilment even as he is for his salvation. He is helped, and sometimes hindered, by his teachers and those around him; yet whatever be the outside influences exerted on him, he is the chief architect of

his own success or failure. Utilizing only his talent and will-power, each man can grow in humanity, enhance his personal worth, and perfect himself.

16. Self-development, however, is not left up to man's option. Just as the whole of creation is ordered toward its creator, so too the rational creature should of his own accord direct his life to God, the first truth and the highest good. Thus human self-fulfilment may be said to sum up our obligations. Moreover, this harmonious integration of our human nature, carried through by personal effort and responsible activity, is destined for a higher state of perfection. United with the life-giving Christ, man's life is newly enhanced; it acquires a transcendent *humanism* which surpasses its nature and bestows new fullness of life. This is the highest goal of human self-fulfilment.

17. Each man is also a member of society; hence he belongs to the community of man. It is not just certain individuals but all men who are called to further the development of human society as a whole. Civilizations spring up, flourish and die. As the waves of the sea gradually creep farther and farther in along the shoreline, so the human race inches its way forward through history. We are the heirs of earlier generations, and we reap benefits from the efforts of our contemporaries; we are under obligation to all men. Therefore we cannot disregard the welfare of those who will come after us to increase the human family. The reality of human solidarity brings us not only benefits but also obligations.

18. Man's personal and collective fulfilment could be jeopardized if the proper scale of values were not maintained. The pursuit of life's necessities is quite legitimate; hence we are duty-bound to do the work which enables us to obtain them: 'If anyone is unwilling to work, do not let him eat.'[16] But the acquisition of worldly goods can lead men to greed, to the unrelenting desire for more, to the pursuit of greater personal power. Rich and poor alike—be they individuals, families or nations—can fall prey to avarice and soul-stifling *materialism.*

19. Neither individuals nor nations should regard the possession of more and more goods as the ultimate objective. Every kind of progress is a two-edged sword. It is necessary if man is to grow as a human being; yet it can also enslave him, if he comes to regard it as the supreme good and cannot look beyond it. When this happens, men harden their hearts, shut out others from their minds and gather together solely for reasons of self-interest rather than out of friendship; dissension and disunity follow soon after. Thus the exclusive pursuit of material possessions prevents man's growth as a human being and stands in opposition to his true grandeur. Avarice, in individuals and in nations, is the most obvious form of stultified moral development.

20. If development calls for an ever-growing number of technical experts, even more necessary still is the deep thought and reflection of wise men in search of a new *humanism,* one which will enable our contemporaries to enjoy the higher values of love and friendship, of prayer and contemplation,[17] and thus find themselves. This is what will guarantee man's authentic development—his transition from less than human conditions to truly human ones.

21. What are less than human conditions? The material poverty of those who lack the bare necessities of life, and the moral poverty of those who are crushed under the weight of their own self-love; oppressive political structures resulting from the abuse of ownership or the improper exercise of power, from the exploitation of the worker or unjust transactions. What are truly human conditions? The rise from poverty to the acquisition of life's necessities; the elimination of social ills; broadening the horizons of knowledge; acquiring refinement and culture. From there one can go on to acquire a growing awareness of other people's dignity, a taste for the spirit of poverty,[18] an active interest in the common good, and a desire for peace. Then man can acknowledge the highest values and God himself, their author and end. Finally and above all, there is faith—God's gift to men of good will—and our loving unity in Christ, who calls all men to share God's life as sons of the living God, the father of all men.

Obstacles to development

22. In the very first pages of scripture we read these words: 'Fill the earth and subdue it.'[19] This teaches us that the whole of creation is for man, that he has been charged to give it meaning by his intelligent activity, to complete and perfect it by his own efforts and to his own advantage. Now if the earth truly was created to provide man with the necessities of life and the tools for his own progress, it follows that every man has the right to glean what he needs from the earth. The recent council reiterated this truth: 'God intended the earth and everything in it for the use of all human beings and peoples. Thus, under the leadership of justice and in the company of charity, created goods should flow fairly to all.'[20] All other rights, whatever they may be, including the rights of property and free trade, are to be subordinated to this principle. They should in no way hinder it; in fact, they should actively facilitate its implementation. Redirecting these rights back to their original purpose must be regarded as an important and urgent social duty.

23. 'He who has the goods of this world and sees his brother in need and closes his heart to him, how does the love of God abide in him?'[21] Everyone knows that the fathers of the Church laid down the duty of the rich towards the poor in no uncertain terms. As St Ambrose put it:'You are not making a gift of what is yours to the poor man, but you are giving him back what is his. You have been appropriating things that are meant to be for the common use of everyone. The earth belongs to everyone, not to the rich.'[22] These words indicate that the right to private property is not absolute and unconditional. No one may appropriate surplus goods solely for his own private use when others lack the bare necessities of life. In short, 'as the fathers of the Church and other eminent theologians tell us, the right of private property may never be exercised to the detriment of the common good.' When 'private gain and basic community needs conflict with one another', it is for the public authorities 'to seek a solution to these questions, with the active involvement of individual citizens and social groups'.[23]

24. If certain landed estates impede the general prosperity because they are extensive, unused or poorly used, or because they bring hardship to peoples

or are detrimental to the interests of the country, the common good sometimes demands their expropriation. Vatican II affirms this emphatically.[24] At the same time it clearly teaches that income thus derived is not for man's capricious use, and that the exclusive pursuit of personal gain is prohibited. Consequently, it is not permissible for citizens who have garnered sizeable income from the resources and activities of their own nation to deposit a large portion of their income in foreign countries for the sake of their own private gain alone, taking no account of their country's interests; in doing this, they clearly wrong their country.[25]

25. The introduction of industrialization, which is necessary for economic growth and human progress, is both a sign of development and a spur to it. By dint of intelligent thought and hard work, man gradually uncovers the hidden laws of nature and learns to make better use of natural resources. As he takes control over his way of life, he is stimulated to undertake new investigations and fresh discoveries, to take prudent risks and launch new ventures, to act responsibly and give of himself unselfishly.

26. However, certain concepts have somehow arisen out of these new conditions and insinuated themselves into the fabric of human society. These concepts present profit as the chief spur to economic progress, free competition as the guiding norm of economics, and private ownership of the means of production as an absolute right, having no limits nor concomitant social obligations. This unbridled liberalism paves the way for a particular type of tyranny, rightly condemned by our predecessor Pius XI, for it results in the 'international imperialism of money'.[26] Such improper manipulations of economic forces can never be condemned enough; let it be said once again that economics is supposed to be in the service of man.[27] But if it is true that a type of *capitalism*, as it is commonly called, has given rise to hardships, unjust practices, and fratricidal conflicts that persist to this day, it would be a mistake to attribute these evils to the rise of industrialization itself, for they really derive from the pernicious economic concepts that grew up along with it. We must in all fairness acknowledge the vital role played by labour systemization and industrial organization in the task of development.

27. The concept of work can turn into an exaggerated mystique. Yet, for all that, it is something willed and approved by God. Fashioned in the image of his creator, 'man must co-operate with him in completing the work of creation and engraving on the earth the spiritual imprint which he himself has received.'[28] God gave man intelligence, sensitivity and the power of thought—tools with which to finish and perfect the work he began. Every worker is, to some extent, a creator—be he artist, craftsman, executive, labourer or farmer. Bent over a material that resists his efforts, the worker leaves his imprint on it, at the same time developing his own powers of persistence, inventiveness and concentration. Further, when work is done in common—when hope, hardship, ambition and joy are shared—it brings together and firmly unites the wills, minds and hearts of men. In its accomplishment, men find themselves to be brothers.[29]

28. Work, too, has a double edge. Since it promises money, pleasure and power, it stirs up selfishness in some and incites others to revolt. On the other

hand, it also fosters a professional outlook, a sense of duty, and love of neighbour. Even though it is now being organized more scientifically and efficiently, it still can threaten man's dignity and enslave him; for work is human only if it results from man's use of intellect and free will. Our predecessor John XXIII stressed the urgent need to restore dignity to the worker and make him a real partner in the common task: 'Every effort must be made to ensure that the enterprise is indeed a true human community, concerned about the needs, the activities and the standing of each of its members.'[30] Considered from a Christian point of view, work has an even loftier connotation. It is directed to the establishment of a supernatural order here on earth,[31] a task that will not be completed until we all unite to form that perfect manhood of which St Paul speaks, 'the mature measure of the fullness of Christ'.[32]

29. We must make haste. Too many people are suffering. While some make progress, others stand still or move backwards; and the gap between them is widening. However, the work must proceed in measured steps if the proper equilibrium is to be maintained. Makeshift agrarian reforms may fall short of their goal. Hasty industrialization can undermine vital institutions and produce social evils, causing a setback to true human values.

30. The injustice of certain situations cries out for God's attention. Lacking the bare necessities of life, whole nations are under the thumb of others; they cannot act on their own initiative; they cannot exercise personal responsibility; they cannot work towards a higher degree of cultural refinement or a greater participation in social and public life. They are sorely tempted to redress these insults to their human nature by violent means.

31. Everyone knows, however, that revolutionary uprisings—except where there is manifest, long-standing tyranny which would do great damage to fundamental personal rights and dangerous harm to the common good of the country—engender new injustices, introduce new inequities and bring new disasters. The evil situation that exists, and it surely is evil, may not be dealt with in such a way that an even worse situation results.

32. We want to be clearly understood on this point: the present state of affairs must be confronted boldly, and its concomitant injustices must be challenged and overcome. Continuing development calls for bold innovations that will work profound changes. The critical state of affairs must be corrected for the better without delay. Everyone must lend a ready hand to this task, particularly those who can do most by reason of their education, their office, or their authority. They should set a good example by contributing part of their own goods, as several of our brother bishops have done.[33] In this way they will be responsive to men's longings and faithful to the Holy Spirit, because 'the ferment of the gospel, too, has aroused and continues to arouse in man's heart the irresistible requirements of his dignity.'[34]

33. Individual initiative alone and the interplay of competition will not ensure satisfactory development. We cannot proceed to increase the wealth and power of the rich while we entrench the needy in their poverty and add to the woes of the oppressed. Organized programmes are necessary for 'directing,

stimulating, co-ordinating, supplying and integrating'[35] the work of individuals and intermediary organizations. It is for the public authorities to establish and lay down the desired goals, the plans to be followed, and the methods to be used in fulfilling them; and it is also their task to stimulate the efforts of those involved in this common activity. But they must also see to it that private initiative and intermediary organizations are involved in this work. In this way they will avoid total collectivization and the dangers of a planned economy which might threaten human liberty and obstruct the exercise of man's basic human rights.

The need to organize

34. Organized programmes designed to increase productivity should have but one aim: to serve human nature. They should reduce inequities, eliminate discrimination, free men from the bonds of servitude, and thus give them the capacity, in the sphere of temporal realities, to improve their lot, to further their moral growth and to develop their spiritual endowments. When we speak of development, we should mean social progress as well as economic growth. It is not enough to increase the general fund of wealth and then distribute it more fairly. It is not enough to develop technology so that the earth may become a more suitable living place for human beings. The mistakes of those who led the way should help those now on the road to development to avoid certain dangers. The reign of technology—*technocracy*, as it is called—can cause as much harm to the world of tomorrow as *liberalism* did to the world of yesteryear. Economics and technology are meaningless if they do not benefit man, for it is he they are to serve. Man is truly human only if he is the master of his own actions and the judge of their worth, only if he is the architect of his own progress. He must act according to his God-given nature, freely accepting its potentials and its claims upon him.

35. We can even say that economic growth is dependent on social progress, the goal to which it aspires; and that basic education is the first objective for any nation seeking to develop itself. Lack of education is as serious as lack of food; the illiterate is a starved spirit. When someone learns how to read and write, he is equipped to do a job and to shoulder a profession, to develop self-confidence and realize that he can progress along with others. As we said in our message to the UNESCO meeting at Tehran, literacy is the 'first and most basic tool for personal enrichment and social integration; and it is society's most valuable tool for furthering development and economic progress.'[36] We also rejoice at the good work accomplished in this field by private initiative, by the public authorities, and by international organizations. These are the primary agents of development, because they enable man to act for himself.

36. Man is not really himself, however, except within the framework of society and there the family plays the basic and most important role. The family's influence may have been excessive at some periods of history and in some places, to the extent that it was exercised to the detriment of the fundamental rights of the individual. Yet time-honoured social frameworks,

proper to the developing nations, are still necessary for a while, even as their excessive strictures are gradually relaxed. The natural family, stable and monogamous—as fashioned by God[37] and sanctified by Christianity—'in which different generations live together, helping each other to acquire greater wisdom and to harmonize personal rights with other social needs, is the basis of society'.[38]

37. There is no denying that the accelerated rate of population growth brings many added difficulties to the problems of development where the size of the population grows more rapidly than the quantity of available resources to such a degree that things seem to have reached an impasse. In such circumstances people are inclined to apply drastic remedies to reduce the birth rate. There is no doubt that public authorities can intervene in this matter, within the bounds of their competence. They can instruct citizens on this subject and adopt appropriate measures, so long as these are in conformity with the dictates of the moral law and the rightful freedom of married couples is preserved completely intact. When the inalienable right of marriage and of procreation is taken away, so is human dignity. Finally, it is for parents to take a thorough look at the matter and decide upon the number of their children. This is an obligation they take upon themselves, before their children already born, and before the community to which they belong—following the dictates of their own consciences informed by God's law authentically interpreted, and bolstered by their trust in him.[39]

38. In the task of development man finds the family to be the first and most basic social structure; but he is often helped by professional organizations. While such organizations are founded to aid and assist their members, they bear a heavy responsibility for the task of education which they can and must carry out. In training and developing individual men, they do much to cultivate in them an awareness of the common good and of its demands upon all.

39. Every form of social action involves some doctrine; and the Christian rejects that which is based on a *materialistic* and *atheistic* philosophy, namely one which shows no respect for a religious outlook on life, for freedom or human dignity. So long as these higher values are preserved intact, however, the existence of a variety of professional organizations and trade unions is permissible. Variety may even help to preserve freedom and create friendly rivalry. We gladly commend those people who unselfishly serve their brothers by working in such organizations.

40. Cultural institutions also do a great deal to further the work of development. Their important role was stressed by the council: '...the future of the world stands in peril unless wiser men are forthcoming. It should also be pointed out that many nations, poorer in economic goods, are quite rich in wisdom and can offer noteworthy advantages to others.'[40] Every country, rich or poor, has a cultural tradition handed down from past generations. This tradition includes institutions required by life in the world, and higher manifestations—artistic, intellectual and religious—of the life of the spirit. When the latter embody truly human values, it would be a great mistake to sacrifice them for the sake of the former. Any group of people who would

consent to let this happen, would be giving up the better portion of their heritage; in order to live, they would be giving up their reason for living. Christ's question is directed to nations also: 'What does it profit a man, if he gain the whole world but suffer the loss of his own soul?'[41]

41. The poorer nations can never be too much on guard against the temptation posed by the wealthier nations. For these nations, with their favourable results from a highly technical and culturally developed civilization, provide an example of work and diligence with temporal prosperity the main pursuit. Not that temporal prosperity of itself precludes the activity of the human spirit. Indeed, with it, 'the human spirit, being less subjected to material things, can be more easily drawn to the worship and contemplation of the creator.'[42] On the other hand, 'modern civilization itself often complicates the approach to God, not for any essential reason, but because it is so much engrossed in worldly affairs.'[43] The developing nations must choose wisely from among the things that are offered to them. They must test and reject false values that would tarnish a truly human way of life, while accepting noble and useful values in order to develop them in their own distinctive way, along with their own indigenous heritage.

42. The ultimate goal is a full-bodied humanism.[44] And does this not mean the fulfilment of the whole man and of every man? A narrow humanism, closed in on itself and not open to the values of the spirit and to God who is their source, could achieve apparent success, for man can set about organizing terrestrial realities without God. But 'closed off from God, they will end up being directed against man. A humanism closed off from other realities becomes inhuman.'[45] True humanism points the way towards God and acknowledges the task to which we are called, the task which offers us the real meaning of human life. Man is not the ultimate measure of man. Man becomes truly man only by passing beyond himself. In the words of Pascal: 'Man infinitely surpasses man.'[46]

II

Obligations upon the wealthy

43. Development of the individual necessarily entails a joint effort for the development of the human race as a whole. At Bombay we said: 'Man must meet man, nation must meet nation, as brothers and sisters, as children of God. In this mutual understanding and friendship, in this sacred communion, we must also begin to work together to build the common future of the human race.'[47] We also urge men to explore concrete and practicable ways of organizing and co-ordinating their efforts, so that available resources might be shared with others; in this way genuine bonds between nations might be forged.

44. This duty concerns first and foremost the wealthier nations. Their obligations stem from the human and supernatural brotherhood of man, and present a threefold obligation: (1) mutual solidarity—the aid that the richer nations must give to developing nations; (2) social justice—the rectification

of trade relations between strong and weak nations; (3) universal charity—the effort to build a more humane world community, where all can give and receive, and where the progress of some is not bought at the expense of others. The matter is urgent, for on it depends the future of world civilization.

45. 'If a brother or a sister be naked and in want of daily food,' says St James, 'and one of you say to them, "Go in peace, be warm and filled," yet you do not give them what is necessary for the body, what does it profit?'[48] Today no one can be unaware of the fact that on some continents countless men and women are ravished by hunger and countless children are undernourished. Many children die at an early age; many more of them find their physical and mental growth retarded. Thus whole populations are immersed in pitiable circumstances and lose heart.

46. Anxious appeals for help have already been voiced. That of our predecessor John XXIII was warmly received.[49] We reiterated his sentiments in our Christmas message of 1963,[50] and again in 1966 on behalf of India.[51] The work of the Food and Agriculture Organization of the United Nations (FAO) has been encouraged by the Holy See and has found generous support. Our own organization, *Caritas Internationalis*, is at work all over the world. Many Catholics, at the urging of our brother bishops, have contributed unstintingly to the assistance of the needy and have gradually widened the circle of those they call neighbours.

47. But these efforts, as well as public and private allocations of gifts, loans and investments, are not enough. It is not just a question of eliminating hunger and reducing poverty. It is not just a question of fighting wretched conditions, though this is an urgent and necessary task. It involves building a human community where men can live truly human lives, free from discrimination on account of race, religion or nationality, free from servitude to other men or to natural forces which they cannot yet control satisfactorily. It involves building a human community where liberty is not an idle word, where the needy Lazarus can sit down with the rich man at the same banquet table.[52] On the part of the rich man, it calls for great generosity, willing sacrifice and diligent effort. Each man must examine his conscience, which sounds a new call in our present times. Is he prepared to support, at his own expense, projects and undertakings designed to help the needy? Is he prepared to pay higher taxes so that public authorities may expand their efforts in the work of development? Is he prepared to pay more for imported goods, so that the foreign producer may make a fairer profit? Is he prepared to emigrate from his homeland if necessary and if he is young, in order to help the emerging nations?

48. The duty of promoting human solidarity also falls upon the shoulders of nations: 'It is a very important duty of the advanced nations to help the developing nations...'[53] This conciliar teaching must be implemented. While it is proper that a nation be the first to enjoy the God-given fruits of its own labour, no nation may dare to hoard its riches for its own use alone. Each and every nation must produce more and better goods and products, so that all its citizens may live truly human lives and so that it may contribute to the

common development of the human race. Considering the mounting indigence of less developed countries, it is only fitting that a prosperous nation set aside some of the goods it has produced in order to alleviate their needs; and that it train educators, engineers, technicians and scholars who will contribute their knowledge and their skill to these less fortunate countries.

49. We must repeat that the superfluous goods of wealthier nations ought to be placed at the disposal of poorer nations. The rule, by virtue of which in times past those nearest us were to be helped in time of need, applies today to all the needy throughout the world. And the prospering peoples will be the first to benefit from this. Continuing avarice on their part will arouse the judgement of God and the wrath of the poor, with consequences no one can foresee. If prosperous nations continue to be jealous of their own advantage alone, they will jeopardize their highest values, sacrificing the pursuit of excellence to the acquisition of possessions. We might well apply to them the parable of the rich man. His fields yielded an abundant harvest and he did not know where to store it: 'But God said to him, "Fool, this very night your soul will be demanded from you..."'[54]

50. If these efforts are to be successful, they cannot be disparate and disorganized; nor should they vie with one another for the sake of power or prestige. The times call for co-ordinated planning of projects and programmes, which are much more effective than occasional efforts promoted by individual good will. As we said above, studies must be made, goals must be defined, methods and means must be chosen, and the work of select men must be co-ordinated; only then will present needs be met and future demands anticipated. Moreover, such planned programmes do more than promote economic and social progress. They give force and meaning to the work undertaken, put due order into human life, and thus enhance man's dignity and his capabilities.

51. A further step must be taken. When we were at Bombay for the Eucharistic Congress, we asked world leaders to set aside part of their military expenditures for a world fund to relieve the needs of impoverished peoples.[55] What is true for the immediate war against poverty is also true for the work of national development. Only a concerted effort on the part of all nations, embodied in and carried out by this world fund, will stop these senseless rivalries and promote fruitful, friendly dialogue between nations.

52. It is certainly all right to maintain bilateral and multilateral agreements. Through such agreements, ties of dependence and feelings of jealousy—holdovers from the era of colonialism—give way to friendly relationships of true solidarity that are based on juridical and political equality. But such agreements would be free of all suspicion if they were integrated into an overall policy of world-wide collaboration. The member nations, who benefit from these agreements, would have less reason for fear or mistrust. They would not have to worry that financial or technical assistance was being used as a cover for some new form of colonialism that would threaten their civil liberty, exert economic pressure on them, or create a new power group with controlling influence.

53. Is it not plain to everyone that such a fund would reduce the need for those other expenditures that are motivated by fear and stubborn pride? Countless millions are starving, countless families are destitute, countless men are steeped in ignorance; countless people need schools, hospitals, and homes worthy of the name. In such circumstances, we cannot tolerate public and private expenditures of a wasteful nature; we cannot but condemn lavish displays of wealth by nations or individuals; we cannot approve a debilitating arms race. It is our solemn duty to speak out against them. If only world leaders would listen to us, before it is too late!

Collaboration among the nations

54. All nations must initiate the dialogue which we called for in our first encyclical, *Ecclesiam Suam*.[56] A dialogue between those who contribute aid and those who receive it will permit a well-balanced assessment of the support to be provided, taking into consideration not only the generosity and the available wealth of the donor nations, but also the real needs of the receiving countries and the use to which the financial assistance can be put. Developing countries will thus no longer risk being overwhelmed by debts whose repayment swallows up the greater part of their gains. Rates of interest and time for repayment of the loan could be so arranged as not to be too great a burden on either party, taking into account free gifts, interest-free or low-interest loans, and the time needed for liquidating the debts. The donors could certainly ask for assurances as to how the money will be used. It should be used for some mutually acceptable purpose and with reasonable hope of success, for there is no question of backing idlers and parasites. On the other hand, the recipients would certainly have the right to demand that no one interfere in the internal affairs of their government or disrupt their social order. As sovereign nations, they are entitled to manage their own affairs, to fashion their own policies, and to choose their own form of government. In other words, what is needed is mutual co-operation among nations, freely undertaken, where each enjoys equal dignity and can help to shape a world community truly worthy of man.

55. This task might seem impossible in those regions where the daily struggle for subsistence absorbs the attention of the family, where people are at a loss to find work that might improve their lot during their remaining days on earth. These people must be given every possible help; they must be encouraged to take steps for their own betterment and to seek out the means that will enable them to do so. This common task undoubtedly calls for concerted, continuing and courageous effort. But let there be no doubt about it, it is an urgent task. The very life of needy nations, civil peace in the developing countries, and world peace itself are at stake.

56. Efforts are being made to help the developing nations financially and technologically. Some of these efforts are considerable. Yet all these efforts will prove to be vain and useless, if their results are nullified to a large extent by the unstable trade relations between rich and poor nations. The latter will have no grounds for hope or trust if they fear that what is being given them with one hand is being taken away with the other.

57. Highly industrialized nations export their own manufactured products, for the most part. Less developed nations, on the other hand, have nothing to sell but raw materials and agricultural crops. As a result of technical progress, the price of manufactured products is rising rapidly and they find a ready market. But the basic crops and raw materials produced by the less developed countries are subject to sudden and wide-ranging shifts in market price; they do not share in the growing market value of industrial products.

This poses serious difficulties for the developing nations. They depend on exports to a large extent for a balanced economy and for further steps toward development. Thus the needy nations grow more destitute, while the rich nations become even richer.

58. It is evident that the principle of free trade, by itself, is no longer adequate for regulating international agreements. It certainly can work when both parties are about equal economically; in such cases it stimulates progress and rewards effort. That is why industrially developed nations see an element of justice in this principle. But the case is quite different when the nations involved are far from equal. Market prices that are *freely* agreed upon can turn out to be most unfair. It must be avowed openly that, in this case, the fundamental tenet of *liberalism* (as it is called), as the norm for market dealings, is open to serious question.

59. The teaching set forth by our predecessor Leo XIII in *Rerum Novarum* is still valid today: when two parties are in very unequal positions, their mutual consent alone does not guarantee a fair contract; the rule of free consent remains subservient to the demands of the natural law.[57] In *Rerum Novarum* this principle was set down with regard to a just wage for the individual worker; but it should be applied with equal force to contracts made between nations: trade relations can no longer be based solely on the principle of free, unchecked competition, for it very often creates an economic dictatorship. Free trade can be called just only when it conforms to the demands of social justice.

60. As a matter of fact, the highly developed nations have already come to realize this. At times they take appropriate measures to restore balance to their own economy, a balance which is frequently upset by competition when left to itself. Thus it happens that these nations often support their agriculture at the price of sacrifices imposed on economically more favoured sectors. Similarly, to maintain the commercial relations which are developing among themselves, especially within a common market, the financial, fiscal and social policy of these nations tries to restore comparable opportunities to competing industries which are not equally prospering.

Overcoming the sickness of society

61. Now in this matter one standard should hold true for all. What applies to national economies and to highly developed nations must also apply to trade relations between rich and poor nations. Indeed, competition should not be eliminated from trade transactions; but it must be kept within limits so that it

operates justly and fairly, and thus becomes a truly human endeavour. Now in trade relations between the developing and the highly developed economies there is a great disparity in their overall situation and in their freedom of action. In order that international trade be human and moral, social justice requires that it restore to the participants a certain equality of opportunity. To be sure, this equality will not be attained at once, but we must begin to work towards it now by injecting a certain amount of equality into discussions and price talks. Here again international agreements on a broad scale can help a great deal. They could establish general norms for regulating prices, promoting production facilities, and favouring certain infant industries. Isn't it plain to everyone that such attempts to establish greater justice in international trade would be of great benefit to the developing nations, and that they would produce lasting results?

62. There are other obstacles to creation of a more just social order and to the development of world solidarity: nationalism and racism. It is quite natural that nations recently arrived at political independence should be quite jealous of their new-found but fragile unity and make every effort to preserve it. It is also quite natural for nations with a long-standing cultural tradition to be proud of their traditional heritage. But this commendable attitude should be further ennobled by love, a love for the whole family of man. Haughty pride in one's own nation disunites nations and poses obstacles to their true welfare. It is especially harmful where the weak state of the economy calls for a pooling of information, efforts and financial resources to implement programmes of development and to increase commercial and cultural interchange.

63. Racism is not the exclusive attribute of young nations, where sometimes it hides beneath the rivalries of clans and political parties, with heavy losses for justice and at the risk of civil war. During the colonial period it often flared up between the colonists and the indigenous population, and stood in the way of mutually profitable understanding, often giving rise to bitterness in the wake of genuine injustices. It is still an obstacle to collaboration among disadvantaged nations and a cause of division and hatred within countries whenever individuals and families see the inviolable rights of the human person held in scorn, as they themselves are unjustly subjected to a regime of discrimination because of their race or their colour.

64. This state of affairs, which bodes ill for the future, causes us great distress and anguish. But we cherish this hope: that distrust and selfishness among nations will eventually be overcome by a stronger desire for mutual collaboration and a heightened sense of solidarity. We hope that the developing nations will take advantage of their geographical proximity to one another to organize on a broader territorial base and to pool their efforts for the development of a given region. We hope that they will draw up joint programmes, co-ordinate investment funds wisely, divide production quotas fairly, and exercise management over the marketing of these products. We also hope that multilateral and broad international associations will undertake the necessary work of organization to find ways of helping needy nations, so that these nations may escape from the fetters now binding them;

so that they themselves may discover the road to cultural and social progress, while remaining faithful to the native genius of their land.

65. That is the goal toward which we must work. An ever more effective world solidarity should allow all peoples to become the artisans of their destiny. Up to now relations between nations have too often been governed by force; indeed, that is the hallmark of past history. May the day come when international relationships will be characterized by respect and friendship, when mutual co-operation will be the hallmark of collaborative efforts, and when concerted effort for the betterment of all nations will be regarded as a duty by every nation. The developing nations now emerging are asking that they be allowed to take part in the construction of a better world, a world which would provide better protection for every man's rights and duties. It is certainly a legitimate demand, so everyone must heed and fulfil it.

66. Human society is sorely ill. The cause is not so much the depletion of natural resources, nor their monopolistic control by a privileged few; it is rather the weakening of brotherly ties between individuals and nations.

67. We cannot insist too much on the duty of giving foreigners a hospitable reception. It is a duty imposed by human solidarity and by Christian charity, and it is incumbent upon families and educational institutions in the host nations. Young people, in particular, must be given a warm reception; more and more families and hostels must open their doors to them. This must be done, first of all, that they may be shielded from feelings of loneliness, distress and despair that would sap their strength. It is also necessary so that they may be guarded against the corrupting influence of their new surroundings, where the contrast between the dire poverty of their homeland and the lavish luxury of their present surroundings is, as it were, forced upon them. And finally, it must be done so that they may be protected from subversive notions and temptations to violence, which gain headway in their minds when they ponder their 'wretched plight'.[58] In short, they should be welcomed in the spirit of brotherly love, so that the concrete example of wholesome living may give them a high opinion of authentic Christian charity and of spiritual values.

68. We are deeply distressed by what happens to many of these young people. They come to wealthier nations to acquire scientific knowledge, professional training, and a high-quality education that will enable them to serve their own land with greater effectiveness. They do get a fine education, but very often they lose their respect for the priceless cultural heritage of their native land.

69. Emigrant workers should also be given a warm welcome. Their living conditions are often inhuman, and they must scrimp on their earnings in order to send help to their families who have remained behind in their native land in poverty.

70. We would also say a word to those who travel to newly industrialized nations for business purposes: industrialists, merchants, managers and representatives of large business concerns. It often happens that in their own land they do not lack a social sense. Why is it, then, that they give in to baser motives of self-interest when they set out to do business in the developing

countries? Their more favoured position should rather spur them on to be initiators of social progress and human betterment in these lands. Their organizational experience should help them to figure out ways to make intelligent use of the labour of the indigenous population, to develop skilled workers, to train engineers and other management men, to foster these people's initiative and prepare them for offices of ever greater responsibility. In this way they will prepare these people to take over the burden of management in the near future. In the meantime, justice must prevail in dealings between superiors and their subordinates. Legitimate contracts should govern these employment relations, spelling out the duties involved. And no one, whatever his status may be, should be unjustly subjected to the arbitrary whim of another.

The commitment of individuals

71. We certainly rejoice over the fact that an ever increasing number of experts are being sent on development missions by private groups, bilateral associations and international organizations. These specialists must not 'act as overlords, but as helpers and fellow workers'.[59] The people of a country soon discover whether their new helpers are motivated by good will or not, whether they want to enhance human dignity or merely try out their special techniques. The expert's message will surely be rejected by these people if it is not inspired by brotherly love.

72. Technical expertise is necessary, but it must be accompanied by concrete signs of genuine love. Untainted by overbearing nationalistic pride or any trace of racial discrimination, experts should learn how to work in collaboration with everyone. They must realize that their expert knowledge does not give them superiority in every sphere of life. The culture which shaped their living habits does contain certain universal human elements; but it cannot be regarded as the only culture, nor can it regard other cultures with haughty disdain. If it is introduced into foreign lands, it must undergo adaptation. Thus those who undertake such work must realize they are guests in a foreign land; they must see to it that they studiously observe its historical traditions, its rich culture, and its peculiar genius. A rapprochement between cultures will thus take place, bringing benefits to both sides.

73. Sincere dialogue between cultures, as between individuals, paves the way for ties of brotherhood. Plans proposed for man's betterment will unite all nations in the joint effort to be undertaken, if every citizen—be he a government leader, a public official, or a simple workman—is motivated by brotherly love and is truly anxious to build one universal human civilization that spans the globe. Then we shall see the start of a dialogue on man rather than on the products of the soil or of technology. This dialogue will be fruitful if it shows the participants how to make economic progress and how to achieve spiritual growth as well; if the technicians take the role of teachers and educators; if the training provided is characterized by a concern for spiritual and moral values, so that it ensures human betterment as well as economic growth. Then the bonds of solidarity will endure, even when the aid programmes are past and gone. Is it not plain to all that closer ties of this sort

will contribute immeasurably to the preservation of world peace?

74. We are fully aware of the fact that many young people have already responded wholeheartedly to the invitation of our predecessor Pius XII, summoning the laity to take part in missionary work.[60] We also know that other young people have offered their services to public and private organizations that seek to aid developing nations. We are delighted to learn that in some nations their requirement of *military duty* can be fulfilled, in part at least, by *social service* or, simply, *service*. We commend such undertakings and the men of good will who take part in them. Would that all those who profess to be followers of Christ might heed his plea: 'I was hungry and you gave me to eat; I was thirsty and you gave me to drink; I was a stranger and you took me in; naked and you covered me; sick and you visited me; I was in prison and you came to me.'[61] No one is permitted to disregard the plight of his brothers living in dire poverty, enmeshed in ignorance and tormented by insecurity. The Christian, moved by this sad state of affairs, should echo the words of Christ: 'I have compassion on the crowd.'[62]

75. Let everyone implore God the Father Almighty that the human race, which is certainly aware of these evils, will bend every effort of mind and spirit to their eradication. To this prayer should be added the resolute commitment of every individual. Each should do as much as he can, as best he can, to counteract the slow pace of progress in some nations. And it is to be hoped that individuals, social organizations and nations will join hands in brotherly fashion—the strong aiding the weak—all contributing their knowledge, their enthusiasm and their love to the task, without thinking of their own convenience. It is the person who is motivated by genuine love, more than anyone else, who pits his intelligence against the problems of poverty, trying to uncover the causes and looking for effective ways of combatting and overcoming them. As a promoter of peace, 'he goes on his way, holding aloft the torch of joy and shedding light and grace on the hearts of men all over the world; he helps them to cross the barriers of geographical frontiers, to acknowledge every man as a friend and brother.'[63]

Support for international organizations

76. Extreme disparity between nations in economic, social and educational levels provokes jealousy and discord, often putting peace in jeopardy. As we told the council fathers on our return from the United Nations: 'We have to devote our attention to the situation of those nations still striving to advance. What we mean, to put it in clearer words, is that our charity toward the poor, of whom there are countless numbers in the world, has to become more solicitous, more effective, more generous.'[64] When we fight poverty and oppose the unfair conditions of the present, we are not just promoting human well-being; we are also furthering man's spiritual and moral development, and hence we are benefiting the whole human race. For peace is not simply the absence of warfare, based on a precarious balance of power; it is fashioned by efforts directed day after day towards the establishment of the ordered universe willed by God, with a more perfect form of justice among men.[65]

77. Nations are the architects of their own development, and they must bear the burden of this work; but they cannot accomplish it if they live in isolation from others. Regional mutual aid agreements among the poorer nations, broader-based programmes of support for these nations, major alliances between nations to co-ordinate these activities—these are the road signs that point the way to national development and world peace.

78. Such international collaboration among the nations of the world certainly calls for institutions that will promote, co-ordinate and direct it, until a new juridical order is firmly established and fully ratified. We give willing and wholehearted support to those public organizations that have already joined in promoting the development of nations, and we ardently hope that they will enjoy ever growing authority. As we told the United Nations General Assembly in New York: 'Your vocation is to bring not just some peoples but all peoples together as brothers....Who can fail to see the need and importance of thus gradually coming to the establishment of a world authority capable of taking effective action on the juridical and political planes?'[66]

79. Some would regard these hopes as vain flights of fancy. It may be that these people are not realistic enough, and that they have not noticed that the world is moving rapidly in a certain direction. Men are growing more anxious to establish closer ties of brotherhood; despite their ignorance, their mistakes, their offences, and even their lapses into barbarism and their wanderings from the path of salvation, they are slowly making their way to the creator, even without adverting to it. This struggle towards a more human way of life certainly calls for hard work and imposes difficult sacrifices. But even adversity, when endured for the sake of one's brothers and out of love for them, can contribute greatly to human progress. The Christian knows full well that when he unites himself with the expiatory sacrifice of the divine saviour, he helps greatly to build up the body of Christ,[67] to assemble the people of God into the fullness of Christ.

80. We must travel this road together, united in minds and hearts. Hence we feel it necessary to remind everyone of the seriousness of this issue in all its dimensions, and to impress upon them the need for action. The moment for action has reached a critical juncture. Can countless innocent children be saved? Can countless destitute families obtain more human living conditions? Can world peace and human civilization be preserved intact? Every individual and every nation must face up to this issue, for it is their problem.

A universal appeal

81. We appeal, first of all, to our sons. In the developing nations and in other countries lay people must consider it their task to improve the temporal order. While the hierarchy has the role of teaching and authoritatively interpreting the moral laws and precepts that apply in this matter, the laity have the duty of using their own initiative and taking action in this area—without waiting passively for directives and precepts from others. They must try to infuse a Christian spirit into people's mental outlook and daily

behaviour, into the laws and structures of the civil community.[68] Changes must be made; present conditions must be improved. And the transformations must be permeated with the spirit of the gospel. We especially urge Catholic men living in developed nations to offer their skills and earnest assistance to public and private organizations, both civil and religious, working to solve the problems of developing nations. They will surely want to be in the first ranks of those who spare no effort to have just and fair laws, based on moral precepts, established among all nations.

82. All our Christian brothers, we are sure, will want to consolidate and expand their collaborative efforts to reduce man's immoderate self-love and haughty pride, to eliminate quarrels and rivalries, and to repress demagoguery and injustice—so that a more human way of living is opened to all, with each man helping others out of brotherly love. Furthermore, we still remember with deep affection the dialogue we had with various non-Christian individuals and communities in Bombay. So once again we ask these brothers of ours to do all in their power to promote living conditions truly worthy of the children of God.

83. Finally, we look to all men of good will, reminding them that civil progress and economic development are the only road to peace. Delegates to international organizations, public officials, gentlemen of the press, teachers and educators—all of you must realize that you have your part to play in the construction of a new world order. We ask God to enlighten and strengthen you all, so that you may persuade all men to turn their attention to these grave questions and prompt nations to work towards their solution. Educators, you should resolve to inspire young people with a love for the needy nations. Gentlemen of the press, your job is to place before our eyes the initiatives that are being taken to promote mutual aid, and the tragic spectacle of misery and poverty that people tend to ignore in order to salve their consciences. Thus at least the wealthy will know that the poor stand outside their doors waiting to receive some left-overs from their banquets.

84. Government leaders, your task is to draw your communities into closer ties of solidarity with all men, and to convince them that they must accept the necessary taxes on their luxuries and their wasteful expenditures in order to promote the development of nations and the preservation of peace. Delegates to international organizations, it is largely your task to see to it that senseless arms races and dangerous power plays give way to mutual collaboration between nations, a collaboration that is friendly, peace-oriented, and divested of self-interest, a collaboration that contributes greatly to the common development of mankind and allows the individual to find fulfilment.

85. It must be admitted that men very often find themselves in a sad state because they do not give enough thought and consideration to these things. So we call upon men of deep thought and wisdom—Catholics and Christians, believers in God and devotees of truth and justice, all men of good will—to take as their own Christ's injunction, 'Seek and you shall find,'[69] Blaze the trails to mutual co-operation among men, to deeper knowledge and more widespread charity, to a way of life marked by true brotherhood, to a human society based on mutual harmony.

86. Finally, a word to those of you who have heard the cries of needy nations and have come to their aid. We consider you the promoters and apostles of genuine progress and true development. Genuine progress does not consist in wealth sought for personal comfort or for its own sake; rather it consists in an economic order designed for the welfare of the human person, where the daily bread that each man receives reflects the glow of brotherly love and the helping hand of God.

87. We bless you with all our heart, and we call upon all men of good will to join forces with you as a band of brothers. Knowing, as we all do, that development means peace these days, what man would not want to work for it with every ounce of his strength? No one, of course. So we beseech all of you to respond wholeheartedly to our urgent plea, in the name of the Lord.

Given in Rome, at St Peter's, on the feast of the Resurrection, 26 March 1967, in the fourth year of our pontificate.

Octagesimo Adveniens

Apostolic letter to His Eminence Cardinal Maurice Roy,
President of the Council for the Laity and of
the Pontifical Commission Justice and Peace to mark the
eightieth anniversary of the encyclical letter Rerum Novarum

Introduction

In 1968 Pope Paul VI published his encyclical on contraception. *Humanae Vitae* proved to be the last encyclical he issued and from then on he seems to have chosen other styles of document—hence *Octagesimo Adveniens* appears as an 'apostolic letter', addressed to the Archbishop of Quebec, rather than as an encyclical. Though Cardinal Roy was technically the addressee, the text of the document, like that of an encyclical, is clearly directed at the whole Catholic world.

It is dated 14 May 1971 and celebrates, as the title indicates, the eightieth anniversary of *Rerum Novarum*. There had been a four-year gap between *Populorum Progressio* and *Octagesimo Adveniens*, and a great deal had happened. It had become clear, for example, that the simple concept of 'development' was not a panacea for the ills of the underdeveloped countries. That fact had been noted in *Populorum Progressio*: it is eminently clear in *Octagesimo Adveniens*. Secondly, there had occurred the second meeting of the Conference of Latin American Bishops. It had taken place in Medellín in Colombia in 1968. Its brief was to apply the teaching of Vatican II to the situation as it existed in Latin America, and it was clear from the outset that such a meeting was to be important, so important, indeed, that the pope himself decided to attend.

But it could never have been envisaged just how important the conclusions of Medellín were to prove to be. Where the popes had talked the language of development, Medellín talked the language of liberation. There was, in other words, an important shift in emphasis from economics to politics. Paul VI made a gesture in the direction of Medellín in *Octagesimo Adveniens*. He recognizes that particular situations need particular remedies, and is ready to admit that popes cannot be abreast of the situation in all parts of the world. He acknowledges the importance of the political dimension, though he stresses that politics cannot be seen as an end in themselves. He turns his attention to urbanization and industrialization not solely as steps in the progress of development, but as occasions for yet further exploitation.

[245]

Proclaiming Justice and Peace

The Latin text of *Octagesimo Adveniens* (OA) is published in AAS 63 (1971) 401-441. The paragraphs have been numbered, but additional numbering is in accordance with the policy outlined in the Editorial Note (p.ix).

Summary

Paras. 1-6: The problems of the modern world, as the pope has encountered them at first hand on his travels, are both common to all and yet particular to diverse parts of the world in the form they take. The Church, too, has diverse opportunities to play a part in the solution of those problems, depending upon its opportunities to operate in the different countries. The local community must decide what it can do in the light of its own circumstances to spread the social message of Christianity. But in any case it is the Church's duty to speak out.

Paras. 7-21: There are a number of new social problems to be faced. A major challenge is presented by urbanization: Christians must strive to humanize the city. Another challenge is presented by young people, a third by the role of women, a fourth by the problem of workers for whom much remains to be done if greater justice and sharing of responsibility are to be achieved. There is also the problem of emigration, of the treatment of emigrant workers, of the family, of the growing power of the media and of danger to the environment.

Paras. 22-36: The aspirations to equality and to participation as two expressions of human dignity and of freedom are constantly growing. Though they are often denied, they seek to promote a democratic view of society. The Christian has a role to play in this, in the organization and life of political society. But a Christian cannot adhere to any ideological system which contradicts the faith and the concept of humanity, or which regards itself as a final or sufficient explanation of everything—such as sociology in some of its forms tries to do, or Marxism. On the other hand Christians must not be misled into an uncritical acceptance of liberalism either: all ideologies must be viewed from the stand point of faith.

Paras. 37-41: Because of the weakness of ideologies there has been a revival of 'utopias'. The appeal to these is often an excuse to avoid concrete tasks, but it is also a way of reawakening the imagination, which is important. People must beware of being manipulated through the advances in science and technology. The human sciences must be supported, however, despite their dangers, for inadequate as they may be they are indispensable as an aid to discovering what is human. Today there is an attempt to replace purely quantitative criteria of what constitutes human progress by qualitative ones.

Paras. 42-47: It is not the role of the Church to propose models, or to oppose existing ones. The most important duty in the realms of justice is to allow each country freely to develop itself. People are yearning for freedom, but this must start with interior freedom if it is to be achieved. Some nations' ambition for power stands in the way of the establishment of institutions to achieve greater justice for all. Political power must have as its aim the achievement of the common good—though in so doing it does not deprive intermediary bodies and individuals of their proper responsibility for achieving the common good. Political life is to be taken seriously. Allowing people to take responsibility and a concrete exercise of their freedom is part of the way towards development. But a Christian must remember that true freedom is to be found in God.

Paras. 48-52: The pope addresses an urgent call to action to all Christians, for words lack weight unless they are backed by effective action. Concretely there exists a legitimate variety of possible options on the part of individuals, and church organizations have a part to play. The word of God will not be proclaimed unless it is accompanied by the witness of the power of the Spirit, working within the actions of Christians in the service of their brothers and sisters.

Venerable brother, greetings and apostolic benediction.

The diversity of the challenge

1. The eightieth anniversary of the publication of the encyclical *Rerum Novarum*, the message of which continues to inspire action for social justice, prompts us to take up again and to extend the teaching of our predecessors, in response to the new needs of a changing world. The Church, in fact, travels forward with humanity and shares its lot in the setting of history. At the same time that she announces to men the good news of God's love and of salvation in Christ, she clarifies their activity in the light of the gospel and in this way helps them to correspond to God's plan of love and to realize the fullness of their aspirations.

2. It is with confidence that we see the Spirit of the Lord pursuing his work in the hearts of men and in every place gathering together Christian communities conscious of their responsibilities in society. On all the continents, among all races, nations and cultures, and under all conditions the Lord continues to raise up authentic apostles of the gospel.
    2.1. We have had the opportunity to meet these people, to admire them and to give them our encouragement in the course of our recent journeys. We have gone into the crowds and have heard their appeals, cries of distress and at the same time cries of hope.
    2.2. These problems of course are particular to each part of the world, but at the same time they are common to all mankind, which is questioning itself about its future and about the tendency and the meaning of the changes taking place. Flagrant inequalities exist in the economic, cultural and political development of the nations: while some regions are heavily industrialized, others are still at the agricultural stage; while some countries enjoy prosperity, others are struggling against starvation; while some peoples have a high standard of culture, others are still engaged in eliminating illiteracy.

Proclaiming Justice and Peace

From all sides there rises a yearning for more justice and a desire for a better guaranteed peace in mutual respect among individuals and peoples.

3. There is of course a wide diversity among the situations in which Christians—willingly or unwillingly—find themselves according to regions, socio-political systems and cultures. In some places they are reduced to silence, regarded with suspicion and as it were kept on the fringe of society, enclosed without freedom in a totalitarian system. In other places they are a weak minority whose voice makes itself heard with difficulty. In some other nations, where the Church sees her place recognized, sometimes officially so, she too finds herself subjected to the repercussions of the crisis which is unsettling society; some of her members are tempted by radical and violent solutions from which they believe that they can expect a happier outcome. While some people, unaware of present injustices, strive to prolong the existing situation, others allow themselves to be beguiled by revolutionary ideologies which promise them, not without delusion, a definitively better world.

General and specific responses

4. In the face of such widely varying situations it is difficult for us to utter a unified message and to put forward a solution which has universal validity. Such is not our ambition, nor is it our mission. It is up to the Christian communities to analyse with objectivity the situation which is proper to their own country, to shed on it the light of the gospel's unalterable words and to draw principles of reflection, norms of judgement and directives for action from the social teaching of the Church. This social teaching has been worked out in the course of history and notably, in this industrial era, since the historic date of the message of Pope Leo XIII on 'the condition of the workers', and it is an honour and joy for us to celebrate today the anniversary of that message. It is up to these Christian communities, with the help of the Holy Spirit, in communion with the bishops who hold responsibility and in dialogue with other Christian brethren and all men of good will, to discern the options and commitments which are called for in order to bring about the social, political and economic changes seen in many cases to be urgently needed.

4.1. In this search for the changes which should be promoted, Christians must first of all renew their confidence in the forcefulness and special character of the demands made by the gospel. The gospel is not out of date because it was proclaimed, written and lived in a different socio-cultural context. Its inspiration, enriched by the living experience of Christian tradition over the centuries, remains ever new for converting men and for advancing the life of society. It is not however to be utilized for the profit of particular temporal options, to the neglect of its universal and eternal message.[1]

5. Amid the disturbances and uncertainties of the present hour, the Church has a specific message to proclaim and a support to give to men in their efforts to take in hand and give direction to their future. Since the period in which the encyclical *Rerum Novarum* denounced in a forceful and imperative

manner the scandal of the condition of the workers in the nascent industrial society, historical evolution has led to an awareness of other dimensions and other applications of social justice. The encyclicals *Quadragesimo Anno*[2] and *Mater et Magistra*[3] already noted this fact.

5.1. The recent council for its part took care to point them out, in particular in the pastoral constitution *Gaudium et Spes*. We ourself have already continued these lines of thought in our encyclical *Populorum Progressio*. 'Today,' we said, 'the principal fact that we must all recognize is that the social question has become world-wide.'[4] 'A renewed consciousness of the demands of the gospel makes it the Church's duty to put herself at the service of all, to help them grasp their serious problem in all its dimensions, and to convince them that solidarity in action at this turning point in human history is a matter of urgency.'[5]

6. It will moreover be for the forthcoming synod of bishops itself to study more closely and to examine in greater detail the Church's mission in the face of grave issues raised today by the question of justice in the world. But the anniversary of *Rerum Novarum*, venerable brother, gives us the opportunity today to confide our preoccupations and thoughts in the face of this problem to you as president of the Pontifical Commission Justice and Peace and of the Council of Laity.

6.1 In this way it is also our wish to offer these bodies of the Holy See our encouragement in their ecclesial activity in the service of men.

7. In so doing, our purpose—without however forgetting the permanent problems already dealt with by our predecessors—is to draw attention to a number of questions. These are questions which because of their urgency, extent and complexity must in the years to come take first place among the preoccupations of Christians, so that with other men the latter may dedicate themselves to solving the new difficulties which put the very future of man in jeopardy. It is necessary to situate the problems created by the modern economy in the wider context of a new civilization. These problems include human conditions of production, fairness in the exchange of goods and in the division of wealth, the significance of the increased needs of consumption and the sharing of responsibility. In the present changes, which are so profound and so rapid, each day man discovers himself anew, and he questions himself about the meaning of his own being and of his collective survival. Reluctant to gather the lessons of a past that he considers over and done with and too different from the present, man nevertheless needs to have light shed upon his future—a future which he perceives to be as uncertain as it is changing—by permanent eternal truths. These are truths which are certainly greater than man but, if he so wills, he can himself find their traces.[6]

I

Urbanization and its consequences

8. A major phenomenon draws our attention, as much in the industrialized countries as in those which are developing: urbanization. After long

centuries, agrarian civilization is weakening. Is sufficient attention being devoted to the arrangement and improvement of the life of the country people, whose inferior and at all times miserable economic situation provokes the flight to the unhappy crowded conditions of the city outskirts, where neither employment nor housing awaits them?

This unceasing flight from the land, industrial growth, continual demographic expansion and the attraction of urban centres bring about concentrations of population, the extent of which is difficult to imagine, for people are already speaking in terms of a 'megalopolis' grouping together tens of millions of persons. Of course ther exist medium-sized towns, the dimension of which ensures a better balance in the population. While being able to offer employment to those that progress in agriculture makes available, they permit an adjustment of the human environment which better avoids the proletarianism and crowding of the great built-up areas.

9. The inordinate growth of these centres accompanies industrial expansion, without being identified with it. Based on technological research and the transformation of nature, industrialization constantly goes forward, giving proof of incessant creativity. While certain enterprises develop and are concentrated, others die or change their location. Thus new social problems are created: professional or regional unemployment, redeployment and mobility of persons, permanent adaptation of workers and disparity of conditions in the different branches of industry. Unlimited competition utilising the modern means of publicity incessantly launches new products and tries to attract the consumer, while earlier industrial installations which are still capable of functioning become useless. While very large areas of the population are unable to satisfy their primary needs, superfluous needs are ingeniously created. It can thus rightly be asked if, in spite of all his conquests, man is not turning back against himself the results of his activity. Having rationally endeavoured to control nature,[7] is he not now becoming the slave of the objects which he makes?

10. Is not the rise of an urban civilization which accompanies the advance of industrial civilization a true challenge to the wisdom of man, to his capacity for organization and to his far-seeing imagination? Within industrial society urbanization upsets both the ways of life and the habitual structures of existence: the family, the neighbourhood, and the very framework of the Christian community. Man is experiencing a new loneliness; it is not in the face of a hostile nature which it has taken him centuries to subdue, but in an anonymous crowd which surrounds him and in which he feels himself a stranger. Urbanization, undoubtedly an irreversible stage in the development of human societies, confronts man with difficult problems. How is he to master its growth, regulate its organization, and successfully accomplish its animation for the good of all? In this disordered growth, new proletariats are born. They instal themselves in the heart of the cities sometimes abandoned by the rich; they dwell on the outskirts—which become a belt of misery besieging in a still silent protest the luxury which blatantly cries out from centres of consumption and waste. Instead of favouring fraternal encounter and mutual aid, the city fosters discrimination and also indifference. It lends itself to new forms of exploitation and of domination whereby some people in speculating on the needs of others derive inadmissible profits. Behind the

façades, much misery is hidden, unsuspected even by the closest neighbours; other forms of misery spread where human dignity founders: delinquency, criminality, abuse of drugs and eroticism.

11. It is in fact the weakest who are the victims of dehumanizing living conditions, degrading for conscience and harmful for the family institution. The promiscuity of working people's housing makes a minimum of intimacy impossible; young couples waiting in vain for a decent dwelling at a price they can afford are demoralized and their union can thereby even be endangered; youth escape from a home which is too confined and seek in the streets compensations and companionships which cannot be supervised. It is the grave duty of those responsible to strive to control this process and to give it direction.

11.1. There is an urgent need to remake at the level of the street, of the neighbourhood or of the great agglomerative dwellings, the social fabric whereby man may be able to develop the needs of his personality. Centres of special interest and of culture must be created or developed at the community and parish levels with different forms of associations, recreational centres, and spiritual and community gatherings where the individual can escape from isolation and form anew fraternal relationships.

12. To build up the city, the place where men and their expanded communities exist, to create new modes of neighbourliness and relationships, to perceive an original application of social justice and to undertake responsibility for this collective future, which is foreseen as difficult, is a task in which Christians must share. To those who are heaped up in an urban promiscuity which becomes intolerable it is necessary to bring a message of hope. This can be done by brotherhood which is lived and by concrete justice. Let Christians, conscious of this new responsibility, not lose heart in view of the vast and faceless society; let them recall Jonah who traversed Nineveh, the great city, to proclaim therein the good news of God's mercy and was upheld in his weakness by the sole strength of the word of almighty God. In the Bible, the city is in fact often the place of sin and pride—the pride of man who feels secure enough to be able to build his life without God and even to affirm that he is powerful against God. But there is also the example of Jerusalem, the holy city, the place where God is encountered, the promise of the city which comes from on high.[8]

Needs of particular groups

13. Urban life and industrial change bring strongly to light questions which until now were poorly grasped. What place, for example, in this world being brought to birth, should be given to youth?

13.1. Everywhere dialogue is proving to be difficult between youth, with its aspirations, renewal and also insecurity for the future, and the adult generations. It is obvious to all that here we have a source of serious conflicts, division and opting out, even within the family, and a questioning of modes of authority, education for freedom and the handing on of values and beliefs, which strikes at the deep roots of society.

13.2. Similarly, in many countries a charter for women which would put an end to an actual discrimination and would establish relationships of equality in rights and of respect for their dignity is the object of study and at times of lively demands. We do not have in mind that false equality which would be in contradiction with woman's proper role, which is of such capital importance, at the heart of the family as well as within society. Developments in legislation should on the contrary be directed to protecting her proper vocation and at the same time recognizing her independence as a person, and her equal rights to participate in cultural, economic, social and political life.

14. As the Church solemnly reaffirmed in the recent council, 'the beginning, the subject and the goal of all social institutions is and must be the human person.'[9] Every man has the right to work, to a chance to develop his qualities and his personality in the exercise of his profession, to equitable remuneration which will enable him and his family 'to lead a worthy life on the material, social, cultural and spiritual level'[10] and to assistance in case of need arising from sickness or age.

14.1. Although for the defence of these rights democratic societies accept today the principle of labour union rights, they are not always open to their exercise. The important role of union organizations must be admitted: their object is the representation of the various categories of workers, their lawful collaboration in the economic advance of society, and the development of the sense of their responsibility for the realization of the common good. Their activity, however, is not without its difficulties. Here and there the temptation can arise of profiting from a position of force to impose, particularly by strikes—the right to which as a final means of defence remains certainly recognized— conditions which are too burdensome for the overall economy and for the social body, or to desire to obtain in this way demands of a directly political nature. When it is a question of public services, required for the life of an entire nation, it is necessary to be able to assess the limit beyond which the harm caused to society becomes inadmissible.

15. In short, progress has already been made in introducing, in the area of human relationships, greater justice and greater sharing of responsibilities. But in this immense field much remains to be done. Further reflection, research and experimentation must be actively pursued, unless one is to be late in meeting the legitimate aspirations of the workers—aspirations which are being increasingly asserted as their education, their consciousness of their dignity and the strength of their organizations increase.

15.1. Egoism and domination are permanent temptations for men. Likewise an ever finer discernment is needed, in order to strike at the roots of newly arising situations of injustice and to establish progressively a justice which will be less and less imperfect. In industrial change, which demands speedy and constant adaptation, those who will find themselves injured will be more numerous and at a greater disadvantage from the point of view of making their voices heard.

15.2. The Church directs her attention to these new 'poor'—the handicapped and the maladjusted, the old, different groups of those on the fringe of society, and so on—in order to recognize them, help them, defend their place and dignity in a society hardened by competition and the attraction of success.

16. Among the victims of situations of injustice—unfortunately no new phenomenon—must be placed those who are discriminated against, in law or in fact, on account of their race, origin, colour, culture, sex or religion. Racial discrimination possesses at the moment a character of very great relevance by reason of the tension which it stirs up both within certain countries and on the international level. Men rightly consider unjustifiable and reject as inadmissible the tendency to maintain or introduce legislation or behaviour systematically inspired by racialist prejudice. The members of mankind share the same basic rights and duties, as well as the same supernatural destiny. Within a country which belongs to each one, all should be equal before the law, find equal admittance to economic, cultural, civil and social life and benefit from a fair sharing of the nation's riches.

17. We are thinking also of the precarious situation of a great number of emigrant workers whose condition as foreigners makes it all the more difficult for them to make any sort of social vindication,* in spite of their real participation in the economic effort of the country that receives them. It is urgently necessary for people to go beyond a narrowly nationalist attitude in their regard and to give them a charter which will assure them a right to emigrate, favour their integration, facilitate their professional advancement and give them access to decent housing where, if such is the case, their families can join them.[11]

17.1. Linked to this category are the people who, to find work, or to escape a disaster or a hostile climate, leave their regions and find themselves without roots among other people.

17.2. It is everyone's duty, but especially that of Christians,[12] to work with energy for the establishment of universal brotherhood, the indispensable basis for authentic justice and the condition for enduring peace: 'We cannot in truthfulness call upon that God who is the father of all if we refuse to act in a brotherly way towards certain men, created in God's image. A man's relationship with God the Father and his relationship with his brother men are so linked together that scripture says: 'He who does not love does not know God' (1 John 4:8).'[13]

Coping with population growth

18. With demographic growth, which is particularly pronounced in the young nations, the number of those failing to find work and driven to misery or parasitism will grow in the coming years unless the conscience of man rouses itself and gives rise to a general movement of solidarity through an effective policy of investment and of organization of production and trade, as well as of education. We know the attention given to these problems within international organizations, and it is our lively wish that their members will not delay bringing their actions into line with their declarations.

18.1. It is disquieting in this regard to note a kind of fatalism which is gaining a hold even on people in positions of responsibility. This feeling sometimes leads to Malthusian solutions inculcated by active propaganda for contraception and abortion. In this critical situation, it must on the contrary be affirmed that the family, without which no society can stand, has a right to the assistance which will assure it of the conditions for a healthy development. 'It is certain,' we said in our encyclical *Populorum Progressio,* 'that public authorities can intervene, within the limit of their competence, by favouring the availability of appropriate information and by adopting suitable measures, provided that these be in conformity with the moral law and that they respect the rightful freedom of married couples. Where the inalienable right to marriage and procreation is lacking, human dignity has ceased to exist.'[14]

19. In no other age has the appeal to the imagination of society been so explicit. To this should be devoted enterprises of invention and capital as important as those invested for armaments or technological achievements. If man lets himself rush ahead without foreseeing in good time the emergence of new social problems, they will become too grave for a peaceful solution to be hoped for.

The power of the media

20. Among the major changes of our times, we do not wish to forget to emphasize the growing role being assumed by the media of social communication and their influence on the transformation of mentalities, of knowledge, of organizations and of society itself. Certainly they have many positive aspects. Thanks to them news from the entire world reaches us practically in an instant, establishing contacts which supersede distances and creating elements of unity among all men. A greater spread of education and culture is becoming possible. Nevertheless, by their very action the media of social communication are reaching the point of representing as it were a new power. One cannot but ask about those who really hold this power, the aims that they pursue and the means they use, and finally, about the effect of their activity on the exercise of individual liberty, both in the political and ideological spheres and in social, economic and cultural life. The men who hold this power have a grave moral responsibility with respect to the truth of the information that they spread, the needs and the reactions that they generate and the values which they put forward. In the case of television, moreover, what is coming into being is an original mode of knowledge and a new civilization: that of the image.

20.1. Naturally, the public authorities cannot ignore the growing power and influence of the media of social communication and the advantages and risks which their use involves for the civic community and for its development and real perfecting.

20.2. Consequently they are called upon to perform their own positive function for the common good by encouraging every constructive expression, by supporting individual citizens and groups in defending the fundamental values of the person and of human society, and also by taking suitable steps to prevent the spread of what would harm the common heritage of values on which orderly civil progress is based.[15]

The environment at risk

21. While the horizon of man is thus being modified according to the images

that are chosen for him, another transformation is making itself felt, one which is the dramatic and unexpected consequence of human activity. Man is suddenly becoming aware that by an ill-considered exploitation of nature he risks destroying it and becoming in his turn the victim of this degradation. Not only is the material environment becoming a permanent menace—pollution and refuse, new illnesses and absolute destructive capacity—but the human framework is no longer under man's control, thus creating an environment for tomorrow which may well be intolerable. This is a wide-ranging social problem which concerns the entire human family.

21.1. The Christian must turn to these new perceptions in order to take on responsibility, together with the rest of men, for a destiny which from now on is shared by all.

Human rights

22. While scientific and technological progress continues to overturn man's surroundings, his patterns of knowledge, work, consumption and relationships, two aspirations persistently make themselves felt in these new contexts, and they grow stronger to the extent that he becomes better informed and better educated: the aspiration to equality and the aspiration to participation, two forms of man's dignity and freedom.

23. Through this statement of the rights of man and the seeking for international agreements for the application of these rights, progress has been made towards inscribing these two aspirations in deeds and structures.[16] Nevertheless various forms of discrimination continually reappear—ethnic, cultural, religious, political and so on. In fact, human rights are still too often disregarded, if not scoffed at, or else they receive only formal recognition. In many cases legislation does not keep up with real situations. Legislation is necessary, but it is not sufficient for setting up true relationships of justice and equality. In teaching us charity, the gospel instructs us in the preferential respect due to the poor and the special situation they have in society: the more fortunate should renounce some of their rights so as to place their goods more generously at the service of others. If, beyond legal rules, there is really no deeper feeling of respect for and service to others, then even equality before the law can serve as an alibi for flagrant discrimination, continued exploitation and actual contempt. Without a renewed education in solidarity, an over-emphasis on equality can give rise to an individualism in which each one claims his own rights without wishing to be answerable for the common good.

23.1. In this field, everyone sees the highly important contribution of the Christian spirit, which moreover answers man's yearning to be loved. 'Love for man, the prime value of the earthly order', ensures the conditions for peace, both social peace and international peace, by affirming our universal brotherhood.[17]

Political life

24. The two aspirations, to equality and to participation, seek to promote a democratic type of society. Various models are proposed, some are tried out,

none of them gives complete satisfaction, and the search goes on between ideological and pragmatic tendencies. The Christian has the duty to take part in this search and in the organization and life of political society. As a social being, man builds his destiny within a series of particular groupings which demand, as their completion and as a necessary condition for their development, a vaster society, one of a universal character, the political society. All particular activity must be placed within that wider society, and thereby it takes on the dimension of the common good.[18] This indicates the importance of education for life in society, in which there are called to mind, not only information on each one's rights, but also their necessary correlative: the recognition of the duties of each one in regard to others. The sense and practice of duty are themselves conditioned by self-mastery and by the acceptance of responsibility and of the limits placed upon the freedom of the individual or of the group.

25. Political activity—need one remark that we are dealing primarily with an activity, not an ideology?—should be the projection of a plan of society which is consistent in its concrete means and in its inspiration, and which springs from a complete conception of man's vocation and of its differing social expressions. It is not for the State or even for political parties, which would be closed unto themselves, to try to impose an ideology by means that would lead to a dictatorship over minds, the worst kind of all. It is for cultural and religious groupings, in the freedom of acceptance which they presume, to develop in the social body, disinterestedly and in their own ways, those ultimate convictions on the nature, origin and end of man and society. In this field, it is well to keep in mind the principle proclaimed at the Second Vatican Council: 'The truth cannot impose itself except by virtue of its own truth, and it makes its entrance into the mind at once quietly and with power.'[19]

The ambiguity of ideology

26. Therefore the Christian who wishes to live his faith in a political activity which he thinks of as service cannot without contradicting himself adhere to ideological systems which radically or substantially go against his faith and his concept of man. He cannot adhere to the Marxist ideology, to its atheistic materialism, to its dialectic of violence and to the way it absorbs individual freedom in the collectivity, at the same time denying all transcendence to man and his personal and collective history; nor can he adhere to the liberal ideology which believes it exalts individual freedom by withdrawing it from every limitation, by stimulating through exclusive seeking of interest and power, and by considering social solidarities as more or less automatic consequences of individual initiatives, not as an aim and a major criterion of the value of the social organization.

27. Is there need to stress the possible ambiguity of every social ideology? Sometimes it leads political or social activity to be simply the application of an abstract, purely theoretical idea; at other times it is thought which becomes a mere instrument at the service of activity as a simple means of a strategy. In both cases is it not man that risks finding himself alienated? The

Christian faith is above and is sometimes opposed to the ideologies, in that it recognizes God, who is transcendent and the creator, and who, through all the levels of creation, calls on man as endowed with responsibility and freedom.

28. There would also be the danger of giving adherence to an ideology which does not rest on a true and organic doctrine, to take refuge in it as a final and sufficient explanation of everything, and thus to build a new idol, accepting at times without being aware of doing so, its totalitarian and coercive character. And people imagine they find in it a justification for their activity, even violent activity, and an adequate response to a generous desire to serve. The desire remains but it allows itself to be consumed by an ideology which, even if it suggests certain paths to man's liberation, ends up by making him a slave.

29. It has been possible today to speak of a retreat of ideologies. In this respect the present time may be favourable for an openness to the concrete transcendence of Christianity. It may also be a more accentuated sliding towards a new positivism: universalized technology as the dominant form of activity, as the overwhelming pattern of existence, even as a language, without the question of its meaning being really asked.

30. But outside this positivism which reduces man to a single dimension even if it be an important one today and by so doing mutilates him, the Christian encounters in his activity concrete historical movements sprung from ideologies and in part distinct from them. Our venerated predecessor Pope John XXIII in *Pacem in Terris* already showed that it is possible to make a distinction: 'Neither can false philosophical teachings regarding the nature, origin and destiny of the universe and of man be identified with historical movements that have economic, social, cultural or political ends, not even when these movements have originated from those teachings and have drawn and still draw inspiration therefrom. Because the teachings, once they are drawn up and defined, remain always the same, while the movements, being concerned with historical situations in constant evolution, cannot but be influenced by these latter and cannot avoid, therefore, being subject to changes, even of a profound nature. Besides, who can deny that those movements, in so far as they conform to the dictates of right reason and are interpreters of the lawful aspirations of the human person, contain elements that are positive and deserving of approval?'[20]

The attraction of socialism

31. Some Christians are today attracted by socialist currents and their various developments. They try to recognize therein a certain number of aspirations which they carry within themselves in the name of their faith. They feel that they are part of that historical current and wish to play a part within it. Now this historical current takes on, under the same name, different forms according to different continents and cultures, even if it drew its inspiration, and still does in many cases, from ideologies incompatible with faith. Careful judgement is called for. Too often Christians attracted by socialism tend to

idealize it in terms which, apart from anything else, are very general: a will for justice, solidarity and equality. They refuse to recognize the limitations of the historical socialist movements, which remain conditioned by the ideologies from which they originated. Distinctions must be made to guide concrete choices between the various levels of expression of socialism: a generous aspiration and a seeking for a more just society, historical movements with a political organization and aim, and an ideology which claims to give a complete and self-sufficient picture of man. Nevertheless, these distinctions must not lead one to consider such levels as completely separate and independent. The concrete link which, according to circumstances, exists between them must be clearly marked out. This insight will enable Christians to see the degree of commitment possible along these lines, while safeguarding the values, especially those of liberty, responsibility and openness to the spiritual, which guarantee the integral development of man.

The challenge of Marxism

32. Other Christians even ask whether an historical development of Marxism might not authorize certain concrete rapprochements. They note in fact that a certain splintering of Marxism, which until now showed itself to be a unitary ideology which explained in atheistic terms the whole of man and the world since it did not go outside their development process. Apart from the ideological confrontation officially separating the various champions of Marxism-Leninism in their individual interpretations of the thought of its founders, and apart from the open opposition between the political systems which make use of its name today, some people lay down distinctions between Marxism's various levels of expression.

33. For some, Marxism remains essentially the active practice of class struggle. Experiencing the ever present and continually renewed force of the relationships of domination and exploitation among men, they reduce Marxism to no more than a struggle—at times with no other purpose—to be pursued and even stirred up on permanent fashion. For others, it is first and foremost the collective exercise of political and economic power under the direction of a single party, which would be the sole expression and guarantee of the welfare of all, and would deprive individuals and other groups of any possibility of initiative and choice. At a third level, Marxism, whether in power or not, is viewed as a socialist ideology based on historical materialism and the denial of everything transcendent. At other times, finally, it presents itself in a more attenuated form, one also more attractive to the modern mind: as a scientific activity, as a rigorous method of examining social and political reality, and as the rational link, tested by history, between theoretical knowledge and the practice of revolutionary transformation. Although this type of analysis gives a privileged position to certain aspects of reality to the detriment of the rest, and interprets them in the light of its ideology, it nevertheless furnishes some people not only with a working tool but also a certitude preliminary to action: the claim to decipher in a scientific manner the mainsprings of the evolution of society.

34. While, through the concrete existing form of Marxism, one can distinguish these various aspects and the questions they pose for the reflection and activity of Christians, it would be illusory and dangerous to reach a point of forgetting the intimate link which radically binds them together, to accept the elements of Marxist analysis without recognizing their relationships with ideology, and to enter into the practice of class struggle and its Marxist interpretations, while failing to note the kind of totalitarian and violent society to which this process leads.

The roots of liberalism

35. On another side, we are witnessing a renewal of the liberal ideology. This current asserts itself both in the name of economic efficiency, and for the defence of the individual against the increasingly overwhelming hold of organizations, and as a reaction against the totalitarian tendencies of political powers. Certainly, personal initiative must be maintained and developed. But do not Christians who take this path tend to idealize liberalism in their turn, making it a proclamation in favour of freedom? They would like a new model, more adapted to present-day conditions, while easily forgetting that at the very root of philosophical liberalism is an erroneous affirmation of the autonomy of the individual in his activity, his motivation and the exercise of his liberty. Hence, the liberal ideology likewise calls for careful discernment on their part.

The dynamism of Christianity

36. In this renewed encounter of the various ideologies, the Christian will draw from the sources of his faith and the Church's teaching the necessary principles and suitable criteria to avoid permitting himself to be first attracted by and then imprisoned within a system whose limitations and totalitarianism may well become evident to him too late, if he does not perceive them in their roots. Going beyond every system, without however failing to commit himself concretely to serving his brothers, he will assert, in the very midst of his options, the specific character of the Christian contribution for a positive transformation of society.[21]

37. Today, moreover, the weaknesses of the ideologies are better perceived through the concrete systems in which they are trying to affirm themselves. Bureaucratic socialism, technocratic capitalism and authoritarian democracy are showing how difficult it is to solve the great human problem of living together in justice and equality. How in fact could they escape the materialism, egoism or constraint which inevitably go with them? This is the source of a protest which is springing up more or less everywhere, as a sign of a deep-seated sickness, while at the same time we are witnessing the re-birth of what it is agreed to call 'utopias'. These claim to resolve the political problem of modern societies better than the ideologies. It would be dangerous to disregard this. The appeal to a utopia is often a convenient excuse for those who wish to escape from concrete tasks in order to take refuge in an imaginary world. To live in a hypothetical future is a facile alibi for rejecting

immediate responsibilities. But it must clearly be recognized that this kind of criticism of existing society often provokes the forward-looking imagination both to perceive in the present the disregarded possibility hidden within it, and to direct itself towards a fresh future; it thus sustains social dynamism by the confidence that it gives to the inventive powers of the human mind and heart; and, if it refuses no overture, it can also meet the Christian appeal. The Spirit of the Lord, who animates man renewed in Christ, continually breaks down the horizons within which his understanding likes to find security and the limits to which his activity would willingly restrict itself; there dwells within him a power which urges him to go beyond every system and every ideology. At the heart of the world there dwells the mystery of man discovering himself to be God's son in the course of a historical and psychological process in which constraint and freedom as well as the weight of sin and the breath of the Spirit alternate and struggle for the upper hand.

37.1. The dynamism of Christian faith here triumphs over the narrow calculations of egoism. Animated by the power of the Spirit of Jesus Christ, the saviour of mankind, and upheld by hope, the Christian involves himself in the building up of the human city, one that is to be peaceful, just and fraternal and acceptable as an offering to God.[22] In fact, 'the expectation of a new earth must not weaken but rather stimulate our concern for cultivating this one. For here grows the body of a new human family, a body which even now is able to give some kind of foreshadowing of the new age.'[23]

The dangers of science

38. In this world dominated by scientific and technological change, which threatens to drag it towards a new positivism, another more fundamental doubt is raised. Having subdued nature by using his reason, man now finds that he himself is as it were imprisoned within his own rationality; he in turn becomes the object of science. The 'human sciences' are today enjoying a significant flowering. On the one hand they are subjecting to critical and radical examination the hitherto accepted knowledge about man, on the grounds that this knowledge seems either too empirical or too theoretical. On the other hand, methodological necessity and ideological presuppositions too often lead the human sciences to isolate, in the various situations, certain aspects of man, and yet to give these an explanation which claims to be complete or at least an interpretation which is meant to be all-embracing from a purely quantitative or phenomenological point of view. This scientific reduction betrays a dangerous presumption. To give a privileged position in this way to such an aspect of analysis is to mutilate man and, under the pretext of a scientific procedure, to make it impossible to understand man in his totality.

39. One must be no less attentive to the action which the human sciences can instigate, giving rise to the elaboration of models of society to be subsequently imposed on men as scientifically tested types of behaviour. Man can then become the object of manipulations directing his desires and needs and modifying his behaviour and even his system of values. There is no doubt that there exists here a grave danger for the societies of tomorrow and for

man himself. For even if all agree to build a new society at the service of men, it is still essential to know what sort of man is in question.

40. Suspicion of the human sciences affects the Christian more than others, but it does not find him disarmed. For, as we ourself wrote in *Populorum Progressio*, it is here that there is found the specific contribution of the Church to civilizations: 'Sharing the noblest aspirations of men and suffering when she sees them not satisfied, she wishes to help them attain their full flowering, and that is why she offers men what she possesses as her characteristic attribute: a global vision of man and of the human race.'[24] Should the Church in its turn contest the proceedings of the human sciences, and condemn their pretentions? As in the case of the natural sciences, the Church has confidence in this research also and urges Christians to play an active part in it.[25] Prompted by the same scientific demands and the desire to know man better, but at the same time enlightened by their faith, Christians who devote themselves to the human sciences will begin a dialogue which promises to be fruitful. Of course, each individual scientific discipline will be able, in its own particular sphere, to grasp only a partial—yet true—aspect of man; the complete picture and the full meaning will escape it. But within these limits the human sciences give promise of a positive function that the Church willingly recognizes. They can even widen the horizons of human liberty to a greater extent than the conditioning circumstances perceived enable one to foresee. They could thus assist Christian social morality, which no doubt will see its field restricted when it comes to suggesting certain models of society, while its function of making a critical judgement and taking an overall view will be strengthened by its showing the relative character of the behaviour and values presented by such and such a society as definitive and inherent in the very nature of man. These sciences are a condition at once indispensable and inadequate for a better discovery of what is human. They are a language which becomes more and more complex, yet one that deepens rather than solves the mystery of the heart of man; nor does it provide the complete and definitive answer to the desire which springs from his innermost being.

Limitations on progress

41. This better knowledge of man makes it possible to pass a better critical judgement upon and to elucidate a fundamental notion that remains at the basis of modern societies as their motive, their measure and their goal: namely, progress. Since the nineteenth century, western societies and, as a result, many others have put their hopes in ceaselessly renewed and indefinite progress. They saw this progress as man's effort to free himself in face of the demands of nature and of social constraints; progress was the condition for and the yardstick of human freedom. Progress, spread by the modern media of information and by the demand for wider knowledge and greater consumption, has become an omnipresent ideology. Yet a doubt arises today regarding both its value and its result. What is the meaning of this never-ending, breathless pursuit of a progress that always eludes one just when one believes one has conquered it sufficiently in order to enjoy it in peace? If it is not attained, it leaves one dissatisfied. Without doubt, there has

been just condemnation of the limits and even the misdeeds of a merely quantitative economic growth; there is a desire to attain objectives of a qualitative order also. The quality and the truth of human relations, the degree of participation and of responsibility, are no less significant and important for the future of society than the quantity and variety of the goods produced and consumed. Overcoming the temptation to wish to measure everything in terms of efficiency and of trade, and in terms of the interplay of forces and interests, man today wishes to replace these quantitative criteria with the intensity of communication, the spread of knowledge and culture, mutual service and a combining of efforts for a common task. Is not genuine progress to be found in the development of moral consciousness, which will lead man to exercise a wider solidarity and to open himself freely to others and to God? For a Christian, progress necessarily comes up against the eschatological mystery of death. The death of Christ and his resurrection and the outpouring of the Spirit of the Lord help man to place his freedom, in creativity and gratitude, within the context of the truth of all progress and the only hope which does not deceive.[26]

III

Seeking answers

42. In the face of so many new questions the Church makes an effort to reflect in order to give an answer, in its own sphere, to men's expectations. If today the problems seem original in their breadth and their urgency, is man without the means of solving them? It is with all its dynamism that the social teaching of the Church accompanies men in their search. If it does not intervene to authenticate a given structure or to propose a ready-made model, it does not thereby limit itself to recalling general principles. It develops through reflection applied to the changing situations of this world, under the driving force of the gospel as the source of renewal when its message is accepted in its totality and with all its demands. It also develops with the sensitivity proper to the Church which is characterized by a disinterested will to serve and by attention to the poorest. Finally, it draws upon its rich experience of many centuries which enables it, while continuing its permanent preoccupations, to undertake the daring and creative innovations which the present state of the world requires.

Economic ties

43. There is need to establish a greater justice in the sharing of goods, both within national communities and on the international level. In international exchanges there is a need to go beyond relationships based on force, in order to arrive at agreements reached with the good of all in mind. Relationships based on force have never in fact established justice in a true and lasting manner, even if at certain times the alternation of positions can often make it possible to find easier conditions for dialogue. The use of force moreover leads to the setting in motion of opposing forces, and from this springs a

climate of struggle which opens the way to situations of extreme violence and to abuses.[27] But, as we have often stated, the most important duty in the realm of justice is to allow each country to promote its own development, within the framework of a co-operation free from any spirit of domination, whether economic or political. The complexity of the problems raised is certainly great, in the present intertwining of mutual dependences. Thus it is necessary to have the courage to undertake a revision of the relationships between nations, whether it is a question of the international division of production, the structure of exchanges, the control of profits, the monetary system,—without forgetting the actions of human solidarity—to question the models of growth of the rich nations and change people's outlooks, so that they may realize the prior call of international duty, and to renew international organizations so that they may increase in effectiveness.

44. Under the driving force of new systems of production, national frontiers are breaking down, and we can see new economic powers emerging, the multinational enterprises, which by the concentration and flexibility of their means can conduct autonomous strategies which are largely independent of the national political powers and therefore not subject to control from the point of view of the common good. By extending their activities, these private organizations can lead to a new and abusive form of economic domination on the social, cultural and even political level. The excessive concentration of means and powers that Pope Pius XI already condemned on the fortieth anniversary of *Rerum Novarum* is taking on a new and very real image.

Desire for independence

45. Today men yearn to free themselves from need and dependence. But this liberation starts with the interior freedom that men must find again with regard to their goods and their powers; they will never reach it except through a transcendent love for man, and, in consequence, through a genuine readiness to serve. Otherwise, as one can see only too clearly, the most revolutionary ideologies lead only to a change of masters; once installed in power in their turn, these new masters surround themselves with privileges, limit freedoms and allow other forms of injustice to become established.

45.1. Thus many people are reaching the point of questioning the very model of society. The ambition of many nations, in the competition that sets them in opposition and which carries them along, is to attain technological, economic and military power. This ambition then stands in the way of setting up structures in which the rhythm of progress would be regulated with a view to greater justice, instead of accentuating inequalities and living in a climate of distrust and struggle which would unceasingly compromise peace.

46. Is it not here that there appears a radical limitation to economics? Economic activity is necessary and, if it is at the service of man, it can be 'a source of brotherhood and a sign of providence'.[28] It is the occasion of concrete exchanges between man, of rights recognized, of services rendered and of dignity affirmed in work. Though it is often a field of confrontation and domination, it can give rise to dialogue and foster co-operation. Yet it runs the risk of taking up too much strength and freedom.[29] This is why the

need is felt to pass from economics to politics. It is true that in the term 'politics' many confusions are possible and must be clarified, but each man feels that in the social and economic field, both national and international, the ultimate decision rests with political power.

46.1. Political power, which is the natural and necessary link for ensuring the cohesion of the social body, must have as its aim the achievement of the common good. While respecting the legitimate liberties of individuals, families and subsidiary groups, it acts in such a way as to create, effectively and for the well-being of all, the conditions required for attaining man's true and complete good, including his spiritual end. It acts within the limits of its competence, which can vary from people to people and from country to country. It always intervenes with care for justice and with devotion to the common good, for which it holds final responsibility. It does not, for all that, deprive individuals and intermediary bodies of the field of activity and responsibility which are proper to them and which lead them to collaborate in the attainment of this common good. In fact, 'the true aim of all social activity should be to help individual members of the social body, but never to destroy or absorb them.'[30] According to the vocation proper to it, the political power must know how to stand aside from particular interests in order to view its responsibility with regard to the good of all men, even going beyond national limits. To take politics seriously at its different levels—local, regional, national and worldwide—is to affirm the duty of man, of every man, to recognize the concrete reality and the value of the freedom of choice that is offered to him to seek to bring about both the good of the city and of the nation and of mankind. Politics are a demanding manner—but not the only one—of living the Christian commitment to the service of others. Without of course solving every problem, it endeavours to apply solutions to the relationships men have with one another. The domain of politics is wide and comprehensive, but it is not exclusive. An attitude of encroachment which would tend to set up politics as an absolute value would bring serious danger. While recognizing the autonomy of the reality of politics, Christians who are invited to take up political activity should try to make their choices consistent with the gospel and, in the framework of a legitimate plurality, to give both personal and collective witness to the seriousness of their faith by effective and disinterested service of men.

Sharing power

47. The passing to the political dimension also expresses a demand made by the man of today: a greater sharing in responsibility and in decision-making. This legitimate aspiration becomes more evident as the cultural level rises, as the sense of freedom develops and as man becomes more aware of how, in a world facing an uncertain future, the choices of today already condition the life of tomorrow. In *Mater et Magistra*[31] Pope John XXIII stressed how much the admittance to responsibility is a basic demand of man's nature, a concrete exercise of his freedom and a path to his development, and he showed how, in economic life and particularly in enterprise, this sharing in responsibilities should be ensured.[32] Today the field is wider, and extends to the social and political sphere in which a reasonable sharing in responsibility

and in decisions must be established and strengthened. Admittedly, it is true that the choices proposed for a decision are more and more complex; the considerations that must be borne in mind are numerous and the foreseeing of the consequences involves risk, even if new sciences strive to enlighten freedom at these important moments. However, although limits are sometimes called for, these obstacles must not slow down the giving of wider participation in working out decisions, making choices and putting them into practice. In order to counterbalance increasing technocracy, modern forms of democracy must be devised, not only making it possible for each man to become informed and to express himself, but also by involving him in a shared responsibility. Thus human groups will gradually begin to share and to live as communities. Thus freedom, which too often asserts itself as a claim for autonomy by opposing the freedom of others will develop in its deepest human reality: to involve itself and to spend itself in building up active and lived solidarity. But, for the Christian, it is by losing himself in God who sets him free that man finds true freedom, renewed in the death and resurrection of the Lord.

II

A call to action

48. In the social sphere, the Church has always wished to assume a double function: first to enlighten minds in order to assist them to discover the truth and to find the right path to follow amid the different teachings that call for their attention; and secondly to take part in action and to spread, with a real care for service and effectiveness, the energies of the gospel. Is it not in order to be faithful to this desire that the Church has sent on an apostolic mission among the workers priests who, by sharing fully the condition of the worker, are at that level the witnesses to the Church's solicitude and seeking?

48.1. It is to all Christians that we address a fresh and insistent call to action. In our encyclical on the Development of Peoples we urged that all should set themselves to the task:'Laymen should take up as their own proper task the renewal of the temporai order. If the role of the hierarchy is to teach and to interpret authentically the norms of morality to be followed in this matter, it belongs to the laity, without waiting passively for orders and directives, to take the initiative freely and to infuse a Christian spirit into the mentality, customs, laws and structures of the community in which they live.'[33] Let each one examine himself, to see what he has done up to now, and what he ought to do. It is not enough to recall principles, state intentions, point to crying injustices and utter prophetic denunciations; these words will lack real weight unless they are accompanied for each individual by a livelier awareness of personal responsibility and by effective action. It is too easy to throw back on others responsibility for injustices, if at the same time one does not realize how each one shares in it personally, and how personal conversion is needed first. This basic humility will rid action of all inflexibility and sectarianism; it will also avoid discouragement in the face of a task which seems limitless in size. The Christian's hope comes primarily from the fact that he knows that the Lord is working with us in the world, continuing in his body which is the Church—and, through the Church, in the whole of mankind—the redemption which was accomplished on the cross and which burst forth in victory on the morning of the resurrection.[34] This hope springs also from the fact that the Christian knows that other men are at work, to undertake actions of justice and peace working for the same ends. For beneath an outward appearance of indifference, in the heart of every man there is a will to live in brotherhood and a thirst for justice and peace, which is to be expanded.

49. Thus, amid the diversity of situations, functions and organizations, each one must determine, in his conscience, the actions which he is called to share in. Surrounded by various currents into which, beside legitimate aspirations, there insinuate themselves more ambiguous tendencies, the Christian must make a wise and vigilant choice and avoid involving himself in collaboration without conditions and contrary to the principles of a true humanism, even in the name of a genuinely felt solidarity. If in fact he wishes to play a specific part as a Christian in accordance with his faith—a part that unbelievers themselves expect of him—he must take care in the midst of his active commitment to clarify his motives and to rise above the objectives aimed at, by taking a more all-embracing view which will avoid the danger of selfish particularism and oppressive totalitarianism.

50. In concrete situations, and taking account of solidarity in each person's life, one must recognize a legitimate variety of possible options. The same Christian faith can lead to different commitments.[35] The Church invites all Christians to take up a double task of inspiring and of innovating, in order to make structures evolve, so as to adapt them to the real needs of today. From Christians who at first sight seem to be in opposition, as a result of starting from differing options, she asks an effort at mutual understanding of the other's positions and motives; a loyal examination of one's behaviour and its correctness will suggest to each one an attitude of more profound charity which, while recognizing the differences, believes nonetheless in the possibility of convergence and unity. 'The bonds which unite the faithful are mightier than anything which divides them.'[36]

50.1. It is true that many people, in the midst of modern structures and conditioning circumstances, are determined by their habits of thought and their functions, even apart from the safeguarding of material interests. Others feel so deeply the solidarity of classes and cultures that they reach the point of sharing without reserve all the judgements and options of their surroundings.[37] Each one will take great care to examine himself and to bring about that true freedom according to Christ which makes one receptive to the universal in the very midst of the most particular conditions.

The Christian witness

51. It is in this regard too that Christian organizations, under their different forms, have a responsibility for collective action. Without putting themselves in the place of the institutions of civil society, they have to express, in their own way and rising above their particular nature, the concrete demands of the

Christian faith for a just, and consequently necessary, transformation of society.[38]

51.1. Today more than ever the word of God will be unable to be proclaimed and heard unless it is accompanied by the witness of the power of the Holy Spirit, working within the action of Christians in the service of their brothers, at the points in which their existence and their future are at stake.

52. In expressing these reflections to you, venerable brother, we are of course aware that we have not dealt with all the social problems that today face the man of faith and men of good will. Our recent declarations—to which has been added your message of a short time ago on the occasion of the launching of the Second Development Decade—particularly concerning the duties of the community of nations in the serious question of the integral and concerted development of man, are still fresh in people's minds. We address these present reflections to you with the aim of offering to the Council of the Laity and the Pontifical Commission Justice and Peace some fresh contributions, as well as an encouragement, for the pursuit of their task of 'awakening the people of God to a full understanding of its role at the present time' and of 'promoting the apostolate on the international level'.[39]

It is with these sentiments, venerable brother, that we impart to you our apostolic blessing.

From the Vatican, 14 May 1971.

Editor's Note

OA 17: In English the common meaning of this word is to justify something by providing proof. Here, however, it has a rather more Latinate sense of asserting and maintaining one's just rights.

Justice in the World

Introduction

One of the results of the Second Vatican Council has been a series of synods. These are gatherings in Rome of representatives of the episcopal conferences around the world together with some *ex officio* members and others appointed by the pope. The first synod met in 1967, the second two years later. The third, devoted to discussion both of the priesthood and of justice in the world, met from 30 September to 6 November 1971. Commentators on Roman Catholic affairs have rarely given high marks to the deliberations of the various synods, but this document, produced at the end of the third one, is an exception. It is a powerful statement not only of the Church's actual involvement in human affairs, but also of its theological justification. The document recognizes that because it is addressed to the whole world, it must necessarily remain at a somewhat general level, but it encourages local churches to interpret its teachings in accord with local needs. The bishops admit that the Church has itself not always been the very best example of that justice which it preaches, and point to specific areas, including the treatment of women and the practice of ecclesiastical courts, where there is much need of improvement. They point out that some of the remedies for injustice and inequality have not had the desired effect. They back a number of initiatives of the United Nations. They urge upon the Church a greater effort in education for justice at every level.

For a longer discussion of the content of Justice in the World (JW) and of its place within Catholic social teaching, see the Introduction, pp.xvi. The Latin text is to be found in AAS 63 (1971) 923-942. Of the Latin text, only the major subdivisions have been kept in this edition. The bishops added an unusually large—for a Vatican document—number of cross-headings, but these have not been retained here. The paragraphs of the Latin text were not numbered, so numbering has been added in accordance with the Editorial Note (p.ix).

Summary

Paras. 1-6: The bishops, gathered in synod, are aware of the forces which oppress people throughout the world. They are also aware of the desire which people have to liberate themselves, and with that desire the Church associates itself, as a constitutive part of its mission.

Paras. 7-12: Technological advance and the need to conserve the world's resources have brought people together, yet there are at the same time forces driving them apart, in particular the unequal distribution of wealth.

Paras. 13-28: The establishment of justice depends upon the will of the poorer nations to develop. Without this will they will become the victims of international economic forces. They must, therefore, take their future into their own hands, and they have a right to participate in their own economic, political and social progress. There are some towards whom action for justice must be especially directed, migrants, for example, farm workers, refugees, those denied religious liberty and other civil rights.

Paras. 29-38: The Old Testament presents God as the liberator of the oppressed, and for the Christian love of neighbour and the pursuit of justice cannot be separated. The Church has both the right and the duty to proclaim justice, but it is not the Church's task to offer solutions to particular problems: that is the role of members of the Church as citizens.

Paras. 39-48: If the Church is to bear witness to justice it must be an example of justice both in the way it treats its members and in the way it administers its possessions.

Paras. 49-58: Education for justice is essential. It should find expression in the family, in schools and so on, and also in the liturgy. The Church's social teaching has been outlined in a number of papal and conciliar documents.

Paras. 59-62: As a sign of that solidarity which all desire, there ought to be co-operation between churches in rich and in poor regions. Roman Catholics ought to co-operate with other Christians, with all who believe in God, and with all those who, even though they do not believe in God, sincerely and honourably seek justice.

Paras. 63-77: The synod recognizes that the recommendations that it makes have to be very general in nature, but if they are to be effective they must be translated into practical action at local level. It gives encouragement to all Christians to work for the kingdom of love and of justice, and calls upon them to co-operate with God in liberating people from sin.

INTRODUCTION

1. Gathered from the whole world, in communion with all who believe in Christ and with the entire human family, and opening our hearts to the Spirit who is making the whole of creation new, we have questioned ourselves about the mission of the people of God to further justice in the world.

The network of domination

2. Scrutinizing the 'signs of the times' and seeking to detect the meaning of emerging history, while at the same time sharing the aspirations and questionings of all those who want to build a more human world, we have

listened to the word of God that we might be converted to the fulfilling of the divine plan for the salvation of the world.

3. Even though it is not for us to elaborate a very profound analysis of the situation of the world, we have nevertheless been able to perceive the serious injustices which are building around the world of men a network of domination, oppression and abuses which stifle freedom and which keep the greater part of humanity from sharing in the building up and enjoyment of a more just and more fraternal world.

The struggle for liberation

4. At the same time we have noted the inmost stirring moving the world in its depths. There are facts constituting a contribution to the furthering of justice. In associations of men and among peoples themselves there is arising a new awareness which shakes them out of any fatalistic resignation and which spurs them on to liberate themselves and to be responsible for their own destiny. Movements among men are seen which express hope in a better world and a will to change whatever has become intolerable.

Justice as part of preaching the gospel

5. Listening to the cry of those who suffer violence and are oppressed by unjust systems and structures, and hearing the appeal of a world that by its perversity contradicts the plan of its creator, we have shared our awareness of the Church's vocation to be present in the heart of the world by proclaiming the good news to the poor, freedom to the oppressed, and joy to the afflicted. The hopes and forces which are moving the world in its very foundations are not foreign to the dynamism of the gospel, which through the power of the Holy Spirit frees men from personal sin and from its consequences in social life.

6. The uncertainty of history and the painful convergences in the ascending path of the human community direct us to sacred history; there God has revealed himself to us, and makes known to us, as it is brought progressively to realization, his plan of liberation and salvation which is once and for all fulfilled in the paschal mystery of Christ. Action on behalf of justice and participation in the transformation of the world fully appear to us as a constitutive dimension of the preaching of the gospel, or, in other words, of the Church's mission for the redemption of the human race and its liberation from every oppressive situation.

I

Justice and world society

Forces promoting unity

7. The world in which the Church lives and acts is held captive by a

tremendous paradox. Never before have the forces working for bringing about a unified world society appeared so powerful and dynamic; they are rooted in the awareness of the full basic equality as well as of the human dignity of all. Since men are members of the same human family, they are indissolubly linked with one another in the one destiny of the whole world, in the responsibility for which they all share.

8. The new technological possibilities are based upon the unity of science, on the global and simultaneous character of communications and on the birth of an absolutely interdependent economic world. Moreover, men are beginning to grasp a new and more radical dimension of unity; for they perceive that their resources, as well as the precious treasures of air and water—without which there cannot be life—and the small delicate biosphere of the whole complex of all life on earth, are not infinite, but on the contrary must be saved and preserved as a unique patrimony belonging to all mankind.

Forces bringing disunity

9. The paradox lies in the fact that within this perspective of unity the forces of division and antagonism seem today to be increasing in strength. Ancient divisions between nations and empires, between races and classes, today possess new technological instruments of destruction. The arms race is a threat to man's highest good, which is life; it makes poor peoples and individuals yet more miserable, while making richer those already powerful; it creates a continuous danger of conflagration, and in the case of nuclear arms, it threatens to destroy all life from the face of the earth. At the same time new divisions are being born to separate man from his neighbour. Unless combatted and overcome by social and political action, the influence of the new industrial and technological order favours the concentration of wealth, power and decision-making in the hands of a small public or private controlling group. Economic injustice and lack of social participation keep a man from attaining his basic human and civil rights.

10. In the last twenty-five years a hope has spread through the human race that economic growth would bring about such a quantity of goods that it would be possible to feed the hungry at least with the crumbs falling from the table, but this has proved a vain hope in underdeveloped areas and in pockets of poverty in wealthier areas, because of the rapid growth of population and of the labour force, because of rural stagnation and the lack of agrarian reform, and because of the massive migratory flow to the cities, where the industries, even though endowed with huge sums of money, nevertheless provide so few jobs that not infrequently one worker in four is left unemployed. These stifling oppressions constantly give rise to great numbers of 'marginal' persons, ill-fed, inhumanly housed, illiterate and deprived of political power as well as of the suitable means of acquiring responsibility and moral dignity.

Inequality of resources

11. Furthermore, such is the demand for resources and energy by the richer

nations, whether capitalist or socialist, and such are the effects of dumping by them in the atmosphere and the sea that irreparable damage would be done to the essential elements of life on earth, such as air and water, if their high rates of consumption and pollution, which are constantly on the increase, were extended to the whole of mankind.

12. The strong drive towards global unity, the unequal distribution which places decisions concerning three-quarters of income, investment and trade in the hands of one third of the human race, namely the more highly developed part, the insufficiency of a merely economic progress, and the new recognition of the material limits of the biosphere—all this makes us aware of the fact that in today's world new modes of understanding human dignity are arising.

The right to development

13. In the face of international systems of domination, the bringing about of justice depends more and more on the determined will for development.

14. In the developing nations and in the so-called socialist world, that determined will asserts itself especially in a struggle for forms of claiming one's rights and self-expression, a struggle caused by the evolution of the economic system itself.

15. This aspiring to justice asserts itself in advancing beyond the threshold at which begins a consciousness of enhancement of personal worth (cf. *Populorum Progressio* 15, AAS 59 (1967) 265) with regard both to the whole man and the whole of mankind. This is expressed in an awareness of the right to development. The right to development must be seen as a dynamic interpenetration of all those fundamental human rights upon which the aspirations of individuals and nations are based.

16. This desire however will not satisfy the expectations of our time if it ignores the objective obstacles which social structures place in the way of conversion of hearts, or even of the realization of the ideal of charity. It demands on the contrary that the general condition of being marginal in society be overcome, so that an end will be put to the systematic barriers and vicious circles which oppose the collective advance towards enjoyment of adequate remuneration of the factors of production, and which strengthen the situation of discrimination with regard to access to opportunities and collective services from which a great part of the people are now excluded. If the developing nations and regions do not attain liberation through development, there is a real danger that the conditions of life created especially by colonial domination may evolve into a new form of colonialism in which the developing nations will be the victims of the interplay of international economic forces. That right to development is above all a right to hope according to the concrete measure of contemporary humanity. To respond to such a hope, the concept of evolution must be purified of those myths and false convictions which have up to now gone with a thought-pattern subject to a kind of deterministic and automatic notion of progress.

The struggle for development

17. By taking their future into their own hands through a determined will for progress, the developing peoples—even if they do not achieve the final goal—will authentically manifest their own personalization. And in order that they may cope with the unequal relationships within the present world complex, a certain responsible nationalism gives them the impetus needed to acquire an identity of their own. From this basic self-determination can come attempts at putting together new political groupings allowing full development to these peoples; there can also come measures necessary for overcoming the inertia which could render fruitless such an effort—as in some cases population pressure; there can also come new sacrifices which the growth of planning demands of a generation which wants to build its own future.

18. On the other hand, it is impossible to conceive true progress without recognizing the necessity—within the political system chosen—of a development composed both of economic growth and participation; and the necessity too of an increase in wealth implying as well social progress by the entire community as it overcomes regional imbalance and islands of prosperity. Participation constitutes a right which is to be applied both in the economic and in the social and political field.

19. While we again affirm the right of people to keep their own identity, we see ever more clearly that the fight against a modernization destructive of the proper characteristics of nations remains quite ineffective as long as it appeals only to sacred historical customs and venerable ways of life. If modernization is accepted with the intention that it serve the good of the nation, men will be able to create a culture which will constitute a true heritage of their own in the manner of a true social memory, one which is active and formative of authentic creative personality in the assembly of nations.

Those in special need

20. We see in the world a set of injustices which constitute the nucleus of today's problems and whose solution requires the undertaking of tasks and functions in every sector of society, and even on the level of the global society towards which we are speeding in this last quarter of the twentieth century. Therefore we must be prepared to take on new functions and new duties in every sector of human activity and especially in the sector of world society, if justice is really to be put into practice. Our action is to be directed above all at those men and nations which because of various forms of oppression and because of the present character of our society are silent, indeed voiceless, victims of injustice.

21. Take, for example, the case of migrants. They are often forced to leave their own country to find work, but frequently find the doors closed in their faces because of discriminatory attitudes, or, if they can enter, they are often obliged to lead an insecure life or are treated in an inhuman manner. The same is true of groups that are less well off on the social ladder such as

workers and especially farm workers who play a very great part in the process of development.

22. To be especially lamented is the condition of so many millions of refugees, and of every group or people suffering persecution—sometimes in institutionalized form—for racial or ethnic origin or on tribal grounds. This persecution on tribal grounds can at times take on the characteristics of genocide.

23. In many areas justice is seriously injured with regard to people who are suffering persecution for their faith, or who are in many ways being ceaselessly subjected by political parties and public authorities to an action of oppressive atheization, or who are deprived of religious liberty either by being kept from honouring God in public worship, or by being prevented from publicly teaching and spreading their faith, or by being prohibited from conducting their temporal affairs according to the principles of their religion.

The denial of human rights

24. Justice is also being violated by forms of oppression, both old and new, springing from restriction of the rights of individuals. This is occurring both in the form of repression by the political power and of violence on the part of private reaction, and can reach the extreme of affecting the basic conditions of personal integrity. There are well-known cases of torture, especially of political prisoners, who besides are frequently denied due process or who are subjected to arbitrary procedures in their trial. Nor can we pass over the prisoners of war who even after the Geneva Convention are being treated in an inhuman manner.

25. The fight against legalized abortion and against the imposition of contraceptives and the pressures exerted against war are significant forms of defending the right to life.

26. Furthermore, contemporary consciousness demands truth in the communications systems, including the right to the image offered by the media and the opportunity to correct its manipulation. It must be stressed that the right, especially that of children and the young, to education and to morally correct conditions of life and communications media is once again being threatened in our days. The activity of families in social life is rarely and insufficiently recognized by state institutions. Nor should we forget the growing number of persons who are often abandoned by their families and by the community: the old, orphans, the sick and all kinds of people who are rejected.

Progress through dialogue

27. To obtain true unity of purpose, as is demanded by the world society of men, a mediatory role* is essential to overcome day by day the opposition, obstacles and ingrained privileges which are to be met with in the advance towards a more human society.

28. But effective mediation involves the creation of a lasting atmosphere of

dialogue. A contribution to the progressive realization of this can be made unhampered by geo-political, ideological or socio-economic conditions or by the generation gap. To restore the meaning of life by adherence to authentic values, the participation and witness of the rising generation of youth is as necessary as communication among peoples.

II

The gospel message and the mission of the Church

God the defender of the poor

29. In the face of the present-day situation of the world, marked as it is by the grave sin of injustice, we recognize both our responsibility and our inability to overcome it by our own strength. Such a situation urges us to listen with a humble and open heart to the word of God, as he shows us new paths towards action in the cause of justice in the world.

30. In the Old Testament God reveals himself to us as the liberator of the oppressed and the defender of the poor, demanding from man faith in him and justice towards man's neighbour. It is only in the observance of the duties of justice that God is truly recognized as the liberator of the oppressed.

Christ links people to God and to each other

31. By his action and teaching Christ united in an indivisible way the relationship of man to God and the relationship of man to other men. Christ lived his life in the world as a total giving of himself to God for the salvation and liberation of men. In his preaching he proclaimed the fatherhood of God towards all men and the intervention of God's justice on behalf of the needy and the oppressed (Luke 6:21-23). In this way he identified himself with his 'least brethren', as he stated: 'As you did it to one of the least of these my brethren, you did it to me' (Matt. 25:40).

32. From the beginning the Church has lived and understood the death and resurrection of Christ as a call by God to conversion in the faith of Christ and in fraternal love, perfected in mutual help even to the point of a voluntary sharing of material goods.

33. Faith in Christ, the son of God and the redeemer, and love of neighbour constitute a fundamental theme of the writers of the New Testament. According to St Paul, the whole of the Christian life is summed up in faith effecting that love and service of neighbour which involve the fulfilment of the demands of justice. The Christian lives under the interior law of liberty, which is a permanent call to man to turn away from self-sufficiency to confidence in God and from concern for self to sincere love of neighbour. Thus takes place his genuine liberation and the gift of himself for the freedom of others.

34. According to the Christian message, therefore, man's relationship to his

neighbour is bound up with his relationship to God; his response to the love of God, saving us through Christ, is shown to be effective in his love and service of men. Christian love of neighbour and justice cannot be separated. For love implies an absolute demand for justice, namely a recognition of the dignity and rights of one's neighbour. Justice attains its inner fullness only in love. Because every man is truly a visible image of the invisible God and a brother of Christ, the Christian finds in every man God himself and God's absolute demand for justice and love.

The Church's duty to uphold justice

35. The present situation of the world, seen in the light of faith, calls us back to the very essence of the Christian message, creating in us a deep awareness of its true meaning and of its urgent demands. The mission of preaching the gospel dictates at the present time that we should dedicate ourselves to the liberation of man even in his present existence in this world. For unless the Christian message of love and justice shows its effectiveness through action in the cause of justice in the world, it will only with difficulty gain credibility with the men of our times.

36. The Church has received from Christ the mission of preaching the gospel message, which contains a call to man to turn away from sin to the love of the Father, universal brotherhood and a consequent demand for justice in the world. This is the reason why the Church has the right, indeed the duty, to proclaim justice on the social, national and international level, and to denounce instances of injustice, when the fundamental rights of man and his very salvation demand it. The Church, indeed, is not alone responsible for justice in the world; however, she has a proper and specific responsibility which is identified with her mission of giving witness before the world of the need for love and justice contained in the gospel message, a witness to be carried out in church institutions themselves and in the lives of Christians.

The limits of what the Church can do

37. Of itself it does not belong to the Church, in so far as she is a religious and hierarchical community, to offer concrete solutions in the social, economic and political spheres for justice in the world. Her mission involves defending and promoting the dignity and fundamental rights of the human person.

Duties of a Christian citizen

38. The members of the Church, as members of society, have the same right and duty to promote the common good as do other citizens. Christians ought to fulfil their temporal obligations with fidelity and competence. They should act as a leaven in the world, in their family, professional, social, cultural and political life. They must accept their responsibilities in this entire area under the influence of the gospel and the teaching of the Church. In this way they testify to the power of the Holy Spirit through their action in the service of men in those things which are decisive for the existence and the future of

humanity. While in such activities they generally act on their own initiative without involving the responsibility of the ecclesiastical hierarchy, in a sense they do involve the responsibility of the Church whose members they are.

III

The practice of justice

Action for justice by individual Christians

39. Many Christians are drawn to give authentic witness on behalf of justice by various modes of action for justice, action inspired by love in accordance with the grace which they have received from God. For some of them, this action finds its place in the sphere of social and political conflicts in which Christians bear witness to the gospel by pointing out that in history there are sources of progress other than conflict, namely love and right. This priority of love in history draws other Christians to prefer the way of non-violent action and work in the area of public opinion.

Justice within the Church

40. While the Church is bound to give witness to justice, she recognizes that anyone who ventures to speak to people about justice must first be just in their eyes. Hence we must undertake an examination of the modes of acting and of the possessions and life-style found within the Church herself.

41. Within the Church rights must be preserved. No one should be deprived of his ordinary rights because he is associated with the Church in one way or another. Those who serve the Church by their labour, including priests and religious, should receive a sufficient livelihood and enjoy that social security which is customary in their region. Lay people should be given fair wages and a system for promotion. We reiterate the recommendations that lay people should exercise more important functions with regard to Church property and should share in its administration.

42. We also urge that women should have their own share of responsibility and participation in the community life of society and likewise of the Church.

43. We propose that this matter be subjected to a serious study employing adequate means: for instance, a mixed commission of men and women, religious and lay people, of differing situations and competence.

44. The Church recognizes everyone's right to suitable freedom of expression and thought. This includes the right of everyone to be heard in a spirit of dialogue which preserves a legitimate diversity within the Church.

45. The form of judicial procedure should give the accused the right to know his accusers and also the right to a proper defence. To be complete, justice should include speed in its procedure. This is especially necessary in marriage cases.

46. Finally, the members of the Church should have some share in the drawing-up of decisions, in accordance with the rules given by the Second Vatican Ecumenical Council and the Holy See, for instance with regard to the setting up of councils at all levels.

The Church's witness to poverty

47. In regard to temporal possessions, whatever be their use, it must never happen that the evangelical witness which the Church is required to give becomes ambiguous. The preservation of certain positions of privilege must constantly be submitted to the test of this principle. Although in general it is difficult to draw a line between what is needed for right use and what is demanded by prophetic witness, we must certainly keep firmly to this principle: our faith demands of us a certain sparingness in use, and the Church is obliged to live and administers its own goods in such a way that the gospel is proclaimed to the poor. If instead the Church appears to be among the rich and the powerful of this world its credibility is diminished.

48. Our examination of conscience now comes to the life-style of all: bishops, priests, religious and lay people. In the case of needy peoples it must be asked whether belonging to the Church places people on a rich island within an ambient of poverty. In societies enjoying a higher level of consumer spending, it must be asked whether our life-style exemplifies that sparingness with regard to consumption which we preach to others as necessary in order that so many millions of hungry people throughout the world may be fed.

Education for justice

49. Christians' specific contribution to justice is the day-to-day life of the individual believer acting like the leaven of the gospel in his family, his school, his work and his social and civic life. Included with this are the perspectives and meaning which the faithful can give to human effort. Accordingly, educational method must be such as to teach men to live their lives in its entire reality and in accord with the evangelical principles of personal and social morality which are expressed in the vital Christian witness of one's life.

50. The obstacles to the progress which we wish for ourselves and for mankind are obvious. The method of education very frequently still in use today encourages narrow individualism. Part of the human family lives immersed in a mentality which exalts possessions. The school and the communications media, which are often obstructed by the established order, allow the formation only of the man desired by that order, that is to say, man in its image, not a new man but a copy of man as he is.

51. But education demands a renewal of heart, a renewal based on the recognition of sin in its individual and social manifestations. It will also inculcate a truly and entirely human way of life in justice, love and simplicity. It will likewise awaken a critical sense, which will lead us to reflect on the society in which we live and on its values; it will make men ready to renounce

these values when they cease to promote justice for all men. In the developing countries, the principal aim of this education for justice consists in an attempt to awaken consciences to a knowledge of the concrete situation and in a call to secure a total improvement; by these means the transformation of the world has already begun.

52. Since this education makes men decidedly more human, it will help them to be no longer the object of manipulation by communications media or political forces. It will instead enable them to take in hand their own destinies and bring about communities which are truly human.

53. Accordingly, this education is deservedly called a continuing education, for it concerns every person and every age. It is also a practical education: it comes through action, participation and vital contact with the reality of injustice.

54. Education for justice is imparted first in the family. We are well aware that not only church institutions but also other schools, trade unions and political parties are collaborating in this.

55. The content of this education necessarily involves respect for the person and for his dignity. Since it is world justice which is in question here, the unity of the human family within which, according to God's plan, a human being is born must first of all be seriously affirmed. Christians find a sign of this solidarity in the fact that all human beings are destined to become in Christ sharers in the divine nature.

A growing understanding of justice

56. The basic principles whereby the influence of the gospel has made itself felt in contemporary social life are to be found in the body of teaching set out in a gradual and timely way from the encyclical *Rerum Novarum* to the letter *Octagesimo Adveniens*. As never before, the Church has, through the Second Vatican Council's constitution *Gaudium et Spes*, better understood the situation in the modern world, in which the Christian works out his salvation by deeds of justice. *Pacem in Terris* gave us an authentic charter of human rights. In *Mater et Magistra* international justice begins to take first place; it finds more elaborate expression in *Populorum Progressio*, in the form of a true and suitable treatise on the right to development, and in *Octagesimo Adveniens* is found a summary of guidelines for political action.

57. Like the apostle Paul, we insist, welcome or unwelcome, that the word of God should be present in the centre of human situations. Our interventions are intended to be an expression of that faith which is today binding on our lives and on the lives of the faithful. We all desire that these interventions should always be in conformity with circumstances of place and time. Our mission demands that we should courageously denounce injustice, with charity, prudence and firmness, in sincere dialogue with all parties concerned. We know that our denunciations can secure assent to the extent that they are an expression of our lives and are manifested in continuous action.

Justice and the liturgy

58. The liturgy, which we preside over and which is the heart of the Church's life, can greatly serve education for justice. For it is a thanksgiving to the Father in Christ, which through its communitarian form places before our eyes the bonds of our brotherhood and again and again reminds us of the Church's mission. The liturgy of the world, catechesis and the celebration of the sacraments have the power to help us to discover the teaching of the prophets, the Lord and the apostles on the subject of justice. The preparation for baptism is the beginning of the formation of the Christian conscience. The practice of penance should emphasize the social dimension of sin and of the sacrament. Finally, the eucharist forms the community and places it at the service of men.

Redistributing the Church's resources

59. That the Church may really be the sign of that solidarity which the family of nations desires, it should show in its own life greater co-operation between the churches of rich and poor regions through spiritual communion and division of human and material resources. The present generous arrangements for assistance between churches could be made more effective by real co-ordination (Sacred Congregation for the Evangelization of Peoples and the Pontifical Council '*Cor Unum*'), through their overall view in regard to the common administration of the gifts of God, and through fraternal solidarity, which would always encourage autonomy and responsibility on the part of the beneficiaries in the determination of criteria and the choice of concrete programmes and their realization.

60. This planning must in no way be restricted to economic programmes; it should instead stimulate activities capable of developing that human and spiritual formation which will serve as the leaven needed for the integral development of the human being.

Co-operation in pursuit of justice

61. Well aware of what has already been done in this field, together with the Scond Vatican Ecumenical Council we very highly commend co-operation with our separated Christian brethren for the promotion of justice in the world, for bringing about development of peoples and for establishing peace. This co-operation concerns first and foremost activities for securing human dignity and man's fundamental rights, especially the right to religious liberty. This is the source of our common efforts against discrimination on the grounds of differences of religion, race and colour, culture and the like. Collaboration extends also to the study of the teaching of the gospel in so far as it is the source of inspiration for all Christian activity. Let the Secretariat for Promoting Christian Unity and the Pontifical Commission Justice and Peace devote themselves in common counsel to developing effectively this ecumenical collaboration.

62. In the same spirit we likewise commend collaboration with all believers in

God in the fostering of social justice, peace and freedom; indeed we commend collaboration also with those who, even though they do not recognize the author of the world, nevertheless, in their esteem for human values, seek justice sincerely and by honourable means.

General recommendations

63. Since the synod is of a universal character, it is dealing with those questions of justice which directly concern the entire human family. Hence, recognizing the importance of international co-operation for social and economic development, we praise above all else the inestimable work which has been done among the poorer peoples by the local churches, the missionaries and the organizations supporting them; and we intend to foster those initiatives and institutions which are working for peace, international justice and the development of man. We therefore urge Catholics to consider well the following propositions:

64. (1). Let recognition be given to the fact that international order is rooted in the inalienable rights and dignity of the human being. Let the United Nations Declaration of Human Rights be ratified by all governments who have not yet adhered to it, and let it be fully observed by all.

65. (2). Let the United Nations—which because of its unique purpose should promote participation by all nations—and international organizations be supported in so far as they are the beginning of a system capable of restraining the armaments race, discouraging trade in weapons, securing disarmament and settling conflicts by peaceful methods of legal action, arbitration and international police action It is absolutely necessary that international conflicts should not be settled by war, but that other methods better befitting human nature should be found. Let a strategy of non-violence be fostered also, and let conscientious objection be recognized and regulated by law in each nation.

66. (3). Let the aims of the Second Development Decade be fostered. These include the transfer of a precise percentage of the annual income of the richer countries to the developing nations, fairer prices for raw materials, the opening of the markets of the richer nations and, in some fields, preferential treatment for exports of manufactured goods from the developing nations. These aims represent first guidelines for a graduated taxation of income as well as for an economic and social plan for the entire world. We grieve whenever richer nations turn their backs on this ideal goal of world-wide sharing and responsibility. We hope that no such weakening of international solidarity will take away their force from the trade discussions being prepared by the United Nations Conference on Trade and Development (UNCTAD).

67. (4). The concentration of power which consists in almost total domination of economics, research, investment, freight charges, sea transport and securities should be progressively balanced by institutional arrangements for strengthening power and opportunities with regard to responsible decision-making by the developing nations and by full and equal participation in international organizations concerned with development.

Their recent *de facto* exclusion from discussions on world trade and also the monetary arrangements which vitally affect their destiny are an example of lack of power which is inadmissible in a just and responsible world order.

68. (5). Although we recognize that international agencies can be perfected and strengthened, as can any human instrument, we stress also the importance of the specialized agencies of the United Nations, in particular those directly concerned with the immediate and more acute questions of world poverty in the field of agrarian reform and agricultural development, health, education, employment, housing, and rapidly increasing urbanization. We feel we must point out in a special way the need for some fund to provide sufficient food and protein for the real mental and physical development of children. In the face of the population explosion we repeat the words by which Pope Paul VI defined the functions of public authority in his encyclical *Populorum Progressio*: 'There is no doubt that public authorities can intervene, within the limit of their competence, by favouring the availability of appropriate information and by adopting suitable measures, provided that these can be in conformity with the moral law and that they absolutely respect the rightful freedom of married couples' (37, AAS 59 (1967) 276).

69. (6). Let the governments continue with their individual contributions to a development fund, but let them also look for a way whereby most of their endeavours may follow multilateral channels, fully preserving the responsibility of the developing nations, which must be associated in decision-making concerning priorities and investments.

70. (7). We consider that we must also stress the new world-wide preoccupation which will be dealt with for the first time in the conference on the human environment to be held in Stockholm in June 1972. It is impossible to see what right the richer nations have to keep up their claim to increase their own material demands, if the consequence is either that others remain in misery or that the danger of destroying the very physical foundations of life on earth is precipitated. Those who are already rich are bound to accept a less material way of life, with less waste, in order to avoid the destruction of the heritage which they are obliged by absolute justice to share with all other members of the human race.

71. (8). In order that the right to development may be fulfilled by action:
    (a) people should not be hindered from attaining development in accordance with their own culture;
    (b) through mutual co-operation, all peoples should be able to become the principal architects of their own economic and social development;
    (c) every people, as active and responsible members of human society, should be able to co-operate for the attainment of the common good on an equal footing with other peoples.

Putting the recommendations into practice

72. The examination of conscience which we have made together, regarding the Church's involvement in action for justice, will remain ineffective if it is

not given flesh in the life of our local churches at all their levels. We also ask the episcopal conferences to continue to pursue the perspectives which we have had in view during the days of this meeting and to put our recommendations into practice, for instance by setting up centres of social and theological research.

73. We also ask that there be recommended to the Pontifical Commission Justice and Peace, the council of the secretariat of the synod and to competent authorities, the description, consideration and deeper study of the wishes and desires of our assembly, and that these bodies should bring to a successful conclusion what we have begun.

IV

A word of hope

The Church's presence among the poor

74. The power of the Spirit, who raised Christ from the dead, is continuously at work in the world. Through the generous sons and daughters of the Church likewise, the people of God is present in the midst of the poor and of those who suffer oppression and persecution; it lives in its own flesh and its own heart the Passion of Christ and bears witness to his resurrection.

75. The entire creation has been groaning till now in an act of giving birth, as it waits for the glory of the children of God to be revealed (cf. Rom. 8:22). Let Christians therefore be convinced that they will yet find the fruits of their own nature and effort cleansed of all impurities in the new earth which God is now preparing for them, and in which there will be the kingdom of justice and love, a kingdom which will be fully perfected when the Lord will come himself.

76. Hope in the coming kingdom is already beginning to take root in the hearts of men. The radical transformation of the world in the paschal mystery of the Lord gives full meaning to the efforts of men, and in particular of the young, to lessen injustice, violence and hatred and to advance all together in justice, freedom, brotherhood and love.

77. At the same time as it proclaims the gospel of the Lord, its redeemer and saviour, the Church calls on all, especially the poor, the oppressed and the afflicted, to co-operate with God to bring about liberation from every sin and to build a world which will reach the fullness of creation only when it becomes the work of man for man.

Editor's Note

JW 27: The meaning of 'mediatory role' is unclear. It is no clearer in the original Latin, though it is evident from the Latin text that *mediatio* is being used in some technical sense.

Evangelii Nuntiandi

*Apostolic exhortation of Pope Paul VI to the bishops,
priests and faithful of the entire Catholic Church on
evangelization in the modern world.*

Introduction

The fourth synod of bishops gathered in Rome at the end of September
1974. Just over 200 people representing episcopal conferences from all
round the world spent a month discussing evangelization in the modern
world. In the end, though a general statement was produced, they failed to
agree on a major text, and handed the topic, together with drafts of their
proposed document, over to Pope Paul. On 8 December 1975 Pope Paul
produced *Evangelii Nuntiandi* whose Latin title, translated as 'On
proclaiming the Gospel', accurately reflects the content of the exhortation.

As the title indicates, it is not primarily a statement of Catholic social
teaching. Nonetheless it is a crucial document for the Church's involvement
in social, political and economic life, for it stresses that salvation 'is
liberation from everything that oppresses man' (EN 9), thus decisively linking
the proclamation of the gospel to concern about the sort of life people have to
live in this world. 'Between evangelization and human advancement—-
development and liberation—there are in fact profound links', the pope says
later on (EN 31), and then goes on to reflect upon this theme.

Pope Paul insists, quite naturally, that proclaiming the good news cannot
be reduced to working for human liberation in the political sense, nor does he
accept that the Church can be identified with any one specific political
expression of human liberation. Indeed, he asserts that any purely temporal
understanding of the concept of liberation contains within itself the seeds of its
own failure. Despite these and other qualifications, however, this apostolic
exhortation firmly commits the Church to the language of liberation, and is a
major step forward.

For further discussion of *Evangelii Nuntiandi* (EN) see the Introduction,
pp.xvii. The Latin text appeared in AAS 68 (1976) 5-76. In the Latin text the
main paragraphs have been numbered, but not subordinate ones, so
additional numbering has been added in accordance with the Editorial Note
(p.ix).

Summary

Paras. 1-16: Is the Church nowadays better equipped to proclaim the gospel? The proclamation of the gospel is a duty placed by Jesus upon the Church. Jesus was himself the first evangelizer. His message was, above all, the proclamation of the kingdom of God. As the kernel of his good news Christ proclaims salvation, the gift of God which liberates people from everything that oppresses them. The kingdom, and salvation, are to be gained through a profound change of mind and heart. Those who accept the good news gather together to seek the kingdom, and in their turn go out to evangelize: those who have received the good news must communicate it. The Church exists in order to preach and teach. It was born of the evangelizing activity of Jesus and the apostles. It was sent out to evangelize while itself remaining in constant need of conversion and renewal if it is to do so credibly. It is the depositary of the good news and gives a mandate to those who go out to spread it. There is, therefore, a very close link between Christ, the Church and evangelization.

Paras. 17-24: To put it briefly, the Church evangelizes when it seeks to convert people's personal and collective consciences, their activities, their lives and the milieux in which they live: their culture must be evangelized. Above all the gospel must be proclaimed by witness, and all Christians are called to do that much. But that witness needs to be explained and justified, and the proclamation is fully developed only when it arouses genuine adherence in those who receive it. The test of that adherence is whether the person who is evangelized goes out to evangelize others.

Paras. 25-39: At the centre of evangelization is the proclamation of salvation in Jesus Christ, a salvation which begins in this life but is fulfilled in the next. It therefore includes the preaching of hope in the promises made by God in the new covenant in Jesus Christ, but it would not be complete did it not also take account of the interplay of the gospel and of people's personal and social lives. There are profound links between evangelization and human advancement both because those to be evangelized are subject to social and economic pressures, and because it is not possible to dissociate the plan of creation from the plan of redemption. There is a temptation to reduce the Church's work for liberation to a purely temporal affair. Were this to happen the Church would lose its fundamental meaning. The liberation proclaimed in evangelization cannot be restricted to economics, politics, social or cultural life. It must reach the whole person, including a person's openness to the absolute. It is important to build structures which are more humane, more just, less oppressive, but the structures will be insufficient if those who live under, or rule over, such structures do not undergo a change of heart and of outlook. The Church rejects violence, and is becoming increasingly conscious of the strictly evangelical means it has to collaborate in liberation. The necessity of ensuring fundamental human rights—among which religious liberty occupies a place of primary importance—is part of this liberation which is bound up with salvation.

Paras. 40-48: The question of how to evangelize is permanently relevant. First and foremost there is witness. Secondly there is preaching, for which modern methods should be used. There is catechetical instruction, again brought up to date. The modern means of communication should be used, but personal contact remains important. The administration of the sacraments has a part to play, so too, despite its limitations, does popular religiosity.

Paras. 49-58: The proclamation of the gospel is to the whole world: to those who have never heard it, to those who have been baptized but live outside the Christian life, to those with an imperfect knowledge of the faith, to those of non-Christian religions—though this must be done with great sensitivity. There is considerable resistance to evangelization both from atheists and other non-believers on the one hand, and from those who do not practise their faith on the other. Basic communities will be places of evangelization for larger communities to the extent that they do not allow themselves to be politically polarized, that they avoid systematic protest or a hypercritical attitude, that they remain in sincere communion and that they never regard themselves as sole beneficiaries or sole agents of evangelization, while growing in missionary consciousness and avoiding sectarianism.

Paras. 59-73: The Church is wholly missionary: evangelization can never be the isolated act of an individual. The Church is universal by vocation and mission, but it is incarnated in different cultures and takes on different forms of expression. Evangelization loses much of its force if it neglects the culture of those to whom it is addressed. But this adaptation must be done without adulterating the content of the message and without the local church losing contact with the universal Church. The successor of Peter is entrusted pre-eminent ministry of teaching the revealed truth, and the bishops, with their clergy, do so in union with him. Religious men and women have a special role as witnesses because of the manner of their lives. The laity have to evangelize the world in which they operate, the world of politics and culture, of the media and so on. The family has its own role to play, so do young people. There is a variety of ministries undertaken by the laity in association with their pastors, and a serious preparation is required by them and by all workers for evangelization.

Paras. 74-82: Evangelization is not possible without the action of the Holy Spirit. Without the Spirit the most convincing dialectic has no power over the heart. If it is to be authentic, evangelizing zeal must spring from holiness of life: the world is calling for evangelizers to speak to it of a God with whom evangelizers should be familiar, and know. Unity among Christians is an instrument of evangelization: division impedes the work of Christ. Taking as a basis the baptism and the faith which are common to all, there should be greater collaboration with Christians with whom there is not yet perfect unity, in order to give greater common witness. The preacher of the gospel will be someone who always seeks the truth which is to be communicated, even at considerable personal cost. And the work of evangelization presupposes in the evangelizer a love for those being evangelized. It would be an error to impose on the consciences of others, but it would be a mark of respect for religious liberty to propose to people's consciences the truth of the gospel, and thereby offer a choice of a way which even non-believers consider noble.

Venerable brothers and dearest sons and daughters, greetings and apostolic benediction.

Proclaiming the gospel: the Church's task

1. There is no doubt that the effort to proclaim the gospel to the people of today, who are buoyed up by hope but at the same time often oppressed by fear and distress, is a service rendered to the Christian community and also to the whole of humanity.

1.1. For this reason the duty of confirming the brethren—a duty which with the office of being the successor of Peter[1] we have received from the Lord, and which is for us a 'daily preoccupation',[2] a programme of life and action, and a fundamental commitment of our pontificate—seems to us all the more noble and necessary when it is a matter of encouraging our brethren in their mission as evangelizers, in order that, in this time of uncertainty and confusion, they may accomplish this task with ever increasing love, zeal and joy.

2. This is precisely what we wish to do here, at the end of this Holy Year during which the Church, 'striving to proclaim the gospel to all people',[3] has had the single aim of fulfilling her duty of being the messenger of the good news of Jesus Christ—the good news proclaimed through two fundamental commands: 'Put on the new self'[4] and 'Be reconciled to God.'[5]

2.1. We wish to do so on this tenth anniversary of the closing of the Second Vatican Council, the objectives of which are definitively summed up in this single one: to make the Church of the twentieth century ever better fitted for proclaiming the gospel to the people of the twentieth century.

2.2. We wish to do so one year after the third* general assembly of the synod of bishops, which, as is well known, was devoted to evangelization; and we do so all the more willingly because it has been asked of us by the synod Fathers themselves. In fact, at the end of that memorable assembly, the Fathers decided to remit to the pastor of the universal Church, with great trust and simplicity, the fruits of all their labours, stating that they awaited from him a fresh forward impulse, capable of creating within a Church still more firmly rooted in the undying power and strength of Pentecost a new period of evangelization.[6]

3. We have stressed the importance of this theme of evangelization on many occasions, well before the synod took place. On 22 June 1973 we said to the Sacred College of Cardinals: 'The conditions of the society in which we live oblige all of us therefore to revise methods, to seek by every means to study how we can bring the Christian message that modern man can find the answer to his questions and the energy for his commitment of human solidarity.'[7] And we added that in order to give a valid answer to the demands of the council which call for our attention, it is absolutely necessary for us to take into account a heritage of faith that the Church has the duty of preserving in its untouchable purity, and of presenting it to the people of our time, in a way that is as understandable and persuasive as possible.

4. This fidelity both to a message whose servants we are and to the people to whom we must transmit it living and intact is the central axis of evangelization. It poses three burning questions, which the 1974 synod kept constantly in mind:

4.1.—In our day, what has happened to that hidden energy of the good news, which is able to have a powerful effect on man's conscience?

4.2.—To what extent and in what way is that evangelical force capable of really transforming the people of this century?

4.3.—What methods should be followed in order that the power of the gospel may have its effect?

4.4. Basically, these inquiries make explicit the fundamental question that the Church is asking herself today and which may be expressed in the following terms: after the council and thanks to the council, which was a time given her by God, at this turning-point of history, does the Church or does she not find herself better equipped to proclaim the gospel and to put it into people's hearts with conviction, freedom of spirit and effectiveness?

5. We çan all see the urgency of giving a loyal, humble and courageous answer to this question, and of acting accordingly. In our 'anxiety for all the churches',[8] we would like to help our brethren and sons and daughters to reply to these inquiries. Our words come from the wealth of the synod and are meant to be a meditation on evangelization. May they succeed in inviting the whole people of God assembled in the Church to make the same meditation; and may they give a fresh impulse to everyone, especially those 'who are assiduous in preaching and teaching',[9] so that each one of them may follow 'a straight course in the message of the truth',[10] and may work as a preacher of the gospel and acquit himself perfectly of his ministry.

5.1. Such an exhortation seems to us to be of capital importance, for the presentation of the gospel message is not an optional contribution for the Church. It is the duty incumbent on her by the command of the Lord Jesus, so that people can believe and be saved. This message is indeed necessary. It is unique. It cannot be replaced. It does not permit either difference, syncretism or accommodation. It is a question of people's salvation. It is the beauty of the revelation that it represents. It brings with it a wisdom that is not of this world. It is able to stir up by itself faith—faith that rests on the power of God.[11] It is truth. It merits having the apostle consecrate to it all his time and all his energies, and to sacrifice for it, if necessary, his own life.

I

The example of Jesus

6. The witness that the Lord gives of himself and that Luke gathered together in his gospel—'I must proclaim the good news of the kingdom of God'[12]—without doubt has enormous consequences, for it sums up the whole mission of Jesus: 'That is what I was sent to do.'[13] These words take on their full significance if one links them with the previous verses, in which Christ has just applied to himself the words of the prophet Isaiah: 'The Spirit of the

Lord has been given to me, for he has anointed me. He has sent me to bring the good news to the poor.'[14]

6.1. Going from town to town, preaching to the poorest—and frequently the most receptive—the joyful news of the fulfilment of the promises and of the covenant offered by God is the mission for which Jesus declares that he is sent by the father. And all the aspects of his mystery—the incarnation itself, his miracles, his teaching, the gathering together of the disciples, the sending out of the twelve, the cross and the resurrection, the permanence of his presence in the midst of his own—were components of his evangelizing activity.

7. During the synod, the bishops very frequently referred to this truth: Jesus himself, the good news of God,[15] was the very first and the greatest evangelizer; he was so through and through: to perfection and to the point of the sacrifice of his earthly life.

7.1. To evangelize: what meaning did this imperative have for Christ? It is certainly not easy to express in a complete synthesis the meaning, the content and the modes of evangelization as Jesus conceived it and put it into practice. In any case the attempt to make such a synthesis will never end. Let it suffice for us to recall a few essential aspects.

8. As an evangelizer, Christ first of all proclaims a kingdom, the kingdom of God; and this is so important that, by comparison, everything else becomes 'the rest', which is 'given in addition'.[16] Only the kingdom therefore is absolute, and it makes everything else relative. The Lord will delight in describing in many ways the happiness of belonging to this kingdom (a paradoxical happiness which is made up of things that the world rejects),[17] the demands of the kingdom and its *Magna Charta*,[18] the heralds of the kingdom,[19] its mysteries,[20] its children,[21] the vigilance and fidelity demanded of whoever awaits its definitive coming.[22]

9. As the kernel and centre of his good news, Christ proclaims salvation, this great gift of God which is liberation from everything that oppresses man but which is above all liberation from sin and the evil one, in the joy of knowing God and being known by him, of seeing him, and of being given over to him. All of this is begun during the life of Christ and definitely accomplished by his death and resurrection. But it must be patiently carried on during the course of history, in order to be realized fully on the day of the final coming of Christ, whose date is known to no one except the Father.[23]

10. This kingdom and this salvation, which are the key words of Jesus Christ's evangelization, are available to every human being as grace and mercy, and yet at the same time each individual must gain them by force—they belong to the violent, says the Lord,[24] through toil and suffering, through a life lived according to the gospel, through abnegation and the cross, through the spirit of the beatitudes. But above all each individual gains them through a total interior renewal which the gospel calls *metanoia*; it is a radical conversion, a profound change of mind and heart.[25]

11. Christ accomplished this proclamation of the kingdom of God through the untiring preaching of a word which, it will be said, has no equal

elsewhere: 'Here is a teaching that is new, and with authority behind it.'[26] 'And he won the approval of all, and they were astonished by the gracious words that came from his lips.'[27] 'There has never been anybody who has spoken like him.'[28] His words reveal the secret of God, his plan and his promise, and thereby change the heart of man and his destiny.

12. But Christ also carries out this proclamation by innumerable signs, which amaze the crowds and at the same time draw them to him in order to see him, listen to him and allow themselves to be transformed by him: the sick are cured, water is changed into wine, bread is multiplied, the dead come back to life. And among all these signs there is the one to which he attaches great importance: the humble and the poor are evangelized, become his disciples and gather together 'in his name' in the great community of those who believe in him. For this Jesus who declared, 'I must preach the good news of the kingdom of God,'[29] is the same Jesus of whom John the Evangelist said that he had come and was to die 'to gather together in unity the scattered children of God'.[30] Thus he accomplishes his revelation, completing it and confirming it by the entire revelation that he makes of himself, by words and deeds, by signs and miracles, and more especially by his death, by his resurrection and by the sending of the Spirit of truth.[31]

13. Those who sincerely accept the good news, through the power of this acceptance and of shared faith, therefore gather together in Jesus' name in order to seek together the kingdom, build it up and live it. They make up a community which is in its turn evangelizing. The command to the twelve to go out and proclaim the good news is also valid for all Christians, though in a different way. It is precisely for this reason that Peter calls Christians 'a people set apart to sing the praises of God',[32] those marvellous things that each one was able to hear in his own language.[33] Moreover, the good news of the kingdom which is coming and which has begun is meant for all people of all times. Those who have received the good news and who have been gathered by it into the community of salvation can and must communicate and spread it.

14. The Church knows this. She has a vivid awareness of the fact that the saviour's words, 'I must proclaim the good news of the kingdom of God,'[34] apply in all truth to herself. She willingly adds with St Paul: 'Not that I boast of preaching the gospel, since it is a duty that has been laid on me; I should be punished if I did not preach it!'[35] It is with joy and consolation that at the end of the great assembly of 1974 we heard these illuminating words: 'We wish to confirm once more that the task of evangelizing all people constitutes the essential mission of the Church.'[36] It is a task and mission which the vast and profound changes of present-day society make all the more urgent. Evangelizing is in fact the grace and vocation proper to the Church, her deepest identity. She exists in order to evangelize, that is to say in order to preach and teach, to be the channel of the gift of grace, to reconcile sinners with God, and to perpetuate Christ's sacrifice in the Mass, which is the memorial of his death and glorious resurrection.

15. Anyone who re-reads in the New Testament the origins of the Church, follows her history step by step and watches her live and act, sees that she is

linked to evangelization in her most intimate being:

15.1.—The Church is born of the evangelizing activity of Jesus and the twelve. She is the normal, desired, most immediate and most visible fruit of this activity: 'Go, therefore, make disciples of all the nations.'[37] Now, 'they accepted what he said and were baptized. That very day about three thousand were added to their number... Day by day the Lord added to their community those destined to be saved.'[38]

15.2.—Having been born consequently out of being sent, the Church in her turn is sent by Jesus. The Church remains in the world when the Lord of glory returns to the father. She remains as a sign—simultaneously obscure and luminous—of a new presence of Jesus, of his departure and of his permanent presence. She prolongs and continues him. And it is above all his mission and his condition of being an evangelizer that she is called upon to continue.[39] For the Christian community is never closed in upon itself. The intimate life of this community—the life of listening to the word and the apostles' teaching, charity lived in a fraternal way, the sharing of bread[40]—this intimate life only acquires its full meaning when it becomes a witness, when it evokes admiration and conversion, and when it becomes the preaching and proclamation of the good news. Thus it is the whole Church that receives the mission to evangelize, and the work of each individual member is important for the whole.

15.3.—The Church is an evangelizer, but she begins by being evangelized herself. She is the community of believers, the community of hope lived and communicated, the community of brotherly love; and she needs to listen unceasingly to what she must believe, to her reasons for hoping, to the new commandment of love. She is the people of God immersed in the world, and often tempted by idols, and she always needs to hear the proclamation of the 'mighty works of God'[41] which converted her to the Lord; she always needs to be called together afresh by him and reunited. In brief, this means that she has a constant need of being evangelized, if she wishes to retain freshness, vigour and strength in order to proclaim the gospel. The Second Vatican Council recalled[42] and the 1974 synod vigorously took up again this theme of the Church which is evangelized by constant conversion and renewal in order to evangelize the world with credibility.

15.4.—The Church is the depositary of the good news to be proclaimed. The promises of the new alliance in Jesus Christ, the teaching of the Lord and the apostles, the word of life, the sources of grace and of God's loving kindness, the path of salvation—all these things have been entrusted to her. It is the content of the gospel, and therefore of evangelization, that she preserves as a precious living heritage, not in order to keep it hidden but to communicate it.

15.5.—Having been sent and evangelized, the Church herself sends out evangelizers. She puts on their lips the saving word, she explains to them the message of which she herself is the depository, she gives them the mandate which she herself has received and she sends them out to preach. To preach not their own selves or their personal ideas,[43] but a gospel of which neither she nor they are the absolute masters and owners, to dispose of it as they wish, but a gospel of which they are the ministers, in order to pass it on with complete fidelity.

16. There is thus a profound link between Christ, the Church and evangelization. During the period of the Church that we are living in, it is she who has the task of evangelizing. This mandate is not accomplished without her, and still less against her.

16.1. It is certainly fitting to recall this fact at a moment like the present one when it happens that not without sorrow we can hear people—whom we wish to believe are well-intentioned but who are certainly misguided in their attitude—continually claiming to love Christ but without the Church, to listen to Christ but not the Church, to belong to Christ but outside the Church. The absurdity of this dichotomy is clearly evident in this phrase of the gospel: 'Anyone who rejects you rejects me.'[44] And how can one wish to love Christ without loving the Church, if the finest witness to Christ is that of St Paul: 'Christ loved the Church and sacrificed himself for her?'[45]

II

The meaning of evangelization

17. In the Church's evangelizing activity there are of course certain elements and aspects to be specially insisted on. Some of them are so important that there will be a tendency simply to identify them with evangelization. Thus it has been possible to define evangelization in terms of proclaiming Christ to those who do not know him, of preaching, of catechesis, of conferring baptism and the other sacraments.

17.1. Any partial and fragmentary definition which attempts to render the reality of evangelization in all its richness, complexity and dynamism does so only at the risk of impoverishing it and even of distorting it. It is impossible to grasp the concept of evangelization unless one tries to keep in view all its essential elements.

17.2. These elements were strongly emphasized at the last synod and are still the subject of frequent study, as a result of the synod's work. We rejoice in the fact that these elements basically follow the lines of those transmitted to us by the Second Vatican Council, especially in *Lumen Gentium, Gaudium et Spes* and *Ad Gentes*.

18. For the Church, evangelizing means bringing the good news into all the strata of humanity, and through its influence transforming humanity from within and making it new: 'Now I am making the whole of creation new.'[46] But there is no new humanity if there are not first of all new persons renewed by baptism[47] and by lives lived according to the gospel.[48] The purpose of evangelization is therefore precisely this interior change, and if it has to be expressed in one sentence the best way of stating it would be to say that the Church evangelizes when she seeks to convert,[49] solely through the divine power of the message she proclaims, both the personal and collective consciences of people, the activities in which they engage, and the lives and concrete milieux which are theirs.

19. Strata of humanity which are transformed: for the Church it is a question not only of preaching the gospel in ever wider geographic areas or to ever

greater numbers of people, but also of affecting and as it were upsetting, through the power of the gospel, mankind's criteria of judgement, determining values, points of interest, lines of thought, sources of inspiration and models of life, which are in contrast with the word of God and the plan of salvation.

20. All this could be expressed in the following words: what matters is to evangelize man's culture and cultures (not in a purely decorative way as it were by applying a thin veneer, but in a vital way, in depth and right to their very roots), in the wide and rich sense which these terms have in *Gaudium et Spes*,[50] always taking the person as one's starting point and always coming back to the relationships of people among themselves and with God.

20.1. The gospel, and therefore evangelization, are certainly not identical with culture, and they are independent in regard to all cultures. Nevertheless, the kingdom which the gospel proclaims is lived by men who are profoundly linked to a culture, and the building up of the kingdom cannot avoid borrowing the elements of human culture or cultures. Though independent of cultures, the gospel and evangelization are not necessarily incompatible with them; rather they are capable of permeating them all without becoming subject to any of them.

20.2. The split between the gospel and culture is without a doubt the drama of our time, just as it was of other times. Therefore every effort must be made to ensure a full evangelization of culture, or more correctly of cultures. They have to be regenerated by an encounter with the gospel. But this encounter will not take place if the gospel is not proclaimed.

21. Above all the gospel must be proclaimed by witness. Take a Christian or a handful of Christians who, in the midst of their own community, show their capacity for understanding and acceptance, their sharing of life and destiny with other people, their solidarity with the efforts of all for whatever is noble and good. Let us suppose that, in addition, they radiate in an altogether simple and unaffected way their faith in values that go beyond current values, and their hope in something that is not seen and that one would not dare to imagine. Through this wordless witness these Christians stir up irresistible questions in the hearts of those who see how they live: Why are they like this? Why do they live in this way? What or who is it that inspires them? Why are they in our midst? Such a witness is already a silent proclamation of the good news and a very powerful and effective one. Here we have an initial act of evangelization. The above questions will perhaps be the first that many non-Christians will ask, whether they are people to whom Christ has never been proclaimed, or baptized people who do not practise, or people who live as nominal Christians but according to principles that are in no way Christian, or people who are seeking, and not without suffering, something or someone whom they sense but cannot name. Other questions will arise, deeper and more demanding ones, questions evoked by this witness which involves presence, sharing, solidarity, and which is an essential element, and generally the first one, in evangelization.[51]

21.1. All Christians are called to this witness, and in this way they can be real evangelizers. We are thinking especially of the responsibility incumbent on immigrants in the country that receives them.

22. Nevertheless this always remains insufficient, because even the finest witness will prove ineffective in the long run if it is not explained, justified—what Peter called always having 'your answer ready for people who ask you the reason for the hope that you all have'[52]—and made explicit by a clear and unequivocal proclamation of the Lord Jesus. The good news proclaimed by the witness of life sooner or later has to be proclaimed by the word of life. There is no true evangelization if the name, the teaching, the life, the promises, the kingdom and the mystery of Jesus of Nazareth, the son of God, are not proclaimed.

22.1. The history of the Church, from the discourse of Peter on the morning of Pentecost onwards, has been intermingled and identified with the history of this proclamation. At every new phase of human history, the Church, constantly gripped by the desire to evangelize, has but one preoccupation: whom to send to proclaim the mystery of Jesus? In what way is this mystery to be proclaimed? How can one ensure that it will resound and reach all those who should hear it? This proclamation—*kerygma*, preaching or catechesis—occupies such an important place in evangelization that it has often become synonymous with it; and yet it is only one aspect of evangelization.

23. In fact the proclamation only reaches full development when it is listened to, accepted and assimilated, and when it arouses a genuine adherence in the one who has thus received it. An adherence to the truths which the Lord in his mercy has revealed; still more, an adherence to a programme of life—a life henceforth transformed—which he proposes. In a word, adherence to the kingdom, that is to say the 'new world' to the new state of things, to the new manner of being, of living, of living in community, which the gospel inaugurates. Such an adherence, which cannot remain abstract and unincarnated, reveals itself concretely by a visible entry into a community of believers. Thus those whose life has been transformed enter a community which is itself a sign of transformation, a sign of newness of life: it is the Church, the visible sacrament of salvation.[53] But entry into the ecclesial community will in its turn be expressed through many other signs which prolong and unfold the sign of the Church. In the dynamism of evangelization, a person who accepts the Church as the word which saves[54] normally translates it into the following sacramental acts: adherence to the Church, and acceptance of the sacraments, which manifest and support this adherence through the grace which they confer.

24. Finally: the person who has been evangelized goes on to evangelize others. Here lies the test of truth, the touchstone of evangelization: it is unthinkable that a person should accept the word and give himself to the kingdom without becoming a person who bears witness to it and proclaims it in his turn.

24.1. To complete these considerations on the meaning of evangelization, a final observation must be made, one which we consider will help to clarify the reflections that follow.

24.2. Evangelization, as we have said, is a complex process made up of varied elements: the renewal of humanity, witness, explicit proclamation, inner adherence, entry into the community, acceptance of signs, apostolic initiative. These elements may appear to be contradictory, indeed mutually exclusive. In fact they are complementary and mutually enriching. Each one must always be seen in relationship with the others. The value of the last synod was to have constantly invited us to relate these elements rather than to place them in opposition one to the other, in order to reach a full understanding of the Church's evangelizing activity. It is this global vision which we now wish to outline, by examining the content of evangelization and the methods of evangelizing and by clarifying to whom the gospel message is addressed and who today is responsible for it.

III

The content of the message

25. In the message which the Church proclaims there are certainly many secondary elements. Their presentation depends greatly on changing circumstances. They themselves also change. But there is the essential content, the living substance, which cannot be modified or ignored without seriously diluting the nature of evangelization itself.

26. It is not superfluous to recall the following points: to evangelize is first of all to bear witness, in a simple and direct way, to God revealed by Jesus Christ, in the Holy Spirit; to bear witness that in his son God has loved the world—that in his incarnate word he has given being to all things and has called men to eternal life. Perhaps this attestation of God will be for many people the unknown God[55] whom they adore without giving him a name, or whom they seek by a secret call of the heart when they experience the emptiness of all idols. But it is fully evangelizing in manifesting the fact that for man the creator is not an anonymous and remote power; he is the father: '...that we should be called children of God; and so we are'.[56] And thus we are one another's brothers and sisters in God.

27. Evangelization will also always contain—as the foundation, centre and at the same time summit of its dynamism—a clear proclamation that, in Jesus Christ, the son of God made man, who died and rose from the dead, salvation is offered to all men, as a gift of God's grace and mercy.[57] And not an immanent salvation, meeting material or even spiritual needs, restricted to the framework of temporal existence and completely identified with temporal desires, hopes, affairs and struggles, but a salvation which exceeds all these limits in order to reach fulfilment in a communion with the one and only divine absolute: a transcendent and eschatological salvation, which indeed has its beginning in this life but which is fulfilled in eternity.

28. Consequently evangelization cannot but include the prophetic proclamation of a hereafter, man's profound and definitive calling, in both continuity and discontinuity with the present situation: beyond time and history, beyond the transient reality of this world, and beyond the things of this world, of which a hidden dimension will one day be revealed—beyond man himself, whose true destiny is not restricted to his temporal aspect but

will be revealed in the future life.⁵⁸ Evangelization therefore also includes the preaching of hope in the promises made by God in the new covenant in Jesus Christ, the preaching of God's love for all men—the capacity of giving and forgiving, of self-denial, of helping one's brother and sister—which, springing from the love of God, is the kernel of the gospel; the preaching of the mystery of evil and of the active search for good. The preaching likewise—and this is always urgent—of the search for God himself through prayer which is principally that of adoration and thanksgiving, but also through communion with the visible sign of the encounter with God which is the Church of Jesus Christ; and this communion in its turn is expressed by the application of those other signs of Christ living and acting in the Church which are the sacraments. To live the sacraments in this way, bringing their celebration to a true fullness, is not, as some would claim, to impede or to accept a distortion of evangelization: it is rather to complete it. For in its totality, evangelization—over and above the preaching of a message—consists in the implantation of the Church, which does not exist without the driving force which is the sacramental life culminating in the eucharist.⁵⁹

29. But evangelization would not be complete if it did not take account of the unceasing interplay of the gospel and of man's concrete life, both personal and social. This is why evangelization involves an explicit message, adapted to the different situations constantly being realized, about the rights and duties of every human being, about family life without which personal growth and development is hardly possible,⁶⁰ about life in society, about international life, peace, justice and development—a message especially energetic today about liberation.

30. It is well known in what terms numerous bishops from all the continents spoke of this at the last synod, especially the bishops from the Third World, with a pastoral accent resonant with the voice of the millions of sons and daughters of the Church who make up those peoples. Peoples, as we know, engaged with all their energy in the effort and struggle to overcome everything which condemns them to remain on the margin of life: famine, chronic disease, illiteracy, poverty, injustices in international relations and especially in commercial exchanges, situations of economic and cultural neo-colonialism sometimes as cruel as the old political colonialism. The Church, as the bishops repeated, has the duty to proclaim the liberation of millions of human beings, many of whom are her own children—the duty of assisting the birth of this liberation, of giving witness to it, of ensuring that it is complete. This is not foreign to evangelization.

Evangelization and liberation

31. Between evangelization and human advancement—development and liberation—there are in fact profound links. These include links of an anthropological order, because the man who is to be evangelized is not an abstract being but is subject to social and economic questions. They also include links in the theological order, since one cannot dissociate the plan of creation from the plan of redemption. The latter plan touches the very

concrete situations of injustice to be combatted and of justice to be restored. They include links of the eminently evangelical order, which is that of charity: how in fact can one proclaim the new commandment without promoting in justice and in peace the true, authentic advancement of man? We ourself have taken care to point this out, by recalling that it is impossible to accept 'that in evangelization one could or should ignore the importance of the problems so much discussed today, concerning justice, liberation, development and peace in the world. This would be to forget the lesson which comes to us from the gospel concerning love of our neighbour who is suffering and in need.'[61]

31.1. The same voices which during the synod touched on this burning theme with zeal, intelligence and courage have, to our great joy, furnished the enlightening principles for a proper understanding of the importance and profound meaning of liberation, such as it was proclaimed and achieved by Jesus of Nazareth and such as it is preached by the Church.

32. We must not ignore the fact that many, even generous Christians who are sensitive to the dramatic questions involved in the problem of liberation, in their wish to commit the Church to the liberation effort are frequently tempted to reduce her mission to the dimensions of a simply temporal project. They would reduce her aims to a man-centred goal; the salvation of which she is the messenger would be reduced to material well-being. Her activity, forgetful of all spiritual and religious preoccupation, would become initiatives of the political or social order. But if this were so, the Church would lose her fundamental meaning. Her message of liberation would no longer have any originality and would easily be open to monopolization and manipulation by ideological systems and political parties. She would have no more authority to proclaim freedom as in the name of God. This is why we have wished to emphasize, in the same address at the opening of the synod, 'the need to restate clearly the specifically religious finality of evangelization. This latter would lose its reason for existence if it were to diverge from the religious axis that guides it: the kingdom of God, before anything else, in its fully theological meaning...'[62]

33. With regard to the liberation which evangelization proclaims and strives to put into practice one should rather say this:

33.1.—It cannot be contained in the simple and restricted dimension of economics, politics, social or cultural life; it must envisage the whole man, in all his aspects, right up to and including his openness to the absolute, even the divine absolute;

33.2.—It is therefore attached to a certain concept of man, to a view of man which it can never sacrifice to the needs of any strategy, practice or short-term efficiency.

34. Hence, when preaching liberation and associating herself with those who are working and suffering for it, the Church is certainly not willing to restrict her mission only to the religious field and dissociate herself from man's temporal problems. Nevertheless she reaffirms the primacy of her spiritual vocation and refuses to replace the proclamation of the kingdom by the proclamation of forms of human liberation; she even states that her contribution to liberation is incomplete if she neglects to proclaim salvation in Jesus Christ.

35. The Church links human liberation and salvation in Jesus Christ, but she never identifies them, because she knows through revelation, historical experience and the reflection of faith that not every notion of liberation is necessarily consistent and compatible with an evangelical vision of man, of things and of events; she knows too that in order that God's kingdom should come it is not enough to establish liberation and to create well-being and development.

35.1. And what is more, the Church has the firm conviction that all temporal liberation, all political liberation—even if it endeavours to find its justification in such a page of the Old or New Testament, even if it claims for its ideological postulates and its norms of action theological data and conclusions, even if it pretends to be today's theology—carries within itself the germ of its own negation and fails to reach the ideal that it proposes for itself, whenever its profound motives are not those of justice in charity, whenever its zeal lacks a truly spiritual dimension and whenever its final goal is not salvation and happiness in God.

36. The Church considers it to be undoubtedly important to build up structures which are more human, more just, more respectful of the rights of the person and less oppressive and less enslaving, but she is conscious that the best structures and the most idealized systems soon become inhuman if the inhuman inclinations of the human heart are not made wholesome, if those who live in these structures or who rule them do not undergo a conversion of heart and of outlook.

37. The Church cannot accept violence, especially the force of arms—which is uncontrollable once it is let loose—and indiscriminate death as the path of liberation, because she knows that violence always provokes violence and irresistibly engenders new forms of oppression and enslavement which are often harder to bear than those from which they claimed to bring freedom. We said this clearly during our journey in Columbia: 'We exhort you not to place your trust in violence and revolution: that is contrary to the Christian spirit, and it can also delay instead of advancing that social uplifting to which you lawfully aspire.'[63] 'We must say and reaffirm that violence is not in accord with the gospel, that it is not Christian; and that sudden or violent changes of structures would be deceitful, ineffective of themselves, and certainly not in conformity with the dignity of the people.'[64]

38. Having said this, we rejoice that the Church is becoming ever more conscious of the proper manner and strictly evangelical means that she possesses in order to collaborate in the liberation of many. And what is she doing? She is trying more and more to encourage large numbers of Christians to devote themselves to the liberation of men. She is providing these Christian 'liberators' with the inspiration of faith, the motivation of fraternal love, a social teaching which the true Christian cannot ignore and which he must make the foundation of his wisdom and of his experience in order to translate it concretely into forms of action, participation and commitment. All this must characterize the spirit of a committed Christian, without confusion with tactical attitudes or with the service of a political system. The Church strives

always to insert the Christian struggle for liberation into the universal plan of salvation which she herself proclaims.

38.1. What we have just recalled comes out more than once in the synod debates. In fact we devoted to this theme a few clarifying words in our address to the Fathers at the end of the Assembly.[65]

38.2. It is to be hoped that all these considerations will help to remove the ambiguity which the word 'liberation' very often takes on in ideologies, political systems or groups. The liberation which evangelization proclaims and prepares is the one which Christ himself announced and gave to man by his sacrifice.

39. The necessity of ensuring fundamental human rights cannot be separated from this just liberation which is bound up with evangelization and which endeavours to secure structures safeguarding human freedoms. Among these fundamental human rights, religious liberty occupies a place of primary importance. We recently spoke of the relevance of this matter, emphasizing 'how many Christians still today, because they are Christians, because they are Catholics, live oppressed by systematic persecution! The drama of fidelity to Christ and of the freedom of religion continues, even if it is disguised by categorical declarations in favour of the rights of the person and of life in society!'[66]

IV

Means of proclaiming the gospel

40. The obvious importance of the content of evangelization must not overshadow the importance of the ways and means.

40.1. This question of 'how to evangelize' is permanently relevant, because the methods of evangelizing vary according to the different circumstances of time, place and culture, and because they thereby present a certain challenge to our capacity for discovery and adaptation.

40.2. On us particularly, the pastors of the Church, rests the responsibility for reshaping with boldness and wisdom, but in complete fidelity to the content of evangelization, the means that are most suitable and effective for communicating the gospel message to the men and women of our times. Let it suffice, in this meditation, to mention a number of methods which, for one reason or another, have a fundamental importance.

41. Without repeating everything that we have already mentioned, it is appropriate first of all to emphasize the following point: for the Church, the first means of evangelization is the witness of an authentically Christian life, given over to God in a communion that nothing should destroy and at the same time given to one's neighbour with limitless zeal. As we said recently to a group of law people, 'Modern man listens more willingly to witnesses than to teachers, and if he does listen to teachers, it is because they are witnesses.'[67] Saint Peter expressed this well when he held up the example of a reverent and chaste life that wins over even without a word those who refuse to obey the word.[68] It is therefore primarily by her conduct and by her life that the

Church will evangelize the world, in other words, by her living witness of fidelity to the Lord Jesus—the witness of poverty and detachment, of freedom in the face of the powers of this world, in short, the witness of sanctity.

42. Secondly, it is not superfluous to emphasize the importance and necessity of preaching. 'And how are they to believe in him of whom they have never heard? And how are they to hear without a preacher?... So faith comes from what is heard and what is heard comes by the preaching of Christ.'[69] This law once laid down by the apostle Paul maintains its full force today.

42.1. Preaching, the verbal proclamation of a message, is indeed always indispensable. We are well aware that modern man is sated by talk; he is obviously often tired of listening and, what is worse, impervious to words. We are also aware that many psychologists and sociologists express the view that modern man has passed beyond the civilization of the word, which is now ineffective and useless, and that today he lives in the civilization of the image. These facts should certainly impel us to employ, for the purpose of transmitting the gospel message, the modern means which this civilization has produced. Very positive efforts have in fact already been made in this sphere. We cannot but praise them and encourage their further development. The fatigue produced these days by so much empty talk and the relevance of many other forms of communication must not however diminish the permanent power of the word, or cause a loss of confidence in it. The word remains ever relevant, especially when it is the bearer of the power of God.[70] This is why St Paul's axiom, 'Faith comes from what is heard,'[71] also retains its relevance: it is the word that is heard which leads to belief.

43. This evangelizing preaching takes on many forms, and zeal will inspire the reshaping of them almost indefinitely. In fact there are innumerable events in life and human situations which offer the opportunity for a discreet but incisive statement of what the Lord has to say in this or that particular circumstance. It suffices to have true spiritual sensitivity for reading God's message in events. But at a time when the liturgy renewed by the council has given greatly increased value to the liturgy of the word, it would be a mistake not to see in the homily an important and very adaptable instrument of evangelization. Of course it is necessary to know and put to good use the exigencies and the possibilities of the homily, so that it can acquire all its pastoral effectiveness. But above all it is necessary to be convinced of this and to devote oneself to it with love. This preaching, inserted in a unique way into the eucharistic celebration, from which it receives special force and vigour, certainly has a particular role in evangelization, to the extent that it expresses the profound faith of the sacred minister and is impregnated with love. The faithful assembled as a paschal church, celebrating the feast of the Lord present in their midst, expect much from this preaching, and will greatly benefit from it provided that it is simple, clear, direct, well adapted, profoundly dependent on gospel teaching and faithful to the magisterium, animated by a balanced apostolic ardour coming from its own characteristic nature, full of hope, fostering belief, and productive of peace and unity. Many parochial or other communities live and are held together thanks to the

Sunday homily, when it possesses these qualities.

43.1. Let us add that, thanks to the same liturgical renewal, the eucharistic celebration is not the only appropriate moment for the homily. The homily has a place and must not be neglected in the celebration of all the sacraments, at para-liturgies, and in assemblies of the faithful. It will always be a privileged occasion for communicating the word of the Lord.

44. A means of evangelization that must not be neglected is that of catechetical instruction. The intelligence, especially that of children and young people, needs to learn through systematic religious instruction the fundamental teachings, the living content of the truth which God has wished to convey to us and which the Church has sought to express in an ever richer fashion during the course of her long history. No one will deny that this instruction must be given to form patterns of Christian living and not to remain only notional. Truly the effort for evangelization will profit greatly—at the level of catechetical instruction given at church, in the schools, where this is possible, and in every case in Christian homes—if those giving catechetical instruction have suitable texts, updated with wisdom and competence, under the authority of the bishops. The methods must be adapted to the age, culture and aptitude of the persons concerned; they must seek always to fix in the memory, intelligence and heart the essential truths that must impregnate all of life. It is necessary above all to prepare good instructors—parochial catechists, teachers, parents—who are desirous of perfecting themselves in this superior art, which is indispensable and requires religious instruction. Moreover, without neglecting in any way the training of children, one sees that present conditions render ever more urgent catechetical instruction, under the form of the catechumenate, for innumerable young people and adults who, touched by grace, discover little by little the face of Christ and feel the need to give themselves to him.

45. Our century is characterized by the mass media or means of social communication, and the first proclamation, catechesis or the further deepening of faith cannot do without these means, as we have already emphasized.

45.1. When they are put at the service of the gospel, they are capable of increasing almost indefinitely the area in which the word of God is heard; they enable the good news to reach millions of people. The Church would feel guilty before the Lord if she did not utilize these powerful means that human skill is daily rendering more perfect. It is through them that she proclaims 'from the housetops'[72] the message of which she is the depository. In them she finds a modern and effective version of the pulpit. Thanks to them she succeeds in speaking to the multitudes.

45.2. Nevertheless the use of the means of social communication for evangelization presents a challenge: through them the evangelical message should reach vast numbers of people, but with the capacity of piercing the conscience of each individual, of implanting itself in his heart as though he were the only person being addressed, with all his most individual and personal qualities, and evoke an entirely personal adherence and commitment.

46. For this reason, side by side with the collective proclamation of the gospel, the other form of transmission, the person-to-person one, remains valid and important. The Lord often used it (for example with Nicodemus, Zacchaeus, the Samaritan woman, Simon the pharisee), and so did the apostles. In the long run, is there any other way of handing on the gospel than by transmitting to another person one's personal experience of faith? It must not happen that the pressing need to proclaim the good news to the multitudes should cause us to forget this form of proclamation whereby an individual's personal conscience is reached and touched by an entirely unique word that he receives from someone else. We can never sufficiently praise those priests who through the sacrament of penance or through pastoral dialogue show their readiness to guide people in the ways of the gospel, to support them in their efforts, to raise them up if they have fallen, and always to assist them with discernment and availability.

47. Yet, one can never sufficiently stress the fact that evangelization does not consist only of the preaching and teaching of a doctrine. For evangelization must touch life: the natural life to which it gives a new meaning, thanks to the evangelical perspectives that it reveals; and the supernatural life, which is not the negation but the purification and elevation of the natural life. This supernatural life finds its living expression in the seven sacraments and in the admirable radiation of grace and holiness which they possess.

47.1. Evangelization thus exercises its full capacity when it achieves the most intimate relationship, or better still a permanent and unbroken intercommunication, between the word and the sacraments. In a certain sense it is a mistake to make a contrast between evangelization and sacramentalization, as is sometimes done. It is indeed true that a certain way of administering the sacraments, without the solid support of catechesis regarding these same sacraments and a global catechesis, could end up by depriving them of their effectiveness to a great extent. The role of evangelization is precisely to educate people in the faith in such a way as to lead each individual Christian to live the sacraments as true sacraments of faith—and not to receive them passively or to undergo them.

48. Here we touch upon an aspect of evangelization which cannot leave us insensitive. We wish to speak about what today is often called popular religiosity.

48.1. One finds among the people particular expressions of the search for God and for faith, both in the regions where the Church has been established for centuries and where she is in the course of becoming established. These expressions were for a long time regarded as less pure and were sometimes despised, but today they are almost everywhere being rediscovered. During the last synod the bishops studied their significance with remarkable pastoral realism and zeal.

48.2. Popular religiosity of course certainly has its limits. It is often subject to penetration by many distortions of religion and even superstitions. It frequently remains at the level of forms of worship not involving a true acceptance by faith. It can even lead to the creation of sects and endanger the true ecclesial community.

48.3. But if it is well oriented, above all by a pedagogy of evangelization, it is rich in values. It manifests a thirst for God which only the simple and poor can know. It makes people capable of generosity and sacrifice even to the point of heroism, when it is a question of manifesting belief. It involves an acute awareness of profound attributes of God: fatherhood, providence, loving and constant presence. It engenders interior attitudes rarely observed to the same degree elsewhere: patience, the sense of the cross in daily life, detachment, openness to others, devotion. By reason of these aspects, we readily call it 'popular piety', that is, religion of the people, rather than religiosity.

48.4. Pastoral charity must dictate to all those whom the Lord has placed as leaders of the ecclesial communities the proper attitude in regard to this reality, which is at the same time so rich and so vulnerable. Above all one must be sensitive to it, know how to perceive its interior dimensions and undeniable values, be ready to help it to overcome its risks of deviation. When it is well oriented, this popular religiosity can be more and more for multitudes of our people a true encounter with God in Jesus Christ.

V

Missionary spirit in the modern world

49. Jesus' last words in St Mark's Gospel confer on the evangelization which the Lord entrusts to his apostles a limitless universality: 'Go out to the whole world; proclaim the good news to all creation.'[73]

49.1. The twelve and the first generation of Christians understood well the lesson of this text and other similar ones; they made them into a programme of action. Even persecution, by scattering the apostles, helped to spread the word and to establish the Church in ever more distant regions. The admission of Paul to the rank of the apostles and his charism as the preacher to the pagans (the non-Jews) of Jesus' coming underlined this universality still more.

50. In the course of twenty centuries of history, the generations of Christians have periodically faced various obstacles to this universal mission. On the one hand, on the part of the evangelizers themselves, there has been the temptation for various reasons to narrow down the field of their missionary activity. On the other hand, there has been the often humanly insurmountable resistance of the people being addressed by the evangelizer. Furthermore, we must note with sadness that the evangelizing work of the Church is strongly opposed, if not prevented, by certain public powers. Even in our own day it happens that preachers of God's word are deprived of their rights, persecuted, threatened or eliminated solely for preaching Jesus Christ and his gospel. But we are confident that despite these painful trials the activity of these apostles will never meet final failure in any part of the world.

50.1. Despite such adversities the Church constantly renews her deepest inspiration, that which comes to her directly from the Lord: To the whole world! To all creation! Right to the ends of the earth! She did this once more at the last synod, as an appeal not to imprison the proclamation of the gospel by limiting it to one sector of mankind or to one class of people or to a single type of civilization. Some examples are revealing.

51. To reveal Jesus Christ and his gospel to those who do not know them has been, ever since the morning of Pentecost, the fundamental programme which the Church has taken on as received from her founder. The whole of the New Testament, and in a special way the Acts of the Apostles, bears witness to a privileged and in a sense exemplary moment of this missionary effort which will subsequently leave its mark on the whole history of the Church.

51.1. She carries out this first proclamation of Jesus Christ by a complex and diversified activity which is sometimes termed 'pre-evangelization' but which is already evangelization in a true sense, although at its initial and still incomplete stage. An almost indefinite range of means can be used for this purpose: explicit preaching, of course, but also art, the scientific approach, philosophical research and legitimate recourse to the sentiments of the human heart.

52. This first proclamation is addressed especially to those who have never heard the good news of Jesus, or to children. But, as a result of the frequent situations of dechristianization in our day, it also proves equally necessary for innumerable people who have been baptized but who live quite outside Christian life, for simple people who have a certain faith but an imperfect knowledge of the foundations of that faith, for intellectuals who feel the need to know Jesus Christ in a light different from the instruction they received as children, and for many others.

53. This first proclamation is also addressed to the immense sections of mankind who practise non-Christian religions. The Church respects and esteems these non-Christian religions because they are the living expression of the soul of vast groups of people. They carry within them the echo of thousands of years of searching for God, a quest which is incomplete but often made with great sincerity and righteousness of heart. They possess an impressive patrimony of deeply religious texts. They have taught generations of people how to pray. They are all impregnated with innumerable 'seeds of the word'[74] and can constitute a true 'preparation for the gospel',[75] to quote a felicitous term used by the Second Vatican Council and borrowed from Eusebius of Caesarea.

53.1. Such a situation certainly raises complex and delicate questions that must be studied in the light of Christian tradition and the Church's magisterium, in order to offer to the missionaries of today and of tomorrow new horizons in their contacts with non-Christian religions.

53.2. We wish to point out, above all today, that neither respect and esteem for these religions nor the complexity of the questions raised is an invitation to the Church to withhold from these non-Christians the proclamation of Jesus Christ. On the contrary the Church holds that these multitudes have the right to know the riches of the mystery of Christ[76]—riches in which we believe that the whole of humanity can find, in unsuspected fullness, everything that it is gropingly searching for concerning God, man and his destiny, life and death, and truth.

53.3. Even in the face of natural religious expressions most worthy of esteem, the Church finds support in the fact that the religion of Jesus, which she proclaims through evangelization, objectively places man in relation with the plan of God, with his living presence and with his action; she thus causes an encounter with the mystery of divine paternity that bends over towards humanity. In other words, our religion effectively establishes with God an authentic and living relationship which the other religions do not succeed in doing, even though they have, as it were, their arms stretched out towards heaven.

53.4. This is why the Church keeps her missionary spirit alive, and even wishes to intensify it in the moment of history in which we are living. She feels responsible before entire peoples. She has no rest so long as she has not done her best to proclaim the good news of Jesus the saviour. She is always preparing new generations of apostles. Let us state this fact with joy at a time when there are not lacking those who think and even say that ardour and the apostolic spirit are exhausted, and that the time of the missions is now past. The synod has replied that the missionary proclamation never ceases and that the Church will always be striving for the fulfilment of this proclamation.

54. Nevertheless the Church does not feel dispensed from paying unflagging attention also to those who have received the faith and who have been in contact with the gospel often for generations. Thus she seeks to deepen, consolidate, nourish and make ever more mature the faith of those who are already called the faithful or believers, in order that they may be so still more.

54.1. This faith is nearly always today exposed to secularism, even to militant atheism. It is a faith exposed to trials and threats, and even more, a faith besieged and actively opposed. It runs the risk of perishing from suffocation or starvation if it is not fed and sustained each day. To evangelize must therefore very often be to give this necessary food and sustenance to the faith of believers, especially through a catechesis full of gospel vitality and in a language suited to people and circumstances.

54.2. The Church also has a lively solicitude for the Christians who are not in full communion with her. While preparing with them the unity willed by Christ, and precisely in order to realize unity in truth, she has the consciousness that she would be gravely lacking in her duty if she did not give witness before them of the fullness of the revelation whose deposit she guards.

55. Also significant is the preoccupation of the last synod in regard to two spheres which are very different from one another but which at the same time are very close by reason of the challenge which they make to evangelization, each in its own way.

55.1. The first sphere is the one which can be called the increase of unbelief in the modern world. The synod endeavoured to describe this modern world: how many currents of thought, values and countervalues, latent aspirations or seeds of destruction, old convictions which disappear and new convictions which arise are covered by this generic name! From the spiritual point of view, the modern world seems to be for ever immersed in what a modern author has termed 'the drama of atheistic humanism'.[77]

55.2. On the one hand one is forced to note in the very heart of this contemporary world the phenomenon which is becoming almost its most striking characteristic: secularism. We are not speaking of secularization, which is the effort, in itself just and legitimate and in no way incompatible with faith or religion, to discover in creation, in each thing or each happening in the universe, the laws which regulate them with a certain autonomy, but with the inner conviction that the creator has placed these laws there. The last council has in this sense affirmed the legitimate autonomy of culture and particularly of the sciences.[78] Here we are thinking of a true secularism: a concept of the world according to which the latter is self-explanatory, without any need for recourse to God, who thus becomes superfluous and an encumbrance. This sort of secularism, in order to recognize the power of man, therefore ends up by doing without God and even by denying him.

55.3. New forms of atheism seem to flow from it: a man-centred atheism, no longer abstract and metaphysical but pragmatic, systematic and militant. Hand in hand with this atheistic secularism, we are daily faced, under the most diverse forms, with a consumer society, the pursuit of pleasure set up as the supreme value, a desire for power and domination, and discrimination of every kind: the inhuman tendencies of this 'humanism'.

55.4. In this same modern world, on the other hand, and this is a paradox, one cannot deny the existence of real stepping-stones to Christianity, and of evangelical values at least in the form of a sense of emptiness or nostalgia. It would not be an exaggeration to say that there exists a powerful and tragic appeal to be evangelized.

56. The second sphere is that of those who do not practise. Today there is a very large number of baptized people who for the most part have not formally renounced their baptism but who are entirely indifferent to it and not living in accordance with it. The phenomenon of the non-practising is a very ancient one in the history of Christianity; it is the result of a natural weakness, a profound inconsistency which we unfortunately bear deep within us. Today however it shows certain new characteristics. It is often the result of the uprooting typical of our time. It also springs from the fact that Christians live in close proximity with non-believers and constantly experience the effects of unbelief. Futhermore, the non-practising Christians of today, more so than those of previous periods, seek to explain and justify their position in the name of an interior religion, of personal independence or authenticity.

56.1. Thus we have atheists and unbelievers on the one side and those who do not practise on the other, and both groups put up a considerable resistance to evangelization. The resistance of the former takes the form of a certain refusal and an inability to grasp the new order of things, the new meaning of the world, of life and of history; such is not possible if one does not start from a divine absolute. The resistance of the second group takes the form of inertia and the slightly hostile attitude of the person who feels that he is one of the family, who claims to know it all and to have tried it all and who no longer believes it.

56.2. Atheistic secularism and the absence of religious practice are found among adults and among the young, among the leaders of society and among the ordinary people, at all levels of education, and in both the old churches and the young ones. The Church's evangelizing action cannot ignore these two worlds, nor must it come to a standstill when faced with them; it must constantly seek the proper means and language for presenting, or re-presenting, to them God's revelation and faith in Jesus Christ.

57. Like Christ during the time of his preaching, like the twelve on the morning of Pentecost, the Church too sees before her an immense multitude of people who need the gospel and have a right to it, for God 'wants everyone to be saved and reach full knowledge of the truth'.[79]

57.1. The Church is deeply aware of her duty to preach salvation to all. Knowing that the gospel message is not reserved to a small group of the initiated, the privileged or the elect but is destined for everyone, she shares Christ's anguish at the sight of the wandering and exhausted crowds 'like sheep without a shepherd' and she often repeats his words: 'I feel sorry for all these people.'[80] But the Church is also conscious of the fact that, if the preaching of the gospel is to be effective, she must address her message to the heart of the multitudes, to communities of the faithful whose action can and must reach others.

Basic communities

58. The last synod devoted considerable attention to these 'small communities', or *communautés de base*, because they are often talked about in the Church today. What are they, and why should they be the special beneficiaries of evangelization and at the same time evangelizers themselves?

58.1. According to the various statements heard in the synod, such communities flourish more or less throughout the Church. They differ greatly among themselves, both within the same region and even more so from one region to another.

58.2. In some regions they appear and develop, almost without exception, within the Church, having solidarity with her life, being nourished by her teaching and united with her pastors. In these cases, they spring from the need to live the Church's life more intensely, or from the desire and quest for a more human dimension such as larger ecclesial communities can only offer with difficulty, especially in the big modern cities which lend themselves both to life in the mass and to anonymity. Such communities can quite simply be in their own way an extension on the spiritual and religious level—worship, deepening of faith, fraternal charity, prayer, contact with pastors—of the small sociological community such as the village, etc. Or again their aim may be to bring together, for the purpose of listening to and meditating on the word, for the sacraments and the bond of the agape, groups of people who are linked by age, culture, civil state or social situation: married couples, young people, professional people, etc., people who already happen to be united in the struggle for justice, brotherly aid to the poor, human advancement. In still other cases they bring Christians together in places where the shortage of priests does not favour the normal life of a parish community. This is all presupposed within communities constituted by the Church, especially individual churches and parishes.

58.3. In other regions, on the other hand, *communautés de base* come together in a spirit of bitter criticism of the Church, which they are quick to stigmatize as 'institutional' and to which they set themselves up in opposition as charismatic communities, free from structures and inspired only by the gospel. Thus their obvious characteristic is an attitude of fault-finding and of rejection with regard to the Church's outward manifestations: her hierarchy, her signs. They are radically opposed to the Church. By following these lines their main inspiration very quickly becomes ideological, and it rarely happens that they do not quickly fall victim to some political option or current of thought, and then to a system, even a party, with all the attendant risks of becoming its instrument.

58.4. The difference is already notable: the communities which by their spirit of opposition cut themselves off from the Church, and whose unity they wound, can well be called *communautés de base*, but in this case it is a strictly sociological name. They could not, without a misuse of terms, be called ecclesial *communautés de base*, even if, while being hostile to the hierarchy, they claim to remain within the unity of the Church. This name belongs to the other groups, those which come together within the Church in order to unite themselves to the Church and to cause the Church to grow.

58.5. These latter communities will be a place of evangelization, for the benefit of the bigger communities, especially the individual churches. And, as we said at the end of the last synod, they will be a hope for the universal Church to the extent:

58.6.—That they seek their nourishment in the word of God and do not allow themselves to be ensnared by political polarization or fashionable ideologies, which are already to exploit their immense human potential;

58.7.—That they avoid the ever present temptation of systematic protest and a hyper-critical attitude, under the pretext of authenticity and a spirit of collaboration;

58.8.—That they remain firmly attached to the local church in which they are inserted, and to the universal Church, thus avoiding the very real danger of becoming isolated within themselves, then of believing themselves to be the only authentic Church of Christ, and hence of condemning the other ecclesial communities;

58.9.—That they maintain a sincere communion with the pastors whom the Lord gives to his Church, and with the magisterium which the Spirit of Christ has entrusted to these pastors;

58.10.—That they never look on themselves as the sole beneficiaries or sole agents of evangelization—or even the only depositaries of the gospel—but, being aware that the Church is much more vast and diversified, accept the fact that this Church becomes incarnate in other ways than through themselves;

58.11.—That they constantly grow in missionary consciousness, fervour, commitment and zeal;

58.12—That they show themselves to be universal in all things and never sectarian.

58.13. On these conditions, which are certainly demanding but also uplifting, the ecclesial *communautés de base* will correspond to their most fundamental vocation: as hearers of the gospel which is proclaimed to them and privileged beneficiaries of evangelization, they will soon become proclaimers of the gospel themselves.

VI

Universal Church, local churches

59. If people proclaim in the world the gospel of salvation, they do so by the command of, in the name of and with the grace of Christ the saviour. 'They will never have a preacher unless one is sent,'[81] wrote he who was without doubt one of the greatest evangelizers. No one can do it without having been sent.

    59.1. But who then has the mission of evangelizing?

    59.2. The Second Vatican Council gave a clear reply to this question: it is upon the Church that 'there rests, by divine mandate, the duty of going out into the whole world and preaching the gospel to every creature'.[82] And in another text: '...the whole Church is missionary, and the work of evangelization is a basic duty of the people of God.'[83]

    59.3. We have already mentioned this intimate connection between the Church and evangelization. While the Church is proclaiming the kingdom of God and building it up, she is establishing herself in the midst of the world as the sign and instrument of this kingdom which is and which is to come. The council repeats the following expression of St Augustine on the missionary activity of the twelve: 'They preached the word of truth and brought forth Church.'[84]

60. The observation that the Church has been sent out and given a mandate to evangelize the world should awaken in us two convictions. The first is this: evangelization is for no one an individual and isolated act; it is one that is deeply ecclesial. When the most obscure preacher, catechist or pastor in the most distant land preaches the gospel, gathers his little community together or administers a sacrament, even alone, he is carrying out an ecclesial act, and his action is certainly attached to the evangelizing activity of the whole Church by institutional relationships, but also by profound invisible links in the order of grace. This presupposes that he acts not in virtue of a mission which he attributes to himself or by a personal inspiration, but in union with the mission of the Church and in her name.

    60.1. From this flows the second conviction: if each individual evangelizes in the name of the Church, who herself does so by virtue of a mandate from the Lord, no evangelizer is the absolute master of his evangelizing action, with a discretionary power to carry it out in accordance with individualistic criteria and perspectives; he acts in communion with the Church and her pastors.

    60.2. We have remarked that the Church is entirely and completely evangelizing. This means that, in the whole world and in each part of the world where she is present, the Church feels responsible for the task of spreading the gospel.

61. Brothers and sons and daughters, at this stage of our reflection, we wish to pause with you at a question which is particularly important at the present time. In the celebration of the liturgy, in their witness before judges and executioners and in their apologetical texts, the first Christians readily expressed their deep faith in the Church by describing her as being spread

throughout the universe. They were fully conscious of belonging to a large community which neither space nor time can limit: 'From the just Abel right to the last of the elect',[85] 'indeed to the ends of the earth',[86] 'to the end of time'.[87]

61.1. This is how the Lord wanted his Church to be: universal, a great tree whose branches shelter the birds of the air,[88] a net which catches fish of every kind[89] or which Peter drew in filled with one hundred and fifty-three big fish,[90] a flock which a single shepherd pastures.[91] A universal Church without boundaries or frontiers except, alas, those of the heart and mind of sinful man.

62. Nevertheless this universal Church is in practice incarnate in the individual churches made up of such or such an actual part of mankind, speaking such and such a language, heirs of a cultural patrimony, of a vision of the world, of an historical past, of a particular human substratum. Receptivity to the wealth of the individual church corresponds to a special sensitivity of modern man.

62.1. Let us be very careful not to conceive of the universal Church as the sum, or, if one can say so, the more or less anomalous federation of essentially different individual churches. In the mind of the Lord the Church is universal by vocation and mission, but when she puts down her roots in a variety of cultural, social and human terrains, she takes on different external expressions and appearances in each part of the world.

62.2. Thus each individual church that would voluntarily cut itself off from the universal Church would lose its relationship to God's plan and would be impoverished in its ecclesial dimension. But, at the same time, a Church *toto orbe diffusa* would become an abstraction if she did not take body and life precisely through the individual churches. Only continual attention to these two poles of the Church will enable us to perceive the richness of this relationship between the universal Church and the individual churches.

63. The individual churches, intimately built up not only of people but also of aspirations, of riches and limitations, of ways of praying, of loving, of looking at life and the world which distinguish this or that human gathering, have the task of assimilating the essence of the gospel message and of transposing it, without the slightest betrayal of its essential truth, into the language that these particular people understand, then of proclaiming it in this language.

63.1. The transposition has to be done with the discernment, seriousness, respect and competence which the matter calls for in the field of liturgical expression,[92] and in the areas of catechesis, theological formulation, secondary ecclesial structures, and ministries. And the word 'language' should be understood here less in the semantic or literary sense than in the sense which one may call anthropological and cultural.

63.2. The question is undoubtedly a delicate one. Evangelization loses much of its force and effectiveness if it does not take into consideration the actual people to whom it is addressed, if it does not use their language, their signs and symbols, if it does not answer the questions they ask, and if it does not have an impact on their concrete life. But on the other hand evangelization risks losing its power and disappearing altogether if one empties or adulterates its content under the pretext of translating it; if, in other words, one sacrifices this reality and destroys the unity without which there is no universality, out of a wish to adapt a universal reality to a local situation. Now, only a Church which preserves the awareness of her universality and shows that she is in fact universal is capable of having a message which can be heard by all, regardless of regional frontiers.

63.3. Legitimate attention to individual churches cannot fail to enrich the Church. Such attention is indispensable and urgent. It responds to the very deep aspirations of peoples and human communities to find their own identity ever more clearly.

64. But this enrichment requires that the individual churches should keep their profound openness towards the universal Church. It is quite remarkable, moreover, that the most simple Christians, the ones who are most faithful to the gospel and most open to the true meaning of the Church, have a completely spontaneous sensitivity to this universal dimension. They instinctively and very strongly feel the need for it, they easily recognize themselves in such a dimension. They feel with it and suffer very deeply within themselves when, in the name of theories which they do not understand, they are forced to accept a church deprived of this universality, a regionalist church, with no horizon.

64.1. As history in fact shows, whenever an individual church has cut itself off from the universal Church and from its living and visible centre—sometimes with the best of intentions, with theological, sociological, political or pastoral arguments, or even in the desire for a certain freedom of movement or action—it has escaped only with great difficulty (if indeed it has escaped) from two equally serious dangers. The first danger is that of a withering isolationism, and then, before long, of a crumbling away, with each of its cells breaking away from it just as it itself has broken away from the central nucleus. The second danger is that of losing its freedom when, being cut off from the centre and from the other churches which gave it strength and energy, it finds itself all alone and a prey to the most varied forces of enslavement and exploitation.

64.2. The more an individual church is attached to the universal Church by solid bonds of communion, in charity and loyalty, in receptiveness to the magisterium of Peter, in the unity of the *lex orandi* which is also the *lex credendi*, in the desire for unity with all the other churches which make up the whole—the more such a church will be capable of translating the treasure of faith into the legitimate variety of expressions of the profession of faith, of prayer and worship, of Christian life and conduct and of the spiritual influence on the people among which it dwells. The more will it also be truly evangelizing, that is to say capable of drawing upon the universal patrimony in order to enable its own people to profit from it, and capable too of communicating to the universal Church the experience and the life of this people, for the benefit of all.

65. It was precisely in this sense that at the end of the last synod we spoke clear words full of paternal affection, insisting on the role of Peter's successor as a visible, living and dynamic principle of the unity between the

Proclaiming Justice and Peace

churches and thus of the universality of the one Church.[93] We also insisted on the grave responsibility incumbent upon us, but which we share with our brothers in the episcopate, of preserving unaltered the content of the Catholic faith which the Lord entrusted to the apostles. While being translated into all expressions, this content must be neither impaired nor mutilated. While being clothed with the outward forms proper to each people, and made explicit by theological expression which takes account of differing cultural, social and even racial milieux, it must remain the content of the Catholic faith just exactly as the ecclesial magisterium has received it and transmits it.

The diversity of the tasks

66. The whole Church therefore is called upon to evangelize, and yet within her we have different evangelizing tasks to accomplish. This diversity of services in the unity of the same mission makes up the richness and beauty of evangelization. We shall briefly recall these tasks.

66.1. First, we would point out in the pages of the gospel the insistence with which the Lord entrusts to the apostles the task of proclaiming the word. He chose them,[94] trained them during several years of intimate company,[95] constituted[96] and sent them out[97] as authorized witnesses and teachers of the message of salvation. And the twelve in their turn sent out their successors who, in the apostolic line, continue to preach the good news.

67. The successor of Peter is thus, by the will of Christ, entrusted with the pre-eminent ministry of teaching the revealed truth. The New Testament often shows Peter 'filled with the Holy Spirit' speaking in the name of all.[98] It is precisely for this reason that St Leo the Great describes him as he who has merited the primacy of the apostolate.[99] This is also why the voice of the Church shows the pope 'at the highest point—*in apice, in specula*—of the apostolate'.[100] The Second Vatican Council wished to reaffirm this when it declared that 'Christ's mandate to preach the gospel to every creature (cf. Mark 16:15) primarily and immediately concerns the bishops with Peter and under Peter.'[101]

67.1. The full, supreme and universal power[102] which Christ gives to his vicar for the pastoral government of his Church is thus specially exercised by the pope in the activity of preaching and causing to be preached the good news of salvation.

68. In union with the successor of Peter, the bishops, who are successors of the apostles, receive through the power of their episcopal ordination the authority to teach the revealed truth in the Church. They are teachers of the faith.

68.1. Associated with the bishops in the ministry of evangelization and responsible by a special title are those who through priestly ordination 'act in the person of Christ'.[103] They are educators of the people of God in the faith and preachers, while at the same time being ministers of the eucharist and of the other sacraments.

68.2. We pastors are therefore invited to take note of this duty, more than any other members of the Church. What identifies our priestly service, gives a profound unity to the thousand and one tasks which claim our attention day by day and throughout our lives, and confers a distinct character on our activities, is this aim, ever present in all our action: to proclaim the gospel of God.[104]

68.3. A mark of our identity which no doubts ought to encroach upon and no objection eclipse is this: as pastors, we have been chosen by the mercy of the supreme pastor,[105] in spite of our inadequacy, to proclaim with authority the word of God, to assemble the scattered people of God, to feed this people with the signs of the action of Christ which are the sacraments, to set this people on the road to salvation, to maintain it in that unity of which we are, at different levels, active and living instruments, and unceasingly to keep this community gathered around Christ faithful to its deepest vocation. And when we do all these things, within our human limits and by the grace of God, it is a work of evangelization that we are carrying out. This includes ourself as pastor of the universal Church, our brother bishops at the head of the individual churches, priests and deacons united with their bishops and whose assistants they are, by a communion which has its source in the sacrament of orders and in the charity of the Church.

69. Religious, for their part, find in their consecrated life a privileged means of effective evangelization.

69.1. At the deepest level of their being they are caught up in the dynamism of the Church's life, which is thirsty for the divine absolute and called to holiness. It is to this holiness that they bear witness. They embody the Church in her desire to give herself completely to the radical demands of the beatitudes. By their lives they are a sign of total availability to God, the Church and the brethren. As such they have a special importance in the context of the witness which, as we have said, is of prime importance in evangelization. At the same time as being a challenge to the world and to the Church herself, this silent witness of poverty and abnegation, of purity and sincerity, of self-sacrifice in obedience, can become an eloquent witness capable of touching also non-Christians who have good will and are sensitive to certain values.

69.2. In this perspective one perceives the role played in evangelization by religious men and women consecrated to prayer, silence, penance and sacrifice. Other religious, in great numbers, give themselves directly to the proclamation of Christ. Their missionary activity depends clearly on the hierarchy and must be co-ordinated with the pastoral plan which the latter adopts. But who does not see the immense contribution that these religious have brought and continue to bring to evangelization? Thanks to their consecration they are eminently willing and free to leave everything and to go and proclaim the gospel even to the ends of the earth. They are enterprising and their apostolate is often marked by an originality, by a genius that demands admiration. They are generous: often they are found at the outposts of the mission, and they take the greatest of risks for their health and their very lives. Truly the Church owes them much.

70. Lay people, whose particular vocation places them in the midst of the world and in charge of the most varied temporal tasks, must for this very reason exercise a very special form of evangelization.

70.1. Their primary and immediate task is not to establish and develop the ecclesial community—this is the specific role of the pastors—but to put to use every Christian and evangelical possibility latent but already present and active in the affairs of the world. Their own field of evangelizing activity is the vast and complicated world of politics, society and economics, but also the world of culture, of the sciences and the arts, of international life, of the mass media. It also includes other realities which are open to evangelization, such as human love, the family, the education of children and adolescents, professional work, suffering. The more gospel-inspired lay people there are engaged in these realities, clearly involved in them, competent to promote them and conscious that they must exercise to the full their Christian powers which are often buried and suffocated, the more these realities will be at the service of the kingdom of God and therefore of salvation in Jesus Christ, without in any way losing or sacrificing their human content but rather pointing to a transcendent dimension which is often disregarded.

71. One cannot fail to stress the evangelizing action of the family in the evangelizing apostolate of the laity. At different moments in the Church's history and also in the Second Vatican Council, the family has well deserved the beautiful name of 'domestic Church'.[106] This means that there should be found in every Christian family the various aspects of the entire Church. Furthermore, the family, like the Church, ought to be a place where the gospel is transmitted and from which the gospel radiates.

71.1. In a family which is conscious of this mission, all the members evangelize and are evangelized. The parents not only communicate the gospel to their children, but from their children they can themselves receive the same gospel as deeply lived by them.

71.2. And such a family becomes the evangelizer of many other families, and of the neighbourhood of which it forms part. Families resulting from a mixed marriage also have the duty of proclaiming Christ to the children in the fullness of the consequences of a common baptism; they have moreover the difficult task of becoming builders of unity.

72. Circumstances invite us to make special mention of the young. Their increasing number and growing presence in society and likewise the problems assailing them should awaken in everyone the desire to offer them with zeal and intelligence the gospel ideal as something to be known and lived. And on the other hand, young people who are well trained in faith and prayer must become more and more the apostles of youth. The Church counts greatly on their contribution, and we ourself have often manifested our full confidence in them.

73. Hence the active presence of the laity in the temporal realities takes on all its importance. One cannot, however, neglect or forget the other dimension: the laity can also feel themselves called, or be called, to work with their pastors in the service of the ecclesial community, for its growth and life, by exercising a great variety of ministries according to the grace and charisms which the Lord is pleased to give them.

73.1. We cannot but experience a great inner joy when we see so many pastors, religious and lay people, fired with their mission to evangelize, seeking ever more suitable ways of proclaiming the gospel effectively. We encourage the openness which the Church is showing today in this direction and with this solicitude. It is an openness to meditation first of all, and then to ecclesial ministries capable of renewing and strengthening the evangelizing vigour of the Church.

73.2. It is certain that, side by side with the ordained ministries, whereby certain people are appointed pastors and consecrate themselves in a special way to the service of the community, the Church recognizes the place of non-ordained ministries which are able to offer a particular service to the Church.

73.3. A glance at the origins of the Church is very illuminating, and gives the benefit of an early experience in the matter of ministries. It was an experience which was all the more valuable in that it enabled the Church to consolidate herself and to grow and spread. Attention to the sources however has to be complemented by attention to the present needs of mankind and of the Church. To drink at these ever inspiring sources without sacrificing anything of their values, and at the same time to know how to adapt oneself to the demands and needs of today—these are the criteria which will make it possible to seek wisely and to discover the ministries which the Church needs and which many of her members will gladly embrace for the sake of ensuring greater vitality in the ecclesial community. These ministries will have a real pastoral value to the extent that they are established with absolute respect for unity and adhering to the directives of the pastors, who are the ones who are responsible for the Church's unity and the builders thereof.

73.4. These ministries, apparently new but closely tied up with the Church's living experience down the centuries—such as catechists, directors of prayer and chant, Christians devoted to the service of God's word or to assisting their brethren in need, the heads of small communities, or other persons charged with the responsibility of apostolic movements—these ministries are valuable for the establishment, life and growth of the Church, and for her capacity to influence her surroundings and to reach those who are remote from her. We owe also our special esteem to all the lay people who accept to consecrate a part of their time, their energies, and sometimes their entire lives, to the service of the missions.

73.5. A serious preparation is needed for all workers for evangelization. Such preparation is all the more necessary for those who devote themselves to the ministry of the word. Being animated by the conviction, ceaselessly deepened, of the greatness and riches of the word of God, those who have the mission of transmitting it must give the maximum attention to the dignity, precision and adaptation of their language. Everyone knows that today the art of speaking takes on a very great importance. How can preachers and catechists neglect this? We earnestly desire that in each individual church the bishops should be vigilant concerning the adequate formation of all the ministers of the word. This serious preparation will increase in them the indispensable assurance and also the enthusiasm to proclaim today Jesus Christ.

VII

Preaching in the power of the Spirit

74. We would not wish to end this encounter with our beloved brethren and sons and daughters without a pressing appeal concerning the interior attitudes which must animate those who work for evangelization.

74.1. In the name of the apostles Peter and Paul, we wish to exhort all those who, thanks to the charisms of the Holy Spirit and to the mandate of the Church, are true evangelizers, to be worthy of this vocation, to exercise it without the reticence of doubt or fear, and not to neglect the conditions that will make this evangelization not only possible but also active and fruitful. These, among many others, are the fundamental conditions which we consider it important to emphasize.

75. Evangelization will never be possible without the action of the Holy Spirit. The Spirit descends on Jesus of Nazareth at the moment of his baptism when the voice of the Father—'This is my beloved son with whom I am well pleased'[107]—manifests in an external way the election of Jesus and his mission. Jesus is 'led by the Spirit' to experience in the desert the decisive combat and the supreme test before beginning this mission.[108] It is 'in the power of the Spirit'[109] that he returns to Galilee and begins his preaching at Nazareth, applying to himself the passage of Isaiah: 'The Spirit of the Lord is upon me.' And he proclaims: 'Today this scripture has been fulfilled.'[110] To the disciples whom he was about to send forth he says, breathing on them: 'Receive the Holy Spirit.'[111] ,

75.1. In fact, it is only after the coming of the Holy Spirit on the day of Pentecost that the apostles depart to all the ends of the earth in order to begin the great work of the Church's evangelization. Peter explains this event as the fulfilment of the prophecy of Joel: 'I will pour out my Spirit.'[112] Peter is filled with the Holy Spirit so that he can speak to the people about Jesus, the son of God.[113] Paul too is filled with the Holy Spirit[114] before dedicating himself to his apostolic ministry, as is Stephen when he is chosen for the ministry of service and later on for the witness of blood.[115] The Spirit, who causes Peter, Paul and the twelve to speak, and who inspires the words that they are to utter, also comes down 'on those who heard the word'.[116]

75.2. It is in the 'consolation of the Holy Spirit' that the Church increases.[117] The Holy Spirit is the soul of the Church. It is he who explains to the faithful the deep meaning of the teaching of Jesus and of his mystery. It is the Holy Spirit who, today just as at the beginning of the Church, acts in every evangelizer who allows himself to be possessed and led by him. The Holy Spirit places on his lips the words which he could not find by himself, and at the same time the Holy Spirit predisposes the soul of the hearer to be open and receptive to the good news and to the kingdom being proclaimed.

75.3. Techniques of evangelization are good, but even the most advanced ones could not replace the gentle action of the Spirit. The most perfect preparation of the evangelizer has no effect without the Holy Spirit. Without the Holy Spirit the most convincing dialectic has no power over the heart of man. Without him the most highly developed schemas resting on a sociological or psychological basis are quickly seen to be quite valueless.

75.4. We live in the Church at a privileged moment of the Spirit. Everywhere people are trying to know him better, as the scripture reveals him. They are happy to place themselves under his inspiration. They are gathering about him; they want to let themselves be led by him. Now if the Spirit of God has a pre-eminent place in the whole life of the Church, it is in her evangelizing mission that he is most active. It is not by chance that the great inauguration of evangelization took place on the morning of Pentecost, under the inspiration of the Spirit.

75.5. It must be said that the Holy Spirit is the principal agent of evangelization: it is he who impels each individual to proclaim the gospel, and it is he who in the depths of consciences causes the word of salvation to be accepted and understood.[118] But it can equally be said that he is the goal of evangelization: he alone stirs up the new creation, the new humanity of which evangelization is to be the result, with that unity in variety which evangelization wishes to achieve within the Christian community. Through the Holy Spirit the gospel penetrates to the heart of the world, for it is he who causes people to discern the signs of the times—signs willed by God—which evangelization reveals and puts to use within history.

75.6. The bishops' synod of 1974, which insisted strongly on the place of the Holy Spirit in evangelization, also expressed the desire that pastors and theologians—and we would also say the faithful marked by the seal of the spirit by baptism—should study more thoroughly the nature and manner of the Holy Spirit's action in evangelization today. This is our desire too, and we exhort all evangelizers, whoever they may be, to pray without ceasing to the Holy Spirit with faith and fervour and to let themselves prudently be guided by him as the decisive inspirer of their plans, their initiatives and their evangelizing activity.

The qualities of an evangelist

76. Let us now consider the very persons of the evangelizers. It is often said nowadays that the present century thirsts for authenticity. Especially in regard to young people it is said that they have a horror of the artificial or false and that they are searching above all for truth and honesty.

76.1. These 'signs of the times' should find us vigilant. Either tacitly or aloud—but always forceful—we are being asked: Do you really believe what you are proclaiming? Do you live what you believe? The witness of life has become more than ever an essential condition for real effectiveness in preaching. Precisely because of this we are, to a certain extent, responsible for the progress of the gospel that we proclaim.

76.2. 'What is the state of the Church ten years after the council?' we asked at the beginning of this meditation. Is she firmly established in the midst of the world and yet free and independent enough to call for the world's attention? Does she testify to solidarity with people and at the same time to the divine absolute? Is she more ardent in contemplation and adoration and more zealous in missionary, charitable and liberating action? Is she ever more committed to the effort to search for the restoration of the complete unity of Christians, a unity that makes more effective the common witness, 'so that the world may believe'?[119] We are all responsible for the answers that could be given to these questions.

76.3. We therefore address our exhortation to our brethren in the episcopate, placed by the Holy Spirit to govern the Church.[120] We exhort the priests and deacons, the bishops' collaborators in assembling the people of God and in animating spiritually the local communities. We exhort the religious, witnesses of a Church called to holiness and hence themselves invited to a life that bears testimony to the beatitudes of the gospel. We exhort the laity: Christian families, youth, adults, all those who exercise a trade or profession, leaders, without forgetting the poor who are often rich in faith and hope—all lay people who are conscious of their evangelizing role in the service of their Church or in the midst of society and the world. We say to all of them: our evangelizing zeal must spring from true holiness of life, and, as the Second Vatican Council suggests, preaching must in its turn make the preacher grow in holiness, which is nourished by prayer and above all by love for the eucharist.[121]

76.4. The world which, paradoxically, despite innumerable signs of the denial of God, is nevertheless searching for him in unexpected ways and painfully experiencing the need of him—the world is calling for evangelizers to speak to it of a God whom the evangelists themselves should know and be familiar with as if they could see the invisible.[122] The world calls for and expects from us simplicity of life, the spirit of prayer, charity towards all, especially towards the lowly and the poor, obedience and humility, detachment and self-sacrifice. Without this mark of holiness, our word will have difficulty in touching the heart of modern man. It risks being vain and sterile.

77. The power of evangelization will find itself considerably diminished if those who proclaim the gospel are divided among themselves in all sorts of ways. Is this not perhaps one of the great sicknesses of evangelization today? Indeed, if the gospel that we proclaim is seen to be rent by doctrinal disputes, ideological polarizations or mutual condemnations among Christians, at the mercy of the latters' differing views on Christ and the Church and even because of their different concepts of society and human institutions, how can those to whom we address our preaching fail to be disturbed, disoriented, even scandalized?

77.1. The Lord's spiritual testament tells us that unity among his followers is not only the proof that we are his but also the proof that he is sent by the Father. It is the test of the credibility of Christians and of Christ himself. As evangelizers, we must offer Christ's faithful not the image of people divided and separated by unedifying quarrels, but the image of people who are mature in faith and capable of finding a meeting-point beyond the real tensions, thanks to a shared, sincere and disinterested search for truth. Yes, the destiny of evangelization is certainly bound up with the witness of unity given by the Church. This is a source of responsibility and also of comfort.

77.2. At this point we wish to emphasize the sign of unity among all Christians as the way and instrument of evangelization. The division among Christians is a serious reality which impedes the very work of Christ. The Second Vatican Council states clearly and emphatically that this division 'damages the most holy cause of preaching the gospel to all men, and it impedes many from embracing the faith'.[123] For this reason, in proclaiming the Holy Year we considered it necessary to recall to all the faithful of the Catholic world that 'before all men can be brought together and restored to the grace of God our father, communion must be re-established between those who by faith have acknowledged and accepted Jesus Christ as the Lord of mercy who sets men free and unites them in the Spirit of love and truth.'[124] And it is with a strong feeling of Christian hope that we look to the efforts being made in the Christian world for this restoration of the full unity willed by Christ, St Paul assures us that 'hope does not disappoint us'.[125] While we still work to obtain full unity from the Lord, we wish to see prayer intensified. Moreover we make our own the desire of the Fathers of the third general assembly of the synod of bishops, for a collaboration marked by greater commitment with the Christian brethren with whom we are not yet united in perfect unity, taking as a basis the foundation of baptism and the patrimony of faith which is common to us. By doing this we can already give a greater common witness to Christ before the world in the very work of evangelization.

77.3. Christ's command urges us to do this; the duty of preaching and of giving witness to the gospel requires this.

78. The gospel entrusted to us is also the word of truth. A truth which liberates[126] and which alone gives peace of heart is what people are looking for when we proclaim the good news to them. The truth about God, about man and his mysterious destiny, about the world; the difficult truth that we seek in the word of God and of which, we repeat, we are neither the masters nor the owners, but the depositaries, the heralds and the servants.

78.1. Every evangelizer is expected to have a reverence for truth, especially since the truth that he studies and communicates is none other than revealed truth and hence, more than any other, a sharing in the first truth which is God himself. The preacher of the gospel will therefore be a person who even at the price of personal renunciation and suffering always seeks the truth that he must transmit to others. He never betrays or hides truth out of a desire to please men, in order to astonish or to shock, nor for the sake of originality or a desire to make an impression. He does not refuse truth. He does not obscure revealed truth by being too idle to search for it, or for the sake of his own comfort, or out of fear. He does not neglect to study it. He serves it generously, without making it serve him.

78.2. We are the pastors of the faithful people, and our pastoral service impels us to preserve, defend, and to communicate the truth regardless of the sacrifices that this involves. So many eminent and holy pastors have left us the example of this love of truth. In many cases it was an heroic love. The God of truth expects us to be the vigilant defenders and devoted preachers of truth.

78.3. Men of learning—whether you be theologians, exegetes or historians—the work of evangelization needs your tireless work of research, and also care and tact in transmitting the truth to which your studies lead you but which is always greater than the heart of men, being the very truth of God.

78.4. Parents and teachers, your task—and the many conflicts of the present day do not make it an easy one—is to help our children and your students to discover truth, including religious and spiritual truth.

79. The work of evangelization presupposes in the evangelizer an ever increasing love for those whom he is evangelizing. That model evangelizer, the apostle Paul, wrote these words to the Thessalonians, and they are a programme for us all: 'With such yearning love we chose to impart to you not only the gospel of God but our very selves, so dear had you become to us.'[127] What is this love? It is much more than that of a teacher; it is the love of a father; and again, it is the love of a mother.[128] It is this love that the Lord expects from every preacher of the gospel, from every builder of the Church.

79.1. A sign of love will be the concern to give the truth and to bring people into unity. Another sign of love will be a devotion to the proclamation of Jesus Christ, without reservation or turning back.

79.2. Let us add some other signs of this love. The first is respect for the religious and spiritual situation of those being evangelized. Respect for their tempo and pace; no one has the right to force them excessively. Respect for their conscience and convictions, which are not to be treated in a harsh manner.

79.3. Another sign of this love is concern not to wound the other person, especially if he or she is weak in faith,[129] with statements that may be clear for those who are already initiated but which for the faithful can be a source of bewilderment and scandal, like a wound in the soul.

79.4. Yet another sign of love will be the effort to transmit to Christians, not doubts and uncertainties born of an erudition poorly assimilated but certainties that are solid because they are anchored in the word of God. The faithful need these certainties for their Christian life; they have a right to them, as children of God who abandon themselves entirely into his arms and to the exigencies of love.

80. Our appeal here is inspired by the fervour of the greatest preachers and evangelizers, whose lives were devoted to the apostolate. Among these we are glad to point out those whom we have proposed to the veneration of the faithful during the course of the Holy Year. They have known how to overcome many obstacles to evangelization.

80.1. Such obstacles are also present today, and we shall limit ourself to mentioning the lack of fervour. It is all the more serious because it comes from within. It is manifested in fatigue, disenchantment, compromise, lack of interest and above all lack of joy and hope. We exhort all those who have the task of evangelizing, by whatever title and at whatever level, always to nourish spiritual fervour.[130]

80.2. This fervour demands first of all that we should know how to put aside the excuses which would impede evangelization. The most insidious of these excuses are certainly the ones which people claim to find support for in such and such a teaching of the council.

80.3. Thus one too frequently hears it said, in various terms, that to impose a truth, be it that of the gospel, or to impose a way, be it that of salvation, cannot but be a violation of religious liberty. Besides, it is added, why proclaim the gospel when the whole world is saved by uprightness of heart? We know likewise that the world and history are filled with 'seeds of the word'; is it not therefore an illusion to claim to bring the gospel where it already exists in the seeds that the Lord himself has sown?

80.4. Anyone who takes the trouble to study in the council's documents the questions upon which these excuses draw too superficially will find quite a different view.

80.5. It would certainly be an error to impose something on the consciences of our brethren. But to propose to their consciences the truth of the gospel and salvation in Jesus Christ, with complete clarity and with a total respect for the free options which it presents—'without coercion, or dishonourable or unworthy pressure'[131]—far from being an attack on religious liberty is fully to respect that liberty, which is offered the choice of a way that even non-believers consider noble and uplifting. Is it then a crime against others' freedom to proclaim with joy a good news which one has come to know through the Lord's mercy?[132] And why should only falsehood and error, debasement and pornography have the right to be put before people and often unfortunately imposed on them by the destructive propaganda of the mass media, by the tolerance of legislation, the timidity of the good and the impudence of the wicked?

80.6. The respectful presentation of Christ and his kingdom is more than the evangelizer's right; it is his duty. It is likewise the right of his fellow men to receive from him the proclamation of the good news of salvation. God can accomplish this salvation in whomsoever he wishes by ways which he alone knows.[133] And yet, if his son came, it was precisely in order to reveal to us, by his word and by his life, the ordinary paths of salvation. And he has commanded us to transmit this revelation to others with his own authority. It would be useful if every Christian and every evangelizer were to pray about the following thought: men can gain salvation also in other ways, by God's mercy, even though we do not preach the gospel to them; but as for us, can we gain salvation if through negligence or fear or shame—what St Paul called 'blushing for the gospel'[134]—or as a result of false ideas we fail to preach it? For that would be to betray the call of God, who wishes the seed to bear fruit through the voice of the ministers of the gospel; and it will depend on us whether this grows into trees and produces its full fruit.

80.7. Let us therefore preserve our fervour of spirit. Let us preserve the delightful and comforting joy of evangelizing, even when it is in tears that we must sow. May it mean for us—as it did for John the Baptist, for Peter and Paul, for the other apostles and for a multitude of splendid evangelizers all through the Church's history—an interior enthusiasm that nobody and nothing can quench. May it be the great joy of our consecrated lives. And may the world of our time, which is searching, sometimes with anguish, sometimes with hope, be enabled to receive the good news not from evangelizers who are dejected, discouraged, impatient or anxious, but from ministers of the gospel whose lives glow with fervour, who have first received the joy of Christ, and who are willing to risk their lives so that the kingdom may be proclaimed and the Church established in the midst of the world.

81. This then, brothers and sons and daughters, is our heartfelt plea. It echoes the voice of our brethren assembled for the third general assembly of the

synod of bishops. This is the task we have wished to give you at the close of a Holy Year which has enabled us to see better than ever the needs and the appeals of a multitude of brethren, both Christians and non-Christians, who await from the Church the word of salvation.

81.1. May the light of the Holy Year, which has shone in the local churches and in Rome for millions of consciences reconciled with God, continue to shine in the same way after the jubilee through a programme of pastoral action with evangelization as its basic feature, for these years which mark the eve of a new century, the eve also of the third millennium of Christianity.

82. This is the desire that we rejoice to entrust to the hands and the heart of the immaculate Blessed Virgin Mary, on this day which is especially consecrated to her and which is also the tenth anniversary of the close of the Second Vatican Council. On the morning of Pentecost she watched over with her prayer the beginning of evangelization prompted by the Holy Spirit: may she be the star of the evangelization ever renewed which the Church, docile to her Lord's command, must promote and accomplish, especially in these times which are difficult but full of hope!

82.1. In the name of Christ we bless you, your communities, your families, all those who are dear to you, in the words which Paul addressed to the Philippians: 'I give thanks to my God every time I think of you—which is constantly, in every prayer I utter—rejoicing, as I plead on your behalf, at the way you have all continually helped to promote the gospel...I hold all of you dear—you who...are sharers of my gracious lot...to defend the solid grounds on which the gospel rests. God himself can testify how much I long for each of you with the affection of Christ Jesus!'[135]

82.2. Given in Rome, at St Peter's, on the solemnity of the Immaculate Conception of the Blessed Virgin Mary, 8 December 1975, in the thirteenth year of our pontificate.

Editor's Note

EN 2.2: There had in fact been four meetings of the synod of bishops, but that of 1969 is described as an 'extraordinary' or 'special' session, rather than a 'general' one.

Redemptor Hominis

*Encyclical letter of Pope John Paul II addressed to
his venerable brothers in the episcopate, to the priests,
the religious families, to the sons and daughters of
the Church, and to all men and women of
good will as he begins his papal ministry.*

Introduction

Cardinal Karol Wojtyla was elected pope on 16 October 1978. This encyclical
letter was issued by him on 4 March 1979 and was clearly intended to lay
down his line of approach to his new office. It is entitled 'The Redeemer of
Man', and is specifically concerned with the redemptive work of Christ, but
the pope also has a good deal to say about the dignity of man and therefore
about human rights, and also about the Church's task in proclaiming the
gospel not in the abstract, but to real, concrete individuals with all the threats
which they face, and within the society which they have inherited.

The scope of the encyclical is wide, and not all of it has been reprinted here.
Even some of the sections which this volume reproduces do not have great
bearing on the social teaching of the Church. They have been included,
however, in order to present the main thrust of the pope's letter, and to avoid
the impression that editorial policy has been unduly selective.

This letter was published after Pope John Paul had returned from the third
conference of the Latin American bishops, held at Puebla, in Mexico, during
January 1979. In the documents which the bishops produced they made great
use of *Evangelii Nuntiandi*, and it is no surprise that John Paul picks up some
of the ideas of Paul VI, in particular the link between the Church's mission
and human progress and development. But the pope's attitude to progress is a
sober, almost a sombre, one, as he points out the dangers, as well as the
advantages, which it brings.

The Latin text of *Redemptor Hominis* (RH) is to be found in AAS 71 (1979)
257-324, and the sections reprinted here, paragraphs 8-17, are to be found
on pp.270-300. Main sections are numbered in the Latin text: subordinate
paragraphs have been given subordinate numbers in accordance with the
Editorial Note (p.ix). Cross-headings have also been added.

A summary of the whole text has been included: those sections in square
brackets have not been reprinted here.

Proclaiming Justice and Peace

Summary

[*Paras. 1-7*: We are approaching the year 2000, and in a way we are in a new
advent, a season of expectation. The act of redemption marked the high point
of history, for God in the form of a man became an actor in that history. It
was to the redeemer that the pope's thoughts were turned when he accepted
the office and entered into the rich inheritance of the recent pontificates. He
had been able closely to observe the activity of Pope Paul VI, who taught all
an intrepid love for the Church, and the Church was the subject of his first
encyclical. He respected every element of the truth in the various criticisms
made of the Church, but he preserved a providential balance. The Church is
now more united in the fellowship of service and in awareness of the
apostolate. The unity springs from the principle of collegiality, given
particular expression in synods and in national episcopal conferences. Pope
Paul took the first difficult steps on the road to Christian unity: John Paul II
pledged to follow his example. There must also be an effort made to come
closer to non-Christian religions. As we approach the second millenium the
question must be: how should we go forward? And our response must be: we
should turn towards Christ, the redeemer of human kind.]

Paras. 8-12: The world God created for human beings recovers in Jesus its
links with the divine source of wisdom and love. Jesus became our
reconciliation with the Father. The God of creation is revealed as the God of
redemption, who is faithful to his love for people and for the world which he
revealed on the day of creation. The redemption has restored dignity to men
and women, and given back meaning to life in the world. In the world's
various religions there are many reflections of the one truth, for the deepest
aspiration of the human spirit is expressed in the quest for God, for the full
meaning of life. We must reveal to the world the dignity each human being
can reach in Christ, the grace of divine adoption and the inner truth of
humanity. The missionary attitude always begins with a feeling of deep
esteem for what is in human beings. Jesus Christ meets people in every age
with the words 'the truth will make you free.' Christ is the one who brings
freedom based on truth.

Paras. 13-17: It is the sole purpose of the Church that everyone may be able
to find Christ, so that Christ may walk with each person. We are speaking not
of an abstract individual but of real, concrete people. This means that the
Church must be aware of the threats which face people. They are afraid that
at least some of what they produce can be turned against them—there is
exploitation for industrial and military purposes, there is the threat to the
environment. Does progress make human life more human? People's
situations in the modern world seem far removed from the objective demands
of the moral order, from the requirements of justice and of social love. In
some countries there is an excess of food, in others starvation, but the
indispensable transformation of the structures of economic life cannot
proceed without a true conversion of mind and heart, and economic progress
must not be allowed to become an end in itself, with everything else
subordinated to it. The Declaration of Human Rights, linked to the
foundation of the United Nations, starts from the welfare of the individual in

the community which, as a fundamental factor in the common good, is an essential criterion for all programmes, systems and regimes. The Church has always taught that the fundamental duty of power is solicitude for the common good, and that is achieved only when all citizens are assured of their rights, including the right to religious freedom together with the right to freedom of conscience. The Church in its activity does not ask for privilege, but for a fundamental right.

[*Paras. 18-22*: Christ's union with human beings is power, and the source of power, and by it people are inwardly transformed with a new life that lasts to eternal life. The Church lives by this truth about human beings. It is the guardian of the great treasure of humanity enriched by the mystery of divine filiation. The Church is united with the Spirit of Christ, the Spirit promised and continuously communicated by the redeemer. Christ promised the Church the special assistance of the Spirit of truth. Love of the truth, and the desire to understand it, must go hand in hand in the Church. The Church's responsibility for divine truth must be shared among all. The Church is built anew by the eucharist. It is the most profound revelation of the human solidarity of Christ's disciples and confessors, though it cannot be reduced to this. But the Christ who calls to the eucharist also exhorts us to penance. In defending the tradition of the sacrament of penance the Church is defending the right to a personal encounter with the crucified Christ. Fidelity to the vocation received from God through Christ involves joint responsibility for the Church. Each member has a special gift, a special form of participation in the Church's saving work, and by fulfilling that task serves others. This is the 'kingly' office of Christ.]

II

Christ and the dignity of human nature

8. The redeemer of the world! In him has been revealed in a new and more wonderful way the fundamental truth concerning creation to which the Book of Genesis gives witness when it repeats several times: 'God saw that it was good.'[38] The good has its source in wisdom and love. In Jesus Christ the visible world which God created for man[39]—the world that, when sin entered, 'was subjected to futility'[40]—recovers again its original link with the divine source of wisdom and love. Indeed, 'God so loved the world that he gave his only son.'[41] As this link was broken in the man Adam, so in the man Christ it was reforged.[42] Are we of the twentieth century not convinced of the overpoweringly eloquent words of the apostle of the gentiles concerning the 'creation [that] has been groaning in travail together until now'[43] and 'waits with eager longing for the revelation of the sons of God',[44] the creation that 'was subjected to futility'? Does not the previously unknown immense progress—which has taken place especially in the course of this century—in the field of man's dominion over the world itself reveal—to a previously unknown degree—that manifold subjection 'to futility'? It is enough to recall

certain phenomena, such as the threat of pollution of the natural environment in areas of rapid industrialization, or the armed conflicts continually breaking out over and over again, or the prospectives of self-destruction through the use of atomic, hydrogen, neutron and similar weapons, or the lack of respect for the life of the unborn. The world of the new age, the world of space flights, the world of the previously unattained conquests of science and technology—is it not also the world 'groaning in travail'[45] that 'waits with eager longing for the revealing of the sons of God'?[46]

8.1. In its penetrating analysis of 'the modern world', the Second Vatican Council reached that most important point of the visible world that is man, by penetrating like Christ the depth of human consciousness and by making contact with the inward mystery of man, which in biblical and non-biblical language is expressed by the word 'heart'. Christ, the redeemer of the world, is the one who penetrated in a unique unrepeatable way into the mystery of man and entered his 'heart'. Rightly therefore does the Second Vatican Council teach: 'The truth is that only in the mystery of the incarnate word does the mystery of man take on light. For Adam, the first man, was a type of him who was to come (Rom. 5:14), Christ the Lord. Christ the new Adam, in the very revelation of the mystery of the Father and of his love, *fully reveals man to himself* and brings to light his most high calling.' And the council continues: 'He who is the "image of the invisible God" (Col. 1:15), is himself the perfect man who has restored in the children of Adam that likeness to God which had been disfigured ever since the first sin. Human nature, by the very fact that it was assumed, not absorbed, in him, has been raised in us also to a dignity beyond compare. For, by his incarnation, he, the son of God, *in a certain way united himself with each man.* He worked with human hands, he thought with a human mind. He acted with a human will, and with a human heart he loved. Born of the Virgin Mary, he has truly been made one of us, like to us in all things except sin,'[47] he, the redeemer of man.

9. As we reflect again on this stupendous text from the council's teaching, we do not forget even for a moment that Jesus Christ, the son of the living God, become our reconciliation with the Father.[48] He it was, and he alone, who satisfied the Father's eternal love, that fatherhood that from the beginning found expression in creating the world, giving man all the riches of creation, and making him 'little less than God',[49] in that he was created 'in the image and after the likeness of God'.[50] He and he alone also satisfied that fatherhood of God and that love which man in a way rejected by breaking the first covenant[51] and the later covenants that God 'again and again offered to man'.[52] The redemption of the world—this tremendous mystery of love in which creation is renewed—[53]is, at its deepest root, the fullness of justice in a human heart—the heart of the first-born son—in order that it may become justice in the hearts of many human beings, predestined from eternity in the first-born son to be children of God[54] and called to grace, called to love. The cross on Calvary, through which Jesus Christ—a man, the son of the Virgin Mary, thought to be the son of Joseph of Nazareth—'leaves' this world, is also a fresh manifestation of the eternal fatherhood of God, who in him draws near again to humanity, to each human being, giving him the thrice holy 'Spirit of truth'.[55]

9.1. This revelation of the Father and outpouring of the Holy Spirit, which stamp an indelible seal on the mystery of the redemption, explain the meaning of the cross and death of Christ. The God of creation is revealed as the God of redemption, as the God who is 'faithful to himself',[56] and faithful to his love for man and the world, which he revealed on the day of creation. He is a love that does not draw back before anything that justice requires in him. Therefore 'for our sake [God] made him [the son] to be sin who knew no sin.'[57] If he 'made to be sin' him who was without any sin whatever, it was to reveal the love that is always greater than the whole of creation, the love that is he himself, since 'God is love'.[58] Above all, love is greater than sin, than weakness, than the 'futility of creation';[59] it is stronger than death; it is a love always ready to raise up and forgive, always ready to go to meet the prodigal son,[60] always looking for 'the revealing of the sons of God',[61] who are called to 'the glory that is to be revealed'.[62] This revelation of love is also described as mercy;[63] and in man's history this revelation of love and mercy has taken a form and a name: that of Jesus Christ.

10. Man cannot live without love. He remains a being that is incomprehensible for himself, his life is senseless, if love is not revealed to him, if he does not encounter love, if he does not experience it and make it his own, if he does not participate intimately in it. This, as has already been said, is why Christ the redeemer 'fully reveals man to himself'. If we may use the expression, this is the human dimension of the mystery of the redemption. In this dimension man finds again the greatness, dignity and value that belong to his humanity. In the mystery of the redemption man becomes newly 'expressed' and, in a way, is newly created. He is newly created! 'There is neither Jew nor Greek, there is neither slave nor free, there is neither male nor female; for you are all one in Christ Jesus.'[64] The man who wishes to understand himself thoroughly—and not just in accordance with immediate, partial, often superficial, and even illusory standards and measures of his being—he must with his unrest, uncertainty and even his weakness and sinfulness, with his life and death, draw near to Christ. He must, so to speak, enter into him with all his own self, he must 'appropriate' and assimilate the whole of the reality of the incarnation and redemption in order to find himself. If this profound process takes place within him, he then bears fruit not only of adoration of God but also of deep wonder at himself. How precious must man be in the eyes of the creator, if he 'gained so great a redeemer',[65] and if God 'gave his only son' in order that man 'should not perish but have eternal life'.[66]

10.1. In reality, the name for that deep amazement at man's worth and dignity is the gospel, that is to say: the good news. It is also called Christianity. This amazement determines the Church's mission in the world and, perhaps even more so, 'in the modern world'. This amazement, which is also a conviction and a certitude—at its deepest root it is the certainty of faith, but in a hidden and mysterious way it vivifies every aspect of authentic humanism—is closely connected with Christ. It also fixes Christ's place—so to speak, his particular right of citizenship—in the history of man and mankind. Unceasingly contemplating the whole of Christ's mystery, the Church knows with all the certainty of faith that the redemption that took place through the cross has definitively restored his dignity to man and given back meaning to his life in the world, a meaning that was lost to a considerable extent because of sin. And for that reason, the redemption was accomplished in the paschal mystery, leading through the cross and death to resurrection.

10.2. The Church's fundamental function in every age and particularly in ours is to direct man's gaze, to point the awareness and experience of the whole of humanity towards the mystery of God, to help all men to be familiar with the profundity of the redemption taking place in Christ Jesus. At the same time man's deepest sphere is involved—we mean the sphere of human hearts, consciences and events.

The Church's mission and human freedom

11. The Second Vatican Council did immense work to form that full and universal awareness by the Church of which Pope Paul VI wrote in his first encyclical. This awareness—or rather self-awareness—by the Church is formed 'in dialogue'; and before this dialogue becomes a conversation, attention must be directed to 'the other', that is to say: the person with whom we wish to speak. The Ecumenical Council gave a fundamental impulse to forming the Church's self-awareness by so adequately and competently presenting to us a view of the terrestial globe as a map of various religions. It showed furthermore that this map of the world's religions has superimposed on it, in previously unknown layers typical of our time, the phenomenon of atheism in its various forms, beginning with the atheism that is programmed, organized and structured as a political system.

11.1. With regard to religion, what is dealt with is in the first place religion as a universal phenomenon linked with man's history from the beginning, then the various non-Christian religions, and finally Christianity itself. The council document on non-Christian religions, in particular, is filled with deep esteem for the great spiritual values, indeed for the primacy of the spiritual, which in the life of mankind finds expression in religion and then in morality, with direct effects on the whole of culture. The Fathers of the Church rightly saw in the various religions as it were so many reflections of the one truth, 'seeds of the word',[67] attesting that, though the routes taken may be different, there is but a single goal to which is directed the deepest aspiration of the human spirit as expressed in its quest for God and also in its quest, through its tending towards God, for the full dimension of its humanity, or in other words for the full meaning of human life. The council gave particular attention to the Jewish religion, recalling the great spiritual heritage common to Christians and Jews. It also expressed its esteem for the believers of Islam, whose faith also looks to Abraham.[68]

11.2. The opening made by the Second Vatican Council has enabled the Church and all Christians to reach a more complete awareness of the mystery of Christ, 'the mystery hidden for ages'[69] in God, to be revealed in time in the man Jesus Christ, and to be revealed continually in every time. In Christ and through Christ God has revealed himself fully to mankind and has definitively drawn close to it; at the same time, in Christ and through Christ man has acquired full awareness of his dignity, of the heights to which he is raised, of the surpassing worth of his own humanity, and of the meaning of his existence.

11.3. All of us who are Christ's followers must therefore meet and unite around him. This unity in the various fields of the life, tradition, structures and discipline of the individual Christian churches and ecclesial communities cannot be brought about without effective work aimed at getting to know each other and removing the obstacles blocking the way to perfect unity. However, we can and must immediately reach and display to the world our unity in proclaiming the mystery of Christ, in revealing the divine dimension and also the human dimension of the redemption, and in struggling with unwearying perserverance for the dignity that each human being has reached and can continually reach in Christ, namely the dignity of both the grace of divine adoption and the inner truth of humanity, a truth which—if in the common awareness of the modern world it has been given such fundamental importance—for us is still clearer in the light of the reality that is Jesus Christ.

11.4. Jesus Christ is the stable principle and fixed centre of the mission that God himself has entrusted to man. We must all share in this mission and concentrate all our forces on it, since it is more necessary than ever for modern mankind. If this mission seems to encounter greater opposition nowadays than ever before, this shows that today it is more necessary than ever and, in spite of the opposition, more awaited than ever. Here we touch indirectly on the mystery of the divine 'economy' which linked salvation and grace with the cross. It was not without reason that Christ said that 'the kingdom of heaven has suffered violence, and men of violence take it by force'[70] and moreover that 'the children of this world are more astute...than are the children of light.'[71] We gladly accept this rebuke, that we may be like those 'violent people of God' that we have so often seen in the history of the Church and still see today, and that we may consciously join in the great mission of revealing Christ to the world, helping each person to find himself in Christ, and helping the contemporary generations of our brothers and sisters, the peoples, nations, states, mankind, developing countries and countries of opulence—in short, helping everyone to get to know 'the unsearchable riches of Christ',[72] since these riches are for every individual and are everybody's property.

12. In this unity in mission, which is decided principally by Christ himself, all Christians must find what already unites them, even before their full communion is achieved. This is apostolic and missionary unity, missionary and apostolic unity. Thanks to this unity we can together come close to the magnificent heritage of the human spirit that has been manifested in all religions, as the Second Vatican Council's declaration *Nostra Aetate* says.[73] It also enables us to approach all cultures, all ideological concepts, all people of good will. We approach them with the esteem, respect and discernment that since the time of the apostles has marked the *missionary* attitude, the attitude *of the missionary*. Suffice it to mention St Paul and, for instance, his address in the Areopagus at Athens.[74] The *missionary* attitude always begins with a feeling of deep esteem for 'what is in man',[75] for what man has himself worked out in the depths of his spirit concerning the most profound and

important problems. It is a question of respecting everything that has been brought about in him by the Spirit, which 'blows where it wills'.[76] The mission is never destruction, but instead is a taking up and fresh building, even if in practice there has not always been full correspondence with this high ideal. And we know well that the conversion that is begun by the mission is a work of grace, in which man must fully find himself again.

12.1. For this reason the Church in our time attaches great importance to all that is stated by the Second Vatican Council in its *Declaration on Religious Freedom*, both the first and the second part of the document.[77] We perceive intimately that the truth revealed to us by God imposes on us an obligation. We have, in particular, a great sense of responsibility for this truth. By Christ's institution the Church is its guardian and teacher having been endowed with a unique assistance of the Holy Spirit in order to guard and teach it in its most exact integrity.[78] In fulfilling this mission, we look towards Christ himself, the first evangelizer,[79] and also towards his apostles, martyrs and confessors. The *Declaration on Religious Freedom* shows us convincingly that, when Christ and, after him, his apostles proclaimed the truth that comes not from men but from God ('My teaching is not mine, but his who sent me,'[80] that is the Father's), they preserved, while acting with their full force of spirit, a deep esteem for man, for his intellect, his will, his conscience and his freedom.[81] Thus the human person's dignity itself becomes part of the content of that proclamation, being included not necessarily in words but by an attitude towards it. This attitude seems to fit the special needs of our times. Since man's true freedom is not found in everything that the various systems and individuals see and propagate as freedom, the Church, because of her divine mission, becomes all the more the guardian of this freedom, which is the condition and basis for the human person's true dignity.

12.2. Jesus Christ meets the man of every age, including our own, with the same words: 'You will know the truth, and the truth will make you free.'[82] These words contain both a fundamental requirement and a warning: the requirement of an honest relationship with regard to truth as a condition for authentic freedom, and the warning to avoid every kind of illusory freedom, every superficial unilateral freedom, every freedom that fails to enter into the whole truth about man and the world. Today also, even after two thousand years, we see Christ as the one who brings man freedom based on truth, frees man from what curtails, diminishes and as it were breaks off this freedom at its root, in man's soul, his heart and his conscience. What a stupendous confirmation of this has been given and is still being given by those who, thanks to Christ and in Christ, have reached true freedom and have manifested it even in situations of external constraint!

12.3. When Jesus Christ himself appeared as a prisoner before Pilate's tribunal and was interrogated by him about the accusation made against him by the representatives of the Sanhedrin, did he not answer: 'For this I was born, and for this I have come into the world, to bear witness to the truth'?[83] It was as if with these words spoken before the judge at the decisive moment he was once more confirming what he had said earlier: 'You will know the truth and the truth will make you free.' In the course of so many centuries, of so many generations, from the time of the apostles on, is it not often Jesus Christ himself that has made an appearance at the side of people judged for the sake of the truth? And has he not gone to death with people condemned for the sake of the truth? Does he ever cease to be the continuous spokesman and advocate for the person who lives 'in spirit and truth'?[84] Just as he does not cease to be it before the Father, he is it also with regard to the history of man. And in her turn the Church, in spite of all the weaknesses that are part of her human history, does not cease to follow him who said: 'The hour is coming, and now is, when the true worshippers will worship the Father in spirit and truth, for such the Father seeks to worship him. God is spirit, and those who worship him must worship in spirit and truth.'[85]

III

The Church as a defender of human beings

13. When we penetrate by means of the continually and rapidly increasing experience of the human family into the mystery of Jesus Christ, we understand with greater clarity that there is at the basis of all these ways that the Church of our time must follow, in accordance with the wisdom of Pope Paul VI,[86] one single way: it is the way that has stood the test of centuries and it is also the way of the future. Christ the Lord indicated this way especially, when, as the Council teaches, 'by his incarnation, he, the son of God, in a certain way *united himself with each man.*'[87] The Church therefore sees its fundamental task in enabling that union to be brought about and renewed continually. The Church wishes to serve this single end: that each person may be able to find Christ, in order that Christ may walk with each person the path of life, with the power of the truth about man and the world that is contained in the mystery of the incarnation and the redemption and with the power of the love that is radiated by that truth. Against a background of the ever increasing historical processes, which seem at the present time to have results especially within the spheres of various systems, ideological concepts of the world and regimes, Jesus Christ becomes, in a way, newly present, in spite of all his apparent absences, in spite of all the limitations of the presence and of the institutional activity of the Church. Jesus Christ becomes present with the power of the truth and the love that are expressed in him with unique unrepeatable fullness in spite of the shortness of his life on earth and the even greater shortness of his public activity.

13.1. Jesus Christ is the chief way for the Church. He himself is our way 'to the Father's house'[88] and is the way to each man. On this way leading from Christ to man, on this way on which Christ unites himself with each man, nobody can halt the Church. This is an exigency of man's temporal welfare and of his eternal welfare. Out of regard for Christ and in view of the mystery that constitutes the Church's own life, the Church cannot remain insensible to whatever serves man's true welfare, any more than she can remain indifferent to what threatens it. In various passages in its documents the Second Vatican Council has expressed the Church's fundamental solicitude that life in 'the world should conform more to man's surpassing dignity'[89] in all its aspects, so as to make that life 'ever more human'.[90] This is the solicitude of Christ himself, the good shepherd of all men. In the name of this solicitude, as we read in the council's pastoral constitution, 'the Church must in no way be confused with the political community, nor bound to any political system. She is at once a sign and a safeguard of the transcendence of the human person.'[91]

13.2. Accordingly, what is in question here is man in all his truth, in his full magnitude. We are not dealing with the 'abstract' man, but the real, 'concrete', 'historical' man. We are dealing with 'each' man, for each one is included in the mystery of the redemption and with each one Christ has united himself for ever through this mystery. Every man comes into the world through being conceived in his mother's womb and being born of his mother, and precisely on account of the mystery of the redemption is entrusted to the solicitude of the Church. Her solicitude is about the whole man and is focused on him in an altogether special manner. The object of her care is man in his unique unrepeatable human reality, which keeps intact the image and likeness of God himself.[92] The Council points out this very fact when, speaking of that likeness, it recalls that 'man is the only creature on earth that God willed for itself.'[93] Man as 'willed' by God, as 'chosen' by him from eternity and called, destined for grace and glory—this is 'each' man, 'the most concrete' man, 'the most real'; this is man in all the fullness of the mystery in which he has become a sharer in Jesus Christ, the mystery in which each one of the four thousand million human beings living on our planet has become a sharer from the moment he is conceived beneath the heart of his mother.

14. The Church cannot abandon man, for his 'destiny', that is to say his election, calling, birth and death, salvation or ̄erdition, is so closely and unbreakably linked with Christ. We are speaking precisely of each man on this planet, this earth that the creator gave to the first man, saying to the man and the woman: 'subdue it and have dominion'.[94] Each man in all the unrepeatable reality of what he is and what he does, of his intellect and will, of his conscience and heart. Man who in his reality has, because he is a 'person', a history of his life that is his own and, most important, a history of his soul that is his own. Man who, in keeping with the openness of his spirit within and also with the many diverse needs of his body and his existence in time, writes this personal history of his through numerous bonds, contacts, situations, and social structures linking him with other men, beginning to do so from the first moment of his existence on earth, from the moment of his conception and birth. Man in the full truth of his existence, of his personal being and also of his community and social being—in the sphere of his own family, in the sphere of society and very diverse contexts, in the sphere of his own nation or people (perhaps still only that of his clan or tribe), and in the sphere of the whole of mankind—this man is the primary route that the Church must travel in fulfilling her mission: *he is the primary and fundamental way for the Church*, the way traced out by Christ himself, the way that leads invariably through the mystery of the incarnation and the redemption.

14.1. It was precisely this man in all the truth of his life, in his conscience, in his continual inclination to sin and at the same time in his continual aspiration to truth, the good, the beautiful, justice and love that the Second

Vatican Council had before its eyes when, in outlining his situation in the modern world, it always passed from the external elements of this situation to the truth within humanity: 'In man himself many elements wrestle with one another. Thus, on the one hand, as a creature he experiences his limitations in a multitude of ways. On the other, he feels himself to be boundless in his desires and summoned to a higher life. Pulled by manifold attractions, he is constantly forced to choose among them and to renounce some. Indeed, as a weak and sinful being, he often does what he would not, and fails to do what he would. Hence he suffers from internal divisions, and from these flow so many and such great discords in society.'[95]

14.2. This man is the way for the Church—a way that, in a sense, is the basis of all the other ways that the Church must walk—because man—every man without any exception whatever—has been redeemed by Christ, and because with man—with each man without any exception whatever—Christ is in a way united, even when man is unaware of it: 'Christ, who died and was raised up for all, provides man'—each man and every man—'with the light and the strength to measure up to his supreme calling.'[96]

14.3. Since this man is the way for the Church, the way for her daily life and experience, for her mission and toil, the Church of today must be aware in an always new manner of man's 'situation'. That means that she must be aware of his possibilities, which keep returning to their proper bearings and thus revealing themselves. She must likewise be aware of the threats to man and of all that seems to oppose the endeavour 'to make human life ever more human'[97] and make every element of this life correspond to man's true dignity—in a word, she must be aware of *all that is opposed* to that process.

Threats and challenges

15. Accordingly, while keeping alive in our memory the picture that was so perspicaciously and authoritatively traced by the Second Vatican Council, we shall try once more to adapt it to the 'signs of the times' and to the demands of the situation, which is continually changing and evolving in certain directions.

15.1. The man of today seems ever to be under threat from what he produces, that is to say from the result of the work of his hands and, even more so, of the work of his intellect and the tendencies of his will. All too soon, and often in an unforeseeable way, what this manifold activity of man yields is not only subjected to 'alienation', in the sense that it is simply taken away from the person who produces it, but rather it turns against man himself, at least in part, through the indirect consequences of its effects returning on himself. It is or can be directed against him. This seems to make up the main chapter of the drama of present-day human existence in its broadest and universal dimension. Man therefore lives increasingly in fear. He is afraid that what he produces—not all of it, of course, or even most of it, but part of it and precisely that part that contains a special share of his genius and initiative—can radically turn against himself; he is afraid that it can become the means and instrument for an unimaginable self-destruction, compared with which all the cataclysms and catastrophes of history known to us seem to fade away. This gives rise to a question: why is it that the power given to man from the beginning by which he was to subdue the earth[98] turns against himself, producing an understandable state of disquiet, of conscious or unconscious fear and of menace, which in various ways is being communicated to the whole of the present-day human family and is manifesting itself under various aspects?

15.2. This state of menace for man from what he produces shows itself in various directions and various degrees of intensity. We seem to be increasingly aware of the fact that the exploitation of the earth, the planet on which we are living, demands rational and honest planning. At the same time, exploitation of the earth not only for industrial but also for military purposes and the uncontrolled development of technology outside the framework of a long-range authentically humanistic plan often bring with them a threat to man's natural environment, alienate him in his relations with nature and remove him from nature. Man often seems to see no other meaning in his natural environment than what serves for immediate use and consumption. Yet it was the creator's will that man should communicate with nature as an intelligent and noble 'master' and 'guardian', and not as a heedless 'exploiter' and 'destroyer'.

15.3. The development of technology and the development of contemporary civilization, which is marked by the ascendancy of technology, demand a proportional development of morals and ethics. For the present, this last development seems unfortunately to be always left behind. Accordingly, in spite of the marvel of this progress, in which it is difficult not to see also authentic signs of man's greatness, signs that in their creative seeds were revealed to us in the pages of the Book of Genesis, as early as where it describes man's creation,[99] this progress cannot fail to give rise to disquiet on many counts. The first reason for disquiet concerns the essential and fundamental question: does this progress, which has man for its author and promoter, make human life on earth 'more human' in every aspect of that life? Does it make it more 'worthy of man'? There can be no doubt that in various aspects it does. But the question keeps coming back with regard to what is most essential—whether in the context of this progress man, as man, is becoming truly better, that is to say more mature spiritually, more aware of the dignity of his humanity, more responsible, more open to others, especially the neediest and the weakest, and readier to give and to aid all.

15.4. This question must be put by Christians, precisely because Jesus Christ has made them so universally sensitive about the problem of man. The same question must be asked by all men, especially those belonging to the social groups that are dedicating themselves actively to development and progress today. As we observe and take part in these processes we cannot let ourselves be taken over merely by euphoria or be carried away by one-sided enthusiasm for our conquests, but we must all ask ourselves, with absolute honesty, objectivity and a sense of moral responsibility, the essential questions concerning man's situation today and in the future. Do all the conquests attained until now and those projected for the future for technology accord with man's moral and spiritual progress? In this context is man, as man, developing and progressing or is he regressing and being degraded in his humanity? In men and 'in man's world', which in itself is a world of moral good and evil, does good prevail over evil? In men and among men is there a growth of social love, of respect for the rights of others—for every man, nation and people—or on the contrary is there an increase of various degrees of selfishness, exaggerated nationalism instead of authentic love of country, and also the propensity to dominate others beyond the limits of one's legitimate rights and merits and the propensity to exploit the whole of material progress and that in the technology of production for the exclusive purpose of dominating others or of favouring this or that imperialism?

15.5. These are the essential questions that the Church is bound to ask herself, since they are being asked with greater or less explicitness by the thousands of millions of people now living in the world. The subject of development and progress is on everybody's lips and appears in the columns of all the newspapers and other publications in all the languages of the modern world. Let us not forget however that this subject contains not only affirmations and certainties but also questions and points of anguished disquiet. The latter are no less important than the former. They fit in with the dialectical nature of human knowledge and even more with the fundamental need for solicitude by man for man, for his humanity, and for the future of people on earth. Inspired by eschatological faith, the Church considers an essential, unbreakably united element of her mission this solicitude for man, for his humanity, for the future of men on earth and therefore also for the course set for the whole of development and progress. She finds the principle of this solicitude in Jesus Christ himself, as the Gospels witness. This is why she wishes to make it grow continually through her relationship with Christ, reading man's situation in the modern world in accordance with the most important signs of our time.

16. If therefore our time, the time of our generation, the time that is approaching the end of the second millennium of the Christian era, shows itself a time of great progress, it is also seen as a time of threat in many forms for man. The Church must speak of this threat to all people of good will and must always carry on a dialogue with them about it. Man's situation in the modern world seems indeed to be far removed from the objective demands of the moral order, from the requirements of justice, and even more of social love. We are dealing here only with that which found expression in the creator's first message to man at the moment in which he was giving him the earth, to 'subdue' it.[100] This first message was confirmed by Christ the Lord in the mystery of the redemption. This is expressed by the Second Vatican Council in those beautiful chapters of its teaching that concern man's 'kingship', that is to say his call to share in the kingly function—the *munus regale*—of Christ himself.[101] The essential meaning of this 'kingship' and 'dominion' of man over the visible world, which the creator himself gave man for his task, consists in the priority of ethics over technology, in the primacy of the person over things, and in the superiority of spirit over matter.

16.1. This is why all phases of present-day progress must be followed attentively. Each stage of that progress must, so to speak, be x-rayed from this point of view. What is in question is the advancement of persons, not just the multiplying of things that people can use. It is a matter—as a contemporary philosopher has said and as the council has stated—not so much of 'having more' as of 'being more'.[102] Indeed there is already a real perceptible danger that, while man's dominion over the world of things is making enormous advances, he lose the essential threads of his dominion and in various ways let his humanity be subjected to the world and become himself something subject to manipulation in many ways—even if the manipulation is often not perceptible directly—through the whole of the organization of community life, through the production system and through pressure from the means of social communication. Man cannot relinquish himself or the place in the visible world that belongs to him; he cannot become the slave of things, the slave of economic systems, the slave of production, the slave of his own products. A civilization purely materialistic in outline condemns man to such slavery, even if at times, no doubt, this occurs contrary to the intentions and the very premises of its pioneers. The present solicitude for man certainly has at its root this problem. It is not a matter here merely of giving an abstract answer to the question: who is man? It is a matter of the whole of the dynamism of life and civilization. It is a matter of the meaningfulness of the various initiatives of everyday life and also of the premises for many civilization programmes, political programmes, economic ones, social ones, state ones, and many others.

16.2. If we make bold to describe man's situation in the modern world as far removed from the objective demands of the moral order, from the exigencies of justice, and still more from social love, we do so because this is confirmed by the well-known facts and comparisons that have already on various occasions found an echo in the pages of statements by the popes, the council and the synod.[103] Man's situation today is certainly not uniform but marked with numerous differences. These differences have causes in history, but they also have strong ethical effects. Indeed everyone is familiar with the picture of the consumer civilization, which consists in a certain surplus of goods necessary for man and for entire societies—and we are dealing precisely with the rich highly developed societies—while the remaining societies—at least broad sectors of them—are suffering from hunger, with many people dying each day of starvation and malnutrition. Hand in hand go a certain abuse of freedom by one group—an abuse linked precisely with a consumer attitude uncontrolled by ethics—and a limitation by it of the freedom of the others, that is to say those suffering marked shortages and being driven to conditions of even worse misery and destitution.

16.3. This pattern, which is familiar to all, and the contrast referred to, in the documents giving their teaching, by the popes of this century, most recently by John XXIII and by Paul VI,[104] represent, as it were, the gigantic development of the parable in the Bible of the rich banqueter and the poor man Lazarus.[105]

16.4. So widespread is the phenomenon that it brings into question the financial, monetary, production and commercial mechanisms that, resting on various political pressures, support the world economy. These are proving incapable either of remedying the unjust social situations inherited from the past or of dealing with the urgent challenges and ethical demands of the present. By submitting man to tensions created by himself, dilapidating at an accelerated pace material and energy resources, and compromising the geo-physical environment, these structures unceasingly make the areas of misery spread, accompanied by anguish, frustration and bitterness.[106]

16.5. We have before us here a great drama that can leave nobody indifferent. The person who, on the one hand, is trying to draw the maximum profit and, on the other hand, is paying the price in damage and injury is always man. The drama is made still worse by the presence close at hand of the privileged social classes and of the rich countries, which accumulate goods to an excessive degree and the misuse of whose riches very often becomes the cause of various ills. Add to this the fever of inflation and the plague of unemployment—these are further symptoms of the moral disorder that is being noticed in the world situation and therefore requires daring creative resolves in keeping with man's authentic dignity.[107]

16.6. Such a task is not an impossible one. The principle of solidarity, in a wide sense, must inspire the effective search for appropriate institutions and mechanisms, whether in the sector of trade, where the laws of healthy competition must be allowed to lead the way, or on the level of a wider and more immediate redistribution of riches and of control over them in order that the economically developing peoples may be able not only to satisfy their essential needs but also to advance gradually and effectively.

16.7. This difficult road of the indispensable transformation of the structures of economic life is one on which it will not be easy to go forward without the intervention of a true conversion of mind, will and heart. The task requires resolute commitment by individuals and peoples that are free and linked in solidarity. All too often freedom is confused with the instinct for individual or collective interest or with the instinct for combat and domination, whatever be the ideological colours with which they are covered. Obviously these instincts exist and are operative, but no truly human economy will be possible unless they are taken up, directed and dominated by the deepest powers in man which decide the true culture of peoples. These are the very sources for the effort which will express man's true freedom and which will be capable of ensuring it in the economic field also. Economic development, with every factor in its adequate functioning, must be constantly programmed and realized within a perspective of universal joint development of each individual and people, as was convincingly recalled by my predecessor Paul VI in *Populorum Progressio*. Otherwise, the category of 'economic progress' becomes in isolation a superior category subordinating the whole of human existence to its partial demands, suffocating man, breaking up society, and ending by entangling itself in its own tensions and excesses.

16.8. It is possible to undertake this duty. This is testified by the certain facts and the results, which it would be difficult to mention more analytically here. However, one thing is certain: at the basis of this gigantic sector it is necessary to establish, accept and deepen the sense of moral responsibility which man must undertake. Again and always man. This responsibility becomes especially evident for us Christians when we recall—and we should always recall it—the scene of the last judgement according to the words of Christ related in Matthew's Gospel.[108]

16.9. This eschatological scene must always be 'applied' to man's history; it must always be made the 'measure' for human acts as an essential outline for an examination of conscience by each and every one: 'I was hungry and you gave me no food...naked and you did not clothe me...in prison and you did not visit me.'[109] These words become charged with even stronger warning when we think that, instead of bread and cultural aid, the new states and nations awakening to independent life are being offered, sometimes in abundance, modern weapons and means of destruction placed at the service of armed conflicts and wars that are not so much a requirement for defending their just rights and their sovereignty but rather a form of chauvinism, imperialism, and neo-colonialism of one kind or another. We all know well that the areas of misery and hunger on our globe could have been made fertile in a short time, if the gigantic investments for armaments at the service of war and destruction had been changed into investments for food at the service of life.

16.10. This consideration will perhaps remain in part an 'abstract' one. It will perhaps offer both 'sides' an occasion for mutual accusation, each forgetting its own faults. It will perhaps provoke new accusations against the Church. The Church, however, which has no weapons at her disposal apart from those of the Spirit, of the word and of love, cannot renounce her proclamation of 'the word...in season and out of season'.[110] For this reason she does not cease to implore each side of the two and to beg everybody in the name of God and in the name of man: Do not kill! Do not prepare destruction and extermination for men! Think of your brothers and sisters who are suffering hunger and misery! Respect each one's dignity and freedom!

Human rights

17. This century has so far been a century of great calamities for man, of great devastations, not only material ones but also moral ones, indeed perhaps above all moral ones. Admittedly it is not easy to compare one age or one century with another under this aspect, since that depends also on changing historical standards. Nevertheless, without applying these comparisons, one still cannot fail to see that this century has so far been one in which people have provided many injustices and sufferings for themselves. Has this process been decisively curbed? In any case, we cannot fail to recall at this point, with esteem and profound hope for the future, the magnificent effort made to give life to the United Nations Organization, an effort conducive to the definition and establishment of man's objective and inviolable rights, with the member states obliging each other to observe them rigorously. This commitment has been accepted and ratified by almost all present-day states, and this should constitute a guarantee that human rights will become throughout the world a fundamental principle of work for man's welfare.

17.1. There is no need for the Church to confirm how closely this problem is linked with her mission in the modern world. Indeed it is at the very basis of social and international peace, as has been declared by John XXIII, the Second Vatican Council, and later Paul VI, in detailed documents. After all, peace comes down to respect for man's inviolable rights—*Opus iustitiae pax*—while war springs from the violation of these rights and brings with it still graver violations of them. If human rights are violated in time of peace, this is particularly painful and from the point of view of progress it represents an incomprehensible manifestation of activity directed against man, which can in no way be reconciled with any programme that describes itself as 'humanistic'. And what social, economic, political or cultural programme could renounce this description? We are firmly convinced that there is no programme in today's world in which man is not invariably brought to the fore, even when the platforms of the programmes are made up of conflicting ideologies concerning the way of conceiving the world.

17.2. If, in spite of these premises, human rights are being violated in various ways, if in practice we see before us concentration camps, violence, torture, terrorism, and discrimination in many forms, this must then be the consequence of the other premises, undermining and often almost annihilating the effectiveness of the humanistic premises of these modern programmes and systems. This necessarily imposes the duty to submit these programmes to continual revision from the point of view of the objective and inviolable rights of man.

17.3. The Declaration of Human Rights linked with the setting up of the United Nations Organization certainly had as its aim not only to depart from the horrible experiences of the last world war but also to create the basis for continual revision of programmes, systems and regimes precisely from this single fundamental point of view, namely the welfare of man—or, let us say, of the person in the community—which must, as a fundamental factor in the common good, constitute the essential criterion for all programmes, systems and regimes. If the opposite happens, human life is, even in time of peace, condemned to various sufferings and, along with these sufferings, there is a development of various forms of domination, totalitarianism, neo-colonialism and imperialism which are a threat also to the harmonious living together of the nations. Indeed, it is a significant fact, repeatedly confirmed by the experiences of history, that violation of the rights of man goes hand in hand with violation of the rights of the nation, with which man is united by organic links as with a larger family.

17.4. Already in the first half of this century, when various state totalitarianisms were developing, which, as is well known, led to the horrible catastrophe of war, the Church clearly outlines her position with regard to these regimes that to all appearances were acting for a higher good, namely the good of the state, while history was to show instead that the good in question was only that of a certain party, which had been identified with the state.[111] In reality, those regimes had restricted the rights of the citizens, denying them recognition precisely of those inviolable human rights that have reached formulation on the international level in the middle of our century. While sharing the joy of all people of good will, of all people who truly love justice and peace, at this conquest, the Church, aware that the 'letter' on its own can kill, while only 'the spirit gives life',[112] must continually ask, together with these people of good will, whether the Declaration of Human Rights and the acceptance of its 'letter' mean everywhere also the actualization of its 'spirit'. Indeed, well-founded fears arise that very often we are still far from this actualization and that at times the spirit of social and public life is painfully opposed to the declared 'letter' of human rights. This state of things, which is burdensome for the societies concerned, would place special responsibility towards these societies and the history of man on those contributing to its establishment.

17.5. The essential sense of the state, as a political community, consists in that the society and people composing it are master and sovereign of their own destiny. This sense remains unrealized if, instead of the exercise of power with the moral participation of the society or people, what we see is the imposition of power by a certain group upon all the other members of the society. This is essential in the present age, with its enormous increase in people's social awareness and the accompanying need for the citizens to have a right share in the political life of the community, while taking account of the real conditions of each people and the necessary vigour of public authority.[113] These therefore are questions of primary importance from the point of view of the progress of man himself and the overall development of his humanity.

17.6. The Church has always taught the duty to act for the common good and, in so doing, has likewise educated good citizens for each state. Furthermore, she has always taught that the fundamental duty of power is solicitude for the common good of society; this is what gives power its fundamental rights. Precisely in the name of these premises of the objective ethical order, the rights of power can only be understood on the basis of respect for the objective and inviolable rights of man. The common good that authority in the state serves is brought to full realization only when all the citizens are sure of their rights. The lack of this leads to the dissolution of society, opposition by citizens to authority, or a situation of oppression, intimidation, violence, and terrorism, of which many examples have been provided by the totalitarianisms of this century. Thus the principle of human rights is of profound concern to the area of social justice and is the measure by which it can be tested in the life of political bodies.

17.7. These rights are rightly reckoned to include the right to religious freedom together with the right to freedom of conscience. The Second Vatican Council considered especially necessary the preparation of a fairly long declaration on this subject. This is the document called *Dignitatis Humanae*,[114] in which is expressed not only the theological concept of the question but also the concept reached from the point of view of natural law, that is to say from the 'purely human' position, on the basis of the premises given by man's own experience, his reason and his sense of human dignity. Certainly the curtailment of the religious freedom of individuals and communities is not only a painful experience but it is above all an attack on man's very dignity, independently of the religion professed or of the concept of the world which these individuals and communities have. The curtailment and violation of religious freedom are in contrast with man's dignity and his objective rights. The council document mentioned above states clearly enough what that curtailment or violation of religious freedom is. In this case we are undoubtedly confronted with a radical injustice with regard to what is particularly deep within man, what is authentically human. Indeed, even the phenomenon of unbelief, a-religiousness and atheism, as a human phenomenon, is understood only in relation to the phenomenon of religion and faith. It is therefore difficult, even from a 'purely human' point of view, to accept a position that gives only atheism the right of citizenship in public and social life, while believers are, as though by principle, barely tolerated or are treated as second-class citizens or are even—and this has already happened—entirely deprived of the rights of citizenship.

17.8. Even if briefly, this subject must also be dealt with, because it too enters into the complex of man's situations in the present-day world and because it too gives evidence of the degree to which this situation is overburdened by prejudices and injustices of various kinds. If we refrain from entering into details in this field in which we would have a special right and duty to do so, it is above all because, together with all those who are suffering the torments of discrimination and persecution for the name of God, we are guided by faith in the redeeming power of the cross of Christ. However, because of my office, I appeal in the name of all believers throughout the world to those on whom the organization of social and public life in some way depends, earnestly requesting them to respect the rights of religion and of the Church's activity. No privilege is asked for, but only respect for an elementary right. Actuation of this right is one of the fundamental tests of man's authentic progress in any regime, in any society, system or milieu.

Dives in Misericordia

Encyclical letter of Pope John Paul II to the bishops, priests and faithful of the entire Catholic Church about the divine mercy.

Introduction

The opening words of Pope John Paul's second encyclical, issued on 30 November 1980, mean 'rich in mercy', and the letter treats movingly of the mercy of God. As in the case of *Redemptor Hominis* only a part of the encyclical has been reproduced.

Of the two sections included the first, paragraphs 5-6, is a revealing discussion of the parable of the prodigal son, what it has to say about human dignity and how people should respect one another. The second section, paragraphs 11-12, picks up the theme of what threatens human kind, something already discussed in *Redemptor Hominis*, and goes on to point out that justice is not enough. Justice, says the pope, can even be destructive, unless it be informed by love.

The Latin text of *Dives in Misericordia* (DM) is to be found in AAS 72 (1980) 1177-1232. The sections reproduced are to be found on pp.1193-1199 and 1212-1217. Once again, only major paragraphs are numbered, and subordinate numbering has been added in accordance with the Editorial Note (p.ix).

A summary of the whole text has been given, with the sections omitted here being indicated by square brackets.

Summary

[*Paras. 1-4*: The more the Church's mission is centred upon men and women, the more it must be directed in Jesus Christ to the Father. Theocentrism and anthropocentrism are linked in the history of the Church. In Christ and through Christ the mercy of God became visible. The truth about God the Father of mercies as it is revealed in Christ shows him to be especially close to people when they are suffering, under threat. Through his life and his actions Jesus revealed that love is present in the world, a love which makes itself particularly noticed in contact with suffering, injustice or poverty. But Jesus demanded too that people live their lives according to love and mercy.]

Paras. 5-6: The ideas of mercy as they are expressed in the Old Testament are echoed by Mary in the Magnificat and, although the word 'mercy' does not itself appear in the text, the parable of the prodigal son exemplifies them. The son received material goods as his inheritance, but more important was his dignity as a son in his father's house. When he returned after squandering his inheritance he realized that he had no right in justice to be more than an employee of his father. But his father is faithful to his fatherhood, faithful to the love he has lavished on his son, and this obliges him to be concerned about the son's dignity. We often see in mercy a relationship of inequality which belittles the recipient of mercy. The parable of the prodigal son shows that the reality is different: the son begins to see himself and his actions in their full truth, and undergoes conversion. Because of this the father seems to forget all the evil which has been committed. Mercy is manifested in its true and proper aspect when it restores to value, promotes and draws good from all the forms of evil existing in the world and in human beings.

[*Paras. 7-10*: In his Passion Jesus deserves mercy from the people to whom he has done good, yet does not receive it. He appeals to the Father whose love he has preached and whose mercy he has borne witness to, but he is not spared. The sins of men and women are compensated for by the suffering of the Man-God, but this justice springs completely from love. It produces the fruits of salvation through which human beings once more have access to the fullness of life and holiness that come from God. Even in the glorification of the son of God in the resurrection the cross remains. It is a witness to the strength of evil. The cross is the most profound condescension of God to men and women, a touch of eternal love upon the most painful wounds of earthly existence. In the eschatological fulfilment mercy will be revealed as love while in human history love must be above all revealed as mercy. Christ's messianic programme, the programme of mercy, becomes the programme of the Church. The words of Mary's Magnificat have a prophetic content that concerns not only the past of Israel but also the whole future of the people of God on earth. The present generation knows that, with the countless possibilities provided by progress, it is in a privileged position. But there is also unease, and a sense of powerlessness.]

Paras. 11-12: There is the fear connected to the prospect of conflict. There is the fear of the abuse of power, of falling victim to oppression. There is also remorse because the inequality between individuals and between nations not only still survives but is increasing. A sense of justice has been reawakened. The Church shares it, but experience shows that justice can even be destructive if love is not allowed to shape human life.

[*Paras. 13-15*: The Church must profess and proclaim God's mercy as it has been handed down by revelation. It lives authentically when it brings people closer to the source of the saviour's mercy, particularly through the eucharist and the sacrament of reconciliation. Knowledge of the God of mercy and of tender love is a constant and inexhaustible source of conversion. People attain the mercy of God to the extent that they are themselves interiorly transformed in the spirit of that love towards their neighbour. This is not just a spiritual transformation, realized once and for all, it is a whole life-style, an essential and continuous characteristic of the Christian vocation. In reciprocal relations, merciful love is never a unilateral act: the one who bestows it is always a beneficiary. The equality brought by justice is always limited to extrinsic goods: love and mercy bring it about that people meet one another in that value which is human nature itself, with the dignity proper to human beings. Mercy is an indispensable element for shaping mutual relationships. Mercy has the power to confer on justice a new content, most simply and most fully expressed in forgiveness. The Church, however, while it proclaims and practises mercy, also must pray for the mercy of God amid the many forms of evil which threaten humanity.]

The mercy of God and the dignity of people

5. At the very beginning of the New Testament, two voices resound in St Luke's Gospel in unique harmony concerning the mercy of God, a harmony which forcefully echoes the whole Old Testament tradition. They express the semantic elements linked to the differentiated terminology of the ancient books. Mary, entering the house of Zechariah, magnifies the Lord with all her soul for 'his mercy', which 'from generation to generation' is bestowed on those who fear him. A little later, as she recalls the election of Israel, she proclaims the mercy which he who has chosen her holds 'in remembrance' from all time.[60] Afterwards, in the same house, when John the Baptist is born, his father Zechariah blesses the God of Israel and glorifies him for performing the mercy promised to our fathers and for remembering his holy covenant.[61]

5.1. In the teaching of Christ himself, this image inherited from the Old Testament becomes at the same time simpler and more profound. This is perhaps most evident in the parable of the prodigal son.[62] Although the word 'mercy' does not appear, it nevertheless expresses the essence of the divine mercy in a particularly clear way. This is due not so much to the terminology, as in the Old Testament books, as to the analogy that enables us to understand more fully the very mystery of mercy, as a profound drama played out between the father's love and the prodigality and sin of the son.

5.2. That son, who receives from the father the portion of the inheritance that is due to him and leaves home to squander it in a far country 'in loose living', in a certain sense is the man of every period, beginning with the one who was the first to lose the inheritance of grace and original justice. The analogy at this point is very wide-ranging. The parable indirectly touches upon every breach of the covenant of love, every loss of grace, every sin. In this analogy there is less emphasis than in the prophetic tradition on the unfaithfulness of the whole people of Israel, although the analogy of the prodigal son may extend to this also. 'When he had spent everything,' the son 'began to be in need,' especially as 'a great famine arose in that country' to which he had gone after leaving his father's house. And in this situation 'he would gladly have fed on' anything, even 'the pods that the swine ate', the swine that he herded for 'one of the citizens of that country'. But even this was refused him.

5.3. The analogy turns clearly toward man's interior. The inheritance that the son had received from his father was a quantity of material goods, but more important than these goods was his dignity as a son in his father's house. The situation in which he found himself when he lost the material goods should have made him aware of the loss of that dignity. He had not thought about it previously, when he had asked his father to give him the part of the inheritance that was due to him, in order to go away. He seems not to be conscious of it even now, when he says to himself: 'How many of my father's hired servants have bread enough and to spare, but I perish here with hunger.'

5.4. He measures himself by the standard of the goods that he has lost, that he no longer 'possesses', while the hired servants in his father's house 'possess' them. These words express above all his attitude to material goods; nevertheless, under their surface is concealed the tragedy of lost dignity, the awareness of squandered sonship.

5.5. It is at this point that he makes the decision: 'I will arise and go to my father, and I will say to him, "Father, I have sinned against heaven and before you; I am no longer worthy to be called your son. Treat me as one of your hired servants." '[63] These are words that reveal more deeply the essential problem. Through the complex material situation in which the prodigal son found himself because of his folly, because of sin, the sense of lost dignity has matured. When he decides to return to his father's house, to ask his father to be received—no longer by virtue of his right as a son, but as an employee—at first sight he seems to be acting by reason of the hunger and poverty that he had fallen into; this motive, however, is permeated by an awareness of a deeper loss: to be a hired servant in his own father's house is certainly a great humiliation and source of shame. Nevertheless, the prodigal son is ready to undergo that humiliation and shame. He realizes that he no longer has any right except to be an employee in his father's house. His decision is taken in full consciousness of what he has deserved and of what he can still have a right to in accordance with the norms of justice. Precisely this reasoning demonstrates that at the centre of the prodigal son's consciousness the sense of lost dignity is emerging, the sense of that dignity that springs from the relationship of the son with the father. And it is with this decision that he sets out.

5.6. In the parable of the prodigal son, the term 'justice' is not used even once; just as in the original text the term 'mercy' is not used either. Nevertheless, the relationship between justice and love that is manifested as mercy is inscribed with great exactness in the content of the gospel parable. It becomes more evident that love is transformed into mercy when it is necessary to go beyond the precise norm of justice—precise and often too narrow. The prodigal son, having wasted the property he received from his father, deserves—after his return—to earn his living by working in his father's house as a hired servant and possibly, little by little, to build up a certain provision of material goods, though perhaps never as much as the amount he had squandered. This would be demanded by the order of justice, especially as the son had not only squandered the part of the inheritance belonging to him, but had also hurt and offended his father by his whole conduct. Since this conduct had in his own eyes deprived him of his dignity as a son, it could not be a matter of indifference to his father. It was bound to make him suffer. It was also bound to implicate him in some way. And yet, after all, it was his own son who was involved, and such a relationship could never be altered or destroyed by any sort of behaviour. The prodigal son is aware of this and it is precisely this awareness that shows him clearly the dignity which he has lost and which makes him honestly evaluate the position that he could still expect in his father's house.

6. This exact picture of the prodigal son's state of mind enables us to understand exactly what the mercy of God consists in. There is no doubt that in this simple but penetrating analogy the figure of the father reveals to us God as father. The conduct of the father in the parable and his whole behaviour, which manifests his internal attitude, enables us to rediscover the individual threads of the Old Testament vision of mercy in a synthesis which is totally new, full of simplicity and depth. The father of the prodigal son is faithful to his fatherhood, faithful to the love that he had always lavished on his son. This fidelity is expressed in the parable not only by his immediate readiness to welcome him home when he returns after having squandered his inheritance; it is expressed even more fully by that joy, that merrymaking for the squanderer after his return, merrymaking which is so generous that it provokes the opposition and hatred of the elder brother, who had never gone far away from his father and had never abandoned the home.

6.1. The father's fidelity to himself—a trait already known by the Old Testament term *hesed*—is at the same time expressed in a manner particularly charged with affection. We read, in fact, that when the father saw the prodigal son returning home 'he had compassion, ran to meet him, threw his arms around his neck and kissed him.'[64] He certainly does this under the influence of a deep affection, and this also explains his generosity towards his son, that generosity which so angers the elder son. Nevertheless, the causes of this emotion are to be sought at a deeper level. Notice, the father is aware that a fundamental good has been saved: the good of his son's humanity. Although the son has squandered the inheritance, nevertheless his humanity is saved. Indeed, it has been, in a way, found again. The father's words to the elder son reveal this: 'It was fitting to make merry and be glad, for this your brother was dead and is alive; he was lost and is found.'[65] In the same Chapter 15 of Luke's Gospel, we read the parable of the sheep that was found[66] and then the parable of the coin that was found.[67] Each time there is an emphasis on the same joy that is present in the case of the prodigal son. The father's fidelity to himself is totally concentrated upon the humanity of the lost son, upon his dignity. This explains above all his joyous emotion at the moment of the son's return home.

6.2. Going on, one can therefore say that the love for the son, the love that springs from the very essence of fatherhood, in a way obliges the father to be concerned about his son's dignity. This concern is the measure of his love, the love of which St Paul was to write: 'Love is patient and kind...love does not insist on its own way; it is not irritable or resentful...but rejoices in the right...hopes all things, endures all things' and 'love never ends.'[68] Mercy—as

Christ has presented it in the parable of the prodigal son—has the interior form of the love that in the New Testament is called *agape*. This love is able to reach down to every prodigal son, to every human misery, and above all to every form of moral misery, to sin. When this happens, the person who is the object of mercy does not feel humiliated, but rather found again and 'restored to value'. The father first and foremost expresses to him his joy that he has been 'found again' and that he has 'returned to life'. This joy indicates a good that has remained intact: even if he is a prodigal, a son does not cease to be truly his father's son; it also indicates a good that has been found again, which in the case of the prodigal son was his return to the truth about himself.

6.3. What took place in the relationship between the father and the son in Christ's parable is not to be evaluated 'from the outside'. Our prejudices about mercy are mostly the result of appraising them only from the outside. At times it happens that by following this method of evaluation we see in mercy above all a relationship of inequality between the one offering it and the one receiving it. And, in consequence, we are quick to deduce that mercy belittles the receiver, that it offends the dignity of man. The parable of the prodigal son shows that the reality is different: the relationship of mercy is based on the common experience of that good which is man, on the common experience of the dignity that is proper to him. This common experience makes the prodigal son begin to see himself and his actions in their full truth (this vision in truth is a genuine form of humility); on the other hand, for this very reason he becomes a particular good for his father: the father sees so clearly the good which has been achieved thanks to a mysterious radiation of truth and love, that he seems to forget all the evil which the son has committed.

6.4. The parable of the prodigal son expresses in a simple but profound way the reality of conversion. Conversion is the most concrete expression of the working of love and of the presence of mercy in the human world. The true and proper meaning of mercy does not consist only in looking, however penetratingly and compassionately, at moral, physical or material evil: mercy is manifested in its true and proper aspect when it restores to value, promotes and draws good from all the forms of evil existing in the world and in man. Understood in this way, mercy constitutes the fundamental content of the messianic message of Christ and the constitutive power of his mission. His disciples and followers understood and practised mercy in the same way. Mercy never ceased to reveal itself, in their hearts and in their actions, as an especially creative proof of the love which does not allow itself to be 'conquered by evil', but overcomes 'evil with good'.[69] The genuine face of mercy has to be ever revealed anew. In spite of many prejudices, mercy seems particularly necessary for our times.

Unease and the distortion of justice

11. Thus, in our world the feeling of being under threat is increasing. There is an increase of that existential fear connected especially, as I said in the encyclical *Redemptor Hominis*, with the prospect of a conflict that in view of today's atomic stockpiles could mean the partial self-destruction of humanity. But the threat does not merely concern what human beings can do

to human beings through the means provided by military technology; it also concerns many other dangers produced by a materialistic society which—in spite of 'humanistic' declarations—accepts the primacy of things over persons. Contemporary man, therefore, fears that by the use of the means invented by this type of society, individuals and the environment, communities, societies and nations can fall victim to the abuse of power by other individuals, environments and societies. The history of our century offers many examples of this. In spite of all the declarations on the rights of man in his integral dimension, that is to say in his bodily and spiritual existence, we cannot say that these examples belong only to the past.

11.1. Man rightly fears falling victim to an oppression that will deprive him of his interior freedom, of the possibility of expressing the truth of which he is convinced, of the faith that he professes, of the ability to obey the voice of conscience that tells him the right path to follow. The technical means at the disposal of modern society conceal within themselves not only the possibility of self-destruction through military conflict, but also the possibility of a 'peaceful' subjugation of individuals, of environments, of entire societies and of nations, that for one reason or another might prove inconvenient for those who possess the necessary means and are ready to use them without scruple. An instance is the continued existence of torture, systematically used by authority as a means of domination and political oppression and practised by subordinates with impunity.

11.2. Together with awareness of the biological threat, therefore, there is a growing awareness of yet another threat, even more destructive of what is essentially human, what is intimately bound up with the dignity of the person and his or her right to truth and freedom.

11.3. All this is happening against the background of the gigantic remorse caused by the fact that, side by side with wealthy and surfeited people and societies, living in plenty and ruled by consumerism and pleasure, the same human family contains individuals and groups that are suffering from hunger. There are babies dying of hunger under their mothers' eyes. In various parts of the world, in various socio-economic systems, there exist entire areas of poverty, shortage and underdevelopment. This fact is universally known. The state of inequality between individuals and between nations not only still exists; it is increasing. It still happens that side by side with those who are wealthy and living in plenty there exist those who are living in want, suffering misery and often actually dying of hunger; and their number reaches tens, even hundreds of millions. This is why moral uneasiness is destined to become even more acute. It is obvious that a fundamental defect, or rather a series of defects, indeed a defective machinery is at the root of contemporary economics and materialistic civilization, which does not allow the human family to break free from such radically unjust situations.

11.4. This picture of today's world in which there is so much evil, both physical and moral, so as to make it a world entangled in contradictions and tensions, and at the same time full of threats to human freedom, conscience and religion—this picture explains the uneasiness felt by contemporary man. This uneasiness is experienced not only by those who are disadvantaged or oppressed, but also by those who possess the privileges of wealth, progress and power. And, although there is no lack of people trying to understand the causes of this uneasiness, or trying to react against it with the temporary means offered by technology, wealth or power, still in the very depth of the human spirit this uneasiness is stronger than all temporary means. This uneasiness concerns—as the analyses of the Second Vatican Council rightly pointed out—the fundamental problems of all human existence. It is linked with the very sense of man's existence in the world, and is an uneasiness for the future of man and all humanity; it demands decisive solutions, which now seem to be forcing themselves upon the human race.

12. It is not difficult to see that in the modern world the sense of justice has been awakening on a vast scale; and without doubt this emphasizes that which goes against justice in relationships between individuals, social groups and 'classes', between individual peoples and states, and finally between whole political systems, indeed between what are called 'worlds'. This deep and varied trend, at the basis of which the contemporary human conscience has placed justice, gives proof of the ethical character of the tensions and struggles pervading the world.

12.1. The Church shares with the people of our time this profound and ardent desire for a life which is just in every aspect, nor does she fail to examine the various aspects of the sort of justice that the life of people and society demands. This is confirmed by the field of Catholic social doctrine, greatly developed in the course of the last century. On the lines of this teaching proceed the education and formation of human consciences in the spirit of justice, and also individual undertakings, especially in the sphere of the apostolate of the laity, which are developing in precisely this spirit.

12.2. And yet it would be difficult not to notice that very often programmes which start from the idea of justice and which ought to assist its fulfilment among individuals, groups and human societies, in practice suffer from distortions. Although they continue to appeal to the idea of justice, nevertheless experience shows that other negative forces have gained the upper hand over justice, such as spite, hatred and even cruelty. In such cases, the desire to annihilate the enemy, limit his freedom or even force him into total dependence, becomes the fundamental motive for action; and this contrasts with the essence of justice, which by its nature tends to establish equality and harmony between the parties in conflict. This kind of abuse of the idea of justice and the practical distortion of it show how far human action can deviate from justice itself, even when it is being undertaken in the name of justice. Not in vain did Christ challenge his listeners, faithful to the doctrine of the Old Testament, for their attitude which was manifested in the words: 'An eye for an eye and a tooth for a tooth.'[111] This was the form of distortion of justice at that time; and today's forms continue to be modelled on it. It is obvious, in fact, that in the name of an alleged justice (for example, historical justice or class justice) the neighbour is sometimes destroyed, killed, deprived of liberty or stripped of fundamental human rights. The experience of the past and of our own time demonstrates that justice alone is not enough, that it can even lead to the negation and destruction of itself, if that deeper power, which is love, is not allowed to shape human life in its various dimensions. It has been precisely historical experience that, among other things, has led to the formulation of the saying: '*Summum ius, summa iniuria'* (The greatest justice, the greatest harm). This statement does not detract from the value of justice and does not minimize the significance of the order that is based upon it; it only indicates, under another aspect, the need to draw from the powers of the spirit which condition the very order of justice, powers which are still more profound.

12.3. The Church, having before her eyes the picture of the generation to which we belong, shares the uneasiness of so many of the people of our time. Moreover, one cannot fail to be worried by the decline of many fundamental values, which constitute an unquestionable good not only for Christian morality but simply for human morality, for moral culture: these values include respect for human life from the moment of conception, respect for marriage in its indissoluble unity and respect for the stability of the family. Moral permissiveness strikes especially at this most sensitive sphere of life and society. Hand in hand with this go the crisis of truth in human relationships, lack of responsibility for what one says, the purely utilitarian relationship between individual and individual, the loss of a sense of the authentic common good and the ease with which this good is alienated. Finally, there is the 'desacralization' that often turns into 'dehumanization': the individual and the society for whom nothing is 'sacred' suffer moral decay, in spite of appearances.

Laborem Exercens

Encyclical letter of Pope John Paul II addressed to his venerable brothers in the episcopate, to the priests, the religious families, to the sons and daughters of the Church, and to all men and women of good will about human work, on the occasion of the ninetieth anniversary of the publication of Rerum Novarum.

Introduction

As he explains at the end of his letter, Pope John Paul's third encyclical had been intended for publication on 15 May 1981, to mark the ninetieth anniversary of *Rerum Novarum*. The assassination attempt prevented this, and he had time to revise the text only after his return from hospital. It appeared, therefore, on 14 September.

Despite the occasion of its publication, *Laborem Exercens* does not even footnote *Rerum Novarum*; other papal and conciliar texts are quoted but rarely. Though the pope is conscious of the tradition to which he is an heir, this encyclical marks a new, and more concrete, style for social teaching. Previous popes had tended to favour a modified form of capitalism. John Paul does not. Like his predecessors, Pope John Paul does not wish to concede that a 'class struggle' is unavoidable; but he accepts that confrontation between classes may be necessary. Though clearly sharing the Church's traditional unease at the thought of women working he insists that 'they should not have to pay for their advancement [in work] by abandoning what is specific to them' (LE 19.4.). He discusses structural injustice and commends, or appears to commend, nationalization of certain industries, provided they truly pass to the control of the people. Above all he emphasizes the priority of the workers over the suppliers of capital.

For a more extensive discussion of *Laborum Exercens* (LE), see the Introduction, pp.xviii. The Latin text appears in AAS 73 (1981) 577-647. Cross-headings have been added, as has subordinate paragraph numbering in accordance with the Editorial Note (p.ix).

Summary

Paras. 0-3: Work means any activity of human beings, whether it be manual or intellectual. It is one of the characteristics that distinguish human beings from other creatures. The ninetieth anniversary of *Rerum Novarum* is being celebrated on the eve of the introduction of new technological, political and economic conditions which will influence the world of work no less than did the industrial revolution. It is not the Church's task to analyse the consequences these changes may have on society, but it is its task to call attention to the dignity and the rights of those who work. The Church's social teaching has, however, broadened its scope over the years since *Rerum Novarum*. In the past it was the class issue which was highlighted. Recently the world dimension has been taken more into account. But throughout the subject of human work has been a constant.

Paras. 4-10: In the very first pages of Genesis is to be found the source of the Church's conviction that work is a fundamental dimension of human life. The first man and woman were told to subdue the earth. Human beings are made in the image of God partly through this mandate received from their creator. It is through work that human beings achieve domination over the earth. In the present age this domination is achieved technologically, which raises a whole set of new questions. The basic ethical one is whether work is for people, or people are for work. There is always a danger of regarding work as a special kind of merchandise or as a force ('the work-force') needed for production. In other words, there is a danger of regarding the worker as an instrument of production rather than as a true maker or creator. This reversal of order is capitalism, and it is this sort of attitude which, in the last century, gave rise to a great burst of solidarity among workers, first and foremost industrial workers, whose activity, dominated by machines, was narrowly specialized, monotonous and depersonalized. It was a reaction against the degradation of man as the subject of work, and from the point of view of social morality the outburst was justified. Worker solidarity has since been able to bring about profound changes. It must be realized that work is a good thing, not only because through it nature is transformed, but also because through it people achieve their fulfilment as human beings. Moreover, it makes it possible for them to found families. Finally, through work people enter into a greater society, an historical and social incarnation of the work of all. Work increases the common good, and thereby adds to the heritage of the whole human family.

Paras. 11-15: The period since *Rerum Novarum* has been characterized by the conflict between capital and labour. This socio-economic conflict found expression in the ideological conflict between liberalism and Marxism and was thereby transformed into a systematic class struggle. We must recall the Church's constant principle: the priority of labour over capital. The first phase of work is the relationship between people and the resources of nature which they find, and do not create. The concept of capital includes the means by which human beings appropriate natural resources, so capital is the result of the historical heritage of human labour. What is included in the concept of capital is a collection of things, and the primacy of people over things must be emphasized. A labour system can be morally legitimate only if it overcomes the opposition between labour and capital. At the most, things condition work: it cannot be that they put people and their work into a position of dependence. To think of labour solely in terms of its economic purpose is the error of economism which is a form of practical materialism and is associated with a materialist philosophy. Behind the conflict between capital and labour lies the issue of the ownership of property—the workers being without the ownership of the means of production and the entrepreneurs having them. The Church's teaching on ownership differs both from the collectivism proclaimed by Marxism and from capitalism, for it insists that there is a right to private property, but that right is subordinated to the right to common use. The means of production cannot be possessed against labour, and they cannot be possessed for possession's sake. In particular circumstances the socialization of certain means of production cannot be excluded. Rigid capitalism that defends the exclusive right to the private ownership of the means of production as if it were an untouchable dogma of economic life is unacceptable. A state take-over of the means of production, however, is not the same thing as socialization of the property. Socialization occurs only when by some means labour is associated with the ownership of capital. Workers desire not only due remuneration, they also want to know that they are working for themselves.

Paras. 16-23: Workers' rights cannot merely be the result of economic systems which are guided chiefly by the criterion of maximum profit. On the contrary, respect for the objective rights of workers must constitute the adequate and fundamental criterion for shaping the economy. When considering the rights of workers with relation to the 'indirect employer' (i.e., all those responsible for the general orientation of labour policy), attention must first be directed to the provision of suitable employment. It is the role of indirect employers to act against unemployment. In this area action should also be taken at an international level. In the last analysis, the justice of a socio-economic system is to be judged by the way in which work is remunerated. Remuneration should correspond to the needs of the worker, either through a family wage or through family allowances or other grants so that only one spouse need work in order to provide for the family's needs. It should be possible for a mother to devote herself entirely to her children. The true advancement of women requires that labour be so structured that they do not have to pay for their advancement by abandoning what is specific to them. There are a number of other rights of workers—to health care, to insurance, to a suitable working environment, to rest. These and other rights give rise to the right of association so that workers may defend their interests. Labour unions are a mouthpiece for the struggle for social justice. Unions will certainly enter politics, understood as a prudent concern for the common good, but they should not be so closely tied to political parties that they become an instrument to be used for something other than their specific role. Workers must have the right to strike, but that right should not be abused, especially not for political purposes. What has been said can be applied to the agricultural sector. The various bodies involved in the world of work should foster the right of the disabled to professional training and suitable productive activity. Likewise, much depends on just legislation to ensure that migrant workers are not exploited—though it is regrettable that people have to emigrate in order to find work.

Paras. 24-27: The Church has a duty to formulate a spirituality of work which will help people to come closer to God through their work, to participate in his salvific plan, and to deepen their friendship with Christ. Through their work, human beings share in the activity of their creator. Inevitably, all work is linked to toil, and this constitutes an announcement of death. By enduring toil in union with Christ crucified for us, people collaborate in the redemption of the human race. They carry the cross daily.

Venerable brothers and dearest sons and daughters, greetings and apostolic benediction.

The nature of human work

0. Through work man must earn his daily bread[1] and contribute to the continual advance of science and technology and, above all, to elevating unceasingly the cultural and moral level of the society within which he lives in community with those who belong to the same family. And work means any activity by man, whether manual or intellectual, whatever its nature or circumstances; it means any human activity that can and must be recognized as work, in the midst of all the many activities of which man is capable and to which he is predisposed by his very nature, by virtue of humanity itself. Man is made to be in the visible universe and image and likeness of God himself,[2] and he is placed in it in order to subdue the earth.[3] From the beginning therefore he is called to work. Work is one of the characteristics that distinguish man from the rest of creatures, whose activity for sustaining their lives cannot be called work. Only man is capable of work, and only man works, at the same time by work occupying his existence on earth. Thus work bears a particular mark of man and of humanity, the mark of a person operating within a community of persons. And this mark decides its interior characteristics; in a sense it constitutes its very nature.

I

1. Since 15 May of the present year was the ninetieth anniversary of the publication by the great pope of the 'social question', Leo XIII, of the decisively important encyclical which begins with the words *Rerum Novarum*, I wish to devote this document to human work and, even more, to man in the vast context of the reality of work. As I said in the encyclical *Redemptor Hominis*, published at the beginning of my service in the see of St Peter in Rome, man 'is the primary and fundamental way for the Church',[4] precisely because of the inscrutable mystery of redemption in Christ; and so it is necessary to return constantly to this way and to follow it ever anew in the various aspects in which it shows us all the wealth and at the same time all the toil of human existence on earth.

1.1. Work is one of these aspects, a perennial and fundamental one, one that is always relevant and constantly demands renewed attention and decisive witness. Because fresh questions and problems are always arising, there are always fresh hopes, but also fresh fears and threats, connected with this basic dimension of human existence: man's life is built up every day from work, from work it derives its specific dignity, but at the same time work contains the unceasing measure of human toil and suffering, and also of the harm and injustice which penetrate deeply into social life within individual nations and on the international level. While it is true that man eats the bread produced by the work of his hands[5]—and this means not only the daily bread by which his body keeps alive but also the bread of science and progress, civilization and culture—it is also a perennial truth that he eats this bread by 'the sweat of his face',[6] that is to say, not only by personal effort and toil but also in the midst of many tensions, conflicts and crises, which, in relationship with the reality of work, disturb the life of individual societies and also of all humanity.

1.2. We are celebrating the ninetieth anniversary of the encyclical *Rerum Novarum* on the eve of new developments in technological, economic and political conditions which, according to many experts, will influence the world of work and production no less than the industrial revolution of the last century. There are many factors of a general nature: the widespread introduction of automation into many spheres of production, the increase in the cost of energy and raw materials, the growing realization that the heritage of nature is limited and that it is being intolerably polluted, and the emergence on the political scene of peoples who, after centuries of subjection, are demanding their rightful place among the nations and in international decision-making. These new conditions and demands will require a reordering and adjustment of the structures of the modern economy and of the distribution of work. Unfortunately, for millions of skilled workers these changes may perhaps mean unemployment, at least for a time, or the need for retraining. They will very probably involve a reduction or a less rapid increase in material well-being for the more developed countries. But they can also bring relief and hope to the millions who today live in conditions of shameful and unworthy poverty.

1.3. It is not for the Church to analyse scientifically the consequences that these changes may have on human society. But the Church considers it her task always to call attention to the dignity and rights of those who work, to condemn situations in which that dignity and those rights are violated, and to help to guide the above-mentioned changes so as to ensure authentic progress by man and society.

Changing emphases in the Church's social teaching

2. It is certainly true that work, as a human issue, is at the very centre of the 'social question' to which, for almost a hundred years, since the publication of the above-mentioned encyclical, the Church's teaching and the many undertakings connected with her apostolic mission have been especially directed. The present reflections on work are not intended to follow a different line, but rather to be in organic connection with the whole tradition

of this teaching and activity. At the same time, however, I am making them, according to the indication in the gospel, in order to bring out from the heritage of the gospel 'what is new and what is old'.[7] Certainly, work is part of 'what is old'—as old as man and his life on earth. Nevertheless, the general situation of man ih the modern world, studied and analysed in its various aspects of geography, culture and civilization, calls for the discovery of the new meanings of human work. It likewise calls for the formulation of the new tasks that in this sector face each individual, the family, each country, the whole human race and finally the Church herself.

2.1. During the years that separate us from the publication of the encyclical *Rerum Novarum*, the social question has not ceased to engage the Church's attention. Evidence of this are the many documents of the magisterium issued by the popes and by the Second Vatican Council, pronouncements by individual episcopates, and the activity of the various centres of thought and of practical apostolic initiatives, both on the international level and at the level of the local churches. It is difficult to list here in detail all the manifestations of the commitment of the Church and of Christians in the social question, for they are too numerous. As a result of the council, the main co-ordinating centre in this field is the Pontifical Commission Justice and Peace, which has corresponding bodies within the individual bishops' conferences. The name of this institution is very significant. It indicates that the social question must be dealt with in its whole complex dimension. Commitment to justice must be closely linked with commitment to peace in the modern world. This twofold commitment is certainly supported by the painful experience of the two great world wars which in the course of the last ninety years have convulsed many European countries and, at least partially, countries in other continents. It is supported especially since World War II, by the permanent threat of a nuclear war and the prospect of the terrible self-destruction that emerges from it.

2.2. If we follow the main line of development of the documents of the supreme magisterium of the Church, we find in them an explicit confirmation of precisely such a statement of the question. The key position, as regards the question of world peace, is that of John XXIII's encyclical *Pacem in Terris*. However, if one studies the development of the question of social justice, one cannot fail to note that, whereas during the period between *Rerum Novarum* and Pius XI's *Quadragesimo Anno* the Church's teaching concentrates mainly on the just solution of the 'labour question' within individual nations, in the next period the Church's teaching widens its horizon to take in the whole world. The disproportionate distribution of wealth and poverty and the existence of some countries and continents that are developed and of others that are not call for a levelling out and for a search for ways to ensure just development for all. This is the direction of the teaching in John XXIII's encyclical *Mater et Magistra*, in the pastoral constitution *Gaudium et Spes* of the Second Vatican Council, and in Paul VI's encyclical *Populorum Progressio*.

2.3. This trend of development of the Church's teaching and commitment in the social question exactly corresponds to the objective recognition of the state of affairs. While in the past the 'class' question was especially highlighted as the centre of this issue, in more recent times it is the 'world' question that is emphasized. Thus, not only the sphere of class is taken into consideration but also the world sphere of inequality and injustice, and as a consequence, not only the class dimension but also the world dimension of the tasks involved in the path towards the achievement of justice in the modern world. A complete analysis of the situation of the world today shows in an even deeper and fuller way the meaning of the previous analysis of social injustices; and it is the meaning that must be given today to efforts to build justice on earth, not concealing thereby unjust structures but demanding that they be examined and transformed on a more universal scale.

3. In the midst of all these processes—those of the diagnosis of objective social reality and also those of the Church's teaching in the sphere of the complex and many-sided social question—the question of human work naturally appears many times. This issue is, in a way, a constant factor both of social life and of the Church's teaching. Furthermore, in this teaching attention to the question goes back much further than the last ninety years. In fact the Church's social teaching finds its source in sacred scripture, beginning with the Book of Genesis and especially in the Gospel and the writings of the apostles. From the beginning it was part of the Church's teaching, her concept of man and life in society, and, especially, the social morality which she worked out according to the needs of the different ages. This traditional patrimony was then inherited and developed by the teaching of the popes on the modern 'social question', beginning with the encyclical *Rerum Novarum*. In this context, study of the question of work, as we have seen, has continually been brought up to date while maintaining that Christian basis of truth which can be called ageless.

3.1. While in the present document we return to this question once more—without however any intention of touching on all the topics that concern it—this is not merely in order to gather together and repeat what is already contained in the Church's teaching. It is rather in order to highlight—perhaps more than has been done before—the fact that human work is a key, probably the essential key, to the whole social question, if we try to see that question really from the point of view of man's good. And if the solution—or rather the gradual solution—of the social question, which keeps coming up and becomes ever more complex, must be sought in the direction of 'making life more human',[8] then the key, namely human work, acquires fundamental and decisive importance.

II

The biblical command: subdue the earth

4. The Church is convinced that work is a fundamental dimension of man's existence on earth. She is confirmed in this conviction by considering the whole heritage of the many sciences devoted to man: anthropology, palaeontology, history, sociology, psychology and so on; they all seem to bear witness to this reality in an irrefutable way. But the source of the Church's conviction is above all the revealed word of God, and therefore

what is a conviction of the intellect is also a conviction of faith. The reason is that the Church—and it is worth while stating it at this point—believes in man: she thinks of man and addresses herself to him not only in the light of historical experience, not only with the aid of the many methods of scientific knowledge, but in the first place in the light of the revealed word of the living God. Relating herself to man, she seeks to express the eternal designs and transcendent destiny which the living God, the creator and redeemer, has linked with him.

4.1. The Church finds in the very first pages of the Book of Genesis the source of her conviction that work is a fundamental dimension of human existence on earth. An analysis of these texts makes us aware that they express—sometimes in an archaic way of manifesting thought—the fundamental truths about man, in the context of the mystery of creation itself. These truths are decisive for man from the very beginning, and at the same time they trace out the main lines of his earthly existence, both in the state of original justice and also after the breaking, caused by sin, of the creator's original covenant with creation in man. When man, who had been created 'in the image of God...male and female',[9] hears the words: 'Be fruitful and multiply, and fill the earth and subdue it,'[10] even though these words do not refer directly and explicitly to work, beyond any doubt they indirectly indicate it as an activity for man to carry out in the world. Indeed, they show its very deepest essence. Man is the image of God partly through the mandate received from his creator to subdue, to dominate, the earth. In carrying out this mandate, man, every human being, reflects the very action of the creator of the universe.

4.2. Work understood as a 'transitive' activity, that is to say an activity beginning in the human subject and directed towards an external object, presupposes a specific dominion by man over 'the earth', and in its turn it confirms and develops this dominion. It is clear that the term 'the earth' of which the biblical text speaks is to be understood in the first place as that fragment of the visible universe that man inhabits. By extension, however, it can be understood as the whole of the visible world in so far as it comes within the range of man's influence and of his striving to satisfy his needs. The expression 'subdue the earth' has an immense range. It means all the resources that the earth (and indirectly the visible world) contains and which, through the conscious activity of man, can be discovered and used for his ends. And so these words, placed at the beginning of the Bible, never cease to be relevant. They embrace equally the past ages of civilization and economy, as also the whole of modern reality and future phases of development, which are perhaps already to some extent beginning to take shape, though for the most part they are still almost unknown to man and hidden from him.

4.3. While people sometimes speak of periods of 'acceleration' in the economic life and civilization of humanity or of individual nations, linking these periods to the progress of science and technology and especially to discoveries which are decisive for social and economic life, at the same time it can be said that none of these phenomena of 'acceleration' exceeds the essential content of what was said in that most ancient of biblical texts. As man, through his work, becomes more and more the master of the earth, and as he confirms his dominion over the visible world, again through his work, he nevertheless remains in every case and at every phase of this process within the creator's original ordering. And this ordering remains necessarily and indissolubly linked with the fact that man was created, as male and female, 'in the image of God'. This process is, at the same time, universal: it embraces all human beings, every generation, every phase of economic and cultural development, and at the same time it is a process that takes place within each human being, in each conscious human being, in each conscious human subject. Each and every individual is at the same time embraced by it. Each and every individual, to the proper extent and in an incalculable number of ways, takes part in the giant process whereby man 'subdues the earth' through his work.

5. This universality and, at the same time, this multiplicity of the process of 'subduing the earth' throw light upon human work, because man's dominion over the earth is achieved in and by means of work. There thus emerges the meaning of work in an objective sense, which finds expression in the various epochs of culture and civilization. Man dominates the earth by the very fact of domesticating animals, rearing them and obtaining from them the food and clothing he needs, and by the fact of being able to extract various natural resources from the earth and the seas. But man 'subdues the earth' much more when he begins to cultivate it and then to transform its products, adapting them to his own use. Thus agriculture constitutes through human work a primary field of economic activity and an indispensable factor of production. Industry in its turn will always consist in linking the earth's riches—whether nature's living resources, or the products of agriculture, or the mineral or chemical resources—with man's work, whether physical or intellectual. This is also in a sense true in the sphere of what are called service industries, and also in the sphere of research, pure or applied.

5.1. In industry and agriculture man's work has today in many cases ceased to be mainly manual, for the toil of human hands and muscles is aided by more and more highly perfected machinery. Not only in industry but also in agriculture we are witnessing the transformations made possible by the gradual development of science and technology. Historically speaking this, taken as a whole, has caused great changes in civilization, from the beginning of the 'industrial era' to the successive phases of development through new technologies, such as the electronics and the microprocessor technology in recent years.

5.2. While it may seem that in the industrial process it is the machine that 'works' and man merely supervises it, making it function and keeping it going in various ways, it is also true that for this very reason industrial development provides grounds for reproposing in new ways the question of human work. Both the original industrialization that gave rise to what is called the worker question and the subsequent industrial and post-industrial changes show in an eloquent manner that, even in the age of ever more mechanized 'work', the proper subject of work continues to be man.

5.3. The development of industry and of the various sectors connected with it, even the most modern electronics technology, especially in the fields of miniaturization, communications and telecommunications and so forth, show how vast is the role of technology, that ally of work that human thought has produced, in the interaction between the subject and object of work (in the widest sense of the word). Understood in this case not as a capacity or aptitude for work, but rather as a whole set of instruments which man uses in his work, technology is undoubtedly man's ally. It facilitates his work, perfects, accelerates and augments it. It leads to an increase in the quantity of things produced by work, and in many cases improves their quality. However, it is also a fact that, in some instances, technology can cease to be man's ally and become almost his enemy, as when the mechanization of work 'supplants' him, taking away all personal satisfaction and the incentive to creativity and responsibility, when it deprives many workers of their previous employment, or when, through exalting the machine, it reduces man to the status of its slave.

5.4. If the biblical words 'subdue the earth' addressed to man from the very beginning are understood in the context of the whole modern age, industrial and post-industrial, then they undoubtedly include also a relationship with technology, with the world of machinery which is the fruit of the work of the human intellect and a historical confirmation of man's dominion over nature.

5.5. The recent stage of human history, especially that of certain societies, brings a correct affirmation of technology as a basic coefficient of economic progress; but at the same time this affirmation has been accompanied by and continues to be accompanied by essential questions concerning human work in relationship to its subject, which is man. These questions are particularly charged with content and tension of an ethical and an ethical and social character. They therefore constitute a continual challenge for institutions of many kinds, for states and governments, for systems and international organizations; they also constitute a challenge for the Church.

6. In order to continue our analysis of work, an analysis linked with the word of the Bible telling man that he is to subdue the earth, we must concentrate our attention on work in the subjective sense, much more than we did on the objective significance, barely touching upon the vast range of problems known intimately and in detail to scholars in various fields and also, according to their specializations, to those who work. If the words of the Book of Genesis to which we refer in this analysis of ours speak of work in the objective sense in an indirect way, they also speak only indirectly of the subject of work; but what they say is very eloquent and is full of great significance.

6.1. Man has to subdue the earth and dominate it, because as the 'image of God' he is a person, that is to say, a subjective being capable of acting in a planned and rational way, capable of deciding about himself and with a tendency to self-realization. As a person, man is therefore the subject of work. As a person he works, he performs various actions belonging to the work process; independently of their objective content, these actions must all serve to realize his humanity, to fulfil the calling to be a person that is his by reason of his very humanity. The principal truths concerning this theme were recently recalled by the Second Vatican Council in the constitution *Gaudium et Spes*, especially in Chapter 1, which is devoted to man's calling.

6.2. And so this 'dominion' spoken of in the biblical text being meditated upon here refers not only to the objective dimension of work, but at the same time introduces us to an understanding of its subjective dimension. Understood as a process whereby man and the human race subdue the earth, work corresponds to this basic biblical concept only when throughout the process man manifests himself and confirms himself as the one who 'dominates'. This dominion, in a certain sense, refers to the subjective dimension even more than to the objective one: this dimension conditions the very ethical nature of work. In fact there is no doubt that human work has an ethical value of its own, which clearly and directly remains linked to the fact that the one who carries it out is a person, a conscious and free subject, that is to say, a subject that decides about himself.

6.3. This truth, which in a sense constitutes the fundamental and perennial heart of Christian teaching on human work, has had and continues to have primary significance for the formulation of the important social problems characterizing whole ages.

6.4. The ancient world introduced its own typical differentiation of people into classes according to the type of work done. Work which demanded from the worker the exercise of physical strength, the work of muscles and hands, was considered unworthy of free men and was therefore given to slaves. By broadening certain aspects that already belonged to the Old Testament, Christianity brought about a fundamental change of ideas in this field, taking the whole content of the gospel message as its point of departure, especially the fact that the one who, while being God, became like us in all things[11] devoted most of the years of his life on earth to manual work at the carpenter's bench. This circumstance constitutes in itself the most eloquent 'gospel of work', showing that the basis for determining the value of human work is not primarily the kind of work being done, but the fact that the one who is doing it is a person. The sources of the dignity of work are to be sought primarily in the subjective dimension, not in the objective one.

6.5. Such a concept practically does away with the very basis of the ancient differentiation of people into classes according to the kind of work done. This does not mean that from the objective point of view human work cannot and must not be rated and qualified in any way. It only means that the primary basis of the value of work is man himself, who is its subject. This leads immediately to a very important conclusion of an ethical nature: however true it may be that man is destined for work and called to it, in the first place work is 'for man' and not man 'for work'. Through this conclusion one rightly comes to recognize the pre-eminence of the subjective meaning of work over the objective one. Given this way of understanding things and presupposing that different sorts of work that people do can have greater or lesser objective value, let us try nevertheless to show that each sort is judged above all by the measure of the dignity of the subject of work, that is to say, the person, the individual who carries it out. On the other hand, independent of the work that every man does, and presupposing that this work constitutes a purpose—at times a very demanding one—of his activity, this purpose does not possess a definitive meaning in itself. In fact, in the final analysis it is always man who is the purpose of the work, whatever work it is that is done by man—even if the common scale of values rates it as the merest 'service', as the most monotonous, even the most alienating work.

Work in its social and personal dimensions

7. It is precisely these fundamental affirmations about work that always emerged from the wealth of Christian truth, especially from the very message of the 'gospel of work', thus creating the basis for a new way of thinking, judging and acting. In the modern period, from the beginning of the industrial age, the Christian truth about work had to oppose the various trends of materialistic and economistic thought.

7.1. For certain supporters of such ideas, work was understood and treated as a sort of 'merchandise' that the worker—especially the industrial worker—sells to the employer, who at the same time is the possessor of the capital, that is to say, of all the working tools and means that make production possible. This way of looking at work was widespread especially in the first half of the nineteenth century. Since then explicit expressions of this sort have almost disappeared and have given way to more human ways of thinking about work and evaluating it. The interaction between the worker and the tools and means of production has given rise to the development of various forms of capitalism—parallel with various forms of collectivism—into which other socio-economic elements have entered as a consequence of new concrete circumstances, of the activity of workers' associations and public authorities, and of the emergence of large transnational enterprises. Nevertheless, the danger of treating work as a special kind of 'merchandise' or as an impersonal 'force' needed for production (the expression 'work-force' is in fact in common use) always exists, especially when the whole way of looking at the question of economics is marked by the premises of materialistic economism.

7.2. A systematic opportunity for thinking and evaluating in this way, and in a certain sense a stimulus for doing so, is provided by the quickening process of the development of a one-sidedly materialistic civilization, which gives prime importance to the objective dimension of work, while the subjective dimension—everything in direct or indirect relationship with the subject of work—remains on a secondary level. In all cases of this sort, in every social situation of this type, there is a confusion or even a reversal of the order laid down from the beginning by the words of the Book of Genesis: man is treated as an instrument of production,[12] whereas he—alone, independent of the work he does—ought to be treated as the effective subject of work and its true maker and creator. Precisely this reversal of order, whatever the programme or name under which it occurs, should rightly be called 'capitalism'—in the sense more fully explained below. Everybody knows that capitalism has a definite historical meaning as a system, an economic and social system, opposed to 'socialism' or 'communism'. But in light of the analysis of the fundamental reality of the whole economic process—first and foremost of the production structure that work is—it should be recognized that the error of early capitalism can be repeated wherever man is in a way treated on the same level as the whole complex of the material means of production, as an instrument and not in accordance with the true dignity of his work—that is to say, where he is not treated as subject and maker, and for this very reason as the true purpose of the whole process of production.

7.3. This explains why the analysis of human work in the light of the works concerning man's 'dominion' over the earth goes to the very heart of the ethical and social question. This concept should also find a central place in the whole sphere of social and economic policy, both within individual countries and in the wider field of international and intercontinental relationships, particularly with reference to the tensions making themselves felt in the world not only between East and West but also between North and South. Both John XXIII in the encyclical *Mater et Magistra* and Paul VI in the encyclical *Populorum Progressio* gave special attention to these dimensions of the modern ethical and social question.

8. When dealing with human work in the fundamental dimension of its subject, that is to say, the human person doing work, one must make at least a summary evaluation of developments during the ninety years since *Rerum Novarum* in relation to the subjective dimension of work. Although the subject of work is always the same, that is to say man, nevertheless wide-ranging changes take place in the objective aspect. While one can say that, by reason of its subject, work is one single thing (one and unrepeatable every time) yet when one takes into consideration its objective directions one is forced to admit that there exist many works, many different sorts of work. The development of human civilization brings continual enrichment in this field. But at the same time, one cannot fail to note that in the process of this development not only do new forms of work appear but also others disappear. Even if one accepts that on the whole this is a normal phenomenon, it must still be seen whether certain ethically and socially dangerous irregularities creep in and to what extent.

8.1. It was precisely one such wide-ranging anomaly that gave rise in the last century to what has been called 'the worker question', sometimes described as 'the proletariat question'. This question and the problems connected with it gave rise to a just social reaction and caused the impetuous emergence of a great burst of solidarity between workers, first and foremost industrial workers. The call to solidarity and common action addressed to the workers—especially to those engaged in narrowly specialized, monotonous and depersonalized work in industrial plants, when the machine tends to dominate man—was important and eloquent from the point of view of social ethics. It was the reaction against the degradation of man as the subject of work and against the unheard-of accompanying exploitation in the field of wages, working conditions and social security for the worker. This reaction united the working world in a community marked by great solidarity.

8.2. Following the lines laid down by the encyclical *Rerum Novarum* and many later documents of the Church's magisterium, it must be frankly recognized that the reaction against the system of injustice and harm that cried to heaven for vengeance[13] and that weighed heavily upon workers in that period of rapid industrialization was justified from the point of view of social morality. This state of affairs was favoured by the liberal socio-political system which in accordance with its 'economistic' premises, strengthened and safeguarded economic initiative by the possessors of capital alone, but did not pay sufficient attention to the rights of the workers, on the grounds that human work is solely an instrument of production, and that capital is the basis, efficient factor and purpose of production.

8.3. From that time, worker solidarity, together with a clearer and more committed realization by others of workers' rights, has in many cases brought about profound changes. Various forms of neo-capitalism or collectivism have developed. Various new systems have been thought out. Workers can often share in running businesses and in controlling their productivity, and in fact do so. Through appropriate associations they exercise influence over conditions of work and pay, and also over social legislation. But at the same time various ideological or power systems and new relationships which have arisen at various levels of society have allowed flagrant injustices to persist or have created new ones. On the world level, the development of civilization and of communications has made possible a more complete diagnosis of the living and working conditions of man globally, but it has also revealed other forms of injustice much more extensive than those which in the last century stimulated unity between workers for particular solidarity in the working world. This is true in countries which have completed a certain process of industrial revolution. It is also true in countries where the main working milieu continues to be agriculture or other similar occupations.

8.4. Movements of solidarity in the sphere of work—a solidarity that must never mean being closed to dialogue and collaboration with others—can be necessary also with reference to the condition of social groups that were not previously included in such movements, but which in changing social systems and conditions of living are undergoing what is in effect 'proletarianization' or which actually already find themselves in a 'proletariat' situation, one which, even if not yet given that name, in fact deserves it. This can be true of certain categories or groups of the working 'intelligentsia', especially when ever wider access to education and an ever increasing number of people with degrees or diplomas in the fields of their cultural preparation are accompanied by a drop in demand for their labour. This unemployment of intellectuals occurs or increases when the education available is not oriented towards the types of employment or service required by the true needs of society, or when there is less demand for work which requires education, at least professional education, than for manual labour, or when it is less well paid. Of course, education in itself is always valuable and an important enrichment of the human person; but in spite of that, 'proletarianization' processes remain possible.

8.5. For this reason there must be continued study of the subject of work and of the subject's living conditions. In order to achieve social justice in the various parts of the world, in the various countries and in the relationships between them, there is a need for ever new movements of solidarity of the workers and with the workers. This solidarity must be present whenever it is called for by the social degrading of the subject of work, by exploitation of the workers and by the growing areas of poverty and even hunger. The Church is firmly committed to this cause for she considers it her mission, her service, a proof of her fidelity to Christ, so that she can truly be the 'Church of the poor'. And the 'poor' appear under various forms; they appear in various places and at various times; in many cases they appear as a result of the violation of the dignity of human work: either because the opportunities for human work are limited as a result of the scourge of unemployment or because a low value is put on work and the rights that flow from it, especially the right to a just wage and to the personal security of the worker and his or her family.

9. Remaining within the context of man as the subject of work, it is now appropriate to touch upon, at least in a summary way, certain problems that more closely define the dignity of human work in that they make it possible to characterize more fully its specific moral value. In doing this we must always keep in mind the biblical calling to 'subdue the earth',[14] in which is expressed the will of the creator that work should enable man to achieve that 'dominion' in the visible world that is proper to him.

9.1. God's fundamental and original intention with regard to man, whom he created in his image and after his likeness,[15] was not withdrawn or cancelled out even when man, having broken the original covenant with God, heard the words: 'In the sweat of your face you shall eat bread.'[16] These words refer to the sometimes heavy toil that from then onwards has accompanied human work; but they do not alter the fact that work is the means whereby man achieves that 'dominion' which is proper to him over the visible world, by 'subjecting' the earth. Toil is something that is universally known, for it is universally experienced. It is familiar to those doing physical work under sometimes exceptionally laborious conditions. It is familiar not only to agricultural workers, who spend long days working the land, which sometimes 'bears thorns and thistles',[17] but also to those who work in mines and quarries, to steelworkers at their blast furnaces, to those who work in builders' yards and in construction work, often in danger of injury or death. It is also familiar to those at an intellectual work-bench; to scientists; to those who bear the burden of grave responsibility for decisions that will have a vast impact on society. It is familiar to doctors and nurses, who spend days and nights at their patients' bedside. It is familiar to women, who sometimes without proper recognition on the part of society and even of their own families bear the daily burden and responsibility for their homes and the upbringing of their children. It is familiar to all workers and, since work is a universal calling, it is familiar to everyone.

9.2. And yet in spite of all this toil—perhaps, in a sense, because of it—work is a good thing for man. Even though it bears the mark of a *bonum arduum*, in the terminology of St Thomas,[18] this does not take away the fact that, as such, it is a good thing for man. It is not only good in the sense that it is useful or something to enjoy, it is also good as being something worthy, that is to say, something that corresponds to man's dignity, that expresses this dignity and increases it. If one wishes to define more clearly the ethical meaning of work, it is this truth that one must particularly keep in mind. Work is a good thing for man—a good thing for his humanity—because through work man not only transforms nature, adapting it to his own needs, but he also achieves fulfilment as a human being and indeed in a sense becomes 'more a human being'.

9.3. Without this consideration it is impossible to understand the meaning of the virtue of industriousness, and more particularly it is impossible to understand why industriousness should be a virtue: for virtue, as a moral habit, is something whereby man becomes good as man.[19] This fact in no way alters our justifiable anxiety that in work, whereby matter gains in nobility, man himself should not experience a lowering of his own dignity.[20] Again, it is well known that it is possible to use work in various ways against man, that it is possible to punish man with the system of forced labour in concentration camps, that work can be made into a means for oppressing man, and that in various ways it is possible to exploit human labour, that is to say, the worker. All this pleads in favour of the moral obligation to link industriousness as a virtue with the social order of work, which will enable man to become in work 'more a human being' and not be degraded by it not only because of the wearing out of his physical strength (which, at least up to a certain point, is inevitable), but especially through damage to the dignity and subjectivity that are proper to him.

10. Having thus confirmed the personal dimension of human work, we must go on to the second sphere of values which is necessarily linked to work. Work constitutes a foundation for the formation of family life, which is a natural right and something that man is called to. These two spheres of values—one linked to work and the other consequent on the family nature of human life—must be properly united and must properly permeate each other. In a way, work is a condition for making it possible to found a family, since the family requires the means of subsistence which man normally gains through work. Work and industriousness also influence the whole process of education in the family, for the very reason that everyone 'becomes a human being' through, among other things, work, and becoming a human being is precisely the main purpose of the whole process of education. Obviously, two aspects of work in a sense come into play here: the one making family life and its upkeep possible, and the other making possible the achievement of the purposes of the family, especially education. Nevertheless, these two aspects of work are linked to one another and are mutually complementary in various points.

10.1. It must be remembered and affirmed that the family constitutes one of the most important terms of reference for shaping the social and ethical order of human work. The teaching of the Church has always devoted special attention to this question, and in the present document we shall have to return to it. In fact, the family is simultaneously a community made possible by work and the first school of work, within the home, for every person.

10.2. The third sphere of values that emerges from this point of view—that of the subject of work—concerns the great society to which man belongs on the basis of particular cultural and historical links. This society—even when it has not yet taken on the mature form of a nation—is not only the great 'educator' of every man, even though an indirect one (because each individual absorbs within the family the contents and values that go to make up the culture of a given nation); it is also a great historical and social incarnation of the work of all generations. All of this brings it about that man combines his deepest human identity with membership of a nation, and intends his work also to increase the common good developed together with his compatriots, thus realizing that in this way work serves to add to the heritage of the whole human family, of all the people living in the world.

10.3. These three spheres are always important for human work in its subjective dimension. And this dimension, that is to say, the concrete reality of the worker, takes precedence over the objective dimension. In the subjective dimension there is realized, first of all, that 'dominion' over the world of nature to which man is called from the beginning according to the words of the Book of Genesis. The very process of 'subduing the earth', that is to say work, is marked in the course of history and especially in recent centuries by an immense development of technological means. This is an advantageous and positive phenomenon, on condition that the objective dimension of work does not gain the upper hand over the subjective dimension, depriving man of his dignity and inalienable rights or reducing them.

III

The priority of labour over capital

11. The sketch of the basic problems of work outlined above draws inspiration from the texts at the beginning of the Bible and in a sense forms the very framework of the Church's teaching, which has remained unchanged throughout the centuries within the context of different historical experiences. However, the experiences preceding and following the publication of the encyclical *Rerum Novarum* form a background that endows that teaching with particular expressiveness and the eloquence of living relevance. In this analysis, work is seen as a great reality with a fundamental influence on the shaping in a human way of the world that the creator has entrusted to man; it is a reality closely linked with man as the subject of work and with man's rational activity. In the normal course of events this reality fills human life and strongly affects its value and meaning. Even when it is accompanied by toil and effort, work is still something good, and so man develops through love for work. This entirely positive and creative, educational and meritorious character of man's work must be the basis for the judgements and decisions being made today in its regard in spheres that include human rights, as is evidenced by the international declarations on work and the many labour codes prepared either by the competent legislative institutions in the various countries or by organizations devoting their social, or scientific and social, activity to the problems of work. One organization fostering such initiatives on the international level is the International Labour Organization, the oldest specialized agency of the United Nations.

11.1. In the following part of these considerations I intend to return in greater detail to these important questions, recalling at least the basic elements of the Church's teaching on the matter. I must however first touch on a very important field of questions in which her teaching has taken shape in this latest period, the one marked and in a sense symbolized by the publication of the encyclical *Rerum Novarum*.

11.2. Throughout this period, which is by no means yet over, the issue of work has of course been posed on the basis of the great conflict that in the age of and together with industrial development emerged between 'capital' and 'labour', that is to say between the small but highly influential group of entrepreneurs, owners or holders of the means of production, and the broader multitude of people who lacked these means and who shared in the process of production solely by their labour. The conflict originated in the fact that the workers put their powers at the disposal of the entrepreneurs and these, following the principle of maximum profit, tried to establish the lowest possible wages for the work done by the employees. In addition there were other elements of exploitation connected with the lack of safety at work and of safeguards regarding the health and living conditions of the workers and their families.

11.3. This conflict, interpreted by some as a socio-economic class conflict, found expression in the ideological conflict between liberalism, understood as the ideology of capitalism, and Marxism, understood as the ideology of scientific socialism and communism, which professes to act as the spokesman for the working class and the world-wide proletariat. Thus the real conflict between labour and capital was transformed into a systematic class struggle conducted not only by ideological means, but also and chiefly by political means. We are familiar with the history of this conflict and with the demands of both sides. The Marxist programme, based on the philosophy of Marx and Engels, sees in class struggle the only way to eliminate class injustices in society and to eliminate the classes themselves. Putting this programme into practice presupposes the collectivization of the means of production so that through the transfer of these means from private hands to the collectivity human labour will be preserved from exploitation.

11.4. This is the goal of the struggle carried on by political as well as ideological means. In accordance with the principle of 'the dictatorship of the proletariat', the groups that as political parties follow the guidance of Marxist ideology aim by the use of various kinds of influence, including revolutionary pressure, to win a monopoly of power in each society in order to introduce the collectivist system into it by eliminating private ownership of the means of production. According to the principal ideologists and leaders of this broad international movement, the purpose of this programme of action is to achieve the social revolution and to introduce socialism and finally the communist system throughout the world.

11.5. As we touch on this extremely important field of issues, which constitute not only a theory but a whole fabric of socio-economic, political and international life in our age, we cannot go into the details nor is this necessary for they are known both from the vast literature on the subject and by experience. Instead we must leave the context of these issues and go back to the fundamental issue of human work, which is the main subject of the considerations in this document. It is clear indeed that this issue, which is of such importance for man—it constitutes one of the fundamental dimensions of his earthly existence and of his vocation—can also be explained only by taking into account the full context of the contemporary situation.

12. The structure of the present-day situation is deeply marked by many conflicts caused by man, and the technological means produced by human work play a primary role in it. We should also consider here the prospect of world-wide catastrophe in the case of a nuclear war, which would have almost unimaginable possibilities of destruction. In view of this situation we must

first of all recall a principle that has always been taught by the Church: the principle of the priority of labour over capital. This principle directly concerns the process of production: In this process labour is always a primary efficient cause, while capital, the whole collection of means of production, remains a mere instrument or instrumental cause. This principle is an evident truth that emerges from the whole of man's historical experience.

12.1. When we read in the first chapter of the Bible that man is to subdue the earth, we know that these works refer to all the resources contained in the visible world and placed at man's disposal. However, these resources can serve man only through work. From the beginning there is also linked with work the question of ownership, for the only means that man has for causing the resources hidden in nature to serve himself and others is his work. And to be able through his work to make these resources bear fruit, man takes over ownership of small parts of the various riches of nature: those beneath the ground, those in the sea, on land or in space. He takes over all these things by making them his work-bench. He takes them over through work and for work.

12.2. The same principle applies in the successive phases of this process, in which the first phase always remains the relationship of man with the resources and riches of nature. The whole of the effort to acquire knowledge with the aim of discovering these riches and specifying the various ways in which they can be used by man and for man teaches us that everything that comes from man throughout the whole process of economic production, whether labour or the whole collection of means of production and the technology connected with these means (meaning the capability to use them in work), presupposes these riches and resources of the visible world, riches and resources that man finds and does not create. In a sense man finds them already prepared, ready for him to discover them and to use them correctly in the productive process. In every phase of the development of his work man comes up against the leading role of the gift made by 'nature', that is to say, in the final analysis, by the creator. At the beginning of man's work is the mystery of creation. This affirmation, already indicated as my starting point, is the guiding thread of this document and will be further developed in the last part of these reflections.

12.3. Further consideration of this question should confirm our conviction of the priority of human labour over what in the course of time we have grown accustomed to calling capital. Since the concept of capital includes not only the natural resources placed at man's disposal, but also the whole collection of means by which man appropriates natural resources and transforms them in accordance with his needs (and thus in a sense humanizes them), it must immediately be noted that all these means are the result of the historical heritage of human labour. All the means of production, from the most primitive to the ultra-modern one—it is man that has gradually developed them: man's experience and intellect. In this way there have appeared not only the simplest instruments for cultivating the earth, but also through adequate progress in science and technology the more modern and complex ones: machines, factories, laboratories and computers. Thus everything that is at the service of work, everything that in the present state of technology constitutes its ever more highly perfected 'instrument', is the result of work.

12.4. This gigantic and powerful instrument—the whole collection of means of production that in a sense are considered synonymous with 'capital'—is the result of work and bears the signs of human labour. At the present stage of technological advance, when man, who is the subject of work, wishes to make use of this collection of modern instruments, the means of production, he must first assimilate cognitively the result of the work of the people who invented those instruments, who planned them, built them and perfected them, and who continue to do so. Capacity for work—that is to say, for sharing efficiently in the modern production process—demands greater and greater preparation and, before all else, proper training. Obviously it remains clear that every human being sharing in the production process, even if he or she is only doing the kind of work for which no special training or qualifications are required, is the real efficient subject in this production process, while the whole collection of instruments, no matter how perfect they may be in themselves, are only a mere instrument subordinate to human labour.

12.5. This truth, which is part of the abiding heritage of the Church's teaching, must always be emphasized with reference to the question of the labour system and with regard to the whole socio-economic system. We must emphasize and give prominence to the primacy of man in the production process, the primacy of man over things. Everything contained in the concept of capital in the strict sense is only a collection of things. Man, as the subject of work and independent of the work he does—man alone is a person. This truth has important and decisive consequences.

13. In the light of the above truth we see clearly, first of all, that capital cannot be separated from labour; in no way can labour be opposed to capital or capital to labour, and still less can the actual people behind these concepts be opposed to each other, as will be explained later. A labour system can be right, in the sense of being in conformity with the very essence of the issue and in the sense of being intrinsically true and also morally legitimate, if in its very basis it overcomes the opposition between labour and capital through an effort at being shaped in accordance with the principle put forward above: the principle of the substantial and real priority of labour, of the subjectivity of human labour and its effective participation in the whole production process, independent of the nature of the services provided by the worker.

13.1. Opposition between labour and capital does not spring from the structure of the production process or from the structure of the economic process. In general the latter process demonstrates that labour and what we are accustomed to call capital are intermingled; it shows that they are inseparably linked. Working at any work-bench, whether a relatively primitive or an ultra-modern one, a man can easily see that through his work he enters into two inheritances: the inheritance of what is given to the whole of humanity in the resources of nature and the inheritance of what others have already developed on the basis of those resources, primarily by developing technology, that is to say, by producing a whole collection of increasingly perfect instruments for work. In working, man also 'enters into the labour of others'.[21] Guided both by our intelligence and by the faith that draws light from the word of God, we have no difficulty in accepting this image, of the sphere and process of man's labour. It is a consistent image, one that is humanistic as well as theological. In it man is the master of the creatures placed at his disposal in the visible world. If some dependence is discovered in the work process, it is dependence on the giver of all the resources of creation and also on other human beings, those to whose work and initiative we owe the perfected and increased possibilities of our own work. All that we can say of everything in the production process which constitutes a whole collection of 'things', the instruments, the capital, is that it conditions man's work; we cannot assert that it constitutes as it were an impersonal 'subject' putting man and man's work into a position of dependence.

13.2. This consistent image, in which the principle of the primacy of person over things is strictly preserved, was broken up in human thought sometimes after a long period of incubation in practical living. The break occurred in such a way that labour was separated from capital and set in opposition to it, and capital was set in opposition to labour, as though they were two impersonal forces, two production factors juxtaposed in the same 'economistic' perspective. This way of stating the issue contained a fundamental error, what we can call the error of economism, that of considering human labour solely according to its economic purpose. This fundamental error of thought can and must be called an error of materialism, in that economism directly or indirectly includes a conviction of the primacy and superiority of the material, and directly or indirectly places the spiritual and the personal (man's activity, moral values and such matters) in a position of subordination to material reality. This is still not theoretical materialism in the full sense of the term, but it is certainly practical materialism, a materialism judged capable of satisfying man's needs not so much on the grounds of premises derived from materialist theory as on the grounds of a particular way of evaluating things and so on the grounds of a certain hierarchy of goods based on the greater immediate attractiveness of what is material.

13.3. The error of thinking in the categories of economism went hand in hand with the formation of a materialist philosophy, as this philosophy developed from the most elementary and common phase (also called common materialism, because it professes to reduce spiritual reality to a superfluous phenomenon) to the phase of what is called dialectical materialism. However, within the framework of the present consideration, it seems that economism had a decisive importance for the fundamental issue of human work, in particular for the separation of labour and capital and for setting them up in opposition as two production factors viewed in the above-mentioned economistic perspective; and it seems that economism influenced this non-humanistic way of stating the issue before the materialist philosophical system did. Nevertheless it is obvious that materialism, including its dialectical form, is incapable of providing sufficient and definitive bases for thinking about human work, in order that the primacy of man over the capital instrument, the primacy of the person over things, may find in it adequate and irrefutable confirmation and support. In dialectical materialism too man is not first and foremost the subject of work and the efficient cause of the production process, but continues to be understood and treated, in dependence on what is material, as a kind of 'resultant' of the economic or production relations prevailing at a given period.

13.4. Obviously the antinomy between labour and capital under consideration here—the antinomy in which labour was separated from capital and set up in opposition to it, in a certain sense on the ontic level as if it were just an element like any other in the economic process—did not originate merely in the philosophy and economic theories of the eighteenth century; rather it originated in the whole of economic and social practice of that time, the time of the birth and rapid development of industrialization, in which what was mainly seen was the possibility of vastly increasing material wealth, means, while the end, that is to say man, who should be served by the means, was ignored. It was this practical error that struck a blow first and foremost against human labour, against the working man, and caused the ethically just social reaction already spoken of above. The same error, which is now part of history and which was connected with the period of primitive capitalism and liberalism, can nevertheless be repeated in other circumstances of time and place if people's thinking starts from the same theoretical or practical premises. The only chance there seems to be for radically overcoming this error is through adequate changes both in theory and in practice, changes in line with the definite conviction of the primacy of the person over things and of human labour over capital as a whole collection of means of production.

The ownership of capital by labour

14. The historical process briefly presented here has certainly gone beyond its initial phase, but it is still taking place and indeed is spreading in the relationships between nations and continents. It needs to be specified further from another point of view. It is obvious that when we speak of opposition between labour and capital, we are not dealing only with abstract concepts or 'impersonal forces' operating in economic production. Behind both concepts there are people, living, actual people: on the one side are those who do the work without being the owners of the means of production, and on the other side those who act as entrepreneurs and who own these means or represent the owner. Thus the issue of ownership or property enters from the beginning into the whole of this difficult historical process. The encyclical *Rerum Novarum*, which has the social question as its theme, stresses this issue also, recalling and confirming the Church's teaching on ownership, on the right to private property even when it is a question of the means of production. The encyclical *Mater et Magistra* did the same.

14.1. The above principle, as it was then stated and as it is still taught by the Church, diverges radically from the programme of collectivism as proclaimed by Marxism and put into practice in various countries in the decades following the time of Leo XIII's encyclical. At the same time it differs from the programme of capitalism practised by liberalism and by the political systems inspired by it. In the latter case, the difference consists in the way the right to ownership or property is understood. Christian tradition has never upheld this right as absolute and untouchable. On the contrary, it has always understood this right within the broader context of the right common to all to use the goods of the whole of creation: the right to private property is subordinated to the right to common use, to the fact that goods are meant for everyone.

14.2. Furthermore, in the Church's teaching, ownership has never been understood in a way that could constitute grounds for social conflict in labour. As mentioned above, property is acquired first of all through work in order that it may serve work. This concerns in a special way ownership of the means of production. Isolating these means as a separate property in order to set it up in the form of 'capital' in opposition to 'labour'—and even to practise exploitation of labour—is contrary to the very nature of these means and their possession. They cannot be possessed against labour, they cannot even be possessed for possession's sake, because the only legitimate title to their possession—whether in the form of private ownership or in the form of public or collective ownership—is that they should serve labour and thus by serving labour that they should make possible the achievement of the first principle of this order, namely the universal destination of goods and the right to common use of them. From this point of view, therefore, in consideration of human labour and of common access to the goods meant for man, one cannot exclude the socialization,* in suitable conditions, of certain means of production. In the course of the decades since the publication of the encyclical *Rerum Novarum*, the Church's teaching has always recalled all these principles, going back to the arguments formulated in a much older tradition, for example, the well-known arguments of the *Summa Theologiae* of St Thomas Aquinas.[22]

14.3. In the present document, which has human work as its main theme, it is right to confirm all the effort with which the Church's teaching has striven and continues to strive always to ensure the priority of work and thereby man's character as a subject in social life and especially in the dynamic structure of the whole economic process. From this point of view the position of 'rigid' capitalism continues to remain unacceptable, namely the position that defends the exclusive right to private ownership of the means of production as an untouchable 'dogma' of economic life. The principle of respect for work demands that this right should undergo a constructive revision both in theory and in practice. If it is true that capital, as the whole of the means of production, is at the same time the product of the work of generations, it is equally true that capital is being unceasingly created through the work done with the help of all these means of production, and these means can be seen as a great work-bench at which the present generation of workers is working day after day. Obviously we are dealing here with different kinds of work, not only so-called manual labour, but also the many forms of intellectual work, including white-collar work and management.

14.4. In the light of the above, the many proposals put forward by experts in Catholic social teaching and by the highest magisterium of the Church take on special significance:[23] proposals for joint ownership of the means of work, sharing by the workers in the management and/or profits of business, so-called shareholding by labour, etc. Whether these various proposals can or cannot be applied concretely, it is clear that recognition of the proper position of labour and the worker in the production process demands various adaptations in the sphere of the right to ownership of the means of production. This is so not only in view of older situations but also, first and foremost, in view of the whole of the situation and the problems in the second half of the present century with regard to the so-called Third World and the various new independent countries that have arisen, especially in Africa but elsewhere as well, in place of the colonial territories of the past.

14.5. Therefore, while the position of 'rigid' capitalism must undergo continual revision in order to be reformed from the point of view of human rights, both human rights in the widest sense and those linked with man's work, it must be stated that from the same point of view these many deeply desired reforms cannot be achieved by an *a priori* elimination of private ownership of the means of production. For it must be noted that merely taking these means of production (capital) out of the hands of their private owners is not enough to ensure their satisfactory socialization. They cease to be the property of a certain social group, namely the private owners, and become the property of organized society, coming under the administration and direct control of another group of people, namely those who, though not owning them, from the fact of exercising power in society manage them on the level of the whole national or the local economy.

14.6. This group in authority may carry out its task satisfactorily from the point of view of the priority of labour; but it may also carry it out badly by claiming for itself a monopoly of the administration and disposal of the means of production and not refraining even from offending basic human rights. Thus, merely converting the means of production into state property in the collectivist systems is by no means equivalent to 'socializing' that property. We can speak of socializing only when the subject character of society is ensured, that is to say, when on the basis of his work each person is fully entitled to consider himself a part owner of the great work-bench at which he is working with everyone else. A way towards that goal could be found by associating labour with the ownership of capital, as far as possible, and by producing a wide range of intermediate bodies with economic, social and cultural purposes; they would be bodies enjoying real autonomy with regard to the public powers, pursuing their specific aims in honest collaboration with each other and in subordination to the demands of the common good, and they would be living communities both in form and in substance in the sense that the members of each body would be looked upon and treated as persons and encouraged to take an active part in the life of the body.[24]

15. Thus the principle of the priority of labour over capital is a postulate of the order of social morality. It has key importance both in the system built on the principle of private ownership of the means of production and also in the systems in which private ownership of these means has been limited even in a radical way. Labour is in a sense inseparable from capital; in no way does it accept the antinomy, that is to say, the separation and opposition with regard to the means of production that has weighed upon human life in recent centuries as a result of merely economic premises. When man works, using all the means of production, he also wishes the fruit of this work to be used by himself and others, and he wishes to be able to take part in the very work process as a sharer in responsibility and creativity at the work-bench to which he applies himself.

15.1. From this spring certain specific rights of workers, corresponding to the obligation of work. They will be discussed later. But here it must be emphasized in general terms that the person who works desires not only due remuneration for his work; he also wishes that within the production process provision be made for him to be able to know that in his work, even on something that is owned in common, he is working 'for himself'. This awareness is extinguished within him in a system of excessive bureaucratic centralization, which makes the worker feel that he is just a cog in a huge machine moved from above, that he is for more reasons than one a mere production instrument rather than a true subject of work with an initiative of his own. The Church's teaching has always expressed the strong and deep conviction that man's work concerns not only the economy but also, and especially, personal values. The economic system itself and the production process benefit precisely when these personal values are fully respected. In the mind of St Thomas Aquinas,[25] this is the principal reason in favour of private ownership of the means of production. While we accept that for certain well-founded reasons exceptions can be made to the principle of private ownership—in our own time we even see that the system of 'socialized ownership' has been introduced—nevertheless the personalist argument still holds good both on the level of principles and on the practical level. If it is to be rational and fruitful, any socialization of the means of production must take this argument into consideration. Every effort must be made to ensure that in this kind of system also the human person can preserve his awareness of working 'for himself'. If this is not done, incalculable damage is inevitably done throughout the economic process, not only economic damage but first and foremost damage to man.

IV

Workers' rights

16. While work, in all its many senses, is an obligation, that is to say a duty, it is also a source of rights on the part of the worker. These rights must be examined in the broad context of human rights as a whole, which are connatural with man and many of which are proclaimed by various international organizations and increasingly guaranteed by the individual states for their citizens. Respect for this broad range of human rights constitutes the fundamental condition for peace in the modern world: peace both within individual countries and societies and in international relations, as the Church's magisterium has several times noted, especially since the encyclical *Pacem in Terris*. The human rights that flow from work are part of the broader context of those fundamental rights of the person.

16.1. However, within this context they have a specific character corresponding to the specific nature of human work as outlined above. It is in keeping with this character that we must view them. Work is, as has been said, an obligation, that is to say, a duty, on the part of man. This is true in all the many meanings of the word. Man must work both because the creator has commanded it and because of his own humanity, which requires work in order to be maintained and developed. Man must work out of regard for others, especially his own family, but also for the society he belongs to, the country of which he is a child and the whole human family of which he is a member, since he is the heir to the work of generations and at the same time a sharer in building the future of those who will come after him in the succession of history. All this constitutes the moral obligation of work understood in its wide sense. When we have to consider the moral rights corresponding to this obligation of every person with regard to work, we must always keep before our eyes the whole vast range of points of reference in which the labour of every working subject is manifested.

16.2. For when we speak of the obligation of work and of the rights of the worker that correspond to this obligation, we think in the first place of the relationship between the employer, direct or indirect, and the worker.

16.3. The distinction between the direct and the indirect employer is seen to be very important when one considers both the way in which labour is actually organized and the possibility of the formation of just or unjust relationships in the field of labour.

16.4. Since the direct employer is the person or institution with whom the worker enters directly into a work contract in accordance with definite conditions, we must understand as the indirect employer many different factors, other than the direct employer, that exercise a determining influence on the shaping both of the work contract and consequently of just or unjust relationships in the field of human labour.

17. The concept of indirect employer includes both persons and institutions of various kinds and also collective labour contracts and the principles of conduct which are laid down by these persons and institutions and which determine the whole socio-economic system or are its result. The concept of 'indirect employer' thus refers to many different elements. The responsibility of the indirect employer differs from that of the direct employer—the term itself indicates that the responsibility is less direct—but it remains a true responsibility: the indirect employer substantially determines one or other facet of the labour relationship, thus conditioning the conduct of the direct employer when the latter determines in concrete terms the actual work contract and labour relations. This is not to absolve the direct employer from his own responsibility, but only to draw attention to the whole network of influences that condition his conduct. When it is a question of establishing an ethically correct labour policy, all these influences must be kept in mind. A policy is correct when the objective rights of the worker are fully respected.

17.1. The concept of indirect employer is applicable to every society and in the first place to the State. For it is the State that must conduct a just labour policy. However, it is common knowledge that in the present system of economic relations in the world there are numerous links between individual states, links that find expression, for instance, in the import and export process, that is to say, in the mutual exchange of economic goods, whether raw materials, semimanufactured goods or finished industrial products. These links also create mutual dependence, and as a result it would be difficult to speak in the case of any state, even the economically most powerful, of complete self-sufficiency or autarky.

17.2. Such a system of mutual dependence is in itself normal. However it can easily become an occasion for various forms of exploitation or injustice and as a result influence the labour policy of individual states; and finally it can influence the individual worker who is the proper subject of labour. For instance the highly industrialized countries, and even more the businesses that direct on a large scale the means of industrial production (the companies referred to as multinational or transnational), fix the highest possible prices for their products, while trying at the same time to fix the lowest possible prices for raw materials or semimanufactured goods. This is one of the causes of an ever increasing disproportion between national incomes. The gap between most of the richest countries and the poorest ones is not diminishing or being stabilized, but is increasing more and more to the detriment, obviously, of the poor countries. Evidently this must have an effect on local labour policy and on the worker's situation in the economically disadvantaged societies. Finding himself in a system thus conditioned, the direct employer fixes working conditions below the objective requirements of the workers, especially if he himself wishes to obtain the highest possible profits from the business which he runs (or from the businesses which he runs, in the case of a situation of 'socialized' ownership of the means of production).

17.3. It is easy to see that this framework of forms of dependence linked with the concept of the indirect employer is enormously extensive and complicated. It is determined, in a sense, by all the elements that are decisive for economic life within a given society and state, but also by much wider links and forms of dependence. The attainment of the worker's rights cannot however be doomed to be merely a result of economic systems which on a larger or smaller scale are guided chiefly by the criterion of maximum profit. On the contrary, it is respect for the objective rights of the worker—every kind of worker: manual or intellectual, industrial or agricultural, etc.—that must constitute the adequate and fundamental criterion for shaping the whole economy, both on the level of the individual society and state and within the whole of the world economic policy and of the systems of international relationships that derive from it.

17.4. Influence in this direction should be exercised by all the international organizations whose concern it is, beginning with the United Nations. It appears that the International Labour Organization and the Food and Agriculture Organization of the United Nations and other bodies too have fresh contributions to offer on this point in particular. Within the individual states there are ministries or public departments and also various social institutions set up for this purpose. All of this effectively indicates the importance of the indirect employer—as has been said above—in achieving full respect for the worker's rights, since the rights of the human person are the key element in the whole of the social moral order.

18. When we consider the rights of workers in relation to the 'indirect employer', that is to say, all the agents at the national and international level that are responsible for the whole orientation of labour policy, we must first direct our attention to a fundamental issue: the question of finding work or, in other words, the issue of suitable employment for all who are capable of it.

The opposite of a just and right situation in this field is unemployment, that is to say, the lack of work for those who are capable of it. It can be a question of general unemployment or of unemployment in certain sectors of work. The role of the agents included under the title of indirect employer is to act against unemployment, which in all cases is an evil and which, when it reaches a certain level, can become a real social disaster. It is particularly painful when it especially affects young people, who after appropriate cultural, technical and professional preparation fail to find work and see their sincere wish to work and their readiness to take on their own responsibility for the economic and social development of the community sadly frustrated. The obligation to provide unemployment benefits, that is to say, the duty to make suitable grants indispensable for the subsistence of unemployed workers and their families, is a duty springing from the fundamental principle of the moral order in this sphere, namely the principle of the common use of goods or, to put it in another and still simpler way, the right to life and subsistence.

18.1. In order to meet the danger of unemployment and to ensure employment for all, the agents defined here as 'indirect employer' must make provision for overall planning with regard to the different kinds of work by which not only the economic life, but also the cultural life of a given society is shaped; they must also give attention to organizing that work in a correct and rational way. In the final analysis this overall concern weighs on the shoulders of the State, but it cannot mean one-sided centralization by the public authorities. Instead, what is in question is a just and rational co-ordination, within the framework of which the initiative of individuals, free groups and local work centres and complexes must be safeguarded, keeping in mind what has been said above with regard to the subject character of human labour.

18.2. The fact of the mutual dependence of societies and states and the need to collaborate in various areas mean that, while preserving the sovereign rights of each society and state in the field of planning and organizing labour in its own society, action in this important area must also be taken in the dimension of international collaboration by means of the necessary treaties and agreements. Here too the criterion for these pacts and agreements must more and more be the criterion of human work considered as a fundamental right of all human beings, work which gives similar rights to all those who work in such a way that the living standard of the workers in the different societies will less and less show those disturbing differences which are unjust and are apt to provoke even violent reactions. The international organizations have an enormous part to play in this area. They must let themselves be guided by an exact diagnosis of the complex situations and of the influence exercised by natural, historical, civil and other such circumstances. They must also be more highly operative with regard to plans for action jointly decided on, that is to say, they must be more effective in carrying them out.

18.3. In this direction, it is possible to actuate a plan for universal and proportionate progress by all in accordance with the guidelines of Paul VI's encyclical *Populorum Progressio*. It must be stressed that the constitutive element in this progress and also the most adequate way to verify it in a spirit of justice and peace, which the Church proclaims and for which she does not cease to pray to the Father of all individuals and of all peoples, is the continual reappraisal of man's work, both in the aspect of its objective finality and in the aspect of the dignity of the subject of all work, that is to say, man. The progress in question must be made through man and for man and it must produce its fruit in man. A test of this progress will be the increasingly mature recognition of the purpose of work and increasingly universal respect for the rights inherent in work in conformity with the dignity of man, the subject of work.

18.4. Rational planning and the proper organization of human labour in keeping with individual societies and states should also facilitate the discovery of the right proportions between the different kinds of employment: work on the land, in industry, in the various services, white-collar work and scientific or artistic work, in accordance with the capacities of individuals and for the common good of each society and of the whole of mankind. The organization of human life in accordance with the many possibilities of labour should be matched by a suitable system of instruction and education aimed first of all at developing mature human beings, but also aimed at preparing people specifically for assuming to good advantage an appropriate place in the vast and socially differentiated world of work.

18.5. As we view the whole human family throughout the world, we cannot fail to be struck by a disconcerting fact of immense proportions: the fact that while conspicuous natural resources remain unused there are huge numbers of people who are unemployed or underemployed and countless multitudes of people suffering from hunger. This is a fact that without any doubt demonstrates that both within the individual political communities and in their relationships on the continental and world levels there is something wrong with the organization of work and employment, precisely at the most critical and socially most important points.

19. After outlining the important role that concern for providing employment for all workers plays in safeguarding respect for the inalienable rights of man in view of his work, it is worth while taking a closer look at these rights, which in the final analysis are formed within the relationship between worker and direct employer. All that has been said above on the subject of the indirect employer is aimed at defining these relationships more exactly, by showing the many forms of conditioning within which these relationships are indirectly formed. This consideration does not however have a purely descriptive purpose; it is not a brief treatise on economics or politics. It is a matter of highlighting the deontological and moral aspect. The key problem of social ethics in this case is that of just remuneration for work done. In the context of the present there is no more important way of securing a just relationship between the worker and the employer than that constituted by remuneration for work. Whether the work is done in a system of private ownership of the means of production or in a system where ownership has undergone a certain 'socialization', the relationship between the employer (first and foremost the direct employer) and the worker is resolved on the basis of the wage, that is, through just remuneration of the work done.

19.1. It should also be noted that the justice of a socio-economic system and, in each case, its just functioning, deserve in the final analysis to be evaluated by the way in which man's work is properly remunerated in the system. Here we return once more to the first principle of the whole ethical and social order, namely the principle of the common use of goods. In every system, regardless of the fundamental relationships within it between capital and labour, wages, that is to say remuneration for work, are still a practical means whereby the vast majority of people can have access to those goods which are intended for common use: both the goods of nature and manufactured goods. Both kinds of goods become accessible to the worker through the wage which he receives as remuneration for his work. Hence in every case a just wage is the concrete means of verifying the justice of the whole socio-economic system and, in any case, of checking that it is functioning justly. It is not the only means of checking, but it is a particularly important one and in a sense the key means.

19.2. This means of checking concerns above all the family. Just remuneration for the work of an adult who is responsible for a family means remuneration which will suffice for establishing and properly maintaining a family and for providing security for its future. Such remuneration can be given either through what is called a family wage—that is, a single salary given to the head of the family for his work, sufficient for the needs of the family without the other spouse having to take up gainful employment outside the home—or through other social measures such as family allowances or grants to mothers devoting themselves exclusively to their families. These grants should correspond to the actual needs, that is, to the number of dependants for as long as they are not in a position to assume proper responsibility for their own lives.

19.3. Experience confirms that there must be a social re-evaluation of the mother's role, of the toil connected with it and of the need that children have for care, love and affection in order that they may develop into responsible, morally and religiously mature and psychologically stable persons. It will redound to the credit of society to make it possible for a mother—without inhibiting her freedom, without psychological or practical discrimination, and without penalizing her as compared with other women—to devote herself to taking care of her children and educating them in accordance with their needs, which vary with age. Having to abandon these tasks in order to take up paid work outside the home is wrong from the point of view of the good of society and of the family when it contradicts or hinders these primary goals of the mission of a mother.[26]

19.4. In this context it should be emphasized that on a more general level the whole labour process must be organized and adapted in such a way as to respect the requirements of the person and his or her forms of life, above all life in the home, taking into account the individual's age and sex. It is a fact that in many societies women work in nearly every sector of life. But it is fitting that they should be able to fulfil their tasks in accordance with their own nature, without being discriminated against and without being excluded from jobs for which they are capable, but also without lack of respect for their family aspirations and for their specific role in contributing, together with men, to the good of society. The true advancement of women requires that labour should be structured in such a way that women do not have to pay for their advancement by abandoning what is specific to them and at the expense of the family, in which women as mothers have an irreplaceable role.

19.5. Besides wages, various social benefits intended to ensure the life and health of workers and their families play a part here. The expenses involved in health care, especially in the case of accidents at work, demand that medical assistance should be easily available for workers and that as far as possible it should be cheap or even free of charge. Another sector regarding benefits is the sector associated with the right to rest. In the first place this involves a regular weekly rest comprising at least Sunday and also a longer period of rest, namely the holiday or vacation taken once a year or possibly in several shorter periods during the year. A third sector concerns the right to a pension and to insurance for old age and in case of accidents at work. Within the sphere of these principal rights there develops a whole system of particular rights which, together with remuneration for work, determine the correct relationship between worker and employer. Among these rights there should never be overlooked the right to a working environment and to manufacturing processes which are not harmful to the workers' physical health or to their moral integrity.

Protecting workers' rights

20. All these rights, together with the need for the workers themselves to secure them, give rise to yet another right: the right of association, that is, to form associations for the purpose of defending the vital interests of those employed in the various professions. These associations are called labour or trade unions. The vital interests of the workers are to a certain extent common for all of them; at the same time, however, each type of work, each profession, has its own specific character which should find a particular reflection in these organizations.

20.1. In a sense, unions go back to the medieval guilds of artisans, in so far as those organizations brought together people belonging to the same craft and thus on the basis of their work. However unions differ from the guilds on this essential point: the modern unions grew up from the struggle of the workers—workers in general but especially the industrial workers—to protect their just rights vis-à-vis the entrepreneurs and the owners of the means of production. Their task is to defend the existential interests of workers in all sectors in which their rights are concerned. The experience of history teaches that organizations of this type are an indispensable element of social life, especially in modern industrialized societies. Obviously this does not mean that only industrial workers can set up associations of this type. Representatives of every profession can use them to ensure their own rights. Thus there are unions of agricultural workers and of white-collar workers; there are also employers' associations. All, as has been said above, are further divided into groups or subgroups according to particular professional specializations.

20.2. Catholic social teaching does not hold that unions are no more than a reflection of the 'class' structure of society and that they are a mouthpiece for a class struggle which inevitably governs social life. They are indeed a mouthpiece for the struggle for social justice, for the just rights of working people in accordance with their individual professions. However, this struggle should be seen as a normal endeavour 'for' the just good: in the present case, for the good which corresponds to the needs and merits of working people associated by profession; but it is not a struggle 'against' others. Even if in controversial questions the struggle takes on a character of opposition toward others, this is because it aims at the good of social justice, not for the sake of 'struggle' or in order to eliminate the opponent. It is characteristic of work that it first and foremost unites people. In this consists its social power: the power to build a community. In the final analysis, both those who work and those who manage the means of production or who own them must in some way be united in this community. In the light of this fundamental structure of all work—in the light of the fact that, in the final analysis, labour and capital are indispensable components of the process of production in any social system—it is clear that even if it is because of their work needs that people unite to secure their rights, their union remains a constructive factor of social order and solidarity, and it is impossible to ignore it.

20.3. Just efforts to secure the rights of workers who are united by the same profession should always take into account the limitations imposed by the general economic situation of the country. Union demands cannot be turned into a kind of group or class 'egoism', although they can and should also aim at correcting—with a view to the common good of the whole of society—everything defective in the system of ownership of the means of production or in the way these are managed. Social and socio-economic life is certainly like a system of 'connected vessels', and every social activity directed toward safeguarding the rights of particular groups should adapt itself to this system.

20.4. In this sense, union activity undoubtedly enters the field of politics, understood as prudent concern for the common good. However, the role of unions is not to 'play politics' in the sense that the expression is commonly understood today. Unions do not have the character of political parties struggling for power; they should not be subjected to the decision of political parties or have too close links with them. In fact, in such a situation they easily lose contact with their specific role, which is to secure the just rights of workers within the framework of the common good of the whole of society; instead they become an instrument used for other purposes.

20.5. Speaking of the protection of the just rights of workers according to their individual professions, we must of course always keep in mind that which determines the subjective character of work in each profession, but at the same time, indeed before all else, we must keep in mind that which conditions the specific dignity of the subject of the work. The activity of union organizations opens up many possibilities in this respect, including their efforts to instruct and educate the workers and to foster their self-education. Praise is due to the work of the schools, what are known as workers' or people's universities and the training programmes and courses which have developed and are still developing this field of activity. It is always to be hoped that, thanks to the work of their unions, workers will not only have more, but above all be more: in other words that they will realize their humanity more fully in every respect.

20.6. One method used by unions in pursuing the just rights of their members is the strike or work stoppage, as a kind of ultimatum to the competent bodies, especially the employers. This method is recognized by Catholic social teaching as legitimate in the proper conditions and within just limits. In this connection workers should be assured the right to strike, without being subjected to personal penal sanctions for taking part in a strike. While admitting that it is a legitimate means, we must at the same time emphasize that a strike remains, in a sense, an extreme means. It must not be abused; it must not be abused especially for 'political' purposes. Furthermore, it must never be forgotten that when essential community services are in question, they must in every case be ensured, if necessary by means of appropriate legislation. Abuse of the strike weapon can lead to the paralysis of the whole of socio-economic life, and this is contrary to the requirements of the common good of society, which also corresponds to the properly understood nature of work itself.

Work: special aspects and problems

21. All that has been said thus far on the dignity of work, on the objective and subjective dimension of human work, can be directly applied to the question of agricultural work and to the situation of the person who cultivates the earth by toiling in the fields. This is a vast sector of work on our planet, a sector not restricted to one or other continent nor limited to the societies which have already attained a certain level of development and progress. The world of agriculture, which provides society with the goods it needs for its daily sustenance, is of fundamental importance. The conditions of the rural population and of agricultural work vary from place to place, and the social position of agricultural workers differs from country to country. This depends not only on the level of development of agricultural technology but also, and perhaps more, on the recognition of the just rights of agricultural workers and, finally, on the level of awareness regarding the social ethics of work.

21.1. Agricultural work involves considerable difficulties, including unremitting and sometimes exhausting physical effort and a lack of appreciation on the part of society, to the point of making agricultural people feel that they are social outcasts and of speeding up the phenomenon of their mass exodus from the countryside to the cities and unfortunately to still more dehumanizing living conditions. Added to this are the lack of adequate professional training and of proper equipment, the spread of a certain individualism and also objectively unjust situations. In certain developing countries, millions of people are forced to cultivate the land belonging to others and are exploited by the big landowners, without any hope of ever being able to gain possession of even a small piece of land of their own. There is a lack of forms of legal protection for the agricultural workers themselves and for their families in case of old age, sickness or unemployment. Long days of hard physical work are paid miserably. Land which could be cultivated is left abandoned by the owners. Legal titles to possession of a small portion of land that someone has personally cultivated for years are disregarded or left defenceless against the 'land hunger' of more powerful individuals or groups. But even in the economically developed countries, where scientific research, technological achievements and state policy have brought agriculture to a very advanced level, the right to work can be infringed when the farm workers are denied the possibility of sharing in decisions concerning their services, or when they are denied the right to free association with a view to their just advancement socially, culturally and economically.

21.2. In many situations radical and urgent changes are therefore needed in order to restore to agriculture—and to rural people—its just value as the basis for a healthy economy, within the social community's development as a whole. Thus it is necessary to proclaim and promote the dignity of work, of all work, but especially of agricultural work in which man so eloquently 'subdues' the earth he has received as a gift from God and affirms his 'dominion' in the visible world.

22. Recently national communities and international organizations have turned their attention to another question connected with work, one full of implications: the question of disabled people. They too are fully human subjects with corresponding innate, sacred and inviolable rights and, in spite of the limitations and sufferings affecting their bodies and faculties, they point up more clearly the dignity and greatness of man. Since disabled people are subjects with all their rights, they should be helped to participate in the life of society in all its aspects and at all the levels accessible to their capacities. The disabled person is one of us and participates fully in the same humanity that we possess. It would be radically unworthy of man and a denial of our common humanity to admit to the life of the community, and thus admit to work, only those who are fully functional. To do so would be to practise a serious form of discrimination, that of the strong and healthy against the weak and sick. Work in the objective sense should be subordinated in this circumstance too to the dignity of man, to the subject of work and not to economic advantage.

22.1. The various bodies involved in the world of labour, both the direct and the indirect employer, should therefore, by means of effective and appropriate measures, foster the right of disabled people to professional training and work so that they can be given a productive activity suited to them. Many practical problems arise at this point, as well as legal and economic ones; but the community, that is to say, the public authorities, associations and intermediate groups, business enterprises and the disabled themselves should pool their ideas and resources so as to attain this goal that must not be shirked: that disabled people may be offered work according to their capabilities, for this is demanded by their dignity as persons and as subjects of work. Each community will be able to set up suitable structures for finding or creating jobs for such people both in the usual public or private enterprises, by offering them ordinary or suitably adapted jobs, and in what are called 'protected' enterprises and surroundings.

22.2. Careful attention must be devoted to the physical and psychological working conditions of disabled people—as for all workers—to their just remuneration, to the possibility of their promotion and to the elimination of various obstacles. Without hiding the fact that this is a complex and difficult task, it is to be hoped that a correct concept of labour in the subjective sense will produce a situation which will make it possible for disabled people to feel that they are not cut off from the working world or dependent upon society, but that they are full-scale subjects of work, useful, respected for their human dignity and called to contribute to the progress and welfare of their families and of the community according to their particular capacities.

23. Finally, we must say at least a few words on the subject of emigration in search of work. This is an age-old phenomenon which nevertheless continues to be repeated and is still today very widespread as a result of the complexities of modern life. Man has the right to leave his native land for various motives—and also the right to return—in order to seek better conditions of life in another country. This fact is certainly not without difficulties of various kinds. Above all it generally constitutes a loss for the country which is left behind. It is the departure of a person who is also a member of a great community united by history, tradition and culture; and that person must begin life in the midst of another society united by a different culture and very often by a different language. In this case, it is the loss of a subject of work, whose efforts of mind and body could contribute to the common good of his own country, but these efforts, this contribution, are instead offered to another society which in a sense has less right to them than the person's country of origin.

23.1. Nevertheless, even if emigration is in some aspect an evil, in certain circumstances it is, as the phrase goes, a necessary evil. Everything should be done—and certainly much is being done to this end—to prevent this material evil from causing greater moral harm; indeed every possible effort should be made to ensure that it may bring benefit to the emigrant's personal, family and social life, both for the country to which he goes and the country which he leaves. In this area much depends on just legislation, in particular with regard to the rights of workers. It is obvious that the question of just legislation enters into the context of the present considerations, especially from the point of view of these rights.

23.2. The most important thing is that the person working away from his native land, whether as a permanent emigrant or as a seasonal worker, should not be placed at a disadvantage in comparison with the other workers in that society in the matter of working rights. Emigration in search of work must in no way become an opportunity for financial or social exploitation. As regards the work relationship, the same criteria should be applied to immigrant workers as to all other workers in the society concerned. The value of work should be measured by the same standard and not according to the difference in nationality, religion or race. For even greater reason the situation of constraint in which the emigrant may find himself should not be exploited. All these circumstances should categorically give way, after special qualifications have of course been taken into consideration, to the fundamental value of work, which is bound up with the dignity of the human person. Once more the fundamental principle must be repeated: the hierarchy of values and the profound meaning of work itself require that capital should be at the service of labour and not labour at the service of capital.

V

The spiritual significance of work

24. It is right to devote the last part of these reflections about human work on the occasion of the ninetieth anniversary of the encyclical *Rerum Novarum* to the spirituality of work in the Christian sense. Since work in its subjective aspect is always a personal action, an *actus personae*, it follows that the whole person, body and spirit, participates in it, whether it is manual or intellectual work. It is also to the whole person that the word of the living God is directed, the evangelical message of salvation in which we find many points which concern human work and which throw particular light on it. These points need to be properly assimilated: an inner effort on the part of the human spirit, guided by faith, hope and charity, is needed in order that through these points the work of the individual human being may be given the meaning which it has in the eyes of God and by means of which work enters into the salvation process on a par with the other ordinary yet particularly important components of its texture.

24.1. The Church considers it her duty to speak out on work from the viewpoint of its human value and of the moral order to which it belongs, and she sees this as one of her important tasks within the service that she renders to the evangelical message as a whole. At the same time she sees it as her particular duty to form a spirituality of work which will help all people to come closer, through work, to God, the creator and redeemer, to participate in his salvific plan for man and the world and to deepen their friendship with Christ in their lives by accepting, through faith, a living participation in his threefold mission as priest, prophet and king, as the Second Vatican Council so eloquently teaches.

25. As the Second Vatican Council says, 'Throughout the course of the centuries, men have laboured to better the circumstances of their lives through a monumental amount of individual and collective effort. To believers, this point is settled: considered in itself, such human activity accords with God's will. For man, created in God's image, received a mandate to subject to himself the earth and all that it contains, and to govern the world with justice and holiness; a mandate to relate himself and the totality of things to him who was to be acknowledged as the lord and creator of all. Thus, by the subjection of all things to man, the name of God would be wonderful in all the earth.'[27]

25.1. The word of God's revelation is profoundly marked by the fundamental truth that man, created in the image of God, shares by his work in the activity of the creator and that, within the limits of his own human capabilities, man in a sense continues to develop that activity and perfects it as he advances further and further in the discovery of the resources and values contained in the whole of creation. We find this truth at the very beginning of sacred scripture in the Book of Genesis, where the creation activity itself is presented in the form of 'work' done by God during 'six days',[28] 'resting' on the seventh day.[29] Besides, the last book of sacred scripture echoes the same respect for what God has done through his creative 'work' when it proclaims: 'Great and wonderful are your deeds, O Lord God the Almighty',[30] this is similar to the Book of Genesis, which concludes the description of each day of creation with the statement: 'And God saw that it was good.'[31]

25.2. This description of creation, which we find in the very first chapter of the Book of Genesis, is also in a sense the first 'gospel of work'. For it shows what the dignity of work consists of: it teaches that man ought to imitate God, his creator, in working, because man alone has the unique characteristic of likeness to God. Man ought to imitate God both in working and also in resting, since God himself wished to present his own creative activity under the form of work and rest. This activity by God in the world always continues, as the words of Christ attest: 'My father is working still';[32] he works with creative power by sustaining in existence the world that he called into being from nothing, and he works with salvific power in the hearts of those whom from the beginning he has destined for 'rest'[33] in union with himself in his 'Father's house'.[34] Therefore man's work too not only requires a rest every 'seventh day',[35] but also cannot consist in the mere exercise of human strength in external action; it must leave room for man to prepare himself, by becoming more and more what in the will of God he ought to be, for the 'rest' that the Lord reserves for his servants and friends.[36]

25.3. Awareness that man's work is a participation in God's activity ought to permeate, as the council teaches, even 'the most ordinary everyday activities. For, while providing the substance of life for themselves and their families, men and women are performing their activities in a way which appropriately benefits society. They can justly consider that by their labour they are unfolding the creator's work, consulting the advantages of their brothers and sisters, and contributing by their personal industry to the realization in history of the divine plan.'[37]

25.4. This Christian spirituality of work should be a heritage shared by all. Especially in the modern age, the spirituality of work should show the maturity called for by the tensions and restlessness of mind and heart. 'Far from thinking that works produced by man's own talent and energy are in opposition to God's power, and that the rational creature exists as a kind of rival to the creator, Christians are convinced that the triumphs of the human race are a sign of God's greatness and the flowering of his own mysterious design. For the greater man's power becomes, the farther his individual and community responsibility extends...People are not deterred by the Christian message from building up the world or impelled to neglect the welfare of their fellows. They are, rather, more stringently bound to do these very things.'[38]

25.5. The knowledge that by means of work man shares in the work of creation constitutes the most profound motive for undertaking it in various sectors. 'The faithful, therefore,' we read in the constitution *Lumen Gentium*, 'must learn the deepest meaning and the value of all creation, and its orientation to the praise of God. Even by their secular activity they must assist one another to live holier lives. In this way the world will be permeated by the spirit of Christ and more effectively achieve its purpose in justice, charity and peace...Therefore, by their competence in secular fields and by their personal activity, elevated from within by the grace of Christ, let them work vigorously so that by human labour, technical skill and civil culture, created goods may be perfected according to the design of the creator and the light of his word.'[39]

26. The truth that by means of work man participates in the activity of God himself, his creator, was given particular prominence by Jesus Christ—the Jesus at whom many of his first listeners in Nazareth 'were astonished, saying, "Where did this man get all this? What is the wisdom given to him?... Is not this the carpenter?" '[40] For Jesus not only proclaimed but first and foremost fulfilled by his deeds the 'gospel', the word of eternal wisdom that had been entrusted to him. Therefore, this was also 'the gospel of work', because he who proclaimed it was himself a man of work, a craftsman like Joseph of Nazareth.[41] And if we do not find in his words a special command to work—but rather on one occasion a prohibition against too much anxiety about work and life[42]—at the same time the eloquence of the life of Christ is unequivocal: he belongs to the 'working world', he has appreciation and respect for human work. It can indeed be said that he looks with love upon human work and the different forms that it takes, seeing in each one of these forms a particular facet of man's likeness with God, the creator and Father. Is it not he who says: 'My father is the vine-dresser,'[43] and in various ways puts into his teaching the fundamental truth about work which is already expressed in the whole tradition of the Old Testament, beginning with the Book of Genesis?

26.1. The books of the Old Testament contain many references to human work and to the individual professions exercised by man: for example, the doctor,[44] the pharmacist,[45] the craftsman or artist,[46] the blacksmith[47]—we could apply these words to today's foundry workers—the potter,[48] the farmer,[49] the scholar,[50] the sailor,[51] the builder,[52] the musician,[53] the shepherd[54] and the fisherman.[55] The words of praise for the work of women are well known.[56] In his parables on the kingdom of God, Jesus Christ constantly refers to human work: that of the shepherd,[57] the farmer,[58] the doctor,[59] the sower,[60] the householder,[61] the servant,[62] the steward,[63] the fisherman,[64] the merchant,[65] the labourer.[66] He also speaks of the various forms of women's work.[67] He compares the apostolate to the manual work of harvesters[68] or fishermen.[69] He refers to the work of scholars too.[70]

26.2. This teaching of Christ on work, based on the example of his life during his years in Nazareth, finds a particularly lively echo in the teaching of the apostle Paul. Paul boasts of working at his trade (he was probably a tent-maker),[71] and thanks to that work he was able even as an apostle to earn his own bread.[72] 'With toil and labour we worked night and day, that we might not burden any of you.'[73] Hence his instructions, in the form of exhortation and command, on the subject of work: 'Now such persons we command and exhort in the Lord Jesus Christ to do their work in quietness and to earn their own living,' he writes to the Thessalonians.[74] In fact, noting that some 'are living in idleness...not doing any work,'[75] the apostle does not hesitate to say in the same context: 'If any one will not work, let him not eat.'[76] In another passage he encourages his readers: 'Whatever your task, work heartily, as serving the Lord and not men, knowing that from the Lord you will receive the inheritance as your reward.'[77]

26.3. The teachings of the 'apostle of the gentiles' obviously have key importance for the morality and spirituality of human work. They are an important complement to the great though discreet gospel of work that we find in the life and parables of Christ, in what Jesus 'did and taught'.[78]

26.4. On the basis of these illuminations emanating from the source himself, the Church has always proclaimed what we find expressed in modern terms in the teaching of the Second Vatican Council: 'Just as human activity proceeds from man, so it is ordered towards man. For when a man works he not only alters things and society, he develops himself as well. He learns much, he cultivates his resources, he goes outside himself and beyond himself. Rightly understood, this kind of growth is of greater value than any external riches which can be garnered... Hence, the norm of human activity is this: that in accord with the divine plan and will, it should harmonize with the genuine good of the human race and allow people as individuals and as members of society to pursue their total vocation and fulfil it.'[79]

26.5. Such a vision of the values of human work, or in other words such a spirituality of work, fully explains what we read in the same section of the council's pastoral constitution with regard to the right meaning of progress: 'A person is more precious for what he is than for what he has. Similarly, all that people do to obtain greater justice, wider brotherhood and a more humane ordering of social relationships has greater worth than technical advances. For these advances can supply the material for human progress, but of themselves alone they can never actually bring it about.'[80]

26.6. This teaching on the question of progress and development—a subject that dominates present-day thought—can be understood only as the fruit of a tested spirituality of human work; and it is only on the basis of such a spirituality that it can be realized and put into practice. This is the teaching and also the programme that has its roots in 'the gospel of work'.

27. There is yet another aspect of human work, an essential dimension of it, that is profoundly imbued with the spirituality based on the gospel. All work, whether manual or intellectual, is inevitably linked with toil. The Book of Genesis expresses it in a truly penetrating manner: the original blessing of work contained in the very mystery of creation and connected with man's elevation as the image of God is contrasted with the curse that sin brought with it: 'Cursed is the ground because of you; in toil you shall eat of it all the days of your life.'[81] This toil connected with work marks the way of human life on earth and constitutes an announcement of death: 'In the sweat of your face you shall eat bread till you return to the ground, for out of it you were taken.'[82] Almost as an echo of these words, the author of one of the wisdom books says: 'Then I considered all that my hands had done and the toil I had spent in doing it.'[83] There is no one on earth who could not apply these words to himself.

27.1. In a sense, the final word of the gospel on this matter as on others is found in the paschal mystery of Jesus Christ. It is here that we must seek an answer to these problems so important for the spirituality of human work. The paschal mystery contains the cross of Christ and his obedience unto death, which the apostle contrasts with the disobedience which from the beginning has burdened man's history on earth.[84] It also contains the elevation of Christ, who by means of death on a cross returns to his disciples in the resurrection with the power of the Holy Spirit.

27.2. Sweat and toil, which work necessarily involves in the present condition of the human race, present the Christian and everyone who is called to follow Christ with the possibility of sharing lovingly in the work that Christ came to do.[85] This work of salvation came about through suffering and death on a cross. By enduring the toil of work in union with Christ crucified for us, man in a way collaborates with the son of God for the redemption of humanity. He shows himself a true disciple of Christ by carrying the cross in his turn every day[86] in the activity that he is called upon to perform.

27.3. Christ, 'undergoing death itself for all of us sinners, taught us by example that we too must shoulder that cross which the world and the flesh inflict upon those who pursue peace and justice'; but also, at the same time, 'appointed Lord by his resurrection and given all authority in heaven and on earth. Christ is now at work in people's hearts through the power of his Spirit... He animates, purifies and strengthens those noble longings too by which the human family strives to make its life more human and to render the whole earth submissive to this goal.'[87]

27.4. The Christian finds in human work a small part of the cross of Christ and accepts it in the same spirit of redemption in which Christ accepted his cross for us. In work, thanks to the light that penetrates us from the resurrection of Christ, we always find a glimmer of new life, of the new good, as if it were an announcement of 'the new heavens and the new earth'[88] in which man and the world participate precisely through the toil that goes with work. Through toil—and never without it. On the one hand this confirms the indispensability of the cross in the spirituality of human work; on the other hand the cross which this toil constitutes reveals a new good springing from work itself, from work understood in depth and in all its aspects and never apart from work.

27.5. Is this new good—the fruit of human work—already a small part of that 'new earth' where justice dwells?[89] If it is true that the many forms of toil that go with man's work are a small part of the cross of Christ, what is the relationship of this new good to the resurrection of Christ? The council seeks to reply to this question also, drawing light from the very sources of the revealed word: 'Therefore, while we are warned that it profits a man nothing if he gains the whole world and loses himself (cf. Luke 9:25), the expectation of a new earth must not weaken but rather stimulate our concern for cultivating this one. For here grows the body of a new human family, a body which even now is able to give some kind of foreshadowing of the new age. Earthly progress must be carefully distinguished from the growth of Christ's kingdom. Nevertheless, to the extent that the former can contribute to the better ordering of human society, it is of vital concern to the kingdom of God.'[90]

27.6. In these present reflections devoted to human work we have tried to emphasize everything that seemed essential to it, since it is through man's labour that not only 'the fruits of our activity', but also 'human dignity, brotherhood and freedom' must increase on earth.[91] Let the Christian who listens to the word of the living God, uniting work with prayer, know the place that his work has not only in earthly progress, but also in the development of the kingdom of God, to which we are all called through the power of the Holy Spirit and through the word of the gospel.

27.7. In concluding these reflections, I gladly impart the apostolic blessing to all of you, venerable brothers and beloved sons and daughters.

27.8. I prepared this document for publication last 15 May on the ninetieth anniversary of the encyclical *Rerum Novarum,* but it is only after my stay in the hospital that I have been able to revise it definitively.

Given at Castelgandolfo, on the feast of the triumph of the cross, 14 September 1981, the third year of the pontificate.

Editor's Note

LE 14.2: In this case 'socialization' clearly means some form of nationalization or state ownership, but see the Introduction, p.xxi, and footnote 26.

Sollicitudo Rei Socialis

An encyclical letter of John Paul II to the bishops, priests, religious and sons and daughters of the Church, and to all those of good will, on the twentieth anniversary of the publication of 'Populorum Progressio'.

Introduction

It has been remarked in the Editor's Introduction to this collection that encyclicals have regularly been issued on anniversaries of *Rerum Novarum*. Paul VI's *Populorum Progressio* was an exception in focusing attention upon the question of development. *Sollicitudo Rei Socialis* was written to commemorate *Populorum Progressio*, and is also devoted almost entirely to problems of development—the chief hindrance to which, Pope John Paul suggests, is the division of the world into the two power blocs of East and West. Though the letter is only dated from the very end of 1987, the events in Eastern Europe of just two years later have radically altered the context in which it was composed. It is difficult not to see in the frequent use of the word 'solidarity' a reference to the Polish Solidarity union, to which John Paul has given considerable encouragement and, it is said, substantial funds. For a more extensive discussion of *Sollicitudo Rei Socialis* (SRS), see the Introduction, pp. xx. The Latin text was published in AAS 80 (1988), pp. 513. The main enumeration is as it appears there, though subordinate paragraph numbers have been added in line with the Editorial Note, p. ix.

Summary

Paras. 1-3: The social teaching of the Church has become a regularly updated doctrinal corpus. An important part of it is *Populorum Progressio*. The present encyclical is to pay homage to that one on its twentieth anniversary, and in so doing to reaffirm the value of the Church's teaching.

Paras. 4-10: Though Paul VI's teaching retains its force, circumstances have changed. It was published two years after the Second Vatican Council, and it took up the synthesis of the Council, especially as expressed in *Gaudium et Spes*. But *Populorum Progressio* also had great originality because it addressed "all people of good will" on the topic of development, because it gave a moral evaluation of the social question, and because it noted that money was being spent for selfish purposes, and particularly on armaments, that should have been spent on development, the new name for peace.

Paras. 11-15: When *Populorum Progressio* was written the outlook for development was hopeful. There has been some progress, but the outlook is now less optimistic. The gap between North and South has persisted and perhaps, according to a range of social indicators, widened, while the right of economic initiative not only of individuals but even of whole nations, is often suppressed; human rights are frequently denied, which is also a form of poverty: underdevelopment is cultural, political and simply human, as well as economic.

Paras. 16-19: The responsibility for this deterioration falls upon the actions of developed nations and upon mechanisms which operate almost automatically to increase their wealth. Yet even inside these nations there are signs of underdevelopment, particularly in homelessness and unemployment. There is also the problem of international debt, which is an obstacle to development.

Paras. 20-25: A further hindrance is the division of the world into two great blocs—the West embracing liberal capitalism, the East Marxist collectivism—out of which has come the division into two opposed armed forces. To both blocs the Church adopts a critical stance, and it is questionable to what extent the two blocs can promote integral development. Countries which have recently achieved independence and are trying to establish their own identity, find themselves caught up in the struggle between these two blocs, each of which has a tendency to imperialism, or to neo-colonialism. The West seems now to be turning in upon itself in selfish isolation, while the East ignores its duty to alleviate human misery. Both attitudes are a desertion of a moral obligation. Other barriers to development are the arms trade, the stockpiling of atomic weapons, the millions of refugees who cannot find a home in a divided world, terrorism. And there is also a demographic problem, which some governments attempt to tackle through campaigns against birth, which is contrary to true development.

Para. 26: There are positive signs, however, such as people's recognition of their own dignity, thanks in part to the United Nations' Declaration of Human Rights; there is a growing recognition, too, of the need for solidarity, a concern for peace, and for the environment. There is a commitment both of people and of institutions to the solving of these problems.

Paras. 27-29: Development is not a straightforward process. It can be set back, as it was by two World Wars, and unless guided by a concern for the true good of the human race it is in any case not enough for happiness. There can also be a form of 'superdevelopment' or 'consumerism'. Simply to 'have' things does not itself perfect the human subject. Development must be directed to the totality of the human vocation—and that includes the vocation to immortality.

Paras. 30-32: According to the Bible, it is the task of human beings to exercise dominion over all other created beings, in obedience to the divine law, a task made more difficult by the Fall. In that context development is a moment in the history of creation, and Christ guides us in our collaboration with God's creative act. The Church wishes to place itself at the service of the divine plan. It is obliged to relieve misery and suffering, to give up superfluous things to provide for those in need. The obligation to commit oneself to development is not just an individual duty: it falls upon societies, nations, Churches as well as upon men and women.

Paras. 33-34: There is a close link between development and human rights on

[393]

an individual, a community, and an international level. Development must also include the cosmos—the question of natural resources, the quality of life, pollution.

Paras 35-38: Development is hindered by 'structural sin', on the one hand the all-consuming desire for profit and on the other the thirst for power. While people fall victims of this double structure of sin, so do whole nations. Even those without explicit faith can recognise that the obstacles to integral development arise from attitudes which human beings can turn into absolute values. For a Christian, overcoming the moral obstacles is a conversion. There has been a transformation of this moral awareness which shows itself in a growing recognition of humanity's interdependence—a commitment to solidarity.

Paras. 39-40: There is solidarity among the poor, alongside whom the Church is called to take its stand. International relations must also be based on a solidarity which helps us to see the other as neighbour or helper, a perspective which excludes exploitation and which leads to peace. Solidarity is a Christian virtue closely allied to charity and is inspired by the Trinity, that supreme model of unity which we call communion. By the exercise of solidarity the structures of sin can be overcome.

Paras. 41-42: While it is not the Church's role to offer technical solutions to underdevelopment, it has something to say in its social teaching about the nature, conditions, requirements and aims of authentic development, and obstacles to its realization. This social teaching is not a third way between liberal capitalism and Marxist collectivism, but an interpretation of reality in the light of the Gospel. The social teaching is part of the evangelizing mission to the Church, the condemnation of injustice part of its prophetic role. Central to the doctrine is the option for the poor; characteristic of it is the principle that the goods of this world are the property of all. This is not to deny the right to private property, but to point out it must be seen as a 'social mortgage'.

Paras. 43-45: Love for the poor must be translated into action, into the reform by the developed nations of international trade, of the financial market, of technological transfer, and of international organizations. Developing nations must also play their part, by allowing their citizens access to wider culture and the free flow of information, by increasing food production and by installing democratic processes. There should also be within particular geographical areas greater collaboration and interdependence among developing nations.

Paras. 46-49: Liberation has emerged, especially in Latin America, as the fundamental category and principle of action: development cannot be merely economic, for that does not set people free. The Church affirms the possibility of overcoming the obstacles placed by sin, and by the structures of sin. There is no justification for despair, pessimism, or inertia. At stake is human dignity, whose defense and promotion has been entrusted to us by the Creator. No temporal achievement can be identified with the Kingdom of God, but nor can this be an excuse for a lack of concern for people at the social, national and international levels. The Kingdom becomes present in the Eucharist above all: in union with God and with each other through the

Eucharist we have the strength to commit ourselves to work for development and for peace. In this task we turn for help to Mary.

Venerable brothers and dear sons and daughters, Health and the apostolic blessing!

I. Introduction

1. The social concern of the church, directed toward an authentic development of man and society which would respect and promote all the dimensions of the human person, has always expressed itself in the most varied ways. In recent years one of the special means of intervention has been the magisterium of the Roman pontiffs which, beginning with the encyclical *Rerum Novarum* of Leo XIII as a point of reference,[1] has frequently dealt with the question and has sometimes made the dates of publication of the various social documents coincide with the anniversaries of that first document.[2]

1.1 The popes have not failed to throw fresh light by means of those messages upon new aspects of the social doctrine of the church. As a result, this doctrine, beginning with the outstanding contribution of Leo XIII and enriched by the successive contributions of the magisterium, has now become an updated doctrinal corpus. It builds up gradually as the church, in the fullness of the word revealed by Christ Jesus[3] and with the assistance of the Holy Spirit (cf. Jn. 14:16, 26; 16:13-15), reads events as they unfold in the course of history. She thus seeks to lead people to respond, with the support also of rational reflection and of the human sciences, to their vocation as responsible builders of earthly society.

2. Part of this large body of social teaching is the distinguished encyclical *Populorum Progressio*,[4] which my esteemed predecessor Paul VI published on March 26, 1967.

2.1 The enduring relevance of this encyclical is easily recognized if we note the series of commemorations which took place during 1987 in various forms and in many parts of the ecclesiastical and civil world. For this same purpose, the Pontifical Justice and Peace Commission sent a circular letter to the synods of the Eastern Catholic churches and to the episcopal conferences asking for ideas and suggestions on the best way to celebrate the enyclical's anniversary, to enrich its teachings and, if need be, to update them. At the time of the 20th anniversary, the same commission organized a solemn commemoration in which I myself took part and gave the concluding address.[5] And now, also taking into account the replies to the above-mentioned circular letter, I consider it appropriate at the close of the year 1987 to devote an encyclical to the theme of *Populorum Progressio*.

3. In this way I wish principally to achieve two objectives of no little importance: on the one hand, to pay homage to this historic document of Paul VI and to its teaching; on the other hand, following in the footsteps of my esteemed predecessors in the See of Peter, to reaffirm the continuity of the social doctrine as well as its constant renewal. In effect, continuity and renewal are a proof of the perennial value of the teaching of the church.

3.1 This twofold dimension is typical of her teaching in the social sphere.

On the one hand it is constant, for it remains identical in its fundamental inspiration, in its 'principles of reflection,' in its 'criteria of judgment,' in its basic 'directives for action'[6] and above all in its vital link with the Gospel of the Lord. On the other hand, it is ever new because it is subject to the necessary and opportune adaptations suggested by the changes in historical conditions and by the unceasing flow of the events which are the setting of the life of people and society.

4. I am convinced that the teachings of the encyclical *Populorum Progressio*, addressed to the people and the society of the '60s, retain all their force as an appeal to conscience today in the last part of the '80s, in an effort to trace the major lines of the present world always within the context of the aim and inspiration of the 'development of peoples', which are still very far from being exhausted. I therefore propose to extend the impact of that message by bringing it to bear, with its possible applications, upon the present historical moment, which is no less dramatic than that of 20 years ago.

4.1 As we well know, time maintains a constant and unchanging rhythm. Today, however, we have the impression that it is passing ever more quickly, especially by reason of the multiplication and complexity of the phenomena in the midst of which we live. Consequently, the configuration of the world in the course of the last 20 years, while preserving certain fundamental constants, has undergone notable changes and presents some totally new aspects.

4.2 The present period of time, on the eve of the third Christian millennium, is characterized by a widespread expectancy rather like a new 'Advent,'[7] which to some extent touches everyone. It offers an opportunity to study the teachings of the encyclical in greater detail and to see their possible future developments.

4.3 The aim of the present reflection is to emphasize, through a theological investigation of the present world, the need for a fuller and more nuanced concept of development, according to the suggestions contained in the encyclical. Its aim is also to indicate some ways of putting it into effect.

II. Originality of the Encyclical *Populorum Progressio*

5. As soon as it appeared, the document of Pope Paul VI captured the attention of public opinion by reason of its originality. In a concrete manner and with great clarity, it was possible to identify the above-mentioned characteristics of continuity and renewal within the church's social doctrine. The intention of rediscovering numerous aspects of this teaching through a careful rereading of the encyclical will therefore constitute the main thread of the present reflections.

5.1 But first I wish to say a few words about the date of publication: the year 1967. The very fact that Pope Paul VI chose to publish a social encyclical in that year invites us to consider the document in relationship to the Second Vatican Council, which had ended on Dec. 8, 1965.

6. We should see something more in this than simple chronological proximity. The encyclical *Populorum Progressio* presents itself, in a certain way, as a document which applies the teachings of the council. It not only makes continual reference to the texts of the council,[8] but its also flows from the

[396]

same concern of the church which inspired the whole effort of the council—and in a particular way the pastoral constitution *Gaudium et Spes*—to coordinate and develop a number of themes of her social teaching.

6.1 We can therefore affirm that the encyclical *Populorum Progressio* is a kind of response to the council's appeal with which the constitution *Gaudium et Spes* begins:

'The joys and the hopes, the griefs and the anxieties of the people of this age, especially those who are poor or in any way afflicted, these too are the joys and hopes, the griefs and anxieties of the followers of Christ. Indeed, nothing genuinely human fails to raise an echo in their hearts.'[9] These words express the fundamental motive inspiring the great document of the council, which begins by noting the situation of poverty and of underdevelopment in which millions of human beings live.

6.2 This poverty and underdevelopment are, under another name, the 'griefs and the anxieties' of today, of 'especially those who are poor.' Before this vast panorama of pain and suffering the council wished to suggest horizons of joy and hope. The encyclical of Paul VI has the same purpose, in full fidelity to the inspiration of the council.

7. There is also the theme of the encyclical which, in keeping with the great tradition of the church's social teaching, takes up again in a direct manner the new exposition and rich synthesis which the council produced, notably in the constitution *Gaudium et Spes*.

7.1 With regard to the content and themes once again set forth by the encyclical, the following should be emphasized: the awareness of the duty of the church as 'an expert in humanity' 'to scrutinize the signs of the times and to interpret them in the light of the Gospel';[10] the awareness, equally profound, of her mission of 'service', a mission distinct from the function of the state even when she is concerned with people's concrete situation;[11] the reference to the notorious inequalities in the situations of those same people;[12] the confirmation of the council's teaching, a faithful echo of the centuries-old tradition of the church regarding the 'universal purpose of goods'[13]; the appreciation of the culture and the technological civilization which contribute to human liberation,[14] without failing to recognize their limits;[15] finally, on the specific theme of development, which is precisely the theme of the encyclical, the insistence on the 'more serious duty' incumbent on the more developed nations 'to help the developing countries.'[16] The same idea of development proposed by the encyclical flows directly from the approach which the pastoral constitution takes to this problem.[17]

7.2 These and other explicit references to the pastoral constitution lead one to conclude that the encyclical presents itself as an application of the council's teaching in social matters to the specific problem of the development and the underdevelopment of peoples.

8. This brief analysis helps us to appreciate better the originality of the encyclical, which can be stated in three points.

8.1 The first is constituted by the very fact of a document, issued by the highest authority of the Catholic Church and addressed both to the church herself and 'to all people of good will,'[18] on a matter which at first sight is solely economic and social: the development of peoples. The term *development* is taken from the vocabulary of the social and economic sciences. From this point of view, the encyclical *Populorum Progressio* follows directly in the line of the encyclical *Rerum Novarum*, which deals with the 'condition of the workers.'[19] Considered superficially, both themes could seem extraneous to the legitimate concern of the church seen as a religious institution—and 'development' even more so than the 'condition of the workers.'

8.2 In continuity with the encyclical of Leo XIII, it must be recognized that the document of Paul VI possesses the merit of having emphasized the ethical and cultural character of the problems connected with development, and likewise the legitimacy and necessity of the church's intervention in this field.

8.3 In addition, the social doctrine of the church has once more demonstrated its character as an application of the word of God to people's lives and the life of society as well as to the earthly realities connected with them, offering 'principles for reflection,' 'criteria of judgment' and 'directives for action.'[20] Here, in the document of Paul VI, one finds these three elements with a prevalently practical orientation, that is, directed toward moral conduct.

8.4 In consequence, when the church concerns herself with the 'development of peoples' she cannot be accused of going outside her own specific field of competence and, still less, outside the mandate received from the Lord.

9. The second point of originality of *Populorum Progressio* is shown by the breadth of outlook open to what is commonly called the 'social question'.

9.1 In fact, the encyclical *Mater et Magistra* of Pope John XXIII had already entered into this wider outlook,[21] and the council had echoed the same in the constitution *Gaudium et Spes*.[22] However, the social teaching of the church had not yet reached the point of affirming with such clarity that the social question has acquired a worldwide dimension[23] nor had this affirmation and the accompanying analysis yet been made into a 'directive for action', as Paul VI did in his encyclical.

9.2 Such an explicit taking up of a position offers a great wealth of content, which it is appropriate to point out.

9.3 In the first place a possible misunderstanding has to be eliminated. Recognition that the 'social question' has assumed a worldwide dimension does not at all mean that it has lost its incisiveness or its national and local importance. On the contrary, it means that the problems in industrial enterprises or in the workers' and union movements of a particular country or region are not to be considered as isolated cases with no connection. On the contrary, they depend more and more on the influence of factors beyond regional boundaries and national frontiers.

9.4 Unfortunately, from the economic point of view the developing countries are much more numerous than the developed ones; the multitudes of human beings who lack the goods and services offered by development are much more numerous than those who possess them.

9.5 We are therefore faced with a serious problem of unequal distribution of the means of subsistence originally meant for everybody, and thus also an unequal distribution of the benefits deriving from them. And this happens not through the fault of the needy people and even less through a sort of inevitability dependent on natural conditions or circumstances as a whole.

9.6 The encyclical of Paul VI, in declaring that the social question has

[398]

acquired worldwide dimensions, first of all points out a moral fact, one which has its foundation in an objective analysis of reality. In the words of the encyclical itself, 'each one must be conscious' of this fact[24] precisely because it directly concerns the conscience, which is the source of moral decisions.

9.7 In this framework, the originality of the encyclical consists not so much in the affirmation, historical in character, of the universality of the social question, but rather in the moral evaluation of this reality. Therefore political leaders and citizens of rich countries considered as individuals, especially if they are Christians, have the moral obligation, according to the degree of each one's responsibility, to take into consideration in personal decisions and decisions of government this relationship of universality, this interdependence which exists between their conduct and the poverty and underdevelopment of so many millions of people. Pope Paul's encyclical translates more succinctly the moral obligation as the 'duty of solidarity';[25] and this affirmation, even though many situations have changed in the world, has the same force and validity today as when it was written.

9.8 On the other hand, without departing from the lines of this moral vision, the originality of the encyclical also consists in the basic insight that the very concept of development, if considered in the perspective of universal interdependence, changes notably. True development cannot consist in the simple accumulation of wealth and in the greater availability of goods and services if this is gained at the expense of the development of the masses and without due consideration for the social, cultural and spiritual dimensions of the human being.[26]

10. As a third point, the encyclical provides a very original contribution to the social doctrine of the church in its totality and to the very concept of development. This originality is recognizable in a phrase of the document's concluding paragraph and which can be considered as its summary as well as its historic label: 'Development is the new name for peace.'[27]

10.1 In fact, if the social question has acquired a worldwide dimension, this is because the demand for justice can only be satisfied on that level. To ignore this demand could encourage the temptation among the victims of injustice to respond with violence, as happens at the origin of many wars. Peoples excluded from the fair distribution of the goods originally destined for all could ask themselves, Why not respond with violence to those who first treat us with violence? And if the situation is examined in the light of the division of the world into ideological blocs—a division already existing in 1967—and in the light of the subsequent economic and political repercussions and dependencies, the danger is seen to be much greater.

10.2 The first consideration of the striking content of the encyclical's historic phrase may be supplemented by a second consideration to which the document itself alludes:[28] How can one justify the fact that huge sums of money, which could and should be used for increasing the development of peoples, are instead utilized for the enrichment of individuals or groups or assigned to the increase of stockpiles of weapons, both in developed countries and in the developing ones, thereby upsetting the real priorities? This is even more serious given the difficulties which often hinder the direct transfer of capital set aside for helping needy countries. If 'development is the new name for peace,' war and military preparations are the major enemy of the integral development of peoples.

10.3 In the light of this expression of Pope Paul VI, we are thus invited to re-examine the concept of development. This of course is not limited to merely satisfying material necessities through an increase of goods while ignoring the sufferings of the many and making the selfishness of individuals and nations the principal motivation. As the Letter of St. James pointedly reminds us: 'What causes wars, and what causes fighting among you? Is it not your passions that are at war in your members? You desire and do not have' (Jas. 4:1-2).

10.4 On the contrary, in a different world, ruled by concern for the common good of all humanity or by concern for the 'spiritual and human development of all' instead of by the quest for individual profit, peace would be possible as the result of a 'more perfect justice among people.'[29]

10.5 Also this new element of the encyclical has a permanent and contemporary value, in view of the modern attitude which is so sensitive to the close link between respect for justice and the establishment of real peace.

III. Survey of the Contemporary World

11. In its own time the fundamental teaching of the encyclical *Populorum Progressio* received great acclaim for its novel character. The social context in which we live today cannot be said to be completely identical to that of 20 years ago. For this reason, I now wish to conduct a brief review of some of the characteristics of today's world in order to develop the teaching of Paul VI's encyclical, once again from the point of view of the 'development of peoples.'

12. The first fact to note is that the hopes for development, at that time so lively, today appear very far from being realized.

12.1 In this regard, the encyclical had no illusions. Its language, grave and at times dramatic, limited itself to stressing the seriousness of the situation and to bringing before the conscience of all the urgent obligation of contributing to its solution. In those years there was a certain widespread optimism about the possibility of overcoming, without excessive efforts, the economic backwardness of the poorer peoples, of providing them with infrastructures and assisting them in the process of industrialization.

12.2 In that historical context, over and above the efforts of each country, the United Nations promoted consecutively two decades of development.[30] In fact, some measures, bilateral and multilateral, were taken with the aim of helping many nations, some of which had already been independent for some time and others—the majority—being states just born from the process of decolonization. For her part, the church felt the duty to deepen her understanding of the problems posed by the new situation in the hope of suporting these efforts with her religious and human inspiration in order to give them a 'soul' and an effective impulse.

13. It cannot be said that these various religious, human, economic and technical initiatives have been in vain, for they have succeeded in achieving certain results. But in general, taking into account the various factors, one

cannot deny that the present situation of the world, from the point of view of development, offers a rather negative impression.

13.1 For this reason, I wish to call attention to a number of general indicators, without excluding other specific ones. Without going into an analysis of figures and statistics, it is sufficient to face squarely the reality of an innumerable multitude of people—children, adults and the elderly—in other words, real and unique human persons who are suffering under the intolerable burden of poverty. There are many millions who are deprived of hope due to the fact that in many parts of the world their situation has noticeably worsened. Before these tragedies of total indigence and need in which so many of our brothers and sisters are living, it is the Lord Jesus himself who comes to question us (cf. Mt. 25:31-46).

14. The first negative observation to make is the persistence and often the widening of the gap between the areas of the so-called developed North and the developing South. This geographical terminology is only indicative, since one cannot ignore the fact that the frontiers of wealth and poverty intersect within the societies themselves, whether developed or developing. In fact, just as social inequalities down to the level of poverty exist in rich countries, so in parallel fashion in the less developed countries one often sees manifestations of selfishness and a flaunting of wealth which is as disconcerting as it is scandalous.

14.1 The abundance of goods and services available in some parts of the world, particularly in the developed North, is matched in the South by an unacceptable delay, and it is precisely in this geopolitical area that the major part of the human race lives.

14.2 Looking at all the various sectors—the production and distribution of foodstuffs, hygiene, health and housing, availability of drinking water, working conditions (especially for women), life expectancy and other economic and social indicators—the general picture is a disappointing one, both considered in itself and in relation to the corresponding data of the more developed countries. The word *gap* returns spontaneously to mind.

14.3 Perhaps this is not the appropriate word for indicating the true reality, since it could give the impression of a stationary phenomenon. This is not the case. The pace of progress in the developed and developing countries in recent years has differed, and this serves to widen the distances. Thus the developing countries, especially the poorest of them, find themselves in a situation of very serious delay.

14.4 We must also add the differences of culture and value systems between the various population groups, differences which do not always match the degree of economic development, but which help to create distances. These are elements and aspects which render the social question much more complex precisely because this question has assumed a universal dimension.

14.5 As we observe the various parts of the world separated by this widening gap and note that each of these parts seems to follow its own path with its own achievements, we can understand the current usage which speaks of different worlds within our one world: the First World, the Second World, the Third World and at times the Fourth World.[31] Such expressions, which obviously do not claim to classify exhaustively all countries, are significant: They are a sign of a widespread sense that the unity of the world, that is, the unity of the human race, is seriously compromised. Such phraseology, beyond its more or less objective value, undoubtedly conceals a moral content before which the church, which is a 'sacrament or sign and instrument...of the unity of the whole human race,'[32] cannot remain indifferent.

15. However, the picture just given would be incomplete if one failed to add to the "economic and social indexes" of underdevelopment other indexes which are equally negative and indeed even more disturbing, beginning with the cultural level. These are illiteracy, the difficulty or impossibility of obtaining higher education, the inability to share in the building of one's own nation, the various forms of exploitation and of economic, social, political and even religious oppression of the individual and his or her rights, discrimination of every type, especially the exceptionally odious form based on difference of race. If some of these scourges are noted with regret in areas of the more developed North, they are undoubtedly more frequent, more lasting and more difficult to root out in the developing and less-advanced countries.

15.1 It should be noted that in today's world, among other rights, the right of economic initiative is often suppressed. Yet it is a right which is important not only for the individual, but also for the common good. Experience shows us that the denial of this right or its limitation in the name of an alleged 'equality' of everyone in society diminishes or in practice absolutely destroys the spirit of initiative, that is to say, the creative subjectivity of the citizen. As a consequence, there arises not so much a true equality as a 'leveling down'. In the place of creative initiative there appears passivity, dependence and submission to the bureaucratic apparatus which, as the only 'ordering' and 'decision-making' body—if not also the 'owner'—of the entire totality of goods and the means of production, puts everyone in a position of almost absolute dependence, which is similar to the traditional dependence of the worker-proletarian in capitalism. This provokes a sense of frustration or desperation and predisposes people to opt out of national life, impelling many to emigrate and also favouring a form of 'psychological' emigration.

15.2 Such a situation has its consequences also from the point of view of the 'rights of individual nations.' In fact, it often happens that a nation is deprived of its subjectivity, that is to say, the 'sovereignty' which is its right, in its economic, political-social and in a certain way cultural significance, since in a national community all these dimensions of life are bound together.

15.3 It must also be restated that no social group, for example a political party, has the right to usurp the role of sole leader, since this brings about the destruction of the true subjectivity of society and of the individual citizens as happens in every form of totalitarianism. In this situation the individual and people become 'objects,' in spite of all declarations to the contrary and verbal assurances.

15.4 We should add here that in today's world there are many other forms of poverty. For are there not certain privations or deprivations which deserve this name? The denial or the limitation of human rights—as for example the right to religious freedom, the right to share in the building of society, the freedom to organize and to form unions or to take initiatives in economic matters—do these not impoverish the human person as much as, if not more than, the deprivation of material goods? And is development which does not take into account the full affirmation of these rights really development on the human level?

15.5 In brief, modern underdevelopment is not only economic, but also cultural, political and simply human as was indicated 20 years ago by the encyclical *Populorum Progressio*. Hence at this point we have to ask ourselves if the sad reality of today might not be, at least in part, the result of a too narrow idea of development, that is, a mainly economic one.

16. It should be noted that in spite of the praiseworthy efforts made in the last two decades by the more developed or developing nations and the international organizations to find a way out of the situation or at least to remedy some of its symptoms, the conditions have become notably worse.

16.1 Responsibility for this deterioration is due to various causes. Notable among them are undoubtedly grave instances of omissions on the part of the developing nations themselves and especially on the part of those holding economic and political power. Nor can we pretend not to see the responsibility of the developed nations, which have not always, at least in due measure, felt the duty to help countries separated from the affluent world to which they themselves belong.

16.2 Moreover, one must denounce the existence of economic, financial and social mechanisms which, although they are manipulated by people, often function almost automatically, thus accentuating the situation of wealth for some and poverty for the rest. These mechanisms, which are manoeuvred directly or indirectly by the more developed countries, by their functioning favour the interests of the people manipulating them. But in the end they suffocate or condition the economies of the less-developed countries. Later on these mechanisms will have to be subjected to a careful analysis under the ethical-moral aspect.

16.3 *Populorum Progressio* already foresaw the possibility that under such systems the wealth of the rich would increase and the poverty of the poor would remain.[33] A proof of this forecast has been the appearance of the so-called Fourth World.

17. However much society worldwide shows signs of fragmentation, expressed in the conventional names First, Second, Third and even Fourth World, their interdependence remains close. When this interdependence is separated from its ethical requirements, it has disastrous consequences for the weakest. Indeed, as a result of a sort of internal dynamic and under the impulse of mechanisms which can only be called perverse, this interdependence triggers negative effects even in the rich countries. It is precisely within these countries that one encounters, though on a lesser scale, the more specific manifestations of underdevelopment. Thus it should be obvious that development either becomes shared in common by every part of the world or it undergoes a process of regression even in zones marked by constant progress. This tells us a great deal about the nature of authentic development: Either all the nations of the world participate or it will not be true development.

17.1 Among the specific signs of underdevelopment which increasingly affect developed countries also, there are two in particular that reveal a tragic situation. The first is the housing crisis. During this International Year of the Homeless proclaimed by the United Nations, attention is focused on the millions of human beings lacking adequate housing or with no housing at all, in order to awaken everyone's conscience and to find a solution to this serious problem with its negative consequences for the individual, the family and society.[34]

17.2 The lack of housing is being experienced universally and is due in large measure to the growing phenomenon of urbanization.[35] Even the most highly developed peoples present the sad spectacle of individuals and families literally struggling to survive without a roof over their heads or with a roof so inadequate as to constitute no roof at all.

17.3 The lack of housing, an extremely serious problem in itself, should be seen as a sign and summing up of a whole series of shortcomings, economic, social, cultural or simply human in nature. Given the extent of the problem, we should need little convincing of how far we are from an authentic development of peoples.

18. Another indicator common to the vast majority of nations is the phenomenon of unemployment and underemployment.

18.1 Everyone recognizes the reality and growing seriousness of this problem in the industrialized countries.[36] While it is alarming in the developing countries, with their high rate of population growth and their large numbers of young people, in the countries of high economic development the sources of work seem to be shrinking, and thus the opportunities for employment are decreasing rather than increasing.

18.2 This phenomenon too, with its series of negative consequences for individuals and for society, ranging from humiliation to the loss of that self-respect which every man and woman should have, prompts us to question seriously the type of development which has been followed over the past 20 years. Here the words of the encyclical *Laborem Exercens* are extremely appropriate: 'it must be stressed that the constitutive element in this progress and also the most adequate way to verify it in a spirit of justice and peace, which the church proclaims and for which she does not cease to pray...is the continual reappraisal of man's work, both in the aspect of its objective finality and in the aspect of the dignity of the subject of all work, that is to say, man.' On the other hand 'we cannot fail to be struck by a disconcerting fact of immense proportions: the fact that...there are huge numbers of people who are unemployed...a fact that without any doubt demonstrates that both within the individual political communities and in their relationships on the continental and world level there is something wrong with the organization of work and employment, precisely at the most critical and socially most important points.'[37]

18.3 This second phenomenon, like the previous one, because it is universal in character and tends to proliferate, is a very telling negative sign of the state and the quality of the development of peoples which we see today.

19. A third phenomenon, likewise characteristic of the most recent period even though it is not met with everywhere, is without doubt equally indicative of the interdependence between developed and less-developed

countries. It is the question of the international debt, concerning which the Pontifical Justice and Peace Commission has issued a document.[38]

19.2 At this point one cannot ignore the close connection between a problem of this kind—the growing seriousness of which was already foreseen in *Populorum Progressio*[39]—and the question of the development of peoples.

19.3 The reason which prompted the developing peoples to accept the offer of abundantly available capital was the hope of being able to invest it in development projects. Thus the availability of capital and the fact of accepting it as a loan can be considered a contribution to development, something desirable and legitimate in itself even though perhaps imprudent and occasionally hasty.

19.4 Circumstances having changed both within the debtor nations and in the international financial market, the instrument chosen to make a contribution to development has turned into a counterproductive mechanism. This is because the debtor nations, in order to service their debt, find themselves obliged to export the capital needed for improving or at least maintaining their standard of living. It is also because, for the same reason, they are unable to obtain new and equally essential financing.

19.5 Through this mechanism the means intended for the development of peoples has turned into a brake upon development instead, and indeed in some cases has even aggravated underdevelopment.

19.6 As the recent document of the Pontifical Justice and Peace Commission states,[40] these observations should make us reflect on the ethical character of the interdependence of peoples. And along similar lines, they should make us reflect on the requirements and conditions, equally inspired by ethical principles, for cooperation in development.

20. If at this point we examine the reasons for this serious delay in the process of development, a delay which has occurred contrary to the indications of the encyclical *Populorum Progressio*, which had raised such great hopes, our attention is especially drawn to the political causes of today's situation.

20.1 Faced with a combination of factors which are undoubtedly complex, we cannot hope to achieve a comprehensive analysis here. However, we cannot ignore a striking fact about the political picture since World War II, a fact which has considerable impact on the forward movement of the development of peoples.

20.2 I am referring to the existence of two opposing blocs, commonly known as the East and the West. The reason for this description is not purely political but is also, as the expression goes, geopolitical. Each of the two blocs tends to assimilate or gather around it other countries or groups of countries, to different degrees of adherence or participation.

20.3 The opposition is first of all political, inasmuch as each bloc identifies itself with a system of organizing society and exercising power which presents itself as an alternative to the other. The political opposition, in turn, takes its origin from a deeper opposition, which is ideological in nature.

20.4 In the West there exists a system which is historically inspired by the principles of the liberal capitalism which developed with industrialization during the last century. In the East there exists a system inspired by the Marxist collectivism which spring from an interpretation of the condition of the proletarian classes made in the light of a particular reading of history.

Each of the two ideologies, on the basis of two very different visions of man and of his freedom and social role, has proposed and still promotes on the economic level antithetical forms of the organization of labour and of the structures of ownership, especially with regard to the so-called means of production.

20.5 It was inevitable that by developing antagonistic systems and centers of power, each with its own forms of propaganda and indoctrination, the ideological opposition should evolve into a growing military opposition and give rise to two blocs of armed forces, each suspicious and fearful of the other's domination.

20.6 International relations, in turn, could not fail to feel the effects of this 'logic of blocs' and of the respective 'spheres of influence.' The tension between the two blocs which began at the end of World War II has dominated the whole of the subsequent 40 years. Sometimes it has taken the form of 'cold war', Sometimes of 'wars by proxy' through the manipulation of local conflicts and sometimes it has kept people's minds in suspense and anguish by the threat of an open and total war.

20.7 Although at the present time this danger seems to have receded yet without completely disappearing, and even though an initial agreement has been reached on the destruction of one type of nuclear weapon, the existence and opposition of the blocs continue to be a real and worrying fact which still colours the world picture.

21. This happens with particularly negative effects in the international relations which concern the developing countries. For as we know the tension between East and West is not in itself an opposition between two different levels of development but rather between two concepts of the development of individuals and peoples, both concepts being imperfect and in need of radical correction. This opposition is transferred to the developing countries themselves and thus helps to widen the gap already existing on the economic level between North and South and which results from the distance between the two worlds: the more-developed one and the less-developed one.

21.1 This is one of the reasons why the church's social doctrine adopts a critical attitude toward both liberal capitalism and Marxist collectivism, for from the point of view of development the question naturally arises: In what way and to what extent are these two systems capable of changes and updating such as to favour or promote a true and integral development of individuals and peoples in modern society? In fact, these changes and updatings are urgent and essential for the cause of a development common to all.

21.2 Countries which have recently achieved independence, and which are trying to establish a cultural and political identity of their own and need effective and impartial aid from all the richer and more developed countries, find themselves involved in and sometimes overwhelmed by ideological conflicts which inevitably create internal divisions, to the extent in some cases of provoking full civil war. This is also because investments and aid for development are often diverted from their proper purpose and used to sustain conflicts, apart from and in opposition to the interests of the countries which ought to benefit from them. Many of these countries are becoming more and more aware of the danger of falling victim to a form of neocolonialism and are trying to escape from it. It is this awareness which, in spite of difficulties, uncertainties and at time contradictions, gave rise to the international movement of non-aligned nations, which, in its positive aspect, would like to affirm in an effective way the right of every people to its own identity, independence and security as well as the right to share, on a basis of equality and solidarity, in the goods intended for all.

22. In the light of these considerations, we easily arrive at a clearer picture of the last 20 years and a better understanding of the conflicts in the Northern Hemisphere, namely between East and West, as an important cause of the retardation or stagnation of the South.

22.1 The developing countries, instead of becoming autonomous nations concerned with their own progress toward a just sharing in the goods and services meant for all, become parts of a machine, cogs on a gigantic wheel. This is often true also in the field of social communications, which, being run by centers mostly in the Northern Hemisphere, do not always give due consideration to the priorities and problems of such countries or respect their cultural makeup. They frequently impose a distorted vision of life and of man, and thus fail to respond to the demands of true development.

22.2 Each of the two blocs harbours in its own way a tendency toward imperialism, as it is usually called, or toward forms of neo-colonialism: an easy temptation to which they frequently succumb as history, including recent history, teaches.

22.3 It is this abnormal situation, the result of a war and of an unacceptably exaggerated concern for security, which deadens the impulse toward united cooperation by all for the common good of the human race, to the detriment especially of peaceful peoples who are impeded from their rightful access to the goods meant for all.

22.4 Seen in this way, the present division of the world is a direct obstacle to the real transformation of the conditions of underdevelopment in the developing and less advanced countries. However, peoples do not always resign themselves to their fate. Furthermore, the very needs of an economy stifled by military expenditure and by bureaucracy and intrinsic inefficiency now seem to favour processes which might mitigate the existing opposition and make it easier to begin a fruitful dialogue and genuine collaboration for peace.

23. The statement in the encyclical *Populorum Progressio* that the resources and investments devoted to arms production ought to be used to alleviate the misery of impoverished peoples[41] makes more urgent the appeal to overcome the opposition between the two blocs.

23.1 Today the reality is that these resources are used to enable each of the two blocs to overtake the other and thus guarantee its own security. Nations which historically, economically and politically have the possibility of playing a leadership role are prevented by this fundamentally flawed distortion from adequately fulfilling their duty of solidarity for the benefit of peoples which aspire to full development.

23.2 It is timely to mention—and it is no exaggeration—that a leadership role among nations can only be justified by the possibility and willingness to contribute widely and generously to the common good.

23.3 If a nation were to succumb more or less deliberately to the temptation to close in upon itself and failed to meet the responsibilities following from its superior position in the community of nations, it would fall seriously short of its clear ethical duty. This is readily apparent in the circumstances of history, where believers discern the dispositions of divine providence, ready to make use of the nations for the realization of its plans, so as to render 'vain the designs of the peoples' (cf. Ps. 33:10).

23.4 When the West gives the impression of abandoning itself to forms of growing and selfish isolation and the East in its turn seems to ignore for questionable reasons its duty to cooperate in the task of alleviating human misery, then we are up against not only a betrayal of humanity's legitimate expectations—a betrayal that is a harbinger of unforeseeable consequences— but also a real desertion of a moral obligation.

24. If arms production is a serious disorder in the present world with regard to true human needs and the employment of the means capable of satisfying those needs, the arms trade is equally to blame.

24.1 Indeed, with reference to the latter it must be added that the moral judgment is even more severe. As we all know, this is a trade without frontiers, capable of crossing even the barriers of the blocs. It knows how to overcome the division between East and West, and above all the one between North and South, to the point—and this is more serious—of pushing its way into the different sections which make up the Southern Hemisphere. We are thus confronted with a strange phenomenon: While economic aid and development plans meet with the obstacle of insuperable ideological barriers and with tariff and trade barriers, arms of whatever origin circulate with almost total freedom all over the world. And as the recent document of the Pontifical Justice and Peace Commission on the international debt points out,[42] everyone knows that in certain cases the capital lent by the developed world has been used in the underdeveloped world to buy weapons.

24.2 If to all this we add the tremendous and universally acknowledged danger represented by atomic weapons stockpiled on an incredible scale, the logical conclusion seems to be this: In today's world, including the world of economics, the prevailing picture is one destined to lead us more quickly toward death rather than one of concern for true development which would lead all toward a 'more human' life, as envisaged by the encyclical *Populorum Progressio*.[43]

24.3 The consequences of this state of affairs are to be seen in the festering of a wound which typifies and reveals the imbalances and conflicts of the modern world: the millions of refugees whom war, natural calamities, persecution and discrimination of every kind have deprived of home, employment, family and homeland. The tragedy of these multitudes is reflected in the hopeless faces of men, women and children who can no longer find a home in a divided and inhospitable world.

24.4 Nor may we close our eyes to another painful wound in today's world: the phenomenon of terrorism, understood as the intention to kill people and destroy property indiscriminately and to create a climate of terror and insecurity, often including the taking of hostages. Even when some ideology or the desire to create a better society is adduced as the motivation for this inhuman behaviour, acts of terrorism are never justifiable. Even less so when, as happens today, such decisions and such actions, which at times lead to real massacres and to the abduction of innocent people who have nothing to do with the conflicts, claim to have a propaganda purpose for furthering a cause. It is still worse when they are an end in themselves, so that murder is committed merely for the sake of killing. In the face of such horror and suffering, the words I spoke some years ago are still true, and I wish to repeat them again: 'What Christianity forbids is to seek solutions...by the way of hatred, by the murdering of defenseless people, by the methods of terrorism.'[44]

25. At this point something must be said about the demographic problem and the way it is spoken of today, following what Paul VI said in his encyclical[45] and what I myself stated at length in the apostolic exhortation *Familiaris Consortio*.[46]

25.1 One cannot deny the existence, especially in the Southern Hemisphere, of a demographic problem which creates difficulties for development. One must immediately add that in the Northern Hemisphere the nature of this problem is reversed: Here the cause for concern is the drop in the birthrate, with repercussions on the aging of the population, unable even to renew itself biologically. In itself, this is a phenomenon capable of hindering development. Just as it is incorrect to say that such difficulties stem solely from demographic growth, neither is it proved that all demographic growth is incompatible with orderly development.

25.2 On the other hand, it is very alarming to see governments in many countries launching systematic campaigns against birth, contrary not only to the cultural and religious identity of the countries themselves but also contrary to the nature of true development. It often happens that these campaigns are the result of pressure and financing coming from abroad, and in some cases they are made a condition for the granting of financial and economic aid and assistance. In any event, there is an absolute lack of respect for the freedom of choice of the parties involved, men and women often subjected to intolerable pressures, including economic ones, in order to force them to submit to this new form of oppression. It is the poorest populations which suffer such mistreatment, and this sometimes leads to a tendency toward a form of racism or the promotion of certain equally racist forms of eugenics.

25.3 This fact too, which deserves the most forceful condemnation, is a sign of an erroneous and perverse idea of true human development.

26. This mainly negative overview of the actual situation of development in the contemporary world would be incomplete without a mention of the coexistence of positive aspects.

26.1 The first positive note is the full awareness among large numbers of men and women of their own dignity and of that of every human being. This awareness is expressed, for example, in the more lively concern that human rights should be respected, and in the more vigorous rejection of their violation. One sign of this is the number of recently established private associations, some worldwide in membership, almost all of them devoted to monitoring with great care and commendable objectivity what is happening internationally in this sensitive field.

26.2 At this level one must acknowledge the influence exercised by the Universal Declaration of Human Rights promulgated some 40 years ago by the United Nations. Its very existence and gradual acceptance by the international community are signs of a growing awareness. The same is to be said, still in the field of human rights, of other juridical instruments issued by the United Nations or other international organizations.[47]

26.3 The awareness under discussion applies not only to individuals, but also to nations and peoples, which, as entities having a specific cultural identity, are particularly sensitive to the preservation, free exercise and promotion of their precious heritage.

26.4 At the same time, in a world divided and beset by every type of conflict, the conviction is growing of a radical interdependence and consequently of the need for a solidarity which will take up interdependence and transfer it to the moral plane. Today, perhaps more than in the past, people are realizing that they are linked together by a common destiny which is to be constructed together if catastrophe for all is to be avoided. From the depth of anguish, fear and escapist phenomena like drugs, typical of the contemporary world, the idea is slowly emerging that the good to which we are all called and the happiness to which we aspire cannot be obtained without an effort and commitment on the part of all, nobody excluded, and the consequent renouncing of personal selfishness.

26.5 Also to be mentioned here, as a sign of respect for life—despite all the temptations to destroy it by abortion and euthanasia—is a concomitant concern for peace, together with an awareness that peace is indivisible. It is either for all or for none. It demands an ever greater degree of rigorous respect for justice and consequently a fair distribution of the results of true development.[48]

26.6 Among today's positive signs we must also mention a greater realization of the limits of available resources and of the need to respect the integrity and the cycles of nature and to take them into account when planning for development, rather than sacrificing them to certain demagogic ideas about the latter. Today this is called ecological concern.

26.7 It is also right to acknowledge the generous commitment of statesmen, politicians, economists, trade unionists, people of science and international officials—many of them inspired by religious faith—who at no small personal sacrifice try to resolve the world's ills and who give of themselves in every way so as to ensure that an ever increasing number of people may enjoy the benefits of peace and a quality of life worthy of the name.

26.8 The great international organizations and a number of the regional organizations contribute to this in no small measure. Their united efforts make possible more effective action.

26.9 It is also through these contributions that some Third World countries, despite the burden of many negative factors, have succeeded in reaching a certain self-sufficiency in food or a degree of industrialization which makes it possible to survive with dignity and to guarantee sources of employment for the active population.

26.10 Thus, all is not negative in the contemporary world nor could it be, for the heavenly Father's providence lovingly watches over even our daily cares (cf. Mt. 6:25-32; 10:23-31; Lk. 12:6-7; 22-30). Indeed, the positive values which we have mentioned testify to a new moral concern, particularly with respect to the great human problems such as development and peace.

26.11 This fact prompts me to turn my thoughts to the true nature of the development of peoples, along the lines of the encyclical which we are commemorating and as a mark of respect for its teaching.

IV. Authentic Human Development

27. The examination which the encyclical invites us to make of the contemporary world leads us to note in the first place that development is not a straightforward process, as it were automatic and in itself limitless, as though, given certain conditions, the human race were able to progress rapidly toward an undefined perfection of some kind.[49]

27.1 Such an idea—linked to a notion of 'progress' with philosophical connotations deriving from the Enlightenment rather than to the notion of 'development'[50] which is used in a specifically economic and social sense— now seems to be seriously called into doubt particularly since the tragic experience of the two world wars, the planned and partly achieved destruction of whole peoples and the looming atomic peril. A naive mechanistic optimism has been replaced by a well-founded anxiety for the fate of humanity.

28. At the same time, however, the 'economic' concept itself, linked to the word *development*, has entered into crisis. In fact there is a better understanding today that the mere accumulation of goods and services, even for the benefit of the majority, is not enough for the realization of human happiness. Nor, in consequence, does the availability of the many real benefits provided in recent times by science and technology, including the computer sciences, bring freedom from every form of slavery. On the contrary, the experience of recent years shows that unless all the considerable body of resources and potential at man's disposal is guided by a moral understanding and by an orientation toward the true good of the human race, it easily turns against man to oppress him.

28.1 A disconcerting conclusion about the most recent period should serve to enlighten us: Side-by-side with the miseries of underdevelopment, themselves unacceptable, we find ourselves up against a form of superdevelopment, equally inadmissible, because like the former it is contrary to what is good and to true happiness. This superdevelopment, which consists in an excessive availability of every kind of material goods for the benefit of certain social groups, easily makes people slaves of 'possession' and of immediate gratification, with no other horizon than the multiplication or continual replacement of the things already owned with others still better. This is the so-called civilization of 'consumption' or 'consumerism,' which involves so much 'throwing away' and 'waste'. An object already owned but now superseded by something better is discarded, with no thought of its possible lasting value in itself nor of some other human being who is poorer.

28.2 All of us experience first hand the sad effects of this blind submission to pure consumerism: in the first place a crass materialism, and at the same time a radical dissatisfaction because one quickly learns—unless one is shielded from the flood of publicity and ceaseless and tempting offers of products—that the more one possesses the more one wants, while deeper aspirations remain unsatisfied and perhaps even stifled.

28.3 The encyclical of Pope Paul VI pointed out the difference, so often emphasized today, between 'having' and 'being,'[51] which had been expressed earlier in precise words by the Second Vatican Council.[52] To 'have' objects and goods does not in itself perfect the human subject unless it contributes to the maturing and enrichment of that subject's 'being,' that is to say, unless it contributes to the realization of the human vocation as such.

28.4 Of course, the difference between 'being' and 'having', the danger inherent in a mere multiplication or replacement of things possessed compared to the value of 'being', need not turn into a contradiction. One of the greatest injustices in the contemporary world consists precisely in this; that the ones who possess much are relatively few and those who possess almost nothing are many. It is the injustice of the poor distribution of the goods and services originally intended for all.

28.5 This then is the picture: There are some people—the few who possess much—who do not really succeed in 'being' because, through a reversal of the hierarchy of values, they are hindered by the cult of having; and there are others—the many who have little or nothing—who do not succeed in realizing their basic human vocation because they are deprived of essential goods.

28.6 The evil does not consist in 'having' as such, but in possessing without regard for the quality and the ordered hierarchy of the goods one has. Quality and hierarchy arise from the subordination of goods and their availability to man's 'being' and his true vocation.

28.7 This shows that although development has a necessary economic dimension since it must supply the greatest possible number of the world's inhabitants with an availability of goods essential for them 'to be', it is not limited to that dimension. If it is limited to this then it turns against those whom it is meant to benefit.

28.8 The characteristics of full development, one which is 'more human' and able to sustain itself at the level of the true vocation of men and women without denying economic requirements, were described by Paul VI.[53]

29. Development, which is not only economic, must be measured and oriented according to the reality and vocation of man seen in his totality, namely, according to his interior dimension. There is no doubt that he needs created goods and the products of industry, which is constantly being enriched by scientific and technological progress. And the ever greater availability of material goods not only meets needs but also opens new horizons. The danger of the misuse of material goods and the appearance of artificial needs should in no way hinder the regard we have for the new goods and resources placed at our disposal and the use we make of them. On the contrary, we must see them as a gift from God and as a response to the human vocation, which is fully realized in Christ.

29.1 However, in trying to achieve true development we must never lose sight of that dimension which is in the specific nature of man, who has been created by God in his image and likeness (cf. Gn. 1:26). It is a bodily and spiritual nature, symbolized in the second creation account by the two elements: the earth, from which God forms man's body, and the breath of life which he breathes into man's nostrils (cf. Gn. 2:7).

29.2 Thus man comes to have a certain affinity with other creatures: He is called to use them and to be involved with them. As the Genesis account says (cf. Gn. 2:15), he is placed in the garden with the duty of cultivating and watching over it, being superior to the other creatures placed by God under his dominion (cf. Gn. 1:25-26). But at the same time man must remain subject to the will of God, who imposes limits upon his use and dominion over things (cf. Gn. 2:16-17), just as he promises him immortality (cf. Gn. 2:9; Wis. 2:23). Thus man, being the image of God, has a true affinity with him too.

29.3 On the basis of this teaching, development cannot consist only in the use, dominion over and indiscriminate possession of created things and the products of human industry, but rather in subordinating the possession, dominion and use to man's divine likeness and to his vocation to immortality. This is the transcendent reality of the human being, a reality which is seen to be shared from the beginning by a couple, a man and a woman (cf. Gn. 1:27), and is therefore fundamentally social.

30. According to Sacred Scripture therefore, the notion of development is not only 'lay' or 'profane,' but is also seen to be, while having a socio-economic dimension of its own, the modern expression of an essential dimension of man's vocation.

30.1 The fact is that man was not created, so to speak, immobile and static. The first portrayal of him, as given in the Bible, certainly presents him as a creature and image, defined in his deepest reality by the origin and affinity that constitute him. But all this plants within the human being—man and woman—the seed and the requirement of a special task to be accomplished by each individually and by them as a couple. The task is 'to have dominion' over the other created beings, 'to cultivate the garden.' This is to be accomplished within the framework of obedience to the divine law and therefore with respect for the image received, the image which is the clear foundation of the power of dominion recognized as belonging to man as the means to his perfection (cf. Gn. 1:26-30; 2:15-16; Wis. 9:2-3).

30.2 When man disobeys God and refuses to submit to his rule, nature rebels against him and no longer recognizes him as its 'master,' for he has tarnished the divine image in himself. The claim to ownership and use of created things remains still valid, but after sin its exercise becomes difficult and full of suffering (cf. Gn. 3:17-26).

30.3 In fact, the following chapter of Genesis shows us that the descendants of Cain build 'a city', engage in sheep farming, practice the arts (music) and technical skills (metallurgy); while at the same time people began to 'call upon the name of the Lord' (cf. Gn. 4:17-26).

30.4 The story of the human race described by Sacred Scripture is, even after the fall into sin, a story of constant achievements which, although always called into question and threatened by sin, are nonetheless repeated, increased and extended in response to the divine vocation given from the beginning to man and to woman (cf. Gn. 1:26-28) and inscribed in the image which they received.

30.5 It is logical to conclude, at least on the part of those who believe in the word of God, that today's 'development' is to be seen as a comment in the story which began at creation, a story which is constantly endangered by reason of infidelity to the Creator's will and especially by the temptation to idolatry. But this 'development' fundamentally corresponds to the first premises. Anyone wishing to renounce the difficult yet noble task of improving the lot of man in his totality, and of all people, with the excuse that the struggle is difficult and that constant effort is required, or simply because of the experience of defeat and the need to begin again, that person would be betraying the will of God, the creator. In this regard, in the encyclical *Laborem Exercens* I referred to man's vocation to work in order to emphasize the idea that it is always man who is the protagonist of development.[54]

30.6 Indeed, the Lord Jesus himself, in the parable of the talents, emphasizes the severe treatment given to the man who dared to hide the gift received: 'You wicked and slothful servant! You knew that I reap where I have not sowed and gather where I have not winnowed?...So take the talent from him, and give it to him who has the 10 talents' (Mt. 25:26-28). It falls to us, who receive the gifts of God in order to make them fruitful, to 'sow' and 'reap.' If we do not, even what we have will be taken away from us.

30.7 A deeper study of these harsh words will make us commit ourselves more resolutely to the duty, which is urgent for everyone today, to work tobether for the full development of others: 'development of the whole human being and of all people.'[55]

31. Faith in Christ, the redeemer, while it illuminates from within the nature of development, also guides us in the task of collaboration. In the Letter of St. Paul to the Colossians, we read that Christ is 'the firstborn of all creation' and that 'all things were created through him' and for him (1:15-16). In fact, 'all things hold together in him,' since 'in him all the fullness of God was pleased to dwell, and through him to reconcile to himself all things' (v.20).

31.1 A part of this divine plan, which begins from eternity in Christ, the perfect 'image' of the Father, and which culminates in him 'the firstborn from the dead' (v.18), is our own history, marked by our personal and collective effort to raise up the human condition and to overcome the obstacles which are continually arising along our way. It thus prepares us to share in the fullness which 'dwells in the Lord' and which he communicates 'to his body, which is the church' (v. 18; cf. Eph. 1:22-23). At the same time sin, which is always attempting to trap us and which jeopardizes our human achievements, is conquered and redeemed by the 'reconciliation' accomplished by Christ (cf. Col. 1:20).

31.2 Here the perspectives widen. The dream of 'unlimited progress' reappears, radically transformed by the new outlook created by Christian faith, assuring us that progress is possible only because God the Father has decided from the beginning to make man a sharer of his glory in Jesus Christ risen from the dead, in whom 'we have redemption through his blood...the forgiveness of our trespasses' (Eph. 1:7). In him God wished to conquer sin and make it serve our greater good,[56] which infinitely surpasses what progress could achieve.

31.3 We can say therefore—as we struggle amid the obscurities and deficiencies of underdevelopment and superdevelopment—that one day this corruptible body will put on incoruptibility, this mortal body immortality (cf. I Cor. 15:54), when the Lord 'delivers the kingdom to God the Father' (v. 24) and all the works and actions that are worthy of man will be redeemed.

31.4 Furthermore, the concept of faith makes quite clear the reasons which impel the church to concern herself wth the problems of development, to consider them a duty of her pastoral ministry and to urge all to think about the nature and characteristics of authentic human development. Through her commitment she desires, on the one hand, to place herself at the service of the divine plan which is meant to order all things to the fullness which dwells in Christ (cf. Col. 1:19) and which he communicated to his body; and on the other hand she desires to respond to her fundamental vocation of being a 'sacrament,' that is to say, 'a sign and instrument of intimate union with God and of the unity of the whole human race.'[57]

31.5 Some fathers of the church were inspired by this idea to develop in original ways a concept of the meaning of history and of human work, directed toward a goal which surpasses this meaning and which is always defined by its relationship to the work of Christ. In other words, one can find in the teaching of the fathers an optimistic vision of history and work, that is to say, of the perennial value of authentic human achievements inasmuch as they are redeemed by Christ and destined for the promised kingdom.[58]

31.6 Thus, part of the teaching and most ancient practice of the church is her conviction that she is obliged by her vocation—she herself, her ministers and each of her members—to relieve the misery of the suffering, both far and near, not only out of her 'abundance' but also out of her 'necessities.' Faced by cases of need, one cannot ignore them in favour of superfluous church ornaments and costly furnishings for divine worship; on the contrary it could be obligatory to sell these goods in order to provide food, drink, clothing and shelter for those who lack these things.[59] As has been already noted, here we are shown a 'hierarchy of values'—in the framework of the right to property—between 'having' and 'being,' especially when the 'having' of a few can be to the detriment of the 'being' of many others.

31.7 In his encyclical Pope Paul VI stands in the line of this teaching, taking his inspiration from the pastoral constitution *Gaudium et Spes*.[60] For my own part, I wish to insist once more on the seriousness and urgency of that teaching, and I ask the Lord to give all Christians the strength to put it faithfully into practice.

32. The obligation to commit oneself to the development of peoples is not just an individual duty and still less an individualistic one, as if it were possible to achieve this development through the isolated efforts of each individual. It is an imperative which obliges each and every man and woman as well as societies and nations. In particular, it obliges the Catholic Church and the other churches and ecclesial communities, with which we are completely willing to collaborate in this field. In this sense, just as we Catholics invite our Christian brethren to share in our initiatives, so too we declare that we are ready to collaborate in theirs and we welcome the invitation presented to us. In this pursuit of integral human development we can also do much with the members of other religions, as in fact is being done in various places.

32.1 Collaboration in the development of the whole person and of every human being is in fact a duty of all toward all and must be shared by the four parts of the world: East and West, North and South; or, as we say today, by the different 'worlds.' If, on the contrary, people try to achieve it in only one part or in only one world, they do so at the expense of the others; and,

[415]

precisely because the others are ignored, their own development becomes exaggerated and misdirected.

32.2 Peoples or nations too have a right to their own full development, which while including—as already said—the economic and social aspects should also include individual cultural identity and openness to the transcendent. Not even the need for development can be used as an excuse for imposing on others one's own way of life or own religious belief.

33. Nor would a type of development which did not respect and promote human rights—personal and social, economic and political, including the rights of nations and of peoples—be really worthy of man.

33.1 Today, perhaps more than in the past, the intrinsic contradiction of a development limited only to its economic element is seen more clearly. Such development easily subjects the human person and his deepest needs to the demands of economic planning and selfish profit.

32.2 The intrinsic connection between authentic development and respect for human rights once again reveals the moral character of development: the true elevation of man in conformity with the natural and historical vocation of each individual is not attained only by exploiting the abundance of goods and services or by having available perfect infrastructures.

33.3 When individuals and communities do not see a rigorous respect for the moral, cultural and spiritual requirements based on the dignity of the person and on the proper identity of each community, beginning with the family and religious societies, then all the rest—availability of goods, abundance of technical resources applied to daily life, a certain level of material well-being—will prove unsatisfying and in the end contemptible. The Lord clearly says this in the Gospel when he calls the attention of all to the true hierarchy of values: 'For what will it profit a man, if he gains the whole world and forfeits his life?' (Mt. 16:26).

33.4 True development, in keeping with the specific needs of the human being—man or woman, child, adult or old person—implies, especially for those who actively share in this process and are responsible for it, a lively awareness of the value of the rights of all and of each person. It likewise implies a lively awareness of the need to respect the right of every individual to the full use of the benefits offered by science and technology.

33.5 On the internal level of every nation, respect for all rights takes on great importance, especially: the right to life at every stage of its existence; the rights of the family as the basic social community or 'cell of society'; justice in employment relationships; the rights inherent in the life of the political community as such; the rights based on the transcendent vocation of the human being, beginning with the right of freedom to profess and practice one's own religious belief.

33.6 On the international level, that is, the level of relations between states or, in present-day usage, between the different 'worlds,' there must be complete respect for the identity of each people, with is own historical and cultural characteristics. It is likewise essential, as the encyclical *Populorum Progressio* already asked, to recognize each people's equal right 'to be seated at the table of the common banquet,'[61] instead of lying outside the door like Lazarus, while 'the dogs come and lick his sores' (cf. Lk. 16:21). Both peoples and individuals must enjoy the fundamental equality[62] which is the basis, for example, of the Charter of the United Nations: the equality which is the basis of the right of all to share in the process of full development.

33.7 In order to be genuine, development must be achieved within the framework of solidarity and freedom, without ever sacrificing either of them under whatever pretext. The moral character of development and its necessary promotion are emphasized when the most rigorous respect is given to all the demands deriving from the order of truth and good proper to the human person. Furthermore the Christian who is taught to see that man is the image of God, called to share in the truth and the good which is God himself, does not understand a commitment to development and its application which excludes regard and respect for the unique dignity of this 'image'. In other words, true development must be based on the love of God and neighbour, and must help to promote the relationships between individuals and society. This is the 'civilization of love' of which Paul VI often spoke.

34. Nor can the moral character of development exclude respect for the beings which constitute the natural world, which the ancient Greeks—alluding precisely to the order which distinguishes it—called the 'cosmos.' Such realities also demand respect, by virtue of a threefold consideration which it is useful to reflect upon carefully. The first consideration is the appropriateness of acquiring a growing awareness of the fact that one cannot use with impunity the different categories of beings, whether living or inanimate—animals, plants, the natural elements—simply as one wishes, according to one's own economic needs. On the contrary, one must take into account the nature of each being and of its mutual connection in an ordered system, which is precisely the 'cosmos.'

34.1 The second consideration is based on the realization—which is perhaps more urgent—that natural resources are limited; some are not, as it is said, renewable. Using them as if they were inexhaustible, with absolute dominion, seriously endangers their availability not only for the present generation but above all for generations to come.

34.2 The third consideration refers directly to the consequences of a certain type of development on the quality of life in the industrialized zones. We all know that the direct or indirect result of industrialization is, ever more frequently, the pollution of the environment, with serious consequences for the health of the population.

34.3 Once again it is evident that development, the planning which governs it and the way in which resources are used must include respect for moral demands. One of the latter undoubtedly imposes limits on the use of the natural world. The dominion granted to man by the Creator is not an absolute power nor can one speak of a freedom to 'use and misuse' or to dispose of things as one pleases. The limitation imposed from the beginning by the Creator himself and expressed symbolically by the prohibition not to 'eat of the fruit of the tree' (cf. Gn. 2:16-17) shows clearly enough that, when it comes to the natural world, we are subject not only to biological laws but also to moral ones, which cannot be violated with impunity.

34.4 A true concept of development cannot ignore the use of the elements of nature, the renewability of resources and the consequences of haphazard industrialization—three considerations which alert our consciences to the moral dimension of development.[63]

V. A Theological Reading Of Modern Problems

35. Precisely because of the essentially moral character of development, it is clear that the obstacles to development likewise have a moral character. If in the years since the publication of Pope Paul's encyclical there has been no development—or very little, irregular or even contradictory development—the reasons are not only economic. As has already been said, political motives also enter in. For the decisions which either accelerate or slow down the development of peoples are really political in character. In order to overcome the misguided mechanisms mentioned earlier and to replace them with new ones which will be more just and in conformity with the common good of humanity, an effective political will is needed. Unfortunately, after analyzing the situation, we have to conclude that this political will has been insufficient.

35.1 In a document of a pastoral nature such as this, an analysis limited exclusively to the economic and political causes of underdevelopment (and, *mutatis mutandis*, of so-called superdevelopment) would be incomplete. It is therefore necessary to single out the moral causes which, with respect to the behaviour of individuals considered as responsible persons, interfere in such a way as to slow down the course of development and hinder its full achievement.

35.2 Similarly, when the scientific and technical resources are available which, with the necessary concrete political decisions, ought to help lead peoples to true development, the main obstacles to development will be overcome only by means of essentially moral decisions. For believers, and especially for Christians, these decisions will take their inspiration from the principles of faith, with the help of divine grace.

36. It is important to note therefore that a world which is divided into blocs, sustained by rigid ideologies and in which instead of interdependence and solidarity different forms of imperialism hold sway, can only be a world subject to structures of sin.

36.1 The sum total of the negative factors working against a true awareness of the universal common good and the need to further it gives the impression of creating, in persons and institutions, an obstacle which is difficult to overcome.[64]

36.2 If the present situation can be attributed to difficulties of various kinds, it is not out of place to speak of 'structures of sin' which, as I stated in my apostolic exhortation *Reconciliatio et Paenitentia*, are rooted in personal sin and thus always linked to the concrete acts of individuals who introduce these structures, consolidate them and make them difficult to remove.[65] And thus they grow stronger, spread and become the source of other sins and so influence people's behavior.

36.3 'Sin' and 'structures of sin' are categories which are seldom applied to the situation of the contemporary world. However, one cannot easily gain a profound understanding of the reality that confronts us unless we give a name to the root of the evils which afflict us.

36.4 One can certainly speak of 'selfishness' and of 'shortsightedness,' of 'mistaken political calculations' and 'imprudent economic decisions.' And in each of these evaluations one hears an echo of an ethical and moral nature. Man's condition is such that a more profound analysis of individuals' actions and omissions cannot be achieved without implying, in one way or another, judgments or references of an ethical nature.

36.5 This evaluation is in itself positive, especially if it is completely consistent and if it is based on faith in God and on his law, which commands what is good and forbids evil.

36.6 In this consists the difference between socio-political analysis and formal reference to 'sin' and the 'structures of sin.' According to this latter viewpoint, there enter in the will of the Triune God, his plan for humanity, his justice and his mercy. The God who is rich in mercy, the redeemer of man, the Lord and giver of life, requires from people clear-cut attitudes which express themselves also in actions or omissions towards one's neighbour. We have here a reference to the 'second tablet' of the Ten Commandments (cf. Ex. 20:12-17; Dt. 5:16-21). Not to observe these is to offend God and hurt one's neighbour, and to introduce into the world influences and obstacles which go far beyond the actions and the brief lifespan of an individual. This also involves interference in the process of the development of peoples, the delay or slowness of which must be judged also in this light.

37. This general analysis, which is religious in nature, can be supplemented by a number of particular considerations to demonstrate that among the actions and attitudes opposed to the will of God, the good of neighbour and the 'structures' created by them, two are very typical: on the one hand, the all-consuming desire for profit, and on the other, the thirst for power, with the intention of imposing one's will upon others. In order to characterize better each of these attitudes, one can add the expression: 'at any price.' In other words, we are faced with the absolutizing of human attitudes with all its possible consequences.

37.1 Since these attitudes can exist independently of each other, they can be separated; however, in today's world both are indissolubly united, with one or the other predominating.

37.2 Obviously, not only individuals fall victim to this double attitude of sin; nations and blocs can do so too. And this favours even more the introduction of the 'structures of sin' of which I have spoken. If certain forms of modern 'imperialism' were considered in the light of these moral criteria, we would see that hidden behind certain decisions, apparently inspired only by economics or politics, are real forms of idolatry: of money, ideology, class, technology.

37.3 I have wished to introduce this type of analysis above all in order to point out the true nature of the evil which faces us with respect to the development of peoples: It is a question of a moral evil, the fruit of many sins which lead to 'structures of sin.' To diagnose the evil in this way is to identify precisely, on the level of human conduct, the path to be followed in order to overcome it.

38. This path is long and complex, and what is more it is constantly threatened because of the intrinsic frailty of human resolutions and achievements and because of the mutability of very unpredictable external circumstances. Nevertheless, one must have the courage to set out on this path and, where some steps have been taken or a part of the journey made, the courage

to go on to the end. In the context of these reflections, the decision to set out or to continue the journey involves, above all, a moral value which men and women of faith recognize as a demand of God's will, the only true foundation of an absolutely binding ethic.

38.1 One would hope that also men and women without an explicit faith would be convinced that the obstacles to integral development are not only economic but rest on more profound attitudes which human beings can make into absolute values. Thus one would hope that all those who, to some degree or other, are responsible for ensuring 'more human life' for their fellow human beings, whether or not they are inspired by a religious faith, will become fully aware of the urgent need to change the spiritual attitudes which define each individual's relationship with self, with neighbour, with even the remotest human communities and with nature itself; and all of this in view of higher values such as the common good or, to quote the felicitous expression of the encyclical *Populorum Progressio*, the full development 'of the whole individual and of all people.'[66]

38.2 For Christians, as for all who recognize the precise theological meaning of the word *sin*, a change of behaviour or mentality or mode of existence is called *conversion*, to use the language of the Bible (cf. Mk. 13:3, 5; Is. 30:15). This conversion specifically entails a relationship to God, to the sin committed, to its consequences and hence to one's neighbour, either an individual or a community. It is God, in 'whose hands are the hearts of the powerful'[67] and the hearts of all, who according to his own promise and by the power of his Spirit can transform 'hearts of stone' into 'hearts of flesh' (cf. Ez. 36:26).

38.3 On the path toward the desired conversion, toward the overcoming of the moral obstacles to development, it is already possible to point to the positive and moral value of the growing awareness of interdependence among individuals and nations. The fact that men and women in various parts of the world feel personally affected by the injustices and violations of human rights committed in distant countries, countries which perhaps they will never visit, is a further sign of a reality transformed into awareness, thus acquiring a moral connotation.

38.4 It is above all a question of interdependence, sensed as a system determining relationships in the contemporary world in its economic, cultural, political and religious elements, and accepted as a moral category. When interdependence becomes recognized in this way, the correlative response as a moral and social attitude, as a 'virtue', is solidarity. This then is not a feeling of vague compassion or shallow distress at the misfortunes of so many people, both near and far. On the contrary, it is a firm and persevering determination to commit oneself to the common good; that is to say, to the good of all and of each individual because we are all really responsible for all.

38.5 This determination is based on the solid conviction that what is hindering full development is that desire for profit and that thirst for power already mentioned. These attitudes and 'structures of sin' are only con-quered—presupposing the help of divine grace—by a diametrically opposed attitude: a commitment to the good of one's neighbor with the readiness, in the Gospel sense, to 'lose oneself' for the sake of the other instead of exploiting him, and to 'serve him' instead of oppressing him for one's own advantage (cf. Mt. 10:40-42; 20-25; Mk. 10:42-45; Lk. 22:25-27).

39. The exercise of solidarity within each society is valid when its members recognize one another as persons. Those who are more influential because they have greater share of goods and common services should feel responsible for the weaker and be ready to share with them all they possess. Those who are weaker, for their part, in the same spirit of solidarity should not adopt a purely passive attitude or one that is destructive of the social fabric, but while claiming their legitimate rights, should do what they can for the good of all. The intermediate groups, in their turn, should not selfishly insist on their particular interests, but respect the interests of others.

39.1 Positive signs in the contemporary world are the growing awareness of the solidarity of the poor among themselves, their efforts to support one another and their public demonstrations on the social scene which, without recourse to violence, present their own needs and rights in the face of the inefficiency or corruption of the public authorities. By virtue of her own evangelical duty, the church feels called to take her stand beside the poor, to discern the justice of their requests and to help satisfy them, without losing sight of the good of groups in the context of the common good.

39.2 The same criterion is applied by analogy in international relationships. Interdependence must be transformed into solidarity, based upon the principle that the goods of creation are meant for all. That which human industry produces through the processing of raw materials, with the contribution of work, must serve equally for the good of all.

39.3 Surmounting every type of imperialism and determination to preserve their own hegemony, the stronger and richer nations must have a sense of moral responsibility for the other nations, so that a real international system may be established which will rest on the foundation of the equality of all peoples and on the necessary respect for their legitimate differences. The economically weaker countries, or those still at subsistence level, must be enabled, with the assistance of other peoples and of the international community, to make a contribution of their own to the common good with their treasures of humanity and culture, which otherwise would be lost forever.

39.4 Solidarity helps us to see the 'other'—whether a person, people or nation—not just as some kind of instrument, with a work capacity and physical strength to be exploited at low cost and then discarded when no longer useful, but as our 'neighbour,' a 'helper' (cf. Gn. 2:18-20), to be made a sharer on a par with ourselves in the banquet of life to which all are equally invited by God. Hence the importance of reawakening the religious awareness of individuals and peoples.

39.5 Thus the exploitation, oppression and annihilation of others are excluded. These facts, in the present division of the world into opposing blocs, combine to produce the danger of war and an excessive preoccupation with personal security, often to the detriment of the autonomy, freedom of decision and even the territorial integrity of the weaker nations situated within the so-called 'areas of influence' or 'safety belts.'

39.6 The 'structures of sin' and the sins which they produce are likewise radically opposed to peace and development, for development, in the familiar expression of Pope Paul's encyclical, is 'the new name for peace.'[68]

39.7 In this way the solidarity which we propose is the path to peace and at the same time to development. For world peace is inconceivable unless the world's leaders come to recognize that interdependence in itself demands the abandonment of the politics of blocs, the sacrifice of all forms of economic, military or political imperialism and the transformation of mutual distrust into collaboration. This is precisely the act proper to solidarity among individuals and nations.

39.8 The motto of the pontificate of my esteemed predecessor Pius XII was *Opus iustitiae pax*: peace as the fruit of justice. Today one could say, with the same exactness and the same power of biblical inspiration (cf. Is. 32:17; Jas. 3:18): *Opus solidaritatis pax*: peace as the fruit of solidarity.

39.9 The goal of peace, so desired by everyone, will certainly be achieved through the putting into effect of social and international justice, but also through the practice of the virtues which favour togetherness and which teach us to live in unity, so as to build in unity, by giving and receiving a new society and a better world.

40. Solidarity is undoubtedly a Christian virtue. In what has been said so far it has been possible to identify many points of contact between solidarity and charity, which is the distinguishing mark of Christ's disciples (cf. Jn. 13:35).

40.1 In the light of faith, solidarity seeks to go beyond itself, to take on the specifically Christian dimensions of total gratuity, forgiveness and reconciliation. One's neighbour is then not only a human being with his or her own rights and a fundamental equality with everyone else, but becomes the living image of God the Father, redeemed by the blood of Jesus Christ and placed under the permanent action of the Holy Spirit. One's neighbour must therefore be loved, even if an enemy, with the same love with which the Lord loves him or her; and for that person's sake one must be ready for sacrifice, even the ultimate one: to lay down one's life for the brethren (cf. 1 Jn. 3:16).

40.2 At that point, awareness of the common fatherhood of God, of the brotherhood of all in Christ—'children of the Son'—and of the presence and life-giving action of the Holy Spirit will bring to our vision of the world a new criterion for interpreting it. Beyond human and natural bonds, already so close and strong, there is discerned in the light of faith a new model of the unity of the human race, which must ultimately inspire our solidarity. This supreme model of unity, which is a reflection of the intimate life of God, one God in three Persons, is what we Christians mean by the word *communion*.

40.3 This specifically Christian communion, jealously preserved, extended and enriched with the Lord's help, is the soul of the church's vocation to be a 'sacrament,' in the sense already indicated.

40.4 Solidarity therefore must play its part in the realization of this divine plan, both on the level of individuals and on the level of national and international society. The 'evil mechanisms' and 'structures of sin' of which we have spoken can be overcome only through the exercise of the human and Christian solidarity to which the church calls us and which she tirelessly promotes. Only in this way can such positive energies be fully released for the benefit of development and peace.

40.5 Many of the church's canonized saints offer a wonderful witness of such solidarity and can serve as examples in the present difficult circumstances. Among them I wish to recall St. Peter Claver and his service to the slaves at Cartagena de Indias, and St. Maximilian Maria Kolbe, who offered his life in place of a prisoner unknown to him in the concentration camp at Auschwitz.

VI. Some Particular Guidelines

41. The church does not have technical solutions to offer for the problem of underdevelopment as such, as Pope Paul VI already affirmed in his encyclical.[69]

41.1 For the church does not propose economic and political systems or programs nor does she show preference for one or the other, provided that human dignity is properly respected and promoted, and provided she herself is allowed the room she needs to exercise her ministry in the world.

41.2 But the church is an 'expert in humanity,'[70] and this leads her necessarily to extend her religious mission to the various fields in which men and women expend their efforts in search of the always relative happiness which is possible in this world, in line with their dignity as persons.

41.3 Following the example of my predecessors, I must repeat that whatever affects the dignity of individuals and peoples, such as authentic development, cannot be reduced to a 'technical' problem. If reduced in this way, development would be emptied of its true content, and this would be an act of betrayal of the individuals and peoples whom development is meant to serve.

41.4 This is why the church has something to say today, just as 20 years ago, and also in the future, about the nature, conditions, requirements and aims of authentic development, and also about the obstacles which stand in its way. In doing so the church fulfills her mission to evangelize, for she offers her first contribution to the solution of the urgent problem of development when she proclaims the truth about Christ, about herself and about man, applying this truth to a concrete situation.[71]

41.5 As her instrument for reaching this goal, the church uses her social doctrine. In today's difficult situation, a more exact awareness and a wider diffusion of the 'set of principles for reflection, criteria for judgment and the directives for action' proposed by the church's teaching[72] would be of great help in promoting both the correct definition of the problems being faced and the best solution to them.

41.6 It will thus be seen at once that the questions facing us are above all moral questions; and that neither the analysis of the problem of development as such nor the means to overcome the present difficulties can ignore this essential dimension.

41.7 The church's social doctrine is not a 'third way' between liberal capitalism and Marxist collectivism nor even a possible alternative to other solutions less radically opposed to one another: Rather, it constitutes a category of its own. Nor is it an ideology, but rather the accurate formulation of the results of a careful reflection on the complex realities of human existence, in society and in the international order, in the light of faith and of the church's tradition. Its main aim is to interpret these realities, determining their conformity with or divergence from the lines of the Gospel teaching on man and his vocation, a vocation which is at once earthly and transcendent;

its aim is thus to guide Christian behaviour. It therefore belongs to the field, not of ideology, but of theology and particularly of moral theology.

41.8 The teaching and spreading of her social doctrine are part of the church's evangelizing mission. And since it is a doctrine aimed at guiding people's behavior, it consequently gives rise to a 'commitment to justice,' according to each individual's role, vocation and circumstances.

41.9 The condemnation of evils and injustices is also part of that ministry of evangelization in the social field which is an aspect of the church's prophetic role. But it should be made clear that proclamation is always more important than condemnation, and the latter cannot ignore the former, which gives it true solidity and the force of higher motivation.

42. Today more than in the past, the church's social doctrine must be open to an international outlook, in line with the Second Vatican Council,[73] the most recent encyclicals[74] and particularly in line with the encyclical which we are commemorating.[75] It will not be superfluous therefore to re-examine an further clarify in this light the characteristic themes and guidelines dealt with by the magisterium in recent years.

42.1 Here I would like to indicate one of them: the option or love of preference for the poor. This is an option or a special form of primacy in the exercise of Christian charity to which the whole tradition of the church bears witness. It affects the life of each Christian inasmuch as he or she seeks to imitate the life of Christ, but it applies equally to our social reponsibilites and hence to our manner of living, and to the logical decisions to be made concerning the ownership and use of goods.

42.3 Today, furthermore, given the worldwide dimension which the social question has assumed,[76] this love of preference for the poor, and the decisions which it inspires in us, cannot but embrace the immense multitudes of the hungry, the needy, the homeless, those without medical care and, above all, those without hope of a better future. It is impossible not to take account of the existence of these realities. To ignore them would mean becoming like the 'rich man' who pretended not to know the beggar Lazarus lying at his gate (cf. Lk. 16:19-31).[77]

42.4 Our daily life as well as our decisions in the political and economic fields must be marked by these realities. Likewise the leaders of nations and the heads of international bodies, while they are obliged always to keep in mind the true human dimension as a priority in their development plans, should not forget to give precedence to the phenomenon of growing poverty. Unfortunately, instead of becoming fewer the poor are becoming more numerous, not only in less developed countries but—and this seems no less scandalous—in the more developed ones too.

42.5 It is necessary to state once more the characteristic principle of Christian social doctrine: The goods of this world are originally meant for all.[78]

42.6 The right to private property is valid and necessary, but it does not nullify the value of this principle. Private property, in fact, is under a 'social mortgage,'[79] which means that it has an intrinsically social function based upon and justified precisely by the principle of the universal destination of goods.

42.7 Likewise, in this concern for the poor, one must not overlook that special form of poverty which consists in being deprived of fundamental human rights, in particular the right to religious freedom and also the right to freedom of economic initiative.

43. The motivating concern for the poor—who are, in the very meaningful term, 'the Lord's poor'[80]—must be translated at all levels into concrete actions, until it decisively attains a series of necessary reforms. Each local situation will show what reforms are most urgent and how they can be achieved. But those demanded by the situation of international imbalance, as already described, must not be forgotten.

43.1 In this respect I wish to mention specifically: the reform of the international trade system, which is mortgaged to protectionism and increasing bilateralism; the reform of the world monetary and financial system, today recognized as inadequate; the question of technological exchanges and their proper use; the need for a review of the structure of the existing international organizations, in the framework of an international juridical order.

43.2 The international trade system today frequently discriminates against the products of the young industries of the developing countries and discourages the producers of raw materials. There exists too a kind of international division of labour, whereby the low-cost products of certain countries which lack effective labor laws or which are too weak to apply them are sold in other parts of the world at considerable profit for the companies engaged in this form of production, which knows no frontiers.

43.3 The world monetary and financial system is marked by an excessive fluctuation of exchange rates and interest rates, to the detriment of the balance of payments and the debt situation of the poorer countries.

43.4 Forms of technology and their transfer constitute today one of the major problems of international exchange and of the grave damage deriving therefrom. There are quite frequent cases of developing countries being denied needed forms of technology or sent useless ones.

43.5 In the opinion of many, the international organizations seem to be at a stage of their existence when their operating methods, operating costs and effectiveness need careful review and possible correction. Obviously, such a delicate process cannot be put into effect without the collaboration of all. This presupposes the overcoming of political rivalries and the renouncing of all desire to manipulate these organizations, which exist solely for the common good.

43.6 The existing institutions and organizations have worked well for the benefit of peoples. Nevertheless, humanity today is in a new and more difficult phase of its genuine development. It needs a greater degree of international ordering, at the service of the societies, economies and cultures of the whole world.

44. Development demands above all a spirit of initiative on the part of the countries which need it.[81] Each of them must act in accordance with its own responsibilities, not expecting everything from the more favoured countries and acting in collaboration with others in the same situation. Each must discover and use to the best advantage its own area of freedom. Each must make itself capable of initiatives responding to its own needs as a society. Each must likewise realize its true needs as well as the rights and duties which

oblige it to respond to them. The development of peoples begins and is most appropriately accomplished in the dedication of each people to its own development, in collaboration with others.

44.1 It is important then that as far as possible the developing nations themselves should favor the self-affirmation of each citizen through access to a wider culture and a free flow of information. Whatever promotes literacy and the basic education which completes and deepens it is a direct contribution to true development, as the encyclical *Populorum Progressio* proposed.[82] These goals are still far from being reached in so many parts of the world.

44.2 In order to take this path, the nations themselves will have to identify their own priorities and clearly recognize their own needs according to the particular conditions of their people, their geographical setting and their cultural traditions.

44.3 Some nations will have to increase food production in order to have always available what is needed for subsistence and daily life. In the modern world—where starvation claims so many victims, especially among the very young—there are examples of not particularly developed nations which have nevertheless achieved the goal of food self-sufficiency and have even become food exporters.

44.4 Other nations need to reform certain unjust structures and in particular their political institutions, in order to replace corrupt, dictatorial and authoritarian forms of government by democratic and participatory ones. This is a process which we hope will spread and grow stronger. For the 'health' of a political community—as expressed in the free and responsible participation of all citizens in public affairs, in the rule of law and in respect for and promotion of human rights—is the *necessary condition and sure guarantee* of 'the whole individual and of all people'.

45. None of what has been said can be achieved without the collaboration of all—especially the international community—in the framework of a solidarity which includes everyone, beginning with the most neglected. But the developing nations themselves have the duty to practice solidarity among themselves and with the neediest countries of the world.

45.1 It is desirable, for example, that nations of the same geographical area should establish forms of cooperation which will make them less dependent on more powerful producers; they should open their frontiers to the products of the area; they should examine how their products might complement one another; they should combine in order to set up those services which each one separately is incapable of providing; they should extend cooperation to the monetary and financial sector.

45.2 Interdependence is already a reality in many of these countries. To acknowledge it in such a way as to make it more operative represents an alternative to excessive dependence on richer and more powerful nations as part of the hoped-for development, without opposing anyone, but discovering and making best use of the country's own potential. The developing countries belonging to one geographical area, especially those included in the term *South* can and ought to set up new regional organizations inspired by criteria of equality, freedom and participation in the comity of nations—as is already happening with promising results.

45.3 An essential condition for global solidarity is autonomy and free self-determination, also within associations such as those indicated. But at the same time solidarity demands a readiness to accept the sacrifices necessary for the good of the whole world community.

VII. Conclusion

46. Peoples and individuals aspire to be free: Their search for full development signals their desire to overcome the many obstacles preventing them from enjoying a 'more human life.'

46.1 Recently, in the period following the publication of the encyclical *Populorum Progressio*, a new way of confronting the problems of poverty and underdevelopment has spread in some areas of the world, especially in Latin America. This approach makes liberation the fundamental category and the first principle of action.

46.2 The positive values as well as the deviations and risks of deviation which are damaging to the faith and are connected with this form of theological reflection and method have been appropriately pointed out by the church's magisterium.[83]

46.3 It is fitting to add that the aspiration to freedom from all forms of slavery affecting the individual and society is something noble and legitimate. This in fact is the purpose of development, or rather liberation and development, taking into account the intimate connection between the two.

46.4 Development which is merely economic is incapable of setting man free; on the contrary, it will end by enslaving him further. Development that does not include the cultural, transcendent and religious dimensions of man and society, to the extent that it does not recognize the existence of such dimensions and does not endeavor to direct its goals and priorities toward the same, is even less conducive to authentic liberation. Human beings are totally free only when they are completely themselves, in the fullness of their rights and duties. The same can be said about society as a whole.

46.5 The principal obstacle to be overcome on the way to authentic liberation is sin and the structures produced by sin as it multiplies and spreads.[84]

46.6 The freedom with which Christ has set us free (cf. Gal. 5:1) encourages us to become the servants of all. Thus the process of development and liberation takes concrete shape in the exercise of solidarity, that is to say, in the love and service of neighbor, especially of the poorest: 'For where trugh and love are missing, the process of liberation results in the death of a freedom which will have lost all support.'[85]

47. In the context of the sad experiences of recent years and of the mainly negative picture of the present moment, the church must strongly affirm the possibility of overcoming the obstacles which by excess or by defect stand in the way of development. And she must affirm her confidence in a true liberation. Ultimately, this confidence and this possibility are based on the church's awareness of the divine promise guaranteeing that our present history does not remain closed in upon itself but is open to the kingdom of God.

47.1 The church has confidence also in man, though she knows the evil of which he is capable. For she well knows that—in spite of the heritage of sin and the sin which each one is capable of committing—there exist in the human person sufficient qualities and energies, a fundamental 'goodness' (cf. Gn. 1:31), because he is the image of the Creator, placed under the redemptive influence of Christ, who 'united himself in some fashion with every man,'[86] and because the efficacious action of the Holy Spirit 'fills the earth' (Wis. 1:7).

47.2 There is no justification then for despair or pessimism or inertia. Though it be with sorrow, it must be said that just as one may sin through selfishness and the desire for excessive profit and power, one may also be found wanting with regard to the urgent needs of multitudes of human beings submerged in conditions of underdevelopment, through fear, indecision and basically, through cowardice. We are all called, indeed obliged, to face the tremendous challenge of the last decade of the second millennium, also because the present dangers threaten everyone: a world economic crisis, a war without frontiers, without winners or losers. In the face of such a threat, the distinction between rich individuals and countries and poor individuals and countries will have little value, except that a greater responsibility rests on those who have more and can do more.

47.3 This is not, however, the sole motive or even the most important one. At stake is the dignity of the human person, whose defense and promotion have been entrusted to us by the Creator, and to whom the men and women at every moment of history are strictly and responsibly in debt. As many people are already more or less clearly aware, the present situation does not seem to correspond to this dignity. Every individual is called upon to play his or her part in this peaceful campaign, a campaign to be conducted by peaceful means in order to secure development in peace, in order to safeguard nature itself and the world about us. The church too feels profoundly involved in this enterprise, and she hopes for its ultimate success.

47.4 Consequently, following the example of Pope Paul VI with his encyclical *Populorum Progressio*,[87] I wish to appeal with simplicity and humility to everyone, to all men and women without exception. I wish to ask them to be convinced of the seriousness of the present moment and of each one's individual responsibility, and to implement—by the way they live as individuals and as families, by the use of their resources, by their civic activity, by contributing to economic and political decisions and by personal commitment to national and international undertakings—the measures inspired by solidarity and love of preference for the poor. This is what is demanded by the present moment and above all by the very dignity of the human person, the indestructible image of God the Creator, which is identical in each one of us.

47.5 In this commitment, the sons and daughters of the church must serve as examples and guides, for they are called upon, in conformity with the program announced by Jesus himself in the synagogue at Nazareth, to 'preach good news to the poor...to proclaim release to the captives and recovering of sight to the blind, to set at liberty those who are oppressed, to proclaim the acceptable year of the Lord' (Lk. 4:18-19). It is appropriate to emphasize the pre-eminent role that belongs to the laity, both men and women, as was reaffirmed in the recent assembly of the synod. it is their task to animate temporal realities with Christian commitment, by which they show that they are witnesses and agents of peace and justice.

47.6 I wish to address especially those who through the sacrament of baptism and the profession of the same Creed share a real, though imperfect, communion with us. I am certain that the concern expresed in this encyclical as well as the motives inspiring it will be familiar to them, for these motives are inspired by the Gospel of Jesus Christ. We can find here a new invitation to bear witness together to our common convictions concerning the dignity of man, created by God, redeemed by Christ, made holy by the Spirit and called upon in this world to live a life in conformity with this dignity.

47.7 I likewise address this appeal to the Jewish people, who share with us the inheritance of Abraham, 'our father in faith' (cf. Rom. 4:11f),[88] and the tradition of the Old Testament, as well as to the Moslems, who, like us, believe in the just and merciful God. And I extend it to all the followers of the world's great religions.

47.8 The meeting held last Oct. 27 in Assisi, the city of St. Francis, in order to pray for and commit ourselves to peace—each one in fidelity to his own religious profession—showed how much peace and, as its necessary condition, the development of the whole person and of all peoples are also a matter of religion and how the full achievement of both the one and the other depends on our fidelity to our vocation as men and women of faith. For it depends, above all, on God.

48. The church well knows that no temporal achievement is to be identified with the kingdom of God, but that all such achievements simply reflect and in a sense anticipate the glory of the kingdom, the kingdom which we await at the end of history when the Lord will come again. But that expectation can never be an excuse for lack of concern for people in their concrete personal situations and in their social, national and international life, since the former is conditioned by the latter, especially today.

48.1 However imperfect and temporary are all the things that can and ought to be done through the combined efforts of everyone and through divine grace at a given moment of history in order to make people's lives 'more human,' nothing will be lost or will have been in vain. This is the teaching of the Second Vatican Council, in an enlightening passage of the pastoral constitution *Gaudium et Spes*: 'When we have spread on earth the fruits of our nature and our enterprise—human dignity, fraternal communion and freedom—according to the command of the Lord and in his Spirit, we will find them once again, cleansed this time from the stain of sin, illumined and transfigured, when Christ presents to his Father an eternal and universal kingdom....Here on earth that kingdom is already present in mystery.'[89]

48.2 The kingdom of God becomes present above all in the celebration of the sacrament of the eucharist, which is the Lord's sacrifice. In that celebration the fruits of the earth and the work of human hands—the bread and wine—are transformed mysteriously, but really and substantially, through the power of the Holy Spirit and the words of the minister, into the body and blood of the Lord Jesus Christ, the Son of God and Son of Mary, through whom the kingdom of the Father has been made present in our midst.

48.3 The goods of this world and the work of our hands—the bread and wine—serve for the coming of the definitive kingdom, since the Lord, through his Spirit, takes them up into himself in order to offer himself to the Father and to offer us with himself in the renewal of his one sacrifice, which anticipates God's kingdom and proclaims its final coming.

48.4 Thus the Lord unites us with himself through the eucharist—sacrament and sacrifice—and he unites us with himself and with one another by a bond stronger than any natural union; and thus united, he sends us into the whole world to bear witness through faith and works to God's love, preparing the coming of his kingdom and anticipating it, though in the obscurity of the present time.

48.5 All of us who take part in the eucharist are called to discover, through this sacrament, the profound meaning of our actions in the world in favor of development and peace; and to receive from it the strength to commit ourselves ever more generously, following the example of Christ, who in this sacrament lays down his life for his friends (cf. Jn. 15:13). Our personal commitment, like Christ's and in union with his, will not be in vain but certainly fruitful.

49. I have called the current Marian year in order that the Catholic faithful may look more and more to Mary, who goes before us on the pilgrimage of faith[90] and with maternal care intercedes for us before her son, our Redeemer. I wish to entrust to her and to her intercession this difficult moment of the modern world and the efforts that are being made and will be made, often with great suffering, in order to contribute to the true development of peoples proposed and proclaimed by my predecessor Paul VI.

49.1 In keeping with Christian piety through the ages, we present to the Blessed Virgin difficult individual situations, so that she may place them before her son, asking that he alleviate and change them. But we also present to her social situations and the international crisis itself, in their worrying aspects of poverty, unemployment, shortage of food, the arms race, contempt for human rights and situations or dangers of conflict, partial or total. In a filial spirit we wish to place all this before her 'eyes of mercy' repeating once more with faith and hope the ancient antiphon: 'Holy Mother of God, despise not our petitions in our necessities, but deliver us always from all dangers, O glorious and blessed Virgin.'

49.2 Mary most holy, our mother and queen, is the one who turns to her son and says: 'They have no more wine' (Jn. 2:3). She is also the one who praises God the Father, because 'he has put down the mighty from their thrones and exalted those of low degree; he has filled the hungry with good things, and the rich he has sent empty away' (Lk. 1:52-53). He maternal concern extends to the personal and social aspects of people's life on earth.[91]

49.3 Before the Most Blessed Trinity, I entrust to Mary all that I have written in this encyclical, and I invite all to reflect and actively commit themselves to promoting the true development of peoples as the prayer of the Mass for this intention states so well:

49.4 'Father, you have given all peoples one common origin, and your will is to gather them as one family in yourself. Fill the hearts of all with the fire of your love, and the desire to ensure justice for all their brothers and sisters. By sharing the good things you give us may we secure justice and equality for every human being, an end to all division and a human society built on love and peace.'[92]

49.5 This, in conclusion, is what I ask in the name of all my brothers and sisters, to whom I send a special blessing as a sign of greeting and good wishes.

49.6 Given in Rome, at St. Peter's, on Dec. 30 of the year 1987, the 10th of my pontificate.

Centesimus Annus

Encyclical on the 100th Anniversary
of 'Rerum Novarum' by Pope John Paul II

Introduction

'The historical experience of the West ... shows that even if the Marxist analysis and its foundation of alienation are false, nevertheless alienation—and the loss of the authentic meaning of life—is a reality in Western societies too,' writes Pope John Paul II in his ninth encyclical, titled *Centesimus Annus* ('The 100th Year'). The encyclical was issued for the centenary of Pope Leo XIII's social encyclical *Rerum Novarum*. The encyclical, made public May 2, is written in the wake of communism's collapse in Eastern Europe and looks to the new things *(rerum novarum)* today influencing the social order. The pope examines strengths and weaknesses of different forms of capitalism and the free market, and he takes up such themes as work, unions and wages, unemployment, profit, atheism, class struggle, freedom and private property. Modern times are witnessing a new form of ownership, the pope writes: 'the possession of know-how, technology and skill.' The poor, in addition to lacking material goods, now lack 'knowledge and training, which prevents them from escaping their state of humiliating subjection.' Human work, he states, 'is becoming increasingly important as the productive factor both of non-material and material wealth.' The pope insists that the human person cannot be understood 'on the basis of economics alone' or defined 'simply on the basis of class membership.' Of the church, he writes: 'Her contribution to the political order is precisely her vision of the dignity of the person revealed in all its fullness in the mystery of the incarnate Word.' The text of the encyclical follows.

Venerable brothers, beloved sons and daughters, health and the apostolic blessing!

1. The centenary of the promulgation of the encyclical which begins with the words 'Rerum Novarum,' [1] by my predecessor of venerable memory Pope Leo XIII, is an occasion of great importance for the present history of the church and for my own pontificate. It is an encyclical that has the distinction of having been commemorated by solemn papal documents from its 40th anniversary to its 90th. It may be said that its path through history has been marked by other documents which paid tribute to it and applied it to the circumstances of the day. [2]

1.1. In doing likewise for the 100th anniversary, in response to requests from many bishops, church institutions and study centers as well as business leaders and workers, both individually and as members of associations, I wish first and foremost to satisfy the debt of gratitude which the whole church owes to this great pope and his 'immortal document.'[3] I also mean to show that the vital energies rising from that root have not been spent with the passing of the years, but rather have increased even more. This is evident from the various initiatives which have preceded and which are to accompany and follow the celebration, initiatives promoted by episcopal conferences, by international agencies, universities and academic institutes, by professional associations and by other institutions and individuals in many parts of the world.

2. The present encyclical is part of these celebrations, which are meant to thank God—the origin of 'every good endowment and every perfect gift' (Jas. 1:17)—for having used a document published a century ago by the See of Peter to achieve so much good and to radiate so much light in the church and in the world. Although the commemoration at hand is meant to honor, it also honors those encyclicals and other documents of my predecessors which have helped to make Pope Leo's encyclical present and alive in history, thus constituting what would come to be called the church's 'social doctrine,' 'social teaching' or even 'social magisterium.'

2.1. The validity of this teaching has already been pointed out in two encyclicals published during my pontificate: on current problems regarding the development of individuals and peoples.[4]

3. I now wish to propose a 'rereading' of Pope Leo's encyclical by issuing an invitation to 'look back' at the text itself in order to discover anew the richness of the fundamental principles which it formulated for dealing with the question of the condition of workers. But this is also an invitation to 'look around' at the 'new things' which surround us and in which we find ourselves caught up, very different from the 'new things' which characterized the final decade of the last century. Finally, it is an invitation to 'look to the future' at a time when we can already glimpse the third millennium of the Christian era, so filled with uncertainties but also with promises—uncertainties and promises which appeal to our imagination and creativity and which reawaken our responsibility as disciples of the 'one teacher' (cf. Mt. 23:8) to show the way, to proclaim the truth and to communicate the life which is Christ (cf. Jn. 14:6).

3.1. A rereading of this kind will not only confirm the permanent value of such teaching, but will also manifest the true meaning of the church's tradition, which, being ever living and vital, builds upon the foundation laid by our fathers in the faith and particularly upon what 'the apostles passed down to the church'[5] in the name of Jesus Christ, who is her irreplaceable foundation (cf. 1 Cor. 3:11).

3.2. It was out of an awareness of his mission as the successor of Peter that Pope Leo XIII proposed to speak out, and Peter's successor today is moved by that same awareness. Like Pope Leo and the popes before and after him, I take my inspiration from the Gospel image of 'the scribe who has been trained for the kingdom of heaven,' whom the Lord compares to 'a householder who brings out of his treasure what is new and what is old' (Mt. 13:52). The treasure is the great outpouring of the church's tradition, which contains 'what is old'—received and passed on from the very beginning—and which enables us to interpret the 'new things' in the midst of which the life of the church and the world unfolds.

3.3. Among the things which become 'old' as a result of being incorporated into tradition and which offer opportunities and material for enriching both tradition and the life of faith, there is the fruitful activity of many millions of people who, spurred on by the social magisterium, have sought to make that teaching the inspiration for their involvement in the world. Acting either as individuals or joined together in various groups, associations and organizations, these people represent a great movement for the defense of the human person and the safeguarding of human dignity. Amid changing historical circumstances, this movement has contributed to the building up of a more just society or at least to the curbing of injustice.

3.4. The present encyclical seeks to show the fruitfulness of the principles enunciated by Leo XIII, which belong to the church's doctrinal patrimony and as such involve the exercise of her teaching authority. But pastoral solicitude also prompts me to propose an analysis of some events of recent history. It goes without saying that part of the responsibility of pastors is to give careful consideration to current events in order to discern the new requirements of evangelization. However, such an analysis is not meant to pass definitive judgments, since this does not fall per se within the magisterium's specific domain.

CHAPTER I

Characteristics of *Rerum Novarum*

4. Toward the end of the last century the church found herself facing a historical process which had already been taking place for some time but which was by then reaching a critical point. The determining factor in this process was a combination of radical changes which had taken place in the political, economic and social fields, and in the areas of science and technology, to say nothing of the wide influence of the prevailing ideologies. In the sphere of politics the result of these changes was a new conception of society and of the state, and consequently of authority itself. A traditional society was passing away and another was beginning to be formed—one which brought the hope of new freedoms, but also the threat of new forms of injustice and servitude.

4.1. In the sphere of economics, in which scientific discoveries and their practical application come together, new structures for the production of consumer goods had progressively taken shape. A new form of property had appeared—capital; and a new form of labor—labor for wages, characterized by high rates of production which lacked due regard for sex, age or family situation and were determined solely by efficiency, with a view to increasing profits.

4.2. In this way labor became a commodity to be freely bought and sold on the market, its price determined by the law of supply and demand without taking into account the bare minimum required for the support of the individual and his family. Moreover, the worker was not even sure of being able to sell 'his own commodity,' continually threatened as he was by unemployment, which in the absence of any kind of social security meant the specter of death by starvation.

4.3. The result of this transformation was a society 'divided into two classes separated by a deep chasm.'[6] This situation was linked to the marked change taking place in the political order already mentioned. Thus the prevailing political theory of the time sought to promote total economic freedom by appropriate laws or, conversely, by a deliberate lack of any intervention. At the same time, another conception of property and economic life was beginning to appear in an organized and often violent form, one which implied a new political and social structure.

4.4. At the height of this clash, when people finally began to realize fully the very grave injustice of social realities in many places and the danger of a revolution fanned by ideals which were then called 'socialist,' Pope Leo XIII intervened with a document which dealt in a systematic way with the 'condition of the workers.' The encyclical had been preceded by others devoted to teachings of a political character; still others would appear later.[7] Here, particular mention must be made of the encyclical *Libertas Praestantissmim*, which called attention to the essential bond between human freedom and truth, so that freedom which refused to be bound to the truth would fall into arbitrariness and end up submitting itself to the vilest of passions to the point of self-destruction. Indeed, what is the origin of all the evils to which *Rerum Novarum* wished to respond if not a kind of freedom which, in the area of economic and social activity, cuts itself off from the truth about man?

4.5. The pope also drew inspiration from the teaching of his predecessors as well as from the many documents issued by bishops, from scientific studies promoted by members of the laity, from the work of Catholic movements and associations, and from the church's practical achievements in the social field during the second half of the 19th century.

5. The 'new things' to which the pope devoted his attention were anything but positive. The first paragraph of the encyclical describes in strong terms the 'new things' *(rerum novarum)* which gave it its name: 'That the spirit of revolutionary change which has long been disturbing the nations of the world should have passed beyond the sphere of politics and made its influence felt in the related sphere of practical economics is not surprising. Progress in industry, the development of new trades, the changing relationship between employers and workers, the enormous wealth of a few as opposed to the poverty of the many, the increasing self-reliance of the workers and their closer association with each other, as well as a notable decline in morality: All these elements have led to the conflict now taking place.'[8]

5.1. The pope and the church with him were confronted, as was the civil community, by a society which was torn by a conflict all the more harsh and inhumane because it knew no rule or regulation. It was the conflict between capital and labor or—as the encyclical puts it—the worker question. It is precisely about this conflict, in the very pointed terms in which it then appeared, that the pope did not hesitate to speak.

5.2. Here we find the first reflection for our times as suggested by the encyclical. In the face of a conflict which set man against man, almost as if they were 'wolves,' a conflict between the extremes of mere physical survival on the one side and opulence on the other, the pope did not hesitate to intervene by virtue of his 'apostolic office,'[9] that is, on the basis of the mission received from Jesus Christ himself to 'feed his lambs and tend his sheep' (cf. Jn. 21:15-17), and to 'bind and loose' on earth for the kingdom of heaven (cf. Mt. 16:19). The pope's intention was certainly to restore peace, and the present-day reader cannot fail to note his severe condemnation, in no uncertain terms, of the class struggle.[10] However, the pope was very much aware that peace is built on the foundation of justice: What was essential to the encyclical was precisely its proclamation of the fundamental conditions for justice in the economic and social situation of the time.[11]

5.3. In this way Pope Leo XIII, in the footsteps of his predecessors, created a lasting paradigm for the church. The church, in fact, has something to say about specific human situations, both individual and communal, national and international. She formulates a genuine doctrine for these situations, a corpus which enables her to analyze social realities, to make judgments about them and to indicate directions to be taken for the just resolution of the problems involved.

5.4. In Pope Leo XIII's time such a concept of the church's right and duty was far from being commonly admitted. Indeed, a twofold approach prevailed: one directed to this world and this life, to which faith ought to remain extraneous; the other directed toward a purely otherworldly salvation, which neither enlightens nor directs existence on earth. The pope's approach in publishing gave the church 'citizenship status' as it were amid the changing realities of public life, and this standing would be more fully confirmed later on. In effect, to teach and to spread her social doctrine pertains to the church's evangelizing mission and is an essential part of the Christian message, since this doctrine points out the direct consequences of that message in the life of society and situates daily work and struggles for justice in the context of bearing witness to Christ the savior. This doctrine is likewise a source of unity and peace in dealing with the conflicts which inevitably arise in social and economic life. Thus it is possible to meet these new situations without degrading the human person's transcendent dignity, either in oneself or in one's adversaries, and to direct those situations toward just solutions.

5.5. Today, at a distance of 100 years, the validity of this approach affords me the opportunity to contribute to the development of Christian social doctrine. The 'new evangelization,' which the modern world urgently needs and which I have emphasized many times, must include among its essential elements a proclamation of the church's social doctrine. As in the days of Pope Leo XIII, this doctrine is still suitable for indicating the right way to respond to the great challenges of today, when ideologies are being increasingly discredited. Now, as then, we need to repeat that there can be no genuine solution of the 'social question' apart from the Gospel and that the 'new things' can find in the Gospel the context for their correct understanding and the proper moral perspective for judgment on them.

6. With the intention of shedding light on the conflict which had arisen between capital and labor, Pope Leo XIII affirmed the fundamental rights of workers. Indeed, the key to reading the encyclical is the dignity of the worker as such and, for the same reason, the dignity of work, which is defined as follows: 'to exert oneself for the sake of procuring what is necessary for the various purposes of life and first of all for self-preservation.'[12] The pope describes work as 'personal, inasmuch as the energy expended is bound up with the personality and is the exclusive property of him who acts and, furthermore, was given to him for his advantage.'[13] Work thus belongs to the vocation of every person; indeed, man expresses and fulfills himself by working. At the same time work has a 'social' dimension through its intimate relationship not only to the family, but also to the common good, since 'it may truly be said that it is only by the labor of workingmen that states grow rich.'[14] These are themes that I have taken up and developed in my encyclical *Laborem Exercens*.[15]

6.1. Another important principle is undoubtedly that of the right to 'private property.'[16] The amount of space devoted to this subject in the encyclical shows the importance attached to it. The pope is well aware that private property is not an absolute value nor does he fail to proclaim the necessary complementary principles such as the universal destination of the earth's goods.[17]

6.2. On the other hand, it is certainly true that the type of private property which Leo XIII mainly considers is land ownership.[18] But this does not mean that the reasons adduced to safeguard private property or to affirm the right to possess the things necessary for one's personal development and the development of one's family, whatever the concrete form which that right may assume, are not still valid today.

6.3. This is something which must be affirmed once more in the face of the changes we are witnessing in systems formerly dominated by collective ownership of the means of production as well as in the face of the increasing instances of poverty or, more precisely, of hindrances to private ownership in many parts of the world, including those where systems predominate which are based on an affirmation of the right to private property. As a result of these changes and of the persistence of poverty, a deeper analysis of the problem is called for, an analysis which will be developed later in this document.

7. In close connection with the right to private property, Pope Leo XIII's encyclical also affirms other rights as inalienable and proper to the human person. Prominent among these, because of the space which the pope devotes to it and the importance which he attaches to it, is the 'natural human right' to form private associations. This means above all the right to establish professional associations of employers and workers or of workers alone.[19] Here we find the reason for the church's defense and approval of the establishment of what are commonly called trade unions: certainly not

because of ideological prejudices or in order to surrender to a class mentality, but because the right of association is a natural right of the human being, which therefore precedes his or her incorporation into political society. Indeed, the formation of unions 'cannot...be prohibited by the state,' because 'the state is bound to protect natural rights, not to destroy them; and if it forbids its citizens to form associations, it contradicts the very principle of its own existence.'[20]

7.1. Together with this right, which—it must be stressed—the pope explicitly acknowledges as belonging to workers or, using his own language, to 'the working class,' the encyclical affirms just as clearly the right to the 'limitation of working hours,' the right to legitimate rest, and the right of children and women[21] to be treated differently with regard to the type and duration of work.

7.2. If we keep in mind what history tells us about the practices permitted or at least not excluded by law regarding the way in which workers were employed, without any guarantees as to working hours or the hygienic conditions of the workplace or even regarding the age and sex of apprentices, we can appreciate the pope's severe statement: 'It is neither just nor human so to grind men down with excessive labor as to stupefy their minds and wear out their bodies.' And referring to the 'contract' aimed at putting into effect 'labor relations'of this sort, he affirms with greater precision that 'in all agreements between employers and workers there is always the condition expressed or understood' that proper rest be allowed proportionate to 'the wear and tear of one's strength.' He then concludes: 'To agree in any other sense would be against what is right and just.'[22]

8. The pope immediately adds another right which the worker has as a person. This is the right to a 'just wage,' which cannot be left to the 'free consent of the parties, so that the employer, having paid what was agreed upon, has done his part and seemingly is not called upon to do anything beyond.'[23] It was said at the time that the state does not have the power to intervene in the terms of these contracts except to ensure the fulfillment of what had been explicitly agreed upon. This concept of relations between employers and employees, purely pragmatic and inspired by a thoroughgoing individualism, is severely censured in the encyclical as contrary to the twofold nature of work as a personal and necessary reality. For if work as something personal belongs to the sphere of the individual's free use of his own abilities and energy, as something necessary it is governed by the grave obligation of every individual to ensure 'the preservation of life.' 'It necessarily follows,' the pope concludes, 'that every individual has a natural right to procure what is required to live; and the poor can procure that in no other way than by what they can earn through their work.'[24]

8.1. A workman's wages should be sufficient to enable him to support himself, his wife and his children. 'If through necessity or fear of a worse evil the workman accepts harder conditions because an employer or contractor will afford no better, he is made the victim of force and injustice.'[25]

8.2. Would that these words, written at a time when what has been called 'unbridled capitalism' was pressing forward, should not have to be repeated today with the same severity. Unfortunately, even today one finds instances of contracts between employers and employees which lack reference to the most elementary justice regarding the employment of children or women, working hours, the hygienic condition of the workplace and fair pay; and this is the case despite the international declarations and conventions on the subject[26] and the internal laws of states. The pope attributed to the 'public authority' the 'strict duty' of providing properly for the welfare of the workers, because a failure to do so violates justice; indeed, he did not hesitate to speak of 'distributive justice.'[27]

9. To these rights Pope Leo XIII adds another right regarding the condition of the working class, one which I wish to mention because of its importance: namely, the right to discharge freely one's religious duties. The pope wished to proclaim this right within the context of the other rights and duties of workers, notwithstanding the general opinion even in his day that such questions pertained exclusively to an individual's private life. He affirms the need for Sunday rest so that people may turn their thoughts to heavenly things and to the worship which they owe to almighty God.[28] No one can take away this human right, which is based on a commandment; in the words of the pope, 'No man may with impunity violate that human dignity which God himself treats with great reverence,' and consequently the state must guarantee to the worker the exercise of this freedom.[29]

9.1. It would not be mistaken to see in this clear statement a springboard for the principle of the right to religious freedom, which was to become the subject of many solemn international declarations and conventions[30] as well as of the Second Vatican Council's well-known declaration and of my own repeated teaching.[31] In this regard, one may ask whether existing laws and the practice of industrialized societies effectively ensure in our own day the exercise of this basic right to Sunday rest.

10. Another important aspect which has many applications to our own day is the concept of the relationship between the state and its citizens. *Rerum Novarum* criticizes two social and economic systems: socialism and liberalism. The opening section, in which the right to private property is reaffirmed, is devoted to socialism. Liberalism is not the subject of a special section, but it is worth noting that criticisms of it are raised in the treatment of the duties of the state.[32] The state cannot limit itself to 'favoring one portion of the citizens,' namely the rich and prosperous, nor can it 'neglect the other,' which clearly represents the majority of society. Otherwise, there would be a violation of that law of justice which ordains that every person should receive his due. 'When there is question of defending the rights of individuals, the defenseless and the poor have a claim to special consideration. The richer class has many ways of shielding itself and stands less in need of help from the state; whereas the mass of the poor have no resources of their own to fall back on and must chiefly depend on the assistance of the state. It is for this reason that wage earners, since they mostly belong to the latter class, should be specially cared for and protected by the government.'[33]

10.1. These passages are relevant today, especially in the face of the new forms of poverty in the world and also because they are affirmations which do not depend on a specific notion of the state or on a particular political theory. Leo XIII is repeating an elementary principle of sound political organization, namely, the more that individuals are defenseless within a given society, the more they require the care and concern of others, and in particular the intervention of governmental authority.

10.2. In this way what we nowadays call the principle of solidarity, the validity of which both in the internal order of each nation and in the international order I have discussed in the encyclical *Sollicitudo Rei Socialis*,[34] is clearly seen to be one of the fundamental principles of the Christian view of social and political organization. This principle is frequently stated by Pope Leo XIII, who uses the term 'friendship,' a concept already found in Greek philosophy. Pope Pius XI refers to it with the equally meaningful term 'social charity.' Pope Paul VI, expanding the concept to cover the many modern aspects of the social question, speaks of a 'civilization of love.'[35]

11. Rereading the encyclical in the light of contemporary realities enables us to appreciate the church's constant concern for and dedication to categories of people who are especially beloved to the Lord Jesus. The contents of the text are an excellent testimony to the continuity within the church of the so-called 'preferential option for the poor,' an option which I defined as a 'special form of primacy in the exercise of Christian charity.'[36] Pope Leo's encyclical on the condition of the workers is thus an encyclical on the poor and on the terrible conditions to which the new and often violent process of industrialization had reduced great multitudes of people. Today in many parts of the world similar processes of economic, social and political transformation are creating the same evils.

11.1. If Pope Leo XIII calls upon the state to remedy the condition of the poor in accordance with justice, he does so because of his timely awareness that the state has the duty of watching over the common good and of ensuring that every sector of social life, not excluding the economic one, contributes to achieving that good while respecting the rightful autonomy of each sector. This should not however lead us to think that Pope Leo expected the state to solve every social problem. On the contrary, he frequently insists on necessary limits to the state's intervention and on its instrumental character inasmuch as the individual, the family and society are prior to the state and inasmuch as the state exists in order to protect their rights and not stifle them.[37]

11.2. The relevance of these reflections for our own day is inescapable. It will be useful to return later to this important subject of the limits inherent in the nature of the state. For now, the points which have been emphasized (certainly not the only ones in the encyclical) are situated in continuity with the church's social teaching and in the light of a sound view of private property, work, the economic process, the reality of the state and, above all, of man himself. Other themes will be mentioned later when we examine certain aspects of the contemporary situation. From this point forward it will be necessary to keep in mind that the main thread and in a certain sense the guiding principle of Pope Leo's encyclical and of all of the church's social doctrine is a correct view of the human person and of his unique value inasmuch as 'man...is the only creature on earth which God willed for itself.'[38] God has imprinted his own image and likeness on man (cf. Gn. 1:26), conferring upon him an incomparable dignity, as the encyclical frequently insists. In effect, beyond the rights which man acquires by his own work, there exist rights which do not correspond to any work he performs but which flow from his essential dignity as a person.

CHAPTER II

Toward the new things of today

12. The commemoration of *Rerum Novarum* would be incomplete unless reference were also made to the situation of the world today. The document lends itself to such a reference because the historical picture and the prognosis which it suggests have proved to be surprisingly accurate in the light of what has happened since then.

12.1. This is especially confirmed by the events which took place near the end of 1989 and at the beginning of 1990. These events, and the radical transformations which followed, can only be explained by the preceding situations, which to a certain extent crystallized or institutionalized Leo XIII's predictions and the increasingly disturbing signs noted by his successors. Pope Leo foresaw the negative consequences—political, social and economic—of the social order proposed by 'socialism,' which at that time was still only a social philosophy and not yet a fully structured movement. It may seem surprising that 'socialism' appeared at the beginning of the pope's critique of solutions to the 'question of the working class' at a time when 'socialism' was not yet in the form of a strong and powerful state, with all the resources which that implies, as was later to happen. However, he correctly judged the danger posed to the masses by the attractive presentation of this simple and radical solution to the 'question of the working class' of the time—all the more so when one considers the terrible situation of injustice in which the working classes of the recently industrialized nations found themselves.

12.2. Two things must be emphasized here: first, the great clarity in perceiving, in all its harshness, the actual condition of the working class—men, women and children; second, equal clarity in recognizing the evil of a solution which, by appearing to reverse the positions of the poor and the rich, was in reality detrimental to the very people whom it was meant to help. The remedy would prove worse than the sickness. By defining the nature of the socialism of his day as the suppression of private property, Leo XIII arrived at the crux of the problem.

12.3. His words deserve to be reread attentively: 'To remedy these wrongs (the unjust distribution of wealth and the poverty of the workers), the socialists encourage the poor man's envy of the rich and strive to do away with private property, contending that individual possessions should become the common property of all...; but their contentions are so clearly powerless to end the controversy that, were they carried into effect, the workingman himself would be among the first to suffer. They are moreover emphatically unjust, for they would rob the lawful possessor, distort the functions of the state and create utter confusion in the community.'[39] The evils caused by the setting up of this type of socialism as a state system—what would later be called 'real socialism'—could not be better expressed.

13. Continuing our reflections and referring also to what has been said in the encyclicals *Laborem Exercens,* and *Sollicitudo Rei Socialis,* we have to add that the fundamental error of socialism is anthropological in nature. Socialism considers the individual person simply as an element, a molecule within the social organism, so that the good of the individual is completely subordinated to the functioning of the socioeconomic mechanism. Socialism likewise maintains that the good of the individual can be realized without reference to his free choice, to the unique and exclusive responsibility which he exercises in the face of good or evil. Man is thus reduced to a series of social relationships, and the concept of the person as the autonomous subject of moral decision disappears, the very subject whose decisions build the social order. From this mistaken conception of the person there arise both a distortion of law, which defines the sphere of the exercise of freedom, and an opposition to private property. A person who is deprived of something he can call 'his own' and of the possibility of earning a living through his own initiative comes to depend on the social machine and on those who control it. This makes it much more difficult for him to recognize his dignity as a person and hinders progress toward the building up of an authentic human community.

13.1. In contrast, from the Christian vision of the human person there necessarily follows a correct picture of society. According to *Rerum Novarum* and the whole social doctrine of the church, the social nature of man is not completely fulfilled in the state, but is realized in various intermediary groups, beginning with the family and including economic, social, political and cultural groups which stem from human nature itself and have their own autonomy, always with a view to the common good. This is what I have called the 'subjectivity' of society which, together with the subjectivity of the individual, was canceled out by 'real socialism.'[40]

13.2. If we then inquire as to the source of this mistaken concept of the nature of the person and the 'subjectivity' of society, we must reply that its first cause is atheism. It is by responding to the call of God contained in the being of things that man becomes aware of his transcendent dignity. Every individual must give this response, which constitutes the apex of his humanity, and no social mechanism or collective subject can substitute for it. The denial of God deprives the person of his foundation and consequently leads to a reorganization of the social order without reference to the person's dignity and responsibility.

13.3. The atheism of which we are speaking is also closely connected with the rationalism of the Enlightenment, which views human and social reality in a mechanistic way. Thus there is a denial of the supreme insight concerning man's true greatness, his transcendence in respect to earthly realities, the contradiction in his heart between the desire for the fullness of what is good and his own inability to attain it, and above all, the need for salvation which results from this situation.

14. From the same atheistic source, socialism also derives its choice of the means of action condemned in *Rerum Novarum,* namely, class struggle. The pope does not, of course, intend to condemn every possible form of social conflict. The church is well aware that in the course of history conflicts of interest between different social groups inevitably arise and that in the face of such conflicts Christians must often take a position, honestly and decisively. The encyclical *Laborem Exercens* moreover clearly recognized the positive role of conflict when it takes the form of a 'struggle for social justice';[41] *Quadragesimo Anno* had already stated that 'if the class struggle abstains from enmities and mutual hatred, it gradually changes into an honest discussion of differences founded on a desire for justice.'[42]

14.1. However, what is condemned in class struggle is the idea that conflict is not restrained by ethical or juridical considerations or by respect for the dignity of others (and consequently of oneself); a reasonable compromise is thus excluded, and what is pursued is not the general good of society, but a partisan interest which replaces the common good and sets out to destroy whatever stands in its way. In a word, it is a question of transferring to the sphere of internal conflict between social groups the doctrine of 'total war,' which the militarism and imperialism of that time brought to bear on international relations. As a result of this doctrine, the search for a proper balance between the interests of the various nations was replaced by attempts to impose the absolute domination of one's own side through the destruction of the other side's capacity to resist, using every possible means, not excluding the use of lies, terror tactics against citizens and weapons of utter destruction (which precisely in those years were beginning to be designed). Therefore class struggle in the Marxist sense and militarism have the same root, namely, atheism and contempt for the human person, which place the principle of force above that of reason and law.

15. *Rerum Novarum* is opposed to state control of the means of production, which would reduce every citizen to being a 'cog' in the state machine. It is no less forceful in criticizing a concept of the state which completely excludes the economic sector from the state's range of interest and action. There is certainly a legitimate sphere of autonomy in economic life which the state should not enter. The state, however, has the task of determining the juridical framework within which economic affairs are to be conducted and thus of safeguarding the prerequisites of a free economy, which presumes a certain equality between the parties such that one party would not be so powerful as practically to reduce the other to subservience.[43]

15.2. In this regard, *Rerum Novarum* points the way to just reforms which can restore dignity to work as the free activity of man. These reforms imply that society and the state will both assume responsibility, especially for protecting the worker from the nightmare of unemployment. Historically, this has happened in two converging ways: either through economic policies aimed at ensuring balanced growth and full employment or through unemployment insurance and retraining programs capable of ensuring a smooth transfer of workers from crisis sectors to those in expansion.

15.3. Furthermore, society and the state must ensure wage levels adequate for the maintenance of the worker and his family, including a certain amount for savings. This requires a continuous effort to improve workers' training and capability so that their work will be more skilled and productive, as well as careful controls and adequate legislative measures to block shameful forms of exploitation, especially to the disadvantage of the most vulnerable workers, of immigrants and of those on the margins of society. The role of trade unions in negotiating minimum salaries and working conditions is decisive in this area.

15.4. Finally, 'humane' working hours and adequate free time need to be guaranteed as well as the right to express one's own personality at the workplace without suffering any affront to one's conscience or personal dignity. This is the place to mention once more the role of trade unions, not only in negotiating contracts, but also as 'places' where workers can express themselves. They serve the development of an authentic culture of work and help workers to share in a fully human way in the life of their place of employment.[44]

15.5. The state must contribute to the achievement of these goals both directly and indirectly. Indirectly and according to the principle of subsidiarity, by creating favorable conditions for the free exercise of economic activity, which will lead to abundant opportunities for employment and sources of wealth. Directly and according to the principle of solidarity, by defending the weakest by placing certain limits on the autonomy of the parties who determine working conditions and by ensuring in every case the necessary minimum support for the unemployed worker.[45]

15.6. The encyclical and the related social teaching of the church had far-reaching influence in the years bridging the 19th and 20th centuries. This influence is evident in the numerous reforms which were introduced in the areas of social security, pensions, health insurance and compensation in the case of accidents, within the framework of greater respect for the rights of workers.[46]

16. These reforms were carried out in part by states, but in the struggle to achieve them the role of the workers' movement was an important one. This movement, which began as a response of moral conscience to unjust and harmful situations, conducted a widespread campaign for reform far removed from vague ideology and closer to the daily needs of workers. In this context its efforts were often joined to those of Christians in order to improve workers' living conditions. Later on this movement was dominated to a certain extent by the Marxist ideology against which *Rerum Novarum* had spoken.

16.1. These same reforms were also partly the result of an open process by which society organized itself through the establishment of effective instruments of solidarity which were capable of sustaining an economic growth more respectful of the values of the person. Here we should remember the numerous efforts to which Christians made a notable contribution in establishing producers', consumers' and credit cooperatives, in promoting general education and professional training, in experimenting with various forms of participation in the life of the workplace and in the life of society in general.

16.2. Thus as we look at the past there is good reason to thank God that the great encyclical was not without an echo in human hearts and indeed led to a generous response on the practical level. Still, we must acknowledge that its prophetic message was not fully accepted by people at the time. Precisely for this reason there ensued some very serious tragedies.

17. Reading the encyclical within the context of Pope Leo's whole magisterium,[47] we see how it points essentially to the socioeconomic consequences of an error which has even greater implications. As has been mentioned, this error consists in an understanding of human freedom which detaches it from obedience to the truth and consequently from the duty to respect the rights of others. The essence of freedom then becomes self-love carried to the point of contempt for God and neighbor, a self-love which leads to an unbridled affirmation of self-interest and which refuses to be limited by any demand of justice.[48]

17.1. This very error had extreme consequences in the tragic series of wars which ravaged Europe and the world between 1914 and 1945. Some of these resulted from militarism and exaggerated nationalism, and from related forms of totalitarianism; some derived from the class struggle; still others were civil wars or wars of an ideological nature. Without the terrible burden of hatred and resentment which had built up as a result of so many injustices both on the international level and within individual states, such cruel wars would not have been possible in which great nations invested their energies and in which there was no hesitation to violate the most sacred human rights, with the extermination of entire peoples and social groups being planned and carried out. Here we recall the Jewish people in particular, whose terrible fate has become a symbol of the aberration of which man is capable when he turns against God.

17.2. However, it is only when hatred and injustice are sanctioned and organized by the ideologies based on them, rather than on the truth about man, that they take possession of entire nations and drive them to act.[49] *Rerum Novarum* opposed ideologies of hatred and showed how violence and resentment could be overcome by justice. May the memory of those terrible events guide the actions of everyone, particularly the leaders of nations in our own time when other forms of injustice are fueling new hatreds and when new ideologies which exalt violence are appearing on the horizon.

18. While it is true that since 1945 weapons have been silent on the European continent, it must be remembered that true peace is never simply the result of military victory, but rather implies both the removal of the causes of war and genuine reconciliation between peoples. For many years there has been in Europe and the world a situation of non-war rather than genuine peace. Half of the continent fell under the domination of a communist dictatorship, while the other half organized itself in defense against this threat. Many peoples lost the ability to control their own destiny and were enclosed within the suffocating boundaries of an empire

in which efforts were made to destroy their historical memory and the centuries-old roots of their culture. As a result of this violent division of Europe, enormous masses of people were compelled to leave their homeland or were forcibly deported.

18.1. An insane arms race swallowed up the resources needed for the development of national economies and for assistance to the less-developed nations. Scientific and technological progress, which should have contributed to man's well-being, was transformed into an instrument of war: Science and technology were directed to the production of ever more efficient and destructive weapons. Meanwhile, an ideology, a perversion of authentic philosophy, was called upon to provide doctrinal justification for the new war. And this war was not simply expected and prepared for, but was actually fought with enormous bloodshed in various parts of the world. The logic of power blocs or empires, denounced in various church documents and recently in the encyclical *Sollicitudo Rei Socialis*,[50] led to a situation in which controversies and disagreements among Third World countries were systematically aggravated and exploited in order to create difficulties for the adversary.

18.2. Extremist groups, seeking to resolve such controversies through the use of arms, found ready political and military support and were equipped and trained for war; those who tried to find peaceful and humane solutions, with respect for the legitimate interests of all parties, remained isolated and often fell victim to their opponents. In addition, the precariousness of the peace which followed World War II was one of the principal causes of the militarization of many Third World countries and the fratricidal conflicts which afflicted them as well as of the spread of terrorism and of increasingly barbaric means of political and military conflict. Moreover, the whole world was oppressed by the threat of an atomic war capable of leading to the extinction of humanity.

18.3. Science used for military purposes had placed this decisive instrument at the disposal of hatred strengthened by ideology. But if war can end without winners or losers in a suicide of humanity, then we must repudiate the logic which leads to it: the idea that the effort to destroy the enemy, confrontation and war itself are factors of progress and historical advancement.[51] When the need for this repudiation is understood, the concepts of 'total war' and 'class struggle' must necessarily be called into question.

19. At the end of World War II, however, such a development was still being formed in people's consciences. What received attention was the spread of communist totalitarianism over more than half of Europe and over other parts of the world. The war, which should have re-established freedom and restored the rights of nations, ended without having attained these goals. Indeed, in a way, for many peoples, expecially those which had suffered most during the war, it openly contradicted these goals. It may be said that the situation which arose has evoked different responses.

19.1. Following the destruction caused by the war, we see in some countries and under certain aspects a positive effort to rebuild a democratic society inspired by social justice, so as to deprive communism of the revolutionary potential represented by masses of people subjected to exploitation and oppression. In general, such attempts endeavor to preserve free-market mechanisms, ensuring by means of a stable currency and the harmony of social relations the conditions for steady and healthy economic growth in which people through their own work can build a better future for themselves and their families. At the same time, these attempts try to avoid making market mechanisms the only point of reference for social life, and they tend to subject them to public control, which upholds the principle of the common destination of material goods.

19.2. In this context, an abundance of work opportunities, a solid system of social security and professional training, the freedom to join trade unions and the effective action of unions, the assistance provided in cases of unemployment, the opportunities for democratic participation in the life of society—all these are meant to deliver work from the mere condition of 'a commodity' and to guarantee its dignity.

19.3. Then there are the other social forces and ideological movements which oppose Marxism by setting up systems of 'national security' aimed at controlling the whole of society in a systematic way in order to make Marxist infiltration impossible. By emphasizing and increasing the power of the state, they wish to protect their people from communism, but in doing so they run the grave risk of destroying the freedom and values of the person, the very things for whose sake it is necessary to oppose communism.

19.4. Another kind of response, practical in nature, is represented by the affluent society or the consumer society. It seeks to defeat Marxism on the level of pure materialism by showing how a free-market society can achieve a greater satisfaction of material human needs than communism, while equally excluding spiritual values.

19.5. In reality, while on the one hand it is true that this social model shows the failure of Marxism to contribute to a humane and better society, on the other hand, insofar as it denies an autonomous existence and value to morality, law, culture and religion, it agrees with Marxism in the sense that it totally reduces man to the sphere of economics and the satisfaction of material needs.

20. During the same period, a widespread process of 'decolonization' occurred by which many countries gained or regained their independence and the right freely to determine their own destiny. With the formal reacquisition of state sovereignty, however, these countries often find themselves merely at the beginning of the journey toward the construction of genuine independence. Decisive sectors of the economy still remain de facto in the hands of large foreign companies which are unwilling to commit themselves to the long-term development of the host country. Political life itself is controlled by foreign powers, while within the national boundaries there are tribal groups not yet amalgamated into a genuine national community. Also lacking is a class of competent professional people capable of running the state apparatus in an honest and just way nor are there qualified personnel for managing the economy in an efficient and responsible manner.

20.1. Given this situation, many think that Marxism can offer a sort of shortcut for building up the nation and the state; thus many variants of socialism emerge with specific national characteristics. Legitimate demands for national recovery, forms of nationalism and also of militarism, principles drawn from ancient popular traditions (which are sometimes in harmony with Christian social doctrine) and Marxist-Leninist concepts and ideas—all these mingle in the many ideologies which take shape in ways that differ from case to case.

21. Last, it should be remembered that after World War II and in reaction to its horrors, there arose a more lively sense of human rights, which found recognition in a number of international documents[52] and, one might say, in the drawing up of a new 'right of nations,' to which the Holy See has constantly contributed. The focal point of this evolution has been the United Nations. Not only has there been a development in awareness of the rights of individuals, but also in awareness of the rights of nations as well as a clearer realization of the need to act in order to remedy the grave imbalances that exist between the various geographical areas of the world. In a certain sense these imbalances have shifted the center of the social question from the national to the international level.[53]

21.1. While noting this process with satisfaction, nevertheless one cannot ignore the fact that the overall balance of the various policies of aid for development has not always been positive. The United Nations, moreover, has not yet succeeded in establishing as alternatives to war effective means for the resolution of international conflicts. This seems to be the most urgent problem which the international community has yet to resolve.

CHAPTER III

The year 1989

22. It is on the basis of the world situation just described and already elaborated in the encyclical *Sollicitudo Rei Socialis* that the unexpected and promising significance of the events of recent years can be understood. Although they certainly reached their climax in 1989 in the countries of Central and Eastern Europe, they embrace a longer period of time and a wider geographical area. In the course of the '80s, certain dictatorial and oppressive regimes fell one by one in some countries of Latin America and also of Africa and Asia. In other cases there began a difficult but productive transition toward more participatory and more just political structures. An important, even decisive, contribution was made by the church's commitment to defend and promote human rights. In situations strongly influenced by ideology, in which polarization obscured the awareness of a human dignity common to all, the church affirmed clearly and forcefully that every individual—whatever his or her personal convictions—bears the image of God and therefore deserves respect. Often the vast majority of people identified themselves with this kind of affirmation, and this led to a search for forms of protest and for political solutions more respectful of the dignity of the person.

22.1. From this historical process new forms of democracy have

[448]

emerged which offer a hope for change in fragile political and social structures weighed down by a painful series of injustices and resentments as well as by a heavily damaged economy and serious social conflicts. Together with the whole church, I thank God for the often heroic witness borne in such difficult circumstances by many pastors, entire Christian communities, individual members of the faithful and other people of good will; at the same time I pray that he will sustain the efforts being made by everyone to build a better future. This is, in fact, a responsibility which falls not only to the citizens of the countries in question, but to all Christians and people of good will. It is a question of showing that the complex problems faced by those peoples can be resolved through dialogue and solidarity rather than by a struggle to destroy the enemy through war.

23. Among the many factors involved in the fall of oppressive regimes, some deserve special mention. Certainly the decisive factor which gave rise to the changes was the violation of the rights of workers. It cannot be forgotten that the fundamental crisis of systems claiming to express the rule and indeed the dictatorship of the working class began with the great upheavals which took place in Poland in the name of solidarity. It was the throngs of working people which foreswore the ideology which presumed to speak in their name. On the basis of a hard, lived experience of work and of oppression, it was they who recovered and in a sense rediscovered the content and principles of the church's social doctrine.

23.1. Also worthy of emphasis is the fact that the fall of this kind of 'bloc' or empire was accomplished almost everywhere by means of peaceful protest, using only the weapons of truth and justice. While Marxism held that only by exacerbating social conflicts was it possible to resolve them through violent confrontation, the protests which led to the collapse of Marxism tenaciously insisted on trying every avenue of negotiation, dialogue and witness to the truth, appealing to the conscience of the adversary and seeking to reawaken in him a sense of shared human dignity.

23.2. It seemed that the European order resulting from World War II and sanctioned by the Yalta agreements could only be overturned by another war. Instead, it has been overcome by the non-violent commitment of people who, while always refusing to yield to the force of power, succeeded time after time in finding effective ways of bearing witness to the truth. This disarmed the adversary, since violence always needs to justify itself through deceit and to appear, however falsely, to be defending a right or responding to a threat posed by others.[54] Once again I thank God for having sustained people's hearts amid difficult trials, and I pray that this example will prevail in other places and other circumstances. May people learn to fight for justice without violence, renouncing class struggle in their internal disputes and war in international ones.

24. The second factor in the crisis was certainly the inefficiency of the economic system, which is not to be considered simply as a technical problem, but rather a consequence of the violation of the human rights to private initiative, to ownership of property and to freedom in the economic sector. To this must be added the cultural and national dimension: It is not

possible to understand man on the basis of economics alone nor to define him simply on the basis of class membership. Man is understood in a more complete way when he is situated within the sphere of culture through his language, history and the position he takes toward the fundamental events of life such as birth, love, work and death. At the heart of every culture lies the attitude man takes to the greatest mystery: the mystery of God. Different cultures are basically different ways of facing the question of the meaning of personal existence. When this question is eliminated, the culture and moral life of nations are corrupted. For this reason the struggle to defend work was spontaneously linked to the struggle for culture and for national rights.

24.1. But the true cause of the new developments was the spiritual void brought about by atheism, which deprived the younger generations of a sense of direction and in many cases led them, in the irrepressible search for personal identity and for the meaning of life, to rediscover the religious roots of their national cultures and to rediscover the person of Christ himself as the existentially adequate response to the desire in every human heart for goodness, truth and life. This search was supported by the witness of those who in difficult circumstances and under persecution remained faithful to God. Marxism had promised to uproot the need for God from the human heart, but the results have shown that it is not possible to succeed in this without throwing the heart into turmoil.

25. The events of 1989 are an example of the success of willingness to negotiate and of the Gospel spirit in the face of an adversary determined not to be bound by moral principles. These events are a warning to those who in the name of political realism wish to banish law and morality from the political arena. Undoubtedly the struggle which led to the changes of 1989 called for clarity, moderation, suffering and sacrifice. In a certain sense, it was a struggle born of prayer, and it would have been unthinkable without immense trust in God, the Lord of history, who carries the human heart in his hands. It is by uniting his own sufferings for the sake of truth and freedom to the sufferings of Christ on the cross that man is able to accomplish the miracle of peace and is in a position to discern the often narrow path between the cowardice which gives in to evil and the violence which, under the illusion of fighting evil, only makes it worse.

25.1. Nevertheless, it cannot be forgotten that the manner in which the individual exercises his freedom is conditioned in innumerable ways. While these certainly have an influence on freedom, they do not determine it; they make the exercise of freedom more difficult or less difficult, but they cannot destroy it. Not only is it wrong from the ethical point of view to disregard human nature, which is made for freedom, but in practice it is impossible to do so. Where society is so organized as to reduce arbitrarily or even suppress the sphere in which freedom is legitimately exercised, the result is that the life of society becomes progressively disorganized and goes into decline.

25.2. Moreover, man, who was created for freedom, bears within himself the wound of original sin, which constantly draws him toward evil and puts him in need of redemption. Not only is this doctrine an integral part of Christian revelation, it also has great hermeneutical value insofar as it helps one to understand human reality. Man tends toward good, but he is also capable of evil. He can transcend his immediate interest and still remain bound to it. The social order will be all the more stable, the more it takes this fact into account and does not place in opposition personal interest and the interests of society as a whole, but rather seeks ways to bring them into fruitful harmony. In fact, where self-interest is violently suppressed, it is replaced by a burdensome system of bureaucratic control which dries up the wellsprings of initiative and creativity. When people think they possess the secret of a perfect social organization which makes evil impossible, they also think that they can use any means, including violence and deceit, in order to bring that organization into being. Politics then becomes a 'secular religion' which operates under the illusion of creating paradise in this world. But no political society—which possesses its own autonomy and laws[55]—can ever be confused with the kingdom of God. The Gospel parable of the weeds among the wheat (cf. Mt. 13:24-30, 36-43) teaches that it is for God alone to separate the subjects of the kingdom from the subjects of the Evil One and that this judgment will take place at the end of time. By presuming to anticipate judgment here and now, man puts himself in the place of God and sets himself against the patience of God.

25.3. Through Christ's sacrifice on the cross, the victory of the kingdom of God has been achieved once and for all. Nevertheless, the Christian life involves a struggle against temptation and the forces of evil. Only at the end of history will the Lord return in glory for the final judgment (cf. Mt. 25:31) with the establishment of a new heaven and a new earth (cf. 2 Pt. 3:13; Rv. 21:1); but as long as time lasts the struggle between good and evil continues even in the human heart itself.

25.4. What sacred Scripture teaches us about the prospects of the kingdom of God is not without consequences for the life of temporal societies, which, as the adjective indicates, belong to the realm of time, with all that this implies of imperfection and impermanence. The kingdom of God, being in the world without being of the world, throws light on the order of human society, while the power of grace penetrates that order and gives it life. In this way the requirements of a society worthy of man are better perceived, deviations are corrected, the courage to work for what is good is reinforced. In union with all people of good will, Christians, especially the laity, are called to this task of imbuing human realities with the Gospel.[56]

26. The events of 1989 took place principally in the countries of Eastern and Central Europe. However, they have worldwide importance because they have positive and negative consequences which concern the whole human family. These consequences are not mechanistic or fatalistic in character, but rather are opportunities for human freedom to cooperate with the merciful plan of God, who acts within history.

26.1. The first consequence was an encounter in some countries between the church and the workers' movement, which came about as a result of an ethical and explicitly Christian reaction against a widespread situation of injustice. For about a century the workers' movement had fallen in part under the dominance of Marxism in the conviction that the working class, in order to struggle effectively against oppression, had to appropriate its economic and materialistic theories.

26.2. In the crisis of Marxism, the natural dictates of the consciences of workers have re-emerged in a demand for justice and a recognition of the dignity of work in conformity with the social doctrine of the church.[57] The worker movement is part of a more general movement among workers and other people of good will for the liberation of the human person and for the affirmation of human rights. It is a movement which today has spread to many countries and which, far from opposing the Catholic Church, looks to her with interest.

26.3. The crisis of Marxism does not rid the world of the situations of injustice and oppression which Marxism itself exploited and on which it fed. To those who are searching today for a new and authentic theory and praxis of liberation, the church offers not only her social doctrine and, in general, her teaching about the human person redeemed in Christ, but also her concrete commitment and material assistance in the struggle against marginalization and suffering.

26.4. In the recent past, the sincere desire to be on the side of the oppressed and not to be cut off from the course of history has led many believers to seek in various ways an impossible compromise between Marxism and Christianity. Moving beyond all that was short-lived in these attempts, present circumstances are leading to a reaffirmation of the positive value of an authentic theology of integral human liberation.[58] Considered from this point of view, the events of 1989 are proving to be important also for the countries of the Third World, which are searching for their own path to development, just as they were important for the countries of Central and Eastern Europe.

27. The second consequence concerns the peoples of Europe themselves. Many individual, social, regional and national injustices were committed during and prior to the years in which communism dominated; much hatred and ill will have accumulated. There is a real danger that these will re-explode after the collapse of dictatorship, provoking serious conflicts and casualties should there be a lessening of the moral commitment and conscious striving to bear witness to the truth which were the inspiration for past efforts. It is to be hoped that hatred and violence will not triumph in people's hearts, especially among those who are struggling for justice, and that all people will grow in the spirit of peace and forgiveness.

27.1. What is needed are concrete steps to create or consolidate international structures capable of intervening through appropriate arbitration in the conflicts which arise between nations, so that each nation can uphold its own rights and reach a just agreement and peaceful settlement vis-a-vis the rights of others. This is especially needed for the nations of Europe, which are closely united in a bond of common culture and an age-old history. A great effort is needed to rebuild morally and economically the countries which have abandoned communism. For a long time the most elementary economic relationships were distorted, and basic virtues of economic life such as truthfulness, trustworthiness and hard work were denigrated. A patient material and moral reconstruction is needed, even as people, exhausted by longstanding privation, are asking their governments for tangible and immediate results in the form of material benefits and an adequate fulfillment of their legitimate aspirations.

27.2. The fall of Marxism has naturally had a great impact on the division of the planet into worlds which are closed to one another and in jealous competition. It has further highlighted the reality of interdependence among peoples as well as the fact that human work by its nature is meant to unite peoples, not divide them. Peace and prosperity, in fact, are goods which belong to the whole human race: It is not possible to enjoy them in a proper and lasting way if they are achieved and maintained at the cost of other peoples and nations by violating their rights or excluding them from the sources of well-being.

28. In a sense, for some countries of Europe the real postwar period is just beginning. The radical reordering of economic systems, hitherto collectivized, entails problems and sacrifices comparable to those which the countries of Western Europe had to face in order to rebuild after World War II. It is right that in the present difficulties the formerly communist countries should be aided by the united effort of other nations. Obviously they themselves must be the primary agents of their own development, but they must also be given a reasonable opportunity to accomplish this goal, something that cannot happen without the help of other countries. Moreover, their present condition, marked by difficulties and shortages, is the result of a historical process in which the formerly communist countries were often objects and not subjects. Thus they find themselves in the present situation not as a result of free choice or mistakes which were made, but as a consequence of tragic historical events which were violently imposed on them and which prevented them from following the path of economic and social development.

28.1. Assistance from other countries, especially the countries of Europe which were part of that history and which bear responsibility for it, represents a debt in justice. But it also corresponds to the interest and welfare of Europe as a whole, since Europe cannot live in peace if the various conflicts which have arisen as a result of the past are to become more acute because of a situation of economic disorder, spiritual dissatisfaction and desperation.

28.2. This need, however, must not lead to a slackening of efforts to sustain and assist the countries of the Third World, which often suffer even more serious conditions of poverty and want.[59] What is called for is a special effort to mobilize resources, which are not lacking in the world as a whole, for the purpose of economic growth and common development, redefining the priorities and hierarchies of values on the basis of which economic and political choices are made. Enormous resources can be made available by disarming the huge military machines which were constructed for the conflict between East and West. These resources could become even more abundant if in place of war reliable procedures for the resolution of conflicts could be set up, with the resulting spread of the principle of arms control and arms reduction also in the countries of the Third World, through the adoption of appropriate measures against the arms trade.[60] But it will be necessary above all to abandon a mentality in which the poor—as individuals and as peoples—are considered a burden, as irksome intruders trying to consume what others have produced. The poor ask for the right to share in enjoying material goods and to make good use of their capacity for work, thus creating a world that is more just and prosperous for all. The advancement of the poor constitutes a great opportunity for the moral, cultural and even economic growth of all humanity.

29. Finally, development must not be understood solely in economic terms, but in a way that is fully human.[61] It is not only a question of raising all peoples to the level currently enjoyed by the richest countries, but rather of building up a more decent life through united labor, of concretely enhancing every individual's dignity and creativity as well as his capacity to respond to his personal vocation and thus to God's call. The apex of development is the exercise of the right and duty to seek God, to know him and to live in accordance with that knowledge.[62] In the totalitarian and authoritarian regimes, the principle that force predominates over reason was carried to the extreme. Man was compelled to submit to a conception of reality imposed on him by coercion and not reached by virtue of his own reason and the exercise of his own freedom. This principle must be overturned and total recognition must be given to the rights of the human conscience, which is bound only to the truth, both natural and revealed. The recognition of these rights represents the primary foundation of every authentically free political order.[63] It is important to reaffirm this latter principle for several reasons:

29.1. a) Because the old forms of totalitarianism and authoritarianism are not yet completely vanquished; indeed there is a risk that they will regain their strength. This demands renewed efforts of cooperation and solidarity between all countries.

29.2. b) Because in the developed countries there is sometimes an excessive promotion of purely utilitarian values, with an appeal to the appetites and inclinations toward immediate gratification, making it difficult to recognize and respect the hierarchy of the true values of human existence.

29.3. c) Because in some countries new forms of religious fundamentalism are emerging which covertly, or even openly, deny to citizens of faiths other than that of the majority the full exercise of their civil and religious rights, preventing them from taking part in the cultural process and restricting both the church's right to preach the Gospel and the rights of those who hear this preaching to accept it and to be converted to Christ. No authentic progress is possible without respect for the natural and fundamental right to know the truth and live according to that truth. The exercise and development of this right includes the right to discover and freely to accept Jesus Christ, who is man's true good.[64]

CHAPTER IV

Private property and the universal destination of material goods

30. In *Rerum Novarum*, of Material Goods, Leo XIII strongly affirmed the

natural character of the right to private property, using various arguments against the socialism of his time.[65] This right, which is fundamental for the autonomy and development of the person, has always been defended by the church up to our own day. At the same time the church teaches that the possession of material goods is not an absolute right and that its limits are inscribed in its very nature as a human right.

30.1. While the pope proclaimed the right to private ownership, he affirmed with equal clarity that the 'use' of goods, while marked by freedom, is subordinated to their original common destination as created goods as well as to the will of Jesus Christ as expressed in the Gospel. Pope Leo wrote: 'Those whom fortune favors are admonished...that they should tremble at the warnings of Jesus Christ...and that a most strict account must be given to the Supreme Judge for the use of all they possess'; and quoting St Thomas Aquinas, he added: 'But if the question be asked how must one's possessions be used, the church replies without hesitation that man should not consider his material possessions as his own, but as common to all,' because 'above the laws and judgments of men stands the law, the judgment of Christ.'[66]

30.2. The successors of Leo XIII have repeated this twofold affirmation: the necessity and therefore the legitimacy of private ownership as well as the limits which are imposed on it.[67] The Second Vatican Council likewise clearly restated the traditional doctrine in words which bear repeating: 'In making use of the exterior things we lawfully possess, we ought to regard them not just as our own but also as common, in the sense that they can profit not only the owners but others too'; and a little later we read: 'Private property or some ownership of external goods affords each person the scope needed for personal and family autonomy, and should be regarded as an extension of human freedom....Of its nature private property also has a social function, which is based on the law of the common purpose of goods.'[68] I have returned to this same doctrine, first in my address to the third conference of the Latin American bishops at Puebla and later in the encyclicals *Laborem Exercens* and *Sollicitudo Rei Socialis*.[69]

31. Rereading this teaching on the right to property and the common destination of material wealth as it applies to the present time, the question can be raised concerning the origin of the material goods which sustain human life, satisfy people's needs and are an object of their rights.

31.1. The original source of all that is good is the very act of God, who created both the earth and man, and who gave the earth to man so that he might have dominion over it by his work and enjoy its fruits (Gn. 1:28). God gave the earth to the whole human race for the sustenance of all its members, without excluding or favoring anyone. This is the foundation of the universal destination of the earth's goods. The earth, by reason of its fruitfulness and its capacity to satisfy human needs, is God's first gift for the sustenance of human life. But the earth does not yield its fruits without a particular human response to God's gift, that is to say, without work. It is through work that man, using his intelligence and exercising his freedom, succeeds in dominating the earth and making it a fitting home. In this way he makes part of the earth his own, precisely the part which he has acquired through work; this is the origin of individual property. Obviously he also has the responsibility not to hinder others from having their own part of God's gift; indeed he must cooperate with others so that together all can dominate the earth.

31.2. In history, these two factors—work and the land—are to be found at the beginning of every human society. However, they do not always stand in the same relationship to each other. At one time the natural fruitfulness of the earth appeared to be and was in fact the primary factor of wealth, while work was, as it were, the help and support for this fruitfulness. In our time, the role of human work is becoming increasingly important as the productive factor both of non-material and of material wealth. Moreover, it is becoming clearer how a person's work is naturally interrelated with the work of others. More than ever, work is work with others and work for others: It is a matter of doing something for someone else. Work becomes ever more fruitful and productive to the extent that people become more knowledgeable of the productive potentialities of the earth and more profoundly cognizant of the needs of those for whom their work is done.

32. In our time in particular there exists another form of ownership which is becoming no less important than land: the possession of know-how, technology and skill. The wealth of the industrialized nations is based much more on this kind of ownership than on natural resources.

32.1. Mention has just been made of the fact that people work with each other, sharing in a 'community of work' which embraces ever widening circles. A person who produces something other than for his own use generally does so in order that others may use it after they have paid a just price mutually agreed upon through free bargaining. It is precisely the ability to foresee both the needs of others and the combinations of productive factors most adapted to satisfying those needs that constitutes another important source of wealth in modern society. Besides, many goods cannot be adequately produced through the work of an isolated individual; they require the cooperation of many people in working toward a common goal. Organizing such a productive effort, planning its duration in time, making sure that it corresponds in a positive way to the demands which it must satisfy and taking the necessary risks—all this too is a source of wealth in today's society. In this way the role of disciplined and creative human work and, as an essential part of that work, initiative and entrepreneurial ability becomes increasingly evident and decisive.[70]

32.2. This process, which throws practical light on a truth about the person which Christianity has constantly affirmed, should be viewed carefully and favorably. Indeed, besides the earth, man's principal resource is man himself. His intelligence enables him to discover the earth's productive potential and the many different ways in which human needs can be satisfied. It is his disciplined work in close collaboration with others that makes possible the creation of ever more extensive working communities which can be relied upon to transform man's natural and human environments. Important virtues are involved in this process such as diligence, industriousness, prudence in undertaking reasonable risks, reliability and fidelity in interpersonal relationships as well as courage in carrying out decisions which are difficult and painful, but necessary both for the overall working of a business and in meeting possible setbacks.

32.3. The modern business economy has positive aspects. Its basis is human freedom exercised in the economic field, just as it is exercised in many other fields. Economic activity is indeed but one sector in a great variety of human activities, and like every other sector, it includes the right to freedom as well as the duty of making responsible use of freedom. But it is important to note that there are specific differences between the trends of modern society and those of the past, even the recent past. Whereas at one time the decisive factor of production was the land and later capital—understood as a total complex of the instruments of production—today the decisive factor is increasingly man himself, that is, his knowledge, especially his scientific knowledge, his capacity for interrelated and compact organization as well as his ability to perceive the needs of others and to satisfy them.

33. However, the risks and problems connected with this kind of process should be pointed out. The fact is that many people, perhaps the majority today, do not have the means which would enable them to take their place in an effective and humanly dignified way within a productive system in which work is truly central. They have no possibility of acquiring the basic knowledge which would enable them to express their creativity and develop their potential. They have no way of entering the network of knowledge and intercommunication which would enable them to see their qualities appreciated and utilized. Thus, if not actually exploited, they are to a great extent marginalized; economic development takes place over their heads, so to speak, when it does not actually reduce the already narrow scope of their old subsistence economies. They are unable to compete against the goods which are produced in ways which are new and which properly respond to needs, needs which they had previously been accustomed to meeting through traditional forms of organization. Allured by the dazzle of an opulence which is beyond their reach and at the same time driven by necessity, these people crowd the cities of the Third World where they are often without cultural roots and where they are exposed to situations of violent uncertainty without the possibility of becoming integrated. Their dignity is not acknowledged in any real way, and sometimes there are even attempts to eliminate them from history through coercive forms of demographic control which are contrary to human dignity.

33.1. Many other people, while not completely marginalized, live in situations in which the struggle for a bare minimum is uppermost. These are situations in which the rules of the earliest period of capitalism still flourish in conditions of 'ruthlessness' in no way inferior to the darkest moments of the first phase of industrialization. In other cases the land is still the central element in the economic process, but those who cultivate it are excluded from ownership and are reduced to a state of quasi-servitude.[71] In these cases it is still possible today, as in the days of *Rerum Novarum*, to speak of inhuman exploitation. In spite of the great changes which have taken place in the more advanced societies, the human inadequacies of capitalism and the resulting domination of things over people are far from disappearing. In fact, for the poor, to the lack of material goods has been added a lack of knowledge and training which prevents them from escaping their state of humiliating subjection.

33.2. Unfortunately, the great majority of people in the Third World still live in such conditions. It would be a mistake, however, to understand this 'world' in purely geographic terms. In some regions and in some social sectors of that world, development programs have been set up which are centered on the use not so much of the material resources available but of the 'human resources.'

33.3. Even in recent years it was thought that the poorest countries would develop by isolating themselves from the world market and by depending only on their own resources. Recent experience has shown that countries which did this have suffered stagnation and recession, while the countries which experienced development were those which succeeded in taking part in the general interrelated economic activities at the international level. It seems therefore that the chief problem is that of gaining fair access to the international market, based not on the unilateral principle of the exploitation of the natural resources of these countries but on the proper use of human resources.[72]

33.4. However, aspects typical of the Third World also appear in developed countries, where the constant transformation of the methods of production and consumption devalues certain acquired skills and professional expertise, and thus requires a continual effort of retraining and updating. Those who fail to keep up with the times can easily be marginalized as can the elderly, the young people who are incapable of finding their place in the life of society and in general those who are weakest or part of the so-called Fourth World. The situation of women too is far from easy in these conditions.

34. It would appear that on the level of individual nations and of international relations the free market is the most efficient instrument for utilizing resources and effectively responding to needs. But this is true only for those needs which are 'solvent' insofar as they are endowed with purchasing power and for those resources which are 'marketable' insofar as they are capable of obtaining a satisfactory price. But there are many human needs which find no place on the market. It is a strict duty of justice and truth not to allow fundamental human needs to remain unsatisfied and not to allow those burdened by such needs to perish. It is also necessary to help these needy people to acquire expertise, to enter the circle of exchange and to develop their skills in order to make the best use of their capacities and resources. Even prior to the logic of a fair exchange of goods and the forms of justice appropriate to it, there exists something which is due to man because he is man, by reason of his lofty dignity. Inseparable from that required 'something' is the possibility to survive and at the same time to make an active contribution to the common good of humanity.

34.1. In Third World contexts, certain objectives stated by *Rerum Novarum* remain valid and in some cases still constitute a goal yet to be reached, if man's work and his very being are not to be reduced to the level of a mere commodity. These objectives include a sufficient wage for the support of the family, social insurance for old age and unemployment, and adequate protection for the conditions of employment.

35. Here we find a wide range of opportunities for commitment and effort in the name of justice on the part of trade unions and other workers' organizations. These defend workers' rights and protect their interests as persons while fulfilling a vital cultural role so as to enable workers to participate more fully and honorably in the life of their nation and to assist them along the path of development.

35.1. In this sense, it is right to speak of a struggle against an economic system, if the latter is understood as a method of upholding the absolute predominance of capital, the possession of the means of production and of the land, in contrast to the free and personal nature of human work.[73] In the struggle against such a system, what is being proposed as an alternative is not the socialist system, which in fact turns out to be state capitalism, but rather a society of free work, of enterprise and of participation. Such a society is not directed against the market, but demands that the market be appropriately controlled by the forces of society and by the state so as to guarantee that the basic needs of the whole of society are satisfied.

35.2. The church acknowledges the legitimate role of profit as an indication that a business is functioning well. When a firm makes a profit, this means that productive factors have been properly employed and corresponding human needs have been duly satisfied. But profitability is not the only indicator of a firm's condition. It is possible for the financial accounts to be in order and yet for the people—who make up the firm's most valuable asset—to be humiliated and their dignity offended. Besides being morally inadmissible, this will eventually have negative repercussions on the firm's economic efficiency. In fact, the purpose of a business firm is not simply to make a profit, but is to be found in its very existence as a community of persons who in various ways are endeavoring to satisfy their basic needs and who form a particular group at the service of the whole of society. Profit is a regulator of the life of a business, but it is not the only one; other human and moral factors must also be considered, which in the long term are at least equally important for the life of a business.

35.3. We have seen that it is unacceptable to say that the defeat of so-called 'real socialism' leaves capitalism as the only model of economic organization. It is necessary to break down the barriers and monopolies which leave so many countries on the margins of development and to provide all individuals and nations with the basic conditions which will enable them to share in development. This goal calls for programmed and responsible efforts on the part of the entire international community. Stronger nations must offer weaker ones opportunities for taking their place in international life, and the latter must learn how to use these opportunities by making the necessary efforts and sacrifices and by ensuring political and economic stability, the certainty of better prospects for the future, the improvement of workers' skills and the training of competent business leaders who are conscious of their responsibilities.[74]

35.4. At present, the positive efforts which have been made along these lines are being affected by the still largely unsolved problem of the foreign debt of the poorer countries. The principle that debts must be paid is certainly just. However, it is not right to demand or expect payment when the effect would be the imposition of political choices leading to hunger and despair for entire peoples. It cannot be expected that the debts which have been contracted should be paid at the price of unbearable sacrifices. In such cases it is necessary to find—as in fact is partly happening—ways to lighten, defer or even cancel the debt compatible with the fundamental right of peoples to subsistence and progress.

36. It would now be helpful to direct our attention to the specific problems and threats emerging within the more advanced economies and which are related to their particular characteristics. In earlier stages of development, man always lived under the weight of necessity. His needs were few and were determined to a degree by the objective structures of his physical makeup. Economic activity was directed toward satisfying these needs. It is clear that today the problem is not only one of supplying people with a sufficient quantity of goods, but also of responding to a demand for quality: the quality of the goods to be produced and consumed, the quality of the services to be enjoyed, the quality of the environment and of life in general.

36.1. To call for an existence which is qualitatively more satisfying is of itself legitimate, but one cannot fail to draw attention to the new responsibilities and dangers connected with this phase of history. The manner in which new needs arise and are defined is always marked by a more or less appropriate concept of man and of his true good. A given culture reveals its overall understanding of life through the choices it makes in production and consumption. It is here that the phenomenon of consumerism ari ses. In singling out new needs and new means to meet them, one must be guided by a comprehensive picture of man which respects all the dimensions of his being and which subordinates his material and instinctive dimensions to his interior and spiritual ones. If, on the contrary, a direct appeal is made to his instincts—while ignoring in various ways the reality of the person as intelligent and free—then consumer attitudes and lifestyles can be created which are objectively improper and often damaging to his physical and spiritual health. Of itself, an economic system does not possess criteria for correctly distinguishing new and higher forms of satisfying human needs from artificial new needs which hinder the formation of a mature personality. Thus a great deal of educational and cultural work is urgently needed, including the education of consumers in the responsible use of their power of choice, the formation of a strong sense of responsibility among producers and among people in the mass media in particular as well as the necessary intervention by public authorities.

36.2. A striking example of artificial consumption contrary to the health and dignity of the human person, and certainly not easy to control, is the use of drugs. Widespread drug use is a sign of a serious malfunction in the social system; it also implies a materialistic and in a certain sense destructive 'reading' of human needs. In this way the innovative capacity of a free economy is brought to a one-sided and inadequate conclusion. Drugs, as well as pornography and other forms of consumerism which exploit the frailty of the weak, tend to fill the resulting spiritual void.

36.3. It is not wrong to want to live better; what is wrong is a style of life which is presumed to be better when it is directed toward 'having' rather than 'being' and which wants to have more not in order to be more, but in order to spend life in enjoyment as an end in itself.[75] It is therefore necessary to create lifestyles in which the quest for truth, beauty, goodness and communion with others for the sake of common growth are the factors which determine consumer choices, savings and investments. In this regard, it is not a matter of the duty of charity alone, that is, the duty to give from one's 'abundance' and sometimes even out of one's needs in order to provide what is essential for the life of a poor person. I am referring to the fact that even the decision to invest in one place rather than another, in one productive sector rather than another, is always a moral and cultural choice. Given the utter necessity of certain economic conditions and of political stability, the decision to invest, that is, to offer people an opportunity to make good use of their own labor, is also determined by an attitude of human sympathy and trust in providence, which reveals the human quality of the person making such decisions.

37. Equally worrying is the ecological question which accompanies the problem of consumerism and which is closely connected to it. In his desire to have and to enjoy rather than to be and to grow, man consumes the resources of the earth and his own life in an excessive and disordered way. At the root of the senseless destruction of the natural environment lies an anthropological error, which unfortunately is widespread in our day. Man, who discovers his capacity to transform and in a certain sense create the world through his own work, forgets that this is always based on God's prior and original gift of the things that are. Man thinks that he can make arbitrary use of the earth, subjecting it without restraint to his will as though it did not have its own requisites and a prior God-given purpose, which man can indeed develop but must not betray. Instead of carrying out his role as a cooperator with God in the work of creation, man sets himself up in place of God and thus ends up provoking a rebellion on the part of nature, which is more tyrannized than governed by him.[76]

37.1. In all this, one notes first the poverty or narrowness of man's outlook, motivated as he is by a desire to possess things rather than to relate them to the truth and lacking that disinterested, unselfish and aesthetic attitude that is born of wonder in the presence of being and of the beauty which enables one to see in visible things the message of the invisible God who created them. In this regard, humanity today must be conscious of its duties and obligations toward future generations.

38. In addition to the irrational destruction of the natural environment, we must also mention the more serious destruction of the human environment, something which is by no means receiving the attention it deserves. Although people are rightly worried—though much less than they should be—about preserving the natural habitats of the various animal species threatened with extinction because they realize that each of these species makes its particular contribution to the balance of nature in general, too little effort is made to safeguard the moral conditions for an authentic 'human ecology.' Not only has God given the earth to man, who must use it with respect for the original good purpose for which it was

given to him, but man too is God's gift to man. He must therefore respect the natural and moral structure with which he has been endowed. In this context, mention should be made of the serious problems of modern urbanization, of the need for urban planning which is concerned with how people are to live and of the attention which should be given to a 'social ecology' of work.

38.1. Man receives from God his essential dignity and with it the capacity to transcend every social order so as to move toward truth and goodness. But he is also conditioned by the social structure in which he lives, by the education he has received and by his environment. These elements can either help or hinder his living in accordance with the truth. The decisions which create a human environment can give rise to specific structures of sin which impede the full realization of those who are in any way oppressed by them. To destroy such structures and replace them with more authentic forms of living in community is a task which demands courage and patience.[77]

39. The first and fundamental structure for 'human ecology' is the family, in which man receives his first formative ideas about truth and goodness, and learns what it means to love and to be loved, and thus what it actually means to be a person. Here we mean the family founded on marriage, in which the mutual gift of self by husband and wife creates an environment in which children can be born and develop their potentialities, become aware of their dignity and prepare to face their unique and individual destiny. But it often happens that people are discouraged from creating the proper conditions for human reproduction and are led to consider themselves and their lives as a series of sensations to be experienced rather than as a work to be accomplished. The result is a lack of freedom, which causes a person to reject a commitment to enter into a stable relationship with another person and to bring children into the world or which leads people to consider children as one of the many 'things' which an individual can have or not have, according to taste, and which compete with other possibilities.

39.1. It is necessary to go back to seeing the family as the sanctuary of life. The family is indeed sacred: It is the place in which life—the gift of God—can be properly welcomed and protected against the many attacks to which it is exposed and can develop in accordance with what constitutes authentic human growth. In the face of the so-called culture of death, the family is the heart of the culture of life.

39.2. Human ingenuity seems to be directed more toward limiting, suppressing or destroying the sources of life—including recourse to abortion, which unfortunately is so widespread in the world—than toward defending and opening up the possibilities of life. The encyclical denounced systematic anti-childbearing campaigns which, on the basis of a distorted view of the demographic problem and in a climate of 'absolute lack of respect for the freedom of choice of the parties involved,' often subject them 'to intolerable pressures...in order to force them to submit to this new form of oppression.'[78] These policies are extending their field of action by the use of new techniques to the point of poisoning the lives of millions of defenseless human beings as if in a form of 'chemical warfare.'

39.3. These criticisms are directed not so much against an economic system as against an ethical and cultural system. The economy in fact is only one aspect and one dimension of the whole of human activity. If economic life is absolutized, if the production and consumption of goods become the center of social life and society's only value, not subject to any other value, the reason is to be found not so much in the economic system itself as in the fact that the entire sociocultural system, by ignoring the ethical and religious dimension, has been weakened and ends by limiting itself to the production of goods and services alone.[79]

39.4. All of this can be summed up by repeating once more that economic freedom is only one element of human freedom. When it becomes autonomous, when man is seen more as a producer or consumer of goods than as a subject who produces and consumes in order to live, then economic freedom loses its necessary relationship to the human person and ends up by alienating and oppressing him.[80]

40. It is the task of the state to provide for the defense and preservation of common goods such as the natural and human environments, which cannot be safeguarded simply by market forces. Just as in the time of primitive capitalism the state had the duty of defending the basic rights of workers, so now, with the new capitalism, the state and all of society have the duty of defending those collective goods which, among others, constitute the essential framework for the legitimate pursuit of personal goals on the part of each individual.

40.1. Here we find a new limit on the market: There are collective and qualitative needs which cannot be satisfied by market mechanisms. There are important human needs which escape its logic. There are goods which by their very nature cannot and must not be bought or sold. Certainly the mechanisms of the market offer secure advantages: They help to utilize resources better; they promote the exchange of products; above all they give central place to the person's desires and preferences, which in a contract meet the desires and preferences of another person. Nevertheless, these mechanisms carry the risk of an 'idolatry' of the market, an idolatry which ignores the existence of goods which by their nature are not and cannot be mere commodities.

41. Marxism criticized capitalist bourgeois societies, blaming them for the commercialization and alienation of human existence. This rebuke is of course based on a mistaken and inadequate idea of alienation derived solely from the sphere of relationships of production and ownership, that is, giving them a materialistic foundation and moreover denying the legitimacy and positive value of market relationships even in their own sphere. Marxism thus ends up by affirming that only in a collective society can alienation be eliminated. However, the historical experience of socialist countries has sadly demonstrated that collectivism does not do away with alienation but rather increases it, adding to it a lack of basic necessities and economic inefficiency.

41.1. The historical experience of the West, for its part, shows that even if the Marxist analysis and its foundation of alienation are false, nevertheless alienation—and the loss of the authentic meaning of life—is a reality in Western societies too. This happens in consumerism, when people are ensnared in a web of false and superficial gratifications rather than being helped to experience their personhood in an authentic and concrete way. Alienation is found also in work when it is organized so as to ensure maximum returns and profits with no concern whether the worker, through his own labor, grows or diminishes as a person, either through increased sharing in a genuinely supportive community or through increased isolation in a maze of relationships marked by destructive competitiveness and estrangement, in which he is considered only a means and not an end.

41.2. The concept of alienation needs to be led back to the Christian vision of reality by recognizing in alienation a reversal of means and ends. When man does not recognize in himself and in others the value and grandeur of the human person, he effectively deprives himself of the possibility of benefiting from his humanity and of entering into that relationship of solidarity and communion with others for which God created him. Indeed, it is through the free gift of self that man truly finds himself.[81] This gift is made possible by the human person's essential 'capacity for transcendence.' Man cannot give himself to a purely human plan for reality, to an abstract ideal or to a false utopia. As a person, he can give himself to another person or to other persons, and ultimately to God, who is the author of his being and who alone can fully accept his gift.[82] A man is alienated if he refuses to transcend himself and to live the experience of self-giving and of the formation of an authentic human community oriented toward his final destiny, which is God. A society is alienated if its forms of social organization, production and consumption make it more difficult to offer this gift of self and to establish this solidarity between people.

41.3. Exploitation, at least in the forms analyzed and described by Karl Marx, has been overcome in Western society. Alienation, however, has not been overcome as it exists in various forms of exploitation, when people use one another and when they seek an ever more refined satisfaction of their individual and secondary needs while ignoring the principal and authentic needs which ought to regulate the manner of satisfying the other ones too.[83] A person who is concerned solely or primarily with possessing and enjoying, who is no longer able to control his instincts and passions or to subordinate them by obedience to the truth, cannot be free: Obedience to the truth about God and man is the first condition of freedom, making it possible for a person to order his needs and desires and to choose the means of satisfying them according to a correct scale of values, so that the ownership of things may become an occasion of growth for him. This growth can be hindered as a result of manipulation by the means of mass communication, which impose fashions and trends of opinion through carefully orchestrated repetition without it being possible to subject to critical scrutiny the premises on which these fashions and trends are based.

42. Returning now to the initial question: Can it perhaps be said that after the failure of communism capitalism is the victorious social system and that capitalism should be the goal of the countries now making efforts to rebuild their economy and society? Is this the model which ought to be

proposed to the countries of the Third World, which are searching for the path to true economic and civil progress?

42.1. The answer is obviously complex. If by 'capitalism' is meant an economic system which recognizes the fundamental and positive role of business, the market, private property and the resulting responsibility for the means of production as well as free human creativity in the economic sector, then the answer is certainly in the affirmative, even though it would perhaps be more appropriate to speak of a 'business economy,' 'market economy' or simply 'free economy.' But if by capitalism is meant a system in which freedom in the economic sector is not circumscribed within a strong juridical framework which places it at the service of human freedom in its totality and which sees it as a particular aspect of that freedom, the core of which is ethical and religious, then the reply is certainly negative.

42.2. The Marxist solution has failed, but the realities of marginalization and exploitation remain in the world, especially the Third World, as does the reality of human alienation, especially in the more advanced countries. Against these phenomena the church strongly raises her voice. Vast multitudes are still living in conditions of great material and moral poverty. The collapse of the communist system in so many countries certainly removes an obstacle to facing these problems in an appropriate and realistic way, but it is not enough to bring about their solution. Indeed, there is a risk that a radical capitalistic ideology could spread which refuses even to consider these problems in the a priori belief that any attempt to solve them is doomed to failure, and which blindly entrusts their solution to the free development of market forces.

43. The church has no models to present; models that are real and truly effective can only arise within the framework of different historical situations through the efforts of all those who responsibly confront concrete problems in all their social, economic, political and cultural aspects as these interact with one another.[84] For such a task the church offers her social teaching as an indispensable and ideal orientation, a teaching which, as already mentioned, recognizes the positive value of the market and of enterprise, but which at the same time points out that these need to be oriented toward the common good. This teaching also recognizes the legitimacy of workers' efforts to obtain full respect for their dignity and to gain broader areas of participation in the life of industrial enterprises so that, while cooperating with others and under the direction of others, they can in a certain sense 'work for themselves'[85] through the exercise of their intelligence and freedom.

43.1. The integral development of the human person through work does not impede but rather promotes the greater productivity and efficiency of work itself, even though it may weaken consolidated power structures. A business cannot be considered only as a 'society of capital goods'; it is also a 'society of persons' in which people participate in different ways and with specific responsibilities, whether they supply the necessary capital for the company's activities or take part in such activities through their labor. To achieve these goals there is still need for a broad associated workers' movement directed toward the liberation and promotion of the whole person.

43.2. In the light of today's 'new things,' we have reread the relationship between individual or private property and the universal destination of material wealth. Man fulfills himself by using his intelligence and freedom. In so doing he utilizes the things of this world as objects and instruments and makes them his own. The foundation of the right to private initiative and ownership is to be found in this activity. By means of his work man commits himself not only for his own sake, but also for others and with others. Each person collaborates in the work of others and for their good. Man works in order to provide for the needs of his family, his community, his nation and ultimately all humanity.[86] Moreover, he collaborates in the work of his fellow employees as well as in the work of suppliers and in the customers' use of goods in a progressively expanding chain of solidarity. Ownership of the means of production, whether in industry or agriculture, is just and legitimate if it serves useful work. It becomes illegitimate, however, when it is not utilized or when it serves to impede the work of others in an effort to gain a profit which is not the result of the overall expansion of work and the wealth of society, but rather is the result of curbing them or of illicit exploitation, speculation or the breaking of solidarity among working people.[87] Ownership of this kind has no justification and represents an abuse in the sight of God and man.

43.3. The obligation to earn one's bread by the sweat of one's brow also presumes the right to do so. A society in which this right is systematically denied, in which economic policies do not allow workers to reach satisfactory levels of employment, cannot be justified from an ethical point of view nor can that society attain social peace.[88] Just as the person fully realizes himself in the free gift of self, so too ownership morally justifies itself in the creation, at the proper time and in the proper way, of opportunities for work and human growth for all.

CHAPTER V

State and culture

44. Pope Leo XIII was aware of the need for a sound theory of the state in order to ensure the normal development of man's spiritual and temporal activities, both of which are indispensable.[89] For this reason, in one passage of *Rerum Novarum* he presents the organization of society according to the three powers—legislative, executive and judicial—something which at the time represented a novelty in church teaching.[90] Such an ordering reflects a realistic vision of man's social nature, which calls for legislation capable of protecting the freedom of all. To that end, it is preferable that each power be balanced by other powers and by other spheres of responsibility which keep it within proper bounds. This is the principle of the 'rule of law,' in which the law is sovereign, and not the arbitrary will of individuals.

44.1. In modern times this concept has been opposed by totalitarianism, which in its Marxist-Leninist form maintains that some people, by virtue of a deeper knowledge of the laws of the development of society or through membership of a particular class or through contact with the deeper sources of the collective consciousness, are exempt from error and can therefore arrogate to themselves the exercise of absolute power. It must be added that totalitarianism arises out of a denial of truth in the objective sense. If there is no transcendent truth, in obedience to which man achieves his full identity, then there is no sure principle for guaranteeing just relations between people. Their self-interest as a class, group or nation would inevitably set them in opposition to one another. If one does not acknowledge transcendent truth, then the force of power takes over and each person tends to make full use of the means at his disposal in order to impose his own interests or his own opinion, with no regard for the rights of others. People are then respected only to the extent that they can be exploited for selfish ends. Thus, the root of modern totalitarianism is to be found in the denial of the transcendent dignity of the human person who, as the visible image of the invisible God, is therefore by his very nature the subject of rights which no one may violate—no individual, group, class, nation or state. Not even the majority of a social body may violate these rights by going against the minority, by isolating, oppressing or exploiting it or by attempting to annihilate it.[91]

45. The culture and praxis of totalitarianism also involve a rejection of the church. The state or the party which claims to be able to lead history toward perfect goodness and which sets itself above all values cannot tolerate the affirmation of an objective criterion of good and evil beyond the will of those in power, since such a criterion, in given circumstances, could be used to judge their actions. This explains why totalitarianism attempts to destroy the church or at least to reduce her to submission, making her an instrument of its own ideological apparatus.[92]

45.1. Furthermore, the totalitarian state tends to absorb within itself the nation, society, the family, religious groups and individuals themselves. In defending her own freedom, the church is also defending the human person, who must obey God rather than men (cf. Acts 5:29), as well as defending the family, the various social organizations and nations—all of which enjoy their own spheres of autonomy and sovereignty.

46. The church values the democratic system inasmuch as it ensures the participation of citizens in making political choices, guarantees to the governed the possibility both of electing and holding accountable those who govern them and of replacing them through peaceful means when appropriate.[93]

46.1. Thus she cannot encourage the formation of narrow ruling groups which usurp the power of the state for individual interests or for ideological ends.

46.2. Authentic democracy is possible only in a state ruled by law and on the basis of a correct conception of the human person. It requires that the necessary conditions be present for the advancement both of the individual through education and formation in true ideals, and of the 'subjectivity' of society through the creation of structures of participation and shared responsibility. Nowadays there is a tendency to claim that agnosticism and skeptical relativism are the philosophy and the basic attitude which correspond to democratic forms of political life. Those who are convinced that they know the truth and firmly adhere to it are considered unreliable from a democratic point of view, since they do not accept that truth is determined by the majority or that it is subject to variation according to different political trends. It must be observed in this regard that if there is no ultimate truth to guide and direct political activity, then ideas and convictions can easily be manipulated for reasons of power. As history demonstrates, a democracy without values easily turns into open or thinly disguised totalitarianism.

46.3. Nor does the church close her eyes to the danger of fanaticism or fundamentalism among those who, in the name of an ideology which purports to be scientific or religious, claim the right to impose on others their own concept of what is true and good. Christian truth is not of this kind. Since it is not an ideology, the Christian faith does not presume to imprison changing sociopolitical realities in a rigid schema, and it recognizes that human life is realized in history in conditions that are diverse and imperfect. Furthermore, in constantly reaffirming the transcendent dignity of the person, the church's method is always that of respect for freedom.[94]

46.4. But freedom attains its full development only by accepting the truth. In a world without truth, freedom loses its foundation and man is exposed to the violence of passion and to manipulation, both open and hidden. The Christian upholds freedom and serves it, constantly offering to others the truth which he has known (cf. Jn. 8:31-32), in accordance with the missionary nature of his vocation. While paying heed to every fragment of truth which he encounters in the life experience and in the culture of individuals and of nations, he will not fail to affirm in dialogue with others all that his faith and the correct use of reason have enabled him to understand.[95]

47. Following the collapse of communist totalitarianism and of many other totalitarian and 'national security' regimes, today we are witnessing a predominance, not without signs of opposition, of the democratic ideal, together with lively attention to and concern for human rights. But for this very reason it is necessary for peoples in the process of reforming their systems to give democracy an authentic and solid foundation through the explicit recognition of those rights.[96] Among the most important of these rights, mention must be made of the right to life, an integral part of which is the right of the child to develop in the mother's womb from the moment of conception; the right to live in a united family and in a moral environment conducive to the growth of the child's personality; the right to develop one's intelligence and freedom in seeking and knowing the truth; the right to share in the work which makes wise use of the earth's material resources, and to derive from that work the means to support oneself and one's dependents; and the right freely to establish a family, to have and to rear children through the responsible exercise of one's sexuality. In a certain sense, the source and synthesis of these rights is religious freedom, understood as the right to live in the truth of one's faith and in conformity with one's transcendent dignity as a person.[97]

47.1. Even in countries with democratic forms of government, these rights are not always fully respected. Here we are referring not only to the scandal of abortion, but also to different aspects of a crisis within democracies themselves, which seem at times to have lost the ability to make decisions aimed at the common good. Certain demands which arise within society are sometimes not examined in accordance with criteria of justice and morality, but rather on the basis of the electoral or financial power of the groups promoting them. With time, such distortions of political conduct create distrust and apathy, with a subsequent decline in the political participation and civic spirit of the general population, which feels abused and disillusioned. As a result, there is a growing inability to situate particular interests within the framework of a coherent vision of the common good. The latter is not simply the sum total of particular interests; rather it involves an assessment and integration of those interests on the basis of a balanced hierarchy of values; ultimately, it demands a correct understanding of the dignity and the rights of the person.[98]

47.2. The church respects the legitimate autonomy of the democratic order and is not entitled to express preferences for this or that institutional or constitutional solution. Her contribution to the political order is precisely her vision of the dignity of the person revealed in all its fullness in the mystery of the incarnate Word.[99]

48. These general observations also apply to the role of the state in the economic sector. Economic activity, especially the activity of a market economy, cannot be conducted in an institutional, juridical or political vacuum. On the contrary, it presupposes sure guarantees of individual freedom and private property as well as a stable currency and efficient public services. Hence the principal task of the state is to guarantee this security so that those who work and produce can enjoy the fruits of their labors and thus feel encouraged to work efficiently and honestly. The absence of stability, together with the corruption of public officials and the spread of improper sources of growing rich and of easy profits deriving from illegal or purely speculative activities, constitutes one of the chief obstacles to development and to the economic order.

48.1. Another task of the state is that of overseeing and directing the exercise of human rights in the economic sector. However, primary responsibility in this area belongs not to the state, but to individuals and to the various groups and associations which make up society. The state could not directly ensure the right to work for all its citizens unless it controlled every aspect of economic life and restricted the free initiative of individuals. This does not mean, however, that the state has no competence in this domain, as was claimed by those who argued against any rules in the economic sphere. Rather, the state has a duty to sustain business activities by creating conditions which will ensure job opportunities, by stimulating those activities where they are lacking or by supporting them in moments of crisis.

48.2. The state has the further right to intervene when particular monopolies create delays or obstacles to development. In addition to the tasks of harmonizing and guiding development, in exceptional circumstances the state can also exercise a substitute function when social sectors or business systems are too weak or are just getting under way and are not equal to the task at hand. Such supplementary interventions, which are justified by urgent reasons touching the common good, must be as brief as possible so as to avoid removing permanently from society and business systems the functions which are properly theirs and so as to avoid enlarging excessively the sphere of state intervention to the detriment of both economic and civil freedom.

48.3. In recent years the range of such intervention has vastly expanded to the point of creating a new type of state, the so-called welfare state. This has happened in some countries in order to respond better to many needs and demands, by remedying forms of poverty and deprivation unworthy of the human person. However, excesses and abuses, especially in recent years, have provoked very harsh criticisms of the welfare state, dubbed the 'social assistance state.' Malfunctions and defects in the social assistance state are the result of an inadequate understanding of the tasks proper to the state. Here again the principle of subsidiarity must be respected: A community of a higher order should not interfere in the internal life of a community of a lower order, depriving the latter of its functions, but rather should support it in case of need and help to coordinate its activity with the activities of the rest of society, always with a view to the common good.[100]

48.4. By intervening directly and depriving society of its responsibility, the social assistance state leads to a loss of human energies and an inordinate increase of public agencies which are dominated more by bureaucratic ways of thinking than by concern for serving their clients and which are accompanied by an enormous increase in spending. In fact, it would appear that needs are best understood and satisfied by people who are closest to them and who act as neighbors to those in need. It should be added that certain kinds of demands often call for a response which is not simply material, but which is capable of perceiving the deeper human need. One thinks of the condition of refugees, immigrants, the elderly, the sick and all those in circumstances which call for assistance such as drug abusers: All these people can be helped effectively only by those who offer them genuine fraternal support, in addition to the necessary care.

49. Faithful to the mission received from Christ, her founder, the church has always been present and active among the needy, offering them material assistance in ways that neither humiliate nor reduce them to mere objects of assistance, but which help them to escape their precarious situation by promoting their dignity as persons. With heartfelt gratitude to God it must be pointed out that active charity has never ceased to be practiced in the church; indeed, today it is showing a manifold and gratifying increase. In this regard, special mention must be made of volunteer work, which the church favors and promotes by urging everyone to cooperate in supporting and encouraging its undertakings. In order to overcome today's widespread individualistic mentality, what is required is a concrete commitment to solidarity and charity, beginning in the family with the mutual support of husband and wife and the care which the different generations give to one another. In this sense the family too can be called a community of work and solidarity. It can happen, however, that when a family does decide to live up fully to its vocation, it finds itself without the necessary support from the state and without

sufficient resources. It is urgent therefore to promote not only family policies, but also those social policies which have the family as their principal object, policies which assist the family by providing adequate resources and efficient means of support both for bringing up children and for looking after the elderly so as to avoid distancing the latter from the family unit and in order to strengthen relations between generations.[101]

49.1. Apart from the family, other intermediate communities exercise primary functions and give life to specific networks of solidarity. These develop as real communities of persons and strengthen the social fabric, preventing society from becoming an anonymous and impersonal mass as unfortunately often happens today. It is in interrelationships on many levels that a person lives and that society becomes more 'personalized.' The individual today is often suffocated between two poles represented by the state and the marketplace. At times it seems as though he exists only as a producer and consumer of goods or as an object of state administration. People lose sight of the fact that life in society has neither the market nor the state as its final purpose, since life itself has a unique value which the state and the market must serve. Man remains above all a being who seeks the truth and strives to live in that truth, deepening his understanding of it through a dialogue which involves past and future generations.[102]

50. From this open search for truth, which is renewed in every generation, the culture of a nation derives its character. Indeed, the heritage of values which has been received and handed down is always challenged by the young. To challenge does not necessarily mean to destroy or reject a priori, but above all to put these values to the test in one's own life and through this existential verification to make them more real, relevant and personal, distinguishing the valid elements in the tradition from false and erroneous ones or from obsolete forms which can be usefully replaced by others more suited to the times.

50.1. In this context, it is appropriate to recall that evangelization too plays a role in the culture of the various nations, sustaining culture in its progress toward the truth and assisting in the work of its purification and enrichment.[103] However, when a culture becomes inward looking and tries to perpetuate obsolete ways of living by rejecting any exchange or debate with regard to the truth about man, then it becomes sterile and is heading for decadence.

51. All human activity takes place within a culture and interacts with culture. For an adequate formation of a culture, the involvement of the whole man is required, whereby he exercises his creativity, intelligence and knowledge of the world and of people. Furthermore, he displays his capacity for self-control, personal sacrifice, solidarity and readiness to promote the common good. Thus the first and most important task is accomplished within man's heart. The way in which he is involved in building his own future depends on the understanding he has of himself and of his own destiny. It is on this level that the church's specific and decisive contribution to true culture is to be found. The church promotes those aspects of human behavior which favor a true culture of peace, as opposed to models in which the individual is lost in the crowd, in which

the role of his initiative and freedom is neglected and in which his greatness is posited in the arts of conflict and war. The church renders this service to human society by preaching the truth about the creation of the world, which God has placed in human hands so that people may make it fruitful and more perfect through their work; and by preaching the truth about the redemption whereby the Son of God has saved mankind and at the same time has united all people, making them responsible for one another. Sacred Scripture continually speaks to us of an active commitment to our neighbor and demands of us a shared responsibility for all of humanity.

51.1. This duty is not limited to one's own family, nation or state, but extends progressively to all mankind, since no one can consider himself extraneous or indifferent to the lot of another member of the human family. No one can say that he is not responsible for the well-being of his brother or sister (cf. Gn. 4:9; Lk. 10:29-37; Mt. 25:31-46). Attentive and pressing concern for one's neighbor in a moment of need—made easier today because of the new means of communication which have brought people closer together—is especially important with regard to the search for ways to resolve international conflicts other than by war. It is not hard to see that the terrifying power of the means of destruction—to which even medium- and small-sized countries have access—and the ever closer links between the peoples of the whole world make it very difficult or practically impossible to limit the consequences of a conflict.

52. Pope Benedict XV and his successors clearly understood this danger.[104] I myself, on the occasion of the recent tragic war in the Persian Gulf, repeated the cry: 'Never again war!' No, never again war, which destroys the lives of innocent people, teaches how to kill, throws into upheaval even the lives of those who do the killing and leaves behind a trail of resentment and hatred, thus making it all the more difficult to find a just solution of the very problems which provoked the war. Just as the time has finally come when in individual states a system of private vendetta and reprisal has given way to the rule of law, so too a similar step forward is now urgently needed in the international community. Furthermore, it must not be forgotten that at the root of war there are usually real and serious grievances: injustices suffered, legitimate aspirations frustrated, poverty and the exploitation of multitudes of desperate people who see no real possibility of improving their lot by peaceful means.

52.1. For this reason, another name for peace is development.[105] Just as there is a collective responsibility for avoiding war, so too there is a collective responsibility for promoting development. Just as within individual societies it is possible and right to organize a solid economy which will direct the functioning of the market to the common good, so too there is a similar need for adequate interventions on the international level. For this to happen, a great effort must be made to enhance mutual understanding and knowledge, and to increase the sensitivity of consciences. This is the culture which is hoped for, one which fosters trust in the human potential of the poor and consequently in their ability to improve their condition through work or to make a positive contribution to economic prosperity. But to accomplish this, the poor—be they individuals or nations—need to be provided with realistic opportunities. Creating such conditions calls for a concerted worldwide effort to promote development, an effort which also involves sacrificing the positions of income and of power enjoyed by the more developed economies.[106]

52.2. This may mean making important changes in established lifestyles in order to limit the waste of environmental and human resources, thus enabling every individual and all the peoples of the earth to have a sufficient share of those resources. In addition, the new material and spiritual resources must be utilized which are the result of the work and culture of peoples who today are on the margins of the international community, so as to obtain an overall human enrichment of the family of nations.

CHAPTER VI

Man is in the way of the church

53. Faced with the poverty of the working class, Pope Leo XIII wrote: 'We approach this subject with confidence and in the exercise of the rights which manifestly pertain to us....By keeping silence we would seem to neglect the duty incumbent on us.'[107] During the last 100 years the church has repeatedly expressed her thinking, while closely following the continuing development of the social question. She has certainly not done this in order to recover former privileges or to impose her own vision. Her sole purpose has been care and responsibility for man, who has been entrusted to her by Christ himself: for this man, who, as the Second Vatican Council recalls, is the only creature on earth which God willed for its own sake, and for which God has his plan, that is, a share in eternal salvation. We are not dealing here with man in the 'abstract,' but with the real, 'concrete,' 'historical' man. We are dealing with each individual, since each one is included in the mystery of redemption and through this mystery Christ has united himself with each one forever.[108] It follows that the church cannot abandon man and that 'this man is the primary route that the church must travel in fulfilling her mission...the way traced out by Christ himself, the way that leads invariably through the mystery of the incarnation and the redemption.'[109]

53.1. This, and this alone, is the principle which inspires the church's social doctrine. The church has gradually developed that doctrine in a systematic way, above all in the century that has followed the date we are commemorating, precisely because the horizon of the church's whole wealth of doctrine is man in his concrete reality as sinful and righteous.

54. Today, the church's social doctrine focuses especially on man as he is involved in a complex network of relationships within modern societies. The human sciences and philosophy are helpful for interpreting man's central place within society and for enabling him to understand himself better as a 'social being.' However, man's true identity is only fully revealed to him through faith, and it is precisely from faith that the

church's social teaching begins. While drawing upon all the contributions made by the sciences and philosophy, her social teaching is aimed at helping man on the path of salvation.

54.1. The encyclical *Rerum Novarum* can be read as a valid contribution to socioeconomic analysis at the end of the 19th century, but its specific value derives from the fact that it is a document of the magisterium and is fully a part of the church's evangelizing mission, together with many other documents of this nature. Thus the church's social teaching is itself a valid instrument of evangelization. As such, it proclaims God and his mystery of salvation in Christ to every human being and for that very reason reveals man to himself. In this light, and only in this light, does it concern itself with everything else: the human rights of the individual and in particular of the 'working class,' the family and education, the duties of the state, the ordering of national and international society, economic life, culture, war and peace and respect for life from the moment of conception until death.

55. The church receives 'the meaning of man' from divine revelation. 'In order to know man, authentic man, man in his fullness, one must know God,' said Pope Paul VI, and he went on to quote St Catherine of Siena, who in prayer expressed the same idea: 'In your nature, O eternal Godhead, I shall know my own nature.'[110]

55.1. Christian anthropology therefore is really a chapter of theology, and for this reason, the church's social doctrine by its concern for man and by its interest in him and in the way he conducts himself in the world 'belongs to the field...of theology and particularly of moral theology.'[111] The theological dimension is needed both for interpreting and solving present-day problems in human society. It is worth noting that this is true in contrast both to the 'atheistic' solution, which deprives man of one of his basic dimensions, namely the spiritual one, and to permissive and consumerist solutions, which under various pretexts seek to convince man that he is free from every law and from God himself, thus imprisoning him within a selfishness which ultimately harms both him and others.

55.2. When the church proclaims God's salvation to man, when she offers and communicates the life of God through the sacraments, when she gives direction to human life through the commandments of love of God and neighbor, she contributes to the enrichment of human dignity. But just as the church can never abandon her religious and transcendent mission on behalf of man, so too she is aware that today her activity meets with particular difficulties and obstacles. That is why she devotes herself with ever new energies and methods to an evangelization which promotes the whole human being. Even on the eve of the third millennium she continues to be 'a sign and safeguard of the transcendence of the human person,'[112] as indeed she has always sought to be from the beginning of her existence, walking together with man through history. The encyclical *Rerum Novarum* itself is a significant sign of this.

56. On the 100th anniversary of that encyclical I wish to thank all those who have devoted themselves to studying, expounding and making better known Christian social teaching. To this end, the cooperation of the local churches is indispensable, and I would hope that the present anniversary

will be a source of fresh enthusiasm for studying, spreading and applying that teaching in various contexts.

56.1. In particular, I wish this teaching to be made known and applied in the countries which following the collapse of 'real socialism' are experiencing a serious lack of direction in the work of rebuilding. The Western countries, in turn, run the risk of seeing this collapse as a one-sided victory of their own economic system and thereby failing to make necessary corrections in that system. Meanwhile, the countries of the Third World are experiencing more than ever the tragedy of underdevelopment, which is becoming more serious with each passing day.

56.2. After formulating principles and guidelines for the solution of the worker question, Pope Leo XIII made this incisive statement: 'Everyone should put his hand to the work which falls to his share, and that at once and straightway, lest the evil which is already so great become through delay absolutely beyond remedy,' and he added, 'In regard to the church, her cooperation will never be found lacking.'[113]

57. As far as the church is concerned, the social message of the Gospel must not be considered a theory, but above all else a basis and a motivation for action. Inspired by this message, some of the first Christians distributed their goods to the poor, bearing witness to the fact that despite different social origins it was possible for people to live together in peace and harmony. Through the power of the Gospel, down the centuries monks tilled the land, men and women religious founded hospitals and shelters for the poor, confraternities as well as individual men and women of all states of life devoted themselves to the needy and to those on the margins of society, convinced as they were that Christ's words 'as you did it to one of the least of these my brethren, you did it to me' (Mt. 25:40) were not intended to remain a pious wish, but were meant to become a concrete life commitment. Today more than ever, the church is aware that her social message will gain credibility more immediately from the witness of actions than as a result of its internal logic and consistency. This awareness is also a source of her preferential option for the poor, which is never exclusive or discriminatory toward other groups. This option is not limited to material poverty, since it is well known that there are many other forms of poverty, especially in modern society—not only economic, but cultural and spiritual poverty as well. The church's love for the poor, which is essential for her and a part of her constant tradition, impels her to give attention to a world in which poverty is threatening to assume massive proportions in spite of technological and economic progress. In the countries of the West, different forms of poverty are being experienced by groups which live on the margins of society, by the elderly and the sick, by the victims of consumerism and even more immediately by so many refugees and migrants. In the developing countries, tragic crises loom on the horizon unless internationally coordinated measures are taken before it is too late.

58. Love for others, and in the first place love for the poor, in whom the church sees Christ himself, is made concrete in the promotion of justice. Justice will never be fully attained unless people see in the poor person,

who is asking for help in order to survive, not an annoyance or a burden, but an opportunity for showing kindness and a chance for greater enrichment. Only such an awareness can give the courage needed to face the risk and the change involved in every authentic attempt to come to the aid of another. It is not merely a matter of 'giving from one's surplus,' but of helping entire peoples which are presently excluded or marginalized to enter into the sphere of economic and human development. For this to happen, it is not enough to draw on the surplus goods which in fact our world abundantly produces; it requires above all a change of lifestyles, of models of production and consumption, and of the established structures of power which today govern societies. Nor is it a matter of eliminating instruments of social organization which have proved useful, but rather of orienting them according to an adequate notion of the common good in relation to the whole human family. Today we are facing the so-called 'globalization' of the economy, a phenomenon which is not to be dismissed, since it can create unusual opportunities for greater prosperity. There is a growing feeling, however, that this increasing internationalization of the economy ought to be accompanied by effective international agencies which will oversee and direct the economy to the common good, something that an individual state, even if it were the most powerful on earth, would not be in a position to do. In order to achieve this result, it is necessary that there be increased coordination among the more powerful countries and that in international agencies the interests of the whole human family be equally represented. It is also necessary that in evaluating the consequences of their decisions, these agencies always give sufficient consideration to peoples and countries which have little weight in the international market, but which are burdened by the most acute and desperate needs and are thus more dependent on support for their development. Much remains to be done in this area.

59. Therefore, in order that the demands of justice may be met and attempts to achieve this goal may succeed, what is needed is the gift of grace, a gift which comes from God. Grace, in cooperation with human freedom, constitutes that mysterious presence of God in history which is providence.

59.1. The newness which is experienced in following Christ demands to be communicated to other people in their concrete difficulties, struggles, problems and challenges, so that these can then be illuminated and made more human in the light of faith. Faith not only helps people to find solutions; it makes even situations of suffering humanly bearable, so that in these situations people will not become lost or forget their dignity and vocation.

59.2. In addition, the church's social teaching has an important interdisciplinary dimension. In order better to incarnate the one truth about man in different and constantly changing social, economic and political contexts, this teaching enters into dialogue with the various disciplines concerned with man. It assimilates what these disciplines have to contribute and helps them to open themselves to a broader horizon aimed at serving the individual person who is acknowledged and loved in the fullness of his or her vocation.

59.3. Parallel with the interdisciplinary aspect, mention should also be made of the practical and as it were experiential dimension of this teaching, which is to be found at the crossroads where Christian life and conscience come into contact with the real world. This teaching is seen in the efforts of individuals, families, people involved in cultural and social life as well as politicians and statesmen to give it a concrete form and application in history.

60. In proclaiming the principles for a solution of the worker question, Pope Leo XIII wrote: 'This most serious question demands the attention and the efforts of others.'[114] He was convinced that the grave problems caused by industrial society could be solved only by cooperation between all forces. This affirmation has become a permanent element of the church's social teaching and also explains why Pope John XXIII addressed his encyclical on peace to 'all people of good will.'

60.1. Pope Leo, however, acknowledged with sorrow that the ideologies of his time, especially liberalism and Marxism, rejected such cooperation. Since then, many things have changed, especially in recent years. The world today is ever more aware that solving serious national and international problems is not just a matter of economic production or of juridical or social organization, but also calls for specific ethical and religious values as well as changes of mentality, behavior and structures. The church feels a particular responsibility to offer this contribution and, as I have written in the encyclical *Sollicitudo Rei Socialis,* there is a reasonable hope that the many people who profess no religion will also contribute to providing the social question with the necessary ethical foundation.[115]

60.2. In that same encyclical I also addressed an appeal to the Christian churches and to all the great world religions, inviting them to offer the unanimous witness of our common convictions regarding the dignity of man, created by God.[116] In fact I am convinced that the various religions, now and in the future, will have a pre-eminent role in preserving peace and in building a society worthy of man.

60.3. Indeed, openness to dialogue and to cooperation is required of all people of good will and in particular of individuals and groups with specific responsibilities in the areas of politics, economics and social life at both the national and international levels.

61. At the beginning of industrialized society, it was 'a yoke little better than that of slavery itself' which led my predecessor to speak out in defense of man. Over the past 100 years the church has remained faithful to this duty. Indeed, she intervened in the turbulent period of class struggle after World War I in order to defend man from economic exploitation and from the tyranny of the totalitarian systems. After World War II, she put the dignity of the person at the center of her social messages, insisting that material goods were meant for all and that the social order ought to be free of oppression and based on a spirit of cooperation and solidarity. The church has constantly repeated that the person and society need not only material goods, but spiritual and religious values as well. Furthermore, as she has become more aware of the fact that too many people live, not in the prosperity of the Western world, but in the poverty of the developing

countries amid conditions which are still 'a yoke little better than that of slavery itself,' she has felt and continues to feel obliged to denounce this fact with absolute clarity and frankness, although she knows that her call will not always win favor with everyone.

61.1. One hundred years after the publication of *Rerum Novarum*, the church finds herself still facing 'new things' and new challenges. The centenary celebration should therefore confirm the commitment of all people of good will and of believers in particular.

62. The present encyclical has looked at the past, but above all it is directed to the future. Like *Rerum Novarum*, it comes almost at the threshold of a new century, and its intention, with God's help, is to prepare for that moment.

62.1. In every age the true and perennial 'newness of things' comes from the infinite power of God, who says: 'Behold, I make all things new' (Rv. 21:5). These words refer to the fulfillment of history, when Christ 'delivers the kingdom to God the Father...that God may be everything to everyone' (1 Cor. 15:24, 28). But the Christian well knows that the newness which we await in its fullness at the Lord's second coming has been present since the creation of the world, and in a special way since the time when God became man in Jesus Christ and brought about a 'new creation' with him and through him (2 Cor. 5:17; Gal. 6:15).

62.2. In concluding this encyclical I again give thanks to Almighty God, who has granted his church the light and strength to accompany humanity on its earthly journey toward its eternal destiny. In the third millennium too, the church will be faithful in making man's way her own, knowing that she does not walk alone but with Christ her Lord. It is Christ who made man's way his own and who guides him, even when he is unaware of it.

62.3. Mary, the mother of the Redeemer, constantly remained beside Christ in his journey toward the human family and in its midst, and she goes before the church on the pilgrimage of faith. May her maternal intercession accompany humanity toward the next millennium in fidelity to him who 'is the same yesterday and today and forever' (cf. Heb. 13:8), Jesus Christ our Lord, in whose name I cordially impart my blessing to all.

62.4. Given in Rome, at St. Peter's, on May 1, the memorial of St. Joseph the Worker, in the year 1991, the 13th of my pontificate.

Footnotes

Note: References preceded by an asterisk have been added for this edition to those appearing in the original document.

Abbreviations

AAS	*Acta Apostolicae Sedis*
CA	*Centesimus Annus*
CCL	*Corpus Christianorum (Series Latina)*
CSEL	*Corpus Scriptorum Ecclesiasticorum Latinorum*
DM	*Dives in Misericordia*
EN	*Evangelii Nuntiandi*
GS	*Gaudium et Spes*
JW	*Justice in the World*
LE	*Laborem Exercens*
MM	*Mater et Magistra*
OA	*Octagesimo Adveniens*
PG	*Patrologia Graeca*
PL	*Patrologia Latina*
PP	*Populorum Progressio*
PT	*Pacem in Terris*
QA	*Quadragesimo Anno*
RH	*Redemptor Hominis*
RN	*Rerum Novarum*
SR	*Sollicitudo Rei Socialis*

The books of the Bible are referred to by the standard abbreviations.

Footnotes

Quadragesimo Anno

1. Encyclical, *Arcanum*, Feb. 10, 1880.
2. Encyclical, *Diuturnum*, June 20, 1881.
3. Encyclical, *Immortale Dei*, Nov. 1, 1885.
4. Encyclical, *Sapientiae Christianae*, Jan. 10, 1890.
5. Encyclical, *Quod Apostolici Muneris*, Dec. 28, 1878.
6. Encyclical, *Libertas*, June 20, 1888.
7. Encyclical, *On the Condition of Workers*, May 15, 1891, *RN 1.3.
8. Encyclical, *On the Conditions of Workers*, cf. *RN 14.
9. Encyclical, *On the Condition of Workers*, cf. *RN2.
10. Encyclical, *On the Condition of Workers*, cf. *RN2.
11. Encyclical, *On the Condition of Workers*, *RN14.
12. Cf. Matt. 7:29.
13. Encyclical, *On the Condition of Workers*, *RN 1.3.
14. St. Ambrose, *De excessu fratris sui Satyri* I, 44.
15. Encyclical, *On the Condition of Workers*, *RN14.
16. Let it be sufficient to mention some of these only: Leo XIII's Apostolic letter *Praeclara*, June 20, 1894, and Encyclical *Graves de Communi*, Jan. 18, 1901; Pius X's Motu Proprio *De Actione Populari Christiana*, Dec. 8, 1903; Benedict XV's Encyclical *Ad Beatissimi*, Nov. 1, 1914; Pius IX's Encyclical *Ubi Arcano*, Dec. 23, 1922, and Encyclical *Rite Expiatis*, Apr. 30, 1926.
17. Cf. *La Hierarchié catholique et le problème social depuis l'Encyclique 'Rerum Novarum,'* 1891-1931, pp. XVI-335; ed. 'Union internationale d'Etudes sociales fondée à Malines, en 1920, sous la présidence du Card. Mercier.' Paris, Éditions 'Spes,' 1931.
18. Isa. 11:12.
19. Encyclical, *On the Condition of Workers*, *RN 33.
20. Encyclical, *On the Condition of Workers*, *RN 38.
21. Encyclical, *On the Condition of Workers*, *RN 48.
22. Encyclical, *On the Condition of Workers*, *RN 56.
23. Encyclical, *On the Condition of Workers*, *RN 57.
24. Pius X, Encyclical, *Singulari Quadam*, Sept. 24, 1912.
25. Cf. the Letter of the Sacred Congregation of the Council to the Bishop of Lille, June 5, 1929.
26. Cf. Rom. 1:14.
27. Cf. Encyclical, *On the Condition of Workers*, *RN 14.
28. Pius XI, Encyclical, *Ubi Arcano*, Dec. 23, 1922.
29. Encyclical, *Ubi Arcano*, Dec. 23, 1922.
30. Encyclical, *On the Condition of Workers*, *RN 20.
31. Encyclical, *On the Condition of Workers*, *RN 21.
32. Encyclical, *On the Condition of Workers*, *RN 7.1.
33. Allocution to the Convention of Italian Catholic Action, May 16, 1926.
34. Encyclical, *On the Condition of Workers*, *RN 7.
35. Encyclical, *On the Condition of Workers*, *RN 11.
36. Encyclical, *On the Condition of Workers*, *RN 47.1.
37. Cf. St. Thomas, *Summa theologica*, II-II, Q. 134.
38. Encyclical, *On the Condition of Workers*, *RN 36.
39. Encyclical, *On the Condition of Workers*, *RN 16.
40. Encyclical, *On the Condition of Workers*, *RN 7.1.
41. II Thess. 3:10.
42. Cf. II Thess. 3:8-10.
43. Encyclical, *On the Condition of Workers*, *RN 4.7.
44. Encyclical, *On the Condition of Workers*, *RN 44.
45. Encyclical, *On the Condition of Workers*, *RN 17.1.
46. Cf. Encyclical, *Casti Connubii*, Dec. 31, 1930.
47. Cf. St. Thomas, *De regimine principum* I, 15; Encyclical, *On the Condition of Workers*, *RN 34-36.

48. Cf. Encyclical, *On the Condition of Workers*, *RN 17.1.
49. St. Thomas, *Contra Gentiles*, III, 71; cf. *Summa theologica*, I, Q. 65.
50. Encyclical, *Immortale Dei*, Nov. 1, 1885.
51. Cf. Encyclical, *On the Condition of Workers*, *RN 55.
52. Eph. 4:16.
53. Encyclical, *On the Condition of Workers*, *RN 16.
54. Cf. Rom. 13:1.
55. Cf. Encyclical, *Diuturnum illud*, June 29, 1881.
56. Encyclical, *Divini illius Magistri*, Dec. 31, 1929.
57. Cf. Jas. 2.
58. II Cor. 8:9.
59. Matt. 11:28.
60. Cf. Luke 12:48.
61. Matt. 16:27.
62. Cf. Matt. 7:24ff.
63. Encyclical, *On the Condition of Workers*, *RN 27.
64. Cf. Matt. 16:26.
65. Cf. Judg. 2:17.
66. Cf. Matt. 7:13.
67. Cf. John 6:69.
68. Cf. Matt. 24:35.
69. Cf. Matt. 6:33.
70. Col. 3:14.
71. Rom. 12:5.
72. I Cor. 12:26.
73. Encyclical, *Ubi Arcano*, Dec. 23, 1922.
74. Cf. Act. 20:28.
75. Cf. Deut. 31:7.
76. Cf. II Tim. 2:3.
77. I Tim. 2:4.
78. Encyclical, *Mens Nostra*, Dec. 20, 1929.
79. Cf. Matt. 16:18.
80. Cf. Luke 16:8.
81. Cf. Phil. 2:21.
82. Apoc. 5:13.

Mater et Magistra

1. Cf. 1 Tim. 3:15.
2. John 14:6.
3. John 8:12.
4. Mark 8:2.
5. *Acta Leonis XIII* XI (1891) 97-144.
6. *Ibid.* p.107.
7. St. Thomas, *De Regimine Principum*, 1, 15.
8. Cf. AAS 23 (1931) 185, *QA 28.
9. Cf. *ibid.* p. 189, *QA 39.
10. *Ibid.* pp. 177-228.
11. Cf. *ibid.* p. 199, *QA 65.
12. Cf. *ibid.* p. 200, *QA 69.
13. Cf. *ibid.* p. 201, *QA 72.
14. Cf. *ibid.* p. 210 *et seq.*, *QA 101ff.
15. Cf. *ibid.* p. 211, *QA 109.
16. Cf. AAS 33 (1941) 196.
17. Cf. *ibid.* p.197.
18. Cf. *ibid.* p.196.
19. Cf. *ibid.* p.198 *et seq.*
20. Cf. *ibid.* p.199.
21. Cf. *ibid.* p.201.
22. Cf. *ibid.* p.202.
23. Cf. *ibid.* p.203.
24. AAS 23 (1931) 203, *QA 79.
25. *Ibid.* p. 203, *QA 79.
26. Cf. *ibid.* p. 222 *et seq.*, *QA 136ff.
27. Cf. AAS 33 (1941) 200.
28. AAS 23 (1931) 195, *QA 53.
29. *Ibid.* p. 198, *QA 61.
30. Broadcast message, 1 September 1944, AAS 36 (1944) 254.
31. *Allocutio*, 8 October 1956, AAS 48 (1956) 799-800.
32. Broadcast message, 1 September 1944, AAS 36 (1944) 253.
33. Broadcast message, 24 December 1942, AAS 35 (1943) 17.
34. Cf. *ibid.* p.20.
35. Encyclical letter *Quadragesimo Anno*, AAS 23 (1931) 214, *QA 114.
36. *Acta Leonis XIII* XI (1891) 114.
37. Matt 6:19-20.
38. Matt. 25:40.
39. Cf. AAS 23 (1931) 202, *QA 75.
40. *Allocutio*, 3 May 1960, AAS 52 (1960) 465.
41. Cf. *ibid.*
42. 1 John 3:16-17.
43. Encyclical letter *Summi Pontificatus*, AAS 31 (1939) 428-29.
44. Gen. 1:28.
45. *Ibid.*
46. *Confessions* 1, 1.
47. Ps. 126:1.
48. AAS 23 (1931) 221 *et seq.*, *QA 134ff.
49. Broadcast message, Christmas Eve, 1953, AAS 46 (1954) 10.
50. Ps. 113:4
51. Matt. 16:26.
52. Ex. 20:8.
53. John 17:15.
54. 1 Cor. 10:31.
55. Col. 3:17.
56. Matt. 6:33.
57. Eph. 5:8.
58. Cf. *ibid.*
59. 1 Cor. 13:4-7.
60. 1 Cor. 12:12.

Pacem in Terris

1. Ps. 8:1.
2. Ps. 103:24.
3. Cf. Gen 1:26.
4. Ps. 8:5-6.
5. Rom. 2:15.
6. Cf. Ps. 18:8-11.
7. Cf. Pius XII's broadcast message, Christmas 1942, AAS 35 (1943) 9-24; and John XXIII's sermon, 4 January 1963, AAS 55 (1963) 89-91.
8. Cf. Pius XI's encyclical letter *Divini Redemptoris*, AAS 29 (1937) 78; and Pius XII's broadcast message, Pentecost, 1 June 1941, AAS 33 (1941) 195-205.
9. Cf. Pius XII's broadcast message, Christmas 1942, AAS 35 (1943) 9-24.
10. *Divinae Institutiones*, lib. IV, c.28.2; PL 6.535.
11. Encyclical Letter *Libertas Praestantissimum, Acta Leonis XIII* VIII (1888) 237-238.
12. Cf. Pius XII's broadcast message, Christmas 1942, AAS 35 (1943) 9-24.
13. Cf. Pius XI's encyclical letter *Casti Connubii*, AAS 22 (1930) 539-592, and Pius XII's broadcast message, Christmas 1942, AAS 35 (1943) 9-24.
14. Cf. Pius XII's broadcast message, Pentecost, 1 June 1941, AAS 33 (1941) 201.
15. Cf. Leo XIII's encyclical letter *Rerum Novarum, Acta Leonis XIII* XI (1891) 128-129, *RN 43.
16. Cf. John XXIII's encyclical letter *Mater et Magistra*, AAS 53 (1961) 422; *MM 84.
17. Cf. Pius XII's broadcast message, Pentecost, 1 June 1941, AAS 33 (1941) 201.
18. John XXIII's encyclical letter *Mater et Magistra*, AAS 53 (1961) 428; *MM 112.
19. Cf. *ibid.* p.430.
20. Cf. Leo XIII's encyclical letter *Rerum Novarum, Acta Leonis XIII* XI (1891) 134-142, *RN 48ff. Piux XI's encyclical letter *Quadragesimo Anno*, AAS 23 (1931) 199-200; *QA 69-71 and Pius XII's encyclical letter *Sertum Laetitiae*, AAS 31 (1939) 635-644.
21. Cf. AAS 53 (1961) 430.
22. Cf. Pius XII's broadcast message, Christmas 1952, AAS 45 (1953) 36-46.
23. Cf. Pius XII's broadcast massage, Christmas 1944, AAS 37 (1945) 12.
24. Cf. Pius XII's broadcast message, Christmas 1942, AAS 35 (1943) 21.
25. Eph. 4:25.
26. Cf. Pius XII's broadcast message, Christmas 1942, AAS 35 (1943) 14.
27. *Summa Theol*, Ia-IIae, q. 19, .4: cf. a.9.
28. Rom. 13: 1-6.
29. *In Epist. ad Rom.* c. 13, vv. 1-2, homil. XXIII; PG 60. 615.
30. Leo XIII's encyclical epistle *Immortale Dei, Acta Leonis XIII* V (1885) 120.
31. Cf. Pius XII's broadcast message, Christmas 1944, AAS 37 (1945) 15.
32. Cf. Leo XIII's encyclical epistle *Diuturnum Illud, Acta Leonis XIII* II (1881) 274.
33. Cf. *ibid.*, p.278, also Leo XII's encyclical epistle *Immortale Dei, Acta Leonis XIII* V (1885) 130.
34. Acts 5:29.
35. *Summa Theol.* Ia-IIae, q.93, a.3 ad 2 um; cf. Pius XII's broadcast message, Christmas 1945, AAS 37 (1946) 5-23.
36. Cf. Leo XIIIs encyclical epistle *Diuturnum Illud, Acta Leonis XIII* II (1881) 271-273; and Pius XII's broadcast message, Christmas 1944, AAS 37 (1945) 5-23.
37. Cf. Pius XII's broadcast message, Christmas 1942, AAS 35 (1943) 13, and Leo XIII's encyclical letter *Immortale Dei, Acta Leonis XIII* V (1885) 120.
38. Cf. Pius XII's encyclical letter *Summi Pontificatus*, AAS 31 (1939) 412-453.
39. Cf. Pius XI's encyclical *Mit Brennender Sorge*, AAS 29 (1937) 159, and his encyclical letter *Divini Redemptoris*, AAS 29(1937) 65-106.
40. Leo XIII, encyclical letter *Immortale Dei, Acta Leonis XIII* V (1885) 121.
41. Cf. Leo XIII, encyclical letter *Rerum Novarum, Acta Leonis XIII* XI (1891) 133–134, *RN 46.
42. Cf. Pius XII, encyclical letter *Summi Pontificatus*, AAS 31 (1939) 433.
43. AAS 53 (1961) 417.
44. Cf. Pius XI, encyclical letter *Quadragesimo Anno*, AAS 23 (1931) 215, *QA 118.
45. Cf. Pius XII, broadcast message, Pentecost, 1 June 1941, AAS 33 (1941) 200.
46. Cf. Pius XI, encyclical letter *Mit Brennender Sorge*, AAS 29 (1937) 159, and his encyclical *Divini Redemptoris*, AAS 29 (1937) 79; and Pius XII, broadcast message, Christmas 1942, AAS 35 (1943) 9-24.
47. Cf. Pius XI, encyclical letter *Divini Redemptoris*, AAS 29 (1937) 81, and Pius XII, broadcast message, Christmas 1942, AAS 35 (1943) 9-24.

Footnotes: Pacem in Terris

48. John XXIII, encyclical letter *Mater et Magistra*, AAS 53 (1961) 415; *MM 59.
49. Cf. Pius XII, broadcast message, Christmas 1942, AAS 35 (1943) 21.
50. Cf. Pius XII, broadcast message, Christmas 1944, AAS 37 (1945) 15-16.
51. Cf. Pius XII, broadcast message, Christmas 1942, AAS 35 (1943) 12.
52. Cf. Leo XIII, apostolic letter *Annum Ingressi*, *Acta Leonis XIII* XXII (1902-1903) 52-80.
53. Wisd. 6:2-4.
54. Cf. Pius XII, broadcast message, Christmas 1941, AAS 34 (1942) 16.
55. Cf. Pius XII, broadcast message, Christmas 1940, AAS 33 (1941) 5-14.
56. *De Civitate Dei*, lib. IV, c. 4; PL 41. 115; cf. Pius XII, broadcast message, Christmas 1939, AAS 32 (1940) 5-13.
57. Cf. Pius XII, broadcast message, Christmas 1941, AAS 34 (1942) 10-21.
58. Cf. John XXIII, encyclical letter *Mater et Magistra*, AAS 53 (1961) 439; *MM 153-155.
59. Cf. Pius XII, broadcast message, Christmas 1941, AAS 34 (1942) 17, and Benedict XV, exhortation to the rulers of the belligerent powers, 1 August 1917, AAS 9 (1917) 418.
60. Cf. Pius XII, broadcast message, 24 August 1939, AAS 31 (1939) 334.
61. AAS 53 (1961) 440-441.
62. Cf. Pius XII, broadcast message, Christmas 1941, AAS 34 (1942) 16-17.
63. John XXIII, encyclical letter *Mater et Magistra*, AAS 53 (1961) 443; *MM 174.
64. Cf. Pius XII, address to Young Members of Italian Catholic Action, Rome, 12 September 1948, AAS 40 (1948) 412.
65. Cf. John XXIII, encyclical letter *Mater et Magistra*, AAS 53 (1961) 454; *MM 226-228.
66. *Ibid.*, p.456; *MM 239.
67. *Ibid.*, p.456; cf Leo XIII, encyclical epistle *Immortale Dei*, *Acta Leonis XIII* V (1885) 128; Pius XI, encyclical letter *Ubi Arcano*, AAS 14 (1922) 698; and Pius XII, address to the Union of International Sodalities of Catholic Women, Rome, 11 September 1947, AAS 39 (1947) 486.
68. Cf. Pius XII, address to Italian workers, Rome, Pentecost, 13 June 1943, AAS 35 (1943) 175.
69. *Miscellanea Augustiniana*...St Augustine, *Sermones post Maurinos Reperti*, Rome, 1930, p.633.
70. Cf. Is. 9:6.
71. Eph. 2:14-17.
72. Responsory at Matins, Feria VI Within the Octave of Easter.
73. John 14:27.

Gaudium et Spes

1. Cf. John 18:37; Matt. 20:28; Mark 10:45.
2. Cf. Rom. 7:14 *et seq.*
3. Cf. 2 Cor. 5:15.
4. Cf. Acts 4:12.
5. Cf. Heb. 13:8.
6. Cf. Col. 1:15.
7. Cf. Gen. 1:26; Wisd. 2:23.
8. Cf. Sir. 17:3-10.
9. Cf. Rom. 1:21-25.
10. Cf. John 8:34.
11. Cf. Dan. 3:57-90.
12. Cf. 1 Cor. 6:13-20.
13. Cf. 1 Kings 16:7; Jer. 17:10.
14. Cf. Sir. 17:7-8.
15. Cf. Rom. 2:14-16.
16. Pius XII, radio address on the correct formation of a Christian conscience in the young, 23 March 1952, AAS (1952), 271.
17. Cf. Matt. 22:37-40; Gal. 5:14.
18. Cf. Sir. 15:14.
19. Cf. 2 Cor. 5:10.
20. Cf. Wisd. 1:13; 2:23-24; Rom. 5:21; 6:23; Jas. 1:15.
21. Cf. 1 Cor. 15:56-67.
22. Cf. Pius XI, encyclical letter *Divini Redemptoris*, 19 March 1937, AAS 29 (1937) 65-106; Pius XII, encyclical letter *Ad Apostolorum Principis*, 29 June 1958, AAS 50 (1958) 601-614; John XXIII, encyclical letter *Mater et Magistra*, 15 May 1961, AAS 53 (1961) 451-453, *MM 212-217; Paul VI, encyclical letter *Ecclesiam Suam*, 6 August 1964, AAS 56 (1964) 651-653.
23. Cf. Second Vatican Council, *Dogmatic Constitution on the Church*, Chapter I, n. 8, AAS 57 (1965) 12.
24. Cf. Phil. 1:27.
25. St Augustine, *Confessions* I, 1: PL 32, 661.
26. Cf. Rom. 5:14. Cf. Tertullian, *De Carnis Resurrectione* 6: 'The shape that the slime of the earth was given was intended with a view to Christ, the future man.', P.2, 282; CSEL 47, p.33, 1. 12-13.
27. Cf. 2 Cor. 4:4.
28. Cf. Second Council of Constantinople, canon 7: 'The divine word was not changed into a human nature, nor was a human nature absorbed by the word', Denzinger 219 (428). Cf. also Third Council of Constantinople: 'For just as his most holy and immaculate human nature, though deified, was not destroyed [*theotheisa ouk anerethe*], but rather remained in its proper state and mode of being', Denzinger 291 (556). Cf. Council of Chalcedon: 'to be acknowledged in two natures, without confusion, change, division, or separation', Denzinger 148 (302).
29. Cf. Third Council of Constantinople: 'and so his human will, though deified, is not destroyed', Denzinger 291 (556).
30. Cf. Heb. 4:15.
31. Cf. 2 Cor. 5:18-19; Col. 1:20-22.
32. Cf. 1 Pet. 2:21; Matt. 16:24; Luke 14:27.
33. Cf. Rom. 8:29; Col. 1:18.
34. Cf. Rom. 8:1-11.
35. Cf. 2 Cor. 4:14.
36. Cf. Phil. 3:10; Rom. 8:17.
37. Cf. Second Vatican Council, *Dogmatic Constitution on the Church*, Chapter 2, n. 16, AAS 57 (1965) 20.
38. Cf. Rom. 8:32.
39. Cf. The Byzantine Easter liturgy.
40. Cf. Rom. 8:15 and Gal. 4:6; cf. also John 1:12 and John 3:1-2.
41. Cf. John XXIII, encyclical letter *Mater et Magistra*, 15 May 1961, AAS 53 (1961) 401-464, and encyclical letter *Pacem in Terris*, 11 April 1963, AAS 55 (1963) 257-304; Paul VI, encyclical letter *Ecclesiam Suam*, 6 August 1964, AAS 54 (1964) 609-659.
42. Cf. Luke 17:33.
43. Cf. St Thomas, 1 Ethica Lect. 1.

44. Cf. John XXIII, encyclical letter *Mater et Magistra*, AAS 53 (1961) 418, *MM 67. CF. also Pius XI, encyclical letter *Quadragesimo Anno*, AAS 23, (1931) 222 *et seq*, *QA 136ff.
45. Cf. John XXIII, encyclical letter *Mater et Magistra*, AAS 53 (1961).
46. Cf. Mark 2:27.
47. Cf. John XXIII, encyclical letter *Pacem in Terris*, AAS 55 (1963) 266, *PT 37.
48. Cf. Jas 2:15-16.
49. Cf. Luke 16:19-31.
50. Cf. John XXIII, encyclical letter *Pacem in Terris*, AAS 55 (1963) 299 and 300, *PT 158-9.
51. Cf. Luke 6:37-38; Matt. 7:1-2; Rom. 2:1-11; 14:10; 14:10-12.
52. Cf. Matt. 5:43-47.
53. Cf. *Dogmatic Constitution on the Church*, Chapter II, n. 9, AAS 57 (1965) 12-13.
54. Cf. Ex. 24:1-8.
55. Cf. Gen. 1:26-27; 9:2-3; Wisd. 9:3.
56. Cf. Ps. 8:7 and 10.
57. Cf. John XXIII encyclical letter *Pacem in Terris*, AAS 55 (1963) 297, *PT 150.
58. Cf. message to all mankind sent by the Fathers at the beginning of the Second Vatican Council, 20 October 1962, AAS 54 (1962) 823.
59. Cf. Paul VI, address to the diplomatic corps, 7 January 1965, AAS 57 (1965) 232.
60. Cf. First Vatican Council, *Dogmatic Constitution on the Catholic Faith*, Chapter III; Denz. 1785-1786 (3004-3005).
61. Cf. Msgr. Pio Paschini, *Vita e Opere di Galileo Galilei*, 2 volumes, Vatican Press (1964).
62. Cf. Matt. 24:13; 13:24-30 and 36-43.
63. Cf. 2 Cor. 6:10.
64. Cf. John 1:3 and 14.
65. Cf. Eph. 1:10.
66. Cf. John 3:6, Rom 5:8-10.
67. Cf. Acts 2:36; Matt. 28:18.
68. Cf. Rom. 15:16.
69. Cf. Acts 1:7.
70. Cf. 1 Cor. 7:31; St. Irenaeus, *Adversus Haereses*, V. 36, PG, VIII, 1221.
71. Cf. 2 Cor. 5:2; 2 Pet. 3:13.
72. Cf. 1 Cor. 2:9; Apoc. 21:4-5.
73. Cf. 1 Cor. 15:42 and 53.
74. Cf. 1 Cor. 13:8, 3:14.
75. Cf. Rom. 8:19-21.
76. Cf. Luke 9:25.
77. Cf. Pius XI, encyclical letter *Quadragesimo Anno*, AAS 23 (1931) 207, *QA 90.
78. Preface of the Feast of Christ the King.
79. Cf. Paul VI, encyclical letter *Ecclesiam Suam*, III, AAS 56 (1964) 637-659.
80. Cf. Titus 3:4; 'love of mankind'.
81. Cf. Eph. 1:3; 5-6; 13-14, 23.
82. Second Vatican Council, *Dogmatic Constitution on the Church*, Chapter 1, n. 8, AAS 57 (1965) 12.
83. *Ibid.*, Chapter II, no. 9 AAS 57 (1965) 14:Cf. n. 8: AAS loc. cit., II.
84. *Ibid.*, Chapter 1, n: 8 AAS 57 (1965) 11.
85. Cf. *ibid.* Chapter IV, n. 38 AAS 57 (1965) 43, with note 120.
86. Cf. Rom. 8:14-17.
87. Cf. Matt. 22-39.
88. *Dogmatic Constitution on the Church*, Chapter II, n. 9, AAS 57 (1956) 12-14.
89. Cf. Pius XII, address to the International Union of Institutes of Archaeology, History and History of Art, 9 March 1956, AAS 48 (1956) 212: 'Its divine founder, Jesus Christ, has not given it any mandate or fixed any end of the cultural order. The goal which Christ assigns to it is strictly religious...The Church must lead men to God, in order that they may be given over to him without reserve...The Church can never lose sight of the strictly religious, supernatural goal. The meaning of all its activities, down to the last canon of its Code, can only co-operate directly or indirectly in this goal.'
90. *Dogmatic Constitution on the Church*, Chapter 1, n. 1, AAS 57 (1965) 5.
91. Cf. Heb. 13:14.
92. Cf. 2 Thes. 3:6-13; Eph. 4:28.

93. Cf. Is. 58:1-12.
94. Cf. Matt. 23:3-23; Mark 7:10-13.
95. Cf. John XXIII, encyclical letter *Mater et Magistra*, IV, AAS 53 (1961) 456-457, *MM 236-241; cf. 1: AAS *loc cit.*, 407, 410-411, *MM 28, 41-44.
96. Cf. *Dogmatic Constitution on the Church*, Chapter III, n. 28, AAS 57 (1965) 35.
97. *Ibid.* n. 28, AAS *loc. cit.*, 35-36.
98. Cf. St. Ambrose, *De Virginitate*, Chapter VIII, n. 48, ML 16, 278.
99. Cf. *Dogmatic Constitution on the Church*, Chapter II, n. 15, AAS 57 (1965) 20.
100. Cf. *Dogmatic Constitution on the Church*, Chapter III, n. 13, AAS 57 (1965) 17.
101. Cf. Justin, *Dialogus cum Tryphene*. Chapter 100; MG 6, 729 (ed. Otto), 1897, pp. 391-393: '...but the greater the number of persecutions which are inflicted upon us, so much the greater the number of other men who become devout believers through the name of Jesus.' Cf. Tertullian, *Apologeticus*, Chapter L, 13: 'Every time you mow us down like grass, we increase in number: the blood of Christians is a seed!' Cf. *Dogmatic Constitution on the Church*, Chapter II, n. 9, AAS 57 (1965) 14.
102. Cf. *Dogmatic Constitution on the Church*, Chapter II, n. 15, AAS 57 (1965) 20.
103. Cf. Paul VI, address given on 3 February 1965.
104. Cf. St. Augustine, *De Bene Coniugali*, PL 40, 375-376 and 394; St Thomas, *Summa Theol.* Suppl. Quaest. 49, art. 3 ad 1; *Decretum pro Armenis*, Denz-Schoen. 1327; Pius XI, encyclical letter *Casti Connubii*, AAS 22 (1930) 547-548; Denz.-Schoen. 3704-3714.
105. Cf. Pius XI, encyclical letter *Casti Connubii*, AAS 22 (1930) 546-547; Denz.-Schoen. 3706.
106. Cf. Osee 2; Jer. 3:6-13; Ezech. 16 and 23; Is. 54.
107. Cf. Matt. 9:15; Mark 2:19-20; Luke 5:34-35; John 3:29; cf. also 2 Cor. 11:2; Eph. 5:25.
108. Cf. Eph. 5:25.
109. Cf. Second Vatican Council, *Dogmatic Constitution on the Church*, AAS 57 (1965) 15-16; 40-41:47.
110. Pius XI, encyclical letter *Casti Connubii*, AAS 22 (1930) 583.
111. Cf. 1 Tim. 5:3.
112. Cf. Eph. 5:32.
113. Cf. Gen. 2:22-24; Prov. 5:18-20; 31:10-31; Tob. 8:4-8; Cant. 1:2-3; 2:16; 4:16-5; 1; 7:8-11; 1 Cor. 7:3-6; Eph. 5:25-33.
114. Cf. Pius XI, encyclical letter *Casti Connubii*, AAS 22 (1930) 547 and 548; Denz.-Schoen. 3707.
115. Cf. 1 Cor. 7:5.
116. Cf. Pius XII, address, *Tra le Visite*, 20 January 1958, AAS 50 (1958) 91.
117. Cf. Piux XI, encyclical letter *Casti Connubii*, AAS 22 (1930); Denz.-Schoen. 3716-3718; Pius XII *Allocutio Conventui Unionis Italicae inter Obstetrices*, 29 October 1951, AAS 43 (1951) 835-854; Paul VI, address to a group of cardinals, 23 June 1964, AAS 56 (1964) 581-589. Certain questions which need further and more careful investigation have been handed over, at the command of the supreme pontiff, to a commission for the study of population, family, and births, in order that, after it fulfils its function, the supreme pontiff may pass judgement. Since the doctrine of the magisterium is such, this holy synod does not intend to propose immediately concrete solutions.
118. Cf. Eph. 5:16; Col. 4:5.
119. Cf. *Sacramentarium Gregorianum*, PL 78, 262.
120. Cf. Rom. 5:15 and 18; 6:5-11; Gal 2:20.
121. Cf. Eph. 5:25-27.
122. Cf. Introductory statement of this constitution, n. 4 *et sqq.*
123. Cf. Col. 3:1-2.
124. Cf. Gen. 1:28.
125. Cf. Prov. 8:30-31.
126. Cf. St Irenaeus, *Adversus Haereses*, III, II, 8 (ed. Sagnard, p.200; cf. ibid., 16, 6, pp.290-291; 21, 10-22, pp. 370-372, 22, 3, p. 378; etc.).
127. Cf. Eph. 1:10.
128. Cf. the words of Pius XI to Father M.D. Roland Gosselin: 'It is necessary never to lose sight of the fact that the objective of the Church is to evangelize, not to civilize. If it civilizes, it is for the sake of evangelization.' (Semaines sociales de France, Versailles, 1936, pp.461-462.)
129. First Vatican Council, *Constitution on the Catholic Faith*, Denzinger 1795, 1799 (3015, 3019). Cf. Pius XI, encyclical letter *Quadragesimo Anno*, AAS 23 (1931) 190, *QA42.
130. Cf. John XXIII, encyclical letter *Pacem in Terris*, AAS 55 (1963) 260, *PT 12.
131. Cf. John XXIII, encyclical letter *Pacem in Terris*, AAS 55 (1963) 283, *PT 57, Pius XII, radio address, 24 December 1941, AAS 34 (1942) 16-17.
132. John XXIII, encyclical letter *Pacem in Terris*, AAS 55 (1963) 260, *PT 13.

Footnotes: Gaudium et Spes

133. Cf. John XXIII, prayer delivered on 11 October 1962, at the beginning of the council, AAS 54 (1962) 792.
134. Cf. *Constitution on the Sacred Liturgy*, n. 123, AAS 56 (1964) 131; Paul VI, discourse to the artists of Rome, AAS 56 (1964) 439-442.
135. Cf. Second Vatican Council, *Decree on Priestly Training and Declaration on Christian Education*.
136. Cf. *Dogmatic Constitution on the Church*, Chapter IV, n. 37, AAS 57 (1965) 42-43.
137. Cf. Pius XII, address on 23 March 1952, AAS 44 (1953) 273; John XXIII, allocution to the Catholic Association of Italian Workers, 1 May 1959, AAS 51 (1959) 358.
138. Cf. Pius XI, encyclical letter *Quadragesimo Anno*, AAS 23 (1931) 90 *et seq*, *QA 41ff. Pius XII, address of 23 March 1952, AAS 44 (1952) 276 *et seq*. John XXIII, encyclical letter *Mater et Magistra*, AAS 53 (1961) 450, *MM 207; Second Vatican Council, *Decree on the Media of Social Communication*, Chapter I, n. 6, AAS 56 (1964) 147.
139. Cf. Matt. 16:26; Luke 16:1-31; Col 3:17.
140. Cf. Leo XIII, encyclical letter *Libertas,* in *Acta Leonis XIII*, t. VIII. p. 220 *et seq*.; Pius XI, encyclical letter AAS 23 (1931), p. 191 et seq. *QA 45ff. Pius XI, encyclical letter *Divini Redemptoris*, AAS 39 (1937) 65 *et seq.*; Pius XII, *Nuntius Nutalicius 1941*, AAS 34 (1942) 10 *et seq.*; John XXIII, encyclical letter *Mater et Magistra*, AAS 53 (1961) 401-464.
141. In reference to agricultural problems cf. especially John XXIII, encyclical letter *Mater et Magistra*, AAS 53 (1961), 431 *et sqq.*, *MM 122-149.
142. Cf. Leo XIII, encyclical letter *Rerum Novarum*, AAS 23 (1890-91) 649 and 662, *RN 17.1, 44; Pius XI, encyclical letter *Quadragesimo Anno*, AAS 23 (1931) 200-201, *QA 70ff, Pius XI, encyclical letter *Divini Redemptoris*, AAS 29 (1937) 92, Pius XII, radio address on Christmas Eve, 1942, AAS 35 (1943) 20; Pius XII, allocution of 13 June 1943, AAS 35 (1943) 172; Pius XII, radio address to the workers of Spain, 11 March 1951, AAS 43 (1951) 215; John XXIII, encyclical letter *Mater et Magistra*, AAS 53 (1961) 419, *MM 71.
143. Cf. John XXIII, encyclical letter *Mater et Magistra*, AAS 53 (1961) 408, 424, 427, *MM 32, 92-93, 109; however, the word *curatione* has been taken from the Latin text of the encyclical letter *Quadragesimo Anno*, AAS 23 (1931) 199, *QA 55. Under the aspect of the evolution of the question cf. also: Pius XII, allocution of 3 June 1950, AAS 42 (1950) 485-488; Paul VI, allocution of 8 June 1964, AAS 56 (1964) 574-579.
144. Cf. Pius XII, encyclical letter *Sertum Laetitiae*, AAS 31 (1939) 642; John XXIII, consistorial allocution AAS 52 (1960) 5-11; John XXIII, encyclical letter *Mater et Magistra*, AAS 53 (1961) 411, *MM 43.
145. Cf. St Thomas. *Summa Theol.*, II-II, I. 32, a. 5 ad 2; *ibid.* q. 66, a. 2; cf. explanation in Leo XIII, encyclical letter *Rerum Novarum*, AAS 23 (1890-91) 651, *RN 20; cf. Also Pius XII, allocution of 1 June 1941, AAS 33 (1941) 199; Pius XII, birthday radio address 1954, AAS 47 (1955) 27.
146. Cf. St. Basil, *Hom. in illud Lucae 'Destruam horrea mea'*, n. 2 (PG 31, 263); Lactantius, *Divinarum Institutionum*, lib. V. on justice (PL 6, 565 B); St. Augustine, *In Ioann. Ev.* tr. 50, n. 6 (PL 35, 1760); St Augustine, *Enarratio in Ps.* CXLVII, 12 (PL 37, 192); St Gregory the Great, *Homiliae in Ev.*, hom. 20 (PL 76, 1165); St Gregory the Great, *Regulae Pastoralis Liber*, pars III, c. 21 (PL 77, 87); St Bonaventure, *In III Sent.* d. 33, dub. 1 (ed. Quaracchi, III, 728); St Bonaventure, *In IV Sent.* d. 15, p. 11, a.2 q.1 (ed. *cit.* IV, 371 b); q. *de superfluo* (ms. Assisi, Bibl. Comun. 186 *et sqq.* 112-aa3); St Albert the Great, *In III Sent.*, d. 33, a.3, sol 1 (ed. Borgnet XXVIII, 611); St Albert the Great, *In IV Sent.* d. 15, a.16 (ed. cit. XXIX, 494-497). As for the determination of what is superfluous in our day and age, cf. John XXIII, radio-television message of 11 September 1962, AAS 54 (1962) 682: 'The obligation of every man, the urgent obligation of the Christian man, is to reckon what is superfluous by the measure of the needs of others, and to see to it that the administration and the distribution of created goods serve the common good.'
147. In that case, the old principle holds true: 'In extreme necessity all goods are common, that is, all goods are to be shared.' On the other hand, for the order, extension, and manner by which the principle is applied in the proposed text, besides the modern authors: cf. St Thomas, *Summa Theol.* II-II, q. 66, 1.7. Obviously, for the correct application of the principle, all the conditions that are morally required must be met.
148. Cf. Gratian *Decretum* C. 21, dist. LXXXVI (ed. Friedberg I, 302). This axiom is also found already in PL 54, 591 A (cf. *In Antonianum* 27 (1952) 349-366).
149. Cf. Leo XIII, encyclical letter *Rerum Novarum*, AAS 23 (1890-91) 643-646; Pius XI, encyclical letter *Quadragesimo Anno*, AAS 23 (1931) 191, *QA 44; Pius XII, radio message of 1 June 1941, AAS 33 (1941) 199; Pius XII, radio message on Christmas Eve 1942, AAS 35 (1943) 17; Pius XII, radio message of 1 September 1944, AAS 36 (1944) 253; John XXIII, encyclical letter *Mater et Magistra*, AAS 53 (1961) 428-429, *MM 111-115.
150. Cf. Pius XI, encyclical letter *Quadragesimo Anno*, AAS 23 (1931) 214, *QA 114; John XXIII, encyclical letter *Mater et Magistra*, AAS 53 (1961) 429, *MM 115-117.

151. Cf. Pius XII, radio message of Pentecost 1941, AAS 44 (1941) 199; John XXIII, encyclical letter *Mater et Magistra*, AAS 53 (1961) 430, *MM 119.
152. For the right use of goods according to the doctrine of the New Testament, cf. Luke 3:11; 10:30 *et sqq.*, 11:41; 1 Pet. 4:3; Mark 8:36; 12:39-41; Jas. 5:1-6; 1 Tim. 6:8; Eph. 4:28; 2 Cor. 8:13; 1 John 3:17 *et sqq.*
153. Cf. John XXIII, encyclical letter *Mater et Magistra*, AAS 53 (1961) 417, *MM 66.
154. Cf. John XXIII, *ibid*, *MM 67.
155. Cf. Rom. 13:1-5.
156. Cf. Rom. 13:5.
157. Cf. Pius XII, radio message, 24 December 1942, AAS 35 (1943) 9-24; 24 December 1944, AAS 37 (1945) 11-17; John XXIII, encyclical letter *Pacem in Terris*, AAS 55 (1963) 263, 271, 277 and 278, *PT 26, 52, 72 and 73.
158. Cf. Pius XII, radio message of 7 June 1941, AAS 33 (1941) 200; John XXIII, encyclical letter *Pacem in Terris*, l.c., p.273 and 274, *PT 60 and 61.
159. Cf. John XXIII, encyclical letter *Mater et Magistra*, AAS 53 (1961) 416, *MM 60.
160. Pius XI, allocution 'Ai dirigenti della Federazione Universitaria Cattolica', *Discorsi di Pio XI* (ed. Bertetto), Turin, vol. 1 (1960), p.743.
161. Cf. Second Vatican Council, *Dogmatic Constitution on the Church*, n. 13, AAS 57 (1965) 17.
162. Cf. Luke 2:14.
163. Eph. 2:16; Col. 1:20-22.
164. Cf. John XIII, encyclical letter *Pacem in Terris*, 11 April 1963, AAS 55 (1963) 291: 'Therefore in this age of ours which prides itself on its atomic power, it is irrational to believe that war is still an apt means of vindicating violated rights', *PT 127.
165. Cf. Pius XII, allocution of 30 September 1954, AAS 46 (1954) 589; radio message of 24 December 1954, AAS 47 (1955) 15 *et sqq.* John XXIII, encyclical letter *Pacem in Terris*, AAS 55 (1963) 286-291, *PT 109-130; Paul VI, allocution to the United Nations, 4 October 1965.
166. Cf. John XXIII, encyclical letter *Pacem in Terris*, where reduction of arms is mentioned, AAS (1963) 287, *PT 112.
167. Cf. 2 Cor. 2:6.
168. Cf. Matt. 7:21.

Populorum Progressio

1. Cf. *Acta Leonis XIII XI (1891) 97-148.*
2. Cf. *AAS 23 (1931) 177-228.*
3. Cf., for example, radio message of 1 June 1941, on the fiftieth anniversary of Leo XIII's encyclical letter *Rerum Novarum*, AAS 33 (1941) 195-205; radio message, Christmas 1942, AAS 35 (1943) 9-24; allocution to Italian Catholic Workers Association, meeting to commemorate *Rerum Novarum*, 14 May 1953, AAS 45 (1953) 402-408.
4. Cf. AAS 53 (1961) 401-464.
5. Cf. AAS 55 (1963) 257-304.
6. Cf. encyclical letter *Mater et Magistra*, AAS 53 (1961) 440, *MM 157.
7. Cf. Pastoral *Constitution on the Church in the World of Today*, n. 63, AAS 58 (1966) 1084 *GS 63.1.
8. Apostolic letter *motu proprio, Catholicam Christi Ecclesiam*, AAS 59 (1967) 27.
9. Cf. Leo XIII, encyclical letter *Rerum Novarum, Acta Leonis XIII*, XI (1891), 98.
10. Cf. *Church in the World of Today*, n. 63, AAS 58 (1966) 1085 *GS 63.2.
11. Cf. Luke 7, 22.
12. Cf. *Church in the World of Today*, n. 3, AAS 58 (1966) 1026 *GS 3.1.
13. Cf. Leo XIII, encyclical letter *Immortale Dei, Acta Leonis XIII* V (1885) 127.
14. *Church in the World of Today*, n. 4, AAS 58 (1966) 1027 *GS 4.
15. Cf. L.J. Lebret, OP, *Dynamique concrète du développement*, Paris: Economie et Humanisme, Les editions ouvrierès (1961), 28.
16. 2 Thes. 3:10.
17. Cf., for example, J. Maritain, *Les conditions spirituelles du progrès et de la paix*, in an anthology entitled *Rencontre des cultures a l'UNESCO sous le signe du Concile Oecuménique Vatican II*, Paris: Mame (1966), 66.
18. Cf. Matt. 5:3.
19. Gen. 1:28.
20. *Church in the World of Today*, n. 69, AAS 58 (1966) 1090 *GS 69.
21. 1 John 3:17.
22. *De Nabute.* c. 12, n.53, PL 14. 747; cf. J.R.Palanque. *Saint Ambroise et l'empire romain*, Paris: de Boccard (1933), 336 *et sqq.*
23. Letter to the 52nd Social Week at Brest, in *L'homme et la révolution urbaine*, Lyon: Chronique sociale (1965), 8-9.
24. *Church in the World of Today*, n. 71, AAS 58 (1966) 1093 *GS 71.5.
25. *Ibid.*, n. 65, AAS 58 (1966) 1086 *GS 65.2.
26. Encyclical letter *Quadragesimo Anno*, AAS 23 (1931) 212.
27. Cf. for example, Colin Clark, *The Conditions of Economic Progress*, 3rd ed., New York: St Martin's Press (1960), 3-6.
28. Letter to the 51st Social Week at Lyon, in *Le travail et les travailleurs dans la societé contemporaine*, Lyon: Chronique sociale (1965), 6.
29. Cf., for example, M.D. Chenu, OP., *Pour une théologie du travail*, Paris: Editions du Seuil (1955) [Eng. tr. *The Theology of Work*, Dublin: Gill, 1963].
30. Encyclical letter *Mater et Magistra*, AAS 53 (1961) 423, *MM 91.
31. Cf. for example, O. van Nell-Breuning, SJ, *Wirtschaft und Gesellschaft*, vol. 1: Grundfragen, Freiburg: Herder (1956), 183-184.
32. Eph. 4:13.
33. Cf., for example, Emmanuel Larrain Errázuriz, Bishop óf Talca, Chile, President of CELAM, *Lettre pastorale sur le développement et la paix*, Paris: Pax Christi (1965).
34. *Church in the World of Today*, n. 26, AAS 58 (1966) 1046 *GS 26.3.
35. John XXIII, encyclical letter *Mater et Magistra*, AAS 53 (1961) 414, *MM 53.
36. *L'Osservatore Romano*, 11 September 1965; La Documentation Catholique, 62 (1965) 1674-1675.
37. Cf. Matt. 19:6.
38. *Church in the World of Today*, n. 52, AAS 58 (1966) 1073, *GS 52.3.
39. *Ibid.*, nos. 50-51, with note 14: AAS 58 (1966), 1070-1073, GS 50-51 with note 116; also n. 87, p. 1110 GS 87.2
40. Cf. *ibid.*, n. 15, AAS 58 (1966) 1036, GS 15.2.
41. Matt. 16:26.
42. *Church in the World of Today*, n. 57, AAS 58 (1966) 1078, *GS 57.3.
43. *Ibid.*, n. 19, AAS 58 (1966) 1039, *GS 19.2.
44. Cf., for example, J. Maritain, *L'humanisme intégral*, Paris: Aubier (1936) [Eng. tr. *True Humanism*, New York: Charles Scribner's Sons (1938)].

45. Cf. H. de Lubac, SJ, *Le drame de l'humanisme athée*, 3rd ed., Paris: Spes (1945), 10 [Eng. tr. *The Drama of Atheistic Humanism*, London: Sheed and Ward (1949), 7].
46. *Pensées*, ed. Brunschvicg, n. 434; cf. Maurice Zundel, *L'homme passe l'homme*, Le Caire: Editions du lien (1944).
47. Cf. Address to representatives of non-Christian religions, 3 December 1964, AAS 57 (1965) 132.
48. Jas. 2: 15-16.
49. Cf. encyclical letter *Mater et Magistra*, AAS 53 (1961) 440 *et sqq.* *MM 158-160.
50. Cf. Christmas message, December 1963, AAS 56 (1964) 57-58.
51. Cf. *Encicliche e discorsi di Paolo VI*, vol. IX: ed. Paoline, Rome (1966), 132-136.
52. Cf. Luke 16:19-31.
53. *Church in the World of Today*, n. 86:AAS 58 (1966) 1109, *GS 86 (b).
54. Luke 12:20.
55. Special message to the world, delivered to newsmen during India visit, 4 December 1964, AAS 57 (1965) 135.
56. Cf. AAS 56 (1964) 639 *et sqq.*
57. Cf. *Acta Leonis XIII*, XI (1891), 131.
58. Cf. Leo XIII, encyclical letter *Rerum Novarum*, Acta Leonis XIII, XI (1891), 98.
59. *Church in the World of Today*, n. 85, AAS 58 (1966) 1108, *GS 85.1.
60. Cf. encyclical letter *Fidei donum*, AAS 49 (1957) 246.
61. Matt. 25:35-36.
62. Mark 8:2.
63. John XXIII, Address upon receiving the Balzan Peace Prize, 10 May 1963, AAS 55 (1963) 455.
64. AAS 57 (1965) 896.
65. Cf. John XXIII, encyclical letter *Pacem in Terris*, AAS 55 (1963) 301, *PT 162.
66. AAS 57 (1965) 880.
67. Eph. 4:12. Cf. Second Vatican Council, *Dogmatic Constitution on the Church*, n.13, AAS 57 (1965) 17.
68. Cf. Second Vatican Council, *Decree on the Apostolate of the Laity*, n. 7, 13, 24, AAS 58 (1966) 843, 849, 856.
69. Luke 11:9.

Octagesimo Adveniens

1. *Gaudium et Spes* 10, AAS 58 (1966) 1033, *GS 10.
2. AAS 23 (1931) 209 *et sqq.*
3. AAS 53 (1961) 429, *MM 115.
4. 3, AAS 59 (1967) 258, *PP 3.
5. *Ibid.*, 1, 257, *PP 1.
6. Cf. 2 Cor 4:17.
7. Cf. *Populorum Progressio*, 25, AAS 59 (1967) 269-270, *PP 25.
8. Cf. Rev. 3:12, 21:2.
9. *Gaudium et Spes* 25, AAS 58 (1966) 1045, *GS 25.
10. *Ibid.*, 67, 1089, *GS 67.1.
11. Cf. *Populorum Progressio*, 69, AAS 59, (1967) 290-291, *PP 69.
12. Cf. Matt. 25:35.
13. *Nostra Aetate*, 5, AAS 58 (1966) 743.
14. 37, AAS 59 (1967) 276, *PP 37.
15. Cf. *Inter Mirifica*, 12, AAS 56 (1964) 149.
16. Cf. *Pacem in Terris*, AAS 55 (1963) 261 *et sqq.*, *PT 15-27.
17. Cf. the message of Pope Paul VI for the World Day of Peace, 1 January 1971, AAS 63. (1971) 5-9.
18. Cf. *Gaudium et Spes*, 74, AAS 58 (1966) 1095-1096, *GS 74.
19. *Dignitatis Humanae*, 1, AAS 58 (1966) 930.
20. AAS 55 (1963) 300, *PT 159.
21. Cf. *Gaudium et Spes*, 11, AAS 58 (1966) 1033, *GS 11.2.
22. Cf. Rom. 15:16.
23. *Gaudium et Spes*, 39, AAS 58 (1966) 1057, *GS 39.1.
24. 13, AAS 59 (1967) 264, *PP 13.
25. Cf. *Gaudium et Spes*, 36, AAS 58 (1966) 1054, *GS 36.1.
26. Cf. Rom 5:5.
27. Cf. *Populorum Progressio*, 56 *et sqq.*, AAS 59 (1967) 285 *et sqq.*, *PP 56-61.
28. Cf. *ibid.*, 86, 299, *PP 86.
29. Cf. *Gaudium et Spes*, 63, AAS 58 (1966) 1085, *GS 63.4.
30. *Quadragesimo Anno*, AAS 23 (1931) 203, *QA 79; cf. *Mater et Magistra*, AAS 53 (1961) 414, 428, *MM 53, 111: *Gaudium et Spes*, 74, 75, 76, AAS 58 (1966) 1095-1100, *GS 74-76.5.
31. AAS 53 (1961) 420-422, *MM 74-84.
32. Cf. *Gaudium et Spes*, 68, 75, AAS 58 (1966) 1089-1090, 1097, *GS 68-68.2, 75.
33. 81, AAS 59 (1967) 296-297, *PP 81.
34. Cf. Matt. 28:30; Phil, 2:8-11.
35. Cf. *Gaudium et Spes*, 43, AAS 58 (1966) 1061, *GS 43.2.
36. *Ibid.*, 92, 1113, *GS 92.1.
37. Cf. 1 Thes, 5:21.
38. Cf. *Lumen Gentium*, 31, AAS 57 (1965) 37-38; *Apostolican Actuositatem*, 5, AAS 58. (1966) 842.
39. *Catholicam Christi Ecclesiam*, AAS 59 (1967) 27 and 26.

Evangelii Nuntiandi

1. Cf. Luke 22:32.
2. 2 Cor. 11:28.
3. Cf. Second Vatican Council, decree on the Church's Missionary Activity *Ad Gentes*, 1, AAS 58 (1966) 947.
4. Cf. Eph. 4:24; 2:15; Col. 3:10; Gal. 3:27; Rom. 13:14; 2 Cor. 5:17.
5. 2 Cor. 5:20.
6. Cf. Paul VI, address for the closing of the third general assembly of the synod of bishops (26 October 1974). AAS 66 (1974) 634-635, 637.
7. Paul VI, address to the College of Cardinals (22 June 1973), AAS 65 (1973) 383.
8. 2 Cor. 11:28.
9. 1 Tim. 5:17.
10. 2 Tim. 2:15.
11. Cf. 1 Cor. 2:5.
12. Luke 4:43.
13. *Ibid.*
14. Luke 4:18; cf. Is 61:1.
15. Cf. Mark 1:1; Rom. 1:1-3.
16. Cf. Matt. 6:33.
17. Cf. Matt. 5:3-12.
18. Cf. Matt. 5-7.
19. Cf. Matt. 10.
20. Cf. Matt. 13.
21. Cf. Matt. 18.
22. Cf. Matt. 24-25.
23. Cf. Matt. 24:36; Acts 1:7; 1 Thes. 5:1-2.
24. Cf. Matt. 11:12; Luke 16:16.
25. Cf. Matt. 4:17.
26. Mark 1:27.
27. Luke 4:22.
28. John 7:46.
29. Luke 4:43.
30. John 11:52.
31. Cf. Second Vatican Council, dogmatic constitution on Divine Revelation *Dei Verbum*, 4: AAS 58 (1966) 818-819.
32. 1 Pet. 2:9.
33. Cf. Acts 2:11.
34. Luke 4:43.
35. 1 Cor. 9:16.
36. 'Declaration of the Synod Fathers', 4: *L'Osservatore Romano* (27 October 1974), p.6.
37. Matt. 28:19.
38. Acts 2:41, 47.
39. Cf. Second Vatican Council, dogmatic constitution on the Church *Lumen Gentium*, 8: AAS 57 (1965) 11; decree on the Church's Missionary Activity *Ad Gentes*, 5: AAS 58 (1966) 951-952.
40. Cf. Acts 2:42-46; 4:32-35; 5:12-16.
41. Cf. Acts 2:11; 1 Pet. 2:9.
42. Cf. decree on the Church's Missionary Activity *Ad Gentes*, 5, 11-12, AAS 58 (1966) 951-952, 959-961.
43. Cf. 2 Cor. 4:5; St Augustine, *Sermo XLVI, De Pastoribus*, CCL XLI, pp.529-530.
44. 10:16; cf. St Cyprian, *De Unitate Ecclesiae*, 14, PL 4, 527; St Augustine, *Enarrat.* 88, *Sermo*, 2, 14: PL 37, 1140: St John Chrysostom, Hom. *de capto Eutropio*, 6: PG 52, 402.
45. Eph, 5:25.
46. Rev. 21:5, cf. 2 Cor. 5:17; Gal. 6:15.
47. Cf. Rom. 6:4.
48. Cf. Eph. 4:23-24; Col. 3:9-10.
49. Cf. Rom. 1:16; 1 Cor. 1:18, 2:4.
50. Cf. 53, AAS 58 (1966) 1075.
51. Cf. Tertullian *Apologeticum*, 39, CCL, 1, pp.150-153; Minucius *Felix, Octavius* 9 and 31, CSLP, Turin 1963², pp.11-13, 47-48.
52. 1 Pet. 3:15.

53. Cf. Second Vatican Council, dogmatic constitution on the Church *Lumen Gentium*, 1, 9. 48, AAS 57 (1965) 5, 12-14. 53-54; pastoral constitution on the Church in the Modern World *Gaudium et Spes*, 42, 45, AAS 58 (1966) 1060-1061, 1065-1066; *GS 42.1-42.2, 45. Decree on the Church's Missionary Activity *Ad Gentes*, 1, 5, AAS 58 (1966) 947, 951-952.
54. Cf. Rom. 1:16; 1 Cor. 1:18.
55. Cf. Acts 17:22-23.
56. 1 John 3:1; cf. Rom. 8:14-17.
57. Cf. Eph. 2:8; 1:16. Cf. Sacred Congregation for the Doctrine of the Faith, *Declaratio ad fidem tuendam in mysteria Incarnationis et SS. Trinitatis e quibusdam recentibus erroribus* (21 February 1972), AAS 64 (1972) 237-241.
58. Cf. 1 John 3:2; Rom. 8:29; Phil. 3:20-21. Cf. Second Vatican Council, dogmatic constitution on the Church *Lumen Gentium*, 48-51, AAS 57 (1965) 53-58.
59. Cf. Sacred Congregation for the Doctrine of the Faith, *Declaratio circa Catholicam Doctrinam de Ecclesia contra non-nullos errores hodiernos tuendam* (24 June 1973), AAS 65 (1973) 396-408.
60. Cf. Second Vatican Council, pastoral constitution on the Church in the Modern World *Gaudium et Spes*, 47-52, AAS 58 (1966) 1067-1074, *GS 47-52.6; Paul VI, encyclical letter *Humanae Vitae*, AAS 60 (1968) 481-503.
61. Paul VI, address for the opening of the third general assembly of the synod of bishops (27 September 1974), AAS 66 (1974) 562.
62. *Ibid.*
63. Paul VI, address to the *campesinos* of Columbia (23 August 1968), AAS 60 (1968) 623.
64. Paul VI, address for the 'Day of Development' at Bogotá (23 August 1968), AAS 60 (1968) 627; St Augustine, *Epistola* 229, 2, PL 33, 1020.
65. Paul VI, address for the closing of the third general assembly of the synod of bishops (26 October 1974), AAS 66 (1974) 637.
66. Address given on 15 October 1975, *L'Osservatore Romano* (17 October 1975).
67. Pope Paul VI, address to the members of the *Consilium de Laicis* (2 October 1974), AAS 66 (1974) 568.
68. Cf. 1 Pet. 3:1.
69. Rom. 10:14, 17.
70. Cf. 1 Cor. 2:1-5.
71. Rom. 10:17.
72. Cf. Matt. 10:27; Luke 12:3.
73. Mark 16:15.
74. Cf. St Justin, 1 *Apol.* 46, 1-4, PG 6, 11 *Apol.* 7 (8) 1-4; 10, 1-3; 13, 3-4; *Florilegium Patristicum* II, Bonn 1911², pp.81, 125, 129, 133; Clement of Alexandria, *Stromata* 1, 19, 91;94, *S. Ch.* pp.117-118; 119-120; Second Vatican Council, decree on the Church's Missionary Activity *Ad Gentes*, 11, AAS 58 (1966) 960; dogmatic constitution on the Church *Lumen Gentium*, 17, AAS 57 (1965) 20.
75. Eusebius of Caesarea, *Praeparatio Evangelica* I, 1, PG 21, 26-28; cf. Second Vatican Council, dogmatic constitution on the Church *Lumen Gentium*, 16, AAS 57 (1965) 21.
76. Cf. Eph. 3:8.
77. Cf. Henri de Lubac, *Le drame de l'humanisme athée*, ed. Spes, Paris, 1945.
78. Cf. pastoral constitution on the Church in the Modern World *Gaudium et Spes*, 59, AAS 58 (1966) 1080, *GS 59.1.
79. 1 Tim. 2:4.
80. Matt. 9:36; 15:32.
81. Rom. 10:15.
82. Declaration on Religious Liberty *Dignitatis Humanae*, 13, AAS 58 (1966) 939; cf. dogmatic constitution on the Church *Lumen Gentium*, 5, AAS 57 (1965) 7-8; decree on the Church's Missionary Activity *Ad Gentes*, 1: AAS 58 (1966) 947.
83. Decree on the Church's Missionary Activity *Ad Gentes*, 35, AAS 58 (1966) 983.
84. St Augustine, *Enarratio in Ps.* 44, 23 CCL XXXVIII, p.510; cf. decree on the Church's Missionary Activity *Ad Gentes*, 1, AAS 58 (1966) 947.
85. St Gregory the Great, *Homil. in Evangelia* 19, 1, PL 76, 1154.
86. Acta 1:8; cf. *Didache* 9, 1, Funk, *Patres Apostolici*, 1, 22.
87. Matt. 28:20.
88. Cf. Matt. 13:32.
89. Cf. Matt. 13:47.
90. Cf. John 21:11.
91. Cf. John 10:1-16.

92. Cf. Second Vatican Council, constitution on the Sacred Liturgy *Sacrosanctum Concilium*, 37-38, AAS 56 (1964) 110; cf. also the liturgical books and other documents subsequently issued by the Holy See for the putting into practice of the liturgical reform desired by the same council.

93. Paul VI, address for the closing of the third general assembly of the synod of bishops (26 October 1974), AAS 66 (1974) 636.

94. Cf. John 15:16; Mark 3:13-19; Luke 6:13-16.

95. Cf. Acts 1:21-22.

96. Cf. Mark 3:14.

97. Cf. Mark 3:14-15; Luke 9:2.

98. Acts 4:8; cf. 2-14; 3:12.

99. Cf. St Leo the Great, *Sermo* 69, 3; *Sermo* 70, 1-3; *Sermo* 94, 3; *Sermo* 95, 2, S.C. 200, pp.50-52; 58-66; 258-260; 268.

100. Cf. First Ecumenical Council of Lyons, constitution *Ad Apostolicae Dignitatis: Conciliorum Oecumenicorum Decreta*, ed. Istituto per le Scienze Religiose, Bologna 1973³, p.278; Ecumenical Council of Vienne, constitution *Ad Providam Christi*, ed. *cit.*, p.343; Fifth Lateran Ecumenical Council, constitution *In Apostolici Culminis*, ed. *cit.*, p.608; constitution *Postquam ad Universalis*, ed. *cit.*, p.609; constitution *Supernae Dispositionis*, ed. *cit.*, p.614; constitution *Divina Disponente Clementia*, ed. *cit.*, p.638.

101. Decree on the Church's Missionary Activity *Ad Gentes*, 38, AAS 58 (1966) 985.

102. Cf. Second Vatican Council, dogmatic constitution on the Church *Lumen Gentium*, 22, AAS 57 (1965) 26.

103. Cf. Second Vatican Council, dogmatic constitution on the Church *Lumen Gentium*, 10, 37, AAS 57 (1965) 14-43; decree on the Church's Missionary Activity *Ad Gentes*, 39, AAS 58 (1966) 986; decree on the Ministry and Life of Priests *Presbyterorum Ordinis*, 2, 12, 13, AAS 58 (1966) 992, 1010, 1011.

104. Cf. 1 Thes. 2:9.

105. Cf. 1. Pet. 5:4.

106. Dogmatic constitution on the Church *Lumen Gentium*, 11, AAS 57 (1965); decree on the Apostolate of the Laity *Apostolicam Actuositatem*, 11, AAS 58 (1966) 848; St John Chrysostom, *In Genesim Serm.* VI, 2; VII, 1, PG 54, 607-68.

107. Matt. 3:17.

108. Matt. 4:1.

109. Luke 4:14.

110. Luke 4:18, 21; cf. Is. 61:1.

111. John 20:22.

112. Acts 2:17.

113. Cf. Acts 4:8.

114. Cf. Acts 9:17.

115. Cf. Acts 6:5, 10; 7:55.

116. Acts 10:44.

117. Acts 9:31.

118. Cf. Second Vatican Council, decree on the Church's Missionary Activity *Ad Gentes*, 4, AAS 58 (1966), pp.950-951.

119. John 17:21.

120. Cf. Acts 20:28.

121. Cf. Decree on the Ministry and Life of Priests *Presbyterorum Ordinis*, 13, AAS 58 (1966) 1011.

122. Cf. Heb. 11:27.

123. Decree on the Church's Missionary Activity *Ad Gentes*, 6, AAS 58 (1966) 954-955; cf. decree on Ecumenism *Unitatis Redintegratio*, 1, AAS 57 (1965) 90-91.

124. Bull *Apostolorum Limina*, VII, AAS 66 (1974) 305.

125. Rom. 5:5.

126. Cf. John 8:32.

127. 1 Thes. 2:8; cf. Phil. 1:8.

128. Cf. 1 Thes. 2:7-11; 1 Cor. 4:15; Gal. 4:19.

129. Cf. 1 Cor. 8:9-13; Rom. 14:15.

130. Cf. Rom. 12:11.

131. Cf. Second Vatican Council, declaration on Religious Liberty *Dignitatis Humanae*, 4, AAS 58 (1966) 933.

132. Cf. *Ibid.*, 9-14, *loc. cit.*, pp.935-940.

Footnotes: Evangelii Nuntiandi

133. Cf. Second Vatican Council, decree on the Church's Missionary Activity *Ad Gentes*, 7, AAS 58 (1966) 955.
134. Cf. Rom. 1:16.
135. Phil. 1:3-4, 7-8.

Redemptor Hominis

38. Cf. Gen. 1 *passim.*
39. Cf. Gen. 1:26-30.
40. Rom. 8:20; cf. 8:19-22; Second Vatican Council, pastoral constitution on the Church in the Modern World *Gaudium et Spes*, 2, 13, AAS 58 (1966) 1026, 1034-1035, *GS 2.1, 13.
41. John 3:16.
42. Cf. Rom. 5:12-21.
43. Rom. 8:22.
44. Rom. 8:19.
45. Rom. 8:22.
46. Rom. 8:19.
47. Second Vatican Council, pastoral constitution on the Church in the Modern World *Gaudium et Spes*, 22, AAS 58 (1966) 1042-1043, *GS 22-22.1.
48. Rom. 5:11; Col. 1:20.
49. Ps. 8:6.
50. Cf. Gen. 1:26.
51. Cf. Gen. 3:6-13.
52. Cf. Eucharistic Prayer IV.
53. Cf. Second Vatican Council, pastoral constitution on the Church in the Modern World *Gaudium et Spes*, 37, AAS 58 (1966) 1054-1055, *GS 37.3.; dogmatic constitution on the Church *Lumen Gentium*, 48, AAS 57 (1965) 53-54.
54. Cf. Rom. 8:29-30; Eph. 1:8.
55. Cf. John 16:13.
56. Cf. 1 Thes. 5:24.
57. 2 Cor. 5:21; cf. Gal. 3:13.
58. 1 John 4:8, 16.
59. Cf. Rom. 8:20.
60. Cf. Luke 15:11-32.
61. Rom. 8:19.
62. Cf. Rom. 8:18.
63. Cf. St Thomas, *Summa Theol*, III, q. 46, a.1, ad 3.
64. Gal. 3:28.
65. *Exsultet* at the Easter Vigil.
66. Cf. John 3:16.
67. Cf. St Justin, I *Apologia*, 46, 1-4; II *Apologia*, 7 (8), 1-4; 10, 1-3; 13, 3-4: *Florilegium Patristicum*, II, Bonn 1911², pp.81, 125, 129, 133; Clement of Alexandria, *Stromata*, I, 19, 91 and 94: *Sources Chrétiennes*, 30, pp.117-118; 119-120; Second Vatican Council, decree on the Church's Missionary Activity *Ad Gentes*, 11, AAS 58 (1966) 960; dogmatic constitution on the Church *Lumen Gentium*, 17, AAS 57 (1965) 21.
68. Cf. Second Vatican Council, declaration on the Church's Relations with Non-Christian Religions *Nostra Aetate*, 3-4, AAS 58 (1966) 741-743.
69. Col. 1:26.
70. Matt. 11:12.
71. Luke 16:8.
72. Eph. 3:8.
73. Cf. Second Vatican Council, declaration *Nostra Aetate*, 1-2, AAS 58 (1966) 740-741.
74. Acts 17:22-31.
75. John 2:25.
76. John 3:8.
77. Cf. AAS 58 (1966) 929-946.
78. Cf. John 14:26.
79. Paul VI, apostolic exhortation *Evangelii Nuntiandi*, 6, AAS 68 (1976) 9, *EN 9.
80. John 7:16.
81. Cf. AAS 58 (1966) 936-938.
82. John 8:32.
83. John 18:37.
84. Cf. John 4:23.
85. John 4:23-24.
86. Cf. Paul VI, encyclical letter *Ecclesiam Suam*, AAS 56 (1964) 609-659.
87. Second Vatican Council, pastoral constitution on the Church in the Modern World *Gaudium et Spes*, 22, AAS 58 (1966) 1042, *GS 22.1.

88. Cf. John 14:1 *et sqq.*
89. Second Vatican Council, pastoral constitution on the Church in the Modern World *Gaudium et Spes*, 91, AAS 58 (1966) 1113, *GS 91.
90. *Ibid.*, 38, *loc. cit.*, 1056, *GS 38.
91. *Ibid.*, 76, *loc. cit.*, 1099, *GS 76.1.
92. Cf. Gen. 1:26.
93. Second Vatican Council, pastoral constitution on the Church in the Modern World *Gaudium et Spes*, 24, AAS 58 (1966) 1045, *GS 24.2.
94. Gen. 1:28.
95. Second Vatican Council, pastoral constitution on the Church in the Modern World *Gaudium et Spes*, 10, AAS 58 (1966) 1032, *GS 10.
96. *Ibid.*, 10, *loc. cit.*, 1033, *GS 10.1.
97. *Ibid.*, 38, *loc. cit.*, 1056,*GS 38; Paul VI, encyclical letter *Populorum Progressio*, 21, AAS 59 (1967) 267-268, *PP 21.
98. Cf. Gen. 1:28.
99. Cf. Gen. 1-2.
100. Gen. 1:28; cf. Second Vatican Council, decree on the Social Communications Media *Inter Mirifica*, 6, AAS 56 (1964) 147; pastoral constitution on the Church in the Modern World *Gaudium et Spes*, 74, 78, AAS 58 (1966) 1095-1096, 1101-1102, *GS 74-74.5, 78-78.5.
101. Cf. Second Vatican Council, dogmatic constitution on the Church *Lumen Gentium*, 10, 36, AAS 57 (1965) 14-15, 41-42.
102. Cf. Second Vatican Council, pastoral constitution on the Church in the Modern World *Gaudium et Spes*, 35, AAS 58 (1966) 1053,*GS 35; Paul VI, address to diplomatic corps (7 January 1965), AAS 57 (1965) 232; encyclical letter *Populorum Progressio*, 14, AAS 59 (1967) 264, PP 14.
103. Cf. Pius XII, radio message on the fiftieth anniversary of Leo XIII's encyclical *Rerum Novarum*, 1 June 1941, AAS 33 (1941) 195-205; Christmas radio message, 24 December 1941, AAS 34 (1942) 10-21; Christmas radio message, 24 December 1942, AAS 35 (1943) 9-24; Christmas radio message, 24 December 1943, AAS 36 (1944) 11-24; Christmas radio message, 24 December 1944, AAS 37 (1945) 10-23; address to the cardinals, 24 December 1945, AAS 38 (1946) 15-25; address to the cardinals, 24 December 1946, AAS 39 (1947) 7-17; Christmas radio message, 24 December 1947, AAS 40 (1948) 8-16; John XXIII, encyclical letter *Mater et Magistra*, AAS 53 (1961) 401-464, encyclical letter *Pacem in Terris*, AAS 55 (1963) 257-304, Paul VI, encyclical letter *Ecclesiam Suam*, AAS 56 (1964) 609-659; address to the general assembly of the United Nations, 4 October 1965, AAS 57 (1965) 877-885; encyclical letter *Populorum Progressio*, AAS 59 (1967) 257-299; address to the *campesinos* of Columbia, 23 August 1968, AAS 60 (1968) 619-623; speech to the general assembly of the Latin-American Episcopate, 24 August 1968, AAS 60 (1968) 639-649; speech to the conference of FAO, 16 November 1970, AAS 62 (1970) 830-838; apostolic letter *Octagesima Adveniens*, AAS 63 (1971) 401-441; address to the cardinals, 23 June 1972, AAS 64 (1972) 496-505; Paul VI, address to the third general conference of the Latin-American Episcopate, 28 January 1979, AAS 71 (1979) 187 *et sqq.*; address to the Indians at Cuilipan, 29 January 1979, *loc. cit.*, 207 *et sqq.*; address to the Guadalajara workers, 30 January 1979, *loc. cit.*, 221 *et sqq.*; address to the Monterrey workers, 31 January 1979, *loc. cit.*, 240-242; Second Vatican Council, declaration on Religious Freedom *Dignitatis Humanae*, AAS 58 (1966) 929-941; pastoral constitution on the Church in the Modern World *Gaudium et Spes*, AAS 58 (1966) 1025-1115; *Documenta Synodi Episcoporum: De Iustitia in Mundo*, AAS 63 (1971) 923-941.
104. Cf. John XXIII, encyclical letter *Mater et Magistra*, AAS 53 (1961) 418 *et sqq.* *MM 68-74; encyclical letter *Pacem in Terris*, AAS 55 (1963) 289 *et sqq.* *PT 121-129; Paul VI, encyclical letter *Populorum Progressio*, AAS 59 (1967) 257-99.
105. Cf. Luke 16:19-31.
106. Cf. John Paul II, homily at Santo Domingo 25 January 1979, 3, AAS 71 (1979) 157 *et sqq.*; address to Indians and *campesinos* at Oaxaca, 30 January 1979, 2, *loc. cit.*, 207 *et sqq.*; address to Monterrey workers, 31 January 1979, 4, *loc. cit.*, 242.
107. Cf. Paul VI, apostolic letter *Octagesima Adveniens*, 42, AAS 63 (1971) 431, *OA 42.
108. Cf. Matt. 25:31-46.
109. Matt. 25:42, 43.
110. 2 Tim. 4:2.
111. Pius XI, encyclical letter *Quadragesimo Anno*, AAS 23 (1931) 213; encyclical letter *Non Abbiamo Bisogno*, AAS 23 (1931) 285-312; encyclical letter *Divini Redemptoris*, AAS 29 (1937) 65-106; encyclical letter *Mit Brennender Sorge*, AAS 29 (1937) 145-147; Pius XII, encyclical letter *Summi Pontificatus*, AAS 31 (1939) 413-435.

112. Cf. 2 Cor 3:6.
113. Cf. Second Vatican Council, pastoral constitution on the Church in the Modern World *Gaudium et Spes*, 31, AAS 58 (1966) 1050, *GS 31.2.
114. Cf. AAS 58 (1966) 929-946.

Dives in Misericordia

60. In both places it is a case of *hesed*, i.e., the fidelity that God manifests to his own love for the people, fidelity to the promises that will find their definitive fulfilment precisely in the motherhood of the mother of God (cf. Luke 1:49-54).
61. Cf. Luke 1:72. Here too it is a case of mercy in the meaning of *hesed*, in so far as in the following sentences, in which Zechariah speaks of the 'tender mercy of our God', there is clearly expressed the second meaning, namely *rahamim* (Latin translation: *visera misericordiae*), which rather identifies God's mercy with a mother's love.
62. Cf. Luke 15:14-32.
63. Luke 15:18-19.
64. Luke 15:20
65. Luke 15:32.
66. Cf. Luke 15:3-6.
67. Cf. Luke 15:8-9.
68. 1 Cor. 13:4-8.
69. Cf. Rom. 12:21.

111. Matt. 5:38.

Laborem Exercens

1. Cf. Ps 127 (128): 2; cf. also Gen 3:17-19; Prov. 10:22; Ex. 1:8-14; Jer 22:13.
2. Cf. Gen. 1:26.
3. Cf. Gen. 1:28.
4. Encyclical letter *Redemptor Hominis*, 14, *AAS 71 (1979) 284-85, RH 14.
5. Cf. Ps. 127 (128):2.
6. Gen 3:19.
7. Cf. Matt. 13:52.
8. Second Vatican Council, pastoral constitution on the Church in the Modern World, *Gaudium et Spes*, 38, *AAS 58 (1966) 1055-6, GS 38.
9. Gen. 1:27.
10. Gen. 1:28.
11. Cf. Heb. 2:17; Phil. 2:5-8.
12. Cf. Pius XI, encyclical letter, *Quadragesimo Anno*, AAS 23 (1931) 221, *QA 135.
13. Deut. 24:15; Jas. 5:4; and also Gen. 4:10.
14. Cf. Gen. 1:28.
15. Cf. Gen. 1:26-27.
16. Gen. 3:19.
17. Heb. 6:8; cf. Gen. 3:18.
18. Cf. *Summa Theol*, I-II, q. 40, a. 1, c.; I-II, q. 34, a. 2, ad. 1.
19. *Ibid.*
20. Cf. *Quadragesimo Anno* AAS 23 (1931) 221-222, *QA 135-6.
21. Cf. John 4:38.
22. On the right to property see *Summa Theol.*, II-II, q. 66, arts. 2 and 6; *De Regimine Principum*, Book 1, Chapters 15 and 17. On the social function of property see *Summa Theol.*, II-II, q. 134, art. 1, ad. 3.
23. Cf. *Quadragesimo Anno*, AAS 23 (1931) 199, *QA 64ff; Second Vatican Council, *Gaudium et Spes*, 68, *AAS 58 (1966) 1089-90, *GS 68.
24. Cf. John XXIII, encyclical letter *Mater et Magistra*, AAS 53 (1961) 419, *MM 73.
25. Cf. *Summa Theol.*, II-II, q. 65, a.2.
26. *Gaudium et Spes*, 67, *AAS 58 (1966) 1088-89, GS 67.2.
27. *Ibid*, 34, *AAS 58 (1966) 1052, GS 34.
28. Cf. Gen. 2:2; Ex. 20:8, 11; Deut. 5:12-14.
29. Cf. Gen. 2:3.
30. Rev. 15:3.
31. Gen. 1:4, 10, 12, 18, 21, 25, 31.
32. John 5:17.
33. Cf. Heb. 4:1, 9-10.
34. John 14:2.
35. Cf. Deut. 5:12-14; Ex. 20:8-12.
36. Cf. Matt. 25:21.
37. *Gaudium et Spes*, 34, *AAS 58 (1966) 1052-53, GS 34.1.
38. *Ibid.*, *GS 34.2.
39. Second Vatican Council, dogmatic constitution on the Church *Lumen Gentium*, 36.
40. Mark 6:2-3.
41. Cf. Matt. 13:55.
42. Cf. Matt. 6:25-34.
43. John 15:1.
44. Cf. Sir. 38:1-3.
45. Cf. *Ibid.*, 38:4-8.
46. Cf. Ex. 31:1-5; Sir. 38:27.
47. Cf. Gen. 4:22; Is. 44:12.
48. Cf. Jer. 18:3-4; Sir 38:29-30.
49. Cf. Gen. 9:20; Is. 5:1-2.
50. Cf. Eccles. 12:9-12; Sir. 39:1-8.
51. Cf. Ps. 107 (108): 23-30; Wisd. 14:2-3a.
52. Cf. Gen. 11:3; 2 Kings 12:12-13; 22:5-6.
53. Cf. Gen. 4:21.
54. Cf. Gen. 4:2; 37:3; Ex. 3:1; 1 Sam. 16:11; *et passim*.
55. Cf. Ezech. 47:10.
56. Cf. Prov. 31:15-27.

Footnotes: Laborem Exercens

57. E.g., John 10:1-16.
58. Cf. Mark 12:1-12.
59. Cf. Luke 4:23.
60. Cf. Mark 4:1-9.
61. Cf. Matt. 13:52.
62. Cf. Matt. 24:45; Luke 12:42-48.
63. Cf. Luke 16:1-8.
64. Cf. Matt. 13:47-50.
65. Cf. Matt. 13:45-46.
66. Cf. Matt. 20:1-16.
67. Cf. Matt. 13:33; Luke 15:8-9.
68. Cf. Matt 9:37; John 4:35-38.
69. Cf. Matt 4:19.
70. Cf. Matt. 13:52.
71. Cf. Acts 18:3.
72. *Ibid.*, 20:34-35.
73. 2 Thes. 3:8. St Paul recognizes that missionaries have a right to their keep: 1 Cor. 9-6-14; Gal. 6:6; 2 Thes. 3:9; cf. Luke 10:7.
74. 2 Thes. 3:12.
75. *Ibid.*, 3:11.
76. *Ibid.*, 3:10.
77. Col. 3:23-24.
78. Cf. Acts 1:1.
79. *Gaudium et Spes*, 35, AAS 58 (1966) 1053, *GS 35-35.1.
80. *Ibid.*, *GS 35.
81. Gen. 3:17.
82. *Ibid.*, 3:19.
83. Eccles. 2:11.
84. Cf. Rom. 5:19.
85. Cf. John 17:4.
86. Cf. Luke 9:23.
87. *Gaudium et Spes*, 38, AAS 58 (1966) 1055-56, *GS38.
88. Cf. 2 Pet. 3:13; Rev. 21:1.
89. Cf. 2 Pet. 3:13.
90. *Gaudium et Spes*, 39, AAS 58 (1966) 1057, *GS 39.1.
91. *Ibid.*, *GS 39.2.

Sollicitudo Rei Socialis

1. Leo XIII, encyclical *Rerum Novarum* (May 15, 1891): *Leonis XIII P.M. Acta*, XI, Rome 1892, pp. 97-144, *RN.
2. Pius XI, encyclical *Quadragesimo Anno* (May 15, 1931): *Acta Apostolicae Sedis* 23 (1931), pp. 177-228 *QA; John XXIII, encyclical *Mater et Magistra* (May 15, 1961): AAS 53 (1961), pp. 401-464 *MM; Paul VI, apostolic letter *Octogesima Adveniens* (May 14, 1971); AAS 63 (1971), pp. 401-441 *OA; John Paul II, encyclical *Laborem Exercens* (Sept. 14, 1981):, AAS 73 (1981), pp. 577-647 *LE. Also, Pius XII delivered a radio message (June 1, 1941) for the 50th anniversary of the encyclical of Leo XIII: AAS 33 (1941), pp. 195-205.
3. Cf. Second Vatican Ecumenical Council, Dogmatic Constitution on Divine Revelation *Dei Verbum*, 4.
4. Paul VI, encyclical *Populorum Progressio* (March 26, 1967): AAS 59 (1967), pp. 257-299, *PP.
5. Cf. L'Osservatore Romano, May 25, 1987.
6. Cf. Congregation for the Doctrine of the Faith, Instruction on Christian Freedom and Liberation *Libertatis Conscientia* (March 22, 1986), 72: AAS 79 (1987), p. 586; *Octogesima Adveniens*, 4, *OA 4.
7. Cf. encyclical *Redemptoris Mater* (March 25, 1987), 3: AAS 79 (1987), pp. 363f; Homily at the Mass of Jan. 1, 1987; L'Osservatore Romano, Jan. 2, 1987.
8. The encyclical *Populorum Progressio* cites the documents of the Second Vatican Council 19 times, and 16 of the references are to the Pastoral Constitution on the Church in the Modern World *Gaudium et Spes*.
9. *Gaudum et Spes*, 1, *GS 4.
10. Ibid., 4 *GS 4; cf. *Populorum Progressio*, 13, *PP 13.
11. Cf. *Gaudium et Spes*, 3 *GS 3; *Populorum Progressio* 13, *PP 13.
12. Cf. *Gaudium et Spes*, 63 *GS 63; *Populorum Progressio*, 9, *PP 9.
13. Cf. *Gaudium et Spes*, 69 *GS 69; *Populorum Progressio*, 22, *PP 22.
14. Cf. *Gaudium et Spes*, 57 *GS 57; *Populorum Progressio*, 41, *PP 41.
15. Cf. *Gaudium et Spes*, 19 *GS 19; *Populorum Progressio*, 41, *PP 41.
16. Cf. *Gaudium et Spes*, 86 *GS 86; *Populorum Progressio*, 48, *PP 48.
17. Cf. *Gaudium et Spes*, 69 *GS 69; *Populorum Progressio*, 14-21, *PP 14–21.
18. Cf. the inscription of the encyclical *Populorum Progressio*.
19. The encyclical *Rerum Novarum* of Leo XIII has as its principal subject 'the condition of the workers,' *RN.
20. *Libertatis Conscientia*, 72; *Octogesima Adveniens*, 4, OA 4.
21. Cf. *Mater et Magistra*, 53, *MM 53.
22. *Gaudium et Spes*, 63, *GS 63.
23. Cf. *Populorum Progressio*, 3, 9, *PP 3. 9.
24. Cf. ibid., 3, *PP 3.
25. Ibid., 48, *PP 48.
26. Cf. ibid., 14: 'Development cannot be limited to mere economic growth. In order to be authentic, it must be complete: integral, that is, it has to promote the good of every man and of the whole man,' *PP 14.
27. Ibid., 87, *PP 87.
28. Cf. ibid, 53, *PP 53.
29. Cf. ibid., 76, *PP 76.
30. The decades referred to are the years 1960-1970 and 1970-1980; the present decade is the third (1980-1990).
31. The expression "Fourth World" is used not just occasionally for the so-called less advanced countries, but also and especially for the bands of great or extreme poverty in countries of medium and high income.
32. Second Vatican Council, Dogmatic Constitution on the Church *Lumen Gentium*, 1.
33. *Populorum Progressio*, 33, *PP 33.
34. It should be noted that the Holy See associated itself with the celebration of this international year with a special document issued by the Pontifical Justice and Peace Commission titled 'What have You Done to Your Homeless Brother? The Church and the Housing Problem' (Dec. 27, 1987).
35. Cf. *Octogesima Adveniens*, 8-9, OA 8-9.
36. A recent U.N. publication titled 'World Economic Survey 1987' provides the most recent data (cf. pp. 8-9). The percentage of unemployed in the developed countries with a market economy jumped from 3 percent of the work force in 1970 to 8 percent in 1986. it now amounts to 29 million people.

37. *Laborem Exercens*, 18, *LE 18.
38. 'At the Service of the Human Community: An Ethical Approach to the International Debt Question' (Dec. 27, 1986).
39. *Populorum Progressio*, 54: 'Developing countries will thus no longer risk being overwhelmed by debts whose repayment swallows up the greater part of their gains. Rates of interest and time for repayment of the loan could be so arranged as not to be too great a burden on either party, taking into account free gifts, interest-free or low interest-loans and the time needed for liquidating the debts,' *PP 54.
40. Cf. 'presentation' of the document 'At the Service of the Human Community: An Ethical Approach to the International Debt Question' (Dec. 27, 1986).
41. Cf. *Populorum Progressio*, 53, *PP 53.
42. 'At the Service of the Human Community', III, 2, 1.
43. Cf. *Populorum Progressio*, 20-21, *PP 20-1.
44. Address at Drogheda, Ireland (Sept. 29, 1979), 5: AAS, 71 (1979), II, p. 1079.
45. Cf. *Populorum Progressio*, 37, *PP 37.
46. Cf. apostolic exhortation *Familiaris Consortio* (Nov. 22, 1981), especially in No. 30: AAS 74 (1982), pp. 115-117.
47. Cf. Human Rights. Collection of International Instruments, United Nations, New York 1983; John Paul II, encyclical *Redemptor Hominis* (March 4, 1979), 17: AAS 71 (1979), p. 296, *RH 17.
48. Cf. *Gaudium et Spes*, 78 *GS 78: *Populorum Progressio*, 76: "To wage war on misery and to struggle against injustice is to promote, along with improved conditions, the human and spiritual progress of all men, and therefore the common good of humanity...Peace is something that is built up day after day in the pursuit of an order intended by God, which implies a more perfect form of justice among men," *PP 76.
49. Cf. *Familiaris Consortio*, 6: 'History is not simply a fixed progression toward what is better, but rather an event of freedom and even a struggle between freedoms.'
50. For this reason the word *development* was used in the encyclical rather that the word *progress*, but with an attempt to give the word *development* its fullest meaning.
51. *Populorum Progressio*, 19: 'Increased possession is not the ultimate goal of nations or of individuals. All growth is ambivalent....The exclusive pursuit of possessions thus becomes an obstacle to individual fulfillment and to man's true greatness...Both for nations and for individual men, avarice is the most evident from of moral underdevelopment', *PP 19; cf. also *Octogesima Adveniens*, 9, *OA 9.
52. Cf. *Gaudium et Spes*, 35 *GS 35; Paul VI, Address to the Diplomatic Corps (Jan. 7, 1965): AAS 57 (1965), p. 232.
53. Cf. *Populorum Progressio*, 20-21, *PP 20-21.
54. Cf. *Laborem Exercens*, 4 *LE 4; *Populorum Progressio*, 15, *PP 15.
55. Ibid., 42, *PP 42.
56. Cf. Easter Proclamation, Roman Missal (1975): 'O happy fault, O necessary sin of Adam, which gained for us so great a Redeemer!'
57. *Lumen Gentium*, 1.
58. Cf. for example, St. Basil the Great, *Regulae fusius tractatae, interrogatio* XXXVII, 1-2: PG 31, 1009-1012; Theodoret of Cyr, *De Providentia, Oratio* VII: PG 83, 665-686; St. Augustine, *De Civitate Dei*, XIX, 17: CCL 48, 683-685.
59. Cf. for example, St. John Chrysostom, *In Evang. S. Matthaei, hom.* 50, 3-4: PG 58, 508-510; St. Ambrose, *De Officiis Ministrorum*, lib. II, XXVIII, 136-140; PL 16, 139-141; St. Possidius, *Vita S. Augustini Episcopi*, XXXIV: PL 32, 53f.
60. *Populorum Progressio*, 23: 'If someone who has the riches of this world sees his brother in need and closes his heart to him, how does the love of God abide in him? (1 Jn. 3:17). It is well known how strong were the words used by the fathers of the church to describe the proper attitude of persons who possess anything toward persons in need.' In the previous number, the pope had cited No. 69 of the pastoral constitution *Gaudium et Spes*, of the Second Vatican Council, *PP 23.
61. Cf. *Populorum Progressio*, 47: 'A world where freedom is not an empty word and where the poor man Lazarus can sit down at the same table with the rich man,' *PP 47.
62. Cf. ibid.: 'It is a question, rather, of building a world where every man, no matter what his race, religion or nationality, can live a fully human life, freed from servitude imposed on him by other men'; cf. also *Gaudium et Spes*, 29, *GS 29. Such *fundamental equality* is one of the basic reasons why the church has always been opposed to every form of racism.
63. Cf. Homily at Val Visdende (July 12, 1987), 5: L'Osservatore Romano, July 13-14, 1987; *Octogesima Adveniens*, 21, *OA 21.
64. Cf. *Gaudium et Spes*, 25, *GS 25.
65. Apostolic exhortation *Reconciliatio et Paenitentia* (Dec. 2 1984), 16: 'Whenever the church

speaks of *situations* of sin or when she condemns as *social sins* certain situations or the collective behavior of certain social groups, big or small, or even of whole nations and blocs of nations, she knows and she proclaims that such cases of *social sin* are the result of the accumulation and concentration of many *personal sins*. It is a case of the very personal sins of those who cause or support evil or who exploit it; of those who are in a position to avoid, eliminate or at least limit certain social evils but who fail to do so out of laziness, fear or the conspiracy of silence, through secret complicity or indifference; of those who take refuge in the supposed impossibility of changing the world and also of those who sidestep the effort and sacrifice required, producing specious reasons of a higher order. The real responsibility, then, lies with individuals. A situation—or likewise an institution, a structure, society itself—is not in itself the subject of moral acts. Hence a situation cannot in itself be good or bad': AAS 77 (1985), p. 217.

66. *Populorum Progressio*, 42, *PP 42.
67. Cf. Liturgy of the Hours, Wednesday of the Third Week of Ordinary Time, Vespers.
68. *Populorum Progressio*, 87, *PP 87.
69. Cf. ibid., 13, 81, *PP 13, 18.
70. Cf. ibid., 13, *PP 13.
71. Cf. Address at the opening of the Third General Conference of Latin American Bishops (Jan. 28, 1979): AAS 71 (1979), pp. 189-196.
72. *Libertatis Conscientia*, 72; *Octogesima Adveniens*, 4, *OA 4.
73. *Gaudium et Spes*, 83-90: 'Building Up the International Community,' *GS 83-90.
74. Cf. *Mater et Magistra* *MM; *Pacem in Terris*, Part 4; *Octogesima Adveniens*, 2-4, *OA 2-4.
75. *Populorum Progressio*, 3, 9, *PP 3, 9.
76. Ibid., 3, *PP 3.
77. Ibid., 47, *PP 47; *Libertatis Conscientia*, 68.
78. Cf *Gaudium et Spes*, 69, *GS 69; *Populorum Progressio*, 22, *PP 22; *Libertatis Conscientia*, 90; St. Thomas Aquinas, *Summa Theol.*, IIa, IIae, q. 66, art. 2.
79. Cf. Address at opening of Third General Conference of Latin American Bishops; *ad limina* address to a group of Polish bishops (Dec. 17, 1987), 6: L'Osservatore Romano, Dec. 18, 1987.
80. Because the Lord wished to identify himself with them (Mt. 25:31-46) and takes special care of them (cf. Ps. 12:6; Lk. 1:52f).
81. *Populorum Progressio*, 55: 'These are the men and women that need to be helped, that need to be convinced to take into their own hands their development, gradually acquiring the means', *PP 55; cf. *Gaudium et Spes*, 86, *GS 86.
82. *Populorum Progressio*, 35: 'Basic education is the first objective of a plan of development.'
83. Cf. *Libertatis Conscientia*, Introduction.
84. *Reconciliatio et Paenitentia*, 15, *Libertatis Conscientia*, 38, 42.
85. *Libertatis Conscientia*, 24.
86. *Gaudium et Spes*, 22, *GS 22; *Redemptor Hominis*, 8, *RH 8.
87. *Populorum Progressio*, 5. "We believe that all men of good will, together with our Catholic sons and daughters and our Christian brethren, can and should agree on this program" *PP 5; cf. also 81-83, 87, *PP 81-83, 87.
88. Cf. Second Vatican Council, Declaration on the Relationship of the Church to Non-Christian Religions, *Nostra Aetate*, 4.
89. *Gaudium et Spes*, 39, *GS 39.
90. Cf. *Lumen Gentium*, 58; *Redemptoris Mater*, 5-6.
91. Cf. Paul VI, apostolic exhortation *Marialis Cultus*, (Feb. 2, 1974), 37: AAS 66 (1974), pp. 148f; John Paul II, Homily at the Shrine of Our lady of Zapopan, Mexico (Jan. 30, 1979), 4: AAS 71 (1979), p. 230.
92. Collect of the Mass 'For the Development of Peoples': Roman Missal, 1975, p. 820.

Centesimus Annus

1. Leo XIII, Encyclical letter *Rerum Novarum* (May 15, 1891): Leonis XIII P.M. Acta, XI, Romae 1892, pp. 97-144.
2. Pius XI, Encyclical letter *Quadragesimo Anno* (May 15, 1931): AAS 23 (1931), pp. 177-228; Pius XII, Radio message of June 1, 1941: AAS 33 (1941), pp. 195-205; John XXIII, Encyclical letter *Mater et Magistra* (May 15, 1961): AAS 53 (1961), pp. 401-464; Paul VI, Apostolic epistle *Octagesimo Adveniens* (May 14, 1971): AAS 63 (1971), pp. 401-441.
3. Cf. *Quadragesimo Anno*, III, *QA 147.
4. Encyclical letter *Laborem Exercens* (Sept. 14, 1981): AAS 73 (1981), pp. 577-647; Encyclical letter *Sollicitudo Rei Socialis* (Dec. 30, 1987): AAS 80 (1988), pp. 513-586.
5. Cf. St. Irenaeus, *Adversus Haereses*, I, 10, 1; III, 4, 1: PG 7, 549f; S. Ch. 264, 154f.; 211, 44-46.
6. *Rerum Novarum*, p. 132, *RN 47.
7. Cf., e.g., Leo XIII, Encyclical epistle, *Arcanum Divinae Sapientiae* (Feb. 10, 1880): Leonis XIII P.M. Acta, II, Romae 1882, pp. 10-40; Encyclical epistle *Diuturnum Illud* (June 29, 1881): ibid., pp. 269-287; Encyclical epistle *Libertas Praestantissimum* (June 20, 1888): Leonis XIII P.M. Acta, VIII, Romae 1889, pp. 212-246; Encyclical epistle *Graves de communi* (Jan. 18, 1901): Leonis XIII P.M. Acta, XXI, Romae 1902, pp. 3-20.
8. *Rerum Novarum*, p. 97, *RN 1f.
9. Ibid., p. 98, *RN 1.3.
10. Cf. ibid., p. 109f. *RN 15–16.
11. Cf. ibid., description of working conditions; 44: anti-Christian workers' associations, pp. 110f., pp. 136f., *RN 17f.; 53.
12. Ibid., pp. 130; cf. also pp. 114f, *RN 45; 22.
13. Ibid., p. 130, *RN 44.
14. Ibid., p. 123, *RN 36.
15. Cf. *Laborem Exercens*, 1, 2, 6, *LE 1.1; 2; 6–6.5.
16. Cf. *Rerum Novarum*, pp. 99-107, *RN 3–13.
17. Cf. ibid., pp. 102f., *RN 7.1–8.
18. Cf. ibid., pp. 101-104, *RN 6–9.
19. Cf. ibid., pp. 134f.; 137f , *RN 48.1f.; 52–54.
20. Ibid., p. 135, *RN 50.
21. Cf. ibid., pp. 128-129, *RN 43.
22. Ibid., p. 129, *RN 43.
23. Ibid., p. 129, *RN 44.
24. Ibid., pp. 130f, *RN 45.
25. Ibid., p. 131, *RN 45.
26. Cf. Universal Declaration of Human Rights.
27. Cf. *Rerum Novarum*, pp. 121-123, *RN 34–7.
28. Cf. ibid., p. 127, *RN 42.
29. Ibid., pp. 126f., *RN 41.1.
30. Cf. Universal Declaration of Human Rights, Declaration on the elimination of every form of intolerance and discrimination based on religion or convictions.
31. Second Vatican Council, Declaration on Religious Freedom *Dignitatis Humanae;* John Paul II, letter to heads of state (Sept. 1, 1980): AAS 72 (1980), pp. 1252-1260; Message for the 1988 World Day of Peace (Jan. 1, 1988): AAS 80 (1988), pp. 278-286.
32. *Rerum Novarum*, pp. 99-105; pp. 130f.; p. 135, *RN 3–12; 46F.; 50.
33. Ibid., p. 125, *RN 38.
34. Cf. *Sollicitudo Rei Socialis*, 38-40; cf. also *Mater et Magistra*, p. 407, *SR 38.4–40.5; *MM 23.
35. Cf. *Rerum Novarum*, pp. 114-116; *Quadragesimo Anno*, III; Paul VI, homily for the closing of the Holy Year (Dec. 25, 1975): AAS 68 (1976), p. 145; Message for the 1977 World Day of Peace (Jan. 1, 1977): AAS 68 (1976), p. 709, *RN 21–24; *QA 96–7.
36. *Sollicitudo Rei Socialis*, 42, *SR 42.1.
37. Cf. *Rerum Novarum*, pp. 101f.; 104f.; 130f.; 136, *RN 7; 10–12; 46f.
38. Second Vatican Council, Pastoral Constitution on the Church in the Modern World, *Gaudium et Spes*, 24, *GS 24.2.
39. *Rerum Novarum*, p. 99, *RN 3.
40. Cf. *Sollicitudo Rei Socialis*, 15, 28, *SR 15.2; 28.3ff.
41. Cf. *Laborem Exercens*, 11-15, *LE 11.2–15.1.
42. *Quadragesimo Anno*, III, 113, *QA 114.

[506]

43. Cf. *Rerum Novarum*, pp. 121-125, *RN 34–41.1.
44. Cf. *Laborem Exercens*, 20; Discourse to the International Labor Organization in Geneva (June 15, 1982): *Insegnamenti* V/2 (1982), pp. 2250-2266; Paul VI, Discourse to the same organization (June 10, 1969): AAS 61 (1969), pp. 491-502, *LE 20ff.
45. Cf. *Laborem Exercens*, 8, *LE 8.1ff.
46. Cf. *Quadragesimo Anno*, 14, *QA 3–15.
47. Cf. *Arcanum Divinae Sapientiae; Diuturnum Illud*; Encyclical epistle *Immortale Dei* (Nov. 1, 1885): Leonis XIII P.M. Acta, V, Romae 1886, pp. 118-150; Encyclical letter *Sapientiae Christianae* (Jan. 10, 1890): Leonis XIII P.M. Acta, X, Romae 1891, pp. 10-41; Encyclical epistle *Quod Apostolici Muneris* (Dec. 28, 1878): Leonis XIII P.M. Acta, I, Romae 1881, pp. 170-183; *Libertas Praestantissimum.*
48. Cf. *Libertas Praestantissimum*, 10. 49. Cf. Message for the 1980 World Day of Peace: AAS 71 (1979), pp. 1572-1580.
50. Cf. *Sollicitudo Rei Socialis*, 20.
51. Cf. John XXIII, encyclical letter *Pacem in Terris*, (April 11, 1963), III: AAS 55 (1963), pp. 286-289, *SR 20.2ff.
52. Cf. Universal Declaration of Human Rights, issued in 1948; *Pacem in Terris*, IV; Final Act of the Conference on Cooperation and Security in Europe, Helsinki, 1975, *PT 130–145.
53. Cf. Paul VI, Encyclical letter *Populorum Progressio* (March 26, 1967), 61-65: AAS 59 (1967), pp. 287-289, *PP 61–65.
54. Cf. Message for the 1980 World Day of Peace, pp. 1572-1580.
55. Cf. *Gaudium et Spes*, 36; 39, *GS 36.1f.; 39.
56. Cf. Apostolic exhortation *Christifideles Laici* (Dec. 30, 1988) 32-44: AAS 81 (1989), 431-481.
57. Cf. *Laborem Exercens*, 20. 58. Cf. Congregation for the Doctrine of the Faith, Instruction on Christian Freedom and Liberation *Libertatis Conscientia* (March 22, 1986): AAS 79 (1987), pp. 554-599, *LE 20.2.
59. Cf. Discourse at the Headquarters of the E.C.W.A. on the occasion of the 10th anniversary of the *Appeal for the Sahel* (Ouagadougou, Burkina Faso, Jan. 29, 1990): AAS 82 (1990), pp. 816-821.
60. Cf. *Pacem in Terris*, III.
61. Cf. *Sollicitudo Rei Socialis*, 27-28; *Populorum Progressio*, 43-44, *PT 112–119.
62. Cf. *Sollicitudo Rei Socialis*, 29-31.
63. Cf. Helsinki Final Act and Vienna Accord; *Libertas Praestantissinum*, 5, * SR 29.1–31–7.
64. Cf. Encyclical letter *Redemptoris Missio*, (Dec. 7, 1990), 7: *L'Osservatore Romano*, Jan. 23, 1991.
65. Cf. *Rerum Novarum*, pp. 99-107; 131-133, *RN 3–13; 45–47.1.
66. Ibid., pp. 111-113f., *RN 19–21.
67. Cf. *Quadragesimo Anno*, II; Pius XII, radio message on June 1, 1941, p. 199; *Mater et Magistra*, pp. 428-429; *Populorum Progressio*, 22-24, *QA 44–46; *MM 104-118; *PP 22–24.
68. *Gaudium et Spes*, 69; 71.
69. Cf. Discourse to Latin American bishops at Puebla (Jan. 28, 1979), III, 4: AAS 71 (1979), pp. 199-201; *Laborem Exercens*, 14; *Sollicitudo Rei Socialis*, 42, *GS 69;71.1; 71.4.
70. Cf. *Sollicitudo Rei Socialis*, 15, *SR 15.1.
71. Cf. *Laborem Exercens*, 21, *LE 21.1.
72. Cf. *Populorum Progressio*, 33-42, *PP 33–42.
73. Cf. *Laborem Exercens*, 7, *LE 7.1f.
74. Cf. ibid., 8, *LE 8.4.
75. Cf. *Gaudium et Spes*, 35; *Populorum Progressio*, 19, *GS 35; *PP 19.
76. Cf. *Sollicitudo Rei Socialis*, 34; Message for the 1990 World Day of Peace: AAS 82 (1990), pp. 147-156, *SR 34.3.
77. Cf. Apostolic exhortation *Reconciliatio et Poenitentia*, (Dec. 2, 1984), 16: AAS 77 (1985), pp. 213-217; *Quadragesimo Anno*, III, *QA 130–131.
78. *Sollicitudo Rei Socialis*, 25, *SR 25.2.
79. Cf. ibid., 34, *SR 34.
80. Cf. *Redemptoris Hominis*, (March 4, 1979), 15: AAS 71 (1979), pp. 286-289, *RH 15.1.
81. Cf. *Gaudium et Spes*, 24, *GS 24.2.
82. Cf. ibid., 41, *GS 41.
83. Cf. ibid., 26, *GS 26.
84. Cf. *Gaudium et Spes*, 36; *Octagesimo Adveniens*, 2-5, *GS 36.1; *OA 2-5.
85. Cf. *Laborem Exercens*, 15, *LE 15.1.
86. Cf. ibid., 10, *LE 10–10.3.
87. Ibid., 14, *LE 14.2.
88. Cf. ibid, 18, *LE 18.

89. Cf. *Rerum Novarum*, pp. 126-128, *RN 39–46.
90. Ibid., pp. 121f., *RN 33f.
91. Cf. *Libertas Praestantissimum*, pp. 224-226.
92. Cf. *Gaudium et Spes*, 76, *GS 76.4.
93. Cf. ibid., 29; Pius XII, Christmas radio message on Dec. 24, 1944: AAS 37 (1945), pp. 10-20.
94. Cf. *Dignitatis Humanae*.
95. Cf. *Redemptoris Missio*, 11.
96. Cf. *Redemptoris Hominis*, 17, *RH 17–17.8.
97. Cf. Message for the 1988 World Day of Peace, pp. 1572-1580; Message for the 1991 World Day of Peace: *L'Osservatore Romano*, Dec. 19, 1990; *Dignitatis Humanae*, 1-2.
98. *Gaudium et Spes*, 26, *GS 26.
99. Cf. ibid., 22, *GS 22–22.5.
100. *Quadragesimo Anno*, I, *QA 23–28.
101. Cf. *Familiaris Consortio* (Nov. 22, 1981), 45: AAS 74 (1982), pp. 136f.
102. Cf. Discourse to UNESCO (June 2, 1980): AAS 72 (1980), pp. 735-752.
103. Cf. *Redemptoris Missio*, 39; 52.
104. Cf. Benedict XV, *Ubi Primum* (Sept. 8, 1914): AAS 6 (1914), pp. 501f.; Pius XI, Radio message to the Catholic faithful and to the entire world (Sept. 29, 1938): AAS 30 (1938), pp. 309f.; Pius XII, Radio message to the entire world (Aug. 24, 1939): AAS 31 (1939), pp. 333-335; *Pacem in Terris*, III; Paul VI, Discourse at the United Nations (Oct. 4, 1965): AAS 57 (1965), pp. 877-885, *PT 94–108.
105. Cf. Populorum Progressio, 76-77, *PP 76–77.
106. Cf. *Familiaris Consortio*, 48.
107. *Rerum Novarum*, p. 107, *RN 14.
108. Cf. *Redemptoris Hominis*, 13, *RH 13.
109. Ibid., 14, *RH 14.
110. Paul VI, Homily at the final public session of the Second Vatican Council (Dec. 7, 1965): AAS 58 (1966), p. 58.
111. *Sollicitudo Rei Socialis*, 41, *SR 41.7.
112. *Gaudium et Spes*, 76; cf. *Redemptor Hominis*, 13, *GS 76.1; *RH 13.1.
113. *Rerum Novarum*, p. 143, *RN 59f.
114. Ibid., p. 107, *RN14.
115. Cf. *Sollicitudo Rei Socialis*, 38, *SR 38.1.
116. Ibid., 47, * SR 47.4–47.8.

Index

The references in this index are to **paragraph numbers** of the documents included in this collection. The titles of the documents are abbreviated in accordance with the Table on page 479. It should be noted that the Index does not cover the Introduction, the introductory matter to the documents, or the footnotes.

Index

Index